INTERNATIONAL BANKING LAW AND REGULATION

International Banking Law and Regulation offers a critical exploration of the legal and regulatory frameworks that govern the global banking sector. Tracing the development of banking from its mediaeval origins to today's complex cross-border financial structures, this book examines how law and regulation underpin financial stability, guide corporate lending, and respond to technological and geopolitical change.

From foundational concepts such as money and payment systems to prudential supervision and corporate governance to the intricacies of syndicated lending, ESG finance, securitisation, and Islamic finance, each chapter considers the evolving interaction between legal norms, financial innovation, and regulatory oversight. Special attention is paid to cross-border lending, crisis management, anti-financial crime frameworks, and creditor hierarchies, with comparative insights from major jurisdictions, including the UK, EU, US, China, India, and Japan.

Written for students of banking and finance law, early-career practitioners, and policymakers, this volume combines legal analysis with a practical, international outlook. It explains how banking law operates across jurisdictions, enabling financial institutions to manage risk, meet regulatory obligations, and support global economic activity.

In a rapidly evolving financial landscape, this book provides a timely and authoritative guide to the legal principles shaping the future of international banking.

Matteo Zambelli is a partner in the corporate and commercial practice of the law firm Zambelli Tassetto, Studio Legale, and an Associate Professor at the University of West London, where he lectures on international banking law, legal aspects of international finance, international arbitration, and international commercial law.

INTERNATIONAL BANKING LAW AND REGULATION

Matteo Zambelli

Routledge
Taylor & Francis Group
LONDON AND NEW YORK

Designed cover image: Bancogiro di Rialto – Gabriele Bella/Fondazione Querini Stampalia

First published 2026
by Routledge
4 Park Square, Milton Park, Abingdon, Oxon OX14 4RN

and by Routledge
605 Third Avenue, New York, NY 10158

Routledge is an imprint of the Taylor & Francis Group, an informa business

British Library Cataloguing-in-Publication Data
A catalogue record for this book is available from the British Library

Library of Congress Cataloging-in-Publication Data
Names: Zambelli, Matteo, author.
Title: International banking law and regulation / Matteo Zambelli.
Description: Abingdon, Oxon [UK] ; New York, NY : Routledge, 2026. | Includes bibliographical references and index.
Identifiers: LCCN 2025024006 | ISBN 9781032662190 (hardback) | ISBN 9781032662183 (paperback) | ISBN 9781032662220 (ebook)
Subjects: LCSH: Banks and banking, International—Law and legislation. | Banks and banking, International—Law and legislation—Great Britain. | Bank loans—Law and legislation. | Banking law.
Classification: LCC K1066 .Z36 2026 | DDC 346/.08215—dc23/eng/20250519 LC record available at https://lccn.loc.gov/2025024006

ISBN: 978-1-032-66219-0 (hbk)
ISBN: 978-1-032-66218-3 (pbk)
ISBN: 978-1-032-66222-0 (ebk)

DOI: 10.4324/9781032662220

Typeset in Baskerville
by Apex CoVantage, LLC

CONTENTS

ABOUT THE AUTHOR

Dr. Matteo Zambelli is a partner in the corporate and commercial practice of the law firm Zambelli Tassetto, Studio Legale, and an associate professor at the University of West London LLM programme where he lectures on the International Banking Law, Legal Aspects of International Finance, International Arbitration, International Commercial Law modules. A well-rounded practitioner, Matteo is admitted to the New York State Bar, the Italian Bar (with higher rights of audience) and as a Solicitor, England and Wales and Solicitor, Ireland (not practising in the jurisdiction).

PREFACE

The international banking landscape is shaped by a complex interplay of laws and regulations. These cross-border interactions underpin modern economies and global trade. This volume explores the evolution of international banking from its origins in mediaeval Italy to the sophisticated financial structures of today, encompassing prudential regulation, ring-fencing, loan and portfolio trading, syndicated lending, derivatives, and Islamic finance. It examines the legal and regulatory mechanisms that have developed alongside financial markets and underpin them, providing an analysis of the principles that govern and guide the financial sector as it adapts to the challenges and demands of international banking.

Directed at both students and practitioners, this book aims to serve as a comprehensive resource on the law, practice, and regulation of international banking. It attempts to offer an accessible exploration of the principles, practices, and developments in this field.

A portion of this volume is devoted to defining the nature of the banking business and the fundamental concepts of money and payment. The book provides detailed coverage of banking regulation, with an emphasis on the UK regime, complemented by a comparative analysis of the EU and US frameworks. It also considers regulatory trends in Japan, India, and China, addressing key developments in anti-money laundering provisions and the impact of international sanctions on banking transactions. Additionally, capital adequacy and liquidity requirements are examined, along with the legal and regulatory regimes governing the ring-fencing of retail banking activities and the resolution of failing banks.

Beyond regulatory issues, the book offers an insight into cross-border corporate banking transactions, including bilateral and syndicated loans, and the international lending arrangements that support them. It explores the structure, legal form, and content of such arrangements, as well as key transaction documents detailing the rights and obligations of the various parties involved. By placing these transactions in a wider legal and commercial context, this volume aims to provide readers with a well-rounded understanding of international banking law and practice.

Each chapter introduces key concepts, develops them, and then expands the analysis through structured content boxes, while the respective concluding sections summarise the main takeaways. This work has been completed with reference to materials available as of 15 March 2025. The views expressed herein are solely my own, and I accept full responsibility for any errors, omissions, or inaccuracies in the text. Finally, I would like to thank my family for their support and understanding: Maggie, Gaia, and Livia.

Dr. Matteo Zambelli
March 2025

CASES

LEGISLATION

UNITED KINGDOM

EUROPEAN UNION

UNITED STATES

INDIA

CHINA

JAPAN

ABBREVIATIONS

AAOIFI	Accounting and Auditing Organization for Islamic Financial Institutions
AML	anti-money laundering
APLMA	Asia Pacific Loan Market Association
BACS	Bankers' Automated Clearing Services
BIS	Bank for International Settlements
BRRD	Bank Recovery and Resolution Directive
CBDC	Central Bank Digital Currencies
CDS	credit default swap
CFTC	Commodity Futures Trading Commission (USA)
CHAPS	Clearing House Automated Payment System
CLOs	collateralised loan obligations
CRD	Capital Requirement Directive
CRR	Capital Requirement Regulation
DCEP	Digital Currency Electronic Payment (China)
EBA	European Banking Authority
EC	European Community
ECB	European Central Bank
EEA	European Economic Area
EMU	Economic and Monetary Union
ESCB	European System of Central Banks
ESG	environmental, social, and governance
ESMA	European Securities and Markets Authority
ESRB	European Systemic Risk Board
EU	European Union
EURIBOR	Euro interbank offered rate
FATCA	Foreign Account Tax Compliance Act (USA)
FATF	Financial Action Task Force
FCA	Financial Conduct Authority
FDIC	Federal Deposit Insurance Corporation (USA)
FED	Federal Reserve (USA)
FSA	Financial Services Authority
FSA	Financial Services Agency (Japan)
FSB	Financial Stability Board
FSCS	Financial Services Compensation Scheme
GLP	Green Loan Principles
HMRC	HM Revenue & Customs
HQLA	high-quality liquid assets
ICMA	International Capital Market Association
ICO	initial coin offering
IIFM	International Islamic Financial Market
IMF	International Monetary Fund
IRB	internal ratings-based approach
ISDA	International Swaps and Derivatives Association
JMLSG	Joint Money Laundering Steering Group

KYC	know your customer
LGD	loss given default
LIBOR	London interbank offered rate
LMA	Loan Market Association
LSTA	Loan Syndications and Trading Association
MLRO	Money Laundering Reporting Officer
NAMA	National Asset Management Agency (Ireland)
OFSI	Office of Financial Sanctions Implementation
OMOs	Open Market Operations
PBoC	People's Bank of China
PRA	Prudential Regulation Authority
PSD	Payment Services Directive
PSR	Payment Systems Regulator
QE	Quantitative Easing
Repos	repurchase agreements
RMB	renminbi
RTGS	real time gross settlement system
SEC	Security and Exchange Commission (USA)
SLLP	Sustainability-Linked Loan Principles
SRR	Special Resolution Regime
SSM	Single Supervisory Mechanism
SWIFT	Worldwide Interbank Financial Telecommunication
TEU	Treaty on the European Union
TFEU	Treaty on the Functioning of the European Union
UCC	Uniform Commercial Code
UNCITRAL	United Nations Commission on International Trade Law
US or USA	United States of America
USD	US Dollar

INTRODUCTION

The international banking landscape is shaped by an amalgamation of historical trajectories, financial innovations, and the proliferation of cross-border interactions – each of which underpins the functioning of contemporary economies and facilitates global trade. This volume offers a critical examination of the principles, regulatory practices, and evolving developments that frame the field of international banking law.

Tracing the evolution of banking from its origins in mediaeval Italy to the sophisticated financial structures of today – such as prudential regulation, ring-fencing, loan and portfolio trading, syndicated lending, derivatives, and Islamic finance – this work examines the legal and regulatory mechanisms that have developed alongside financial markets and that underpin their functioning. Each chapter considers the principles designed to regulate and guide the financial sector as it adapts to the challenges and demands of international banking and of sophisticated financial constructs.

The legal and regulatory framework analysed in this book serves as the foundation for financial growth, enabling commerce while striving to safeguard market participants, the public, and the wider economy. A clear and predictable legal infrastructure allows financial institutions to manage risks, respond effectively to crises, and evolve in line with technological and social advancements. To this end, the book explores the critical role of regulatory bodies through an international and comparative perspective, examining the legal frameworks governing credit institutions and the unique challenges of maintaining stability in an increasingly interconnected global market.

THE EVOLUTION OF BANKING AND ITS REGULATORY FRAMEWORK

The origins of banking can be traced back millennia, with each historical era contributing to developments that have shaped today's legal and regulatory frameworks and market practices. Chapter 1 explores this evolution, beginning with the mediaeval banking systems of Italy and the development of banking up to the 20th century. It examines the foundations of modern (Western) banking principles and touches upon some of the principles of Islamic finance, and considers the role of the Bank of England, whose supervisory practices have had a lasting influence on contemporary banking models. The chapter also traces the development of commercial, investment, and central banking frameworks across key financial jurisdictions, including the UK, the US, Europe, India, China, and Japan.

By outlining this historical trajectory, Chapter 1 provides essential context for understanding banking law, demonstrating how banks have evolved into complex institutions requiring formal regulatory oversight. Additionally, light is shed on modern banking practices and financial notions through an historical exploration of how such practices developed. This is because banking law and practices have a history, and we need to understand that history in order to appreciate the notions that underpin such practices, how such legal constructs have developed over time and how they work.

DOI: 10.4324/9781032662220-1

UNDERSTANDING MONEY, PAYMENT SYSTEMS, AND DIGITAL INNOVATION

Chapter 2 explores the central role of money and payment systems in the global economy, examining their legal character from early forms of currency to the emergence of digital finance. The evolution of money reflects broader shifts in commerce, with early currencies such as gold and silver deriving value from their intrinsic worth, while the introduction of fiat currency created a legal construct in which, over time, value is based on government backing rather than tangible assets. Payment systems have similarly evolved, moving from paper-based instruments such as cheques and bank drafts to sophisticated digital platforms that facilitate instantaneous cross-border transactions.

The regulatory implications of digital assets, cryptocurrencies, and blockchain technologies, which present both opportunities and challenges for international banking, are examined. This discussion provides a foundation for later chapters that examine how substantive laws and regulatory frameworks are adapting to these technological developments.

By offering an analysis of the legal aspects of money, payment obligations, and financial transaction mechanisms, this chapter highlights the intersection of traditional and dematerialised payment systems across various jurisdictions. In doing so, it illustrates the rapidly evolving nature of money, where digital innovation continues to reshape international banking law and the broader financial landscape.

REGULATORY FRAMEWORKS

Chapter 3 examines the regulatory framework governing the banking sector in the UK, tracing its historical development, key legislative reforms, and responses to both global and domestic financial crises. An overview of early banking regulation, which was initially shaped by the Bank of England's informal oversight before prudential measures were introduced to enhance financial stability, is provided. Significant milestones in this evolution include the Banking Act 1979, which formalised licensing and supervisory requirements, and the Financial Services and Markets Act 2000[1] (**FSMA**), which established a unified regulatory framework for the financial services sector.

A focus is the transformative impact of the 2007–2009 global financial crisis, which led to the enactment of the Banking Act 2009[2] and the introduction of the Special Resolution Regime (**SRR**). This framework was designed to manage failing banks and mitigate systemic risk, reinforcing the UK's crisis management capabilities. The chapter also considers post-Brexit reforms, particularly the Financial Services and Markets Act 2023,[3] which aims to strengthen the competitiveness and regulatory independence of the UK's financial services sector.

Another central theme is the legal definition of a bank under English law and its practical implications. It compares the UK's regulatory approach with that of other major jurisdictions, such as the EU, US, Japan, India, and China.

1 2000 Chapter 8.
2 2009 Chapter 1.
3 2023 Chapter 29.

CORPORATE GOVERNANCE AND FINANCIAL CRIME

Chapter 4 explores governance in banking, which extends beyond the conventional corporate organisation and management's oversight due to the systemic importance of financial institutions. Given their role in maintaining financial stability, banks require governance structures that prioritise accountability, risk management, and ethical conduct. The chapter touches upon the Senior Managers and Certification Regime, which codifies individual accountability within UK financial institutions, ensuring that senior executives can be held responsible for governance failures. It also considers the influence of environmental, social, and governance (**ESG**) criteria in banking, reflecting the increasing emphasis on sustainable finance and ethical corporate practices.

Chapter 5 analyses the UK's legal and regulatory framework for tackling financial crime and financial misconduct, covering key areas such as money laundering, terrorist financing, bribery, corruption, sanctions violations, and fraud.

An international perspective is provided with regard to the approach of different jurisdictions such as the European Union, the United States, and China on issues of anti-corruption standards, anti-terrorism, and money laundering. The chapter concludes by exploring the responsibilities of financial institutions in implementing UK, EU, US, and other international sanctions regimes, with enforcement mechanisms through international systems such as SWIFT.

PRUDENTIAL SUPERVISION

The prudential regulatory framework governing credit institutions represents a core component of this book.

Chapter 6 provides insights into the prudential measures that safeguard banks against potential losses, examining critical regulatory mechanisms such as capital requirements, liquidity ratios, and risk management standards. These prudential regulations, derived largely from the Basel Accords (as implemented in the relevant jurisdiction), are designed to ensure that banks maintain adequate capital buffers, thus enhancing their ability to absorb losses. The challenges and importance of maintaining effective supervision within a globalised banking system, especially in times of crisis, are finally addressed.

BANKS' RECOVERY AND RESOLUTION

Chapter 7 delves into the frameworks for bank recovery and resolution and on the cross-border implications of a bank's failure. The UK's ring-fencing regime and recovery frameworks, which include mechanisms for the orderly resolution of distressed banks to protect depositors and minimise systemic disruption, are outlined. The analysis extends to comparable frameworks in key global economies, including the United States, the European Union, China, India, and Japan.

The discussion on bank resolution underscores the international effort to harmonise recovery frameworks. Global regulatory bodies, such as the Financial Stability Board (**FSB**) and the European Union's Single Resolution Mechanism, seek to ensure that banks can fail safely without relying on taxpayer-funded bailouts. This alignment of standards across jurisdictions exemplifies the globalisation of banking regulation, highlighting the importance of cooperative regulatory frameworks.

AN INTRODUCTION TO BANK LOAN FINANCING

Chapter 8 explores the fundamental concepts and structures of bank loan financing, with particular emphasis on the increasingly cross-border nature of these transactions.

It provides an overview of loan structures, ranging from simple bilateral loans to complex syndicated loan facilities, highlighting the role of financial institutions, intermediaries, and regulatory frameworks in facilitating the flow of funds between lenders and borrowers across multiple jurisdictions. It underscores the interplay between legal, financial, and regulatory considerations, offering insights into how international bank financing is structured to balance risk, efficiency, and compliance in an increasingly interconnected financial landscape.

This chapter examines some of the key risks faced by a lender within the context of selected European jurisdictions, including France, Germany, Ireland, and Italy, as well as China, India, and Japan, highlighting the regulatory, tax, and legal challenges that foreign lenders must navigate. By analysing these key markets, the chapter provides insights into the diverse legal frameworks that shape international lending practices.

THE DYNAMICS OF LENDING AND CREDIT FACILITIES

Chapters 9, 10, and 11 provide an examination of corporate loan facilities, secured and unsecured lending, and syndicated loans, addressing both the legal and operational dimensions of bank financing. These chapters explore the full spectrum of loan structures, from bilateral loans to complex syndicated facilities, emphasising the significance of loan documentation and security arrangements in protecting lenders and ensuring repayment.

A key focus is the distinction between secured and unsecured lending, with an analysis of the various forms of collateral and security interests available under English law and the Uniform Commercial Code (**UCC**) in the United States. The chapters also examine the role of syndicated loans, which allow multiple lenders to share credit risk when financing a single borrower. Syndicated lending has become a central feature of modern cross-border finance, particularly in large-scale infrastructure, energy, and acquisition financing. The discussion on loan syndication highlights how banks collaborate to structure complex financing arrangements, manage risk exposure, and ensure efficient capital allocation across global markets.

INTERCREDITOR DEEDS AND SECURITY TRUSTS

Chapter 12 examines some of the mechanisms used to establish creditor priorities in finance transactions, with a particular focus on intercreditor deeds, deeds of priority, and subordination agreements. It explores the structures that create different tiers of priority among creditor groups and outlines the typical clauses found within these agreements. Special attention is given to the provisions governing the relationship between senior and junior debt in leveraged finance transactions while acknowledging that similar clauses are commonly found in deeds of priority and subordination agreements. Additionally, the function and significance of security trusts, where security over a borrower's or obligor's assets is held for the benefit of multiple finance parties, and the role of security trustees in finance transactions is considered.

ALTERNATIVE FINANCING MODELS AND THE ROLE OF ESG

Chapter 13 examines the significance of ESG criteria in lending practices and the increasing role of alternative financing models in the modern financial landscape. Sustainable finance, including green and sustainability-linked loans, has become an important factor for financial institutions (albeit this trend has been somewhat reversed since the end of 2024), enabling them to align lending activities with environmental and social objectives.

The chapter then considers three critical areas of international banking and practice: the use of derivatives in loan transactions, the role of loan agreements in project finance transactions, and the issuance of legal opinions within financing arrangements, incorporating perspectives from both English and US law.

SECURITISATION, CLOS, ISLAMIC FINANCE, AND REPOS

The book concludes with Chapter 14, which explores alternative financing methods that complement traditional bank lending. While conventional lending remains fundamental to financial markets, instruments such as securitisation, collateralised loan obligations (**CLO**s), Islamic finance, and repurchase agreements (**repos**) offer sophisticated alternatives that address diverse capital needs and regulatory challenges.

Each of these alternative financing models operates within distinct regulatory frameworks designed to enhance transparency, protect investors, and mitigate systemic risks. The chapter underscores their importance in modern global finance, highlighting how banks must navigate increasingly complex regulatory environments while meeting the evolving demands of diverse client bases and investment strategies.

In conclusion, by offering an analysis of the laws governing international banking and the innovations transforming the industry, this volume is intended to be a resource for students, practitioners, and policymakers. It seeks to equip readers with a deeper understanding of the legal principles underpinning modern corporate and commercial banking activities across multiple jurisdictions, enabling them to navigate the complexities of financial regulation and assess the role of law in ensuring stability, promoting governance standards, and supporting economic growth in an increasingly interconnected global market.

CHAPTER 1

INTRODUCTION TO INTERNATIONAL BANKING LAW

OVERVIEW

The origins of banking law and regulation are deeply rooted in the need to manage and protect the financial transactions that underpin commerce. Over the centuries, this legal fabric has evolved significantly, influenced by commercial practices. Initially, banking was governed by custom and informal standards of good practice, which gradually gave way to more formalised legal frameworks as trade expanded internationally and became more complex.

This chapter provides an historical overview of the development of corporate banking, beginning with the Venetian banks of the Middle Ages and tracing it through to the establishment of US investment banks in the 20th century. As banking practices became more sophisticated, the legal and regulatory frameworks governing them evolved. The chapter will also introduce key banking terms and explore the essential characteristics of banks as financial institutions. It concludes with a perspective on the structure of the banking industry in the UK, US, Europe, and Asia.

1 THE HISTORY OF BANKING

Banks have always played a central role in facilitating trade and commerce. The ability to safely transfer wealth, manage deposits, and extend credit has been essential to the development of both national economies and international trade. To understand modern banking, it is important to consider its historical roots and how early banking practices laid the groundwork for the financial institutions we know today. It is also important to grasp the progression of the legal constructs that support such banking practices since the history of the law, and of the common law in particular, is an intensely historical process. The evolution of law is characterised by incremental change, typically occurring after periods of stability and generally confined to modifications of existing legal principles. This gradual development ensures that the legal system retains continuity, allowing the evolving law to function as a "carrier of history", preserving past legal traditions while adapting to new circumstances.[1]

The genesis of modern commercial banking can be traced back to mediaeval Italy, particularly in cities such as Florence, Venice, and Genoa.[2] These were bustling centres of trade, where merchants from across Europe and the Mediterranean gathered to buy and sell goods. The growing need for secure financial transactions gave rise to the establishment of the earliest merchant banks, which initially provided basic services such as currency exchange and deposit-taking. The legal frameworks governing these early banks were relatively unsophisticated, relying on local statutes and customs. However, as trade routes expanded and commerce became more globalised, the need for more structured and comprehensive legal frameworks became apparent.

1 Lipton, P., 'The Utilisation of Evolutionary Concepts in Legal History: Company Law as a Case Study' (2020) 46(1) *Monash University Law Review* 58, p. 61.

2 The evolution of banking from the mediaeval Italian city-states to modern-day financial systems highlights significant continuities and innovations; see Fratianni, M. and Spinelli, F., 'Italian City-States and Financial Evolution' (2006) 10 *European Review of Economic History* 257.

DOI: 10.4324/9781032662220-2

The 19th and early 20th centuries saw a proliferation of national banking laws aimed at ensuring the stability and integrity of domestic banking systems. Countries developed their own banking regulations, often tailored to their unique economic circumstances. However, the Great Depression of the 1930s revealed the limitations of purely national approaches to banking regulation. The collapse of several major banks, combined with widespread economic turmoil, highlighted the need for stringent regulation of financial institutions.

The post-World War II period marked a significant turning point in the evolution of international banking law. In the latter half of the 20th century, the pace of globalisation accelerated, driven by rapid advancements in technology and the liberalisation of financial markets. Multinational banks emerged as powerful players in the global economy, with branches and subsidiaries operating in multiple countries.

2 WHAT IS BANKING?

Banking has evolved from simple systems of money storage and lending into a complex global network that facilitates the movement of capital across borders. The fundamental function of banks – accepting deposits and issuing loans – has remained consistent throughout history, but the way in which these functions are carried out has grown increasingly sophisticated.

Banking in ancient times was a relatively simple affair involving the safekeeping of valuable commodities and the issuance of loans. The earliest known banking practices date back to Mesopotamia, where temples and palaces served as repositories for grain, precious metals, and other valuable commodities.[3] The priests who managed these repositories acted as early bankers, extending credits to farmers and merchants in exchange for interest.

In ancient India, money lending was a well-established practice by the 7th century BCE. The Manusmriti, a legal text from that period, provided guidelines for lending at interest, with specific rates determined by the borrower's caste.[4] These early laws highlight the long-standing tradition of regulating financial transactions through legal frameworks.[5] The concept of charging interest – known as usury (see further on) – became acceptable in India in the 2nd century BCE, with strict limits placed on the rates that could be charged.

The Greeks also engaged extensively in the practice of banking. Around 600 BCE, the introduction of a standardised coinage system in Athens revolutionised trade, making it easier for merchants to conduct transactions across the Mediterranean. These early Greek bankers, known as *trapezitai*, provided loans to merchants, facilitated the exchange of currencies, and managed deposits on behalf of their clients. The Romans followed suit, developing a sophisticated network of banks that extended across their vast empire. Roman bankers introduced innovative financial instruments, such as the *chirographum*, a form of promissory note, which played a crucial role in facilitating long-distance trade and enabling complex financial transactions.

The Roman legal system further reinforced the stability and reliability of banking practices by establishing a comprehensive framework for contract enforcement and dispute resolution. This legal structure fostered confidence in economic activity and laid the groundwork for many principles that continue to influence modern banking and commercial law.

3 Naik, J., 'Beginning of the Early Banking Industry in Mesopotamia Civilization from 8th Century B.C.E.' (10 January 2014).

4 Suri, K., Jaggi, Y. and Choudhary, S., 'A Study on Dynamics of Banking Sector in India' (2022) 9(8) *International Journal of Multidisciplinary Research and Development* 29, p. 31.

5 "*Interest on money-loans stipulated at one time shall not exceed the double; in the case of grains, fruits, wool and beasts of burden, it shall not go beyond the quintuple*". Ibid., Verse 8.151.

The Roman financial practices also contributed to the fundamental banking lexicon: the term "**credit**" originates from the Latin word "*creditum*", meaning "that which is entrusted or loaned", derived from "*credere*", meaning "to trust or entrust". This concept extends beyond a mere exchange of money for a future promise of repayment; it functions as a "currency of reputation",[6] serving as a mechanism through which trust is conveyed to others.

Following the decline of the Roman Empire, banking activities in Europe experienced a downturn, but they revived in the Middle Ages. During this period of time, both custom and law influenced the forms of payment that were widely accepted as media of exchange. While paper money was used in China, Europe relied predominantly on metallic coinage, with governments designating certain coins as legal tender. Banking in Europe evolved not from moneylending or pawnbroking but from the manual exchange of coins. With their deep knowledge of both local and foreign currencies, moneychangers could distinguish legitimate from counterfeit coins, assess their value, and manage exchange rates.

These early bankers managed to bring order in the chaotic world of currency by creating bank currency – a more reliable alternative to physical coins. When coins were deposited, the banker evaluated them based on weight and quality, crediting the depositor's account with an agreed-upon value in the local money of account. This credit constituted a claim that could be paid out in specie or transferred to another party. Credit transfers allowed for the circulation of money without the need for physical coinage to change hands, facilitating trade and reducing the risks associated with transporting large sums of money. This fiduciary system relied on the banker's solvency.

This "faith" was, in international banking transactions, quite fittingly placed in the Knights Templar, a religious military order. Pilgrims travelling to the Holy Land could deposit money with the Templars at one location and receive a letter of credit, which could be redeemed at another Templar commandery along their journey.[7] The Templars' network of commanderies provided a secure method for transferring funds across long distances, laying the groundwork for modern letters of credit used in international trade today.[8] This early form of international banking was a critical innovation in the mediaeval period.

A **letter of credit** (also referred to as a documentary credit) is a contractual undertaking by a bank to make payment to a seller in connection with the export of specified goods upon presentation of stipulated documents relating to those goods. It is issued at the request of the buyer (the *applicant*) in favour of the seller (the *beneficiary*). The issuing bank undertakes this obligation independently of the underlying contract of sale. Today, letters of credit are typically governed by the Uniform Customs and Practice for Documentary Credits, 2007 Revision, International Chamber of Commerce (ICC) Publication No. 600 (UCP 600).

6 Muldrew, 'Interpreting the Market: The Ethics of Credit and Community Relations in Early Modern England' (May 1993) 18(2) *Social History* 173.
7 Ferris, E., 'The Financial Relations of the Knights Templars to the English Crown' (1902) 8(1) *The American Historical Review* 1, p. 1.
8 Buckley, R. and Nixon, J., 'The Role of Reputation in Banking' (2009) *UNSWLRS* 18, p. 38.

While the Knights Templar supported pilgrims in their travels to Jerusalem, trade and commerce in the Italian peninsula flourished. This financial success was built upon republican political institutions and the rule of law.[9]

3 THE ORIGINS AND EVOLUTION OF BANKING IN THE ITALIAN CITY-STATES

The Italian city-states of Venice, Florence, and, at a later stage, Genoa were instrumental in the development of modern banking practices. The rise of banking in these cities was driven by the growth of international trade, as merchants required secure and efficient financial systems to manage the increasingly complex transactions that characterised commerce during the Middle Ages and Renaissance periods. The Italian banking systems not only facilitated the movement of goods but also paved the way for the development of financial instruments that are still in use today, such as bills of exchange, giro accounts, letters of credit, and public banks.

The term **bankruptcy** has its origins in the Latin phrase "banca rupta", which translates to "broken bench". This phrase traces back to the Italian city-states' banking system, where money changers and bankers would conduct their business on benches (banca) in the marketplace. If a banker or money changer were unable to meet their financial obligations or were found insolvent, their bench would be physically broken as a public sign of their failure. This symbolic act signalled that the individual could no longer operate, as their "bench" was literally and figuratively "broken".

This visual representation of failure not only closed the banker's business but also served as a warning to others about the importance of financial soundness and integrity.

3.1 The Development of Banking in Venice

Venice is regarded as one of the earliest centres of modern banking and as Europe's leading laboratory for lending practices.[10] It is not coincidental that this is the city where the most famous moneylender (Shylock in Shakespeare's The Merchant of Venice) in Western literature was based.

Known for its extensive trading networks, Venice established itself as a centre for commerce as early as the 12th century. Merchants from across Europe and the Mediterranean would gather there to trade, creating the need for a secure method of handling money across long distances. Venetian merchants began to rely on money changers (known as *campsores*) to exchange currencies and facilitate transactions between different regions.

The introduction of Arabic numerals to Venice around the 13th century revolutionised the city's financial and commercial practices. These numerals, which replaced the cumbersome Roman system, allowed for more efficient calculations, improving accounting, trade, and banking. The ability to calculate interest, loans, and exchanges quickly led to the rise of

9 Fratianni, M. and Spinelli, F., 'Italian City-States and Financial Evolution' (2006) 10 *European Review of Economic History* 262.

10 Ferguson, N., *The Ascent of Money: A Financial History of the World* (The Penguin Press, 2008), p. 34.

more sophisticated financial institutions. Classical and biblical moral discourses on debt were progressively abandoned also as a result of "the faceless relations of algebra".[11]

By the late 13th century, the role of money changers had evolved into something closer to modern banking. Money changers accepted deposits from merchants and issued credit, creating a system whereby claims to these deposits could be transferred between parties without the physical exchange of coinage. The *moneta di banco*, or bank money, was a widely used substitute for minted coin in Venice and traditionally represented a credit balance held with a local banker, which could be transferred for the benefit of another account. Over time, these money changers evolved into full-fledged *banchieri*, or bankers, whose primary role was to facilitate credit transfers and maintain detailed records of transactions. These bankers were often private individuals, meaning that the transfer process, known as *scritta*, had a fiduciary[12] character and required the recipient's consent. Furthermore, such transfers had to be backed by a real deposit made by the payer in actual money, ensuring the integrity and reliability of the system.

One of the most significant contributions to banking was the development of **double-entry accounting** or accounting according to the Venetian method (*el modo de Venegia* or *alla viniziana*).[13] This system was first documented by the Italian mathematician Luca Pacioli in his 1494 work *Summa de Arithmetica, Geometria, Proportioni et Proportionalità*. His mathematical encyclopaedia, which contains his "Venetian" bookkeeping treatise, revolutionised the way financial transactions were recorded.[14]

As Pacioli noted, double-entry accounting requires that: "*you shall make two different entries in the ledger; that is one in the debit and the other in the credit*".[15]

The adoption of double-entry accounting in Venice had a profound impact on the city's banking system, as it allowed banks to maintain accurate and reliable records of their transactions; as, once again, Pacioli puts it: "*good written evidence as to debits and credits in the handwriting of the clerks in those institutions*".[16] This was particularly important in a city where international trade was a key part of the economy, and this system provided a theoretical explanation of economic events. Double-entry accounting became the standard for businesses and banks worldwide and remains fundamental to modern financial reporting. The ability to maintain clear and transparent financial records helped build trust among merchants and investors, both in Venice and abroad. Over time, this "Venetian" method it enabled capitalism to flourish, changing the economies of the world forever.[17]

All financial records rely on double-entry bookkeeping; such records are employed for the preparation of **financial statements,** which, in turn, are concerned with classifying, measuring, and recording the transactions of a business.

11 Appleby, J., *Economic Thought and Ideology in Seventeenth-Century England* (Princeton University Press, 1978).

12 The etymology of this word also comes from Latin fiduciarius "entrusted, held in trust" and from fiducia "trust, confidence, reliance" in law, from the root of fidere "to trust". In Roman law, fiducia was "a right transferred in trust" in the paper currency sense since its value depended on the trust of the public.

13 Anonymous, 'The Oldest Example of Double-Entry Bookkeeping' (1930) 4(4) *Bulletin of the Business Historical Society* 11–13.

14 Gleeson-White, J., *Double Entry: How the Merchants of Venice Created Modern Finance* (W.W. Norton & Co, 2012), p. 108.

15 Gleeson-White, J., *Double Entry: How the Merchants of Venice Created Modern Finance* (W.W. Norton & Co, 2012), p. 104.

16 Gleeson-White, J., *Double Entry: How the Merchants of Venice Created Modern Finance* (W.W. Norton & Co, 2012), p. 107.

17 Gleeson-White, J., *Double Entry: How the Merchants of Venice Created Modern Finance* (W.W. Norton & Co, 2012), p. 8.

Venetian bankers were also instrumental in refining the use of bills of exchange. These financial instruments allowed merchants to transfer large sums of money across long distances without the need for transporting coinage, which was both risky and cumbersome. The bill of exchange functioned as a credit instrument that could be redeemed at different locations, making international trade safer and more efficient. This innovation became one of the most important tools for cross-border trade in Europe.

A **bill of exchange** is an unconditional order in writing, addressed by one person to another, signed by the person giving it, requiring the person to whom it is addressed to pay on demand or at a fixed or determinable future time a sum certain in money to or to the order of a specified person, or to bearer.[18]

The chartering of the Banco di Rialto in 1587 marked a turning point in the history of banking. The Banco di Rialto was operated under the authority of the Venetian Senate, providing a formal and secure structure for the deposit and transfer of funds. Unlike private family-run banks, the Banco di Rialto was a public institution, giving it an added layer of legitimacy and security.[19] This model of state-backed banking became influential across Europe, inspiring similar institutions in cities like Amsterdam and London.

The Banco di Rialto contributed to the development of ledger-based banking, or giro banking. Giro banking allowed merchants to transfer funds between accounts without the physical exchange of money, using ledgers (*partite*) maintained by the bank. The giro system between *partite* – the process of crediting and debiting accounts held by different operators – was protected and guaranteed by the State. This ensured that transactions were conducted in high-quality currency of the correct weight, thereby maintaining trust and stability in financial dealings. As these *partite* were used for payments arising from exchange transactions, the purchase of goods, and other commercial activities, the *moneta di banco* became a widely accepted means of expressing the value of financial obligations, serving both public institutions and private merchants in their commercial transactions.[20]

Giro banking became the precursor to modern payment systems and was crucial in reducing transaction times and costs.[21]

Banco Giro[22] was established in 1619 to manage Venice's floating debt. The Banco Giro functioned as an issuing bank, much like the later Bank of England, but with one key distinction. While the Bank of England issued banknotes, the Banco Giro issued bookkeeping entries as a form of money transfer and credit settlement. The deposits held at the Banco Giro, similar to

18 Section 3(1) of the Bills of Exchange Act 1882, UK Public General Acts 1882 c. 61 (Regnal. 45_and_46_Vict).

19 For historical insights on the Venetian banking system and its regulatory frameworks, see Mueller, R., *The Venetian Money Market: Banks, Panics, and the Public Debt, 1200–1500* (Johns Hopkins University Press, 2019).

20 Ammanati, F., 'Notes on Venetian Monetary History from the Mediaeval to the Early Modern Era' in *Competition in the European Book Market* in Nuovo, A., Proot, J. and Booton, D. (eds.) (The Golden Compasses, 2023), p. 201.

21 Lane, F., 'Venetian Bankers, 1496–1533: A Study in the Early Stages of Deposit Banking' (1937) 45(2) *Journal of Political Economy* 187–206, p. 187.

22 To date the porch, that surrounds half of Campo San Giacomo in the Rialto neighborhood in Venice is named (*sotoportego del Banco Giro*) after the presence of the headquarters of the public bank, known as Banco Giro.

those at the Banco di Rialto, carried a premium over physical currency, reflecting the same underlying economic principles that favoured stable, reliable bank money over fluctuating coinage.[23]

3.2 Regulation of Banking in Venice

The regulation of banking in Venice was initially informal, relying on customs and the oversight of local magistrates. However, as commerce became more complex, the need for formal regulation grew. For commercial banks, the authority to license bankers in Venice fell under the jurisdiction of the *Consoli dei Mercanti*, who were also responsible for overseeing bankruptcies and the liquidation of banks. Notably, the records in a banker's account books, particularly their journal, were treated as legal evidence by the *Consoli* and other courts. These entries were regarded with the same weight as notarial contracts or even court judgments.[24] Since banking was critical to Venice's flourishing commerce, the government recognised the need for prudential regulation to ensure stability and trust in its financial institutions. The justification for a stringent set of rules was and still is firmly rooted in the significant damage that banking crises can inflict on the wider economic environment.[25]

Prudential regulation refers to the set of laws, rules, and frameworks designed to ensure the stability and soundness of the financial system by managing risks taken by banks and financial institutions. The primary objective is to safeguard depositors, maintain financial stability, and prevent bank failures that could lead to broader economic crises.

In 1270, bankers were required to post bonds, though this mandate was allowed to lapse over time and was reintroduced decisively in 1455. A 1322 law highlights legislative concern over the fact that banks did not maintain 100% reserves (they were practising fractional reserve banking), prompting a rule that required bankers to redeem deposits on demand within three days and in cash rather than with claims on other banks.[26]

Unlike Siena and Florence, Venice did not have limited liability for bankers, meaning that a banker's personal assets provided additional security beyond the bond. However, this was still deemed inadequate. In 1404, a law limited bankers' investments to 150% of their assessed assets (a debt-to-equity ratio in modern finance terminology), though it had little impact.

In modern contexts, that proportion would be perceived as very conservative as, unlike most other industries, a bank's balance sheet is highly **leveraged**: a bank's liabilities consist almost exclusively of debt with a low percentage of their own capital.[27]

23 Fratianni, M. 'The Evolutionary Chain of International Financial Centers' *MoFiR Working Paper No. 6* (2008), p. 10.

24 A comparable situation exists in modern-day UK law, where section 3 of the Bankers' Books Evidence Act of 1879 allows copies of entries from a banker's book to be accepted as prima facie evidence in legal proceedings.

25 Mahmood, S. K., 'The Long and Short of U.S. Bank Regulations: From the Great Depression to the 2023 Bank Failures' *SSRN* (30 April 2024), available at https://ssrn.com/abstract=4571248 or http://dx.doi.org/10.2139/ssrn.4571248 (accessed in February 2025), p. 1.

26 Martin, F., *Money* (Vintage Books, 2013), p. 105.

27 Kern, A., *Principles of Banking Regulation* (Cambridge University Press, 2019) at [4.2].

Other laws prohibited bankers from trading in commodities or lending for silver purchases, but these restrictions proved difficult to enforce.

By the 14th century, the Venetian Senate had taken a more active role in overseeing banking activities. However, until 1524, Venice lacked comprehensive internal or external regulation and supervision of the banking system. That year, the *Provveditori sopra Banchi* (bank supervisors) was established in response to the rapid expansion of banks and the devaluation of bank money relative to cash. In 1526, prudential regulations were tightened by assigning one supervisor per bank, tasked with inspecting the banks daily and ensuring parity between bank money and cash. Bankers were required to pay depositors on demand, in cash, without delay. Bank money was also declared legal tender, except when specific agreements for "out of bank" payments were stipulated.

The establishment of the Banco di Rialto was also a response to regulatory needs. Banco di Rialto operated under strict government oversight, ensuring that it held sufficient reserves to meet depositor demands. This was a key regulatory requirement to prevent bank runs and protect the integrity of the banking system. The bank's public status and the oversight provided by the Venetian government helped ensure its stability, making it a model for public banking systems across Europe.

The Importance of Legal Certainty in Venetian Banking

The link between law and finance is inextricable. It would not be possible to conceive a financial system or a financial instrument without a legal system to support it or a legal infrastructure to enable the enforcement of related rights.

Venice's rise as a major financial centre during the Middle Ages and Renaissance was underpinned by the concept of legal certainty[28] in its banking and commercial transactions. The stability of Venetian law was crucial in attracting merchants and bankers from across Europe and the Mediterranean, fostering a thriving financial environment. Economic activity, productivity, and innovation can only flourish in an environment that guarantees secure property rights and effective freedom of contract, as Adam Smith observed more than two centuries ago.[29] Without legal certainty, as Shakespeare would put it, the commercial and financial foundations of Venice will crumble: *"Will much impeach the justice of the state/Since that the trade and profit of the city/consisteth of all nations"*.[30]

Venetian regulators also provided comprehensive protections for both creditors and debtors, reducing the risks associated with lending and borrowing. Creditors benefited from legal certainty, as they could lend money with confidence and assured that the courts would enforce repayment obligations. At the same time, debtors were safeguarded against arbitrary or excessive demands from lenders, ensuring that the legal system maintained a balanced approach to financial transactions.

28 The legal stability of the Venetian government (run by merchants for merchants) relying on "*a prince not subject to the variations and failures that arise from death, but a constant and immortal senate; a prince who rules himself by laws and caution rather than violence and desires*". Speech of Senator Tommaso Contarini in Velde, F., 'Early Public Banks' (2014) *SSRN Electronic Journal* 19.

29 Lord Neuberger's inaugural Harbour Lecture at Gray's Inn: From barretry, maintenance and champerty to litigation funding [2013] *UKSpeech* 130508 (8 May 2013), at [9].

30 Act 3, Scene 3 of Shakespeare's The Merchant of Venice.

The city's commitment to legal certainty and regulatory stability allowed it to maintain its status as a leading financial centre well into the 16th century.[31] It was this predictability and transparency that contributed to the long-term success of Venetian banking institutions and set an early standard for modern financial systems.

3.3 Florence: The Rise of the Medici Bank

Florence was another key player in the development of modern banking, particularly through the rise of the Medici family, whose banking dynasty became one of the most powerful in Europe. The Medici Bank, founded in 1397 by Giovanni di Bicci de' Medici, expanded rapidly, establishing branches in major European cities such as London, Brussels, Rome, and Paris. Such a bank was unique in its use of the holding company structure, where different branches were semi-independent but linked through shared ownership and control.[32] This system allowed the Medici family to manage a vast financial empire while minimising risk by decentralising operations.

The success of the Medici Bank was due not only to its innovative organisational structure but also to its ability to serve both private merchants and powerful rulers. They lent to princes, monarchs, and the Church, including Pope John XXIII, which solidified their influence within both religious and political circles.

The Medici Bank's fall in the late 15th century was precipitated by a combination of poor management, bad debts, and political unrest. However, its legacy as a pioneer of modern banking practices, particularly in terms of its organisational structure and the use of financial instruments, set the foundations for modern banking systems and played a key role in the development of the Renaissance economy.

Banca Grossa

In the Florentine banking system, the term "*banca grossa*" referred to the large-scale commercial banks that operated in Florence during the late Middle Ages and the Renaissance. Their extensive networks, significant financial resources, and close ties to ruling elites made them integral to the economic and political landscape of the time.

One of the defining characteristics of *banca grossa* was their international reach. These institutions established **branches** in major European cities such as London, Bruges, Avignon, and Venice, enabling them to engage in cross-border trade finance, currency exchange, and the management of international remittances. This vast network allowed them to facilitate global commerce and provide essential financial services to merchants, governments, and religious institutions across Europe.

Unlike smaller banks that primarily focused on local trade and small-scale lending, *banca grossa* were engaged in large-scale financial operations. They provided credit to monarchs, popes, and wealthy merchants, financed long-distance trade, and acted as moneylenders to governments, funding military campaigns and infrastructure projects.

31 "As Shakespeare wrote, "*there is no power in Venice can alter a decree established: "twill be recorded for a precedent, and many an error by the same example will rush into the state*". Opinion of Advocate General Colomer in *Regione Siciliana v Commission (Regional policy)* [2006] EUECJ C-417/04 at [52].

32 Parks, T., *Medici Money: Banking, Metaphysics and Art in Fifteenth-Century Florence* (Profile Books, 2006), p. 32.

These banks dealt with substantial sums of money and played a crucial role in the trade of wool, silk, and precious metals, which were key commodities in the mediaeval economy.

Structurally, *banca grossa* operated as partnerships, with wealthy merchants pooling their resources to invest in large ventures. This collective investment model was a precursor to modern companies, where multiple investors held equity stakes in a financial institution. Profits were shared among partners. This approach enabled these banks to support ambitious commercial and political enterprises while mitigating financial exposure.

Beyond their commercial activities, these banks had a profound impact on politics and society. The families (Bardi, Peruzzi, and Medici) that owned and managed *banca grossa* were not merely financial powerhouses but also major political players. The Medici family, for example, used their banking success to secure political dominance in Florence, influencing governance and patronising art, architecture, and intellectual pursuits that shaped the Renaissance. Their financial network extended to European courts and the papacy, giving them unprecedented control over economic and political affairs.

Despite their success, many *banca grossa* ultimately collapsed due to a combination of factors. One of the primary causes was default on loans, as seen in the 14th-century bankruptcies of the Peruzzi and Bardi banks, which suffered catastrophic losses after Edward III of England failed to repay large loans. In addition to loan defaults, these banks were highly exposed to market risks, including fluctuations in international trade, political instability, and economic crises. Wars, shifting trade routes, and financial mismanagement created conditions that even these large institutions struggled to withstand. Despite their ultimate decline, their influence on banking, finance, and economic governance endured. Their legacy is still reflected in the global banking practices of today.

3.4 Genoa: The Casa di San Giorgio

In Genoa, the development of banking was driven by the need to manage public and private debt. The Casa di San Giorgio, founded in 1407, was one of the earliest public banks and played a critical role in managing the city's finances. Originally established to oversee the collection of taxes and manage Genoa's public debt, it gradually expanded into commercial banking. It issued bills of exchange and provided credit to merchants, much like its counterparts in Venice and Florence.[33]

The Casa di San Giorgio was notable for its governance structure, which allowed creditors to participate in the management of the institution. This system of shared governance gave the bank a level of stability that many privately-owned banks lacked. Moreover, it mastered important financial practices, such as the use of Venetian ledger-based accounting, which became standard practice in European banking.[34]

33 Roberds, W. and Velde, F. R., 'Early Public Banks' *FRB Atlanta Working Paper No. 2014–9* (1 August 2014), p. 9.

34 Arrighi, G., *The Long Twentieth Century: Money, Power, and the Origins of Our Times* (Verso, 2010), p. 116.

The concepts of *depositum regulare* and *depositum irregulare* were fundamental to early banking, as they defined the legal and practical framework governing bank deposits. These distinctions clarified the rights and obligations of both depositors and bankers, influencing the evolution of banking law.[35]

A *depositum regulare* referred to a deposit in which the depositor retained full ownership of the specific assets, usually coins, placed with the bank for safekeeping. The banker, acting as a custodian, was prohibited from using the deposited assets for any other purpose. The depositor retained the right to reclaim the exact same assets at any time, and the banker was held liable for any loss or damage unless it occurred through no fault of their own, such as in cases of theft without negligence.

By contrast, a *depositum irregulare* involved the deposit of fungible assets, typically money, which the banker was permitted to use. In this arrangement, the ownership of the money is transferred to the bank, allowing it to lend or invest the funds as part of its normal business operations. However, the bank was legally bound to repay the equivalent value to the depositor upon demand rather than the exact same coins. This effectively meant that the depositor was extending a loan to the bank, trusting that their funds would be returned when required.

The distinction between these two forms of deposit was crucial in early banking, as it established who bore the risk associated with the deposited assets. In a *depositum regulare*, the banker was responsible for safeguarding the assets, bearing the risk of loss if they failed to protect them. In a *depositum irregulare*, however, the depositor assumed a different kind of risk, as the bank owned and used the funds, meaning that the depositor's ability to reclaim their money depended on the bank's financial stability.

These principles remain highly relevant in modern banking law. The concept of custody of assets seen in *depositum regulare* is reflected in services such as safety deposit boxes or securities custodian services, where banks safeguard customers' valuables without using them. Meanwhile, *depositum irregulare* was the precursor of modern-day demand deposits, where customers deposit money into bank accounts, allowing banks to utilise those funds while maintaining the obligation to repay the equivalent sum on demand.

4 THE PROHIBITION ON CHARGING INTEREST (USURY)

One of the most significant legal and moral issues in the early development of banking was the prohibition against charging interest, known as usury. The Greek philosopher Aristotle argued that usury was both unproductive and unnatural and, therefore, inherently unjust.[36] While he acknowledged that the creation and accumulation of wealth should be encouraged, he maintained that money should not be lent solely for the purpose of generating profit. Instead, he viewed money as a neutral medium of exchange rather than a commodity to be

35 Mueller, R., *The Venetian Money Market: Banks, Panics, and the Public Debt, 1200–1500* (Johns Hopkins University Press, 2019), p. 10.

36 "*As this is so, usury is most reasonably hated, because its gain comes from money itself and not from that for the sake of which money was invented. For money was brought into existence for the purpose of exchange, but interest increases the amount of the money itself. . . consequently this form of the business of getting wealth is of all forms the most contrary to nature*". Aristotle, *Politics* 1.1258b.

exploited for financial gain.[37] Under Roman law, while simple interest was available in a variety of situations, such as late payment of a debt, interest upon interest was (under Justinian) forbidden in all circumstances.[38]

After the fall of the Roman Empire, religious doctrine considered the charging of interest on loans as inherently exploitative.[39] This concept was deeply embedded in Christianity, Islam, and Judaism, with theological arguments against profiting from another person's misfortune or financial need. In many cases, these prohibitions had to be circumvented in creative ways, especially in commercial hubs like Venice, Florence, and later Amsterdam and London, where trade could not function efficiently without some form of interest-bearing loans.

4.1 Christian Doctrines Against Usury

The Church was a major force behind the prohibition of usury in Europe throughout the Middle Ages. Based on a combination of Biblical injunctions and the writings of Aristotle and Thomas Aquinas,[40] the Church viewed the charging of interest as sinful. Following Aristotle's teaching, it was argued that money was barren and could not, by its nature, increase.[41] Charging interest was, therefore, considered unnatural, as it made money generated more money without labour or productive activity. These philosophical and theological positions were echoed in the Canon Law of the Church, which explicitly forbade usury.

The Third Lateran Council (1179) and the Second Council of Lyon (1274) both reinforced the Church's stance, decreeing that anyone found guilty of usury would be excommunicated and barred from receiving a Christian burial. This strict interpretation made the practice of banking difficult for Christians, leading to the marginalisation of banking activities to certain groups, such as Jewish lenders, who were not bound by the same restrictions when lending to individuals belonging to different faiths.

Jewish moneylenders, such as Shylock in The Merchant of Venice, could avail themselves of an exemption from the biblical prohibition of usury outlined, amongst others, in Exodus 22:25 where it says: "*If you lend money to any of my people with you who is poor, you shall not be like a moneylender to him, and you shall not exact interest from him*". Or in Deuteronomy, "*Thou shalt not lend upon usury to thy brother; usury of money; usury of victuals; usury of anything that is lent upon usury*". (23:19). While these verses strictly prohibited profiting from loans among brethren, a significant loophole appeared in Deuteronomy 23:20, offering a strategic avenue for Jewish moneylenders. The verse states,

37 Applegarth, P., 'Credit and Unconscionability – the Rise and Fall of Statutes', speech delivered for the WA Lee Equity Lecture 2020, Supreme Court of Queensland, Brisbane (QSC)' (2020) *Queensland Judicial Scholarship* 13, p. 3.

38 Dig. 22.1.29; Cod. 2.11.20; Cod. 4.32.28.

39 In Early Mediaeval India (A.D. 400-1200), it was recommended that interest on secured loans be capped at 15% per annum, while interest on unsecured loans could be charged up to 60% per annum. In China, the maximum permissible rate of interest was 3% per month, and the punishment for exceeding this limit was between 40 and 100 strokes with a light cane.

40 "*Of the Sin of Usury, Which is Committed in Loans: To take usury for money lent is unjust in itself, because this is to sell what does not exist, and this evidently leads to inequality which is contrary to justice*". St. Thomas Aquinas, Summa Theologica, trans. Fathers of the English Dominican Province (R. T. Washburne, Ltd., 1918), pp. 330–340, reprinted in Cave, R. C. and Coulson, H. H., *A Source Book for Mediaeval Economic History* (The Bruce Publishing Co., 1936; reprint ed., Biblo & Tannen, 1965), p. 182.

41 McKeon, R. (ed.), *The Basic Works of Aristotle* (Modern Library, 2009), p. 1141.

Unto a stranger thou mayest lend upon usury; but unto thy brother thou shalt not lend upon usury, that the Lord thy God may bless thee in all that thou settest thine hand to in the land whither thou goest to possess it.

This scriptural provision allowed for the extension of interest-bearing loans to non-Jews, providing a way for certain European Jews to engage in such financial practices despite being viewed with disapproval within their own community.

However, even Christian money lenders were instrumental in circumventing the prohibitions on interest.

Circumventing the Doctrine Against Usury

A fairly common method to circumvent the restrictions on usury in Mediaeval Europe without formally violating Christian principles was the use of **bills of exchange**. Originally designed to facilitate international trade, these financial instruments allowed lenders to include interest in the form of currency exchange fees.[42] For instance, a loan made in one currency could be repaid in another currency at a future date, with the difference in exchange rates concealing the interest charged. Since the transaction technically involved a currency exchange rather than a direct loan with interest, it bypassed the strict prohibitions on usury.[43] The root of the matter was the fact that exchange rates were fluctuating. In theory, a bank could also take a loss. Therefore, as long as there was an element of **risk**, theologians did not recognise this business as a loan with interest but as a currency exchange.[44] The Church did not, however, sanction the practice known as the **dry exchange** (*cambio secco*),[45] which involved a transaction of exchange and re-exchange without any actual money being transferred internationally.[46] This arrangement was perceived as a concealed loan, particularly when the exchange rates were predetermined. The pretence became even more transparent if the supposed third party was either another branch of the same bank or entirely fictitious.[47]

Because of the importance of the usury prohibition, bills of exchange were the most reliable credit instrument for providing liquidity in the most developed commercial and financial centres. They became widely accepted in commercial hubs like Venice, Florence, and Genoa, where economic realities demanded flexible financial instruments despite the moral and legal limitations imposed by the Church.[48]

In England, the "*mediaeval dodges of the prohibition of usury*"[49] gave rise to several financial arrangements that had a lasting influence on the development of the common law.

42 Chancellor, E., *The Price of Time: The Real Story of Interest* (Penguin Books, 2023).
43 de Roover, R., 'What Is Dry Exchange? A Contribution to the Study of English Mercantilism' (1944) 52(3) *Journal of Political Economy* 252.
44 Parks, T., *Medici Money: Banking, Metaphysics and Art in Fifteenth-Century Florence* (Profile Books, 2006), pp. 43–45.
45 de Roover, R., 'What Is Dry Exchange? A Contribution to the Study of English Mercantilism' (1944) 52(3) *Journal of Political Economy* 252.
46 Marsilio, C., 'Four Times a Year for So Many Years': The Italian Exchange Fairs during the 16th–17th Century: Comparing Financial Institutions' (2010) 36(2) *Bankhistorisches Archiv. Banking and Finance in Historical Perspective* 151–165.
47 Spufford, P., *Handbook of Mediaeval Exchange* (The Royal Historical Society, 1986).
48 Parks, T., *Medici Money: Banking, Metaphysics and Art in Fifteenth-Century Florence* (Profile Books, 2006), pp. 43–45.
49 Contract and Commercial Law Committee New Zealand, Working paper on the reform of the Moneylenders Act 1908 [1971] *NZCCLRCom* 7 at [13] and [14].

One such device was the mortgage or gage, which allowed a debtor to transfer land to a financier for an agreed period without paying rent. In return, the financier would lease the land back to the debtor for a similar period, usually one year less than the term of the mortgage, at an agreed rent. Although this rent was often calculated as a percentage of the loan amount, it was not formally classified as interest.[50] This structure effectively disguised interest payments within a land transaction, enabling lenders to circumvent usury laws.

Another common method involved concealing a loan within a fictitious sale. Under this arrangement, a debtor would purchase a chattel from the financier, providing a promissory note or "writing obligatory" for the full price. At the same time, the debtor would agree to re-sell the chattel back to the financier at a lower price. The difference between the two amounts effectively functioned as interest on the loan. This practice became widespread, prompting legislative intervention.

To prevent such disguised lending, section 2 of the Bill Against Usury (37 Hen. VIII, c.9 (1545)) prohibited the sale of goods with an agreement to repurchase them at a lower price within three months. Both of these methods illustrate how early financiers circumvented restrictions on charging interest, influencing the evolution of contract and property law in England.

4.2 The Decline of Usury Laws in Europe

As trade and commerce expanded across Europe during the 16th century, attitudes towards usury began to change. The need for capital to finance long-distance trade, exploration, and emerging industrial ventures made interest-bearing loans essential. Gradually, religious prohibitions were either ignored or adapted to accommodate the changing economic realities. The growth of secular law during this period played a significant role in this shift.

By the 17th century, many European countries had passed laws that allowed for the charging of interest, albeit within certain limits. For example, in England, through the Usury Act of 1571, it was conceded that usury up to 10% would not necessarily be prosecuted. In effect, this was taken as toleration, and although the clergy still preached disapproval, a necessary business practice had been freed from an anachronistic law. The abolition of the usury laws in Britain, through the Usury Laws Repeal Act 1884, can be regarded as a significant milestone in the history of deregulation and a triumph of free-market economic theory, which upheld the principle of freedom of contract.[51] This shift was based on the belief that restricting or prohibiting usury was unnecessary, as market forces were considered sufficient to regulate lending practices.[52] An interesting reading is the Marquess of Lansdowne's comments on the second reading of the Usury Laws Repeal Bill:

> *it might be in the recollection of their Lordships that the inconveniences which had been found to result from the operation of the laws against usury had been so many and so great that, notwithstanding strong prejudices on the*

50 This practice, which persisted until the 16th century, is illustrated in Pollock and Maitland's History of English Law (1898, vol. II, p. 123).

51 Contract and Commercial Law Committee New Zealand, Working paper on the reform of the Moneylenders Act 1908 [1971] *NZCCLRCom* 7 at [7].

52 Lee, J., 'Should Interest Rates Be Regulated or Abolished? The Case for the Abolition of Usury' (2017) 8 *The Western Australian Jurist* 227, p. 230.

> *subject of usury and usurers, it had been found necessary to relax those laws from time to time. At the time of the great commercial failures in the years 1836 and 1837 it was found that the greatest relief which was experienced from the pressure was the result of a provision which had been introduced not long previously into the Act for the renewal of the Bank Charter, enabling the Bank of England to charge a higher rate of interest than those fixed by the usury laws. In consequence of this, ho (the Marquess of Lansdowne) had been induced to take charge of a Bill in that House, by which, with respect to bills of exchange, and other securities of that description, the rate of interest was indefinitely extended. This he had proposed as a permanent Act; but considerable apprehension was expressed as to the probable effect of such a law; and it was only passed at that time as a temporary measure. Nor at the end of that time were these apprehensions removed, although the difficulties and inconveniences which had been anticipated were not found to result from it. People could not be brought to believe that money was as much a commodity as any ordinary article of produce – that its value must be regulated, like the value of any other commodity, by the ordinary principles of demand and supply – and that it was as impossible to fix the rate of interest at which it should be lent as to fix the price at which corn and butter should be sold.*[53]

The shift in legal frameworks paved the way for the modern banking systems that emerged in Europe and laid the foundation for the development of corporate finance and investment banking. By the mid-19th century, most European countries had repealed all legislation against usury, which had traditionally been defined as the charging of excessive interest.

The Merchant of Venice and Early Banking Practices

William Shakespeare's *The Merchant of Venice* provides a dramatic exploration of early banking practices and the moral and legal dilemmas surrounding money lending in the 16th century. At the heart of the play is the character of Shylock, a Jewish moneylender, who enters into a contract with the merchant Antonio, lending him 3,000 ducats under an unusual and extreme condition: if Antonio fails to repay the loan, Shylock will be entitled to a pound of his flesh.[54] This narrative underscores certain aspects of the era's approach to moneylending, contractual obligations, and usury laws, offering insights into the legal and financial landscape of early modern Europe.

During this period, Jewish moneylenders became central figures in financial transactions, often facing discrimination and restrictive legal conditions as a result.

The bond between Shylock and Antonio is a striking illustration of how contracts were legally binding and strictly enforced, even when the terms were morally questionable or extreme. However, the play's resolution, in which the court ultimately denies Shylock's claim, reflects the evolving tension between legal formalism and equitable

53 Hansard, Lords Chambers, Usury Laws Repeal Bill, Volume 135: debated on Monday 24 July 1854, Order of the Day for the Second Reading read, Column 582.

54 "*The Merchant of Venice, which was written at a time when the equitable jurisdiction to relieve against liability under such bonds was in its infancy, relatively speaking; and it certainly did not follow from the fact that a bond was said to be 'forfeit' that relief against forfeiture could be granted. If the law had been that developed in 1597, the story line of the play would have been a flop, because every judge in Venice, applying English law, would have been able to grant Antonio relief against the forfeiture of his pound of flesh. You will recall that Shylock was offered by Bassanio not just the amount of his loan in repayment of the debt but three times the outstanding money, and so the circumstances for granting relief were present, if the bond could be regarded as security for performance of the primary obligation to repay 3000 ducats. But Shylock insists on his right to have performance of the obligation in the bond. The way that the words 'forfeit' and 'penalty' are used gives an indication that these concepts were interchangeable in English law at the time. After Balthazar (Portia in disguise) has expounded on the quality of mercy, Shylock responds: 'My deeds upon my head! I crave the law, The penalty and forfeit of my bond'. Balthazar declares that 'This bond is forfeit' and a little later that 'He shall have nothing but the penalty'; and 20 lines later 'Thou shalt have nothing but the forfeiture'*". in The 8th Annual Property Law Lecture at the School of Law and Social Justice in the University of Liverpool: Mr Justice Fancourt, Vice-Chancellor of the County Palatine of Lancaster: "Forfeiture, Penalties and Damages in Property Law" [2023] *UKSpeech* 6XCWS (10 March 2023) at [9] and [10].

justice in early modern legal systems. This development hints at the growing influence of equity and fairness in contractual disputes, foreshadowing modern legal principles that aim to prevent exploitative or unconscionable agreements.

Antonio's willingness to accept such a perilous contract also underscores the high-risk nature of credit and trade in the period. The play highlights how market risks, economic fluctuations, and reliance on credit made commerce a precarious endeavour, exposing merchants to significant personal and financial vulnerability.

4.3 Islamic Law and Prohibition of Riba

Historically, Islamic banking has been characterised as simply "interest-free" banking, a term that fails to capture its complexity, adaptability, and commercial viability. However, this description does reflect its underlying principles of social justice and protection from exploitation, which are central to its ethical framework. Lending in Islam (*Qarḍ Hasan*) is regarded as a charitable act designed to assist those in financial need. From a legal perspective, once a lender advances funds to a borrower, ownership of the money is transferred, and the lender waives any right to impose an additional charge or interest. The borrower, in turn, is only required to repay the capital sum, ensuring that the transaction remains free from financial exploitation and aligned with Islamic principles of fairness and mutual benefit.[55]

On this basis, the prohibition of *riba* – a term that encompasses all forms of interest – is absolute and continues to this day. Islamic teachings, as set out in the Quran and the Hadith, maintain that charging interest is exploitative and unfair, as it leads to unjust enrichment. The Quran condemns riba explicitly, stating that "*those who devour usury will not stand except as stands one whom Satan by his touch hath driven to madness*" (Quran, 2:275). Moreover, it is provided in Sura II, 275–79 that:

> *Allah has made buying and selling lawful and has made the taking of interest unlawful. Remember, therefore, that he who desists because of the admonition that has come to him from his Lord, may retain what he has received in the past; and his affair is committed to Allah. But those who revert to the practice, they are the inmates of the fire; therein shall they abide. . . . O Ye who believe, be mindful of your duty to Allah and relinquish your claim to what remains of interest, if you are truly believers. But if you do not, then beware of war from the side of Allah and his Messenger. If, however, you desist, you will still have your capital sums; thus you will commit no wrong, nor suffer any wrong yourself.*[56]

Since *riba* generates income without any real labour or productive contribution,[57] it is considered economically unproductive from an Islamic perspective.[58] Therefore, lending for profit or with any conditions that commercially benefit the lender is strictly prohibited in Islamic finance, even when the charge is framed as a penalty for unauthorised borrowing or late payment. This is even more so since, in principle, banks are expected to exercise leniency, allowing debtors to reschedule their debts without imposing further financial burdens, and they should certainly avoid making such charges a routine practice.

55 Farrar, S., 'Accommodating Islamic Banking and Finance in Australia' (2011) 34(1) *UNSW Law Journal* 413, p. 416.

56 In *Beximco Pharmaceuticals Ltd & Ors v Shamil Bank of Bahrain EC* [2004] EWCA Civ 19 at [3].

57 "*Riba, or usury, is prohibited under Islamic law and this prohibition extends beyond the taking of interest on money to obtaining the fruits of another person's labour*". in *Glencore International AG v Metro Trading International Inc* [2000] EWHC 199 (Comm) at [138].

58 Khanfar, N., 'The Applicability of the Islamic Mortgage Contract under English Law' (2009) *Urban Economics & Regional Studies eJournal*.

Islamic finance also interprets opportunistic lending as unfair, particularly in cases where the borrower is an entrepreneur seeking to establish a business since only the lender is guaranteed a financial return. Similarly, lending to a borrower with a particular financial need could be seen as exploitative, as it takes advantage of their vulnerability.[59] This concern for protecting the financially vulnerable is also evident in Islamic prohibitions on gambling (*maysir*) and contracts involving excessive uncertainty (*gharar*). While restrictions on gambling are not unique to Islamic law[60] – as common law also renders gambling contracts unenforceable[61] – as a result of the combined effect of these prohibitions, both conventional insurance and the investment in preferred shares are generally impermissible as they only participate in profit and do not bear loss.[62]

Beyond safeguarding the financially weak and vulnerable, Sharia transactional law (*al-muʿāmalāt*) imposes strict rules to ensure that all financial dealings are fair, transparent, and conducted with scrupulous honesty.

Islamic banking, which continues to operate without interest, has developed alternative financial mechanisms to allow for the growth of capital. Lawful gains can be generated through charging fees, leasing, asset trading, and profit-and-loss investment activities. Islamic banks, therefore, are permitted to charge fees for safeguarding their clients' money under the concept of *waḍīʿah*, for remitting funds through *ḥawālah*, and for acting on behalf of clients in financial transactions under the principle of *wakālah*. These include profit-sharing arrangements, such as *mudarabah* and *musharakah*, where the lender and borrower share the profits and losses of an enterprise, rather than one party receiving fixed interest regardless of the outcome of the venture. Historically, these mechanisms have ensured that banks operated within Sharia-compliant frameworks, generating revenue through permissible financial activities rather than interest-based transactions.

5 THE SPREAD OF BANKING BEYOND ITALY

The banking practices developed in Venice, Florence, and Genoa spread across Europe, influencing the development of banking in other countries.

59 The verses of the Qur'an that refer to loans are Verses 282 and 283 of Chapter 2 Surat Al Baqarah contain references to the notion of fairness and borrower's protection: "*O believers! When you contract a loan for a fixed period of time, commit it to writing. Let the scribe maintain justice between the parties. The scribe should not refuse to write as Allah has taught them to write. They will write what the debtor dictates, bearing Allah in mind and not defrauding the debt*". In *Al Jaber v Al Ibrahim & Anor* [2023] EWHC 2831 (Comm) at [334].

60 Buckley, R., 'Reconceptualizing the Regulation of Global Finance' (2016) 36(2) *Oxford Journal of Legal Studies* 242, p. 246.

61 The Gaming Act 1845 in the United Kingdom made gaming houses illegal and gaming or wagering agreements unenforceable. In the US, the General Obligations Law of the State of New York provided under section 5-401 that "*'[a]ll wagers, bets or stakes, made to depend upon any . . . unknown or contingent event whatever shall be unlawful'. Further, section 5-411 provided that '[a]ll contracts for or on account of any money or property, wagered, bet or staked, as provided in Section 5-401, shall be void'*".

62 See, for example, Fiqh Council of North America, Investing in the Stock Market at [1] and [2] "*A share represents an undivided share in the capital of a corporation, just as it represents an undivided share in its assets and its associated rights, once the capital is converted into tangible items, benefits, rights, debts and so on. Shares are of two types – common shares and preferred shares. Common shares participate in both profit and loss and are permissible. Preferred shares participate only in profit and do not bear loss, and they are impermissible*". Available at https://fiqhcouncil.org/wp-content/uploads/2024/11/Investing-in-the-Stock-Market.pdf (accessed in March 2025).

5.1 Banking in Barcelona

The city of Barcelona also played a critical role in the development of European banking during the Middle Ages. Its prominence as a commercial hub in the Crown of Aragon and its strategic position on the Mediterranean trade routes made it an ideal location for financial innovations. By the 13th century, Barcelona's merchants and financiers were crucial in facilitating commerce throughout the Mediterranean and beyond, especially between the Iberian Peninsula, North Africa, and the East.

A key development in Barcelona's financial history was the establishment of the Taula de Canvi, which was one of the earliest examples of a public bank in Europe outside Italy. Founded in 1401, it was originally designed to support municipal finance, particularly the management of public debt. It was created during a period of economic expansion in Barcelona, where both the city and the Crown of Aragon were heavily involved in trade and warfare, requiring more sophisticated financial infrastructure to manage the increasing flow of money.

The Taula de Canvi operated similarly to the Banco di Rialto in Venice. It received deposits from both individuals and institutions, and it issued letters of credit and bills of exchange, which allowed for the secure transfer of funds across long distances. Its primary function was to facilitate the financing of trade and government expenditures, particularly in the context of military campaigns and naval expeditions. The bank was also tasked with managing public debt, issuing bonds, and securing loans to fund the city's growth and defensive needs.

The Taula de Canvi's governance was closely tied to the municipal authorities of Barcelona, ensuring that its operations were transparent and that its activities were aligned with the city's financial goals. The bank's success contributed to Barcelona's standing as a financial and commercial centre, particularly during the 15th century.

5.2 Amsterdam: The Bank of Amsterdam (Wisselbank)

The Bank of Amsterdam, or Wisselbank, was founded in 1609 and is considered one of the most significant financial institutions in the history of modern banking. As Amsterdam emerged as a critical centre for international trade during the Dutch Golden Age, the establishment of a reliable, state-backed financial institution was essential to support the city's thriving commerce.

Historical Context of the Wisselbank's Establishment

By the early 17th century, Amsterdam had become a vital hub for European trade, attracting merchants from across the globe. However, one of the primary challenges facing the city's economy was the chaotic state of its currency system. Merchants arriving in Amsterdam from different parts of Europe brought with them various coins of differing values, purities, and weights. This made trading cumbersome and opened the door to fraud, as some coins were debased or clipped, meaning their actual value was lower than their face value. These issues created inefficiencies in the settlement of commercial transactions, particularly at a time when Amsterdam's economic activity was flourishing due to its strategic position in European and global trade routes.

The Wisselbank was patterned after the Banco di Rialto in Venice.[63] Its primary function was to simplify the process of currency exchange by accepting deposits of various foreign currencies, which were then converted into bank money – a more stable and reliable unit of account backed by the bank's reserves. This innovation allowed merchants to conduct their business without having to worry about the fluctuating values of foreign coins, significantly streamlining the payment and settlement processes.

Refinement of Centralised Ledger Banking

A key instrument employed by the Bank of Amsterdam was the ledger-based banking system pioneered in Venice (giro banking).[64] Giro banking, as discussed previously, allowed merchants and individuals to deposit their wealth with the bank and then conduct transactions by transferring credits between accounts without the need for physical money to change hands. Depositors received a form of bank money, a stable form of credit that could be transferred on paper, thus avoiding the risks and costs associated with transporting large sums of gold or silver.

Unlike private banks of the time, which were often unstable and prone to collapse, the Wisselbank was backed by the city of Amsterdam, giving it a level of credibility and trust unmatched by other financial institutions. The giro system allowed for transactions to be settled quickly and securely, as payments could be made simply by adjusting entries in the bank's ledgers. As a result, Amsterdam became the financial heart of Europe during much of the 17th century, and the Wisselbank model inspired the establishment of similar institutions in other financial centres, such as Hamburg and London.

The Role of the Wisselbank in Global Trade

During the Dutch Golden Age, the Wisselbank became the banking institution of choice for governments, merchants, and other financial institutions across Europe. Its strong reputation for maintaining sufficient reserves and its policy of strictly regulating withdrawals ensured its stability. The bank money issued by the Wisselbank became a trusted medium of exchange in international trade, and the bank played a key role in financing Dutch commerce. By the mid-17th century, the Dutch controlled a substantial portion of European trade, including the vital routes to the East Indies, and the Wisselbank provided the financial infrastructure necessary to support this dominance.[65]

Additionally, the Wisselbank was a precursor to modern **central banking** institutions. While it did not directly manage monetary policy in the way that central banks do today, its role in regulating the supply of bank money and providing a reliable financial environment had a similar effect. The bank's policies helped mitigate the effects of financial panics and economic downturns, acting as a stabilising force in the broader European economy.

63 Fratianni, M., 'The Evolutionary Chain of International Financial Centers' *MoFiR Working Paper No. 6* (2008), p. 19.

64 "*Giro banks did not come into existence until the late sixteenth century, at Venice in 1584 and at Amsterdam in 1609.*" in Lane, F., 'Venetian Bankers, 1496–1533: A Study in the Early Stages of Deposit Banking' (1937) 45(2) *Journal of Political Economy* 187–206, p. 187.

65 Arrighi, G., *The Long Twentieth Century: Money, Power, and the Origins of Our Times* (Verso, 2010), p. 212.

Decline of the Wisselbank

Despite its early success and its transformative impact on European finance, the Bank of Amsterdam's fortunes began to decline in the late 18th century. The bank's downfall was precipitated by several factors, including poor management of its reserves and the broader political instability caused by the Napoleonic Wars. By this time, newer financial centres, such as London, were beginning to eclipse Amsterdam in terms of economic influence. In addition, the Wisselbank's strict adherence to its bullion reserves became a liability in an era of growing financial innovation, as it was unable to respond flexibly to the changing demands of the global economy.

6 ENGLAND

Banking in England developed relatively late compared to other European countries. While London's goldsmiths[66] are often regarded as the "pioneers of English banking and finance",[67] they did not begin their banking activities until the early 17th century, long after banking had already taken root in other countries in Continental Europe.

Significant modernisation of English banking did not occur until the final decades of the 17th century, spurred by the sweeping changes brought about by the Puritan or bourgeois revolution. This period of rapid economic and political transformation opened new opportunities for banking and finance in England, laying the groundwork for the establishment of more structured banking institutions. The upside to the freer availability of credit was the expansion of England's economy.[68] The downside was financial failure and its effects across the trading classes generally. As commercial relationships became more complex, the need for the law to shore up business confidence grew. Thus, security and order had become obvious goals.[69]

The creation of the Bank of England marked the start of a more centralised monetary system in England in a market that was fragmented. Over time, it played an increasingly critical role in shaping domestic and international finance, advancing the development of modern central banking.

6.1 The Early Role of the Bank of England: Financing Government Debt

The Bank of England was established in 1694, less than 30 years after the creation of Sveriges Riksbank, the world's oldest central bank, to raise funds for the War of the Grand Alliance against France. Chartered by an Act of Parliament as "The Governor and Company of the Bank of England", it was created as a private joint-stock company with limited liability whose

66 Goldsmiths, who had a long-standing tradition of handling bullion, only started engaging in the manual exchange of coins and accepting deposits of money and valuables in the late 16th century. However, these services were rudimentary, as the deposits were typically treated as nonfungible and were offered primarily for safekeeping, rather than for broader financial services. Even then, such banking practices were far from widespread.

67 Powell, T., *The Evolution of the Money Market, 1385–1915: An Historical and Analytical Study of the Rise and Development of Finance as a Centralised, Coordinated Force* (1915).

68 Kern, A., *Principles of Banking Regulation* (Cambridge University Press, 2019) at [1.7].

69 Quilter, M., 'Bankruptcy and Order' (2013) 39(1) *Monash University Law Review* 189, p. 199.

charter would be subject to periodic renewal and renegotiation. The Court of Directors, tasked with managing the Bank, had Sir John Houblon, a prominent city merchant and the grandson of a French Huguenot refugee, as its first Governor. His leadership reflected the cosmopolitan nature of London's financial community, which was about to become a major player in global finance.

The Bank's initial capital did not consist of cash; rather, it came from government notes. Subscribers (shareholders) to the Bank, numbering 1,268 in total, had lent the government £1.2 million at an interest rate of 8%, with an additional annuity of £4,000 and the privilege of operating as a banking company for a term of 12 years. These government bonds (or rather bonds of the Bank of England issued on behalf of the government) are called "Gilt-edged" or simply "gilts".[70]

Each renewal of the Bank's charter presented the Crown with an opportunity to negotiate further favourable financing. Investors provided the capital in exchange for the bank's shares and the right to issue banknotes. These banknotes, representing a promise to pay the bearer on demand, were effectively government-backed currency, and their issuance marked the beginning of modern paper money in England.[71]

The Bank of England was granted several privileges that distinguished it from other banks.

During the 18th and 19th centuries, banking in England was subject to the Bubble Act of 1720, which placed significant restrictions on joint-stock companies, including banks. One of the key restrictions was the limitation on the number of partners in a banking firm, which was capped at six partners. This restriction applied to private banks and was meant to prevent the rise of large financial institutions that could pose a systemic risk[72] or challenge the government's control over monetary policy. As a result, most banks operating in England during this period were small, family-owned firms that operated with limited capital.

However, the Bank of England was able to escape this limitation due to its unique charter granted by Parliament. This gave the Bank a significant advantage over private banks, as it could raise large amounts of capital through the issuance of shares. With access to more capital, it was able to engage in large-scale operations and expand its influence, providing a level of stability and liquidity that smaller banks could not match. As the Bank of England grew, it became the primary institution for managing the national debt, overseeing the issuance of currency, and acting as a lender of last resort to other banks,[73] which eventually led to its status as the central bank of England. For example, during the South Sea Bubble crisis in 1720, where speculative investments caused a financial collapse, the Bank of England's ability to issue banknotes provided the Crown with a mechanism to raise funds without

70 Hablutzel, P., 'British Banks' Role in U.K. Capital Markets since the Big Bang' (1992) 68 *Chicago-Kent Law Review* 365.

71 Kern, A., *Principles of Banking Regulation* (Cambridge University Press, 2019) at [1.14].

72 Systemic risk can be defined as "*a risk of disruption to financial services that is caused by an impairment of all or parts of the financial system and has the potential to have serious negative consequences for the real economy*". Guidance to Assess the Systemic Importance of Financial Institutions, Markets and Instruments: Initial Considerations Report to the G-20 Finance Ministers and Central Bank Governors Prepared by Staff of the International Monetary Fund and the Bank for International Settlements, and the Secretariat of the Financial Stability Board October 2009.

73 "*By ensuring that banks had sufficient liquidity to meet requests to exchange bank deposits for cash, the frequency and severity of banking crises were reduced and the resulting system helped bridge the gap between outside and inside money. The gap was further closed by the growing moves towards the central bank's monopoly as sole issuer of banknotes and the legal establishment of state-backed paper money as legal tender*" in Lane, P., 'The Digital Euro: Maintaining the Autonomy of the Monetary System' *Keynote Speech by Philip R. Lane, Member of the Executive Board of the ECB, University College Cork Economics Society Conference 2025*, available at www.ecb.europa.eu/press/key/date/2025/html/ecb.sp250320_1~41c9459722.en.html (accessed in March 2025).

directly taxing citizens, making it an indispensable tool for wartime finance and domestic development.

6.2 The Bank Charter Act and Monopoly on Note Issuance

One of the most important developments in the history of the Bank of England was the Bank Charter Act 1844, which granted the Bank of England the exclusive right to issue banknotes in England and Wales. This act centralised the issuance of currency, giving the Bank of England a virtual monopoly on the creation of money. This move was seen as a way to bring stability to the English monetary system, as previously, many private banks issued their own notes, often leading to over-issuance and inflation.

The Bank Charter Act 1844 also required that the issuance of banknotes be backed by gold reserves, a policy that helped maintain public confidence in the bank's currency. This system of gold-backed currency remained in place until the gold standard was abandoned in the 20th century. The Act marked the beginning of modern central banking in England, establishing the Bank of England as the primary institution responsible for monetary control and regulation of the currency.

6.3 Lender of Last Resort and Financial Stability

As the English economy expanded during the Industrial Revolution, the number of private banks also grew, many of which lacked the liquidity needed to survive financial shocks. The Bank of England began to provide emergency funding to these banks during times of financial crises, thereby preventing bank failures from spreading through the economy. This role was formalised in the mid-19th century after the Overend, Gurney and Company crisis of 1866, during which the Bank of England's intervention was essential in preventing a broader economic collapse. Overend, Gurney & Company, a major discount house, collapsed due to excessive risk-taking. The panic that followed spread to other financial institutions, threatening the stability of the entire banking system. The Bank of England stepped in to provide emergency liquidity, stabilising the market and preventing a broader economic collapse.[74]

Its role as a lender of last resort became a cornerstone of modern central banking policy, with central banks across the world adopting similar practices to stabilise their financial systems. The Bank of England's ability to inject liquidity into the economy during times of crisis helped ensure the stability of the banking sector, particularly during times of war, economic recession, or financial speculation.

The Bank of England established its role as the **lender of last resort**, a pivotal function which ensures that, in times of financial crisis, the Bank provides emergency liquidity to banks facing short-term funding shortages, thus enabling banks with temporary liquidity problems to meet their obligations, thereby preventing bank runs and

74 Sowerbutts, R. and Schneebalg, M., 'The Demise of Overend Gurney' *The Bank of England Quarterly Bulletin* 2016 Q2, available at www.bankofengland.co.uk/-/media/boe/files/quarterly-bulletin/2016/the-demise-of-overend-gurney.pdf (accessed in March 2025).

maintaining trust in the financial system. This role is crucial to modern central banking and has been adopted by central banks worldwide.

The two World Wars posed significant challenges for the Bank of England. During World War I, the Bank played a key role in managing war finance and dealing with the suspension of the gold standard. In World War II, it was instrumental in financing the war effort and stabilising the post-war economy.

On 1 March 1946, the Bank of England was nationalised under the Bank of England Act 1946, which made HM Treasury the sole shareholder; however, the legal continuity of "The Governor and Company of the Bank of England" was under its Royal Charter.[75] The management of the Bank's affairs was entrusted to the Court of Directors, whose members were appointed by the Sovereign.

7 BANKING IN SCOTLAND

Banking in Scotland has a long and distinctive history, marked by the early development of joint-stock banking and the practice of issuing banknotes by private banks.

7.1 The Bank of Scotland and the Royal Bank of Scotland

The Bank of Scotland, established in 1695, was the first bank to be chartered by the Scottish Parliament. Its primary purpose was to promote trade and industry in Scotland by providing loans and facilitating currency exchange. The Royal Bank of Scotland was later founded in 1727 and quickly became one of the largest and most influential banks in the country.

Unlike in England, where the Bank of England held a monopoly on issuing currency, Scottish banks retained the right to issue their own notes, a practice that continues to this day. Further, in contrast with the Bank of England note issue, which was in large denominations, making it unsuitable for commerce other than for large concerns, Scottish banks placed emphasis on credit decisions. The system established by the Bank of Scotland Act of 1695 provided mechanisms for building a substantial basis of credit on a relatively small capital by the issue of paper money.

7.2 The Development of Joint-Stock Banking

Scotland is also credited with the early development of joint-stock banking, which allowed banks to raise large amounts of capital by issuing shares to multiple investors. This innovation made it easier for banks to finance large-scale projects and industrial ventures, and it laid the foundation for the expansion of banking throughout the country. This system was more stable than the English system, which relied heavily on private banks restrained by the six-partner rule until the 19th century.

75 Section 1 of the Act.

Scottish banks also pioneered the development of branch banking by establishing networks of branches throughout the country to serve rural and urban customers better. The Bank of Scotland and the Royal Bank of Scotland appeared to adopt a broadly aligned strategy in this regard. The Royal Bank established an office in Glasgow in 1783, while the Bank of Scotland had, by 1780, opened several branches across various parts of Scotland, including Dumfries, Kelso, Kilmarnock, Inverness, Ayr, and Stirling. In certain locations, these branches operated in direct competition with the offices of provincial banks. The expansion of branch networks enabled both banks to compete effectively in meeting the demand for credit, thereby facilitating the expansion of their bank note issuance.

7.3 The Influence of Scottish Banking on Global Finance

In May 1728, Edinburgh merchant William Hog and his bank devised a novel method to stabilise his working capital. They agreed in advance that, whenever necessary, Hog could temporarily withdraw more funds from his account than he held in it. In doing so, William Hog became the world's first recipient of a cash credit – the precursor to the modern **overdraft**. Conventional loans were required to be secured by some form of asset; however, the newly introduced cash credits depended solely on the personal bond of the applicant, supported by the guarantees of two or more individuals willing to vouch for him. Within the close-knit business community of 1720s Edinburgh, it was relatively straightforward for the bank to ascertain the character and reliability of its clients, and the likelihood of both the applicant and his guarantors simultaneously defaulting was considered to be quite low.[76]

An **overdraft** is an uncommitted revolving loan facility which may be drawn down and repaid by the borrower at any time and is, in almost all cases, repayable on demand (that is, the lending bank may require repayment or a reduction of the facility to zero, at any time).

Scottish banking practices had a significant influence on the development of banking in other parts of the world, particularly in the United States and Canada. Scottish emigrants who settled in North America brought with them their knowledge of banking, and many played important roles in establishing early financial institutions in these regions.

The Scottish Banking System and the Right to Issue Banknotes

One of the most distinctive features of the Scottish banking system is the continued practice of issuing private banknotes. Unlike England, where the Bank of England holds a monopoly on currency issuance, Scottish banks such as the Bank of Scotland, the Royal Bank of Scotland, and Clydesdale Bank have retained the right to issue their own notes. These banknotes are legal tender in Scotland and are widely accepted

76 See www.natwestgroup.com/heritage/history-100/objects-by-theme/serving-our-customers/overdraft-authorisation-1728.html (accessed in March 2025).

throughout the UK. This practice remains a unique aspect of the country's financial heritage.

8 BANKING IN THE UNITED STATES

The development of banking in the United States followed a different trajectory than in Europe, largely due to the country's federal system and the political challenges associated with centralising financial authority.[77]

8.1 The Early US Banking System: State vs. Federal Control

The first attempt to establish a central bank in the United States came with the founding of the First Bank of the United States in 1791, modelled by the Bank of England. However, the Jeffersonian view that a central bank was incompatible with the ideals of a democratic republic led to the dissolution of the bank in 1811. A similar fate befell the Second Bank of the United States, which was chartered in 1816 but was ultimately dismantled in 1836 due to opposition from President Andrew Jackson, who viewed the institution as a threat to states' rights and economic independence.

Following the demise of the Second Bank, from 1837 to 1863, the United States entered a period known as the Free Banking Era, during which state-chartered banks operated independently, often issuing their own currencies. This fragmented system lacked uniform regulation and was prone to instability, culminating in multiple bank failures during the Panic of 1837 and subsequent economic crises. It wasn't until the establishment of the National Banking Act of 1863, which introduced a system of federally chartered banks, that the US banking system began to stabilise.

8.2 The Creation of the Federal Reserve System

The creation of the Federal Reserve System in 1913 was a crucial moment in the development of US banking. It was established in response to the Panic of 1907, which exposed the fragility of the US banking system and the dangers of operating without a central authority to manage liquidity and provide emergency funds. The Federal Reserve's mandate was to act as a lender of last resort, regulate the money supply, and provide a secure financial environment.

The Introduction of Deposit Insurance

New York led an early initiative to protect depositors from banks' failures through the introduction of the New York Safety Fund in 1829.

During the Great Depression in the 1930s, the US banking sector experienced widespread panic as thousands of banks failed, leading to a massive loss of deposits

77 Schweikart, L., 'U.S. Commercial Banking: A Historiographical Survey' (1991) 65(3) *The Business History Review* 606–661.

and public trust. The introduction of deposit insurance was a direct response to this crisis. In 1933, under the Banking Act (also known as the **Glass-Steagall Act**), the US Congress created the Federal Deposit Insurance Corporation (**FDIC**)[78] to provide deposit insurance and restore public confidence in the banking system following numerous bank collapses in the 1920s and 1930s. Initially conceived as a temporary agency, the FDIC was later made permanent through the Banking Act of 1935.

Deposit insurance not only helped restore confidence in the US banking system but also contributed to the resilience of banks during financial crises. The presence of insured deposits reduced the likelihood of bank runs, where large numbers of customers withdraw their funds simultaneously out of fear of insolvency. This innovation remains a feature of the US banking system today, with coverage now extending to $250,000 per depositor per bank, safeguarding individual and business accounts alike.[79]

This mechanism was later adopted globally, serving as a model for deposit insurance systems in various countries around the world.

8.3 The Role of US Investment Banks in Global Finance

Investment banking in the United States grew in prominence during the late 19th and early 20th centuries, with institutions such as J.P. Morgan, Goldman Sachs, and Lehman Brothers playing key roles in financing major industrial projects. These banks helped fuel the rapid expansion of the railroad industry, steel production, and other sectors of the US economy. Investment banks also facilitated the issuance of corporate bonds, helped companies go public, and were instrumental in the consolidation of industries through mergers and acquisitions.

Following the First World War, the United States experienced a period of unprecedented prosperity marked by robust economic growth and record-low unemployment. This era of economic expansion catalysed significant investment in financial markets through various channels. The widespread availability of financial innovations, such as investment trusts, democratised investment opportunities, allowing many Americans to diversify their portfolios and participate in the growing economy. Commercial banking organisations were permitted to function as "universal banks", operating as organisations "*that can engage, directly or through affiliates, in all aspects of the banking, securities, and life insurance businesses*".[80]

In the years leading up to the October 1929 stock market crash, investment trusts raised extraordinary sums of equity. These funds were primarily channelled into securities but were also deployed to finance brokers' loans, which fuelled speculative margin lending. Companies benefitting from increasing profits allocated some of their retained earnings to

78 See www.fdic.gov/90years (accessed in March 2025).

79 In 2010, the FDIC Board of Directors adopted a final rule amending its insurance regulations (12 C.F.R. Part 330) and advertising regulations (12 C.F.R. Part 328) to conform with provisions of the Dodd-Frank Wall Street Reform and Consumer Protection Act, which permanently increased the standard maximum deposit insurance amount from $100,000 to $250,000. As of 1 April 2024, the maximum insurance coverage for a trust owner with five or more beneficiaries is $1,250,000 per owner for all trust accounts (including POD/ITF, revocable, and irrevocable trusts) held at the same bank.

80 See Wilmarth, A. E., Jr., 'The Transformation of the US Financial Services Industry, 1975–2000: Competition, Consolidation, and Increased Risks' (2002) 2 *University of Illinois Law Review* 215 at [223] n. 23.

loans for brokers. At the same time, banks saw substantial growth in deposits, enabling them to extend more credit, a portion of which ultimately financed brokers and speculative trading activities.[81]

As the stock market continued its meteoric rise, it drew in a growing number of speculators, both domestic and international, further inflating the speculative bubble.

In the aftermath of the 1929 crash of the New York Stock Exchange, the US Congress viewed the activities of banks and their securities affiliates as a fundamental cause of the economic boom and crash. Congressman Henry Steagall, for example, declared that the entry of banks into the securities markets produced a situation in which:

> *[o]ur great banking system was diverted from its original purposes into investment activities, and its service devoted to speculation and international high finance. . . . Agriculture, commerce, and industry were forgotten. Bank deposits and credit resources were funneled into the speculative centers of the country for investment in stocks operation and in market speculation. Values were lifted to fictitious levels.*[82]

The collapse of long-term lending relationships amplified the Great Depression.

During the 1930s, these concerns were addressed by insulating commercial banks from investment banking activity, most prominently in the Glass-Steagall Act. This separation ceased to be effective with the passage of the Gramm-Leach-Bliley Act of 1999.

During the 20th century, US investment banks expanded their influence globally. The post-World War II era, in particular, saw the rise of New York as a major global financial centre. American investment banks were key players in international finance, underwriting the reconstruction of Europe and financing the expansion of multinational corporations.

9 FRENCH BANKING

Banking in France began to take shape during the Middle Ages, with the establishment of Italian merchant bankers in Paris, who facilitated loans and financial services for the French monarchy and wealthy nobles. These Italian banks introduced letters of credit and bills of exchange, which made long-distance trade safer and more efficient. These practices were quickly adopted in France, laying the groundwork for the country's early financial systems.

King Louis IX of France, in the 13th century, instituted reforms that regulated money-lending and banking practices, particularly in response to concerns about usury. This early form of financial regulation established the foundation for French banking law, ensuring that banking activities were subject to the oversight of the monarchy.

9.1 The Establishment of Early Public Banks: The Royal Mint and the Banque Générale

One of the earliest public financial institutions in France was the Royal Mint (*Monnaie Royale*), which was established to oversee the minting of coins and ensure the stability of the French currency. The centralisation of currency production helped build trust in French coinage and facilitated domestic and international trade. However, France's reliance on metallic currency – particularly gold and silver – led to periodic shortages of liquidity, especially during times of war.

81 Wilmarth, A. E., Jr., 'The Transformation of the US Financial Services Industry, 1975–2000: Competition, Consolidation, and Increased Risks' (2002) 2 *University of Illinois Law Review* 215.

82 77 Cong. Rec. 3725-26 (remarks of Sen. Glass) at [3835].

The first true bank of France was the Banque Générale, founded in 1716 by John Law, a Scottish adventurer and economic theorist with close ties to the regent of France, the Duke d'Orléans, which was authorised to issue paper money. The following year, John Law established the Compagnie d'Occident (Company of the West), securing exclusive rights to develop France's vast territories in the Mississippi River valley. Over time, Law's enterprise expanded rapidly, acquiring monopolies over the French tobacco trade and the African slave trade. By 1719, under the name **Compagnie des Indes** (Company of the Indies), it had become the sole controller of France's colonial commerce.

Law's influence over France's economy grew significantly. He assumed control of tax collection and the minting of currency, effectively managing both the nation's financial system and foreign trade. Enthusiasm for investment in the Compagnie des Indes soared, pushing share prices from 500 to 18,000 livres – levels wholly disconnected from the company's actual performance. By 1719, Law had issued around 625,000 shares and merged the Banque Générale with the Compagnie. His strategy was to address the enormous national debt inherited from the reign of Louis XIV by exchanging shares in the company for state-issued public securities, known as *billets d'état*, which also surged in value.

This led to a period of speculation and a broader stock market boom across Europe. The French government capitalised on the public's enthusiasm by printing large quantities of paper money, which was eagerly accepted by creditors since it could be used to purchase more shares. However, the excessive issuance of paper currency soon triggered rampant inflation. As confidence in the currency and *billets d'état* eroded, both began to decline sharply. At the same time, the anticipated profits from the company's colonial operations failed to materialise, undermining the entire scheme.

By 1720, the intertwined nature of the company's finances and the state's economic policy led to a dramatic collapse, causing widespread panic and a loss of trust in paper money. This event set back the development of central banking in France for decades.[83] The substantial debts accumulated by the Compagnie and the Banque were assumed by the French state, which was forced to raise taxes in order to service the liabilities. The episode remains one of the earliest and most striking examples of speculative excess and financial instability in modern economic history.

9.2 The Banque de France: A Central Pillar of French Banking

The modernisation of French banking began with the creation of the Banque de France in 1800 by Napoleon Bonaparte. The primary purpose of the bank was to stabilise the French currency following the economic turbulence of the French Revolution. The Banque de France was tasked with issuing banknotes, managing the money supply, and acting as the government's banker. Over time, it became the central institution responsible for regulating the French banking system.[84]

Initially, the Banque de France was a private entity, with shares owned by wealthy French families and financial institutions. However, it operated under close government supervision, and Napoleon granted it a monopoly on the issuance of banknotes in Paris. Over the course of the 19th century, the bank expanded its note-issuing powers across the country, eventually gaining a nationwide monopoly on banknote issuance by 1848.

83 Chancellor, E., *The Price of Time: The Real Story of Interest* (Penguin Books, 2023).
84 Ferguson, N., *The Ascent of Money: A Financial History of the World* (The Penguin Press, 2008), p. 82.

The Banque de France played a role in bringing financial stability to the French economy during times of financial crisis, such as the Panic of 1847 when a global economic downturn led to widespread financial instability. The bank provided liquidity to French financial institutions, acting as a lender of last resort, a role that would become central to modern central banking. Its ability to maintain public confidence in the French currency made it a crucial institution in the development of the modern financial system.

In the late 19th century, the Banque de France expanded its powers further, becoming an essential part of the international gold standard. The bank's role in managing foreign exchange reserves and maintaining the value of the franc was key to its participation in the global financial system. By the 20th century, the Banque de France had evolved into a full-fledged central bank responsible for regulating the French financial system, managing inflation, and overseeing monetary policy.

The Banque de France's influence extended well beyond France, particularly in the interwar period. After World War I, France, like many other countries, faced severe economic challenges, including war debt and hyperinflation. The Banque de France played a critical role in restoring the economy by managing the money supply and supporting reconstruction efforts.

9.3 The Rise of French Merchant Banks

During the 19th century, France experienced the rise of merchant banking, spurred by the demands of an industrialising economy and the expansion of global trade. French merchant banks played a crucial role in financing large infrastructure projects, such as railways, and in supporting the growth of industrial enterprises, both within France and internationally. Two key institutions during this period were Crédit Mobilier and Banque de Paris et des Pays-Bas (Paribas).[85]

Founded in 1852 by the Pereire brothers, Crédit Mobilier was one of the most influential investment banks in France during the 19th century. The Pereire brothers, Émile and Isaac Pereire envisioned a new type of financial institution that would finance large-scale public works projects and industrial development. Crédit Mobilier became a pioneer in project financing, raising capital by issuing long-term bonds and investing heavily in industries such as railroads, mining, and public infrastructure.

> **Project finance** is a distinct financing method used for the development of large-scale infrastructure or industrial projects, whereby the funding is secured primarily on the basis of the project's own merits rather than the creditworthiness of the sponsors or lenders. Typically structured as a transaction involving long-term, non-recourse loans – meaning that lenders rely on the project's future cash flows for repayment and have limited or no recourse to the sponsors' assets.

Crédit Mobilier quickly became instrumental in financing France's industrial revolution; its innovative approach to financing allowed it to fund some of the most ambitious infrastructure projects of the 19th century.

85 Cassis, Y. (ed.), *Finance and Financiers in European History, 1880–1960* (Cambridge University Press, 1992).

However, its aggressive expansion and speculative investments eventually led to its downfall. The bank became overexposed to risky ventures, and its eventual collapse in the 1860s marked the end of an era for French merchant banking. Nevertheless, its legacy in project financing and infrastructure development influenced the later evolution of investment banking in France and abroad.

Founded in 1872, **Banque de Paris et des Pays-Bas**, commonly known as Paribas, was another major player in the development of French investment banking. Paribas emerged in the aftermath of the Franco-Prussian War, a period when France was seeking to rebuild its economy and finance public projects. The bank was formed through a merger of Parisian and Dutch banks, which allowed it to tap into international markets and finance a range of global ventures.

Paribas became particularly influential in international finance, underwriting foreign government bonds and playing a leading role in financing railway construction, public utilities, and industrial enterprises throughout Europe, the Middle East, and Latin America.

10 GERMAN BANKING

The roots of German banking can be traced back to the Holy Roman Empire during the late Middle Ages, when wealthy merchant families, such as the Fuggers, began to engage in banking activities. The Fugger family, who rose to prominence in the 15th and 16th centuries, operated one of the most powerful banking houses in Europe. The Augsburg-based firm was among the most diversified international commercial enterprises of the early modern period. Its success rested upon a remarkable ability to integrate various operational domains, including production, trade, logistics, services, and banking.

While the success of families like the Fuggers and the Welsers marked the early development of private banking in the German-speaking territories,[86] this early phase of banking was largely confined to wealthy merchants and traders, with little in the way of a formalised national banking system due to the fragmented nature of the empire.

10.1 The Rise of Joint-Stock Banks in the 19th Century

The 19th century was a turning point for German banking as the Industrial Revolution swept across Europe. In response to the growing capital needs of industry, Germany saw the rise of joint-stock banks, which allowed for the pooling of resources from multiple investors to finance large industrial ventures. These banks were instrumental in financing the rapid industrialisation of Germany, particularly in the steel, coal, and railway sectors.

The establishment of universal banks – banks that combined commercial banking (deposit-taking and lending) with investment banking (equity financing, underwriting, and issuing securities) – was a key feature of the German banking system during this period. These universal banks, such as Deutsche Bank, founded in 1870, and Dresdner Bank, played a central role in the financing of Germany's industrial giants like Krupp and Siemens. By taking ownership stakes in industrial companies and serving on their boards, these banks not

86 Ehrenberg, R., *Capital and Finance in the Age of the Renaissance: A Study on the Fuggers and Their Connections* (Kelley, 1985).

only provided financial capital but also strategic direction, integrating banking and industry in a way that was unique to Germany.[87]

10.2 The Role of Regional and Cooperative Banks

In addition to the large joint-stock and universal banks, regional banks and cooperative banks played a crucial role in supporting the development of small and medium-sized enterprises (SMEs) and the agricultural sector. Regional banks, known as Landesbanken, were often state-owned institutions that provided funding to local governments and businesses. Cooperative banks, or Volksbanken, emerged in the mid-19th century to provide credit to farmers and small businesses that were often underserved by the larger commercial banks.

These cooperative banks were based on mutual principles and were designed to support local communities by pooling resources and providing affordable credit. The strength of these institutions reflected the German economy's decentralised structure, with a strong emphasis on regional development and local banking networks.

11 UNIFIED CENTRAL BANKING IN CONTINENTAL EUROPE – THE EUROPEAN CENTRAL BANK

The idea of a unified central banking system in Europe emerged in the latter half of the 20th century, driven by the increasing economic interdependence of European countries. The Treaty of Rome in 1957, which established the European Economic Community, laid the groundwork for deeper economic integration. However, it was not until the Maastricht Treaty of 1992 that the foundation for a single currency and a centralised monetary authority was formalised. Such Treaty established the framework for the Economic and Monetary Union (**EMU**) and led to the creation of the European Central Bank (**ECB**) in 1998. The ECB was tasked with managing monetary policy for the Eurozone, controlling inflation, and ensuring price stability across member states that adopted the euro. It represented a shift from national monetary sovereignty to a supranational institution designed to oversee the economic stability of the entire Eurozone. The ECB, in collaboration with national central banks, forms the European System of Central Banks (**ESCB**), further consolidating its role as a pivotal institution in European monetary governance.

12 BANKING IN ASIA: CHINA, JAPAN, AND INDIA

Asia has a long and rich history of banking and finance, with each country developing its own distinct system of banking in response to unique historical, cultural, and economic factors. The evolution of banking in China, Japan, and India reflects both the influence of indigenous practices and the impact of European colonialism and international financial developments. Today, these three countries play significant roles in the global banking system, with each contributing unique innovations and structures to the international financial landscape.[88]

87 Kern, A., *Principles of Banking Regulation* (Cambridge University Press, 2019) at [1.54].
88 Nishimura, S., Suzuki, T. and Michie, R. (eds.), *The Origins of International Banking in Asia: The Nineteenth and Twentieth Centuries* (Oxford University Press, 2012).

12.1 Banking in China

The origins of banking in China date back more than 1,000 years, with early forms of moneylending, currency exchange, and financial management being practiced long before the establishment of modern banking institutions.

During the Tang (618–907 AD) and Song Dynasties (960–1279 AD), China's economy was driven by commerce, particularly along the Silk Road and other trade routes. This increased the need for secure and efficient financial systems. In response, during the Tang Dynasty, China became the first country to introduce paper money, or *jiaozi*, which was initially issued by private merchants and later regulated by the state.[89]

By the late Qing Dynasty in the 19th century, China's banking system began to modernise as it opened up to foreign influence. Foreign banks, particularly from Europe and the United States, began to establish a presence in China, particularly in treaty ports like Shanghai, and they introduced Western banking practices into China's financial system.

The first modern bank in China was the Imperial Bank of China, established in 1897. This marked the beginning of China's integration into the international banking system. The bank was soon followed by the creation of other state-run institutions, such as the Bank of China, which was established in 1912 following the fall of the Qing Dynasty and the establishment of the Republic of China. The Bank of China became the central bank and was instrumental in stabilising China's currency and managing public finances during a turbulent political period.

In 1949, the establishment of the People's Republic of China led to the nationalisation of the banking sector. The People's Bank of China was established in 1948, just before the Communist Party took power, and it became the country's central bank, overseeing the national economy and managing monetary policy. During the Maoist era, banking was controlled by the state, and financial institutions were primarily used to support government-directed economic planning.

China's financial sector underwent significant reform starting in the 1980s, as the country began to transition from a centrally planned economy to a more market-oriented one. The People's Bank of China retained its role as the central bank, but several large state-owned commercial banks were established to handle banking services for individuals and businesses. These included the Industrial and Commercial Bank of China, the China Construction Bank, the Bank of China, and the Agricultural Bank of China.

12.2 Banking in Japan

Japan's banking system is sophisticated and well-developed, with deep roots in the country's industrialisation and post-war economic expansion. Modern banking in Japan began in the late 19th century, following the Meiji Restoration, a period of rapid industrialisation and modernisation. Since then, Japan has become one of the world's largest economies, and its banks have played a crucial role in financing both domestic industries and international trade.[90]

89 Lane, P., 'The Digital Euro: Maintaining the Autonomy of the Monetary System' *Keynote Speech by Philip R. Lane, Member of the Executive Board of the ECB, University College Cork Economics Society Conference 2025*, available at www.ecb.europa.eu/press/key/date/2025/html/ecb.sp250320_1~41c9459722.en.html (accessed in March 2025).

90 Ferguson, N., *The Ascent of Money: A Financial History of the World* (The Penguin Press, 2008), p. 53.

Prior to the Meiji Restoration in 1868, Japan's financial system was largely based on feudal practices, with local merchants and moneylenders providing credit within specific regions. However, following the restoration of imperial rule, the Japanese government sought to modernise the country's economy by adopting Western financial practices.

The Bank of Japan was established in 1882 as the country's central bank, tasked with issuing currency and overseeing the money supply. In addition to the central bank, several private banks were established, including the Mitsui Bank and the Sumitomo Bank, which were connected to powerful zaibatsu (large industrial conglomerates). These banks provided the capital necessary for Japan's industrialisation and the growth of its economy during the late 19th and early 20th centuries.

Following World War II, Japan's banking system played a critical role in the country's rapid economic recovery and post-war boom. The Japanese government, working in close coordination with the Bank of Japan, implemented policies that encouraged banks to lend to key industries, such as steel, automobiles, and electronics, which were central to Japan's export-driven economic growth. Japanese banks, particularly the city banks, provided the financing that allowed Japan to become one of the world's leading industrial powers by the 1960s.

Japan's post-war financial system was characterised by close relationships between banks and corporations, a structure often referred to as main bank relationships. In this system, banks had a significant influence over the management and operations of the companies they lent to, creating a strong link between the banking and industrial sectors.

By the late 20th century, Japanese banks had grown to become some of the largest financial institutions in the world. This period saw the rise of megabanks, formed through mergers between major banks. Some of the largest Japanese banks today include the Mitsubishi UFJ Financial Group, Sumitomo Mitsui Banking Corporation, and Mizuho Financial Group. These banks provide a full range of financial services, including commercial and investment banking, and are heavily involved in international finance.

12.3 Banking in India

India's banking system has a long and complex history, shaped by its colonial past and its post-independence economic development.[91]

Modern banking in India began with the establishment of the Bank of Hindustan in 1770, during the British colonial period. Over the next century, several other banks were established, including the Bank of Bengal in 1806, the Bank of Bombay in 1840, and the Bank of Madras in 1843. These three banks were eventually merged to form the Imperial Bank of India in 1921, which later became the State Bank of India, the largest bank in the country today.

Since 1913, John Maynard Keynes, then serving as an officer within the British Administration in India, had advanced a proposal for the creation of a "State Bank". This institution was envisaged as performing both central banking and commercial banking functions, reflecting the prevailing understanding of central banking roles in colonial contexts. Keynes proposed that the governance of the proposed bank be entrusted to a Central Board,

91 Ferguson, N., *The Ascent of Money: A Financial History of the World* (The Penguin Press, 2008), p. 263.

which would include the Governor, a Deputy Governor, a representative of the Government, and three or more non-voting assessors.

Although Keynes's proposal did not materialise at the time, it provided an early conceptual framework for India's monetary and financial governance. The Reserve Bank of India was established under the Reserve Bank of India Act 1934.

Following India's independence in 1947, the country's banking sector underwent significant reforms. The Reserve Bank of India played a key role in stabilising India's financial system during the early years of independence and continues to be the primary regulator of the banking industry.

In 1969, the Indian government nationalised 14 major private sector banks in an effort to expand banking services to rural areas and to ensure that credit was available to the agricultural and industrial sectors. This marked a major shift in India's banking landscape, as the government sought to use banks as instruments of economic development. A second wave of nationalisation in 1980 further expanded the role of public sector banks, bringing more than 90% of the banking industry under government control.

In the 1990s, as part of India's broader economic liberalisation program, the government introduced a series of reforms aimed at opening up the banking sector to private and foreign investment. This included the licensing of new private sector banks, such as HDFC Bank and ICICI Bank, which have since grown to become some of the largest banks in the country.

13 MERCHANT BANKING

Merchant banking refers to the provision of financial services by banks that primarily cater to merchants engaged in international trade. These banks specialised in trade finance, underwriting of loans, foreign exchange services, and, later, investment banking. The history of merchant banking dates back to the Middle Ages and Renaissance, where it played a pivotal role in the development of modern banking and global commerce.[92]

13.1 Merchant Banking in England

Having emerged in the Italian city-states during the 12th and 13th centuries, the practice of merchant banking spread beyond Italy and became especially prominent in England during the 18th and 19th centuries. With the rise of the British Empire and the expansion of global trade, London emerged as one of the world's leading financial centres. Prominent merchant banks, such as Barings,[93] Hambros, Rothschild, and Lazard, established themselves as the key financiers of international trade and investment.[94]

They specialised in financing international commerce by providing trade finance, including loans for the transportation of goods, insurance against losses at sea, and underwriting of bonds for governments and large corporations. They also played a central role in

92 Ferguson, N., *The Ascent of Money: A Financial History of the World* (The Penguin Press, 2008), p. 274.

93 "*The Barings group collapsed on 27th February 1995. Plc and BSL are now in insolvent liquidation. The immediate cause of the collapse was unauthorised and loss-making trading by Nicholas Leeson, who was the general manager of BFS from 1992 until he disappeared shortly before 27th February 1995*" in *Barings Plc and Anor v. Coopers & Lybrand and Ors* [2001] EWHC Ch 461 at [6].

94 Ferguson, N., *The World's Banker: The History of the House of Rothschild* (Weidenfeld & Nicolson, 1999).

the issuance of government debt, helping finance public infrastructure projects, wars, and colonial expansion.

By the 19th century, these banks, while still involved in trade finance, began to expand their operations into corporate finance and investment banking, helping governments and businesses raise capital through the issuance of bonds and shares. Their ability to attract investors from across Europe and their involvement in major financial transactions cemented their status as powerful institutions in the global economy.[95]

13.2 Merchant Banking and the Rise of Global Finance

Merchant banking's influence extended far beyond trade. The Rothschild family, for example, became one of the most powerful merchant banking dynasties in Europe, financing major governments and facilitating vast international infrastructure projects. Their ability to underwrite large public and private debt issues, provide financial advice, and manage the wealth of Europe's elite positioned them at the centre of international finance.[96]

Merchant banks were also key players in the development of international bond markets. By the 19th century, the issuance of government bonds by merchant banks became an essential method for governments to raise funds for public works, military campaigns, and other large-scale projects. Merchant banks acted as intermediaries, underwriting these bonds and facilitating their sale to investors, often across multiple countries.

13.3 Merchant Banking's Transition to Investment Banking

In the United States, merchant banking in its traditional sense came to an end on Wall Street during the Great Depression. As noted previously, the Glass-Steagall Act imposed a strict separation between commercial banking and underwriting activities, requiring banks to choose between engaging in investment banking or commercial banking. They were no longer permitted to operate in both sectors.[97] Moreover, as global finance evolved in the 20th century, many merchant banks expanded their services and gradually transformed into investment banks.

In Britain, merchant banks, until the 1980s, could be broadly divided into two categories: acceptance houses and issuing houses. Issuing houses specialised in bringing new issues of shares to the Stock Exchange for sale. Acceptance houses originated in the late 1700s and initially operated as true merchants trading their own capital, often derived from the trading, import, or export of goods. Some acceptance houses owned their own ships, which were subsequently utilised by other merchants. During this period, they financed traders through acceptance credit, enabling bills of exchange to be drawn by the trader on the house. Over time, acceptance houses expanded their range of activities to include foreign exchange, money management, loans for current and capital transactions, capital issues, and the underwriting of their clients' bond and share issuances.

The distinction between merchant banking and investment banking began to blur, particularly in the United States. These institutions diversified their offerings to include services such as mergers and acquisitions, asset management, and capital markets advisory.

The Big Bang deregulation of 1986 in London further accelerated the shift, allowing merchant banks to operate as universal banks, engaging in both commercial and investment banking

95 Wechsberg, J., *The Merchant Bankers* (Little, Brown and Company, 1966).
96 Ferguson, N., *The Ascent of Money: A Financial History of the World* (The Penguin Press, 2008), pp. 73–79.
97 Wechsberg, J., *The Merchant Bankers* (Little, Brown and Company, 1966), p. 284.

activities. This deregulation brought many international investment banks into London, transforming the City of London into a global hub for investment banking services. This evolution ultimately led to the establishment of the London Investment Banking Association (which was then merged into the Association for Financial Markets in Europe),[98] whose members participated in a broad spectrum of activities.

By the late 20th century, many traditional merchant banks either evolved into full-service investment banks or were absorbed into larger financial institutions. In the United Kingdom, prominent merchant banks like Barings eventually collapsed or were acquired by other banks due to mismanagement and exposure to financial risks. The growth of corporate finance, venture capital, and private equity also shifted the focus of what was traditionally considered merchant banking into other areas of finance.

While the term "merchant bank" has largely fallen out of use in the 21st century, its legacy remains in modern investment banking which has been shaped by US institutions like J.P. Morgan and Goldman Sachs, which would become global powerhouses. The fundamental role of facilitating large-scale trade finance, advising governments and corporations, and providing financial services to international clients has been absorbed into the practices of today's global financial institutions.

Merchant banking played a pivotal role in shaping global finance. One of its key contributions was in trade finance, where merchant banks provided essential services to merchants engaged in long-distance trade. By offering letters of credit, bills of exchange, and loans, they helped reduce the risks associated with cross-border commerce, enabling the expansion of global trade networks.

Beyond commercial transactions, merchant banks were instrumental in government bond issuance, assisting governments in raising funds for public works, infrastructure projects, and military campaigns. Through the underwriting of sovereign bonds and their placement with international investors, these institutions played a crucial role in the financing of state-led initiatives.

In corporate finance, merchant banks laid the foundation for modern financial advisory services, guiding companies in raising capital, facilitating mergers and acquisitions, and supporting international business expansion. Their expertise helped businesses navigate complex financial landscapes, contributing to the development of structured and sophisticated corporate financing mechanisms.

The influence of merchant banks extended far beyond individual transactions, as their global banking networks – exemplified by institutions such as Rothschild and Barings – were fundamental in integrating international markets. By fostering financial connectivity across borders, these institutions helped establish the foundations of modern financial systems and international banking law.

14 CONCLUSION

The history of banking, particularly in the context of international banking law, reveals a long process of evolution driven by economic necessity and the development of legal frameworks

98 The Association for Financial Markets in Europe (AFME) was formed in November 2009 through the merger of the London Investment Banking Association (LIBA) and the European arm of the Securities Industries and Financial Markets Association (SIFMA).

to support financial transactions. From the earliest banks in Mesopotamia and Rome to the sophisticated financial institutions of the Italian city-states, the evolution of banking reflects the growing complexity of global commerce. The rise of public banks, such as the Banco di Rialto in Venice, and private banking dynasties, like the Medici family in Florence, played a pivotal role in shaping the financial systems we rely on today and paved the way for modern central and investment banks. The Bank of England, the model on which most modern central banks have been based, owes a great deal to its predecessors.

As banking practices evolved, so did the legal fabric that governed them. Early banking regulation was largely informal, relying on local statutes and customs, but as trade and commerce expanded, the need for more comprehensive and standardised legal frameworks became apparent. The early banking practices examined in this Chapter laid the groundwork for the credit institutions we know today.

While the banking landscape is ever-changing, a constant feature for the success of its practices was the existence of a sound and predictable legal and regulatory framework that would promote financial innovation and would foster financial stability.

CHAPTER 2

THE NATURE OF MONEY AND PAYMENT

OVERVIEW

The nature of money and the mechanics of payment are fundamental to the framework of modern financial transactions. Historically, money has transitioned through various forms, from physical commodities like gold and silver coins to modern fiat currencies and, more recently, to dematerialised forms or digital assets such as cryptocurrencies. This chapter delves into the legal foundations governing money, the obligations that arise from payments, the mechanisms that facilitate money transmission, and the emerging role of digital assets in the global economy, all within the context of international banking law.

In addressing the legal definition of money, we explore its dual role as both a store of value and a unit of account, as well as its evolution under different legal and economic frameworks. This chapter considers the role of legal tender provisions, which define the obligations of parties to accept certain forms of money in payment of debts, and how these laws shape the enforceability of transactions across jurisdictions.

Payment mechanisms have undergone a significant transformation, moving from paper-based systems like cheques and bank drafts to sophisticated, technology-driven platforms that operate in real time. An examination of the legal structures surrounding traditional methods, such as banknotes and cheques, and contrasts these with the complexities of dematerialised payment systems, digital wallets, blockchain technology,[1] and cryptocurrencies is provided. From the traditional dominance of banknotes to the advent of Central Bank Digital Currencies (**CBDCs**), the mechanisms by which money is transmitted continue to evolve.

This chapter provides an analysis of these transformations, outlining the legal frameworks governing money and payments while underscoring the importance of legal systems' continuous alignment with financial innovation.

1 MONEY

The concept of money, as it is commonly understood today, did not arise in a vacuum but rather evolved through the centuries.[2]

The transition from a barter economy, where goods and services were exchanged directly, to a monetary system based on the use of commodity money (such as gold or silver) was driven by the need to establish effective economic interactions.

Over time, the legal framework surrounding money has also evolved from basic trade standards in ancient economies to complex modern financial regulations. In the earliest economies, money was typically tied to the value of the materials used to make it, such as precious metals. However, as economies expanded and became more complex, the idea of **fiat money** emerged – a currency that derives its value not from an underlying physical commodity but from a government decree.[3]

1 Wood, P., *International Loans, Bonds, Guarantees and Legal Opinions* (Sweet & Maxwell, 2019) at [46-041].
2 Brindle, M. and Cox, R. (eds.), *Law of Bank Payments* (Sweet & Maxwell, 2017), Chapter 2.
3 Bamford, C., *Principles of International Finance Law* (Oxford University Press, 2015), p. 12.

DOI: 10.4324/9781032662220-3

1.1 The Functions of Money: Legal and Economic Perspectives

As Raffaele Mattioli once remarked: "*Money means nothing unless it is being used*".[4] It is, therefore, important to understand what use money has in the economy. Money serves as the foundation of all modern economies, performing four key functions that enable economic transactions, commercial activities, and financial systems to operate efficiently.[5] These applications – **medium of exchange**, **store of value**, **unit of account**, and **standard of deferred payment** – are essential to both legal and economic frameworks.[6] The relationship between these functions and legal definitions of money has evolved over centuries, reflecting changes in technology, trade, and international finance.[7]

1.2 Medium of Exchange

A fundamental function of money is its role as a medium of exchange. In simple terms, this means that it is used as an intermediary in transactions between buyers and sellers. Historically, economies operated on a barter system, where goods and services were exchanged directly. Such systems are inherently inefficient, as they require a double coincidence of real wants – the need for both parties to have what the other desires. In contrast, money provides a universally accepted means of exchange, simplifying trade by enabling individuals and businesses to conduct transactions without requiring an exact match of wants.[8]

In this context, economists have described money as a "veil" that conceals the underlying real bilateral exchange ratios.[9] As a result, monetary analysis has traditionally focused on identifying the commodity best suited to serve as a universal intermediary or benchmark while assuming that money itself had minimal influence on the exchange and production relationships within the economy.[10]

In this context, coins and, at a later stage, bank notes were employed as intermediary instruments to facilitate the purchase of goods and services.

This function can be performed either by a medium which is legal tender, meaning that if one offers to repay in full a debt in legal tender, the creditor cannot sue the creditor for failing

4 Wechsberg, J., *The Merchant Bankers* (Little, Brown and Company, 1966), p. 246.
5 Martin, F., *Money* (Vintage Books, 2013), pp. 3–31.
6 Lane, P., 'The Digital Euro: Maintaining the Autonomy of the Monetary System' *Keynote Speech by Philip R. Lane, Member of the Executive Board of the ECB, University College Cork Economics Society Conference 2025*, available at www.ecb.europa.eu/press/key/date/2025/html/ecb.sp250320_1~41c9459722.en.html (accessed in March 2025).
7 Sebastianutti, P., 'What Is This Thing Called International Financial Law? Part 3' (2009) 3(3) *Law and Financial Markets Review* 248.
8 Berentsen, A. and Rocheteau, G., 'The Role of Money in Double Coincidence Environments' *University of Lausanne, Faculty HEC, DEEP, Cahiers de Recherches Economiques du Departement d'Econometrie et d'Economie politique (DEEP)* (2000).
9 According to the Economist Steven Stolle the practice of barter was still prevalent in the US frontier throughout the 18th century; however, money was not absent from the equation. "*Citing the accounts of 'Nimrod Warden' who recorded that he had 'bartered with a north-country merchant 6 Hhds [abbreviation for hogshead] of claret at £10 per Hhd for 40 pieces of linen cloth at 30s per piece.' . . . The north-country merchant did not swap cloth for wine, he paid sixty pounds' worth of cloth for sixty pounds' worth of wine. If one quantity had a higher agreed-upon value than the other, a scratch in the account book rectified credit or debt to be settled another time or folded into another transaction where the discrepancy would be absorbed." "Just because money was . . . absent did not mean that it played no part in exchanges*" in Kregel, J., 'The Economic Problem: From Barter to Commodity Money to Electronic Money' *Levy Institute Working Paper No. 982* (2021), p. 9.
10 Kregel, J., 'The Economic Problem: From Barter to Commodity Money to Electronic Money' *Levy Institute Working Paper No. 982* (2021), p. 5.

to repay it,[11] or by "private money" used as a means of payment within a particular community. The latter could function as a medium of exchange, even in the absence of state backing as a fiat currency, effectively serving as a complementary currency operating alongside the national currency and trading at par with it.

In legal terms, coins are classified as personal chattels[12] or tangible movable property (that is, **choses in possession**), whereas banknotes are promissory notes payable to the bearer.[13] Consequently, banknotes are considered documentary intangibles (or **choses in action**),[14] as the paper form represents a legally enforceable promise to pay.[15] Historically, banknotes were mere receipts documenting a customer's deposit of coins with the bank or the amount of a loan advanced by the bank. Over time, they became transferable by delivery, similar to coins,[16] and redeemable by the new holder. Eventually, banknotes ceased to be regarded merely as claims for payment in coin form and evolved into an independent medium of exchange.[17]

This legal framework ensures that money retains its utility as a medium of exchange.[18] However, as we move towards a cashless society – with increasing reliance on digital transactions – the traditional understanding of legal tender is being challenged.[19] Alternative payment systems[20] such as Apple Pay and Google Pay[21] bypass the use of physical money entirely, raising important questions about how the legal status of money will adapt to the changing landscape of financial technology (fintech).

1.3 Store of Value

The second essential function of money is its role as a store of value. This means that money can be saved and retrieved in the future, maintaining its value over time. For any asset to

11 *Gordon v Strange* (1847) 1 Ex 447 (Exch).

12 See, for example, Sections 4 and 5, Bills of Sale Act 1878 or (Section 3, Inheritance and Trustees Powers Act 2014.

13 Crockett, A., *Money: Theory, Policy and Institutions* (Thomas Nelson & Sons Ltd, 1973), p. 17.

14 **Chose in action**: the collection of personal rights over property that can only be asserted or enforced through legal action, rather than by physical possession, such as a cash balance held in a bank account or funds owed under a bond. Choses in action are a creation of English common law and equity, and have been transmitted throughout the common law world, including jurisdictions such as the United States, Canada, and Australia. They continue to hold significance within English law.

15 Bridge, M., *Personal Property Law* (Oxford University Press, 2015), p. 19.

16 See dissenting opinion of Mr Justice Clifford in the US case of *Knox v. Lee (Legal Tender Cases)* (79 U.S. 457 [1871]): "*Money, in the constitutional sense, means coins of gold and silver fabricated and stamped by authority of law as a measure of value, pursuant to the power vested in Congress by the Constitution*".

17 Bamford, C., *Principles of International Finance Law* (Oxford University Press, 2015), p. 137.

18 Fox, D., *Property Rights in Money* (Oxford University Press, 2008), p. 10.

19 Martin, F., *Money* (Vintage Books, 2013), p. 275.

20 See Financial Conduct Authority Discussion Paper (DP22/5) 'The potential competition impacts of Big Tech entry and expansion in retail financial services' published on October 2022 at p. 18, at [3.1]: "*We consider alternative payment networks or 'rails' (card schemes, interbank and potentially crypto or central bank digital currencies), technology or services which complement payment networks (such as digital wallets, Apple Pay and Google Pay) and alternative consumer uses, such as payments for goods and services (remotely and in-person) and peer-to-peer transfers*" and at p. 18 at [3.5]: "*Apple Pay and Google Pay operate a technology layer, providing identity authentication and verification services for consumers. This is not regulated as payment initiation, as it is outsourced by service providers. Apple Pay operates by producing a token on the device (stored in the 'Secure Element' chip) whereas Google Pay uses 'Host Card Emulation' to generate tokens online.*" at www.fca.org.uk/publication/discussion/dp22-5.pdf (accessed in March 2025).

21 "*An estimated 14% of point-of-sale terminal transactions and 38% of e-commerce transactions, by value, involved a digital wallet in 2023*": the Financial Conduct Authority (FCA) and Payment Systems Regulator (PSR) Call for Information "Big tech and digital wallets", CP24/9, July 2024 at https://psr.org.uk/media/yqinyhhn/cp24-9-cfi-digital-wallets-july-2024-v2.pdf (accessed in March 2025), p. 4.

function effectively as a store of value, it must not lose its purchasing power significantly over time due to inflation or other economic fluctuations.

Historically, money derived its value from the physical commodities (such as gold or silver) used to mint coins. These commodity-based currencies had intrinsic value, meaning that the coins themselves were worth something independently of their use as money.

With paper money, the linkage with a commodity of intrinsic value was maintained, leading in the 19th century to the formal development of the gold standard.[22] The gold standard was a monetary system where countries committed to exchanging paper money for a fixed quantity of gold. One of the key benefits of such a system was to shield central bankers from political pressures to expand the money supply.[23]

Before the First World War, most of the Western world, including the United States, Great Britain, and most European countries, adhered to the gold standard. In the United States, the Resumption Act of 1879 reinstated the gold standard, while the Gold Standard Act of 1900 formally established gold as the ultimate measure of value.[24] The First World War almost brought it to an end. Although none of the warring nations demonetised gold or refused to purchase it at a fixed price, neither did they strictly adhere to the principles of the gold standard. After the conflict, the restoration of the gold standard became a paramount objective for economic policymakers aimed at achieving monetary stability.[25] Gold served as an anchor for both the monetary and economic systems, imposing the maintenance of parity as a constraint on economic policy.

During the first half of the 20th century, however, the link with gold was finally severed for most countries (on 21 September 1931 for the UK).[26] The abandonment of a monetary system based directly or indirectly on gold resulted from the significant economic imbalances that emerged between the two world wars. As a result, most economies transitioned to fiat money (see later on) – money is backed by the government's promise to uphold its value.

The post-World War II international monetary system became known as the Bretton Woods system, named after the 1944 conference in Bretton Woods, New Hampshire, where representatives from 44 countries convened.[27]

Under the Bretton Woods system, the exchange rates of foreign currencies were fixed relative to the US dollar, which was itself pegged to gold at the congressionally established price of $35 per ounce.[28] This committed the United States to supply dollar reserves by running a continuous balance of payments deficit. In practice, the system evolved into a fixed-rate dollar standard. Parity adjustments with other currencies were allowed only in cases of "fundamental disequilibrium".

22 The Resumption of Cash Payments Act 1819 marked Britain's return to the gold standard, following the suspension of gold and silver convertibility under the Bank Restriction Act 1797. This earlier Act had introduced the use of paper money in response to the financial strains of the French Revolutionary Wars.

23 Robertson, D. H., *Money, Cambridge Economic Handbooks II*, revised edition, reprinted 1937, with new preface, reprinted 1946 (Nisbet, 1928a), p. 122.

24 Crabbe, L., 'The International Gold Standard and U.S. Monetary Policy from World War I to the New Deal' (June 1989) *Federal Reserve Bulletin* 423.

25 "*On July 31, the New York Stock Exchange joined the world's other major exchanges in closing its doors, thus easing pressure on the gold standard by preventing the export of gold arising from foreign sales of U.S. corporate securities.*" in Crabbe, L., 'The International Gold Standard and U.S. Monetary Policy from World War I to the New Deal' (June 1989) *Federal Reserve Bulletin* 424.

26 "On Monday, September 21, 1931, the British abandoned the gold standard." in Crabbe, L., 'The International Gold Standard and U.S. Monetary Policy from World War I to the New Deal' (June 1989) *Federal Reserve Bulletin* 434.

27 U.S. Department of State Office of the Historian, 'The Bretton Woods Conference 1944' available at https://history.state.gov/milestones/1937-1945/bretton-woods (accessed in March 2025).

28 Altamura, C. E., *European Banks and the Rise of International Finance: The Post-Bretton Woods Era* (Routledge, 2016).

By 1961, outstanding dollar claims surpassed the US government's gold reserves. This gold shortfall raised doubts about the United States' ability to honour its commitment to convert dollars into gold at the official price. On 15 August 1971, President Richard Nixon unveiled his New Economic Policy, aimed at fostering "a new prosperity without war". Informally referred to as the "Nixon Shock", this initiative signalled the beginning of the end for the Bretton Woods system. The first directive was to close the gold window, preventing foreign governments from exchanging their dollars for gold. This effectively transformed the international monetary system into a fiat-based system. Although the Smithsonian Agreement,[29] introduced a few months later, sought to preserve pegged exchange rates, the Bretton Woods system ultimately collapsed shortly thereafter. As a result, even the indirect linkage between fiat currency and precious bullion was removed.

The US case of *Milam v. United States*, 524 F.2d 629 (9th Cir. 1974) illustrates the practical implications of a currency that is legal tender but is fully detached from precious metals. Milam sought to compel the Federal Reserve Board to redeem a $50 Federal Reserve note in gold or silver. However, the Ninth Circuit Court of Appeals rejected his claim and remarked: "*While we agree that golden eagles, double eagles and silver dollars were lovely to look at and delightful to hold, we must at the same time recognize that time marches on . . . [Milam] is entitled to redeem his [Federal Reserve] note, but not in precious metal*".

Absent the link to precious metals, for fiat money to function as a reliable store of value, governments must manage the money supply carefully to prevent excessive inflation, which erodes the value of money over time. Central banks, such as the Bank of England[30] and the Federal Reserve[31] in the United States, play a crucial role[32] in this process. They control inflation through tools such as interest rate adjustments, open market operations, and quantitative easing. These mechanisms help ensure that money retains its value, thereby allowing it to continue functioning as a store of value in the economy.

In this context, electronic money represents a digital alternative to traditional coins and banknotes. It is commonly linked to an electronic device, such as a mobile phone (e.g., Apple Pay) or a card-based product. Such products electronically store monetary value as represented by a claim on the issuer, issued upon receipt of funds for the purpose of making payment transactions.[33] Additionally, electronic money may take the form of "digital cash",

29 In December 1971, monetary authorities from the world's leading developed nations convened in Washington, DC, in a futile attempt to salvage the Bretton Woods global monetary system.

30 The Bank of England operates under two statutory objectives: (a) Financial Stability Objective: The Bank of England's financial stability objective is "*to protect and enhance the stability of the financial system of the United Kingdom*" (section 2A(1), Bank of England Act 1998). The Court of Directors of the Bank of England is responsible for determining the strategy to achieve this objective (section 9A(1), Bank of England Act 1998); and (b) Monetary Policy Objective: The monetary policy objective aims to maintain price stability and, subject to that, to support the government's economic policy (section 11, Bank of England Act 1998). HM Treasury defines what constitutes price stability and provides guidance on the government's economic policy (section 12, Bank of England Act 1998). The formulation of monetary policy is the responsibility of the Bank of England's Monetary Policy Committee (section 13(1), Bank of England Act 1998).

31 For the US Federal Reserve System's legislative 'monetary policy objectives' see Federal Reserve Act 1913, s 2A.: "*The Board of Governors of the Federal Reserve System and the Federal Open Market Committee shall maintain long run growth of the monetary and credit aggregates commensurate with the economy's long run potential to increase production, so as to promote effectively the goals of maximum employment, stable prices, and moderate long-term interest rates*".

32 Goals reflected, with varying precision, in some central bank's legal 'mandates': Federal Reserve Act of 1913 (US), s. 2A; Treaty on the Functioning of the European Union, Art. 127; Bank of England Act 1998 (UK), s, 11.

33 See Article 2(2) of Directive 2009/110 and *Case* C-661/22, *ABC Projektai: Judgment* of the *Court* (*Fifth Chamber*) of *22 February 2024, at [46].*

allowing individuals to upload funds from a bank account or credit card into an internet-based account, which can then be utilised for the payment of goods and services (e.g., PayPal).

In recent years, cryptocurrencies have emerged as alternative stores of value. Out of such cryptocurrencies, Bitcoin,[34] in particular, has been compared to digital gold because of its limited supply and decentralised nature. However, the remarkable volatility of cryptocurrencies has raised concerns about their viability as stores of value. Unlike fiat currencies, which are backed by government authority and supported by central banks passing as legal tender in payment of debts, cryptocurrencies are exposed to substantial fluctuations based on market sentiment, speculation, and regulatory developments.

1.4 Unit of Account

Money also functions as a unit of account, meaning that it provides a common standard for measuring the value of goods and services.[35] Without a standard unit of account, it would be difficult to compare the value of different products, services, or debts, making economic activity less efficient.

By providing a consistent parameter, money allows businesses and consumers to compare prices easily, keep financial records, and make informed economic decisions. In addition, by using money as a unit of account, individuals and companies can express debts, credits, and other financial obligations in clear, quantifiable terms.

Professor Mann, a legal theorist, coined the following definition of money, which seems to approximate to a common modern legal understanding of the term with respect to the notion of unit of account:

> *It is suggested that in law the quality of money is to be attributed to chattels which, issued by the authority of the law and denominated with reference to a unit of account, are meant to serve as universal means of exchange in the state of issue.*[36]

34 "*In October 2008 a famous paper, generally referred to as the 'Bitcoin White Paper', was published. Its actual title was Bitcoin: A Peer-to-Peer Electronic Cash System. The named author is 'Satoshi Nakamoto', which was a pseudonym. Dr Wright claims he is Satoshi Nakamoto. This is a hotly disputed claim and does not matter in this case. The White Paper proposed a new online electronic cash system. The fact it is cash is important (and that is why the word 'coin' is in the name bitcoin). The thing about physical cash is that it cannot be spent twice. Once I have handed over a physical coin to buy something from a shopkeeper, they now have it and I no longer do. I cannot spend it again. In the language of possession, before the transaction I possessed the token (and nobody else) while afterwards it is possessed by the shopkeeper. This characteristic of a physical coin is a key part of what allows the recipient of that token, and therefore everyone else, to place trust in the token's value. Electronic payment systems, which of course existed in 2008 as the White Paper acknowledged, solve the double spending problem in a different way because the payment systems are run by financial institutions, which both parties have to trust. The point of the White Paper was to propose a scheme using cryptographic methods to solve the double spending problem and create a form of electronic cash which does not rely on third party financial institutions. Since then a number of different systems have been developed. Dr Wright maintains that the original bitcoin, and the only one properly so-called, is that held though the BSV Network.*" in *Tulip Trading Limited (A Seychelles Company) v Bitcoin Association For BSV & Ors* [2023] EWCA Civ 83 at [17] to [20].

35 According to Prof. Luigi Einaudi "*Books and pamphlets and statutes of the ninth to the eighteenth century are unintelligible if one does not bear in mind the distinction between money of account or imaginary money and effective or coined money. Usually the money of account was called libra, livre, lira. Men kept accounts, drew instruments of debt, sold and bought goods and securities and property rights in imaginary money, which they never saw. Coins had strange names, they poured into each country from all parts of the world, were gold and silver and half silver dresses, were minted at home or by foreign princes. They made no difference to people who continue to talk and negotiate and keep accounts in libras*" in Einaudi, L., 'The Theory of Imaginary Money from Charlemagne to the French Revolution' in *Enterprise and Secular Change: Readings* in Lane, F. and Riemersma, J. (eds.), *Economic History* (Homewood, 1953), p. 257. Silvestri, P., 'Luigi Einaudi's "Scienza delle Finanze" or the Science of Good Government' (2023) 30(5) *The European Journal of the History of Economic Thought* 764–790.

36 Mann, F. A., *The Legal Aspect of Money: With Special Reference to Comparative Private and Public International Law* (Oxford University Press, 1992).

The legal importance of money as a unit of account can be seen in its role in contracts, where financial obligations must be stated in precise monetary terms. For commercial and loan agreements, money serves as the standard for determining the amount payable. In the context of cross-border transactions, money as a unit of account becomes particularly significant. Exchange rates must be clearly defined in contracts, ensuring that all parties know the amount payable and how it translates across different currencies.

The rise of digital money and cryptocurrencies presents new challenges to the traditional unit of account function. Cryptocurrencies are often volatile, making it difficult to use them as stable units of account. For example, businesses accepting payments in Bitcoin must often adjust their prices frequently to account for fluctuations in Bitcoin's value, which can vary substantially over the course of a single day.[37]

Stablecoins – cryptocurrencies that are pegged to the value of fiat currencies – attempt to solve this problem by maintaining a stable value relative to a reference currency, such as the US dollar.[38]

1.5 Standard of Deferred Payment

The final key function of money is its use as a standard of deferred payment. This refers to the ability of money to serve as the agreed measure for settling debts or obligations that are due in the future.

In credit-based economies, this role is critical, as it allows businesses and individuals to enter into agreements for future or deferred payments with the confidence that the value of money will remain stable over time. This function is closely tied to the store of value function, as money must hold its value over time to serve effectively as a standard for deferred payments.[39]

The legal authority to create private credit money is subject to the extensive regulatory framework governing banks, which provide statutory permissions for deposit-taking and credit issuance. It is also shaped by the general principles of contract, debt, and property law.[40]

The legal treatment of money as a standard of deferred payment is seen most clearly in contracts involving debts and financial obligations. A debt refers to a specific sum of money, established by agreement and ascertainable at the time payment becomes due.[41] While the contract does not need to specify an exact monetary amount, it must clearly indicate the payable sum and the due date.[42]

37 Bamford, C., *Principles of International Finance Law* (Oxford University Press, 2015), p. 13.

38 Tether (USDT) is a prominent example of a stablecoin designed to maintain parity with the dollar, making it more viable as a unit of account in digital transactions. "*Tether tokens are assets that move across the blockchain just as easily as other digital currencies but that are pegged to real-world currencies on a 1-to-1 basis*" https://tether.to/en/how-it-works (accessed in March 2025).

39 "*In a recent literature review on the use and holdings of cash, Shy (2023) documents that: (i) the bulk of cash is held for store of value purposes, (ii) cash holdings sharply increase in times of high economic uncertainty and perceived bank instability, and (iii) a significant proportion of the population holds cash as a store of value.*" in Muñoz, M. and Soons, O., 'Public Money as a Store of Value, Heterogeneous Beliefs and Banks: Implications of CBDC' *Working Paper Series No 146*, p. 1.

40 For UK statutory framework, see Financial Services and Markets Act 2000 (UK), ch 3; for US federal banking legislation, see 12 USC chapter 2; for the; for the general law which applies to the creation of deposits by commercial banks, see Cranston, R., Avgouleas, E., van Zwieten, K., Hare, C. and van Sante, T., *Principles of Banking Law* (Oxford University Press, 2018), p. 160; *Bank of Marin v England* 385 US 99, 101 (1966); *Citizens Bank of Maryland v Stumf* 516 US 16, 21 (1995); *Foley v Hill* (1848) 2 HLC 28.

41 "*An accruing debt, therefore, is a debt not yet actually payable, but a debt which is represented by an existing obligation.*" *Webb v Stenton* (1883) 11QBD 518.

42 Hudson, A., *The Law on Financial Derivatives* (Sweet & Maxwell, 2017) at [12-07].

The requirement for clarity regarding the terms agreed upon by the parties in order to be able to enforce a deferred payment obligation is exemplified by the English case of *Libyan Arab Foreign Bank v Bankers Trust Co* [1989] QB 728, where the court reaffirmed that creditors are entitled to demand payment in the currency specified in the agreement unless the parties stipulate for an alternative arrangement.[43] This legal principle is crucial for ensuring that parties in a financial agreement can rely on money as a stable and enforceable means of settling future obligations. This also implies that a claim in money debt[44] may be settled even if the contractual amount is expressed in foreign currency or, perhaps, digital currency.[45]

The use of digital currencies for deferred payments is still in its early stages, but it raises complex legal and financial issues. Some blockchain platforms are attempting to crystallise the settlement in Bitcoins through the use of smart contracts – self-executing contracts with the terms of the agreement directly written into code. In other terms, smart contracts are performed automatically without human intervention. They can automatically enforce the terms of a deferred payment, potentially reducing the risk of non-payment. However, smart contracts could also present legal challenges, including in terms of enforceability and jurisdiction.[46]

2 FIAT MONEY

Fiat money is the cornerstone of the modern monetary system. Unlike commodity-based currency, which has intrinsic value derived from a physical commodity, fiat money is valuable because of a government's decree. Its worth is not based on the material it is made from but on the trust and confidence placed in the issuing authority, typically the government or central bank. Fiat money is regulated by legal frameworks and statutory provisions that define how it is created and issued and the amount of currency in circulation, ensuring economic stability and public trust in such currency.

In England and other common law jurisdictions, the concept of fiat money has evolved through both statutory and case law frameworks.

In particular, the Currency and Bank Notes Act 1954 is fundamental to the regulation of fiat money. Section 1 of the Act[47] provides that Bank of England notes are to be treated as legal tender, meaning they must be accepted as a means of payment in the settlement of debts. In the United States, the Supreme Court in the *Legal Tender Cases*, 110 U.S. 421 (1884) confirmed that

43 "*Given that a foreign currency debtor is entitled to choose between discharging his obligations in foreign currency or sterling, I consider that he should not be entitled to choose the route which is blocked and then claim that his obligation is discharged or suspended. I prefer the view that he must perform in one way or the other; so long as both routes are available he may choose; but if one is blocked, his obligation is to perform in the other.*" Ibid. at [766].

44 For the purposes of Section 303(1)(a) of the Corporation Tax Act 2009 "*a money debt is a debt which – (a) falls to be settled – (i) by the payment of money, (ii) by the transfer of a right to settlement under a debt which is itself a money debt or (iii) by the issue or transfer of any share in any company*".

45 "*Where a contract expressly provides for the payment of a sum in a foreign currency, the obligation is a money obligation and breach of it gives rise primarily to a claim in debt, whether the obligation is by way of repayment of money loaned, payment for goods or services or payment for other currencies*". *Camdex International Ltd v Bank of Zambia & Anor* [1997] EWCA Civ 798.

46 The self-executing smart contract cannot be unscrambled in the same way as a traditional contract because it is not possible to annul it and halt its performance in the course of execution.

47 "*The Bank of England may issue bank notes of such denominations as the Treasury may approve and shall not issue any other bank notes, and any bank notes issued under this section may be put into circulation in Scotland and Northern Ireland as well as in England and Wales. All bank notes issued under this section shall be legal tender in England and Wales, and all such notes of denominations of less than five pounds shall be legal tender in Scotland and Northern Ireland*".

> *the impressing upon the Treasury notes of the United States the quality of being a legal tender in payment of private debts is an appropriate means, conducive and plainly adapted to the execution of the undoubted powers of Congress, consistent with the letter and spirit of the Constitution, and therefore within the meaning of that instrument, "necessary and proper for carrying into execution the powers vested by this Constitution in the government of the United States".*

Furthermore, the Bank Charter Act 1844[48] played a historic role in shaping the regulation of fiat money in the UK. The Act limited the right to issue banknotes solely to the Bank of England, marking the centralisation of currency issuance and control. Section 11 of the Act prohibited private banks from issuing their own banknotes in England and Wales, cementing the Bank of England's monopoly over the issuance of fiat currency.

Judicial decisions have also played a significant role in interpreting the statutory framework governing fiat money. One of the foundational cases in furthering its legal understanding is *Moss v Hancock* [1899] 2 QB 111, where Justice Darling defined money as "*that which passes freely from hand to hand throughout the community in final discharge of debts and full payment for commodities*". This definition reflects the accepted notion of fiat money as something that holds value by virtue of its widespread acceptability and use in economic transactions. The case also highlights the critical distinction between legal tender and other forms of money. While only certain types of money (such as banknotes and coins issued by a central bank) may be considered legal tender, many other instruments (like cheques, digital payment systems, and electronic tokens) are widely used in commerce, but their acceptance is dependent on mutual agreement between parties.

2.1 The Creation and Issuance of Fiat Money

The process of creating fiat money is controlled by central banks, such as the Bank of England or the Federal Reserve in the United States, which have exclusive authority to issue and regulate the national currency. Their primary objective is to ensure the stability of the currency and manage the money supply in response to economic conditions.

Central banks generate fiat money through the issuance of banknotes and coins, as well as through the management of the digital money supply. In the UK, the Currency and Bank Notes Act 1954 provides the Bank of England with the authority to issue physical money and controls the design, distribution, and management of banknotes. The Bank of England's Notes Department is responsible for ensuring that enough banknotes are in circulation to meet public demand while also maintaining the quality and security of the currency.

2.2 Monetary Policy and the Regulation of Fiat Money

Fiat money is regulated primarily through monetary policy[49] tools, which are used by central banks to control the money supply, stabilise prices, and manage economic growth. Monetary policy is primarily implemented through a range of tools designed to regulate economic activity, control inflation, and manage liquidity. Contrary to the conventional view that banks

48 "*An Act to regulate the Issue of Bank Notes, and for giving to the Governor and Company of the Bank of England certain Privileges for a limited Period.*": Bank Charter Act 1844 (7 & 8 Vict. c. 32).

49 Monetary policy refers to measures implemented by a country's central bank or government to regulate the supply of money within the economy and to influence borrowing costs.

receive deposits from household savings and subsequently lend them out, it is, in fact, the process of bank lending that gives rise to deposits.

Under normal conditions, the central bank does not determine the quantity of money circulating in the economy, nor is central bank money merely "multiplied up" into further loans and deposits in a mechanical fashion. While commercial banks do indeed create money through lending, they are not at liberty to do so without constraint. Their lending activities are circumscribed by both market discipline and prudential regulation. In a competitive banking environment, banks must remain profitable, which imposes natural limits on the extent of their lending. Furthermore, regulatory frameworks impose additional constraints to ensure the resilience of the financial system.

The recipients of newly created money – whether households or businesses – may also influence the total stock of money. For example, if borrowers use funds to repay existing debts, this process effectively results in the "destruction" of money, thereby reducing the overall money supply.

Ultimately, monetary policy serves as the overarching constraint on money creation. The Bank of England seeks to ensure that the quantity of money in the economy is aligned with its objective of maintaining low and stable inflation. In ordinary times, it implements monetary policy by setting the interest rate on central bank reserves, which in turn affects a wide spectrum of interest rates across the economy, including those applicable to bank loans. In the UK, the Bank of England's Monetary Policy Committee is responsible for setting the base rate, which directly impacts the interest rates charged by commercial banks. Another monetary tool is Open Market Operations (**OMO**s), where the central bank buys or sells government securities to regulate the money supply. When the central bank purchases government bonds, it injects liquidity into the economy as banks receive payment for the bonds, increasing their capacity to lend and invest. Conversely, when the central bank sells government bonds, money is withdrawn from circulation, reducing liquidity and curbing inflationary pressures.

In exceptional circumstances – such as when interest rates approach their lower bound – money creation and economic spending may remain insufficient to achieve the central bank's monetary policy objectives. In such cases, one potential policy response is to engage in asset purchases, commonly referred to as "quantitative easing" (**QE**). QE aims to inject money into the economy more directly by acquiring financial assets, primarily from non-bank financial institutions. The immediate consequence of QE is an increase in the level of bank deposits held by those institutions, replacing the assets they have sold. These institutions, seeking to rebalance their portfolios, are likely to reinvest in higher-yielding assets. This process supports asset prices and, in turn, stimulates spending and investment within the economy.

QE was extensively used by the Bank of England,[50] the Federal Reserve, and the European Central Bank (**ECB**) following the 2008 financial crisis and the COVID-19 pandemic to stabilise the economy,[51] demonstrating its role as an effective policy measure in times of economic distress. Although QE results in the creation of new central bank reserves, these reserves are not central to the transmission mechanism. The effectiveness of QE lies not in the reserves themselves, but in the broader economic responses it catalyses, particularly in financial markets and in the behaviour of private sector agents.

50 See the initial authorisation of the asset purchase program in January 2009 (Letter from Darling to King (last page)): www.bankofengland.co.uk/-/media/boe/files/letter/2009/chancellor-letter-290109 (accessed in March 2025).

51 Kokkinis, A. and Miglionico, M., *Banking Law: Private Transactions and Regulatory Frameworks* (Routledge, 2021), p. 245.

The Financial Services and Markets Act 2023 introduced a new levy on the Bank of England to fund its monetary policy and financial stability functions, replacing the previous cash ratio deposit scheme. This levy reflects the broader objective of ensuring that the Bank of England can continue to oversee financial stability in a rapidly evolving digital economy. Additionally, FSMA 2023 granted new secondary objectives to the Financial Conduct Authority (**FCA**) and the Prudential Regulation Authority (**PRA**), requiring them to focus on advancing long-term UK economic growth and international competitiveness in line with broader financial sector reforms.

2.3 Fiat Money Regulation in the European Union

Central banking in Europe was historically instrumental to the issuance and management of national currencies. Against this historical backdrop, the establishment of the EMU at the close of the 20th century marked a unique development. It introduced a new monetary framework characterised by the adoption of a single currency across much of Europe.

The transfer of monetary policy to the supranational level necessitated significant reforms to the European central banking system. This included the creation of a new supranational monetary authority, the ECB, and the integration of national central banks within the Eurozone into a European central banking structure. This structure comprises the European System of Central Banks (**ESCB**) and, within it, the Eurosystem – a sub-set representing the euro area. These developments reflect the supranationalisation of central banking in Europe.

Therefore, in the Eurozone, the creation and regulation of fiat money are governed by the legal framework surrounding the ECB and the euro. The Treaty on the Functioning of the European Union (**TFEU**),[52] particularly Articles 127 to 133,[53] establishes the ECB's mandate to maintain price stability and oversee monetary policy across the Eurozone.[54] The euro, introduced in 1999 as an accounting currency and as physical money in circulation in 2002, serves as the single fiat currency for 20[55] of the 27 EU member states.[56]

The ECB has the exclusive right to authorise the issuance of euro banknotes within the Eurozone. Regulation (EC) No 974/98 on the introduction of the euro provides the legal framework for the euro's use, declaring it as legal tender across participating member states. The ECB's role in regulating the euro is similar to the Bank of England's role with the sterling;[57] however, the ECB must navigate the complexity of managing a single currency across multiple economies, each with distinct fiscal policies.

52 OJ C 326, 26.10.2012, p. 47.

53 See also protocol (No 4) on the Statute of the European System of Central Banks and of the European Central Bank (European Central Bank Statute), Art 16.

54 Bamford, C., *Principles of International Finance Law* (Oxford University Press, 2015), p. 33.

55 Although all EU countries are part of the Economic and Monetary Union (EMU), 20 of them have replaced their national currencies with the single currency – the euro. These EU countries form the euro area, also known as the eurozone: Austria, Belgium, Croatia, Cyprus, Estonia, Finland, France, Germany, Greece, Ireland, Italy, Latvia, Lithuania, Luxembourg, Malta, the Netherlands, Portugal, Slovakia, Slovenia, and Spain.

56 The 27 EU Member States are: Austria, Belgium, Bulgaria, Croatia, Republic of Cyprus, Czech Republic, Denmark, Estonia, Finland, France, Germany, Greece, Hungary, Ireland, Italy, Latvia, Lithuania, Luxembourg, Malta, Netherlands, Poland, Portugal, Romania, Slovakia, Slovenia, Spain, and Sweden.

57 "As central bank money is issued directly by the central bank, from an accounting perspective, it is backed by the assets of the central bank. That is, the Eurosystem can increase the supply of euro 'outside' money by crediting the reserve accounts held by commercial banks at the central bank in exchange for assets. This can be done by providing a loan to a bank (strictly, a temporary collateralised loan under its refinancing operations) or by acquiring bonds". Lane, P., 'The Digital Euro: Maintaining the Autonomy

During the Eurozone debt crisis of 2009–2012, the ECB implemented a series of emergency measures, including the Outright Monetary Transactions program, which allowed the ECB to purchase government bonds from struggling member states. Within the context of ruling on a challenge to the legality of such program, the European Court of Justice (ECJ) in *Gauweiler and Others v Deutscher Bundestag (Case C-62/14)*[58] summarised the role of the ECB as follows:

> *The ECB is the institution on which the Treaties confer responsibility for the exercise of the Union's exclusive competence in respect of monetary policy. The ECB and the national central banks constitute the ESCB, whose principal task, notwithstanding any measures that may be taken in "support of economic policy", is to ensure "price stability". Therefore, unlike other central banks, the ECB is characterised by the fact that it is constrained to a clear mandate that is closely linked to anti-inflationary goals . . . . Besides the fact that it must strictly adhere to the objective of ensuring price stability, a further characteristic of the ECB is that it has a high degree of functional as well as organic independence.*[59]

2.4 Fiat Money in the United States

In the United States, fiat money is created and regulated by the Federal Reserve, which was established under the Federal Reserve Act of 1913. The Act provides the Federal Reserve with the authority to issue Federal Reserve Notes, which serve as the nation's fiat currency. These notes are backed by the full faith and credit of the US government.

The US dollar's role as the world's dominant reserve currency, as a legacy of the Bretton Woods system, gives the Federal Reserve significant influence over global monetary policy. Like the Bank of England, the Federal Reserve uses a variety of tools to regulate the money supply, including setting the federal funds rate (the interest rate at which banks lend to each other) and conducting open market operations.

The United States Supreme Court case *Knox v. Lee (Legal Tender Cases)* (79 U.S. 457 [1871]) provides a crucial judicial interpretation of the constitutionality of fiat money. It upheld the legality of fiat currency, ruling that Congress had the authority to issue paper money as legal tender,[60] especially during times of national emergency, such as the Civil War. This case affirmed the federal government's power to create fiat money, laying the groundwork for the modern monetary system in the United States.

---

of the Monetary System' *Keynote Speech by Philip R. Lane, Member of the Executive Board of the ECB, University College Cork Economics Society Conference 2025*, available at www.ecb.europa.eu/press/key/date/2025/html/ecb.sp250320_1~41c9459722.en.html (accessed in March 2025).

58 Reference for a preliminary ruling – Economic and monetary policy – Decisions of the Governing Council of the ECB on a number of technical features regarding the Eurosystem's outright monetary transactions in secondary sovereign bond markets – Articles 119 TFEU and 127 TFEU – Powers conferred on the ECB and the European System of Central Banks – Monetary policy transmission mechanism – Maintenance of price stability – Proportionality – Article 123 TFEU – Prohibition of monetary financing of Member States in the euro area.

59 Opinion of Advocate General Cruz Villalòn delivered on 14 January 2015 (Case C 62/14).

60 "*It was said there can be no question of the power of this government to emit bills of credit; to make them receivable in payment of debts to itself; to fit them for use by those who see fit to use them in all the transactions of commerce; to make them a currency uniform in value and description, and convenient and useful for circulation. Here the substantive power to tax was allowed to be employed for improving the currency. It is not easy to see why, if state bank notes can be taxed out of existence for the purposes of indirectly making United States notes more convenient and useful for commercial purposes, the same end may not be secured directly by making them a legal tender.*" at page 79 U. S. 544.

2.5 Fiat Money in China

China's monetary system is controlled by the People's Bank of China, which manages the supply of the renminbi (**RMB**), China's fiat currency. Unlike most central banks, the People's Bank of China operates under a direct governmental influence, reflecting China's state-driven economic model.

Statutorily, the issuance of fiat currency in China is governed by the Law of the People's Republic of China on the People's Bank of China, which grants the People's Bank of China the exclusive right to issue RMB and regulate its supply to ensure financial stability. China has developed the Digital Currency Electronic Payment,[61] also known as the digital yuan,[62] which is designed to coexist with physical RMB.

2.6 Fiat Money in India

The rupee is India's fiat currency, and the Reserve Bank of India has exclusive authority over its issuance and management.[63] The Reserve Bank of India's statutory mandate includes maintaining price stability while promoting growth and ensuring that the supply of money aligns with the economy's needs.

A significant example of fiat money regulation in India is the demonetisation policy of 2016, when the government, in coordination with the Reserve Bank of India, invalidated certain high-denomination currency notes to target black money, corruption, and counterfeit currency. This policy highlighted the extensive power of the government and the Reserve Bank of India in managing the money supply and regulating fiat money in the economy.

2.7 Fiat Money in Japan

In Japan, fiat money is issued by the Bank of Japan, which operates under the Bank of Japan Act 1942. The Japanese yen is the country's fiat currency, and the Bank of Japan is tasked with maintaining price stability and regulating the money supply through monetary policy. Japan, in the past, has faced unique challenges in managing deflation, which has persisted for decades,[64] prompting the Bank of Japan to adopt an aggressive quantitative easing policy similar to the one implemented by the Federal Reserve and the Bank of England to respond to financial crises.

This policy has been supported by statutory provisions that grant the Bank of Japan wide-ranging powers to intervene in financial markets to achieve its monetary policy goals.

61 See 'The IMF's Central Bank Digital Currency (CBDC) Virtual Handbook' available at www.imf.org/en/Topics/fintech/central-bank-digital-currency/virtual-handbook (accessed in March 2025).

62 See what follows.

63 The Reserve Bank of India Act 1934 describes its main functions as "*to regulate the issue of Bank Notes and keeping of reserves with a view to securing monetary stability in India and generally to operate the currency and credit system of the country to its advantage.*" This preamble indicates the two core functions of the Reserve Bank of India: (i) the issue of currency; and (ii) monetary authority.

64 Nishizaki, K., Sekine, T., Ueno, Y. and Kawai, Y., 'Chronic Deflation in Japan' (2014) *Asian Economic Policy Review* 9.

3 CRYPTOCURRENCIES: CHALLENGES AND INNOVATIONS

Cryptocurrencies represent a substantial development in the realm of money. Unlike traditional fiat currencies, cryptocurrencies are decentralised, meaning they are not issued or regulated by any central authority, such as a government or central bank. Nevertheless, insofar as they facilitate the payment for goods and services through the transfer of value, they ought to be recognised as a formal medium of exchange.[65] However, their classification within the traditional boundaries of private law presents challenges, as they do not neatly align with existing categories. Cryptocurrencies are, by their nature, intangible assets and thus cannot be subject to possession in the traditional legal sense.[66]

They consist of a sequence of data that represents a transactional output of value associated with the public key of the individual entitled to utilise it. They rely on blockchain technology to function. Blockchain is a Distributed Ledger Technology (DLT) system. The European Securities and Markets Authority (**ESMA**) has characterised such systems as records of electronic transactions maintained by a shared or "distributed" network of participants, commonly referred to as "nodes".[67] They rely on cryptographic techniques, which are employed both to store assets securely and to validate transactions recorded on distributed ledgers. In practice, it means that copies of the blockchain are maintained by multiple individuals or organisations, with no single copy acting as the master or lead version, thereby making the system distributed and decentralised.[68] Blockchains can be either publicly or privately distributed and may be publicly or privately owned.

The most well-known cryptocurrency is Bitcoin, which was introduced in 2009 by an anonymous entity known as Satoshi Nakamoto. Bitcoin was designed to be a peer-to-peer digital currency that could be transferred between users without the need for intermediaries like banks. This decentralisation has made cryptocurrencies attractive for individuals seeking greater privacy and autonomy in their financial transactions.

However, the rise of cryptocurrencies has posed significant challenges for regulators. Because they operate outside the traditional financial system, cryptocurrencies are often seen as a tool for illicit activities, such as money laundering and tax evasion. Additionally, their volatile nature has raised concerns about their suitability as a stable store of value.

3.1 The Legal Nature of Cryptocurrencies

Unlike fiat money, cryptocurrencies do not derive their value from a government decree or a physical commodity.

The Basel Committee on Banking Supervision's Basel Framework, scope and definitions (SCO60 – Cryptoassets exposures)[69] defines *cryptoassets*

65 Bridge, M., Gullifer, L., McMeel, G. and Low, K., *The Law of Personal Property* (Sweet & Maxwell, 2017), p. 163.
66 *The Environment Agency v Churngold Recycling Ltd* [2014] EWCA Civ 909.
67 Financial Markets Law Committee, Fintech: Issues of Legal Complexity (June 2008), p. 61; European Securities Markets Authority, The Distributed Ledger Technology Applied to Securities Markets (7 February 2017), p. 4.
68 The concept of "self-proving" allows users to verify the correctness of the data on a blockchain simply by examining it, ensuring it has not been tampered with. This provides transparency and significantly reduces or eliminates the need for intermediaries and physical documentation in areas where blockchain technology is applied.
69 Effective as of 1 January 2025.

as private digital assets that depend on cryptography and distributed ledger technologies (DLT) or similar technologies. Digital assets are a digital representation of value, which can be used for payment or investment purposes or to access a good or service.[70]

According to the European Banking Authority, a virtual currency is

a digital representation of value that is neither issued by a central bank or public authority nor necessarily attached to a fiat currency, but is used by natural or legal persons as a means of exchange and can be transferred, stored or traded electronically.[71]

In the UK, cryptocurrencies are not recognised as legal tender, but they have been classified as property under common law.

The Jurisdiction Taskforce of the Law Society's LawTech Delivery Panel[72] recognised that digital assets possess the necessary characteristics to qualify as property. This recognition drew upon the decision of the Singapore International Commercial Court in *B2C2 Ltd v Quoine Pte Ltd* [2019] SGHC(I) 03, where the judge referenced the definition of property rights set out by the House of Lords in *National Provincial Bank v Ainsworth* [1965] AC 1175, 1248: property "*must be definable, identifiable by third parties, capable in its nature of assumption by third parties, and have some degree of permanence or stability*". The judge in *B2C2* concluded that cryptocurrencies satisfied all these criteria. On appeal, the Singapore Court of Appeal[73] observed, obiter, that "*there may be much to commend the view that cryptocurrencies should be capable of assimilation into the general concepts of property*".[74] A similar position was adopted in New Zealand in *Ruscoe v Cryptopia Ltd (In Liquidation)* [2020] NZHC 728, where the court held that property rights in cryptocurrency are indeed possible.

The preceding recognition has now been endorsed by case law in England. In *AA v Persons Unknown* [2019] EWHC 3556 (Comm), where the High Court recognised Bitcoin as property. This case arose from a ransomware attack where Bitcoin was demanded as payment. The court ruled that Bitcoin could be classified as property under English law, thus subject to proprietary injunctions. The court's decision was significant in establishing that digital assets like cryptocurrencies, though not legal tender, have real-world value and are capable of being owned and transferred like other assets.

In the Court of Appeal decision in *Tulip Trading Ltd v Van der Laan* [2023] EWCA Civ 83, Birss LJ endorsed the view that digital assets could constitute property:

In the bitcoin scheme transactions are recorded in a ledger or database known as a blockchain, with each network having its own ledger. The blockchain constitutes a public registry recording every transaction. A given amount of bitcoin is simply a number held at a certain digital address. A transaction simply involves reducing the value at one address and correspondingly increasing it at another. Whether new addresses are created in this process does not matter for present purposes, as different cryptocurrencies work in different ways. The amounts held at every address are public, but the identity of the parties is not. The blockchain does not reveal the relationship between the digital addresses and any persons.

Each digital address is associated with a pair of public and private cryptographic keys. The public key identifies the address on the network. The relevant private key is the means by which bitcoin can be dealt with. The holder of the private key uses it to cryptographically sign a record of the transaction moving bitcoin from one

70 'SCO60 – Cryptoassets Exposures' at [60.1], available at www.bis.org/basel_framework/chapter/SCO/60.htm?inforce=20250101&published=20221216 (accessed in March 2025).

71 Opinion on virtual currencies – EBA/Op/2014/08 on 4 July 2014.

72 The LawTech Delivery Panel, Legal statement on cryptoassets and smart contracts, UK Jurisdiction Taskforce, 18 November 2019, available at https://technation.io/wp-content/uploads/2019/11/6.6056_JO_Cryptocurrencies_Statement_FINAL_WEB_111119-1.pdf (accessed in March 2025).

73 *Quoine Pte Ltd v B2C2 Ltd* [2020] SGCA(I) 02.

74 Ibid. at [144].

> *address to another. The record is called a cryptographic hash. The public/private key pair means that the person signing with the private key is proving that they are associated with the public key (and so the address), without revealing the private key itself. The hash ensures that any attempt to alter the record would be noticeable, because even the smallest change would alter the hash. For each network there are devices on the network that undertake "mining". This is the means whereby transactions are validated. The latest transactions are gathered together into a block, which also includes a hash of the previous block (hence each block is chained to its predecessor, making a "blockchain"). . . . The signing of the hashed transaction record with users' private keys in the first place, and the incorporation of these records into a hashed chain of blocks produced by the proof of work, solves the double spending problem. This characteristic of bitcoin does not emerge as a matter of law or convention, it is a characteristic which arises as a matter of fact from the way the software works. As a result it is meaningful to describe bitcoin not merely as something which is transferable but as "rivalrous" . . . . For a transferable thing to be rivalrous, the holding of it by one person necessarily prevents another from holding that very thing at the same time. Because the holder cannot double spend their bitcoin, such that it is rivalrous, the cryptoasset can be said to be capable of assumption by a third party . . . . Thus . . . a cryptoasset such as bitcoin is property.*[75]

These rulings align cryptocurrencies with the UK's broader legal framework for digital assets, and, as a result, regulatory bodies like the FCA have taken steps to bring certain types of cryptocurrency activities under their regulatory perimeter, especially with respect to combating financial crime.

3.2 Statutory Provisions Governing Cryptocurrencies in the UK

The UK has progressively developed a regulatory framework for cryptocurrencies, focused primarily on anti-money laundering (**AML**) and know your customer (**KYC**) obligations. The Money Laundering, Terrorist Financing and Transfer of Funds (Information on the Payer) Regulations 2017,[76] as amended by the Fifth Anti-Money Laundering Directive (**5AMLD**),[77] extended AML and KYC requirements to cryptocurrency exchanges and wallet providers. These businesses must register with the FCA and implement measures to identify users and monitor transactions to prevent cryptocurrencies from being used for illicit purposes such as money laundering, terrorism financing, or tax evasion.

The FCA's Cryptocurrency Derivatives Ban

In January 2021, the FCA imposed a ban[78] on the sale of cryptocurrency derivatives and exchange-traded notes to retail consumers. The FCA expressed concerns about the extreme volatility of cryptocurrencies, the lack of reliable valuations, and the risks of market manipulation. The ban was part of a broader effort to protect consumers from losing money on speculative products, as cryptocurrencies such as Bitcoin often experience dramatic price swings. The FCA's ban is illustrative of the UK's cautious

75 In *Tulip Trading Limited (A Seychelles Company) v Bitcoin Association For BSV & Ors* [2023] EWCA Civ 83 at [21] to [24].

76 S.I. 2017 No. 692, as amended by The Financial Services and Markets Act 2023 (Addition of Relevant Enactments) Regulations 2024 (S.I. 2024/1347).

77 Directive (EU) 2018/843 of the European Parliament and of the Council of 30 May 2018 amending Directive (EU) 2015/849 on the prevention of the use of the financial system for the purposes of money laundering or terrorist financing, and amending Directives 2009/138/EC and 2013/36/EU.

78 www.fca.org.uk/news/press-releases/fca-bans-sale-crypto-derivatives-retail-consumers (accessed in March 2025).

approach to regulating cryptocurrencies, ensuring that while innovation is encouraged, consumer protection remains a top priority.[79]

3.3 Cryptocurrency Regulation in the European Union

In the European Union, as in other jurisdictions, cryptocurrencies were first defined from a tax perspective. In *Skatteverket v David Hedqvist*, Case C-264/14 ECLI:EU:C:2015:718,[80] the ECJ ruled that the exchange of traditional currencies for Bitcoin and vice versa constituted a "supply of services" under the EU VAT Directive[81] and was therefore exempt from value-added tax (**VAT**). It was held:

> *The "bitcoin" virtual currency, being a contractual means of payment, cannot be regarded as a current account or a deposit account, a payment or a transfer. Moreover, unlike a debt, cheques and other negotiable instruments referred to in Article 135(1)(d) of the VAT Directive, the "bitcoin" virtual currency is a direct means of payment between the operators that accept it.*

This clarified the treatment of cryptocurrency transactions for VAT purposes and set an important precedent for how cryptocurrencies could be classified within the EU legal and regulatory framework.

More recently, in an attempt to keep pace with technological developments, it has taken significant steps to create a unified regulatory framework for cryptocurrencies through the Markets in Cryptoassets Regulation (EU) 2023/1114 (**MiCA**).[82] MiCA was adopted in 2023 to establish a harmonised legal regime for the issuance and trading of cryptoassets across EU member states. It aims to enhance consumer protection, ensure market integrity, and mitigate financial stability risks posed by the growing use of cryptocurrencies.

MiCA defines cryptoassets as "*a digital representation of value or rights that can be transferred and stored electronically, using distributed ledger technology or similar technology*".[83] Under MiCA, issuers of cryptoassets must comply with strict disclosure requirements and ensure that appropriate safeguards are in place to protect investors. The regulation also introduces capital requirements for stablecoin issuers and mandates regular reporting on the assets backing stablecoins[84] to ensure transparency and financial stability.

79 This level of protection has been enhanced with the enactment of the Digital Markets, Competition and Consumers Act 2024 which has introduced substantial reforms to the enforcement of consumer protection law (Part 3 of the Act) and consumer rights and dispute resolution (Part 4). The Act gave the Competition and Markets Authority new direct enforcement powers, which will operate in parallel with a court-based enforcement regime. Pursuant to the Digital Markets, Competition and Consumers Act 2024 (Commencement No. 2) Regulations 2025, certain provisions of the Digital Markets, Competition and Consumers Act 2024 have come into force on 6 April 2025 while further provisions, relating to consumer savings, will come into force on 1 January 2026.

80 *Skatteverket v David Hedqvist*, Case C-264/14 ECLI:EU:C:2015:718.

81 Council Directive 2006/112/EC of 28 November 2006 on the common system of value added tax.

82 Regulation (EU) 2023/1114 of the European Parliament and of the Council of 31 May 2023 on markets in crypto-assets, and amending Regulations (EU) No 1093/2010 and (EU) No 1095/2010 and Directives 2013/36/EU and (EU) 2019/1937.

83 Pursuant to Article 3(1)(5) of MiCA.

84 Under preamble (41) of MiCA: the "*so-called algorithmic 'stablecoins' that aim to maintain a stable value in relation to an official currency, or in relation to one or several assets, via protocols, that provide for the increase or decrease in the supply of such crypto-assets in response to changes in demand*".

3.4 The US Approach to Cryptocurrency Regulation

The United States has taken a more fragmented approach to cryptocurrency regulation, with multiple agencies overseeing different aspects of the market.

In its 2014 guidance[85] as to how US federal tax principles apply to various transactions relating to cryptoassets the IRS has defined virtual currency as

> *a digital representation of value that functions as a medium of exchange, a unit of account, and/or a store of value. In some environments, it operates like "real" currency – i.e., the coin and paper money of the United States or of any other country that is designated as legal tender, circulates, and is customarily used and accepted as a medium of exchange in the country of issuance – but it does not have legal tender status in any jurisdiction. Virtual currency that has an equivalent value in real currency, or that acts as a substitute for real currency, is referred to as "convertible" virtual currency.*[86]

The Commodity Futures Trading Commission (**CFTC**) has classified Bitcoin and other cryptocurrencies as commodities, subjecting them to regulation under the Commodity Exchange Act of 1936. This classification was crystallised in *CFTC v My Big Coin Pay, Inc.* 334 F. Supp. 3d 492 (D. Mass. 2018), where the court ruled that cryptocurrencies fell under the CFTC's jurisdiction.

In parallel, the Securities and Exchange Commission (**SEC**) expressed the view that certain cryptocurrencies may qualify as securities, especially when they are used in initial coin offerings (**ICO**s). Section 2(a)(1) of the Securities Act of 1933 and Section 3(a)(10) of the Securities Exchange Act of 1934 each define the term "security" by enumerating a range of financial instruments, including "stock", "note", and "bond". A cryptocurrency should not fall within any of the commonly recognised categories listed in these statutory definitions, as it does not, among other things, generate a yield or confer rights to future income, profits, or assets of a business. In this respect, a cryptocurrency does not, in and of itself, constitute a security. However, both statutory provisions also include "investment contracts" within the definition of a security, and a cryptocurrency could be offered and sold as part of such a contract.

The *Howey Test*, established in *SEC v W.J. Howey Co.* (328 U.S. 293 [1946]), is used to determine whether a transaction constitutes an investment contract and, therefore, a security. In assessing the economic realities of a transaction, the test examines whether there is an investment in a common enterprise made with a reasonable expectation of profits to be derived from the entrepreneurial or managerial efforts of others.[87] This analysis focuses on the substance of the arrangement rather than its form, considering whether the investor relies on the efforts of others for the generation of returns. Since the decision in *Howey*, federal courts have clarified that the "efforts of others" element under the test is satisfied when the efforts undertaken by parties other than the investor are unquestionably significant and constitute essential managerial efforts that determine the success or failure of the enterprise.[88]

In *Landreth Timber Co. v. Landreth*, 471 U.S. 681, 689 (1985), the United States Supreme Court indicated that in assessing whether an instrument constitutes a security, the Court has emphasised that "form should be disregarded for substance", as stated in *Tcherepnin v. Knight*, 389 U.S. 332, 336 (1967), and that the focus should be on the economic realities underpinning the transaction rather than the label attached to the instrument, as reaffirmed in *United Housing Foundation, Inc. v. Forman*, 421 U.S. 837, 849 (1975).

85 Notice 2014-21 available at www.irs.gov/pub/irs-drop/n-14-21.pdf (accessed in March 2025).
86 See Section 2 of Notice 2014-21 available at www.irs.gov/pub/irs-drop/n-14-21.pdf (accessed in March 2025).
87 *Forman*, 421 U.S. at [852].
88 See, e.g., *SEC v. v. Glenn W. Turner Enterprises, Inc.*, 474 F.2d 476, 482 (9th Cir. 1973).

The SEC has aggressively pursued ICOs that fail to comply with US securities laws, arguing that many tokens issued in ICOs meet the definition of a security under the Howey Test.

In *SEC v. Shavers et al*, No. 4:2013cv00416 – Document 23 (E.D. Tex. 2013), the court examined whether Bitcoin investments constituted securities under the Securities Act of 1933. In this case, the defendant operated a Ponzi scheme that promised high returns on Bitcoin investments. The court ruled that Bitcoin investments met the criteria of the Howey Test and thus qualified as securities, subject to SEC regulation. This case was one of the first to address the regulatory classification of Bitcoin and set a precedent for how cryptocurrencies could be treated under securities law in the US.

In February 2025,[89] the SEC's Division of Corporation Finance issued a staff statement outlining its views on "meme coins".[90] In this statement, the Division expressed the view that transactions involving the types of meme coins addressed in the statement do not constitute offers or sales of securities within the meaning of the federal securities laws.[91] Consequently, individuals participating in the offer and sale of such meme coins are not required to register their transactions with the Commission under the Securities Act of 1933, nor are they obliged to rely on any of the exemptions from registration provided by that Act. As a result, purchasers and holders of meme coins do not benefit from the protections afforded by federal securities laws.

3.5 Cryptocurrencies in China: A Tightening Regulatory Grip

China has taken a much stricter approach to cryptocurrency regulation. The People's Bank of China has implemented a series of measures that effectively ban the use of cryptocurrencies within the country. In 2017, the People's Bank of China prohibited ICOs, and in 2021, it intensified its crackdown by declaring all cryptocurrency-related transactions, including trading, mining, and fundraising, to be illegal. The ban reflects China's concerns over financial stability, money laundering, and capital outflows.

Despite the ban on private cryptocurrencies, China has been a pioneer in the development of CBDCs. The Digital Currency Electronic Payment (**DCEP**), also known as the digital yuan, is a state-backed digital currency being piloted across several cities in China. The People's Bank of China views the digital yuan as a way to modernize the payment system while maintaining control over the currency, distinguishing it from decentralised cryptocurrencies like Bitcoin.

89 See 'SEC' Staff Statement on Meme Coins, Division of Corporation Finance' (27 February 2025), available at www.sec.gov/newsroom/speeches-statements/staff-statement-meme-coins#_ftn2 (accessed in March 2025).

90 "*A 'meme coin' is a type of crypto asset inspired by internet memes, characters, current events, or trends for which the promoter seeks to attract an enthusiastic online community to purchase the meme coin and engage in its trading. Although individual meme coins may have unique features, meme coins typically share certain characteristics. Meme coins typically are purchased for entertainment, social interaction, and cultural purposes, and their value is driven primarily by market demand and speculation. In this regard, meme coins are akin to collectibles. Meme coins also typically have limited or no use or functionality*". in SEC' Staff Statement on Meme Coins, Division of Corporation Finance (27 February 2025), available at www.sec.gov/newsroom/speeches-statements/staff-statement-meme-coins#_ftn2 (accessed in March 2025).

91 "*The offer and sale of meme coins does not involve an investment in an enterprise nor is it undertaken with a reasonable expectation of profits to be derived from the entrepreneurial or managerial efforts of others. First, meme coin purchasers are not making an investment in an enterprise. That is, their funds are not pooled together to be deployed by promoters or other third parties for developing the coin or a related enterprise. Second, any expectation of profits that meme coin purchasers have is not derived from the efforts of others. That is, the value of meme coins is derived from speculative trading and the collective sentiment of the market, like a collectible. Moreover, the promoters of meme coins are not undertaking (or indicating an intention to undertake) managerial and entrepreneurial efforts from which purchasers could reasonably expect profit*".

3.6 Cryptocurrency Regulation in India

India's approach to cryptocurrency regulation has been marked by uncertainty and evolving legal frameworks. While the Reserve Bank of India issued a circular prohibiting banks from dealing with cryptocurrency exchanges, the Supreme Court, in *Internet and Mobile Association of India v Reserve Bank of India* (2020) INSC 264, has set aside such circular, declaring that the blanket ban on cryptocurrency-related banking services was unconstitutional. The court ruled that the Reserve Bank of India's action was disproportionate and that cryptocurrencies should not be outright banned but regulated.[92]

Since the Supreme Court ruling, India has been exploring potential regulatory frameworks for cryptocurrencies. Draft legislation, such as the Cryptocurrency and Regulation of Official Digital Currency Bill, has proposed banning private cryptocurrencies while introducing a government-backed CBDC. However, the regulatory future of cryptocurrencies in India remains uncertain as lawmakers continue to debate the best approach to balancing innovation with financial stability.

3.7 Japan: A Proactive Regulatory Approach

Japanese financial regulation generally follows a three-tiered structure. At the top level is primary legislation, which forms the statutory foundation of the regulatory framework. Beneath this is subordinate legislation, comprising government ordinances and cabinet office ordinances, which give effect to the primary laws and provide more detailed regulatory provisions. At the third level are supervisory policies and administrative guidelines, commonly referred to as "Supervisory Policies". Although originally intended to serve as expressions of the regulatory authorities' interpretative stance, in practice, these policies often operate as *de facto* rules, shaping regulatory expectations and influencing compliance behaviour within the financial sector. Within this layered regulatory framework, Japan has regulated cryptocurrencies. The Payment Services Act 2009 (**PSA**) provides the legal framework for cryptocurrency exchanges in Japan. The PSA classifies cryptocurrencies as cryptoassets and requires cryptoexchanges to register with the Financial Services Agency. Furthermore, the Financial Services Agency regulates cryptocurrency exchanges, ensuring that they implement robust AML and KYC procedures, provide adequate consumer protections, and maintain operational transparency.

Japan's proactive regulatory stance was prompted by the 2014 Mt. Gox exchange collapse, in which hackers stole approximately 850,000 Bitcoin, leading to significant financial losses for investors. Following this incident, the Financial Services Agency introduced stricter regulations, including mandatory audits, consumer protection measures, and cybersecurity standards for exchanges. In 2018, a series of further cyberattacks resulted in the misappropriation of funds amounting to approximately \$580 million. These incidents prompted significant regulatory developments in Japan, including the establishment of the Japan Virtual

92 "*It is no doubt true that RBI has very wide powers in view of the special place and role that it has in the economy of the country. These powers can be exercised both in the form of preventive as well as curative measures. But the availability of power is different from the manner and extent to which it can be exercised. While we have recognised the power of RBI to take a pre-emptive action, we are testing in this part of the order the proportionality of such measure, for the determination of which RBI needs to show at least some semblance of any damage suffered by its regulated entities. But there is none. When the consistent stand of RBI is that they have not banned VCs and when the Government of India is unable to take a call despite several committees coming up with several proposals including two draft bills (Crypto-token Regulation Bill 2018 and Banning of Cryptocurrency and Regulation of Official Digital Currency Bill, 2019), both of which advocated exactly opposite positions, it is not possible for us to hold that the impugned measure is proportionate.*"

Currency Exchange Association – a self-regulatory body aimed at enhancing oversight of the cryptoasset sector. In response to the attacks, Japanese authorities introduced stricter regulatory measures by amending the PSA and the Financial Instruments and Exchange Act 1948.

Under the PSA, a Crypto Asset Exchange Service Provider intending to handle a new crypto asset is required to provide prior notification to the Financial Services Agency. In addition to this statutory obligation, the self-regulatory framework established by the Japan Virtual and Crypto Assets Exchange Association – a self-regulatory organisation formally recognised under the PSA – imposes further requirements. Specifically, a member Crypto Asset Exchange Service Provider seeking to engage in transactions involving a new crypto asset must first undertake an internal assessment of the asset in question. This process is designed to ensure that the crypto asset meets the requisite standards of security, compliance, and suitability before being made available to customers. Japan's approach has been seen as a model for balancing innovation with regulation, providing a secure environment for cryptocurrency trading while protecting consumers.

4 THE RISE OF STABLECOINS

In response to the volatility of cryptocurrencies, a new class of digital assets known as stablecoins has emerged. Stablecoins are digital assets that operate on blockchain networks or other distributed ledger technologies, designed to maintain a stable value[93] by being pegged to the value of a fiat currency or another reference asset.

This stability is a defining characteristic, and developers have employed different mechanisms to achieve it. One of the most common approaches is fiat-backed stablecoins, where each token is backed by reserves of fiat currency, such as the US dollar. Examples include Tether (USDT)[94] and USD Coin (USDC),[95] which are often redeemable on a 1:1 basis for the underlying currency. The value of these stablecoins is maintained by ensuring that the issuer holds equivalent fiat reserves.

Another category is commodity-backed stablecoins, which are pegged to the value of physical commodities such as gold. A notable example is Paxos Gold (PAXG),[96] which maintains parity with physical gold holdings. These stablecoins enable investors to gain exposure to commodity prices without directly holding the underlying asset.

A different model is algorithmic stablecoins, which do not rely on direct asset backing but instead use algorithms and smart contracts to automatically adjust token supply in response to fluctuations in demand, thereby maintaining price stability. This category has faced significant scrutiny, particularly following the collapse of TerraUSD in 2022.[97]

The rapid rise of stablecoins has prompted financial regulators worldwide to assess how these digital assets should be classified and regulated.

The Financial Services and Markets Act 2023 (**FSMA 2023**) significantly reshaped the regulatory landscape for digital assets, introducing new provisions that bring stablecoins, referred to as "digital settlement assets", under formal UK regulation. Stablecoins, particularly those used as a means of payment, are now subject to regulatory oversight by the FCA. In particular, UK banks that hold stablecoins are required to implement comprehensive risk

93 Under preamble (41) of MiCA they "*aim to maintain a stable value in relation to an official currency*".
94 See https://tether.to/en/ (accessed in March 2025).
95 See www.circle.com/usdc (accessed in March 2025).
96 See www.paxos.com/pax-gold (accessed in March 2025).
97 See www.sec.gov/newsroom/press-releases/2024-212 (accessed in March 2025).

management frameworks capable of addressing financial, operational, legal, cybersecurity, and reputational risks. These frameworks are subject to ongoing scrutiny by the FCA or PRA. This move integrates stablecoins into the UK's broader financial services framework, recognising their growing role in modern payments. Moreover, stablecoin issuers must comply with stricter prudential and operational requirements to ensure consumer protection and financial stability. This approach is complemented by case law: in *D'Aloia v Persons Unknown & Ors* [2024] EWHC 2342 (Ch), the High Court held that a digital stablecoin, USD Tether, constituted property for the purposes of the law of England and Wales, although it was neither a chose in possession nor a chose in action.

In the European Union, MiCA introduced specific categories for stablecoins, known as "asset-referenced tokens" and "e-money tokens", and imposed regulatory obligations on issuers, including capital requirements, governance rules, and the need to maintain adequate reserves.

The E-money Directive 2009/110/EC already regulates electronic money institutions, and certain stablecoins that function like electronic money may be subject to this regime. Under MiCA, stablecoin issuers must ensure that their tokens are backed by reserves that are sufficiently liquid to meet redemption demands, similar to how banks are required to maintain liquidity for deposits. MiCA also addresses consumer protection by imposing disclosure obligations and ensuring that users have legal recourse in case of issuer insolvency. Moreover, banks must incorporate stablecoin holdings into their broader risk management frameworks. These must address the same categories of risk and are reviewed regularly by the institutions' external auditors. Any deficiencies may trigger heightened regulatory scrutiny by the relevant supervisory authorities.

Moreover, AML and counter-terrorist financing (**CTF**) regulations also play a crucial role in the regulatory landscape for stablecoins. The 5AMLD in the EU extends AML obligations to crypto-asset service providers, including those dealing in stablecoins (see Chapter 5). An additional regulatory concern connected to stablecoins is the protection of users, particularly in cases where the issuer becomes insolvent or fails to maintain sufficient reserves. Regulatory frameworks such as MiCA in the EU address this by requiring stablecoin issuers to hold adequate reserves, maintain transparency, and provide users with legal recourse.

In other jurisdictions, absent a comprehensive legal framework, the classification of stablecoins determines how they will be regulated.

In the United States, the President's Working Group on Financial Markets issued a report in 2021[98] emphasising the need for comprehensive federal legislation to regulate stablecoins, particularly in terms of financial stability, consumer protection, and AML compliance. Without such comprehensive federal legislation, the classification often depends on whether the stablecoin meets the definition of a security under the Securities Act of 1933 or the *Howey Test*. Fiat-backed stablecoins, which are often marketed as stable stores of value and not as investments offering profit may fall outside the scope of this definition. In contrast, in *Reves v Ernst & Young*, 494 U.S. 56 (1990), the Supreme Court further refined the test for securities by outlining the "family resemblance test". This test applies to instruments that do not clearly fit traditional categories of securities but resemble securities based on their function and the expectations of the investing public. Stablecoins marketed for investment purposes could potentially be classified as securities under this broader interpretation. The Commodity Futures Trading Commission has also asserted jurisdiction over certain stablecoins, particularly algorithmic stablecoins.

98 See https://home.treasury.gov/system/files/136/StableCoinReport_Nov1_508.pdf (accessed in March 2025).

Furthermore, issuing stablecoins may subject the issuer to money transmission laws, which require entities transmitting money to be licensed. The Financial Crimes Enforcement Network (**FinCEN**), under the Bank Secrecy Act of 1970, has provided guidance stating that administrators or exchangers of stablecoins may be considered money transmitters, requiring registration and compliance with AML regulations.

In the case of *Ripple Labs, Inc. v FinCEN* (2015), Ripple Labs settled[99] with FinCEN over allegations that it had failed to register as a money services business while selling its native currency, XRP. Although XRP is not a stablecoin, this case illustrates the regulatory expectations that stablecoin issuers might face regarding money transmission and AML compliance. Such obligations for stablecoin issuers arise under the Bank Secrecy Act, with FinCEN overseeing compliance. The Anti-Money Laundering Act of 2020 (**AMLA 2020**) further strengthens these requirements, expanding the definition of "financial institutions" to include certain cryptocurrency-related businesses, potentially including stablecoin issuers.

Consumer protection laws under the Dodd-Frank Wall Street Reform and Consumer Protection Act may also apply, particularly if stablecoins are treated as securities or financial products. The Consumer Financial Protection Bureau (**CFPB**) has a mandate to protect consumers in financial transactions, and its regulatory purview may extend to stablecoin issuers, depending on how the tokens are used. Furthermore, the STABLE Act (Stablecoin Tethering and Bank Licensing Enforcement Act of 2020) was introduced, requiring stablecoin issuers to obtain banking charters and hold reserves equivalent to their issued tokens. This has placed stablecoins under a more stringent regulatory regime akin to traditional financial institutions, ensuring that they are subject to the same oversight as banks.

Tether[100] (USDT) is one of the most widely used stablecoins. Tether is purportedly backed by reserves of US dollars, which are meant to ensure its value remains stable at $1 per token. However, Tether has faced legal challenges regarding the transparency of its reserves. In 2021, Tether reached a settlement with the New York Attorney General's Office over allegations that it had misrepresented the nature of its backing assets.

5 PAYMENT

Payments form a fundamental pillar of a thriving financial sector, playing a crucial role in facilitating commerce, trade, and economic activity. The ability to make and receive payments is an essential aspect of daily life, ensuring the smooth functioning of businesses and financial transactions. In 2023 alone, the UK recorded 48.1 billion transactions,[101] underscoring the scale and importance of an efficient and reliable payment infrastructure in supporting economic growth and financial stability.

However, while payment is a crucial notion in banking and financial transactions, it is somewhat difficult to define:

> *The word "paid" is more slippery. Unquestionably, it is no longer confined to the delivery of cash or its equivalent. In ordinary speech it now embraces transactions which involve the crediting and debiting of*

99 www.justice.gov/sites/default/files/opa/press-releases/attachments/2015/05/05/settlement_agreement.pdf (accessed in March 2025).

100 See https://tether.to/en/ (accessed in March 2025).

101 See *UK Finance's Payments Market Report 2024*, p. 7. available at www.ukfinance.org.uk/system/files/2024-07/Summary%20UK%20Payment%20Markets%202024.pdf (accessed in March 2025).

> *accounts by electronic means, not only transfers between bank accounts by payment cards and direct debits, but also dealings with credit cards and similar instruments. Conditional payment by cheque would also be covered, at any rate outside a strictly legal context.*[102]

Payment, therefore, refers to the process of money transmission, which can be defined as *"an act, initiated by the payer or payee, involving the placement, transfer, or withdrawal of funds, regardless of any underlying obligations between the payer and payee"*.[103] Within the context of a payment transaction, it also signifies the fulfilment or discharge of an obligation to pay, which may or may not include the actual transfer of money.

There are various means by which an obligation to pay may be discharged, with the most common method being the transfer of money to the payee, either through the banking system, by the physical delivery of coins or banknotes, or by employing digital payment. Moreover, parties may agree on non-cash consideration.

A number of issues commonly arise in relation to payment, including the currency in which payment must be made, the timing of payment, arrangements for deferred consideration (such as instalment payments), and retention mechanisms (such as escrow arrangements).[104]

For example, in the absence of contractual provisions to the contrary, if a US Dollar payment is required under the contract, the customer is entitled to demand such payment in cash: *"[w]here the fundamental obligation is to make payment, and where it is possible to make such payment, then the bank must do so"*.[105] Furthermore, where the money of account is denominated in a foreign currency, the debtor has the option to pay either in that currency or in sterling at the prevailing exchange rate in London on the day of payment.

5.1 Payment as the Transmission of Money: Payment Systems

Payments are typically processed through a payment system. Traditionally, such systems were paper-based, relying on cheques and cash. However, advances in technology have transformed them, leading to the rise of electronic payment systems, mobile payments, and blockchain-based transactions.[106]

Payment systems are mechanisms that facilitate the transfer of money between individuals and businesses.[107] The legal basis for the regulation of payment systems is found in the Payment Services Regulations 2017[108] (**PSRs 2017**), which transposed the EU Payment Services Directive (**PSD2**)[109] in the UK. The PSRs 2017 set out the legal framework for the provision of payment services and regulate payment institutions, including banks, payment service providers (PSPs), and e-money institutions.

102 In *Charter Reinsurance Company Ltd v Fagan & Ors* [1996] UKHL 21 per Lord Mustill.
103 See definition of "payment transaction" within The Payment Services Regulations 2017 S.I. 2017 No. 752.
104 An escrow agreement is a contract setting out the terms and conditions by which an independent third party (an escrow agent) holds and eventually distributes funds to an intended recipient once certain prescribed conditions have been fulfilled.
105 *Libyan Arab Foreign Bank v Bankers Trust Co* [1989] QB 728 at [281].
106 Feyen, E., Frost, J., Gambacorta, L., Natarajan, H. and Saal, M., 'Fintech and the Digital Transformation of Financial Services: Implications for Market Structure and Public Policy' *BIS Papers No. 117* (2021).
107 See s. 41 Meaning of "payment system" of the Financial Services (Banking Reform) Act 2013.
108 S.I. 2017 No. 752.
109 Directive (EU) 2015/2366 of the European Parliament and of the Council of 25 November 2015 on payment services in the internal market, amending Directives 2002/65/EC, 2009/110/EC and 2013/36/EU and Regulation (EU) No 1093/2010, and repealing Directive 2007/64/EC.

To offer payment services[110] in the UK, an institution must fall within one of the categories specified in the definition of a "payment service provider" under regulation 2(1) of the PSRs 2017. It is a criminal offence to provide payment services without the required authorisation.[111] This offence is punishable by imprisonment, a fine, or both.

As noted previously, a "payment transaction" is defined in regulation 2(1) of the PSRs 2017 as *"an act, initiated by the payer or payee, of placing, transferring or withdrawing funds, irrespective of underlying obligations between the payer and payee"*.[112]

This definition does not capture arrangements for the physical movement of cash, securities settlement systems approved in connection with section 785 of the Companies Act 2006, and clearing systems operated by recognised clearing houses. A clearing system facilitates the transmission of payment instructions among its members and the settlement of these instructions by debiting or crediting the members' accounts held within such a system.

The preceding exclusion is particularly relevant since, unless a debtor and creditor hold accounts with the same bank, actual payment will be made through the relevant "clearing system". Clearing payments between the debtor and creditor occurs when the existing debtor-creditor relationship is unconditionally and irrevocably discharged, giving way to a new debtor-creditor relationship between the creditor and their bank. An unconditional credit to the creditor's account indicates the creditor's bank's acknowledgment of this new relationship.

Each clearing system operates according to its own "clearing cycle", which must be completed before the creditor's bank is contractually authorised, in relation to the debtor's bank, to credit the creditor's account unconditionally.

Clearing systems are regulated by the Payment Systems Regulator (**PSR**), which was established under the Financial Services (Banking Reform) Act 2013.

The Role of the PSR

In *R (on the application of Barclays Bank plc) v Payment Systems Regulator* [2020] EWHC 1614 (Admin), the High Court considered the extent of the PSR's powers under the Financial Services (Banking Reform) Act 2013. Barclays challenged the PSR's decision requiring changes to certain aspects of payment systems, arguing that the regulator had overstepped its authority. The court upheld the PSR's decision, affirming its broad discretion to intervene in payment systems to ensure competition, efficiency, and security.

The PSR oversees key clearing systems, including CHAPS (Clearing House Automated Payment System), Bacs (Bankers' Automated Clearing Services), and the Faster Payments Service, each of which plays a distinct role in the financial system.

110 The definition of "payment services" under the PSRs 2017 includes "operating a payment account," as outlined in regulation 2(1) and Schedule 1, paragraphs 1(a) and (b). The FCA provides non-binding guidance on the scope of the PSRs in Chapter 15 of its Perimeter Guidance Manual (PERG), which includes specific interpretations of the term "payment services" in PERG 15.3.

111 Under regulation 138 of the PSRs 2017.

112 The PSRs 2017 differentiate between authorised and unauthorised transactions. Under regulation 67(1), a payment transaction is considered authorised by the payer only if the payer has provided consent to the transaction either before execution or, if agreed, after execution. The method of providing consent must comply with the terms agreed between the paying bank and the payer, typically outlined in the account's terms and conditions. The FCA, at [8.221] of its Payment Services and Electronic Money Approach Document (Approach Document), advises that consent to execute a payment transaction may be provided in various ways. These include written consent, using a payment card and PIN, through a website, by telephone, or by using a password.

CHAPS[113] operates as a real-time gross settlement system (**RTGS**), facilitating high-value payments between banks and financial institutions. Unlike systems that process transactions in batches, it settles payments individually and immediately, making it essential for large financial transfers. Its counterparts in other jurisdictions include T2[114] in the European Union and Fedwire[115] in the United States. The legal significance of CHAPS was examined in *Tidal Energy Ltd v Bank of Scotland Plc* [2014] EWCA Civ 1107, where the Court of Appeal considered whether an instruction to make a CHAPS payment is satisfied when funds are sent to the bank maintaining the account identified by number and sort code in the instruction, even if the named beneficiary does not match the account holder.[116]

Bacs, in contrast, is designed for bulk payments, such as direct debits and direct credits, making it a widely used system for processing salaries, utility bills, and recurring payments. It provides a cost-effective and efficient mechanism for handling high volumes of lower-value transactions.[117]

Finally, the Faster Payments Service enables near-instantaneous electronic payments, offering a secure and rapid method for consumers and businesses to transfer funds.

5.2 Banking Payment Systems

Understanding the mechanics of money transmission within existing banking payment systems is essential.[118] Such a system is an organised arrangement for transferring monetary value between participants who are *deposit takers*.[119] This transfer may be conducted physically, such as through paper cheques or electronically. Transfers can occur immediately or as deferred payments.[120] The infrastructure supporting these systems includes technical networks, payment messages, and the rules and agreements governing interactions among participating agents.

113 See Brindle, M. and Cox, R. (eds.), *Law of Bank Payments* (Sweet & Maxwell, 2017), paras 3-002-3.006.

114 T2 is the RTGS system owned and operated by the Eurosystem that replaced TARGET2 on 20 March 2023. Central banks and commercial banks can submit payment orders in euros to T2, where these transactions are processed and settled in central bank money – funds held in an account with a central bank.

115 The Federal Reserve Banks operate the Fedwire Funds Service, an RTGS that allows participants to initiate funds transfers that are immediate, final, and irrevocable upon processing. Depository institutions and other eligible financial institutions holding an account with a Federal Reserve Bank can participate in the Fedwire Funds Service.

116 It was held: "*In my judgment, the customer's instruction made by execution of this specific 'CHAPS transfer' request form, and in particular the giving of the confirmation 'You are hereby authorised to effect these instructions . . . by transmission through the Clearing House Automated Payments System' was an instruction to make a payment transfer in accordance with the current CHAPS Scheme Rules and as the CHAPS transfer system is currently operated in accordance with the usual practice adopted by the participating clearing bankers.*" at [48] and "*CHAPSCo does not prescribe the basis on which payments are processed by the members of the scheme, apart from stating that payments should be processed within the maximum inwards payment transmission time of 1.5 hours. Since at least 2007, all of the major UK clearing banks have processed and routed electronic payments to a customer's account, including CHAPS payments, on the basis of sort code (or bank identifier code) and account number, but not account or beneficiary name. This is reflected by the Payment Council's guidance note entitled 'Payment Services Regulations – Industry Best Practice' which states 'payments executed via CHAPS are processed on sort code and account number – "the unique identifier"'. Banks are expected to process the vast majority of CHAPS payments on a 'straight-through' basis (ie without manual checks) in order to meet the short time-scale that is the hallmark of CHAPS*". at [54].

117 Ellinger, E. P., Lomnicka, E. and Hare, C., *Ellinger's Modern Banking Law* (Oxford University Press, 2011), p. 581.

118 Wood, P., *International Loans, Bonds, Guarantees and Legal Opinions* (Sweet & Maxwell, 2019) at [46-029].

119 Armour, J., Awrey, D., Davies, P., Enriques, L., Gordon, J., Mayer, C. and Payne, J., *Principles of Financial Regulation* (Oxford University Press, 2016), p. 281.

120 See Brindle, M. and Cox, R. (eds.), *Law of Bank Payments* (Sweet & Maxwell, 2017), paras 3-002-3.006.

HHJ Paul Matthews in *Terna Energy Trading DOO v Revolut Ltd* [2024] EWHC 1419 (Comm) provides a helpful summary of the functioning of payment mechanisms within such system:

> *It is necessary to describe briefly the payment mechanisms involved. This is not a case where A makes a payment to B using banknotes or coins, or even bank drafts. In modern commercial banking transactions, no such chattels change hands. Instead, accounts of customers with the same or, more likely, different banks are debited and credited to produce the impression that money has moved. But no money in fact moves at all. It is just a series of reciprocal credits and debits. As lawyers, at least, know, bank accounts do not actually hold money, or funds. Such accounts instead amount to a claim on the bank by the customer, a chose in action. At any one time, there is a single sum due from the bank to the customer (assuming that the account is in credit). The bank will discharge its debt to its customer, in whole or in part, by honouring the instructions of its customer to "transfer" all or part of its customer's credit to the account of a third party with another bank. It does this by agreeing with that other bank to a debit in its own account with that other bank (or a third bank – eg the Bank of England – at which both have accounts) and a corresponding credit to the third party's account with that other bank (or the third bank, as the case may be). . . . A bank ("A") which has a corresponding relationship with another ("B") will have an account with that bank. Bank B will refer to this as a vostro account (what is owed by it to the other: a liability). Bank A will maintain a mirror image record of the same account, known as a nostro account (what is owed to it by the other: an asset). (Any retail banking customer who notes credits and debits to, and keeps a running balance of the state of, his or her bank account is unknowingly maintaining a nostro account.) So the latter is simply a suspense account, used for reconciliation. The position is not in principle different for international transfers, though it is more complicated, because there are often more correspondent banks involved, and more than one possible applicable law. . . . Most such transfers are instituted, verified and recorded by the SWIFT messaging system: . . . (However, SWIFT is not itself a payment system).*[121]

Payment systems can be broadly categorised into pure payment systems and embedded payment systems, each serving a distinct function within the financial infrastructure.[122] Pure payment systems, such as CHAPS and Fedwire in the US, which provide RTGS for high-value financial transfers,[123] are designed solely to manage the transfer of money, operating independently from any other contractual obligations. Their primary function is to facilitate the movement of funds between parties without being tied to the settlement of underlying transactions.

In contrast, embedded payment systems integrate the payment process with the settlement of other obligations, ensuring that both payment and contract performance occur within the same framework. These systems are commonly found in financial markets and trading platforms, where payment is intrinsically linked to the completion of a broader transaction. Delivery-versus-Payment (**DvP**) systems, used in securities settlement, and Payment-versus-Payment (**PvP**) mechanisms, employed in foreign exchange markets, exemplify this approach by ensuring that financial obligations are met simultaneously with the corresponding transfer of assets.

An interbank payment system refers to an arrangement designed to facilitate or regulate the transfer of money between banks and building societies, often through electronic payment systems. Inter-bank payment systems are predominantly owned jointly by their largest users, namely the major UK incumbent banks.

The Banking Act 2009 defines inter-bank payment systems as mechanisms facilitating or controlling the transfer of money (including credit) or digital settlement assets between banks and building societies.[124] However, for the purposes of the Banking Act 2009, internal

121 Ibid. at [18] and [19].
122 Brindle, M. and Cox, R. (eds.), *Law of Bank Payments* (Sweet & Maxwell, 2017), Chapter 1.
123 Kern, A., *Principles of Banking Regulation* (Cambridge University Press, 2019) at [1.34].
124 See section 182 of the Banking Act 2009.

banking systems and correspondent banking arrangements are excluded from this definition. A correspondent bank is a credit institution that provides services on behalf of another financial institution. Correspondent banks[125] are typically used by financial institutions to conduct business in jurisdictions where they lack their own branch network or do not offer the required services provided by such correspondent banks. Where payments between customers of two banks in different countries and currencies require settlement by means of matching inter-bank payments, the matching payments are known as "cover payments".[126]

In the world of international banking and finance, efficient and secure payment systems are essential to ensure the smooth operation of financial markets. Two key components of this infrastructure are RTGS systems and private clearinghouses, such as the Continuous Linked Settlement (**CLS**) Bank for foreign exchange transactions or the Clearing House Interbank Payments System (**CHIPS**).[127] These systems play a vital role in settling large-value and time-sensitive payments, helping to mitigate settlement risk and ensure the stability of the global financial system.

5.3 Essential Features of RTGS Systems

An RTGS system is a high-value payment system in which the settlement of funds occurs in real time and on a gross basis.[128] It plays a crucial role in modern financial infrastructure; they ensure that transactions are settled in real time, ensuring that once processed, payments are final and cannot be reversed.

Unlike net settlement systems,[129] where transactions are aggregated and settled at the end of a business day, RTGS systems operate on a gross settlement basis, meaning that each transaction is settled individually. This method significantly reduces counterparty risk, as the bank initiating a payment is not reliant on receiving funds from other banks before the settlement can be completed.

RTGS systems are typically operated by central banks, forming the backbone of a country's payment infrastructure. They facilitate the transfer of large sums between banks and are commonly used for interbank lending, securities settlements, and other time-sensitive financial transactions. Given their systemic importance, central banks oversee RTGS systems to ensure operational efficiency and financial stability.

As RTGS transactions are settled continuously throughout the day, they also play a vital role in liquidity management. Banks participating in RTGS systems must maintain sufficient

125 Correspondent banking is defined in the Joint Money Laundering Steering Group's anti-money laundering (AML) and counter-terrorist financing (CTF) guidance (in chapter 16 of Part II) as: "*the provision of banking-related services by one bank (the 'Correspondent') to another bank (the 'Respondent'), involving the execution of payments processed by the Correspondent on behalf of the underlying customer(s) of the Respondent. This enables the Respondent to provide its own customers with cross-border products and services that it cannot provide them with itself, typically due to a lack of an international network.*"

126 When the same bank (e.g., a New York bank) acts as the correspondent for all the banks involved, settlement occurs entirely in-house through transfers recorded in the correspondent bank's books. The accounts held by banks with their foreign correspondents for these purposes are referred to as "nostro" accounts (from the perspective of the holding bank) or "vostro" accounts (from the perspective of the foreign correspondent bank). A credit is recorded in the creditor bank's "nostro" account (or "vostro" account from the correspondent bank's perspective), while a corresponding debit is recorded in the debtor bank's "nostro/vostro" account. In such cases, foreign clearing (e.g., New York clearing) is not required.

127 A New York computerised network through which cheques are cleared. Most Eurodollar transactions are cleared through CHIPS.

128 Armour, J., Awrey, D., Davies, P., Enriques, L., Gordon, J., Mayer, C. and Payne, J., *Principles of Financial Regulation* (Oxford University Press, 2016), p. 397.

129 See discussion on set-off and netting later.

balances with the central bank to meet their settlement obligations. To support banks in managing liquidity, many central banks provide intra-day credit or overdraft facilities, ensuring that banks can meet their payment obligations efficiently while minimising disruptions to the broader financial system.

While RTGS systems handle the domestic settlement of large-value payments, private clearinghouses like CLS Bank[130] provide critical services for settling cross-border and foreign exchange (FX) transactions.[131]

CLS Bank is a specialised financial institution that offers a global settlement service designed to eliminate settlement risk in the foreign exchange market by using a PvP mechanism. CLS facilitates the settlement of transactions in major currencies, including the US dollar, euro, pound sterling, and Japanese yen, operating under the oversight of central banks across multiple jurisdictions.

CLS' PvP mechanism ensures that both sides of an FX transaction are settled simultaneously. This significantly reduces the risk of one party defaulting on its payment obligations after the counterparty has already made its transfer. Settlement takes place directly across the books of CLS Bank, ensuring that once a transaction is processed, it is final and irrevocable. This feature helps to reduce settlement risk, particularly Herstatt Risk,[132] which refers to the risk that one party to an FX transaction will make payment while the counterparty fails to do so. This risk became widely recognised following the collapse of Herstatt Bank, which exposed the vulnerabilities of non-synchronised FX settlements.[133] By ensuring that both legs of an FX transaction are settled simultaneously, CLS reduces exposure to settlement risk.

Participation in CLS is limited to member banks, which submit their FX transactions for settlement through the system. To maintain stability and ensure the smooth functioning of the settlement process, these members must hold sufficient balances in the relevant currencies with CLS Bank. Moreover, CLS operates within a five-hour settlement window, overlapping with the opening hours of the world's major financial centres. This intra-day settlement framework enables the continuous settlement of FX transactions across time zones, allowing global financial institutions to manage their liquidity and foreign exchange exposure more effectively.

Beyond mitigating risk, CLS enhances operational efficiency by consolidating multiple FX transactions into a single streamlined process, thereby reducing the overall costs associated with foreign exchange trade settlements. This reduces the necessity for banks to hold large currency reserves across multiple accounts in different jurisdictions. Furthermore, CLS improves liquidity management by allowing banks to consolidate their FX settlements, minimising the requirement to maintain high liquidity levels in multiple currencies throughout the day.

The Structure and Functioning of the SWIFT Network

The Society for Worldwide Interbank Financial Telecommunication (**SWIFT**) is a global messaging network that enables secure financial communications between banks and financial institutions worldwide. Established in 1973 by a consortium of 239

130 www.cls-group.com/about/# (accessed in March 2025).
131 Bamford, C., *Principles of International Finance Law* (Oxford University Press, 2015), p. 88.
132 Armour, J., Awrey, D., Davies, P., Enriques, L., Gordon, J., Mayer, C. and Payne, J., *Principles of Financial Regulation* (Oxford University Press, 2016), p. 396.
133 Kern, A., *Principles of Banking Regulation* (Cambridge University Press, 2019) at [1.35].

banks from 15 countries, SWIFT was created with the aim of standardising financial messaging and reducing the operational risks and inefficiencies associated with earlier systems such as Telex.

SWIFT operates as a secure messaging platform, allowing financial institutions to send and receive information concerning financial transactions in a standardised and reliable manner. Importantly, SWIFT does not manage funds or execute payments; rather, it facilitates the secure transmission of payment instructions, securities trade details, and other financial communications between institutions. It provides a comprehensive set of message formats covering various types of financial transactions, including payment transfers, foreign exchange transactions, securities trades, and trade finance. Among the most widely used message types are the MT103, which is employed for customer transfers, and the MT202, which enables interbank transfers. These standardised message formats promote the efficient processing of financial transactions across borders:

> *there are two different methods of making payment when there are more than two banks (the Sending Bank and the Receiving Bank) involved, such as where each has a correspondent bank in New York through which USD payments have to be made. These two methods are known as the Cover Method and the Serial Method. The latter involves a series of payments between a chain of banks, one after the other, with funds moving only on receipt from the previous bank in the chain. That process takes time and is not well suited to "same day value" transfers. The Cover Method is a quicker process and involves the Sending Bank sending an MT 103 STP to the beneficiary's bank (ie, the Receiving Bank) at the same time as sending an MT 202 COV to the Sending Bank's correspondent bank in New York.*[134]

SWIFT has an extensive global reach, connecting over 11,500 institutions in more than 200 countries. In 2022 alone, SWIFT recorded an average daily volume of approximately 44.8 million messages.[135]

In the context of cross-border payments, SWIFT plays a pivotal role in facilitating correspondent banking relationships. Correspondent banks act as intermediaries in executing payments across different countries, enabling banks to conduct transactions in foreign currencies and navigate diverse regulatory environments. Through these relationships, banks maintain Nostro and Vostro accounts with one another, which allow funds to be transferred using the accounts of the correspondent banks, thereby ensuring the smooth execution of international payments.

In the case of *Malayan Banking Berhad v Barclays Bank PLC* [2019] SGHC(I) 04, the Singapore International Commercial Court held that where a bank sends a SWIFT MT 103 STP Single Customer Credit Transfer message ("MT 103 STP") to another bank to initiate a funds transfer, and the receiving bank acts upon that MT 103 STP, an implied contract arises between the two banks, under which the sending bank is unconditionally obliged to reimburse the receiving bank for the amount of the transfer.

SWIFT vs. Settlement Systems

It is essential to distinguish SWIFT from payment and settlement systems. Although SWIFT provides the messaging infrastructure that enables the secure and standardised

134 *Malayan Banking Berhad v Barclays Bank PLC* [2019] SGHC(I) 04 at [33].
135 See www.swift.com/about-us/discover-swift/fin-traffic-figures (accessed in March 2025).

transmission of financial instructions, it does not itself process or settle transactions. The actual settlement of funds is carried out through other mechanisms, such as RTGS systems or private clearinghouses.

Despite not handling the movement of funds, SWIFT's robust and centralised infrastructure makes it a critical element of the global financial system.

5.4 Open Banking and Digital Payment Platforms

The UK has been at the forefront of payment system innovations, particularly with the implementation of Open Banking. Open Banking, implemented through the PSRs 2017, allows third-party providers to access customers' bank account data (with their consent) to provide tailored financial services. This innovation has transformed the UK's payment landscape by enabling new players to offer payment services that directly compete with traditional banks.

In particular, digital payment platforms like Apple Pay, Google Pay, and PayPal have gained widespread adoption, allowing consumers to make contactless payments using mobile devices. These platforms are regulated under the PSRs 2017.

Open Banking and PSD2 in the UK

Open Banking is a regulatory initiative designed to foster competition and innovation in the financial services sector. Under PSD2, banks are required to share customer account data with third-party providers, allowing these providers to develop new financial products and services. For example, fintech companies can offer services like account aggregation, enabling users to view multiple accounts from different banks in one interface. Open Banking has also facilitated the rise of new payment methods, such as account-to-account transfers, which provide an alternative to traditional card payments.[136]

5.5 Payment Systems Regulation in the European Union

As noted previously, the UK open banking initiative is based on the EU PSD2. Such a directive was conceived as an instrument to govern payment services across the EU. PSD2 was designed to increase competition and innovation in the payments sector by allowing third-party providers, such as fintech companies, to access consumers' bank account information (with their consent) and offer payment services directly to them.

PSD2 also introduced stricter security requirements for online payments (applicable to any online provider), including the implementation of strong customer authentication, which mandates two-factor authentication for online transactions. This requirement has been considered in *Bundeskammer für Arbeiter und Angestellte v ING-DiBa Direktbank Austria Niederlassung*

136 BCG [2024], BCG, 'Fortune Favors the Bold' *Global Payments Report* (October 2024), p. 20 available at https://web-assets.bcg.com/21/ac/d3f46d0144d98059ccbe9506483a/2024-global-payments-report-october-2024.pdf (accessed in March 2025).

der ING-DiBa AG (Case C-191/17).[137] In this case, the ECJ ruled that the terms of a payment account agreement must comply with the requirements set out in PSD2. The case involved Deutsche Bank's terms for online payments, which were found to contravene PSD2's provisions on transparency and consumer rights. The ruling underscored the importance of PSD2 in harmonising payment system regulations across the EU and ensuring that payment service providers adhere to high standards of transparency and consumer protection.

5.6 Payment Systems Regulation in the United States

In the United States, payment systems are overseen by various federal and state regulatory bodies, with the Federal Reserve playing a key role in managing and regulating payment infrastructure. The adoption of faster payment systems is fairly recent. The first instant payment system, RTP, has been operational since 2017 and processes a minimal proportion of US retail payments. This ecosystem has been invigorated by the Fedwire Service in July 2023.

The Federal Reserve operates Fedwire, a real-time gross settlement system similar to CHAPS, which processes large-value payments between banks and financial institutions. The Automated Clearing House (ACH) network, governed by NACHA (the National Automated Clearing House Association), is used for processing bulk payments, including payroll, government benefits, and business-to-business payments.

The Dodd-Frank Wall Street Reform and Consumer Protection Act 2010 introduced significant changes to the regulation of payment systems in the US, including the Durbin Amendment, which capped interchange fees for debit card transactions. In *NACS v. Board of Governors of the Federal Reserve System* (746 F.3d 474 [D.C. Cir. 2014]), merchants challenged the Federal Reserve's implementation of the Durbin Amendment, arguing that the cap on debit card interchange fees was set too high, allowing banks to charge merchants excessive fees. The court ultimately upheld the Federal Reserve's rule, emphasising that the regulatory framework established by the Dodd-Frank Act granted the Federal Reserve broad discretion to set fee caps. This case illustrates the balancing act between regulating payment systems to protect consumers and merchants while ensuring financial institutions remain competitive.

5.7 Payment Systems Innovation and Regulation in China

China's payment systems have undergone significant transformation, driven by the rapid adoption of mobile payment platforms like Alipay and WeChat Pay. These platforms dominate China's digital payment landscape, allowing consumers to make payments using mobile apps that integrate with bank accounts and e-wallets. The People's Bank of China regulates the country's payment systems and has introduced measures to ensure that mobile payment platforms operate securely and transparently.[138] The Payment and Settlement System Regulations govern payment services in China, providing the legal framework for the operation of payment institutions and the oversight of payment activities.

137 Case C-191/17: Judgment of the Court (Fifth Chamber) of 4 October 2018 (request for a preliminary ruling from the Oberster Gerichtshof – Austria).

138 Aurazo, J., Frost, J. and Kosse, A., 'Faster Digital Payments: Global and Regional Perspectives' *BIS Papers No. 152* (December 2024), available at www.bis.org/publ/bppdf/bispap152.pdf (accessed in March 2025).

5.8 Payment Systems in India: UPI and Regulatory Developments

India has experienced a rapid transformation in its payment systems, largely driven by the government-backed Unified Payments Interface (UPI). UPI is a real-time payment system that facilitates instant money transfers between bank accounts using mobile devices.

The Payment and Settlement Systems Act 2007 provides the legal framework for regulating payment systems in India. The Reserve Bank of India, under this Act, has broad regulatory authority over payment systems, including the power to issue guidelines for the operation of payment service providers and to oversee the security and efficiency of payment systems.

In *Aadhaar Judgment* (*Justice K.S. Puttaswamy v Union of India* [2018] 1 SCC 809), the Supreme Court of India upheld the legality of the *Aadhaar* biometric identification system while limiting its mandatory use for certain services, including banking and payment systems. The judgment clarified that payment systems must comply with data protection laws, ensuring that users' personal data is safeguarded while facilitating access to digital payment services. The case underscored the need for balancing innovation in payment systems with the protection of fundamental rights, such as privacy.

5.9 Payment Systems in Japan: Regulation and Innovation

Japan's payment systems are regulated by the Bank of Japan, which operates the Zengin System,[139] a payment network that handles interbank transfers and real-time settlements. The legal framework for payment services is provided by the Payment Services Act,[140] which was amended in 2016 to include provisions for regulating cryptocurrency exchanges. The Payment Services Act was further amended in 2022 to introduce a formal definition of "Electronic Payment Instruments", with the primary objective of capturing stablecoins within a clear regulatory framework and establishing a statutory regime for trust companies that issue stablecoins in the form of trust beneficial rights. The 2022 amendment also clarified the scope of what constitutes an "electronic payment instruments exchange service" and an "electronic payments handling service" – terms used to describe intermediary activities relating to both stablecoins and existing forms of electronic money. Finally, the Payment Services Act sets out requirements for registration, security, and consumer protection, ensuring that payment systems operate securely and efficiently.

5.10 Blockchain and Payment Systems

Blockchain-based payment systems have the potential to streamline cross-border payments by reducing the need for intermediaries such as correspondent banks.

The regulatory landscape for blockchain-based payment systems has been further clarified by FSMA 2023, which brings certain cryptoassets under the UK financial regulatory perimeter. This new legal framework treats cryptoassets as financial instruments for regulatory purposes when used within payment systems. The FCA now has enhanced powers to regulate cryptoasset-based payment systems, ensuring compliance with AML and consumer protection requirements. This aligns with the global trend of integrating cryptoassets into formal financial systems while addressing the unique risks posed by decentralised technologies.

139 See www.zengin-net.jp/en/zengin_net/pdf/pamphlet_e.pdf (accessed in March 2025).
140 (Act No. 59 of 2009).

Blockchain's Role in Cross-Border Payments

Traditional cross-border payments can take days to settle and incur high fees due to the involvement of multiple intermediaries. Blockchain technology offers an alternative by enabling peer-to-peer transactions without intermediaries. Ripple,[141] a blockchain-based platform, allows for real-time settlement of cross-border payments, reducing transaction times from several days to a matter of seconds. This technology has been particularly useful for businesses operating in multiple countries, allowing them to transfer funds quickly and cost-effectively.

6 CENTRAL BANK DIGITAL CURRENCIES

In a technologically driven environment, central banks around the world are exploring the possibility of issuing their own CBDCs.[142] CBDCs are digital or virtual currencies issued by a sovereign central bank as a digital equivalent of a specific denomination of fiat currency, such as the US dollar or GBP. The value of CBDCs remains stable, fluctuating only in line with the movements of the underlying fiat currency relative to other fiat currencies.

6.1 The Legal Framework for CBDCs in the UK

The Bank of England and HM Treasury have been actively exploring the potential introduction of a CBDC, commonly referred to as the "digital pound" or "Britcoin". While the British legal framework for CBDCs is still evolving, several statutory provisions, along with policy and consultation papers, have already laid the groundwork for its potential implementation.

While the Bank of England has the authority to issue physical currency and to oversee systemically important payment systems, the introduction of a CBDC raises the question of whether additional legislative authority would be required for the issuance of digital currency.

In February 2023, the Bank of England and HM Treasury issued a joint consultation paper outlining the potential design of the "digital pound". The paper sketches foundational principles for the possible introduction of a CBDC, emphasising the need for legislation to establish its legal status as central bank money, ensuring it holds the same standing as physical cash. FSMA 2023 further enhances the Bank of England's authority, ensuring that both private digital currencies and CBDCs are integrated into the wider payment infrastructure under appropriate regulatory oversight. FSMA 2023 grants the Bank of England powers to manage and regulate digital assets, ensuring full integration with the existing RTGS system. This framework also addresses concerns about financial disintermediation, proposing limits on individual holdings of digital pounds to protect liquidity within the banking sector. The

141 In December 2020 (see www.sec.gov/files/litigation/complaints/2020/comp-pr2020-338.pdf – accessed in March 2025) in the US the SEC filed an action against Ripple Labs and two of its executives alleging that the company and two top executives raised money through the distribution and sale of XRP, which the SEC claims was a security. Ripple replied that XRP was not a security and that the SEC had no authority to regulate it as one. The case was settled.

142 Armelius, H., Guibourg, G., Johansson, S. and Schmalholz, J., 'E-Krona Design Models: Pros, Cons and Trade-Offs' (2020) (2) *Sveriges Riksbank Economic Review* 80–96.

Bank of England has confirmed that any digital currency would be fully integrated with the RTGS system to ensure efficient and secure payments, reinforcing the role of CBDCs within its statutory framework. Additionally, concerns about privacy and data protection may necessitate the development of new legislation governing the handling of personal financial information related to CBDCs, particularly under the Data Protection Act 2018.[143]

6.2 The Legal Framework for CBDCs in the US

The US has adopted a cautious approach towards the development of CBDCs. The Federal Reserve (**Fed**), alongside other key regulatory bodies, has been actively researching and conducting pilot programmes to explore the feasibility of a US CBDC, commonly referred to as the "digital dollar". However, no statutory provisions have yet been enacted to explicitly authorise the issuance of a CBDC.

The Fed operates under the Federal Reserve Act of 1913, which grants it the authority to issue physical currency and regulate monetary policy. While this statute provides the Fed with broad powers to manage the nation's currency supply, the introduction of a digital currency would likely require additional legislative approval. In 2022, Executive Order 14067[144] – aimed at developing a digital assets policy plan and organising federal regulators' efforts in that area – initiated a comprehensive review of digital assets, including CBDCs. In January 2025, the Presidential Executive Order entitled "Strengthening American Leadership in Digital Financial Technology" (**2025 Executive Order**)[145] was issued, the stated objective of which is to support the responsible advancement of blockchain technology while, at the same time, it prohibited federal agencies from exploring the development of CBDCs. CBDCs are defined in the 2025 Executive Order as "*a form of digital money or monetary value, denominated in the national unit of account, that is a direct liability of the central bank*".

6.3 The Digital Euro

The development of CBDCs in the European Union is being led by the ECB as part of a broader strategy to modernise the European payment landscape. The digital euro is envisioned as a digital form of central bank money designed to complement physical currency while ensuring a secure and efficient retail payment method for both consumers and businesses.

The ECB's initiative aims to support monetary sovereignty by providing a centralised, stable digital currency; offer privacy in transactions while ensuring compliance with AML and CTF regulations; and enhance payment system resilience, particularly in scenarios where private digital currencies might pose risks to the financial system.[146] It is perceived as "*a unique opportunity to overcome the persistent fragmentation in retail payment systems across the euro area. Unlike*

143 2018 c. 12.

144 www.presidency.ucsb.edu/documents/executive-order-14067-ensuring-responsible-development-digital-assets (accessed in March 2025).

145 www.whitehouse.gov/presidential-actions/2025/01/strengthening-american-leadership-in-digital-financial-technology/ (accessed in March 2025).

146 "*The Digital Euro Regulation aims at limiting the digital euro's store of value function, in particular by imposing holding limits. Lower or equal holding limits would apply to residents outside the euro area than to residents in the euro area.*" See ECB note: Digital euro outside the euro area, p. 2, available at https://data.consilium.europa.eu/doc/document/WK-1026-2025-INIT/en/pdf (accessed in March 2025).

single-nation currency systems, the monetary union faces distinct challenges due to diverse legacy national standards and a non-unified retail payment system".[147]

The legal and regulatory framework for the digital euro would be rooted in existing European treaties and regulations, with the TFEU providing key provisions that could facilitate its introduction. Article 128(1) TFEU grants the ECB the exclusive authority to authorise the issuance of banknotes. While traditionally applied to physical currency, this provision could be extended to encompass digital forms of central bank money, reinforcing the ECB's mandate in monetary policy and financial stability. Additionally, Article 127(2) TFEU outlines the ECB's mandate to ensure the smooth operation of payment systems, a crucial rationale for the digital euro's development. The ECB Statute, specifically Article 16 of the Statute of the ESCB, provides the ECB with the authority to issue currency, a power that could be extended to digital currencies, subject to appropriate legislative adaptation.

The European Commission has introduced a legislative proposal to formally establish the digital euro, providing the necessary legal framework for its issuance, distribution, and use across the Eurozone.[148] This proposal addresses the operational aspects of the digital euro, including its distribution via commercial banks and other PSPs, as well as its status as legal tender within the eurozone.

Existing judicial decisions related to digital currencies and financial regulation could also provide useful guidance with respect to the digital euro. In *Skatteverket v David Hedqvist*, Case C-264/14 ECLI:EU:C:2015:718,[149] the EU Court of Justice clarified the legal stance on the VAT treatment of cryptocurrencies, a ruling that may influence the regulatory classification of the digital euro. Furthermore, the *Schrems II*[150] decisions on data protection, although not directly concerning digital assets, are likely to shape how personal data associated with digital euro transactions will be handled, particularly in cross-border contexts.

The ECB is also working with global institutions, including the Bank for International Settlements (**BIS**),[151] to ensure that the digital euro aligns with international standards for CBDC interoperability and cross-border payment efficiency.

6.4 Legal Framework Governing CBDC in China

China has taken a leading role in the development and implementation of a CBDC, with its Digital Currency Electronic Payment, commonly known as the e-CNY, representing the most advanced attempt globally to deploy a fully operational CBDC. The People's Bank

147 Lane, P., 'The Digital Euro: Maintaining the Autonomy of the Monetary System' *Keynote Speech by Philip R. Lane, Member of the Executive Board of the ECB, University College Cork Economics Society Conference 2025*, available at www.ecb.europa.eu/press/key/date/2025/html/ecb.sp250320_1~41c9459722.en.html (accessed in March 2025).

148 www.ecb.europa.eu/euro/digital_euro/progress/shared/pdf/ecb.deprp202412.en.pdf (accessed in March 2025).

149 *Skatteverket v David Hedqvist*, Case C-264/14 ECLI:EU:C:2015:718.

150 Judgment of the Court (Grand Chamber) of 16 July 2020, ECLI:EU:C:2020:559. In its July 2020 *Schrems II* judgment, the Court of Justice of the European Union (CJEU) invalidated the European Commission's Privacy Shield Decision due to concerns over intrusive US surveillance programmes, rendering personal data transfers based on the Privacy Shield Decision unlawful. Additionally, the Court imposed stricter conditions for data transfers relying on standard contractual clauses (SCCs). Data controllers and processors intending to use SCCs must ensure that the level of data protection afforded to individuals is essentially equivalent to that guaranteed under the General Data Protection Regulation (GDPR) and the EU Charter of Fundamental Rights (CFR). Where necessary, supplementary measures must be implemented to address deficiencies in the legal protections of third countries. If such measures cannot guarantee adequate protection, operators are required to suspend the transfer of personal data outside the EU.

151 See Central Bank Digital Currencies: Ongoing Policy Perspectives (May 2023), available at www.bis.org/publ/othp65.pdf (accessed in March 2025).

of China has spearheaded the project, designing the e-CNY as a digital form of the RMB, China's official fiat currency.

The People's Bank of China's authority to issue and manage China's currency is derived from a number of foundational legislative acts, including the Law of the People's Republic of China on the People's Bank of China (**PBoC Law**)[152] and the Law on the Renminbi.[153] These statutes establish the People's Bank of China's central role in currency issuance and monetary policy. With the introduction of the e-CNY, these frameworks have been amended to incorporate digital currency, recognising it as a legal form of RMB. These amendments granted the People's Bank of China explicit authority to issue digital RMB alongside traditional paper currency. Article 16 of the PBoC Law confirms that RMB, whether physical or digital, is the sole legal tender in China, reinforcing the requirement for its mandatory acceptance in commercial transactions.

The Law on the Renminbi mandates that all businesses and individuals in China must accept RMB as legal tender, extending this obligation to the e-CNY. With its legal status enshrined, the e-CNY enjoys the same standing as physical cash, ensuring its widespread adoption under existing currency and payment system laws.[154]

The regulatory framework for the e-CNY is closely tied to China's broader financial and payment system regulations. The Regulations on the Administration of Payment Services of Non-Financial Institutions (2010), alongside the Measures for the Administration of AML and CTF, play a central role in governing the digital payments ecosystem in which the e-CNY operates. Financial institutions in China are required to integrate the e-CNY into their payment infrastructure, and the People's Bank of China has developed partnerships with major state-owned banks to support the deployment and circulation of the e-CNY.

The e-CNY operates under a two-tier model, where the People's Bank of China issues the digital currency to authorised intermediaries, such as state-owned banks, which then distribute it to the public. This structure ensures that the People's Bank of China retains control over the issuance and value of the digital currency while leveraging the existing financial system for its distribution and management.

Unlike decentralised cryptocurrencies such as Bitcoin, the e-CNY is fully traceable and controlled by the People's Bank of China. Chinese authorities have described the e-CNY as incorporating "controllable anonymity", meaning that while transactions between users may retain some level of privacy, the People's Bank of China retains the ability to trace transactions for regulatory and law enforcement purposes, particularly for AML and CTF compliance. The Cybersecurity Law of the People's Republic of China[155] and the Data Security Law of the People's Republic of China[156] provide the legal basis for the handling of personal data associated with e-CNY transactions. However, these laws also grant the Chinese government broad authority to access and control financial data, raising concerns about privacy and government surveillance, particularly among international observers.

152 Unofficial translation available at www.pbc.gov.cn/english/130733/2941519/2015082610501049304.pdf (accessed in March 2025).

153 See also 'Regulations of the People's Republic of China on the Administration of Renminbi (2018 Amended)' unofficial translation available at http://camlmac.pbc.gov.cn/english/130733/3858845/index.html (accessed in March 2025).

154 Working Group on E-CNY Research and Development of the People's Bank of China, 'Progress of Research & Development of E-CNY in China' *BIS Papers No 123* (2021), available at www.bis.org/publ/bppdf/bispap123_e.pdf (accessed in March 2025).

155 Unofficial translation available at https://digichina.stanford.edu/work/translation-cybersecurity-law-of-the-peoples-republic-of-china-effective-june-1-2017/ (accessed in March 2025).

156 Unofficial translation available at https://digichina.stanford.edu/work/translation-data-security-law-of-the-peoples-republic-of-china/ (accessed in March 2025).

China has also explored the cross-border applications of the e-CNY, aiming to reduce reliance on the US dollar in international trade and promote the internationalisation of the RMB. However, the use of the e-CNY outside China poses legal challenges, particularly given China's capital controls and regulatory restrictions on currency movement. The People's Bank of China has conducted trials in cooperation with other countries and international organisations to test the cross-border interoperability of the e-CNY. Notably, China has participated in the BIS multi-CBDC bridge project, which sought to develop a multi-CBDC platform designed to be shared among participating central banks and commercial banks. This platform was built on distributed ledger technology to facilitate instant cross-border payments and settlement, ensuring greater efficiency, security, and transparency in international financial transactions.[157]

7 THE LEGAL NATURE OF DEBT AND PAYMENT OBLIGATIONS

Debt is the natural link between money and payment. It represents a legally enforceable obligation where one party, the debtor, is required to pay a specified sum of money to another party, the creditor. The legal character of this obligation is shaped by common law principles, statutory provisions, and contractual agreements that govern the creation, enforcement, and discharge of debt.

7.1 The Nature of Debt as a Legal Obligation

A debt typically relates to a fixed and ascertainable sum of money that is due from one party to another. As articulated in *Webb v Stenton* (1883) 11 QBD 518, the essence of a debt is the obligation to pay a specific sum, which distinguishes it from other contractual obligations, such as the provision of goods or services. A debt is typically created by contract, though it may also arise through statutory provisions or court orders. In loan agreements, the debt is created when the borrower agrees to repay a specified sum, often with interest, over a predetermined timeframe. The loan agreement details the terms of repayment, the timing of payments, and the remedies available to the lender in case of default. The key feature of debt is that it involves a sum certain, payable either immediately or at a future date, and its enforceability is governed by the terms of the contract or statutory law.

In *Re George Inglefield Ltd* [1933] Ch 1, while dealing with the essential differences between a sale and a secured loan, the court concluded that it is not in doubt that an obligation to repay a debt is a contractual duty and failure to meet such an obligation constitutes a breach of contract. However, since the financing, in that instance, was provided by way of a sale and purchase the seller was not, by reason only of having sold the assets, required to account to the purchaser for any loss incurred by the purchaser on a resale of the assets sold.[158]

At common law, debts are classified as a type of chose in action,[159] meaning that a creditor cannot take possession of the debt without the cooperation of the debtor or through legal

157 See www.bis.org/about/bisih/topics/cbdc/mcbdc_bridge.htm (accessed in March 2025).

158 "*[I]n a transaction of sale the vendor is not entitled to get back the subject-matter of the sale by returning to the purchaser the money that has passed between them. In the case of a mortgage or charge, the mortgagor is entitled, until he has been foreclosed, to get back the subject-matter of the mortgage or charge by returning to the mortgagee the money that has passed between them*" in *Re George Inglefield Ltd* [1933] Ch 1 at p. 27.

159 *New York Life Insurance Co v Public Trustee* [1924] 2 Ch 101.

proceedings. As such, a creditor's right requires enforcement through legal mechanisms if the debtor fails to make payment. This principle was highlighted in the conceptual distinction between ownership of property and entitlement to a claim, as discussed in *Libyan Arab Foreign Bank v Bankers Trust Co* [1989] QB 728, where the court examined the nature of payment obligations under letters of credit and confirmed that the creditor does not have immediate control over the debt until enforcement mechanisms are applied.

7.2 Tender and Discharge of Debt

A debt is generally discharged when the debtor makes payment in accordance with the terms of the contract. The payment must be unconditional and in full. If the creditor were to refuse tender of the full amount, the debtor may be discharged from the obligation. In *Startup v Macdonald* (1843) 6 Man & G 593, the court held that tendering the correct amount in accordance with the contract terms discharges the debtor's obligation, even if the creditor refuses to accept the payment. This principle underscores that once a valid offer to pay is made, the debtor's liability is discharged.

On the other hand, part-payment of a debt may not discharge the entire obligation even if the creditor were to accept the part-payment as full satisfaction of the debt. The reason lies in the principles governing consideration.

Debt Settlement and the Role of Consideration

The rule in *Pinnel's Case* [1602] 5 Co Rep 117a is a longstanding principle in English law which states that part-payment of a debt on the due date does not discharge the entire debt unless additional consideration is given.[160]

Foakes v Beer [1884] UKHL confirmed the principle that part-payment of a debt does not discharge the debtor's obligation unless fresh consideration is provided. In this case, despite Mrs. Beer agreeing to accept instalment payments from Dr. Foakes, the court ruled that since no additional consideration was provided, Mrs. Beer was entitled to claim interest on the debt. This ruling highlights the strict requirements for legally binding settlements of debt obligations and the importance of consideration in any agreement to modify debt terms. However, in *Welby v Drake* ([1825] 1 Car & P 557), the court ruled that if a creditor accepts a third party's payment in full satisfaction of a debt, the debt is discharged. This case illustrates the distinction between part-payment by the debtor and third-party payment, where the latter can constitute full settlement due to the involvement of a third party acting as a separate entity. Also, Section 92 of the Bills of Exchange Act 1882 provides an exception to this rule in the context of negotiable instruments. It allows for the discharge of a bill of exchange or promissory note by part-payment if the holder accepts it in satisfaction of the entire debt.

160 Payment of part of an undisputed claim does not constitute valid consideration for waiving the balance of the claim, as the debtor is merely fulfilling an existing contractual obligation. Conversely, relinquishing even a weak argument can constitute valid consideration for a settlement, provided the dispute is genuine, as demonstrated in *Simantob v Shavleyan* [2019] EWCA Civ 1105.

The mode of payment is an important aspect of discharging a debt. At common law, the creditor is entitled to insist on payment in legal tender unless otherwise agreed. In *Fielding v Corry* (1858) 4 H & N 387, the court held that a creditor could refuse payment by cheque and demand payment in legal tender unless the contract expressly allowed for alternative methods of payment. In modern banking transactions, electronic transfers are used to discharge payment obligations, and many contracts provide for such methods. However, unless the contract specifies otherwise, the creditor retains the right to demand payment in legal tender.

7.3 The Situs of Debt and Payment Obligations

All property, whether tangible or intangible, has a situs for legal purposes. The situs of a debt is a key consideration in determining the jurisdiction and enforceability of payment obligations, particularly in cross-border financial transactions. Since, as noted previously, a debt is to be considered a chose in action, the same generally are situate in the country where they are properly recoverable or can be enforced.

The *situs* of a debt is inextricably linked to the law governing that debt, as recognised by well-established principles of private international law.[161] As articulated in *Martin v Nadel* [1906] 2 KB 26, debts or choses in action are generally situated in the jurisdiction where they are properly recoverable or capable of being enforced.[162] This principle has been reaffirmed by the Supreme Court in *Taurus Petroleum Limited v State Oil Marketing Company of the Ministry of Oil, Republic of Iraq* [2017] UKSC 64, which clarified that the situs of a debt is the residence of the debtor (the bank in this case), rather than the place of payment.

In essence, a debt or chose in action is deemed to be situated in the country where it is enforceable, and as stated in *Société Eram Shipping Co Ltd v Cie Internationale de Navigation* [2003] UKHL 30; [2004] 1 AC 260,[163] it can only be discharged according to the law of that place. As a matter of English law, "the place of performance" for the purpose of a cross-border payment obligation is the contractual place of performance (*Litasco SA v Banque El Amana SA* [2025] EWHC 312 (Comm)).[164] If the debt cannot be recovered or enforced in a particular jurisdiction, it cannot be said to be situated there (*Richardson v Richardson* [1927] P 228).[165]

The general presumption is that a debt is properly recoverable or enforceable in the place of residence or domicile of the debtor. This presumption has long been recognised, since *New York Life Insurance Co v Public Trustee* [1924] 2 Ch 101.[166] It is possible to interpret this line of authority as supporting the proposition that the debtor's residence determines the *situs* of the debt on the basis that it is the place where the debt is typically recoverable. However, to equate the *situs* of a debt simply with the debtor's residence or domicile may risk obscuring the true purpose of the concept – namely, to identify the jurisdiction in which the law governing the debt will determine whether it has been discharged, and to ascertain the legal system under which the existence and extent of the debt must be adjudicated.[167]

161 This principle is affirmed in a long line of authority, including *Ellis v M'Henry* (1871) LR 6 CP 228; *Martin v Nadel* [1906] 2 KB 26, 29; *Swiss Bank Corp v Boehmische Industrial Bank* [1923] 1 KB 673, 684; and *Société Eram Shipping Co Ltd v Cie Internationale de Navigation* [2003] UKHL 30.
162 *Dicey* defines "*lex loci solutionis*" at [1-028] as the "*law of the country where a contract is to be performed or where a debt is to be paid*".
163 At [107].
164 At [83].
165 At [235]–[236].
166 At [115], [119]–[120].
167 At [82].

As stipulated in *Hardy Exploration & Production (India) Inc v Government of India* [2018] EWHC 1916 (Comm), the general presumption may be displaced where it is shown that the debt is properly recoverable in a jurisdiction other than that of the debtor's residence or domicile. This may arise, for instance, when the parties have entered into a "special agreement" or where there exists an "exclusive right of suit" in favour of a different jurisdiction. The overarching purpose of identifying the *situs* in this manner is to ensure legal certainty and to protect debtors and third parties from the risk of double liability.

7.4 Interest on Debt and the Late Payment of Commercial Debts (Interest) Act 1998

Generally, at common law, there is no interest on debts unless the contract or the customs of the trade provide that there should be.[168] Similarly, there can be interest, simple or compound,[169] on a debt, but only if the contract under which the debt arises, or the usage of the trade, so provides. In contractual relationships, compound interest is only awarded where the contract, or the usage of a trade, provides for it.[170]

There are various particular situations where statutory interest is payable as of right. The Late Payment of Commercial Debts (Interest) Act 1998 (**Late Payment Act**) inserts an implied term into business-to-business contracts for the supply of goods and services, providing creditors with a statutory right to claim simple interest on late payments, as well as a fixed sum and reasonable recovery costs.[171] The Late Payment Act sets the interest rate at 8% above the Bank of England base rate, compensating creditors for the delayed receipt of funds. The statutory interest starts accruing after 30 days from the date of delivery, invoice, or acceptance of goods or services unless a different payment term has been contractually agreed upon. Moreover,

> *interest only runs on the obligation of the purchaser of goods or services to pay the price of those goods or services to the supplier; it does not run on an obligation of the supplier to refund the price to the purchaser in the case of a total failure of consideration.*[172]

Furthermore, the resulting statutory right can be displaced if the contract includes an express interest clause or an alternative "substantial remedy" for late payment, as confirmed in *Yuanda (UK) Co Ltd v WW Gear Construction Ltd* [2010] EWHC 720 (TCC). In this case, the court considered whether a lower contractual interest rate could substitute for the statutory rate. The court held that a substantial remedy for late payment must offer adequate compensation and deterrence to meet the statutory standard.[173]

168 *London, Chatham and Dover Railway Co v South Eastern Railway Co* [1893] AC 429 (HL).
169 Compound interest being interest upon interest.
170 It may also be awarded: (a) in trust and constructive trust cases, where the claim has a proprietary flavour and the defendant has applied the money in trade, so that the award is seeking to represent the gain made by the defendant rather than the loss to the claimant; (b) in the form of special damages to cover compound interest paid by the claimant as a result of the defendant's wrongful act or omission; and (c) in arbitration cases, though the principles on which arbitrators should award compound interest have yet to emerge.
171 The EU Directive 2000/35/EC of the European Parliament and of the Council of 29 June 2000 on combating late payment in commercial transactions was adopted with respect to late payments in commercial transactions.
172 *Howell v Lerwick Commercial Mortgage Corporation Ltd* [2015] EWHC 1177 (Ch) at [20].
173 For interest to be claimed on a debt, it must qualify as a "qualifying debt," which refers to an agreement to pay the whole or part of a contract price. This applies to contractual rights to claim specific sums,

7.5 Default and Remedies for Non-Payment

When a debtor fails to comply with the terms of payment, they are in default, which triggers various remedies for the creditor. These remedies include suing for the debt, claiming interest, enforcing security interests, or initiating insolvency proceedings. It is a well-established principle that a creditor is entitled to sue for the unpaid sum and recover any additional costs or damages caused by the debtor's failure to pay.[174]

If the debtor is unable to pay their debts, the creditor can initiate insolvency proceedings under the Insolvency Act 1986. Section 123 of the Insolvency Act provides that a debtor is insolvent if they are unable to pay their debts as they fall due or if their liabilities exceed their assets. This provision allows creditors to petition for a debtor's bankruptcy or the winding-up of a company if the debtor is unable to meet their financial obligations (default and insolvency claims are discussed in Chapters 9, 10, and 13).

8 SET-OFF AND NETTING

Set-off and netting are indispensable mechanisms in financial transactions, particularly in loan agreements and banking. Both concepts serve to reduce counterparty risk by allowing payment obligations to be offset or netted, especially in cases of default or insolvency. In loan agreements and banking transactions, set-off rights are either created under common law or included contractually, while netting is often employed in more complex financial transactions, such as derivatives and multi-party lending.[175]

8.1 Set-Off and Banking Transactions

Set-off is the right of a party to offset mutual debts, meaning that instead of each party paying the gross amount owed, the payment obligations are offset to produce a net amount owed by one party to the other. Set-off can be either legal, equitable, or contractual and is essential in protecting creditors by reducing the risk of non-payment.[176]

Legal set-off is a common law right that applies when both parties have mutual, liquidated debts that are due and payable. This principle was confirmed in *Roxburghe v Cox* (1881) 17 Ch D 520. In banking transactions, this principle allows a lender to set off amounts held in a borrower's account against unpaid loan obligations. For example, if a borrower defaults on a loan, the lender can apply funds from the borrower's deposit account to reduce the outstanding loan amount.

A distinct form of set-off available to banks is Banker's set-off, also known as the right to combine accounts (which is discussed in more detail in Chapter 3). This principle ensures that banks can manage credit risk effectively by using funds from one account to offset liabilities from another. However, the accounts must be of the same nature, and both debts must be

such as those arising from loss and expense claims, but it does not extend to claims for damages for breach of contract.

174 *White v City of London Brewery Co* (1889) 42 Ch D 237.

175 Goode, R. and van Zwieten, K., *Principles of Corporate Insolvency Law* (Sweet & Maxwell, 2019), Chapter 9, Section 1.

176 Goode, R. and van Zwieten, K., *Principles of Corporate Insolvency Law* (Sweet & Maxwell, 2019), Chapter 9, Section 2.

due before the set-off can be exercised.[177] This allows a bank to consolidate multiple accounts held by the same customer and treat them as a single account. In practice, banks frequently rely on the right to combine accounts to mitigate losses when a customer defaults on a loan. Moreover, loan agreements often include specific set-off clauses that provide additional rights beyond those available under common law. They allow lenders to expand the scope of set-off, making it easier to apply funds held in any account of the borrower against their outstanding debts under the loan.[178]

Equitable set-off applies where there is a close connection between the claims, making it inequitable for one party to enforce its claim without taking the other into account. This type of set-off is broader than legal set-off, allowing parties to offset obligations even when the debts arise from different transactions, provided they are closely related. In *Hanak v Green* [1958] 2 QB 9, the court ruled that equitable set-off can be invoked where it would be manifestly unfair to enforce a debt without recognising the counter-obligation. In the context of banking transactions, equitable set-off could arise where a borrower has a claim against the lender for breach of contract, which is closely related to the underlying loan agreement. In such cases, the borrower may set off the damages resulting from the lender's breach against the outstanding loan amount, thereby reducing the debt owed to the lender.

Contractual set-off allows the parties to agree that payments due between them may be offset. Accordingly, where both parties to a transaction have payments due, they may agree contractually that, instead of making separate payments, the party owing the larger amount will pay the difference between the two sums due.[179] Under such an arrangement, payments due in the same currency and on the same day are aggregated, with the smaller total deducted from the larger. The party owing the larger sum then pays the balance. This approach enables the parties to reduce or eliminate their liabilities to one another and offers the administrative benefit of minimising the number of payments required. In commercial contracts, boilerplate provisions[180] often specify whether set-off is permitted or prohibited. In financial transactions, it is standard practice to prohibit set-off by the borrower or security provider.[181]

Contractual terms that exclude or limit the right of set-off are enforceable and not contrary to public policy, as stipulated in *Halesowen Presswork & Assemblies Ltd v Westminster Bank Ltd* [1971] 1 QB 1. This possibility was further confirmed by the Court of Appeal in *Coca-Cola Financial Corporation v Finsat International Ltd* [1998] QB 43, where it was held that:

> *In general English law permits the parties to a contract to include in it such terms as they consider to be appropriate. This freedom of contract is subject to a measure of control based on grounds of public policy and to some statutory restrictions such as those contained in the Unfair Contract Terms Act 1977.*[182]

These provisions are frequently agreed upon to ensure that each party's entitlement under the contract is not rendered contingent upon the finanscial stability or continuing solvency of the other. The subsequent insolvency of one party does not constitute a valid reason to dilute or displace the agreed exclusion of set-off or counterclaim rights.[183]

177 A bank may invoke banker's set-off only if both accounts involved are current or running accounts. This means that the balances on the accounts, whether in credit or debit, must be payable either on demand or with reasonably short notice.
178 Wood, P., *International Loans, Bonds, Guarantees and Legal Opinions* (Sweet & Maxwell, 2019) at [18-010].
179 Wood, P., *Project Finance, Securitisations and Subordinated Debt* (Sweet & Maxwell, 2019) at [11-037].
180 Boilerplate provisions are standard clauses in a contract.
181 Goode, R. and van Zwieten, K., *Principles of Corporate Insolvency Law* (Sweet & Maxwell, 2019), Chapter 9, Section 3.
182 At page 52.
183 *Kaupthing Singer and Friedlander Ltd, Re* [2009] EWHC 740 (Ch) at [23].

However, such terms must be drafted with particularly clear wording (*BOC Group plc v Centeon LLC* [1999] 1 All ER (Comm) 53).[184] This principle was emphasised in *Lehman Brothers Commodity Services Inc v Credit Agricole Corporate and Investment Bank* [2011] EWHC 1390 (Comm) in the context of a standby letter of credit. The judgment clarified that if the parties intend to prohibit set-off in relation to a standby letter of credit, an express prohibition must be included within the letter of credit itself. In this respect, in *AMC III Purple BV v Amethyst Radiotherapy Ltd* [2019] EWHC 1503, the Commercial Court examined a provision that stipulated as follows: "*All payments to be made by the Borrower under the Finance Documents shall be calculated and be made without (and free and clear of any deduction for) set-off or counterclaim*". The clause excluding set-off in the supplemental loan facility agreement provided: "*Each payment to be made by the [borrower] under this Agreement will be made in full, without any set-off or deduction*". The court followed the 2013 Court of Appeal's ruling in *Caterpillar (NI) Ltd (formerly known as FG Wilson (Engineering) Ltd) v John Holt & Company (Liverpool) Ltd* [2013] EWCA Civ 1232 and held, in respect of the facility agreement, that even if the borrower had valid cross-claims against the lender it was not entitled to set them off against any interest payments falling due nor make any deduction from those payments because of the cross-claims.[185]

Insolvency set-off arises in cases of liquidation, administration, or bankruptcy, mandating an account of mutual dealings between the creditor and the insolvent party. It is automatic and cannot be excluded by contract (*National Westminster Bank Ltd v Halesowen Presswork and Assemblies Ltd* [1972] 1 All ER 641). Under rule 14.25 of the Insolvency (England and Wales) Rules 2016 (**IR 2016**),[186] insolvency set-off applies in a liquidation where mutual dealings have taken place between the company and a creditor prior to the company's entry into liquidation. However, not all debts qualify as mutual dealings for the purpose of set-off, and certain exclusions apply. Insolvency set-off also applies during an administration if the administrators issue a notice of their intention to make a distribution to creditors, as provided under rule 14.24 of the IR 2016.

Rule 14.25 of the IR 2016 mandates that an account be taken of the sums due as a result of mutual dealings between the company and its creditors. The amounts owed by the company to the creditor and vice versa are set off against each other, leaving only the net balance to be claimed by the liquidator or proved for by the creditor.[187]

Debts incurred or agreed to be acquired after the company has entered liquidation are not eligible for set-off. Similarly, debts incurred or acquired through assignment are excluded if the creditor was aware that a decision was being sought from creditors on the nomination of a liquidator under section 100 of the Insolvency Act 1986 or if a winding-up petition was pending at the time. Additionally, debts that arose during an administration immediately preceding the liquidation do not qualify for set-off. A further exclusion applies where a creditor incurred or acquired a debt with notice that an administration had immediately preceded the liquidation. These exclusions serve to ensure that only genuine pre-liquidation mutual

184 In *BOC Group plc v Centeon LLC* [1999] 1 All ER (Comm) 53 the following wording was not effective to exclude set-off: "*The Purchaser's obligations to make payments . . . shall be absolute and unconditional and shall not be affected by [various specific matters relating to the outcome of the project] or by any other matter whatsoever*". ("*The Purchaser's obligations to make payments . . . shall be absolute and unconditional and shall not be affected by [various specific matters relating to the outcome of the project] or by any other matter whatsoever*").

185 "*Similar wording was considered in Caterpillar v John Holt where Longmore LJ said (at [36]) '"Any" must mean what it says.' I consider that the effect of the clause used is to prevent an equitable as well as a legal set-off.*" per Mr Justice Butcher at [40].

186 (SI 2016/1024).

187 Goode, R. and van Zwieten, K., *Principles of Corporate Insolvency Law* (Sweet & Maxwell, 2019), Chapter 9, Section 4.

dealings are considered for insolvency set-off, preventing creditors from structuring transactions to gain an unfair advantage during the liquidation process.

Liquidation set-off is an automatic process that takes effect from the commencement of liquidation. In a compulsory liquidation, this occurs from the date of the presentation of the winding-up petition, while in a voluntary liquidation, it corresponds to the date of the shareholders' resolution to wind up the company. On this date, assets are notionally treated as realised and distributed simultaneously, even though the actual collection of amounts due or payment of dividends to creditors occurs at a later stage.[188]

8.2 Netting and Banking Transactions

Netting refers to the process of offsetting multiple obligations between two parties to create a single net obligation. Netting is a more comprehensive tool than set-off and is commonly used in complex financial transactions, particularly in derivatives and syndicated loans, to reduce the number of payment flows and overall exposure between parties. It plays a fundamental role in managing financial transactions by consolidating payment obligations, reducing counterparty risk, and streamlining settlement processes.

Netting differs from set-off in that it applies to **executory contracts**, where both parties still have outstanding payment or delivery obligations, rather than to partially performed contracts involving unpaid debt (this should be contrasted with **non-executory contracts** or claims, which arise in situations where one party has already fulfilled its obligations, leaving only the other party's payment outstanding).

Payment netting (also known as settlement or bilateral netting) consolidates multiple payment obligations into a single net amount. In loan agreements, this mechanism may be used to simplify payments between lenders and borrowers. For example, in syndicated loans (see Chapter 11), where a borrower may have multiple payment obligations to different lenders, payment netting reduces the number of payments made by netting them into a single amount.[189]

Close-out netting[190] occurs when all outstanding obligations between parties are terminated upon a default or insolvency event, and the net balance is calculated and paid. This is a crucial mechanism in derivatives transactions (see Chapter 13) governed by the International Swaps and Derivatives Association (ISDA) Master Agreement,[191] which provides detailed

188 *Re Dynamics Corporation of America* [1976] 1 WLR 757.

189 Hudson, A., *The Law on Financial Derivatives* (Sweet & Maxwell, 2017) at [17-21].

190 Under Regulation 3 of the Financial Collateral Arrangements (No 2) Regulations 2003 (SI 2003/3226), a close-out netting provision is defined: "*a term of a financial collateral arrangement, or of an arrangement of which a financial collateral arrangement forms part, or any legislative provision under which on the occurrence of an enforcement event, whether through the operation of netting or set-off or otherwise –*

(a) the obligations of the parties are accelerated to become immediately due and expressed as an obligation to pay an amount representing the original obligation's estimated current value or replacement cost, or are terminated and replaced by an obligation to pay such an amount; or

(b) an account is taken of what is due from each party to the other in respect of such obligations and a net sum equal to the balance of the account is payable by the party from whom the larger amount is due to the other party".

191 Netting of Payments is described in the 2002 ISDA Master Agreement is considered as follows: "*Netting of Payments. If on any date amounts would otherwise be payable:– (i) in the same currency; and (ii) in respect of the same Transaction, by each party to the other, then, on such date, each party's obligation to make payment of any such amount will be automatically satisfied and discharged and, if the aggregate amount that would otherwise have been payable by one party exceeds the aggregate amount that would otherwise have been payable by the other party, replaced by an obligation upon the party by which the larger aggregate amount would have been payable to pay to the other party the excess of the larger aggregate amount over the smaller aggregate amount*".

provisions for close-out netting. In loan agreements, close-out netting is often invoked when a borrower defaults, allowing the lender to terminate the loan and offset any outstanding obligations to determine the final payment.[192]

Unlike payment netting, which can be applied on a rolling basis to contracts settling on the same day, close-out netting applies to contracts with different settlement dates and brings dealings between the counterparties to an end. Close-out netting serves as a precursor to applying set-off across multiple executory contracts before their settlement dates. It typically involves three stages: first, the termination of unperformed contracts, which may occur automatically or through the issuance of a notice; second, the valuation of each party's gains and losses, calculated by referencing the replacement cost of the terminated transactions, factoring in the difference between the original cost of opening the position and the cost of entering a replacement contract on the settlement date (if higher); and third, the application of set-off to produce a single net balance owed by one party to the other.

To enable close-out netting, an executory contract should make future payments conditional upon the non-occurrence of specified events of default and provide for termination of the contract either automatically or at the discretion of the non-defaulting party if such events occur. The contract should also include detailed provisions for valuing unperformed obligations. These provisions must comply with the common law requirement that any termination payment represents a genuine and reasonable estimate of the loss rather than a penalty and must also address the non-defaulting party's duty to mitigate losses.[193]

The contract may stipulate that, upon termination, all unperformed obligations are to be valued, with profits and losses arising from that valuation set off against one another to produce a single net amount owed by one party to the other (based on which party owes the greater sum). Such a provision requires the valuation to account for profits and losses realised by either party, irrespective of which party's default triggered the termination. This mechanism is known as close-out netting on a "two-way payment" basis.[194]

Under English law, there is a general perception that allowing a defaulting party to benefit from its own default is contrary to natural justice.[195] Consequently, the courts are not predisposed to favour the two-way payment basis over the walk-away basis. However, contractual parties are free to agree on an executory contract that incorporates a two-way payment basis. Provided that the terms governing the two-way payment mechanism are clear and unambiguous, the courts will uphold its validity.

For example, the High Court in *Britannia Bulk plc v Pioneer Navigation Ltd and another* [2011] EWHC 692 (Comm)[196] confirmed that the two-way payment basis of determining which party is entitled to receive a close-out amount under the 1992 ISDA master agreement operated without regard to fault. The selected close-out method required the out-of-the-money, non-defaulting party to pay an in-the-money, defaulting party following the early termination of the agreement. The court held that despite the common law principle that a defaulting party should not be allowed to profit from its default by selecting a specific close-out arrangement, the parties had consciously agreed to contract on that basis.

192 Goode, R. and van Zwieten, K., *Principles of Corporate Insolvency Law* (Sweet & Maxwell, 2019), Chapter 9, Section 3.

193 Hudson, A., *The Law on Financial Derivatives* (Sweet & Maxwell, 2017) at [17-37].

194 Goode, R. and van Zwieten, K., *Principles of Corporate Insolvency Law* (Sweet & Maxwell, 2019), Chapter 9, Section 3.

195 *Cassir, Moore & Co Ltd v Eastcheap Dried Food Co* [1962] 1 Lloyd's Rep 408.

196 And also in *Pioneer Freight Futures Company Ltd v TMT Asia Ltd* [2011] EWHC 778 (Comm). The decision in *Britannia Bulk plc v Pioneer Navigation Ltd and another* [2011] EWHC 692 (Comm) was upheld by the Court of Appeal in *Lomas and others v JFB Firth Rixson Inc and others* [2012] EWCA Civ 419.

It should be noted that a non-defaulting party is not obliged to continue performing under a contract that has been repudiated due to its counterparty's default (even where the default was determined by insolvency).[197] This may lead to the non-defaulting party realising a profit it would not have otherwise made if the contract had continued, or alternatively, suffering a loss as a result of the default. If the executory contract is structured on a walk-away basis, the non-defaulting party is not required to account for any profit it has made. At the same time, the defaulting party is obligated to compensate the non-defaulting party for any losses incurred. Conversely, the non-defaulting party is not required to compensate the defaulting party for any losses it may sustain due to the cessation of the non-defaulting party's performance.

Novation netting replaces multiple contractual obligations with a single net obligation. This form of netting is frequently used in syndicated loans and large-scale banking transactions. By novating existing obligations into a single contract, both borrowers and lenders can reduce administrative complexity and streamline their obligations.

8.3 Statutory and Regulatory Framework for Set-Off and Netting

The enforceability of set-off and netting in financial transactions is supported by statutory frameworks that protect these rights, particularly in insolvency scenarios.

Under the Financial Collateral Arrangements (No. 2) Regulations 2003 (**FCAR**), a close-out netting provision included in security documents relating to security over cash, financial instruments, or credit claims (such as claims arising from loans made by credit institutions), as defined under regulation 3 of FCAR, remains enforceable even if one of the parties is subject to winding-up proceedings or reorganisation measures (regulation 12(1), FCAR). Regulation 12(1) of FCAR does not apply if, at the time the collateral-taker entered into the financial arrangement, the collateral-taker knew or should have known about the commencement of winding-up proceedings or reorganisation measures in relation to the collateral-provider (regulation 12(2)(a)). For these purposes, winding-up proceedings are deemed to commence when a court issues a winding-up order, and reorganisation measures are deemed to commence upon the appointment of an administrator, whether by court order or otherwise (regulation 12(3)).[198]

If regulation 12(1) does not apply, the mandatory set-off rules set out in rules 14.24 and 14.25 of the IR 2016 will override any close-out netting provision where a party to the provision is subject to winding-up proceedings or, in certain circumstances, administration proceedings.[199]

There is uncertainty as to whether regulation 12(1) of FCAR applies to close-out netting provisions involving more than two parties. This uncertainty stems from the language used in the definition of a close-out netting provision in Regulation 3, which includes phrases such as "from each party to the other" and "other party". These terms arguably suggest that regulation 12(1) is intended to apply exclusively to close-out netting provisions between two parties, raising questions about its applicability in multi-party arrangements.

197 *Shipton Anderson & Co (1927) Ltd v Micks Lambert & Co* [1936] 2 All ER 1032.

198 A collateral-taker cannot be deemed, in this context, to have knowledge of voluntary winding-up proceedings or the implementation of a Company Voluntary Arrangement (CVA) involving the collateral-provider.

199 Hudson, A., *The Law on Financial Derivatives* (Sweet & Maxwell, 2017) at [16-34].

Thus, the multilateral netting may not be covered by FCAR. This uncertainty is of particular relevance in industries such as airlines, electricity, and payment handling, where participants often join industry clearing systems, such as the IATA ticketing clearance system, the electricity pool netting system, or a payment clearing system. These schemes typically involve agreements for multilateral netting, whereby all claims between members are consolidated so that each participant owes or is owed a single net balance by the other members. However, such arrangements are vulnerable in the event of insolvency, as multilateral netting involves the set-off of non-mutual claims, effectively using third-party assets to settle another party's debts or obligations. In *British Eagle International Airlines Ltd v Air France* [1975] 2 All ER 390, the House of Lords held that, in cases of insolvency, the principle of insolvency set-off supersedes multilateral netting, ensuring the application of mutual claims only.

Within the context of banking institutions in financial difficulties, the Banking Act 2009 establishes a special resolution regime, granting the Bank of England, the PRA, the FCA, and His Majesty's Treasury (the authorities) a range of tools to safeguard financial stability. This regime enables the effective resolution of failing banks, building societies, investment firms, banking group companies, and central counterparties while ensuring the protection of depositors, client assets, taxpayers, and the broader economy. Within this context, partial property transfers under the Banking Act 2009 are subject to restrictions imposed by secondary legislation, ensuring that certain types of contractual arrangements are adequately protected. The Banking Act 2009 (Restriction of Partial Property Transfers) Order 2009[200] provides comprehensive protection for set-off and netting arrangements, ensuring that property covered by a counterparty's set-off and netting arrangement with a bank cannot be "split up" through the exercise of a partial property transfer. However, to maintain the flexibility needed for partial transfers in the interests of financial stability and depositor protection, the Order includes several exceptions to this protection, referred to as "excluded rights" and "excluded liabilities". These exceptions include rights and liabilities associated with deposits held in account classes or brands primarily used or marketed to depositors eligible for compensation under the Financial Services Compensation Scheme, which covers most individuals and small businesses.[201] Additionally, subordinated debt issued by the failing bank or its counterparty is also excluded from the protection.[202]

9 CONCLUSION

The legal nature of money and the systems that facilitate payment mechanisms are foundational to modern financial transactions and global trade. Money, in its various forms –

200 S.I. 2009 No. 322.

201 Additionally, the Financial Services (Banking Reform) Act 2013 introduced a ring-fence around retail deposits held by UK banks, primarily through a new Part IXB of FSMA, with the aim of separating certain core banking services critical to individuals and small and medium-sized enterprises (SMEs) from wholesale and investment banking services. The main rules relating to the ring-fencing regime are set out in the Ring-fenced Bodies part of the PRA Rulebook. The PRA's rules on netting arrangements state that: "*A ring-fenced body must not enter into a netting arrangement if the effect of the netting arrangement is to permit a person, other than a member of the ring-fenced body's group, to offset its liabilities to the ring-fenced body against its claims on any member of the ring-fenced body's group that is not a ring-fenced affiliate in the event of default of any party to the netting arrangement.*" In Chapter 14, Ring-fenced Bodies, Netting Arrangements.

202 Banking Act 2009, section 3: "*rights and liabilities between P and a banking institution are protected if they are rights and liabilities which either P or the banking institution is entitled to set-off or net under a set-off arrangement, netting arrangement or title transfer financial collateral arrangement which P has entered into with the banking institution so long as they are not excluded rights or excluded liabilities.*"

whether traditional fiat currency or emerging digital assets – operates under complex legal frameworks designed to ensure stability, functionality, and trust in the financial system.

As payment systems have evolved from paper-based instruments to technologically advanced systems such as digital wallets and blockchain, the legal landscape has expanded to address new challenges posed by digital innovation. The regulation of payments and financial transactions is different across jurisdictions, although the common denominator is an attempt to strike a balance between fostering innovation and maintaining regulatory oversight to protect consumers and the financial system.

Moreover, the rise of cryptocurrencies and CBDCs introduced significant changes to the understanding of money and payment mechanisms. Cryptocurrencies, in particular, challenge traditional definitions of money, leading to varying regulatory approaches worldwide. Meanwhile, the potential (although the digital Yuan is already a reality) introduction of CBDCs by central banks could represent a substantial development that could transform monetary systems by enhancing payment efficiency. Payment efficiency is also fostered by mechanisms that allow for debt reduction and mitigate default risks, such as set-off and netting.

The legal and regulatory environment must continue to adapt to these developments, ensuring that payment systems remain secure, efficient, and responsive to the evolving demands of the global economy.

CHAPTER 3

BANKING REGULATION IN THE UK

OVERVIEW

This chapter outlines the regulatory framework governing the UK banking sector, addressing its historical evolution and the impact of significant global and domestic crises on key legislative reforms. It begins by exploring the early regulatory landscape, marked by the Bank of England's informal oversight and the gradual development of statutory frameworks aimed at ensuring financial stability. It traces key milestones in this evolution, such as the Banking Act 1979, which introduced formal licensing and supervisory regimes, and the Financial Services and Markets Act 2000 (**FSMA**).[1]

The chapter then reviews the global financial crisis of 2007–2009 and the resulting Banking Act 2009, which introduced the Special Resolution Regime (**SRR**), allowing for the orderly resolution of failing banks to prevent systemic risk. The discussion also covers the post-Brexit reforms, including the Financial Services and Markets Act 2023 (**FSMA 2023**).

A core aspect of the chapter is the definition of a bank under English law. The practical implications of this definition for entities engaged in core banking activities, particularly deposit-taking and lending, are addressed. The ramifications of this characterisation are also considered with respect to the European Union, the US, Japan, India, and China. Once a credit institution has been defined, its privileges and its obligations towards customers will be considered.

1 THE EVOLUTION OF UK BANKING REGULATION

The evolution of banking regulation in the United Kingdom reflects the country's historical, economic, and financial developments over the centuries. From informal governance by the Bank of England to comprehensive statutory frameworks post-financial crises, banking regulation has adapted to mitigate systemic risks, protect consumers, and ensure financial stability.

1.1 Early Beginnings: Informal Oversight by the Bank of England

For centuries, the Bank of England, which was chartered as a private entity, acted as a quasi-regulator, supervising the banking industry informally and promoting trust and confidence in the financial system. During this period, banking practices were largely governed by private law, particularly the law of contract.

The development of a more structured regulatory environment began in the 19th century, coinciding with the rapid industrialisation of Britain and the expansion of its financial markets. The Joint Stock Banks Act of 1826 marked a turning point, allowing the establishment of joint-stock banks, which were larger and more diversified than the small private entities that had previously dominated the market. These developments also set the stage for more formalised regulatory frameworks.

1 Kokkinis, A. and Miglionico, M., *Banking Law: Private Transactions and Regulatory Frameworks* (Routledge, 2021), p. 12.

DOI: 10.4324/9781032662220-4

The Bank Charter Act 1844 (**Peel's Act**) was a critical moment in the regulation of the UK banking sector. It gave the Bank of England exclusive rights to issue banknotes in England and Wales, marking the first statutory intervention in the UK's monetary system. The Bank of England's role was thus expanded to a central bank with the mandate to regulate the money supply.

However, the Peel's Act did not cover any other form of banking regulation, such as deposit-taking or lending. The banking sector operated under the assumption that market forces, coupled with the Bank of England's role as lender of last resort, would ensure stability. This assumption held sway until significant banking crises forced a more interventionist regulatory stance.

It should be noted that the Bank of England's role as lender of last resort was fundamentally shaped by the conception advanced by Walter Bagehot in his seminal work Lombard Street, published in 1873. Bagehot argued that, in times of financial crisis, a central bank should intervene by lending freely, but at a high or penalty rate of interest, and only against sound or 'good' collateral. This approach was intended to restore confidence in the financial system while minimising moral hazard by ensuring that assistance was made available solely to solvent institutions facing temporary liquidity shortages.

1.2 The Banking Act 1979: Formal Licensing and Supervision

The formal regulation of banking in the United Kingdom commenced with the Banking Act 1979, which established a statutory licensing regime for deposit-taking institutions. Prior to the enactment of this legislation, control over banking was exercised informally by the Bank of England, supplemented by various statutory provisions that conferred privileges on banks recognised by the Board of Trade and the Bank of England.[2]

The drive to establish a formal supervisory system gained momentum following the publication of a White Paper in 1976 and the adoption of the First Council Directive on the coordination of banking regulations (77/780/EEC).[3] These developments laid the groundwork for a new statutory framework for banking supervision within the United Kingdom.[4]

The enactment of the Banking Act 1979 was prompted by a series of banking failures in the 1970s, including the collapse of London and County Securities in 1973, which exposed weaknesses in the informal regulatory framework. However, the Banking Act 1979 did not provide a comprehensive definition of what constituted "banking business" or a "bank". The Act's primary focus was on protecting depositors rather than imposing prudential controls on banking activities. While it marked the beginning of formal bank regulation, it was still relatively limited in scope.

Following the enactment of the Banking Act 1979, the law prioritised preserving the status quo to safeguard the Bank of England's interests, but this approach gave rise to longer-term tensions. These tensions became evident in 1984 with the "Johnson Matthey Bankers affair".[5]

2 Ellinger, E., Lomnicka, E. and Hare, C., *Ellinger's Modern Banking Law* (Oxford University Press, 2011), p. 31.
3 First Council Directive 77/780/EEC of 12 December 1977 on the coordination of the laws, regulations, and administrative provisions relating to the taking up and pursuit of the business of credit institutions.
4 As Lord Hope aptly summarised it in *Three Rivers District Council v. Governor and Company of The Bank of England* [2001] UKHL 16 at [18].
5 Whitworth, A., 'The Banking Act 1979 and Johnson Matthey Bankers' in *Regulating Banks: The Politics of Instability* (Agenda Publishing, 2021), pp. 77–100.

1.3 The Johnson Matthey Crisis and the Banking Act 1987

The failure of Johnson Matthey Bankers in 1984, caused by mismanagement and risky lending practices, shook the confidence of the financial markets and demonstrated the need for stronger regulatory controls. The government's intervention, through the Bank of England, to prevent the collapse from destabilising the entire financial system highlighted the systemic risks posed by individual bank failures. The crisis highlighted the need for proactive oversight, and it triggered a comprehensive review of the UK's banking supervisory framework.[6]

In response, the Banking Act 1987 was introduced to tighten the regulatory framework.[7] This Act gave the Bank of England enhanced powers to supervise banks, including the authority to revoke banking licenses and vet shareholders of UK banks.[8] It also introduced a deposit protection scheme, providing greater security for depositors.[9] The Act expanded the Bank of England's powers of investigation and imposed stricter requirements on banks to manage risks. Finally, it eliminated the dual classification of "recognised banks" and "licensed deposit-takers", replacing it with a unified category of "authorised institutions" to simplify regulation and reduce public confusion.

1.4 The BCCI Scandal and the Collapse of Barings Bank – Regulatory Reforms

> *The rise and fall of the Bank of Credit and Commerce International SA ("the Bank") was the greatest scandal in the history of banking. The Bank had a short but eventful life. It was hopelessly insolvent from at least 1986. . . . The Bank started business in the UK in 1972. In 1980 the Bank became a licensed deposit taker under the Banking Act 1979 and later an authorised institution under the Banking Act 1987 and accordingly regulated by the Bank of England. At the beginning of 1990 it had 2,300 employees. In 1990 the Bank was reorganised and in the course of such restructuring some 900 staff in England were made redundant. The High Court in England on the petition of the Bank of England made orders on the 5th July 1991 for the appointment in England and Wales of Mr Morris, Mr Lyle and Mr Richards as provisional liquidators of the Bank ("the Provisional Liquidators"). The business of the Bank was immediately closed, and the employees were placed on "gardening leave" pending a final decision as to the future of the Bank.*[10]

The Bank of Credit and Commerce International SA (**BCCI**) had established a complex organisational structure and obtained authorisation in two jurisdictions, Luxembourg and the Cayman Islands, neither of which possessed the capacity to effectively supervise the bank

6 As Lord Hope aptly summarised it in *Three Rivers District Council v. Governor and Company of The Bank of England* [2001] UKHL 16 at [20]: "*In September 1984 the effectiveness of the existing statutory regime was called into question by the collapse of Johnson Matthey Bankers. In the light of that debacle a further White Paper was produced and the enactment of a new statute, which was to become the Banking Act 1987, was proposed. The system introduced by the 1979 Act was to be both strengthened and simplified. In place of the dual system of recognition and licensing a single system of authorisation was to be introduced with restrictions on the use of banking names. The Bank was to be required to establish a committee to be known as the Board of Banking Supervision which was to include six independent members as well as three members ex officio. Various other changes were to be made to the powers and duties of the Bank as regulatory authority*".

7 "*An Act to make new provision for regulating the acceptance of deposits in the course of a business, for protecting depositors and for regulating the use of banking names and descriptions . . . and for purposes connected with those matters*".

8 Section 1(1) of the Banking Act creates the Bank's supervisory power. The section states: "The [Bank] shall have the powers conferred on it by this Act and the duty generally to supervise the institutions *authorised by it in the exercise of those powers*".

9 Section 1(2) provides: "It shall be the duty of the [Bank] to keep under review the operation of this Act and developments in the field of banking which appear to it to be relevant to the exercise of its powers and the discharge of its duties".

10 *Bank of Credit & Commerce International SA v Ali* [1999] EWHC 846 (Ch) at [1] and [2].

as a whole. Meanwhile, the centre of its operations was located in a third jurisdiction, the United Kingdom, which did not actively engage in its supervision.

BCCI collapsed due to fraudulent activities carried out by senior staff, effectively making it a large-scale criminal money laundering operation. In response to this failure, the Bank of England exercised its supervisory authority to commission an inquiry,[11] which was undertaken by Lord Justice Bingham. The findings of the inquiry were detailed in the Bingham Report,[12] published in October 1992.[13] The report presented several recommendations, which can be broadly categorised into three key areas: the prohibition of opaque financial structures, the detection and prevention of fraud, and the improvement of information flow to supervisory authorities. The report emphasised that "*the most important single lesson of this debacle is that banking group structures which deny supervisors a clear view of how business is conducted should be outlawed*".[14] It also recommended that the Bank of England be granted explicit statutory powers to refuse or revoke a bank's authorisation in cases where proper supervision is not feasible.[15]

A further banking scandal erupted in 1995. The collapse of Barings Bank due to unauthorised derivatives trading by Nick Leeson further demonstrated the limitations of the regulatory framework in preventing high-risk activities within banks.[16] Mr Leeson's concealed trading activities incurred losses of approximately £827 million, leading to the bank's insolvency. The Bank of England was criticised for not detecting the risks sooner.

The Report of the Board of Banking Supervision Inquiry into the collapse of Barings[17] concluded that the failure was due to inadequate internal risk management and regulatory oversight. An attempt to address such limitation resulted in the notice[18] issued by The Bank of England in October 1997 introducing new obligations under the Financial Institutions (Prudential Supervision) Regulations 1996, which provided that the Bank of England were to refuse any application for authorisation by a credit institution if the existence of a close link between the applicant and any other party would impede the Bank of England's ability to

11 The investigation which Bingham LJ conducted was a private and not a statutory inquiry.
12 Inquiry into the Supervision of the Bank of Credit and Commerce International (HC Paper (1992–93) No 198.
13 The closure of BCCI on 5 July 1991 generated significant concern within the financial community. Many criticised the timing of the action, deeming it long overdue, while others, including depositors, employees, and shareholders, condemned the closure as being unduly hasty. In response to these concerns, Lord Justice Bingham was promptly commissioned to conduct an inquiry into the supervision of BCCI under the Banking Acts. His mandate included assessing whether the actions taken by the UK authorities were appropriately timed and offering recommendations for future regulatory improvements. The establishment of the inquiry was formally announced on 19 July 1991, and Lord Justice Bingham submitted his report to the Chancellor of the Exchequer and the Governor of the Bank of England in July 1992.
14 Inquiry into the Supervision of the Bank of Credit and Commerce International (HC Paper (1992–93) No 198.
15 Chiu, I. and Wilson, J., *Banking Law and Regulation* (Oxford University Press, 2019), p. 237.
16 "Barings Plc and other companies within the group were placed in administration on 26 February 1995. Barings Brothers & Co Limited ('Old Barings') was a banking subsidiary of Barings Plc. On the following day, the Chancellor of the Exchequer made a statement to the House of Commons ('the Statement') in which he said that losses in excess of £600 million had been incurred due to unauthorised dealings on exchanges in the Far East. He acknowledged that the House would be concerned to know how such events could occur without Old Barings, the exchanges or the regulators learning of them. He stated that he was determined to address that question rigorously and to review the regulatory system thoroughly": per Lord Wolfe in *Barings Plc & Ors v Co Lybrand & Ors* [2000] EWCA Civ 148, at [20].
17 Return to an order of the Honourable the House of Commons dated 18 July 1995 for the Report of the Board of Banking Supervision inquiry into the circumstances of the collapse of Barings available at https://assets.publishing.service.gov.uk/media/5a7ca783ed915d6969f46688/0673.pdf (accessed in March 2025).
18 Bank of England Supervision and Surveillance Notice to Credit Institutions authorised under the Banking Act 1987; United Kingdom Administrative Arrangements of Implementation of the Close Links Provision of the Post-BCCI Directive, Number: S&S/1996/9 issued on 31 October 1996.

carry out its supervisory duties effectively. Similarly, the authorisation of already authorised credit institutions could have been revoked by the Bank of England on the same grounds.

Furthermore, the collapse of Barings set the stage for further regulatory reforms, focusing on improving corporate governance, internal controls, and the supervisory role of regulators.

In 1997, the newly elected labour government introduced substantial changes to the regulation of the banking industry, fundamentally reshaping the supervisory framework for financial institutions and the role of the Bank of England. The latter was granted autonomy in setting monetary policy; a move formalised through the Bank of England Act 1998. This legislation set out three principal objectives: establishing a statutory mandate for the Bank of England regarding monetary policy,[19] reforming the constitution and responsibilities of the Court of Directors, and transferring regulatory and supervisory responsibilities for the banking sector to a single regulator, the Financial Services Authority (**FSA**).[20]

The establishment of the FSA marked a shift away from the previous fragmented system of sector-specific regulators, consolidating regulatory oversight under a single body. This reform aimed to provide a more consistent and comprehensive framework for financial market regulation. However, certain aspects of banking regulation, including the regulation of deposit-taking businesses, the Deposit Protection Scheme, banking names and descriptions, oversight of overseas institutions with representative offices, and the collection and disclosure of financial information, remained governed by the Banking Act 1987.[21]

1.5 The Financial Services and Markets Act 2000

The next major development in banking regulation came with the introduction of FSMA, which created a unified framework for regulating financial services, including banking, insurance, and investment. FSMA marked a radical change in the UK's regulatory structure, confirming the FSA as the single regulator for financial services.[22]

Under Part IV of FSMA, banks were required to obtain authorisation from the FSA to carry out regulated activities such as accepting deposits. To obtain authorisation, an individual or entity had to meet certain threshold conditions, which included demonstrating that their resources were adequate for the regulated activity in question. The permission so granted could have been subject to any requirements the Financial Services Agency deemed appropriate.[23]

FSMA has also introduced the principles for business, which require banks to operate with integrity, treat customers fairly, and manage risks prudently. The Act also established the

19 Section 13 of the Bank of England Act 1998 assigned operational responsibility for monetary policy to the Monetary Policy Committee, an independent committee of the Bank of England.

20 The reasons for transferring supervisory functions from the Band of England to the FSA were as follows: (a) the reputation of the City had been consistently undermined by scandals such as Robert Maxwell's fraud and the collapses of BCCI and Barings Banks, with the Bank of England's supervisory role being severely criticised in Lord Bingham's Report following the BCCI collapse and Lord Wolff's Report after Barings; (b) the implementation of EU legislation necessitated this reform; (c) regulatory responsibilities had been shifted from the Department of Trade and Industry to the Treasury in 1992; and (d) the growing pressures of globalisation required a more coordinated approach.

21 The Banking Act 1987 was later replaced by the Financial Services and Markets Act 2000.

22 Chiu, I. and Wilson, J., *Banking Law and Regulation* (Oxford University Press, 2019), p. 238.

23 "*Since the enactment of the 2000 Act, the FSA has been responsible for the supervision of banks. The scheme of regulation, so far as relevant, is as follows. Accepting deposits in the UK is a regulated activity which cannot be done without permission from the FSA under Part IV of the 2000 Act. An authorised person must satisfy certain threshold conditions, which include the condition that his resources must in the opinion of the FSA be adequate in relation to the regulated activity in question. Permission granted by the FSA may be subject to such requirements as the FSA considers appropriate*" per Lord Justice Richards in *Kaupthing Bank HF, R (on the application of) v HM Treasury* [2009] EWHC 2542 (Admin) at [10].

Financial Ombudsman Service to resolve disputes between consumers and financial institutions to enhance consumer protection.

1.6 The Global Financial Crisis of 2007–2009 and the Banking Act 2009

The Global Financial Crisis of 2007–2009 exposed critical weaknesses in the global financial system. The crisis, which began with the collapse of the US subprime mortgage market, quickly spread to the UK, leading to the failure of Northern Rock in 2007. Northern Rock's reliance on short-term wholesale funding to finance its mortgage business made it vulnerable when liquidity in the money markets dried up.[24] In response to the crisis, on 12 December 2007, five central banks around the world (including the Bank of England and the US Federal Reserve) took coordinated action to inject further liquidity into the global banking system. Northern Rock was nationalised on 17 February 2008, and its shareholders ultimately got nothing.[25]

> *On 11 March 2008 central banks announced further coordinated action to tackle the crisis, including the Bank of England extending its existing liquidity support operations and extending repo operations, and the US Federal Reserve announcing the Term Securities Lending Facility (under which it would make longer dated loans against a broad range of eligible collateral). On 14 March 2008, in response to rumours that Bear Stearns was experiencing liquidity problems, the Federal Reserve Bank of New York announced it was providing liquidity supplies to Bear Stearns and on 16 March 2008 JP Morgan agreed to acquire Bear Stearns. The US Federal Reserve ran a programme to enable banks facing liquidity issues to access short term money: originally the term was overnight. The programme was called "the Discount Window". On the same day that JP Morgan announced it would acquire Bear Stearns, the US Federal Reserve extended the maximum Discount Window term to 90 days and announced the establishment of "the Primary Dealer Credit Facility" (which provided US broker dealers access to overnight liquidity for the first time since The Great Depression).*[26]

> *The financial crisis began to deepen in early September 2008. On 7 September 2008 "Fannie Mae" and "Freddie Mac" were taken into "conservatorship" by the US Federal Housing Finance Agency. This affected US markets, but was not globally disruptive. Then on 10 September 2008 Lehman Brothers announced losses of $3.9 billion in the 3 months to August 2008. There were crisis talks in New York over the weekend. On Monday 15 September 2008 Lehman Brothers filed for Chapter 11 Bankruptcy in the USA and Merrill Lynch (widely perceived to be the next potential casualty) was taken over by Bank of America.*[27]

Lehman Brothers was the largest bankruptcy in United States history[28] and triggered a shockwave that reverberated through financial markets worldwide. This event confirmed that perhaps there were no institutions that were "too big to fail", and that it could not be assumed that governments would always provide a "bail-out". The instant reaction was that the wholesale funding markets virtually closed as each market participant viewed each other market participant with deepening suspicion. Term loans would continue to mature, but they would only be replaced in the market with "overnight" money that required daily refinancing.

24 Plenderleith, I., 'Review of the Bank of England's Provision of Emergency liquidity Assistance in 2008–09' (2012) *Documents 8450.*
25 Per Sir Alastair Norris in *Sharp & Other Claimants Listed in the GLO Register v Blank & Ors* [2019] EWHC 3096 (Ch) at [83].
26 Per Sir Alastair Norris in *Sharp & Other Claimants Listed in the GLO Register v Blank & Ors* [2019] EWHC 3096 (Ch) at [83].
27 Per Sir Alastair Norris in *Sharp & Other Claimants Listed in the GLO Register v Blank & Ors* [2019] EWHC 3096 (Ch) at [127] and [128].
28 Marketwatch, Lehman folds with record $613 billion debt, 15 September 2008.

By late September 2008, the world financial system was in "melt down", and banking shares had collapsed.[29]

The impact of the financial crisis was particularly acute for Iceland's three major banks: Kaupthing, Glitnir, and Landsbanki. Landsbanki operated in the United Kingdom as a branch of the Icelandic bank, raising retail internet deposits under the brand name Icesave.[30] Concerns about the banks' ability to meet their liabilities were escalating.[31]

On the 29th of September 2008, the Icelandic Government acquired a controlling 75% stake in Glitnir. However, the nationalisation of Glitnir further exacerbated the crisis of confidence in Iceland's banking sector, leading to a net withdrawal of deposits from the country's banks. In an extraordinary and unprecedented step, the British government invoked anti-terrorism legislation to freeze the assets of Icelandic banks operating in the United Kingdom.[32] These powers were conferred by sections 4 and 14 of Schedule 3 to the Anti-Terrorism, Crime and Security Act 2001, which requires that

> *the Treasury believe that action to the detriment of the United Kingdom's economy (or part of it) has been or is likely to be taken by certain persons who are the government of or resident of a country or territory outside the United Kingdom.*

In his statement on 8 October 2008, the UK Chancellor announced that the FSA had determined that Kaupthing Singer & Friedlander, a UK-based subsidiary of the Icelandic Kaupthing Bank, did not "meet its threshold conditions and was likely to be unable to meet its obligations to depositors".[33] Consequently, the FSA concluded that Kaupthing was in default for the purposes of the Financial Services Compensation Scheme. The Chancellor also stated that he had exercised powers under the Banking (Special Provisions) Act 2008 to transfer the majority of Kaupthing's retail deposits to the Dutch bank ING. The remainder of the business was placed into administration. The transfer of the retail deposit books was facilitated with financial support from HM Treasury and the Financial Services Compensation Scheme.

In this context, the UK government was forced to provide liquidity support to the country's major banks, such as the Royal Bank of Scotland and Lloyds Banking Group, through emergency liquidity assistance (**ELA**) from the Bank of England. At its peak, this support amounted to £61.5 billion.[34] The crisis underscored the need for a more robust regulatory framework to manage failing banks and prevent systemic risks.[35]

29 Per Lord Justice Richards in *Kaupthing Bank HF, R (on the application of) v HM Treasury* [2009] EWHC 2542 (Admin) at [13].

30 Prior to the financial crisis, Landsbanki introduced high-interest online savings accounts under the name 'Icesave' in the UK and the Netherlands. These accounts quickly gained popularity, attracting billions in deposits, primarily from British citizens, owing to their exceptionally high interest rates. When the financial crisis struck, Iceland's government found itself cut off from international financial markets, leaving it unable to support its severely overleveraged banks. As a result, the banks, including Landsbanki, were placed into receivership.

31 Proctor, C., *The Law and Practice of International Banking* (Oxford University Press, 2015) at [13.17].

32 Landsbanki Freezing Order 2008 (SI 2008/2668).

33 HM Treasury press release, Kaupthing Singer & Friedlander, 8 October 2008.

34 Plenderleith, I., 'Review of the Bank of England's Provision of Emergency Liquidity Assistance in 2008–09' (2012) *Documents 8450* 4.

35 In this context "*was the 'credit crunch', the great disruption in the funding markets resulting (most immediately) from the collapse of Lehman Brothers that had occurred on 15 September 2008, which brought home to markets that banks might fail and which generated what became unprecedented turbulence in global financial markets. The Bank of England ('Bank of England' or 'the Bank'), HM Treasury ('the Treasury') and the Financial Services Authority ('FSA'), who together tried to maintain the integrity and overall health of UK markets (and were together known as 'the Tripartite') determined to restore confidence in the banking sector by providing an unprecedented package of financial support. The announcement came on 8 October 2008. The key elements were (a) measures to provide sufficient short-term liquidity to enable banks to lend in the real economy; and (b) a requirement that banks should strengthen their balance sheets by raising more capital (in which exercise the Treasury would participate) with the object that banks should increase what was known technically*

The Banking Act 2009 was introduced to address these challenges, establishing the Special Resolution Regime (**SRR**), a framework that supported the continuity of critical banking services and minimised systemic risk during insolvency events. The SRR gave the authorities powers to intervene early in the resolution of banks, with options to transfer assets to a private purchaser, a bridge bank, or place the bank into temporary public ownership. The Act also introduced reforms to strengthen depositor protection, including enhancements to the Financial Services Compensation Scheme.

The crisis also led to significant international regulatory reforms, such as the Basel III Accord,[36] which introduced stricter capital requirements and liquidity standards for banks. The nature of the Bank of England's lender of last resort function has been fundamentally transformed since 2008. In terms of providing liquidity support, the Bank of England is structured to provide it to the banking sector, most notably through the Discount Window Facility. However, in situations where the Bank of England determines that such support is not the appropriate course of action, the authorities have now acquired the capability to resolve a bank in an orderly manner using the SRR.[37]

1.7 The Vickers Report and the Banking Reform Act 2013

The Vickers Report, published by the Independent Commission on Banking in 2011,[38] recommended structural reforms to the UK banking sector to prevent a repeat of the financial crisis.[39] One of the report's key recommendations was the introduction of ring-fencing, which would separate retail banking from investment banking to protect depositors from the risks associated with more speculative activities.[40] This recommendation was enacted through the Financial Services (Banking Reform) Act 2013, which mandated the creation of Ring-Fenced Banks (**RFB**s).

Under the ring-fencing regime, retail banks that accepted deposits from individuals and small businesses would have been required to be legally and operationally distinct from investment banking activities. The aim was to protect essential banking services, such as

as 'the Core Tier 1 ratio'. This latter element was to be the subject of further discussion with individual banks. The participation of the Government in the recapitalisation process meant that the detailed proposals would need the approval of the European Commission: and that had the potential to require each participating bank to submit a restructuring plan to address issues arising from the receipt of State aid. There followed (on 12 and 13 October 2008) what was called at trial 'the Recapitalisation Weekend'". Per Sir Alastair Norris in *Sharp & Other Claimants Listed in the GLO Register v Blank & Ors* [2019] EWHC 3096 (Ch) at [16].

36 www.bis.org/bcbs/basel3.htm (accessed in March 2025).

37 Plenderleith, I., 'Review of the Bank of England's Provision of Emergency Liquidity Assistance in 2008–09' (2012) *Documents 8450* 15.

38 'The Independent Commission on Banking: Final Report Recommendations' (September 2011), available at https://webarchive.nationalarchives.gov.uk/ukgwa/20131003105424/https:/hmt-sanctions.s3.amazonaws.com/ICB%20final%20report/ICB%2520Final%2520Report%5B1%5D.pdf (accessed in March 2025).

39 Ibid. at p. 6: "*The recommendations in this report aim to create a more stable and competitive basis for UK banking in the longer term. That means much more than greater resilience against future financial crises and removing risks from banks to the public finances. It also means a banking system that is effective and efficient at providing the basic banking services of safeguarding retail deposits, operating secure payments systems, efficiently channelling savings to productive investments, and managing financial risk. To those ends there should be vigorous competition among banks to deliver the services required by well-informed customers. These goals for UK banking are wholly consistent with maintaining the UK's strength as a pre-eminent centre for banking and finance, and are positive for the competitiveness of the UK economy. They also contribute to financial stability internationally, especially in Europe*".

40 In his Speech in April 2011 Sir John Vickers summarised his proposals: "*Structural reform, in sharp form, would end universal banking and require retail banking and wholesale and investment banking to be carried out by separate banks. This would aim to isolate retail banking services and taxpayers from the risks of global wholesale and investment banking. The Commission's focus is on a combination of these capital and structural approaches, in moderate form*". Speech by Sir John Vickers 11 April 2011.

deposit-taking and payments, from the risks associated with complex financial activities like derivatives trading.[41] The Bank of England and the Prudential Regulation Authority (**PRA**) could play central roles in supervising compliance with the ring-fencing requirements, ensuring that banks maintain the necessary separation between their retail and investment activities.

Another substantial change was the transition of banking regulation to a dual regulation system. In the context of UK financial services regulation, "dual regulation"[42] refers to the division of regulatory responsibilities between two regulators: the PRA and the Financial Conduct Authority (**FCA**).[43]

The PRA, a part of the Bank of England, oversees the prudential regulation of deposit-taking institutions, insurers, and systemically important investment firms.[44] In contrast, the FCA is responsible for the conduct regulation of all financial firms and the prudential regulation of firms not regulated by the PRA for prudential purposes.[45] This framework is often described as the "twin peaks" model of supervision.

On 1 April 2013, in accordance with the Financial Services Act 2012, the FSA was abolished, and the majority of the FSA's functions were transferred to the FCA[46] and the PRA. On the same date, the Bank of England took over the FSA's responsibilities for financial market infrastructures, and the Financial Policy Committee[47] was established on a statutory basis.

In addition to changing the UK financial regulation supervisory model, the Financial Services Act 2012 also introduced a statutory framework designed to manage financial crises, outlining the respective roles of HM Treasury and the Bank of England.[48]

41 "*The ring-fencing legislation was enacted in response to the 2008–2009 financial crisis, with a view to strengthening UK banks and providing additional protection to their retail and small business customers. A new Part 9B of FSMA was introduced by section 4(1) of the Financial Services (Banking Reform) Act 2013 ('FSBRA'). Part 9B will take effect from 1st January 2019. It requires UK financial institutions to separate and ring-fence 'core activities' from 'excluded activities' (sections 142A and 142G of FSMA). The only activity so far designated as a core activity is accepting deposits (section 142B of FSMA)*". per Sir Geoffrey Vos in *Barclays Bank Plc And Woolwich Plan Managers Ltd, Re* [2018] EWHC 472 at [10].

42 Chiu, I. and Wilson, J., *Banking Law and Regulation* (Oxford University Press, 2019), p. 248.

43 "*The Financial Conduct Authority is responsible for the statutory regulation of the United Kingdom's financial markets. This includes protecting and enhancing the integrity of the United Kingdom financial system and ensuring the stability and orderly functioning of financial markets. The Authority's powers are derived from the Financial Services and Markets Act 2000 ('the Act'), as amended by the Financial Services Act 2012*". per Lord Sumption in *Financial Conduct Authority v Macris* [2017] UKSC 19 at [2].

44 These firms are referred to as PRA-authorised firms and also as dual-regulated firms because, while the PRA regulates prudential issues, the FCA acts as these firms' conduct regulator.

45 "Prudential" regulation relates to the safety and soundness of financial institutions (such as regulatory capital or resolution requirements), while "conduct" regulation relates to the way in which financial institutions treat their customers.

46 "*The Financial Services Act 2012, amongst other things, changed the name of the Authority from the Financial Services Authority, the name of its predecessor. The Authority is responsible for regulation of financial firms and maintaining the integrity of financial markets in the United Kingdom*": per Lord Justice Fraser *in Financial Conduct Authority v Seiler & Anor* [2024] EWCA Civ 852 at [9].

47 The Financial Policy Committee (FPC) is a committee of the Court of Directors of the Bank of England and is tasked with overseeing macro-prudential regulation. This role involves addressing prudential regulation concerns across the entirety of the UK financial system, distinguishing it from the micro-prudential focus of the PRA, which supervises individual firms. Unlike the PRA and the FCA, the FPC does not have direct regulatory responsibility for specific types of firms. The FPC's objective is to support the Bank of England in achieving its financial stability mandate, as set out in the Banking Act 2009. It does so by identifying, monitoring, and addressing systemic risks – defined as risks to the stability of the UK financial system as a whole or to a significant part of it. To fulfil its mandate, the FPC has access to a range of macro-prudential tools designed to address emerging threats to UK financial stability. While the FPC determines whether a specific tool should be deployed, its application to regulated firms is managed by the PRA and, where necessary, the FCA.

48 The crisis management framework depends on close collaboration between the Bank of England and HM Treasury. While the Bank of England is responsible for the majority of regulatory and resolution measures in response to an emerging financial crisis, HM Treasury retains control over any decisions involving

1.8 Post-Brexit Regulatory Reforms: The Financial Services and Markets Act 2023

The UK's departure from the European Union on 31 January 2020 (Brexit) brought significant changes to its regulatory landscape. The European Union (Withdrawal) Act 2018 ensured that EU-derived legislation would be retained in UK law, but the government sought to adapt these regulations to suit the UK's post-Brexit financial services sector.

In this context, the Financial Services and Markets Act 2023 (**FSMA 2023**) represented a major overhaul of the UK's financial regulatory framework post-Brexit. It introduced a mechanism for revoking retained EU law related to financial services and set the stage for the UK's regulators to create bespoke rules tailored to the needs of the domestic financial system. FSMA 2023 also introduced provisions for regulating digital settlement assets, such as stablecoins, reflecting the growing importance of fintech and innovation in financial services.

2 DEFINING A BANK

As outlined previously, the legal framework governing UK banks and their activities is extensive and stratified. Nevertheless, the definition of a bank remains complex and somewhat inconsistent.

The UK regulatory approach is typically activity-based rather than entity-based, meaning that the definition of a "bank" for any specific purpose is generally determined by the activities the institution undertakes.[49] Therefore, determining what constitutes a "bank" is essential for determining which entities fall within the appropriate regulatory framework.[50] Historically, the definition of what constitutes a "bank" or "banking business" in England has evolved through case law, identifying the essential characteristics of banking activity. Additionally, English law and retained EU law provide a framework for categorising institutions such as "credit institutions" for regulatory purposes, underscoring the critical function that legal definitions serve in the oversight of financial services.

A landmark case in defining a bank under English law is *United Dominions Trust Ltd v Kirkwood* [1966] 2 QB 431 (CA),[51] where the Court of Appeal, led by Lord Denning, developed a three-part test to identify an entity as a bank.[52] To be classified as such, an institution must

the use of public funds. In October 2017, HM Treasury released the latest version of its Memorandum of Understanding on resolution planning and financial crisis management. This agreement, reached between HM Treasury and the Bank of England, including the Bank of England in its role as the PRA, outlines their respective responsibilities and collaborative processes

49 The Independent Commission on Banking (ICB) provided a useful analysis of banking activities in an issues paper published in September 2010 (ICB: Issues Paper: Call for Evidence: September 2010).

50 Ellinger, E. P., Lomnicka, E. and Hare, C., *Ellinger's Modern Banking Law* (Oxford University Press, 2011), p. 81.

51 "*United Dominions Trust Ltd. ('U.D.T.') is a large public company which describes itself as 'bankers' carrying on business at United Dominions House, Eastcheap, in the City of London. It is an important financial house. It lends big sums of money to various people. It has a high standing and includes the Bank of England amongst its shareholders. It also owns all the shares in a wholly-owned subsidiary called United Dominions Trust (Commercial) Ltd.*". Ibid., per Lord Denning at [440]. In this instance, the court found that while the defendant company engaged in some financial activities, it failed to satisfy all the criteria for a bank under this test and thus could not claim the regulatory exemptions applicable to banks. Lord Denning's judgement in this case remains a guiding authority, establishing that for an entity to qualify as a bank, it must comprehensively perform these core functions. The case underscores the practical significance of this classification, particularly in relation to regulatory exemptions and statutory protections.

52 The Privy Council judgement in *Bank of Chettinad Ltd of Colombo v Income Tax Commissioner of Colombo* [1948] AC 378, which defined a bank as "a company which carries on as its principal business the accepting of

perform three core functions: (i) accepting deposits from customers; (ii) collecting and paying cheques on behalf of customers; and (iii) maintaining current accounts where debits and credits are recorded.[53]

While these activities are significant in shaping the common law definition of banking, they do not establish definitive boundaries for what may constitute banking business under common law, as indicated in *Royal Bank of Canada v Inland Revenue Commissioners* [1972] Ch 665.[54]

The decline in the use of cheques presents particular challenges in applying the common law definition of a bank. If interpreted strictly, the definition would exclude any deposit-taking institution that neither accepts nor issues cheques.[55] However, in *Sekers Fabrics Ltd v Clydesdale Bank Plc* [2021] CSOH 89, the court recognised that ordinary banking operations now encompass the electronic transfer of money and the maintenance of systems to support such transfers.[56] This indicates that the courts would likely adopt a flexible approach to this aspect of the definition if it were revisited in future litigation.[57] Similarly, in Ireland in *Woodchester/UDT Bank* [1992] IECA 6, it was acknowledged that "*Banks may generally be described as being in the business of accepting deposits and making loans. In reality the market is somewhat more differentiated than this . . . these distinctions are becoming less important over time*". In Australia, the High Court of Australia considered the definition of a bank in *Commissioners of the State Savings Bank of Victoria v Permewan Wright & Co Ltd* (1914) 19 CLR 457. Justice Isaacs held that banking activities primarily involve the collection of deposits and the granting of loans, which are fundamental to the bank's business model. The court emphasised the transactional nature of banking, focusing on the movement of money between depositors and borrowers.

The common law definition of a bank does not extend to building societies. However, section 12(3) of the Building Societies Act 1997 provides that where a building society engages in activities that form part of the provision of a banking service, it is to be treated as a "bank", a "banker", and as conducting the business of banking.

While case law provides foundational definitions, statutory provisions play a significant role in identifying and regulating banking institutions. The Bank of England summarised its approach to the regulatory definition of a bank in an article published in September 2019. It was indicated:

> *What this [the regulatory definition of a "bank"] means is that all banks in the UK have obtained permission from the financial regulators to accept deposits . . . . This may not be the only (regulated or unregulated) activity*

deposits of money on current account or otherwise, subject to withdrawal by cheque, draft or order", was adopted as the starting point.

53 "*The first is that the banking transactions which he carries out in the course of his business must not be negligible in size and number when compared with the rest of his business. The second is that the transactions relied upon as constituting the accepting of deposits of money from customers on running account must be genuinely of this legal nature and not a mere disguise for transactions of a different legal nature. The court must look to the true nature of the transactions, not merely to their form*". Ibid., per Lord Denning at [466].

54 At p. 679.

55 Lord Denning in *United Dominions Trust Ltd v Kirkwood* seemed to have considered this issue not so central to his analysis "*I do not find it necessary to decide whether it is still possible to carry on the business of banking without undertaking the payment of cheques drawn on the customer's account (which in itself also entails a right in the customer to withdraw moneys from the account upon demand without prior notice) and/or the collection of cheques for the customer (which in itself also entails the acceptance by the banker of payment of moneys into the account by his customer). The real question in this case is whether upon the evidence U.D.T. has proved that it accepts to any significant extent "deposits" of money from customers on running account at all*", per Lord Denning at [466].

56 "*As technology has developed, the transfer of money by electronic means and the maintenance of systems to facilitate such transfers fall within ordinary banking operations, as do a customer's communications with its banker's staff in relation to such transfers*". in *Sekers Fabrics Ltd v Clydesdale Bank Plc* [2021] CSOH 89 at [14].

57 Ellinger, E. P., Lomnicka, E. and Hare, C., *Ellinger's Modern Banking Law* (Oxford University Press, 2011), p. 80.

> *a bank undertakes but it is the minimum activity all banks do. Apart from banks, the only other firms that have permission to accept deposits in the UK are credit unions, friendly societies . . . and building societies . . ., so if a UK firm accepts deposits and does not have the special characteristics that make it a credit union, friendly society or a building society, it is a bank.*[58]

In this context, FSMA provides the principal regulatory framework for financial services, including banking. Section 19 of FSMA,[59] also known as the "general prohibition", stipulates that no person may conduct a regulated activity in the UK unless they are an authorised or exempt person. Breaching this prohibition is a criminal offence, punishable by fines or imprisonment, and agreements entered into in breach of this rule may be unenforceable.[60] By enforcing the general prohibition, FSMA ensures that only vetted institutions can engage in regulated banking activities. Such activities would include accepting deposits – a hallmark of banking as defined under The Financial Services and Markets Act 2000 (Regulated Activities) Order 2001 (**RAO**).[61] The RAO stipulates that accepting deposits means receiving deposits or other repayable funds from the public and using those funds to grant credit or finance other banking operations.

Generally, an activity is regulated if, in addition to being of a specified kind, it is carried on by way of business[62] and it relates to an investment of a specific nature unless otherwise stipulated.[63] In making such a determination, one should consider several indicators, including (a) the degree of continuity of the activity; (b) whether such activity has a commercial element to it; (c) the scale of the activity; and (d) the proportion that the activity bears to other unregulated activities carried on. In *Edgelow v MacElwee* [1918] 1 KB 205, when considering the activity of money lending, it was held that

> *a man does not become a money-lender merely because he may upon one or two isolated occasions lend money to a stranger. There must be more than occasional and disconnected loans. There must be a business of money lending and the word "business" imports the notion of system, repetition and continuity.*[64]

In a similar context, Irish case law has established that one isolated transaction does not of itself constitute the "carrying on of a business".[65] In *Helden v Strathmore Ltd* [2010] EWHC 2012 (Ch), upon review of factual circumstances where a "sizeable number of loans", "*made over a period of years and with some regularity*" pursuant to which "*substantial amounts were advanced*" "*with a view to profit*", the Court came "*to the conclusion that the lending . . . was 'carried on by way of business' within the meaning of section 22*"[66] of FSMA.

58 Bank of England: *Quarterly Bulletin* 2019 Q3: How banks are authorised in the UK.
59 "*(1) No person may carry on a regulated activity in the United Kingdom, or purport to do so, unless he is – (a) an authorised person; or (b) an exempt person. (2) The prohibition is referred to in this Act as the general prohibition*".
60 A person who breaches the general prohibition under FSMA commits a criminal offence and may be subject to a term of imprisonment of up to two years, an unlimited fine, or both, as provided under section 23(1) FSMA. Where the contravention is committed by a company, individual officers of that company – including directors, chief executives, managers, company secretaries and shadow directors – may also be held criminally liable if the offence was committed with their consent or connivance, or resulted from their neglect, pursuant to section 400(1) FSMA. Equivalent provisions extend to partners in partnerships and to officers or members of unincorporated associations, as set out in sections 400(3) and 400(6) FSMA.
61 The Financial Services and Markets Act 2000 (Regulated Activities) Order 2001 (S.I. 2001/544).
62 "*[W]hether one or two transactions make a business depends upon the circumstances of each case. I take the test to be this: if an isolated transaction, which if repeated would be a transaction in business, is proved to have been undertaken with the intent that it should be the first of several transactions, that is, with an intent of carrying on a business, then it is a first transaction in an existing business. The business exists from the time of the commencement of that transaction with the intent that it should be one of a series*", in *Re Griffen, ex p Board of Trade* (1890) 60 LJQB 235.
63 Section 22, FSMA.
64 *Edgelow v MacElwee* [1918] 1 KB 205.
65 *Cripps Warburg v Cologne Investment Company Ltd, Aran Friendly Society* [1980] IR 321.
66 At [89].

To illustrate the risks of an approach that could give rise to an unexpected judicial interpretation, one should consider the decision of *The Argo Fund Ltd v Essar Steel Ltd* [2005] EWHC 600 (Comm), where it was held that an investment fund was to be considered as a financial institution under a loan agreement, which required that the transfer of the original lenders' participation in the syndicated loan could only be made to either a "*bank or other financial institution*". During the restructuring negotiations between the defaulting borrower and some members of the syndicate, a Cayman mutual fund investment company acquired large participation in the loan from other parties to the original financing agreement. Subsequently, the Cayman fund issued proceedings against the borrower, claiming debt or damages for breach of the agreement. The defaulting party counterclaimed that any transfer of debt to the Cayman fund was invalid since the latter was not a "*bank or other financial institution*". The court held that the loan agreement limited the class of entities to whom syndicate members could transfer their rights and obligations to those falling within the previously-mentioned definition but did not restrict the entities to those providing finance in the primary lending market. It further considered that the Cayman fund shared these key characteristics with a bank:

a) It was a lender in the secondary market (i.e., it acquired debt from the original parties to financing arrangements);
b) It had a "lending office" and kept accounts evidencing money lent to the defaulting party;
c) It had the financial, technical and legal expertise required to participate in large financing transactions; and
d) It was an entity "*having a legally recognised form or being, which carries on its business in accordance with the laws of its place of creation and business and whose business concerns commercial finance*".[67]

Thus, in the end, it had the characteristics of a "bank or other financial institution". This approach now seems out of touch with the UK CRR, which stipulates that one of the fundamental characteristics of a credit institution, as a bank is defined under the UK's retained version of the Capital Requirements Regulation (575/2013)[68] (**UK CRR**), is taking deposits from the public and granting credits, thus establishing the functional scope of banking activities. It should be noted that, for entities intending to operate as banks in the UK, compliance with FSMA's regulatory framework is mandatory. Such entities must obtain authorisation under Part 4A of FSMA.

2.1 Part 4A Authorisation

Part 4A of FSMA establishes the authorisation process essential for firms seeking to conduct regulated activities within the UK's financial system. To engage in core activities such as accepting deposits, investment dealing as principal, or conducting insurance business, firms must obtain Part 4A permission.[69]

67 Ibid. per Mr Justice Aikens, at [38].
68 Regulation (EU) No 575/2013 of the European Parliament and of the Council of 26 June 2013 on prudential requirements for credit institutions and investment firms and amending Regulation (EU) No 648/2012, as amended by Capital Requirements Regulation (CRR) II (Regulation (EU) 2019/876).
69 Proctor, C., *The Law and Practice of International Banking* (Oxford University Press, 2015) at [1.10].

To begin the Part 4A authorisation process, a firm must assess its eligibility to determine whether it satisfies certain prerequisites, including the appropriate legal structure, a sustainable business model, and a capable management team. Generally, an authorised entity must be either a UK-incorporated company or, for foreign entities, establish a UK branch or subsidiary. Moreover, the firm's business model must demonstrate viability and compliance with UK banking laws, especially regarding deposit acceptance and loan provision. Equally important, the firm's senior managers must meet the FCA's "fit and proper" standards, evidencing sufficient skills, experience, and integrity for managing a banking institution.[70]

Obtaining a Part 4A authorisation involves submitting an application detailing the firm's intended regulated activities, financial stability, governance framework, and risk management systems. The application is jointly assessed by the PRA, which examines the prudential soundness of the applicant, and the FCA, which evaluates its conduct practices, customer protection mechanisms, and governance. This assessment can extend up to 12 months, underscoring the thoroughness of the process.

Once submitted, the application is scrutinised against specific threshold conditions outlined in Schedule 6 of FSMA. These conditions verify that the firm possesses adequate financial resources, including capital and liquidity, as mandated by the UK CRR and by the provisions of Directive 2013/36/EU (CRD IV),[71] as amended by Directive (EU) 2019/878, which have been implemented into UK law, whereby a CRR firm is required to maintain, at all times, capital resources that are equal to or exceed the applicable base capital resources requirement. For banks, the requirement is €5 million. Small specialist banks and building societies must hold capital equal to the higher of €1 million or £1 million.

Further, the suitability of the firm's management team is examined, with senior personnel subject to rigorous "fit and proper" evaluations. An effective governance framework is also essential, with the PRA concentrating on financial risk management while the FCA ensures that the firm's culture and conduct align with consumer protection standards.

Following authorisation, firms must adhere to ongoing regulatory obligations. These include maintaining capital and liquidity levels as prescribed by the PRA, meeting FCA conduct requirements to ensure customer fairness, and submitting regular reports detailing financial performance, risk management, and compliance with prudential standards. Continuous supervisory engagement, including reviews, on-site inspections, and senior management interviews, is also part of the post-authorisation oversight by both the PRA and FCA.

In cases where an authorised institution breaches its regulatory obligations, the PRA or FCA can take enforcement actions, which may involve varying or revoking its Part 4A permission. Part 4A authorisation is thus not merely an administrative formality but a statutory requirement enabling banks and credit institutions to legally engage in regulated financial activities, with non-compliance carrying significant legal and financial repercussions.

Absent a valid Part 4A permission, breaching Section 19 of FSMA can result in serious consequences. An agreement entered into by an unauthorised individual engaging in a regulated activity in contravention of the general prohibition is unenforceable against the other contracting party.[72] Agreements entered into by authorised persons in the course of their

70 For a recent decision on the fit and proper person requirements to carry on a business as cryptoassets exchange provider, see *Moneybrain Ltd v The Financial Conduct Authority* [2022] UKUT 257 (TCC).

71 Directive 2013/36/EU of the European Parliament and of the Council of 26 June 2013 on access to the activity of credit institutions and the prudential supervision of credit institutions and investment firms, amending Directive 2002/87/EC and repealing Directives 2006/48/EC and 2006/49/EC, as amended by CRD V (Directive (EU) 2019/878).

72 Section 26, FSMA.

authorised business may likewise be unenforceable if they result from a third party's unauthorised performance of regulated activities.[73]

The FCA may, in certain circumstances, determine that it is just and equitable for an agreement to be enforced or for money paid (or property transferred) under the agreement to be retained.[74]

Moreover, the breaching party may be subject to penalties, including civil liability, criminal sanctions, and injunctions. Civil penalties for unauthorised activities under Section 26 allow affected customers to recover losses incurred through contracts with unauthorised firms, with courts able to declare such transactions void.

From a criminal perspective, breaching Section 19 constitutes a criminal offence under Section 23 of FSMA, carrying potentially unlimited fines or imprisonment for up to two years on indictment. The FCA has extensive powers to investigate and prosecute unauthorised activity, ensuring robust consumer protection and maintaining the UK's financial market integrity. It can seek injunctions under Sections 380 and 382 to prevent unauthorised firms from operating and impose restitution orders to compensate clients affected by unlawful practices.

In sum, the authorisation and ongoing supervision under Part 4A FSMA reflect a comprehensive regulatory framework designed to uphold the integrity, stability, and security of the UK's financial system. By imposing rigorous authorisation criteria, mandating continuous prudential and conduct oversight, and providing exemptions where justified, FSMA ensures that regulated financial institutions operate safely, innovatively, and responsibly within the broader market. This regulatory landscape, supported by the dual oversight of the PRA and FCA, provides a robust mechanism for adapting to market changes and addressing potential risks, while the provisions for civil, criminal, and administrative enforcement reinforce the importance of compliance in sustaining the UK's reputation as a secure and reliable financial hub.

A Different Type of Bank: Investment Banks

The rise of investment banks – which focus on securities issuance, trading, and corporate finance – has challenged traditional definitions of banking.

Generally, unlike retail banks, investment or merchant banks do not operate an extensive branch network and are not members of the clearing companies. As noted by Jacobson J in *Australian Securities and Investments Commission v Citigroup Global Markets Australia Pty Limited (No 4)* [2007] FCA 963, investment banks focus on advisory services, underwriting securities, and engaging in proprietary trading. While these activities do not involve traditional banking functions such as deposit-taking, they nonetheless play a critical role in the broader financial system.[75]

From a regulative perspective, firms engaging in investment banking activities without authorisation to accept deposits are governed by a range of differing definitions.

73 section 27, FSMA. The question of whether an agreement was unenforceable under section 27 of FSMA was among the issues considered in *Adams v Options Sipp UK LLP (formerly Carey Pensions UK LLP) and Financial Conduct Authority* [2020] EWHC 1229 (Ch).

74 Section 28A(3), FSMA. A recent case that examined the interpretation of "just and equitable" within the context of section 28 of FSMA was *Kinled Investments Ltd v Zopa Group Ltd* [2022] EWHC 1194 (Comm) (27 May 2022).

75 Proctor, C., *The Law and Practice of International Banking* (Oxford University Press, 2015) at [3.01].

However, due to their systemic importance, such firms are generally subject to a level of regulation and supervision akin to that applied to deposit-taking banks.

The definition of investment banks varies considerably across legal and regulatory contexts. However, two key elements are commonly present. First, a non-deposit-taking investment bank is generally categorised as a type of investment firm. Under the UK's retained version of the Markets in Financial Instruments Regulation (600/2014) (**UK MiFIR**), an investment firm is defined as a person whose regular occupation or business involves providing one or more investment services to third parties, performing one or more investment activities on a professional basis, or both, as set out in Article 2 of UK MiFIR. For these purposes, the terms "investment services" and "investment activities" are those listed in Part 3 of Schedule 2 to the Financial Services and Markets Act 2000 (Regulated Activities Order) 2001 (**RAO**).

Secondly, a non-deposit-taking investment bank will typically, though not invariably, hold permission under the Financial Services and Markets Act 2000 (FSMA) to deal in investments as principal. This regulated activity, as defined in Article 14 of the RAO, encompasses a range of functions, including proprietary trading and market-making.

3 UNITED STATES

In the United States, the term "bank" is defined and interpreted through a complex interplay of federal and state laws, statutory definitions, and judicial interpretations. The designation of an institution as a bank generally hinges on its involvement in deposit-taking and lending activities, though the specific criteria vary depending on regulatory context. Federal legislation such as the Bank Holding Company Act of 1956 (**BHCA**), the Federal Reserve Act of 1913, and the National Bank Act of 1863, along with pertinent case law, establish the overarching legal framework defining a bank under US law.

The BHCA is a primary federal statute governing the definition of a "bank" for regulatory purposes. Section 2(c) of the BHCA specifies that a "bank" is any institution that: (i) accepts deposits which depositors may legally withdraw on demand; and (ii) engages in the business of making commercial loans.[76]

This dual requirement – deposit-taking coupled with lending – forms the foundation of federal banking law, delineating banks from other financial entities like credit unions, savings associations, and non-bank financial institutions. Importantly, this definition underpins the Federal Reserve's regulatory scope, as entities controlling one or more banks are deemed bank holding companies and, as such, fall under the BHCA's provisions.

Case law has further refined the parameters of what constitutes a bank, particularly when the distinction between banks and non-bank financial institutions is disputed.

In *NationsBank of North Carolina, N.A. v. Variable Annuity Life Insurance Co. (VALIC)* [1995] 513 U.S. 251, the US Supreme Court considered whether national banks could sell annuities. Although the case primarily focused on this issue, the ruling affirmed that banks may engage in activities beyond traditional deposit-taking and lending. The Court held that annuities

76 Section 2(c) of the Bank Holding Company Act of 1956 defines "bank" as any institution "which (1) accepts deposits that the depositor has a legal right to withdraw on demand, and (2) engages in the business of making commercial loans".

could be offered as part of a national bank's broader investment services, thereby indicating that the permissible scope of banking activities can extend beyond core functions in certain circumstances. While in *Board of Governors of the Federal Reserve System v. Dimension Financial Corporation* [1986] 474 U.S. 361, the Supreme Court addressed the concept of a "non-bank bank" and whether an institution providing only deposit or lending services – but not both – could circumvent bank holding company regulations under the BHCA. The Court ruled that an entity must engage in both accepting demand deposits and making loans to qualify as a "bank" under the BHCA. This decision reinforced the statute's strict dual-function requirement, preventing financial institutions from exploiting regulatory loopholes to avoid banking supervision.

In addition to the BHCA, regulatory definitions of a bank are provided by the National Bank Act of 1863 and the Federal Reserve Act of 1913. The National Bank Act defines national banks as institutions chartered by the Office of the Comptroller of the Currency (**OCC**), with authorisation to perform the "business of banking". While the Act lacks an exhaustive definition of this term, judicial interpretations have construed "business of banking" expansively to include various financial services beyond deposit-taking and lending, thereby enabling national banks to offer diverse financial products as the industry has advanced. Supervised by the OCC, national banks must adhere to federal banking laws and regulations.

The Federal Reserve Act governs the establishment and operations of the Federal Reserve System, defining "member banks" as those national or state-chartered institutions participating in the Federal Reserve System. Although the Act does not precisely define a "bank", it presumes banks to be institutions conducting conventional banking activities, including deposit-taking and lending, subject to the Federal Reserve's oversight. For an institution to qualify as a member bank, it must meet the Federal Reserve's capital adequacy standards, reserve requirements, and other regulatory conditions.

3.1 Statutory Exemptions and Hybrid Institutions

Several types of US financial institutions engage in banking activities but are not classified as banks under the BHCA due to specific statutory exemptions. Savings and Loan Associations, governed by the Home Owners' Loan Act of 1934, primarily focus on residential mortgage lending and savings deposits. While they perform functions similar to those of banks, they are subject to a separate regulatory framework and are overseen by the Federal Deposit Insurance Corporation (FDIC), which distinguishes them from traditional banks.

Credit Unions operate as member-owned cooperatives, offering savings, credit, and other financial services exclusively to their members. Established under the Federal Credit Union Act 1934,[77] these institutions fall under the supervision of the National Credit Union Administration (NCUA) and are not classified as banks under the BHCA. Industrial Loan Companies (ILCs) engage in deposit-taking and lending but avoid classification under the BHCA by limiting their commercial lending activities. This exemption allows non-financial corporations to own and operate ILCs, thereby falling outside the scope of the general restrictions on bank ownership by commercial entities.

77 [Chapter 750; 48 Stat. 1216; 12 U.S.C. 1751 et seq.].

The US Dual Banking System

The United States operates a dual banking system, allowing financial institutions to be chartered and regulated at both federal and state levels. This structure creates a complex regulatory environment in which banks may be subject to oversight by multiple authorities. At the federal level, key regulatory bodies include the OCC, which charters and supervises national banks, and the Federal Reserve Board (**FRB**), which oversees bank holding companies and state-chartered member banks. The FDIC is responsible for deposit insurance and the regulation of state-chartered non-member banks, while the Consumer Financial Protection Bureau (**CFPB**) oversees consumer protection regulations for financial institutions with assets exceeding $10 billion.

Alongside these federal regulators, state banking agencies play a significant role in supervising state-chartered institutions, adding another layer of oversight. While each regulatory body has distinct responsibilities, its jurisdiction often overlaps, ensuring a comprehensive supervisory framework that covers a wide range of financial activities and entities.

3.2 National and State Banks

National Banks are federally chartered by the OCC pursuant to the authorities granted under the National Bank Act of 1864.[78] They engage in a broad range of activities, including lending, deposit-taking, and currency exchange, and are identified by the inclusion of "National Association" (N.A.) in their names. The Federal Reserve and the FDIC share secondary regulatory responsibilities for these institutions. National banks enjoy significant latitude in conducting banking activities, including securities transactions, credit card issuance, and leasing.

State Banks, by contrast, are chartered under state law and subject to dual regulation from both state and federal authorities. While primary oversight is conducted by state banking agencies, these institutions may also be regulated by the FDIC if non-member or the FRB if a state member bank. State banks have flexibility in certain activities permitted by state law, but they are generally restricted from engaging in any activity that national banks cannot undertake unless granted specific FDIC approval. Like national banks, state banks must adhere to lending limits, though these are governed by state law.

3.3 Bank Holding Companies and Financial Holding Companies

A Bank Holding Company (**BHC**) is any corporation or entity that owns or controls one or more banks falling under the regulatory jurisdiction of the FRB. Formed under state law, BHCs must comply with the BHCA and FRB's Regulation Y,[79] which imposes capital ade-

78 See www.occ.gov/publications-and-resources/publications/comptrollers-licensing-manual/files/background-investigations-licensing-manual.pdf (accessed in March 2025) for the Comptroller's Licensing Manual – Background Investigations, which outlines the procedures that banks must follow when submitting applications and notices to the OCC. These procedures do not constitute substantive rules that define the criteria for decision-making. Instead, they set out the steps a bank must undertake to enable the OCC to assess whether the bank has satisfied the substantive requirements prescribed by existing statutes and regulations. In accordance with the Administrative Procedure Act, the OCC may issue guidance on licensing matters, specifying mandatory procedural steps that a bank must follow to facilitate the OCC's assessment of an application or notice. See 5 USC 553(b)(A).

79 Reg. Y, 49 FR 818, 5 January 1984.

quacy, reporting, and compliance obligations. BHCs also bear a "source of strength" obligation, meaning they must support their subsidiary banks financially and managerially.

Under the Gramm-Leach-Bliley Act,[80] certain BHCs qualify as Financial Holding Companies (**FHCs**), permitting them to expand into broader financial services, including securities underwriting, insurance, and merchant banking. To maintain FHC status, all subsidiary depository institutions must remain well-capitalised and well-managed, meeting the standards set under the Community Reinvestment Act.

3.4 Limited Purpose Institutions and Thrifts

The US financial landscape also includes various limited-purpose institutions that engage in specific financial activities but do not meet the full criteria of a bank under the BHCA. These entities, often termed non-bank banks, are generally regulated by the FDIC and relevant state agencies. Examples include Industrial Loan Companies (ILCs), credit card banks, and limited-purpose trust companies.

Thrifts, such as savings and loan associations and savings banks, are specialised institutions governed by the Home Owners' Loan Act of 1934 and focus primarily on residential mortgage lending. They are subject to the Qualified Thrift Lender test, mandating that at least 65% of their assets be invested in residential mortgages or similarly qualified investments. Thrifts are overseen by the OCC if federally chartered and by the FDIC if state-chartered.

Thrift Holding Companies which own thrift institutions are regulated by the FRB. Post-GLBA, these entities face restrictions on non-financial activities unless previously exempted. Following the Dodd-Frank Act, thrift holding companies became subject to consolidated capital requirements and must uphold the "source of strength" obligation toward their subsidiary thrifts.

4 THE DEFINITION OF A BANK IN EU LAW

In the European Union, a "credit institution" is defined as an undertaking engaged in "taking deposits or other repayable funds from the public and granting credits for its own account".[81] For an entity to meet this definition, two primary activities must be regularly performed: accepting deposits or similar repayable funds from the public and engaging in credit-granting on its own account rather than as an intermediary for others. Together, the CRR and CRD IV establish a harmonised framework designed to safeguard the stability of financial institutions and protect depositor interests.[82]

EU case law has also played a critical role in interpreting the statutory criteria for credit institutions, especially where ambiguities exist regarding the scope of activities qualifying as core banking functions. In *Landbrugsbanken v Commission* [1993] ECR I-5073, the European Court of Justice (ECJ) clarified that entities must engage in both deposit-taking and lending as core business activities to be considered credit institutions. Occasional or incidental lending or solely providing financial advice does not meet the threshold. However, in *European Commission v Kingdom of Spain* (C-286/02) [2004] ECR I-8219, the ECJ held that

80 Pub. L. No. 106-102, 113 Stat. 1338.
81 Article 4(1)(1)(a), CRR.
82 In practice, deposit-taking banks will fall within the scope of Article 4(1)(1)(a) of the definition, while non-deposit-taking investment banks will be covered under Article 4(1)(1)(b) of the CRR.

even institutions primarily engaged in deposit-taking but only occasionally involved in lending could still fall under the credit institution designation. This ruling underscored deposit-taking as a central component, with even limited lending qualifying an institution as a credit institution.[83]

The core elements defining a credit institution – deposit-taking and lending – carry specific implications. Deposit-taking requires an institution to accept funds repayable to the public, encompassing traditional deposits and a broader array of financial instruments, such as certificates of deposit and certain public borrowings. Lending, by contrast, must involve credit granted on the institution's own account, meaning it assumes the associated credit risk. Institutions acting solely as intermediaries do not meet this criterion.

Exemptions to the credit institution definition under the CRR and CRD IV include certain state entities, central banks, and specific public-sector organisations, which may engage in deposit-taking yet operate without profit motives. Additionally, non-deposit-taking institutions like investment firms are regulated through frameworks such as the Markets in Financial Instruments Directive II (MiFID II)[84] and the Investment Firm Regulation (IFR),[85] reflecting distinct regulatory needs given their operational focus.

The authorisation and supervision process for credit institutions reflects the EU's commitment to financial stability. Article 8(1)[86] of CRD IV mandates that any entity operating as a credit institution must be authorised by the appropriate national authority within its Member state of establishment, after which it is subject to stringent prudential regulations concerning capital adequacy, governance, and liquidity. The supervisory responsibilities are shared between the ECB, under the Single Supervisory Mechanism (**SSM**), for the Eurozone's most significant institutions and national authorities overseeing less significant credit institutions. This dual supervisory structure ensures a harmonised approach across Member States, promoting consistency while accommodating the needs of diverse financial landscapes.

Passporting in the EU

The freedoms of establishment and service provision are pivotal for business mobility within the EU. As a result of such freedoms, once an entity is established in one EU country, it can avail itself of the so-called "passporting".

Passporting refers to the exercise of the right, commonly known as the single market passport or a single licence, which allows a firm authorised under certain EU financial services legislation to conduct financial services activities in another EEA member state based on its home state authorisation.[87] This right enables firms to operate either through a branch in the host member state (the right of establishment) or on a cross-border services basis without the need for a physical presence in the host state (a services passport).[88]

83 Haentjens, M. and De Gioia-Carabellese, P., *European Banking and Financial Law* (Routledge, 2015), p. 90.
84 Directive 2014/65/EU.
85 Regulation (EU) 2019/2033 of the European Parliament and of the Council of 27 November 2019 on the prudential requirements of investment firms and amending Regulations (EU) No 1093/2010, (EU) No 575/2013, (EU) No 600/2014 and (EU) No 806/2014.
86 "Member States shall require credit institutions to obtain authorisation before commencing their activities. Without prejudice to Articles 10 to 14, they shall lay down the requirements for such authorisation and notify EBA".
87 Ellinger, E. P., Lomnicka, E. and Hare, C., *Ellinger's Modern Banking Law* (Oxford University Press, 2011), p. 71.
88 Haentjens, M. and De Gioia-Carabellese, P., *European Banking and Financial Law* (Routledge, 2015), p. 99.

Deposit-taking banks and other credit institutions established in the EEA benefit from passporting rights under CRD IV, allowing them to provide services across EEA jurisdictions without requiring separate authorisation in each host state.

5 REGULATORY FRAMEWORKS FOR BANKS IN JAPAN, CHINA, AND INDIA

5.1 Japan

In Japan, the regulatory framework is established by the Banking Act,[89] which defines the operational scope of banks and sets forth licensing and supervisory requirements. The Financial Services Agency oversees compliance with the Act, focusing on enforcing standards that safeguard Japan's financial sector.

According to Article 2, Paragraph 1 of the Banking Act, a bank is defined as: "*A bank means a person who engages in the business of accepting deposits, savings or instalment savings and using such funds to make loans or discount bills*". If a person intends to engage solely in the lending of funds without accepting deposits, registration as a money-lending business under the Money Lending Business Act[90] will suffice. A banking licence is required for lending activities only when they are carried out in conjunction with the acceptance of deposits. Similarly, if a person wishes to provide only fund transfer services, registration under the Payment Services Act[91] will also be enough. However, it should be noted that the Payment Services Act requires the regulator's approval, in addition to registration, where a person intends to provide fund transfer services exceeding JPY 1 million per transaction.[92]

5.2 China

In China, the legal framework defining and regulating banks is primarily established under the Commercial Bank Law of the People's Republic of China.[93] This law lays out the fundamental structure and operational mandates of commercial banks, with the People's Bank of China[94] and the China Banking and Insurance Regulatory Commission (**CBIRC**) jointly overseeing the supervision and regulation of these institutions to ensure stability and compliance within the banking sector.

Under Article 2 of the Commercial Bank Law, a commercial bank is defined as: "A financial institution that absorbs public deposits, extends loans, and handles settlements and other financial services".

This statutory definition emphasises the central functions of commercial banks, which include deposit-taking, lending, and financial settlements. Specifically, commercial banks are

89 (Act No. 59 of 1 June 1981).
90 (Act No. 32 of 1983).
91 (Act No. 59 of 2009).
92 Hideaki, S., 'Japan: Law & Practice' in *Chambers Global Practice Guides: Banking Regulation 2024*, Nagashima Ohno & Tsunematsu (Chambers and Partners, 2024), available at www.noandt.com/wp-content/uploads/2024/01/cp_gpg_BankingRegulation_2024_Japan_LawPractice.pdf (accessed in March 2025).
93 Initially adopted in 1995 and subsequently amended in 2003 and 2015.
94 See www.pbc.gov.cn/en/3688066/3688080/index.html (accessed in March 2025).

responsible for absorbing public deposits, thus providing a secure means for individuals and businesses to store funds.

5.3 India

In India, the statutory framework defining a bank is established by the Banking Regulation Act 1949, a key legislative act that outlines the regulation of banks and banking companies under the supervision of the Reserve Bank of India. The Act provides a comprehensive legal foundation for the operation and governance of banks in India, ensuring their stability and promoting sound banking practices across the sector.

Section 5(b) of the Banking Regulation Act offers a precise definition of "banking", stating: "*Banking means the accepting, for the purpose of lending or investment, of deposits of money from the public, repayable on demand or otherwise, and withdrawable by cheque, draft, order, or otherwise*". By virtue of the definition of the term "banking" set out in section 5(b) of the Banking Regulation Act 1949, an institution or business entity that does not accept deposits of money from the public – whether for the purposes of lending or investment – cannot be classified as a banking company. While a banking company may be engaged in both accepting deposits and extending credit, a financial institution whose activities are limited solely to the business of lending would fall outside the statutory definition of a "banking company" under the 1949 Act.[95]

The Act further elaborates on what constitutes a "banking company" in Section 5(c), defining it as: "A company which transacts the business of banking in India". Under this framework, only institutions engaging in core banking activities as defined under Section 5(b) are recognised as banking companies, emphasising their role in handling public funds and offering financial services essential to the economic infrastructure.

In the 2022 Supreme Court decision of *Nedumpilli Finance Company Limited vs State of Kerala & Ors* (Civil Appeal No. 5233 of 2012), where the issue before the court was whether non-banking financial companies (NBFCs) regulated by the Reserve Bank of India in terms of provisions of the Reserve Bank of India Act, 1934 could also be regulated by respective State enactments, it was held that the Reserve Bank of India Act, 1934 adopts a comprehensive and integrated approach to the regulation of banking, money lending, and the broader operation of the country's currency and credit system. The statute constitutes a complete code in itself, vesting the Reserve Bank of India with extensive powers to oversee and regulate all critical aspects of NBFCs throughout their existence – from inception to dissolution. An NBFC is not permitted to commence or carry on business without first being registered under the Reserve Bank of India Act, 1934, and the entirety of its lifecycle – from "the womb to the tomb" – is subject to the regulatory oversight of the Reserve Bank of India.[96]

The Parliament of India has delegated broad and comprehensive powers to the Reserve Bank of India to issue secondary legislation. This includes directives, circulars, and administrative policies, all of which carry statutory force and are binding upon all banks from time to time. Through this delegation, the Reserve Bank of India is fully empowered to regulate

95 *Nedumpilli Finance Company Limited vs State of Kerala & Ors* (Civil Appeal No. 5233 of 2012).

96 "*Once it is found that Chapter IIIB of the RBI Act provides a supervisory role for the RBI to oversee the functioning of NBFCs, from the time of their birth (by way of registration) till the time of their commercial death (by way of winding up), all activities of NBFCs automatically come under the scanner of RBI. As a consequence, the single aspect of taking care of the interest of the borrowers which is sought to be achieved by the State enactments gets subsumed in the provisions of Chapter IIIB*". Ibid. at [6.19].

the banking sector by setting legally enforceable standards and practices, thereby playing a central role in maintaining monetary and financial stability.[97]

6 THE BANKER-CUSTOMER RELATIONSHIP

The relationship between a banker and a customer is central to the functioning of the banking industry, establishing mutual rights and duties shaped by both statutory and common law principles. At common law, an individual or entity that holds an account with a bank, whether it is a current account or a deposit account, is considered a customer of that bank.[98]

A bank may offer services, such as investment advice, to individuals or entities that do not hold an account with it. However, it remains unclear whether such persons would be regarded as customers of the bank for the purposes of common law. Although there is no case law directly addressing this issue, it is suggested that a bank-customer relationship could arise with respect to such services. As a result, common law duties, including the duty of confidentiality, may apply.[99]

The banker-customer relationship is an intricate blend of contractual rights, statutory duties, and equitable principles designed to foster trust and accountability within the financial system. There is no settled consensus regarding the categorisation and labelling of these duties,[100] as judges and academics have addressed them in various ways, at times grouping certain duties together and, at other times, drawing distinctions between them.[101]

It is fairly clear, however, that – absent specific circumstances where the bank has assumed responsibilities beyond the ordinary scope of deposit-taking and lending (such as providing advice or undertaking a discretionary role in the management of the customer's assets) – the relationship between a bank and its customer is not typically fiduciary in nature, particularly in relation to deposit-taking and lending services.[102] "*The relation between banker and customer is that of debtor and creditor, with a super–added obligation on the part of the banker to honour the customer's cheques if the account is in credit*".[103] Hence, the relationship between a bank and its customer remains a commercial one based on a contract.[104]

6.1 The Duty to Repay

As the relationship may begin with the customer's act of depositing money, a debtor-creditor arrangement would ensue. The court in *Foley v Hill (1848)* 2 HLC 28 noted that "*money, when*

97 *Keshav Lal Khemchang & Sons Pvt. Ltd & Ors. Vs Union of India* [2015] 4 SCC 770.

98 *Great Western Railway Co v London & County Banking Co Ltd* [1901] AC 414, at pages 420 and 421.

99 Cranston, R., Avgouleas, E., van Zwieten, K., Hare, C. and van Sante, T., *Principles of Banking Law* (Oxford University Press, 2018), suggests this interpretation at page 190.

100 Hudson, A., *The Law of Finance* (Sweet & Maxwell, 2013) at [29-03].

101 For example, US 12 U.S. Code § 1431 (Powers and duties of banks) stipulates: "*(a) Each Federal Home Loan Bank shall have power, subject to rules and regulations prescribed by the Director, to borrow and give security therefor and to pay interest thereon, to issue debentures, bonds, or other obligations upon such terms and conditions as the Director may approve, and to do all things necessary for carrying out the provisions of this chapter and all things incident thereto*".

102 "*The relationship between banker and customer has long been established as essentially one of debtor and creditor*". Per Justice Roger Giles in *Aegis Resources DMCC v Union Bank Of India (DIFC) Branch* [2020] DIFC CFI 004 at [54]: this is a judgement of the Dubai International Financial Centre Courts.

103 Per Lord Chancellor (Finlay) in *London Joint Stock Bank, Ltd v. Macmillan & Arthur* [1919] UKHL 367.

104 *JP Morgan Chase Bank v Springwell Navigation Corp* [2008] EWHC 1186 (Comm), at [573], affirmed in *Springwell Navigation Corp v JP Morgan Chase Bank* [2010] EWCA Civ 1221. See also *Philipp v Barclays Bank UK plc* [2023] UKSC 25.

paid into a bank, ceases altogether to be the money of the principal; it is then the money of the banker, who is bound to return an equivalent sum when demanded". Thus, the bank does not hold the deposit on any other basis than a contractual one since it assumes a repayment obligation as a debt owed to the customer. Such an obligation does not arise where there are insufficient funds in the customer's account to honour the payment or where the overdraft facilities agreed upon by the bank are insufficient to cover it.[105]

In *Joachimson v Swiss Bank Corp* [1921] 3 K.B. 110, Atkin LJ stated[106] that a customer must demand repayment at the branch of the bank where their account is maintained, and the bank is only obliged to make repayments at that specific branch. While these statements no longer reflect contemporary banking practice, they remain binding legal principles.[107] It has been suggested, however, that in practice, these requirements are overridden by express or implied agreements between the bank and the customer.[108]

The limitation period for a customer's demand for repayment begins to run from the date the demand is made. However, the balance of a customer's account becomes immediately payable, without the need for a demand, upon the termination of the bank-customer relationship. This includes situations where a bank has entered liquidation.[109]

6.2 Duty to Comply with Their Customers' Instructions

Beyond this core debtor-creditor framework, banks are obligated to honour their customers' instructions by making payments in accordance with the terms of the customer's mandate.[110] Therefore, as highlighted in *Joachimson v Swiss Bank Corporation* [1921] 3 KB 110, banks must process payments and instructions according to the terms set by the customer, provided that such instructions are within the agreed account limits and are clear and unambiguous. When a bank fails in this duty, such as by wrongfully dishonouring a cheque, it can be held liable for breach of contract. In *Kpohraror v Woolwich Building Society* [1996] CLC 510, damages were awarded to the customer for injury to their credit reputation following the wrongful dishonour of a cheque, underscoring the potential reputational impact on customers, particularly traders, when banks do not comply with mandates. In *Philipp v Barclays Bank UK plc* [2023] UKSC 25, the Supreme Court clarified that a bank's "mandate" refers to the terms under which the bank is authorised and agrees to execute its customer's instructions to make payments. A bank may seek to modify the legal consequences of paying on a forged cheque or acting on an equivalent fraudulent payment instruction through express provisions in its contract with the customer. In *Tai Hing Cotton Mill Ltd v Liu Chong Hing Bank Ltd [1986] AC 80*, Lord Scarman referred to this approach as an attempt to "increase the severity of their terms of business".[111]

Within this context, one could consider the Canadian[112] decision of *Du v Jameson Bank* [2017] ONSC 2422, where Du's conduct of a foreign currency exchange account included giving wire transfer instructions to the bank by email; his email account was hacked and

105 *Marzetti v Williams and another* (1830) 1 B.& Ad. 415 at page 424; *Bank of New South Wales v Laing* [1954] AC 135 at p. 154.
106 At pp. 127, 129, and 130.
107 *Khalifeh v Blom Bank s.a.l* [2020] EWHC 2427 (QB) at [36].
108 Ellinger, E. P., Lomnicka, E. and Hare, C., *Ellinger's Modern Banking Law* (Oxford University Press, 2011), p. 123.
109 *Re Russian Commercial and Industrial Bank* [1955] Ch. 148 at p. 157.
110 *Paget's Law of Banking* (15th ed.) at [23.1].
111 At [106].
112 A decision of the Ontario Superior Court of Justice.

fraudulent instructions were sent and complied with. It was held that the bank was not in breach of contract because:

> *The agreement between the parties identified the risks associated with this account, namely operating on the basis of electronic communications. The agreement made it clear that Du assumed the duty of care in relation to that risk. Furthermore, the agreement established standard of care [sic] by which Jameson could be held responsible; namely 'gross negligence' or 'wilful misconduct'.*[113]

Therefore, failure to act according to the terms of its mandate would expose a credit institution to potential liability. In avoiding such potential liability, banks have the right to demand clarity and completeness as stipulated in *London Joint Stock Bank, Ltd v. Macmillan & Arthur* [1919] UKHL 367.[114] Should a bank breach its mandate, even the presence of contractual terms purporting to exclude the bank's liability may not suffice as the decision of the Dubai International Financial Centre Courts in *Aegis Resources DMCC v Union Bank Of India (DIFC) Branch* [2020] DIFC CFI 004 has exemplified. In this case, a bank made a payment to a fraudster based on emailed payment instructions that appear to originate from its customer but were, in fact, sent by a fraudster who has hacked into the customer's e-mail system, underscore that

> *Unless the terms of its contracts with Aegis entitled it to do so, the Bank acted outside its mandate in paying out on the fraudulent payment instructions. The terms of the contracts did not entitle the Bank to do so if it acted negligently, which it did.*[115]

Consequently, the court was satisfied that the bank had acted in breach of its mandate and *Quincecare* duty by acting on the fraudulent payment instructions.

The *Quincecare* duty, as articulated in *Barclays Bank plc v Quincecare Ltd* [1992] 4 All ER 363,[116] obliges a banker to refrain from executing an order if and for as long as the banker is "put on inquiry". This occurs when the banker has reasonable grounds (though not necessarily proof) to believe that the order is an attempt to misappropriate the company's funds.[117] In *Quincecare*, a bank agreed to lend £400,000 to a company, but the company's Chairman fraudulently misappropriated £340,000 by instructing the bank to transfer the funds to solicitors, who then passed them to him. The bank sought repayment from the company, while the company counterclaimed for its losses, alleging the bank had breached its duty of care. The counterclaim failed because the court found that the bank had not been put on inquiry regarding the fraudulent instruction. It was confirmed that it is an implied term of the contract between a bank and its customer that the bank will exercise reasonable skill and care when executing payment orders. This duty also exists in tort and must be balanced against the bank's obligation to execute valid instructions promptly. Lord Steyn J explained that if a

113 At [68].

114 "*The consequences of such negligence fall alone upon the party guilty of it, namely, the customer. It appears to me that a crucial consideration in a case such as the present is this, namely, what is the point of time at which these respective obligations meet. The point of time is the presentation of the cheque. Not until that moment is the banker confronted with any mandate or order, and in my opinion the responsibility for the cheque and all that has happened to it between its signature and its presentation is not and ought not to be laid upon the banker. If at that moment three things are satisfied – namely, (1) that the cheque is duly signed, (2) that its appearance and statement of contents present no reasonable ground for suspicion, and (3) there are customer's funds available – then the banker is bound to pay. But if a banker were bound to inquire in regard to every cheque with quite genuine signatures what had been their history from the time that the customer lifted his pen from the cheque until the time when it was presented at the bank, banking business would be greatly impeded or impossible, and in my humble view it would be subjected to risks for which there is no foundation in legal principle*", at p. 382.

115 At [1].

116 At [376].

117 See *Sekers Fabrics Ltd v Clydesdale Bank Plc* [2021] CSOH 89 at [9].

bank knows an instruction is dishonest, wilfully ignores obvious dishonesty, or recklessly fails to make necessary inquiries, it will be liable.[118]

However, in most cases, the key question is what level of suspicion is sufficient to place a bank under a duty to investigate further. It was emphasised that the law should not impose an overly burdensome obligation on banks that would hinder the efficient execution of transactions. At the same time, it must ensure that banks do not facilitate fraud. The appropriate balance, he concluded, is that a bank must refrain from executing an order if it has reasonable grounds – though not necessarily proof – to believe that the instruction is an attempt to misappropriate company funds. The *Quincecare* duty was later affirmed in *Singularis Holdings Ltd v Daiwa Capital Markets Europe Ltd* [2019] UKSC 50, where Lady Hale summarised the principle. In that case, a director had fraudulently instructed the bank to transfer company funds for his own purposes. The Supreme Court found that any reasonable bank would have identified the glaring signs of fraud and, therefore, had a duty to investigate before executing the transfer.

It should be noted that the previously mentioned decision of the DIFC Court in *Aegis Resources DMCC* can be contrasted with the reasoning adopted by the English High Court *in Philipp v Barclays Bank UK plc* [2021] EWHC 10 (Comm), as well as the judgement of the Hong Kong Court of First Instance in *Luk Wing Yan v CMB Wing Lung Bank Ltd* [2021] HKCFI 279 where the courts in each instance rejected the claims, holding that the purpose of the *Quincecare* duty is to safeguard the customer from the wrongful conduct of a trusted agent rather than an unknown third party as in *Aegis Resources DMCC*. In particular, in *Philipp v Barclays Bank UK Plc,* it was held that the *Quincecare* duty had

> *no application to a situation where, as in the present case, the customer is a victim of APP fraud. In this situation the validity of the instruction is not in doubt. Provided the instruction is clear and is given by the customer personally or by an agent acting with apparent authority, no inquiries are needed to clarify or verify what the bank must do. The bank's duty is to execute the instruction and any refusal or failure to do so will prima facie be a breach of duty by the bank.*

However, even in England – outside the limited scope of the *Quincecare* duty – a bank's broader duty of care (discussed later) in the context of executing payment instructions could be held to apply.

The importance of the bank's duty to comply with its customers' instructions was examined in also in *Terna Energy Trading doo v Revolut Ltd* [2024] EWHC 1419 (Comm), where it was concluded that a bank's status as the debtor of the customer does not preclude an enrichment claim unless it is demonstrated that the bank has disbursed the funds in accordance with the customer's instructions and without notice of the payer's claim. This analysis was recently

118 "*How are these conflicting duties to be reconciled in a case where the customer suffers loss because it is subsequently established that the order to transfer money was an act of misappropriation of money by the director or officer? If the bank execute the order knowing it to be dishonestly given, shutting its eyes to the obvious fact of the dishonesty or acting recklessly in failing to make such inquiries as an honest and reasonable man would make, no problem arises: the bank will clearly be liable. But in real life such a stark situation seldom arises. The critical question is: what lesser state of knowledge on the part of the bank will oblige the bank to make inquiries as to the legitimacy of the order? In judging where the line is to be drawn there are countervailing policy considerations. The law should not impose too burdensome an obligation on bankers, which hampers the effective transacting of banking business unnecessarily. On the other hand, the law should guard against the facilitation of fraud, and exact a reasonable standard of care in order to combat fraud and to protect bank customers and innocent third parties. To hold that a bank is only liable where it has displayed a lack of probity would be much too restrictive an approach. On the other hand, to impose liability whenever speculation might suggest dishonesty would impose wholly impractical standards on bankers. In my judgment the sensible compromise, which strikes a fair balance between competing considerations, is simply to say that a banker must refrain from executing an order if and for as long as the banker is 'put on inquiry' in the sense that he has reasonable grounds (although not necessarily proof) for believing that the order is an attempt to misappropriate the funds of the company*" at [366] and [367].

endorsed by Deputy Judge Richard Farnhill in *D'Aloia v Persons Unknown & Ors* [2024] EWHC 2342 (Ch). In that case, the court found that a cryptocurrency exchange was enriched at the point of receipt of funds.

6.3 The Duty of Confidentiality

The bank's duty of confidentiality is another critical aspect of this relationship. Jurisdictions like Switzerland and Luxembourg have historically offered stringent secrecy protections, notably enshrined in Swiss law through Article 47 of the Swiss Federal Banking Act, which historically safeguarded customer confidentiality. However, these secrecy privileges have faced substantial erosion as countries adhere to global anti-money laundering (AML) and tax transparency initiatives, which mandate disclosures under specific circumstances to combat financial crimes.

In England, the nature of the banks' duty of confidentiality was defined in *Tournier v National Provincial and Union Bank of England* [1924] 1 KB 461, where the Court of Appeal established that there is an implied term in the contract between a bank and its customer which prohibits the bank from disclosing information about the customer's affairs without their consent, except in certain circumstances. Despite its age, this case remains the cornerstone of the legal principles governing the duty of confidentiality specifically applicable to banks.[119] Since the duty of confidentiality arises from common law,[120] it applies to institutions that meet the common law definition of a bank, as established in *United Dominions Trust Ltd v Kirkwood* [1966] 2 QB 431.

The case of *Tournier* concerned information held by a bank about a customer who maintained an account with the institution. It remains uncertain to what extent courts in England and Wales would be willing to extend the duty of confidentiality to customers who do not hold an account with the bank in question. However, in *CF Partners (UK) LLP v Barclays Bank plc* [2014] EWHC 3049 (Ch), the court indicated its willingness to consider extending the application of the duty to a bank's broader activities. In that case, the court examined the duty in the context of the bank's investment banking division.

It remains uncertain whether courts in the United Kingdom will extend the duty of confidentiality to other financial institutions that accept deposits, such as building societies and credit unions. However, the Financial Ombudsman Service (FOS) takes the view that an implied duty of confidentiality applies to building societies as well as banks.[121] In any event, like banks, these institutions are also bound by the equitable duty of confidentiality.[122]

The duty of confidentiality encompasses information relating to a customer's bank account, including details of whether the account has a debit or credit balance, the amount of the balance, the transactions passing through the account, and any securities provided in respect of the account.[123] It also extends to information acquired by the bank from sources other than the customer's own account, provided the information is obtained "in the character

119 Proctor, C., *The Law and Practice of International Banking* (Oxford University Press, 2015) at [43.11].
120 Hudson, A., *The Law of Finance* (Sweet & Maxwell, 2013) at [29-10].
121 FOS: Ombudsman News: Issue 45.
122 Banks are also subject to the general equitable duty of confidence, as established in *Coco v AN Clark (Engineers) Ltd* [1969] RPC 41 and *Attorney General v Guardian Newspapers Ltd (No 2)* ("Spycatcher") [1988] 3 W.L.R. 776. In practice, this means that even if the *Tournier* duty of confidence does not apply, a bank may still be held liable under the equitable duty of confidence.
123 *Tournier*: Atkin LJ at page 485.

of banker" – that is, where a customer relationship exists between the bank and the individual concerned.[124]

The duty does not apply to information about the customer's affairs that the bank obtained "before the relation of banker and customer was in contemplation" or after the bank-customer relationship had ceased.[125] Similarly, the duty does not extend to information disclosed to a person who already possesses the information or could reasonably be expected to have it.[126]

The duty of confidentiality applies both during the period in which a customer maintains an account with the bank[127] and after the account has become inactive or has been closed.[128] It is generally assumed that the duty continues following the death of the customer.

The duty arises as an implied term in the contract between the bank and its customer.[129] As an implied term, it can be overridden by explicit provisions concerning confidentiality in the contract between the bank and its customer. The duty of confidentiality is subject to certain qualifications, or exceptions, as outlined by Bankes LJ in *Tournier*,[130] and these have been affirmed and expanded upon in subsequent case law. The four exceptions are as follows:

i) Disclosure made under compulsion of law;[131]
ii) Disclosure made in the public interest;[132]
iii) Disclosure made to protect the bank's own interests;[133] and
iv) Disclosure made with the express or implied consent of the customer.[134]

If any one of these exceptions applies, the duty of confidentiality does not arise.[135] The *Tournier* exceptions, supported by the Proceeds of Crime Act 2002, permit disclosures necessary for regulatory and anti-money laundering compliance. In *Price Waterhouse v BCCI Holdings* [1992] BCCLC 583, disclosure was deemed essential for investigating BCCI's collapse, demonstrating the balance between public interest and confidentiality in cases involving regulatory bodies.

If a bank breaches its duty of confidentiality, or if the court is satisfied that the bank is about to do so, the customer may seek one or both of the following remedies: damages for breach of contract or an account of profits and an injunction to prevent an anticipated breach of confidence. The amount of damages awarded for a breach of this duty can be substantial, depending on the nature of the disclosed information and the extent of the losses suffered. For instance, in *Jackson and another v Royal Bank of Scotland* [2005] UKHL 3, the bank was ordered

124 *Tournier:* Bankes LJ at page 474; *Barclays Bank plc v Taylor* [1989] 1 WLR 1066 at page 1070.
125 *Tournier:* Scrutton LJ at page 481; Atkin LJ at page 485.
126 *Christofi v Barclays* [2000] 1 W.L.R. 937.
127 *Tournier: Bankes* LJ at page 473.
128 *Tournier:* Bankes LJ at page 473; Atkin LJ at page 485.
129 *Tournier:* Scrutton LJ at page 480; Atkin LJ at page 486.
130 At p. 473.
131 There is no obligation to notify the customer about the disclosure of confidential information to a third party where the compulsion of law exception applies (*Barclays Bank plc v Taylor* [1989] 1 WLR 1066).
132 In *Libyan Arab Foreign Bank v Bankers Trust Co* [1989] QB 728, the court suggested that the public duty exception to the duty of confidentiality could potentially apply to disclosures made to the Federal Reserve Bank of New York in connection with compliance with US sanctions.
133 In *Sunderland v Barclays Bank Ltd* (1938) 5 LDAB, the bank successfully contended that it was entitled, in order to protect its reputation, to disclose information to the plaintiff's husband regarding the insufficiency of funds in the plaintiff's account to honour cheques drawn on it.
134 A bank is required to obtain the customer's consent before providing a credit reference, as there is no implied consent from customers for banks to disclose such information (*Turner v Royal Bank of Scotland plc* [1999] 3 WLUK 446).
135 *El Jawhary v Bank of Credit and Commerce International SA* [1993] B.C.L.C. 396 at [400]; *Barclays Bank plc v Taylor* [1989] 1 WLR 1066 at p. 1074.

to pay damages to the customer for loss of profit after the disclosure of confidential information caused the customer to lose business.

A breach of a customer's confidentiality may also amount to a breach of the bank's regulatory obligations. Under the General Organisational Requirements section of the PRA Rulebook, the PRA requires banks to establish, implement, and maintain systems and procedures that are adequate to ensure the security, integrity, and confidentiality of information, including customer information (General Organisational Requirements 2.4). Equivalent requirements are provided under the FCA's Senior Management Arrangements, Systems and Controls (**SYSC**) module. Additionally, a bank that discloses confidential information in breach of its duty must also consider the FCA's general principle, as set out in its *Principles for Businesses*, which requires regulated firms to pay due regard to the interests of their customers and to treat them fairly (PRIN 2.1.1R).

Finally, banks are considered controllers of their customers' personal data under the retained EU law version of the General Data Protection Regulation ((EU) 2016/679) (**UK GDPR**)[136] and the Data Protection Act 2018. The obligations imposed on banks by data protection legislation, along with certain exemptions available under the UK GDPR, overlap with their duty of confidentiality. This means that banks must ensure compliance with both their regulatory obligations regarding confidentiality and the broader requirements of data protection law when handling customer information.[137]

Banking Confidentiality in Japan

In Japan, banks' duty of confidentiality has been established and developed primarily through case law. The Supreme Court of Japan has consistently held that financial institutions owe their customers a duty of confidentiality, which arises either from business practices or an agreement between the financial institution and its customer. Under this principle, banks are prohibited from disclosing information related to customer transactions, credit risk assessments, or any other customer-related information to third parties unless there is a valid justification for such disclosure.[138]

Furthermore, Article 12–2, Paragraph 2 of the Banking Act explicitly mandates that banks must handle customer information appropriately when acquired in the course of providing financial services. This statutory provision reinforces the duty of confidentiality by imposing a regulatory obligation on banks to ensure that customer data is managed securely and responsibly.

In addition to the legal framework, supervisory guidance issued by the Financial Services Agency further strengthens confidentiality obligations. Section III-3-3-3 of the Comprehensive Guidelines for Supervision of Major Banks[139] emphasises that the Financial Services Agency will assess whether banks have established an adequate information management system.

136 Kokkinis, A. and Miglionico, M., *Banking Law: Private Transactions and Regulatory Frameworks* (Routledge, 2021), p. 95.

137 Proctor, C., *The Law and Practice of International Banking* (Oxford University Press, 2015) at [43.66].

138 Hideaki, S., 'Japan: Law & Practice' in *Chambers Global Practice Guides: Banking Regulation 2024*, Nagashima Ohno & Tsunematsu (Chambers and Partners, 2024), p. 13.

139 Provisional translation available at www.fsa.go.jp/common/law/guide/en_city.pdf (accessed in March 2025).

5.4 Duty to Exercise Skill and Care

A bank, when performing its obligations under its contractual relationship with a customer, has an implied duty to generally exercise reasonable skill and care. This duty extends to handling communications received from the customer concerning their banking business.[140] Whereas "*the limits of a banker's business cannot be laid down as a matter of law. The nature of such a business must in each case be a matter of fact and, accordingly, cannot be treated as if it were a matter of pure law*".[141]

More specifically, a credit institution owes a duty of care and skill in handling customer accounts, particularly regarding cheque collection, deposits, and payment execution. This requirement for accuracy and diligence was underscored in *London Joint Stock Bank Ltd v MacMillan* [1978] AC 777, where the court stressed the need for careful processing of mandates to prevent errors and protect customer interests. Additionally, banks must render regular and accurate accounts to customers, providing transparency over transactions and account balances. This obligation extends to observing any countermanded instructions, as recognised in *Hilton v Westminster Bank Ltd* [1926] 1 KB 361,[142] which held that banks must comply with a customer's instruction to stop payment before it is processed, provided the instruction is clear and timely.

In essence, in addition to the *Quincecare* duty,

> *Where a bank is "put on inquiry" in the sense of having reasonable grounds for believing that a payment instruction given by an agent purportedly on behalf of the customer is an attempt to defraud the customer, this duty requires the bank to refrain from executing the instruction without first making inquiries to verify that the instruction has actually been authorised by the customer. If the bank executes the instruction without making such inquiries and the instruction proves to have been given without the customer's authority, the bank will be in breach of duty. It will also in making the payment be acting outside the scope of its own authority from the customer and will therefore not be entitled to debit the payment to the customer's account.*[143]

Such a general duty of care was held to apply in *CCP Graduate School Ltd v National Westminster Bank PLC & Anor* [2024] EWHC 581 (KB), where there was a discrepancy in the CHAPS payment instructions. Due to fraud, the unique identifiers, namely the account number and sort code, incorrectly referred to the fraudster's account at Santander, while the payee name accurately identified the intended recipient, a subsidiary of JPMorgan. Master Brown considered it at least arguable that a bank may owe a tortious duty to attempt the retrieval and/or freezing of a payment affected by authorised push payment (APP) fraud. Being a tortious duty,[144] it could potentially be owed not only by the paying bank but also by the receiving bank.

Further, such a general duty does not arise simply as a result of the banker-customer relationship. In *Larsson v Revolut Ltd* [2024] EWHC 1287 (Ch), Mr Larsson was deceived into making SWIFT transfers from his UBS account to five Revolut accounts that had been fraudulently opened in his name. He alleged that Revolut had breached duties owed to him by failing to implement and operate adequate fraud-prevention systems. Zacaroli J summarily

140 *Selangor United Rubber Estates Ltd v Cradock (No. 3)* [1968] 1 WLR 1555, at [61].
141 In *Woods v Martins Bank Ltd and another* [1959] 1 QB 55 at [63] at [70].
142 At [362].
143 *Philipp v Barclays Bank UK plc* [2023] UKSC 25 at [97] and [100].
144 "*[T]he recognition by the Supreme Court in Philipp that there could be a duty of retrieval (at [115] to [119], see above). That duty, it might be argued, was not expressed or to be seen in terms of a contractual obligation (not perhaps on its face being necessary for the business efficacy of the contract) but a duty in tort*". Ibid. per Master Brown at [19].

dismissed the argument that such a duty could arise contractually simply because Mr. Larsson also happened to hold an account at Revolut.

Finally, the customer, too, has key responsibilities in this relationship, with a primary duty to avoid fraud. For instance, in *London Joint Stock Bank Ltd v MacMillan* [1978] AC 777, the customer was found liable for failing to exercise reasonable care when issuing a cheque, which subsequently facilitated fraud by a clerk. The court held that customers are responsible for ensuring their instructions do not inadvertently enable fraudulent activity. Furthermore, customers must promptly report any forgeries or fraudulent transactions on their accounts. In *Greenwood v Martins Bank Ltd* [1933] AC 51, a delay in notifying the bank of forged cheques led to the customer being stopped from recovering the lost funds, emphasising the importance of timely reporting in cases of forgery.

6.5 The Regulatory Framework: FSMA and Conduct of Business Rules

The banker-customer relationship is also governed by statutory regulation, particularly under FSMA. FSMA introduced a comprehensive regulatory framework for the conduct of financial services, including banking. Under FSMA, the FCA is responsible for regulating the conduct of banks and ensuring that they treat customers fairly.

FSMA and the Regulation of Banker-Customer Relationships

FSMA establishes a comprehensive regulatory framework that governs both the financial stability of institutions and their conduct towards customers. It imposes statutory obligations on banks to ensure compliance with both prudential and conduct-related standards.[145] This dual regulatory approach – prudential regulation overseen by the PRA and conduct regulation enforced by the FCA – requires banks to maintain financial stability while simultaneously ensuring fair treatment of customers and adherence to prescribed behavioural standards.

Prudential regulation, as administered by the PRA under FSMA, focuses on the financial soundness of banks, which has a direct impact on the security of customer funds. This oversight plays a critical role in reinforcing trust within the banker-customer relationship, ensuring that financial institutions remain stable enough to honour deposits, extend credit responsibly, and manage risks effectively.[146]

Alongside prudential regulation, FSMA mandates conduct regulation, which falls within the remit of the FCA. The FCA's statutory objectives include consumer protection, maintaining market integrity, and promoting effective competition in the interests of consumers. To fulfil these objectives, the FCA implements a range of rules and guidance, most notably through the Conduct of Business Sourcebook (**COBS**), which outlines the standards banks must adhere to when providing financial services to customers. This regulatory framework ensures that banks engage with customers fairly, transparently, and in accordance with consumer protection principles, thereby enhancing confidence in the financial system.

145 Hudson, A., *The Law of Finance* (Sweet & Maxwell, 2013) at [31-13].

146 Ellinger, E. P., Lomnicka, E. and Hare, C., *Ellinger's Modern Banking Law* (Oxford University Press, 2011), p. 123.

Conduct of Business Rules and Their Impact on the Banker-Customer Relationship

One of the central principles within COBS is the duty to treat customers fairly (**TCF**), as outlined in COBS 2.1.1. This principle requires banks to ensure fair treatment throughout the customer lifecycle, from account opening to closure and during the resolution of disputes. By embedding TCF within FSMA's regulatory framework, COBS strengthens the common law duties of confidentiality, care, and proper execution of instructions, offering additional statutory safeguards against exploitative practices and unfair treatment.

The duty of disclosure and transparency, set out in COBS 4.2.1R, imposes a legal obligation on banks to provide clear, fair, and non-misleading information. This statutory obligation supports the common law duty to conform to the customer's mandate, ensuring that contractual agreements are based on informed consent. Failure to provide adequate disclosures may result in claims of misrepresentation or unfair terms, with the FCA empowered to impose fines or sanctions for non-compliance.

COBS 9.2.1R further mandates that banks assess the suitability of financial products and services for customers. This requirement is particularly significant in investment, lending, and financial advisory contexts, where banks must evaluate a customer's financial position, risk tolerance, and objectives before recommending a product. The suitability obligation reinforces the common law duty of care.

The introduction of the Senior Managers and Certification Regime (**SM&CR**) under FSMA further reinforces accountability within banks. This regime requires senior executives to take personal responsibility for ensuring regulatory compliance, particularly concerning customer interactions. COBS 2.2[147] references the general conduct requirements that overlap with the SM&CR, making senior managers directly accountable for upholding transparency, fairness, and consumer protection. The SM&CR imposes individual liability on executives, reinforcing common law duties and ensuring that banks align their policies with regulatory expectations.

Additionally, FSMA and COBS contain specific provisions to protect vulnerable customers. Under COBS 4.1, banks must exercise the utmost care when dealing with individuals who may be at risk of financial harm due to age, disability, mental health, or other vulnerabilities. FCA guidance emphasises the need for tailored support and proactive measures to safeguard these customers. This regulatory focus extends the bank's common law duty of care, requiring financial institutions to take additional steps beyond the minimum legal obligations to prevent financial harm to vulnerable individuals.

Overall, the COBS framework under FSMA enhances the common law banker-customer relationship by embedding statutory duties that promote fairness, transparency, and consumer protection.

7 BANKERS' PRIVILEGES

As Lord Denning noted in *United Dominions Trust Ltd*: "*Bankers are a privileged class. They are exempt from the vexatious restrictions which are imposed on other moneylenders. They are an exclusive circle to which entry is limited*".[148]

147 See www.handbook.fca.org.uk/handbook/COCON/2/2.html (accessed in March 2025).
148 *United Dominions Trust Ltd v Kirkwood* [1966] 2 QB 431 (CA) per Lord Denning at page 441.

Bankers' privileges are a collection of legal rights, protections, and exemptions that empower banks to conduct business efficiently while managing risks and maintaining compliance with regulatory frameworks. They generally encompass, albeit with variations across jurisdictions, the right to exercise particular powers, exemptions from specific liabilities, and unique legal protections that bolster banking operations within the financial system. In England, these privileges, rooted in common law principles and statutory frameworks, underpin the banking sector's stability and operational resilience.

Such privileges include a restriction on the use of the terms "bank" or "banking" when incorporating a company under the Companies Act 2006, as a letter or email of non-objection from the FCA must be provided. Furthermore, under Section 24(1)(a) of FSMA,[149] it would be a criminal offence to employ such terms if the corporate entity were not an authorised person.[150]

In addition to the right to use the term "bank" in a name, one key privilege is the right of set-off, which permits banks to offset balances across a customer's accounts to recover outstanding debts. This right enables banks to transfer funds from a credit account to cover deficits in another, allowing the bank to manage its risk exposure effectively. In England, a bank can only invoke a banker's set-off if the accounts are current or running accounts, that is, where the balance on the account, whether positive or negative, is payable on demand or on reasonably short notice.[151] This is a self-help remedy and, therefore, can be exercised without litigation. There are distinct mandatory statutory provisions governing set-off in cases of liquidation, administration, and bankruptcy. As noted in Chapter 2, the existence of a mandatory insolvency set-off scheme does not, in itself, exclude the application of other forms of set-off, such as banker's set-off.[152] However, in practice, these other forms of set-off will only need to be considered where insolvency set-off does not apply – for instance, when determining residual liabilities between the debtor and creditor following the application of insolvency set-off or in circumstances where one form of set-off falls outside the scope of the other.

As an additional privilege, accounts maintained by a bank are, under the Bankers' Books Evidence Act 1879 (as amended),[153] prima facie evidence of the borrower's indebtedness to the bank.[154] This evidentiary privilege is counterweighted by a potentially wide-ranging administrative burden.[155] Under Section 7 of the Bankers' Books Evidence Act 1879, a bank may be subject to extensive powers of inspections or production by third-party litigants:

> *On the application of any party to a legal proceeding a court or judge may order that such party be at liberty to inspect and take copies of any entries in a banker's book for any of the purposes of such proceedings.*

However, in *Meng v HSBC Bank Plc* [2021] EWHC 342 (QB), one of the few cases to shed light on the issue, the High Court refused to make an order under section 7 of the Bankers' Books Evidence Act 1879 requiring the respondent British banks to provide documents to the applicant for potential use in Canadian extradition proceedings. It was held that Section 7

149 "*A person who is neither an authorised person nor, in relation to the regulated activity in question, an exempt person is guilty of an offence if he – (a) describes himself (in whatever terms) as an authorised person*".

150 Ellinger, E. P., Lomnicka, E. and Hare, C., *Ellinger's Modern Banking Law* (Oxford University Press, 2011), p. 89.

151 *Re Willis, Percival, & Co, ex p Morier* (1879) LR 12 ChD 491.

152 Proctor, C., *The Law and Practice of International Banking* (Oxford University Press, 2015) at [36.05].

153 It should be noted in section 7 of Bankers' Books Evidence Act 1879.

154 Pursuant to Section 3: "*Subject to the provisions of this Act, a copy of any entry in a banker's book shall in all legal proceedings be received as prima facie evidence of such entry, and of the matters, transactions, and accounts therein recorded*".

155 Ellinger, E., Lomnicka, E. and Hare, C., *Ellinger's Modern Banking Law* (Oxford University Press, 2011), p. 88.

extended only to proceedings in the UK and, in any event, was limited to transactional records and not records of meetings.[156]

It is worth noting that, with respect to the disclosure of banking documents in the US, banks can avail themselves of the bank examiner privilege. This is a doctrine established under federal common law. It protects communications between banks and their examiners, aiming to encourage the full and frank disclosures necessary for the effective supervision of banks.[157] The bank examiner privilege is designed to safeguard the integrity of the regulatory process and foster an environment in which regulatory agencies and banks can communicate openly and candidly (*In re Bankers Trust Co.* 61 F.3d 465, 471 (6th Cir. 1995)). The effectiveness of bank supervision relies heavily on the quality of communication between the regulated banking institution and the regulatory agency (*In re Subpoena Served Upon Comptroller of Currency* 967 F.2d 630, 633–34 (D.C. Cir. 1992)).

The banker's lien[158] is another significant privilege, providing banks with a general right to retain possession of a customer's property until the customer fulfils their debt obligations.

> *The so-called banker's lien is an example of this rule of law, and in this case the decisions establish that a banker has a lien over all such negotiable securities of the customer as are lawfully in his possession, and are subject to his control, but this lien may be excluded by agreement, express or implied.*[159]

Thus, a banker's lien is generally implied by law rather than established through explicit agreement, a characteristic that distinguishes it from other forms of liens requiring formalized contracts. At its core, a banker's lien allows a bank to hold customer property as security for debts. Unlike possessory liens, which are limited to specific property related to a particular debt, a banker's lien is more comprehensive, extending to any assets in the bank's possession unless otherwise agreed.[160]

Bankers' liens can be classified as either general or particular. A general lien permits the bank to retain possession of all customer property in its control as security for any outstanding debt, irrespective of the debt's origin. Conversely, a particular lien is narrower in scope, allowing the bank to hold only the specific property tied to the debt in question.

English law presumes a general lien in the banker-customer relationship, a presumption that may only be overridden by explicit terms agreed upon by the parties. This principle was firmly established in *Brandao v Barnett* (1846) 136 E.R. 207, where the court affirmed that banks inherently possess a general lien on all securities deposited in the normal course of business unless there is an express agreement or circumstance negating this right.

The scope of a banker's lien includes property or assets deposited with the bank in the ordinary course of business. Typically, this encompasses negotiable instruments, such as

156 "*Section 9 has always referred to 'the ordinary business of the bank' and that 'ordinary business' can change in its nature over time, just as the mode of record-keeping can change. Section 9 as enacted referred to 'all other books used in the ordinary business of the bank' and in Barker (Barker v Wilson [1980] 1 WLR 884) the Divisional Court had decided that 'book' would include 'microfilm' and any other 'methods which modern technology makes available' (see 887D, G-H). The section 9 language was in due course amended to say 'other records used in the ordinary business of the bank' and Parliament added the words 'whether those records are in written form or are kept on microfilm, magnetic tape or any other form of mechanical or electronic data retrieval mechanism' (at [22]), the phrase 'entries in' in 'other records used in the ordinary business of the bank' in section 9(2), read with section 7, means transactional records. It does not include non-transactional records maintained for regulatory compliance*". Per Mr Justice Fordham at [28].

157 *Wultz v Bank of China Ltd.* 61 F Supp 3d 272, 281 (SDNY 2013).

158 A **lien** is a right that entitles a party to retain possession of assets until a debt owed to them has been paid. This right may arise in several ways: through equity; through the operation of law, whether legal or common law (a legal lien); as a result of contractual agreement, where the lien is bargained for or extended as a matter of contract (a contractual lien); or by virtue of a statutory provision (a statutory lien).

159 *Horsbrugh (Robertson's Trustee) v. Royal Bank of Scotland* [1890] ScotLR 28_35 per Lord M'Laren.

160 Ellinger, E., Lomnicka, E. and Hare, C., *Ellinger's Modern Banking Law* (Oxford University Press, 2011), p. 864.

cheques, bills of exchange, promissory notes, and securities like share certificates. However, assets deposited for a specific, limited purpose fall outside the scope of a general lien, as such deposits are deemed inconsistent with the lien's application. In *Re Bowes, Earl of Strathmore v Vane* (1886) 33 Ch D 586, the court determined that a bank could apply its lien to a share certificate deposited as security for a particular loan. Since no express agreement limited the bank's lien, it could assert the lien over the certificate for other debts. This case clarified that unless an asset is designated for a specific purpose, a banker's lien extends to all property within the bank's control, serving as collateral for the customer's debts.

Property subject to a banker's lien includes any valuable asset deposited by the customer in the course of ordinary banking business, so long as the property is held by the bank in its capacity as a banker. The bank cannot, however, assert a lien over property it holds outside its usual role, nor can it claim a lien over assets held in a fiduciary capacity, such as trust assets. In *Re London and Globe Finance Corporation* [1902] Ch 416, the court ruled that a bank could not apply a lien to securities held for a purpose unrelated to the customer's debt, reinforcing that the bank's lien is limited to assets associated with the customer's banking relationship and not with assets held for other purposes.

While much of the law surrounding bankers' liens is grounded in common law, certain statutory provisions indirectly influence their application, primarily through consumer protections and fair banking practices. In this respect, FSMA affects bankers' liens by regulating banks' conduct, particularly through COBS. As noted previously, this framework imposes obligations on banks to treat customers fairly, requiring clear communication regarding the existence and implications of any lien over customer property. Should a bank assert a lien without fully informing the customer, this ambiguity could constitute a violation of the conduct rules, especially where consumers' understanding of their rights is concerned.

Bankers' liens are also subject to the provisions of insolvency law, particularly under the Insolvency Act 1986. If a customer becomes insolvent, a bank may attempt to exercise its lien over assets in its possession to satisfy outstanding debts. However, such lien is subordinated to the principles of insolvency set-off, which may override a bank's general lien in favour of statutory mechanisms under the Insolvency Act. This principle was highlighted in *Stein v Blake* [1996] AC 243 (HL), where the House of Lords affirmed that statutory insolvency set-off takes precedence over contractual or equitable claims, including a banker's lien. In insolvency cases, banks' ability to assert a lien is also limited by the Insolvency Act's requirements to treat creditors equitably, with priority rules dictating the distribution of assets within the insolvent estate.[161]

Moreover, an express agreement between the bank and the customer can exclude the lien's application; if such an agreement is in place, the bank cannot assert a lien over those designated assets. This was demonstrated in *Re Bowes*,[162] where the court respected the explicit terms of an agreement that limited the bank's lien rights. The bank's lien is also conditional on lawful possession; if assets are obtained under duress, fraud, or in a fiduciary role, the lien does not apply.

Liens are not registrable under the Companies Act 2006, as the obligation to register only applies to charges that are "created by" a company within the meaning of section 859A(1) of the Companies Act 2006. Since liens arise by operation of law rather than through deliberate creation, they fall outside the scope of the registration requirements. There is a risk, however, that a court could interpret a contractual lien as a mortgage or charge (*Re Lehman Brothers*

161 Proctor, C., *The Law and Practice of International Banking* (Oxford University Press, 2015) at [36.08].
162 *Re Bowes, Earl of Strathmore v Vane* (1886) 33 Ch D 586.

International (Europe) (In Administration) [2012] EWHC 2997 (Ch)). Where a contract purports to grant a lien, the court will examine the substance of the provision rather than its form.

8 CONCLUSION

The historical development of UK banking regulation, from the informal oversight of the Bank of England to the creation of comprehensive statutory frameworks, highlights the need for structured and effective supervision to ensure financial stability. Milestones such as the Bank Charter Act 1844, the Banking Act 1979, and FSMA represent key points in the shift towards more formal and centralised regulation of banking activities. Each of these reforms came in response to specific crises, demonstrating the substantially reactive nature of banking regulation.

Crucial pieces of legislation like FSMA have not only reshaped how financial services are regulated in the UK but also established a broader framework that integrates banking, insurance, and investments under a unified regulatory structure. FSMA provided a foundation for regulatory bodies like the FSA (and later the PRA and the FCA) to supervise the industry. As such foundations were shaken during the global financial crisis of 2007–2009, the Banking Act 2009 and the SRR were introduced to address the fault lines that had emerged.

Moreover, the ring-fencing reforms introduced through the Banking Reform Act 2013 demonstrated a commitment to protecting retail banking activities from the risks associated with investment banking. The UK's decision to leave the European Union has further reshaped the regulatory framework, particularly with the enactment of FSMA 2023. The post-Brexit regulatory reforms reflect the UK's ambition to diverge from the EU's regulatory structure while simultaneously reinforcing its status as a global financial hub. These reforms have not only allowed the UK to create bespoke rules tailored to its financial sector but have also opened up opportunities for innovation in areas such as digital assets and fintech.

Throughout this regulatory evolution, the banker-customer relationship has remained central to the operation of the banking industry. The legal foundation of this relationship, as articulated through case law, underscores the debtor-creditor nature of banking while also recognising the importance of duties such as confidentiality, care, and skill. The introduction of statutory regulations such as FSMA has further codified and augmented these common law duties, ensuring that banks are held to high standards of consumer protection and transparency.

Finally, in the EU, the definition of a credit institution, grounded in the CRR and CRD IV, captures the essential banking functions of deposit-taking and credit-granting (the same two essential functions characterise banks in Japan, China, and India). Through this precise classification, the EU enforces a prudential framework that extends robust oversight to institutions managing public funds, reinforcing financial stability and depositor protection. Also, the US regulatory framework for banking institutions is highly nuanced, balancing strict statutory definitions with regulatory flexibility to accommodate a diverse array of financial entities. This complex system is reinforced by dual regulation at federal and state levels, involving primary and secondary regulatory authorities that address both general and specialised aspects of financial oversight.

CHAPTER 4

BANK ORGANISATION, GOVERNANCE, AND INDIVIDUAL RESPONSIBILITIES

OVERVIEW

Since banks differ from ordinary firms in that their failure poses a greater risk to society, potentially triggering contagion in other parts of the financial system, disrupting its operation and adversely affecting the ability of businesses to obtain finance,[1] their governance structures embrace robust frameworks that promote sound decision-making, accountability, risk management, and adherence to regulatory standards. Banks should be governed in a manner that ensures they are not only profitable but also safe, sound, and sustainable.

Governance reforms globally, particularly in major financial hubs such as the UK, EU, US, and Asia, have converged on the importance of individual accountability, effective oversight, and – to some extent – the integration of environmental, social, and governance (**ESG**) factors. This chapter explores banks' corporate governance frameworks across key jurisdictions, with a particular focus on the statutory provisions, regulations, and case law that shape them.

In the UK, governance has evolved significantly. The introduction of the Senior Managers and Certification Regime (**SMCR**) was particularly important in creating a clear framework of individual accountability that requires senior managers to take responsibility for key areas of the business. Importantly, governance is no longer limited to financial performance but encompasses broader societal responsibilities, as evidenced by the significance of ESG-related obligations.

However, it is crucial to note that corporate governance in credit institutions is not uniform across jurisdictions. While the UK and, to some extent, the EU resort to a principles-based approach, other jurisdictions, such as the US, China, and India, have developed frameworks that reflect their regulatory philosophies and economic structures. This chapter examines these differences and identifies the common themes that underpin effective governance in the banking sector.

1 CORPORATE GOVERNANCE

The UK's first code on corporate governance was introduced by the Cadbury Committee in 1992 and it provided what is still widely regarded as the classic definition of corporate governance. Although the environment in which companies, shareholders, and stakeholders operate has continued to evolve, the definition remains highly influential:

> *Corporate governance is the system by which companies are directed and controlled. Boards of directors are responsible for the governance of their companies. The shareholders' role in governance is to appoint the directors and the auditors and to satisfy themselves that an appropriate structure is in place. The responsibilities of the board include setting the company's strategic aims, providing the leadership to put them into effect, supervising the management of the business and reporting to shareholders on their stewardship.*[2]

1 Armour, J., Awrey, D., Davies, P., Enriques, L., Gordon, J., Mayer, C. and Payne, J., *Principles of Financial Regulation* (Oxford University Press, 2016), p. 374.

2 At [2.5] of The final report of the Committee on the Financial Aspects of Corporate Governance as published on 1 December 1992, available at www.icaew.com/-/media/corporate/files/library/subjects/corporate-governance/financial-aspects-of-corporate-governance.ashx (accessed in March 2025).

DOI: 10.4324/9781032662220-5

The first code of corporate governance did not advance any specific considerations for banks. This is because regulatory authorities have consistently affirmed that the governance of banking institutions is, and should be, distinct from that of other corporate entities.

This peculiarity arises from the unique credit and liquidity functions that banks perform, which are essential to financial stability and the broader economy. Moreover, the systemic importance of banking institutions necessitates a framework that prioritises prudential oversight, risk management, and regulatory compliance.[3]

To achieve this objective, an extensive framework of regulations and supervisory guidance has been developed, imposing additional governance requirements on banking institutions. Consequently, unlike directors of non-financial corporations, who are generally expected to prioritise shareholder value, bank directors must balance the interests of multiple stakeholders. Such stakeholders normally include depositors, who rely on the institution's financial stability; the deposit insurance fund,[4] which indirectly bears risks associated with banking failures; creditors; and financial regulators. The overarching principle of "ensuring" the safety and soundness of the institution thus shapes governance decisions in the banking sector, reinforcing its distinctive regulatory and supervisory framework.[5]

The responsibility for governance and risk management within financial institutions rests primarily with their boards and senior management. Boards of directors are expected to exercise robust, independent oversight of executive management in fulfilling these responsibilities. The 2007–2008 global financial crisis revealed significant deficiencies in the governance and risk management practices of companies within the financial services sector.[6] In particular, it exposed the ways in which existing corporate governance frameworks failed to act as an effective safeguard against poor decision-making. These shortcomings were most pronounced in banks and investment firms. In the years preceding the financial crisis, many non-executive directors (**NED**s) appointed to the boards of financial institutions struggled to perform this role effectively.[7] In particular, they failed to identify and mitigate instances of excessive risk-taking. The crisis also exposed weaknesses in the control of remuneration within financial institutions and in the exercise of ownership rights by shareholders. These issues further contributed to poor governance and exacerbated systemic vulnerabilities.

Internationally, the crisis led to a renewed focus on effective corporate governance by organisations such as the Organisation for Economic Cooperation and Development (OECD), the Financial Stability Board (FSB), and the Basel Committee on Banking Supervision (BCBS). Specifically, it prompted the adoption of Basel III, which introduced enhancements to the international framework for prudential and capital regulation for banks and investment firms.

In the UK, a range of initiatives has been undertaken to strengthen corporate governance both generally and specifically within the financial services sector. Sector-specific initiatives included the 2009 review of corporate governance in banks and other financial institutions

3 See Lee, P., 'Directors' Duty to Monitor: Experience in the Banking Sector – Part I' (2016) 133 *The Banking Law Journal* 405.

4 The Financial Services Compensation Scheme (FSCS).

5 Adams, R. and Mehran, H., 'Is Corporate Governance Different for Bank Holding Companies?' (2003) 9 *FRBNY Economic Policy Review* 123.

6 Armour, J., Awrey, D., Davies, P., Enriques, L., Gordon, J., Mayer, C. and Payne, J., *Principles of Financial Regulation* (Oxford University Press, 2016), p. 375.

7 "*Given that the formulation of that strategy was a fundamental role of the Board of Northern Rock, overseen by some directors who had been there since its demutualisation, the failure of that strategy must also be attributed to the Board. The non-executive members of the Board, and in particular the Chairman of the Board, the Chairman of the Risk Committee and the senior non-executive director, failed in the case of Northern Rock*", in House of Commons Treasury Committee. The Run on the Rock. London: HMSO; 2008.

led by Sir David Walker, the work of the Parliamentary Commission on Banking Standards, and the aspects of the Turner Review addressing the future of financial services regulation and supervision with respect to governance and risk management. These efforts subsequently informed and shaped the work programmes of the UK regulators.[8] Likewise, at the European level, many of the legislative initiatives introduced in the aftermath of the financial crisis incorporated substantial corporate governance elements.[9]

2 CORPORATE GOVERNANCE IN THE UK BANKING SECTOR

Corporate governance in the UK banking sector operates within a multifaceted legal and regulatory environment,[10] blending statutory law, regulatory frameworks, and non-binding governance principles to create a robust system aimed at safeguarding financial stability, promoting accountability, and ensuring compliance.[11]

The Companies Act 2006 provides the overarching principles of corporate governance across all UK companies, including banks. The Act, in codifying the fiduciary duties of directors, seeks to align the interests of directors with those of shareholders and other stakeholders, ensuring long-term business success, accountability, and adherence to regulatory standards. Moreover, under the Companies Act 2006, there is an emphasis on the reporting and documentation of environmental factors in corporate decision-making, for example, in sections 414C, 414CZA, and 426B. Such emphasis is also reflected in secondary legislation such as the Companies (Miscellaneous Reporting) Regulations 2018 and the Occupational Pension Schemes (Investment) Regulations 2005.

In addition to the Companies Act 2006, UK banks are governed by an extensive range of sector-specific regulations and rules overseen by the Prudential Regulation Authority (**PRA**) and the Financial Conduct Authority (**FCA**). The PRA Rulebook and the FCA Handbook contain detailed governance requirements tailored to the banking and financial services sectors, addressing the unique risks and operational complexities that banks face. These regulations set out stringent requirements on capital adequacy, liquidity, risk management, and internal controls designed to protect consumers, enhance market integrity, and mitigate systemic risks.

A key element of corporate governance in the banking sector is the SMCR, which – when introduced in 2016 – represented a shift in the regulatory approach to governance, placing greater emphasis on the personal responsibilities of individual senior managers. This regime ensures that governance failures are not solely attributed to collective board oversight but are also linked to individual failings, thereby fostering a culture of accountability, integrity, and proactive risk management within banks.

8 Ferreira, C., Jenkinson, N. and Wilson, C., 'From Basel I to Basel III: Sequencing Implementation in Developing Economies' (2019) *WP/19/127* 16.

9 Key examples include the Directive 2013/36/EU (CRD IV), Directive 2009/138/EC (Solvency II), Directive (2009/65/EC) (UCITS IV), Directive 2011/61/EU (AIFMD), Directive 2014/65/EU (MiFID II), and the Investment Firms Directive ((EU) 2019/2034.

10 Armour, J., Awrey, D., Davies, P., Enriques, L., Gordon, J., Mayer, C. and Payne, J., *Principles of Financial Regulation* (Oxford University Press, 2016), p. 288.

11 Kokkinis, A. and Miglionico, M., *Banking Law: Private Transactions and Regulatory Frameworks* (Routledge, 2021), p. 226.

The role of non-binding governance codes, particularly the UK Corporate Governance Code[12] and the Wates Corporate Governance Principles for Large Private Companies,[13] complements the statutory and regulatory frameworks by providing best practice guidance for boards to ensure "*that their companies are well managed and aligned behind a clear purpose*".[14]

The UK Corporate Governance Code[15] promotes boardroom effectiveness, ethical conduct, and long-term sustainable performance by requiring banks to focus on leadership, accountability, remuneration, and relations with stakeholders. For banks, this often translates into setting a clear risk appetite, ensuring robust internal control mechanisms, and fostering a risk-aware culture from the top down. The code also encourages diversity in board composition, recognising that a mix of skills, perspectives, and experiences can enhance decision-making processes and risk oversight.

The Financial Reporting Council (**FRC**), which oversees the UK Corporate Governance Code, regularly reviews governance practices in the banking sector, ensuring that institutions are transparent about how they meet their governance obligations or explaining any deviations from recommended practices.

As the UK banking sector continues to evolve in response to emerging challenges such as climate-related financial risks, cybersecurity threats, and the growing importance of ESG considerations, corporate governance frameworks are adapting to ensure that boards are equipped to address these risks. Banks are increasingly expected to incorporate ESG factors into their business strategies and risk management frameworks, aligning their operations with broader societal and environmental goals. Moreover, the FCA and PRA view diversity, equity, and inclusion (**DEI**)[16] as essential for the effective governance of financial institutions. In 2023, both regulators consulted on proposals to introduce a new regulatory framework on DEI,[17] recognising that a lack of diversity and an exclusionary culture can contribute to groupthink, weaken decision-making, and reduce effective challenges, ultimately affecting outcomes for consumers and financial markets. Groupthink, in particular, presents a significant governance risk, as it can result in poor decision-making and a failure to act in the best interests of consumers. It arises when individuals within a group conform to a dominant perspective without considering alternative viewpoints or without feeling comfortable challenging the prevailing consensus. This dynamic can undermine firms' ability to identify and address critical risks, as decision-making processes may overlook key factors due to a lack of diverse perspectives and constructive challenges. By fostering a more inclusive and diverse workplace, firms can mitigate these risks, enhance governance, and ensure more balanced and informed decision-making.

Financial reporting has also been expanded to the field of ESG standards. In this context, a significant development is the consolidation of key sustainability frameworks and organisations, aimed at addressing the proliferation of reporting standards. In particular, the establishment of the International Sustainability Standards Board (**ISSB**) by the International Financial Reporting Standards (**IFRS**) Foundation represents a major step towards global standardisation. In 2023,

12 Available at https://media.frc.org.uk/documents/UK_Corporate_Governance_Code_2024_a2hmQmY.pdf (accessed in March 2025).

13 See https://media.frc.org.uk/documents/The_Wates_Corporate_Governance_Principles_for_Large_Private_Companies.pdf (accessed in March 2025).

14 'The Wates Corporate Governance Principles for Large Private Companies' (2018), p. 1.

15 See the UK Corporate Governance Code 2024, published by the FRC on 22 January 2024 and available at https://media.frc.org.uk/documents/UK_Corporate_Governance_Code_2024_kRCm5ss.pdf (accessed in March 2025).

16 Also referred to as diversity and inclusion (D&I) or equity, diversity, and inclusion (EDI) – encompasses a broad spectrum of issues, including discrimination, equality law, environmental, social, and governance (ESG) considerations, and equal opportunities.

17 See www.fca.org.uk/news/press-releases/fca-and-pra-propose-measures-boost-diversity-and-inclusion-financial-services (accessed in March 2025).

the ISSB introduced new sustainability disclosure standards, aligning them with the financial reporting requirements set by the International Accounting Standards Board: IFRS S1 and IFRS S2. IFRS S1 provides a comprehensive framework for companies to disclose sustainability-related risks and opportunities to investors, thereby enhancing transparency and consistency in corporate sustainability reporting. IFRS S2 is intended to be used in conjunction with IFRS S1 and focuses specifically on climate-related disclosures. Additionally, the ISSB introduced the *Proposed IFRS Sustainability Disclosure Taxonomy*, designed to reflect the disclosure obligations set out in IFRS S1 and IFRS S2, further facilitating structured and comparable sustainability reporting. Following the publication of these standards, numerous jurisdictions have adopted or announced plans to implement mandatory disclosure requirements aligned with the ISSB framework. Countries that have taken steps in this direction include India, Australia, Costa Rica, Hong Kong, Japan, Nigeria, Singapore, Canada, the UK, and Turkey. This widespread adoption underscores the significant commitment to harmonising sustainability reporting and integrating ESG considerations into corporate financial disclosures. The European Union, on the other hand, has developed a significant regulatory framework for disclosure within the Union.[18] It should be noted, however, that since 2025, this perspective has somewhat changed internationally (particularly in the US).[19] This unexpected change in approach underscores the fact that governance in the banking sector must remain dynamic and adaptable.

2.1 The UK Corporate Governance Code

The UK Corporate Governance Code[20] is a cornerstone of governance for listed companies, including banks. Although the Code is not legally binding, it operates on a "comply or explain" basis, meaning that banks must either comply with the provisions of the Code or explain any deviations.

A key principle of the Code is that the board of directors is collectively responsible for the long-term success of the company. This aligns with the duties codified under the Companies Act 2006, and in the banking sector, it has far-reaching implications. For instance, *Re Barings plc (No 5)* [1999] 1 BCLC 433 underscored the importance of robust internal controls and risk management. In this case, the failure of Barings Bank was attributed to inadequate oversight by its senior managers, particularly in relation to the activities of rogue trader Nick Leeson. The court emphasised that directors must ensure that governance structures are capable of detecting and managing risks before they materialise into crises.

The UK Corporate Governance Code further demands transparency and accountability. In particular, it requires banks to have independent NEDs who can provide oversight and challenge the decisions of executive management. The importance of this independent oversight was highlighted in the *Okpabi v Royal Dutch Shell* [2021] UKSC 3 case, where the UK

18 The Taxonomy Regulation (EU) 2020/852 established an EU-wide classification system or taxonomy intended to provide businesses and investors with a common language to identify to what degree economic activities can be considered environmentally sustainable or green. It also imposes disclosure requirements for certain financial services firms and large public-interest entities.

19 President Donald Trump issued Executive Order 14151 titled "Ending Radical and Wasteful Government DEI Programs and Preferencing" on 20 January 2025. This executive order seeks to end DEI throughout the federal government.

20 The January 2024 version of the Code (2024 Code) applies to financial years beginning on or after 1 January 2025 (with the exception of Provision 29 of the 2024 Code which is applicable for financial years beginning on or after 1 January 2026).

Supreme Court considered the liability of a parent company for the actions of its subsidiary.[21] The Court held that parent companies may owe a duty of care where they exercise significant control over the operations of their subsidiaries. This case reinforces the need for effective governance and oversight within complex banking groups, where failures in one part of the organisation can have systemic consequences.

Furthermore, in holding England as the proper place in which to bring a claim against both a UK-domiciled company and its Zambian subsidiary for environmental damage abroad, the Supreme Court in *Vedanta Resources plc v Lungowe* [2019] UKSC 20 has raised important questions about whether parent companies can be liable alongside their non-UK subsidiaries for adverse human rights impacts occurring abroad. The decisions in *Okpabi* and *Lungowe* highlight the growing importance of corporate governance in managing environmental and social risks and they have implications for banks, especially those with global operations, as they reinforce the need for robust governance structures that ensure subsidiaries comply with ESG standards.

2.2 Directors' Duties Under the Companies Act 2006

Directors' duties, as defined under the Companies Act 2006, play a critical role in ensuring robust corporate governance and effective risk management of credit institutions. The responsibilities of directors are significantly amplified in the banking sector due to the regulatory and compliance obligations, exposure to financial crime risks, and the need to maintain financial stability. These duties, set out in sections 171 to 177 of the Companies Act 2006, are shaped by additional sector-specific regulations such as the SMCR, FSMA, and Directive 2013/36/EU as implemented in the UK (**CRD IV**).[22] Furthermore, the emerging focus on ESG[23] factors has broadened the scope of directors' responsibilities in ensuring sustainable and responsible banking practices.

For example, in *ClientEarth v Shell Plc & Ors (Re Prima Facie Case)* [2023] EWHC 1137 (Ch), ClientEarth, a non-profit environmental law organisation with a minority shareholding in Shell, the multinational oil and gas company, attempted (unsuccessfully) to establish a prima facie case in a derivative claim[24] against the company's directors in relation to alleged breaches

21 "*On 12 February 2021 – see Okpabi v RDS and SPDC [2021] UKSC 3, the Supreme Court held that the Claimants had an arguable case that RDS owed them a common law duty of care so as properly to found jurisdiction against SDPC, its foreign subsidiary company, as a necessary and proper party to the proceedings. The claims were remitted to the High Court for determination of the outstanding jurisdictional challenges. The challenges were finally resolved by agreement in April 2021 and it is now accepted that the court has jurisdiction to determine the claims*". per Mr Justice O'Farrell DBE in *Alame & & Ors v Royal Dutch Shell Plc & Anor* [2022] EWHC 989 (TCC).

22 Directive (EU) 2019/878 of the European Parliament and of the Council of 20 May 2019 amending Directive 2013/36/EU as regards exempted entities, financial holding companies, mixed financial holding companies, remuneration, supervisory measures and powers, and capital conservation measures. See also The Capital Requirements Regulations 2013, SI 2013 No. 3115, as amended.

23 Environmental, social, and governance (ESG) is a broad term encompassing a wide range of environmental, social, and governance factors that investors use to assess the behaviour and practices of entities under consideration for investment. The term ESG is commonly favoured within the investment community when referring to these factors to evaluate corporate behaviour, assess the long-term financial performance of companies, and manage risk effectively. The older terms, corporate social responsibility (CSR) or corporate responsibility (CR), are still occasionally used to describe a wide range of socially responsible behaviours adopted by businesses.

24 Under S. 260(3) of the Companies Act 2006. The procedure for derivative claims involves two stages. Initially, the claimant must establish a prima facie case. Thereafter, the court must decide whether to grant permission for the claim to proceed. In determining whether to grant such permission, the court must take into account a range of considerations, including whether the claimant is acting in good faith, the importance that a hypothetical director – acting in accordance with their duty to promote the success of the company – would attach to pursuing the claim, the likelihood of ratification of the

of the duties included the duty to promote the success of the company under s.172 and the duty to exercise reasonable care, skill, and diligence under s.174, regarding Shell's climate change risk management strategy. While the claimant was ultimately unsuccessful, the case highlights the heightened focus on sustainability factors when assessing directors' performance.

Duty to Act Within Powers (Section 171)

Section 171 of the Companies Act 2006 requires directors to act within their powers and only for proper purposes. In the context of banks and credit institutions, this duty ensures that directors' decisions align with the company's constitution and relevant legal and regulatory framework, including sector-specific regulations like the CRD V, Basel III, and SMCR.

For instance, when issuing capital instruments or making decisions regarding lending policies, directors must ensure that such actions comply with the bank's constitution, corporate governance policies, and regulatory requirements regarding capital adequacy and liquidity. Failure to do so can result in regulatory sanctions and expose the directors to personal liability. In *Howard Smith Ltd v Ampol Petroleum Ltd* [1974] AC 821, the court held that directors must exercise their powers for a proper purpose. In a banking context, this means that decisions to issue shares, raise capital, or restructure debt must be made to strengthen the bank's capital base or enhance its risk profile rather than for any personal or improper motives.

Similarly, directors must ensure that decisions regarding the bank's participation in M&A or other strategic transactions are conducted for the benefit of the institution and its stakeholders and not for personal gain or to entrench the position of certain individuals or groups. These decisions must align with the bank's broader strategic objectives, and directors must exercise independent judgement (section 173) and avoid conflicts of interest (section 175) when making them.

Duty to Promote the Success of the Company (Section 172)

Section 172 imposes a duty on directors to act in a way they believe, in good faith, would promote the success of the company for the benefit of its shareholders as a whole. For banks and credit institutions, the duty to promote success extends beyond generating profits for shareholders – it encompasses the broader goal of managing risks prudently, protecting the interests of depositors, ensuring capital adequacy, and fostering a compliance culture that prevents financial crime and mitigates regulatory risks.[25] Directors must consider the long-term consequences of their decisions, including the bank's ability to weather financial crises and maintain its standing in the market. Moreover, directors should consider the impact of their company's operations on the environment and the community, as a result, credit institutions are expected to integrate ESG considerations into their risk management and decision-making processes.

In the context of financial crime risk management, the duty to promote success is closely linked to the bank's obligations under the Bribery Act 2010, Criminal Finances Act 2017, and

alleged breach, and whether the claimant could alternatively bring the claim in their own right. While the claimant does not need to have been a shareholder at the time the cause of action arose, they must hold shares in the company at the time of bringing the claim.

25 Clarke, B., 'Duty of Care, Skill and Diligence – from Warm Baths to Hot Water' (2016) 56 *Irish Jurist* 139–160.

the Economic Crime and Corporate Transparency Act 2023 (**ECCT Act**). These acts place significant responsibilities on directors to ensure that the bank has effective compliance and risk management systems in place. Failure to implement adequate prevention procedures can lead to criminal liability for the bank and, by extension, the directors, particularly in cases where senior management failed to act to prevent financial crime. The ECCT Act, for instance, introduces new offences related to the failure of large organisations to prevent commercial fraud, increasing the personal risk faced by directors in the banking sector.

Directors must demonstrate top-level commitment to managing financial crime risk and ensure that compliance systems are robust and proportionate to the size, scale, and complexity of the institution. The GC100, the representative body of FTSE 100 general counsel and company secretaries, Guidance on Directors' Duties[26] highlights the importance of directors receiving timely and accurate information to assess risks effectively and promote the company's success. For credit institutions, this means that directors must regularly review the institution's risk profile, compliance with financial crime regulations, and response to regulatory changes.

Duty to Exercise Independent Judgement (Section 173)

Section 173 of the Companies Act 2006 requires directors to exercise independent judgement. In the banking sector, this duty is particularly important because of the potential for conflicts of interest, particularly in large institutions with complex client and stakeholder relationships. Directors must act independently in the best interests of the bank, even if this conflicts with the interests of other group companies or external stakeholders.

For instance, directors must ensure that their decisions regarding lending practices, investments, or capital market transactions are made independently of undue influence from major shareholders, clients, or even regulators. In *Duomatic Ltd, Re* [1969] 2 Ch. 365, the court held that directors must act independently, even when following the instructions of shareholders, provided that the company's constitution allows them to delegate powers. In a banking context, this principle ensures that directors prioritise the institution's financial health and regulatory compliance over external pressures.

When engaging in complex financial transactions, such as derivatives trading or syndicated loans,[27] directors must exercise their independent judgement to assess the risks and benefits objectively. They must ensure that these transactions align with the bank's risk appetite and regulatory obligations under frameworks like CRD V and Basel III. Failure to do so could expose the bank to undue risk and undermine its financial stability.

Duty to Exercise Reasonable Care, Skill, and Diligence (Section 174)

The duty to exercise reasonable care, skill, and diligence under section 174 of the Companies Act 2006 is particularly relevant in the context of banks and credit institutions, given the complexity of financial products and the regulatory environment in which they operate. Directors must meet both an objective and subjective standard of care, requiring them to act with the level of care expected from someone in their position and to apply their own expertise and experience to the decision-making process.

26 GC100, Guidance on Directors' Duties: Section 172 and Stakeholder Considerations (October 2018).
27 See Chapters 13 and 11, respectively.

This means that directors must be well-versed in the bank's financial operations, regulatory requirements, and risk management systems. They must engage actively with risk management frameworks and ensure that the credit institution complies with its capital adequacy, liquidity, and leverage ratio requirements.

Directors must also be diligent in supervising internal investigations into financial crime or regulatory breaches. In cases where senior executives are implicated in misconduct, the board must ensure that the investigation is independent and that directors are not influenced by potential conflicts of interest.

Duty to Avoid Conflicts of Interest (Section 175)

The duty to avoid conflicts of interest under section 175 is essential for directors in the banking sector, where potential conflicts often arise due to the complexity of client relationships, cross-directorships, and related-party transactions.[28] Directors must ensure that their personal interests or relationships do not conflict with their duty to act in the best interests of the credit institution.

For example, in *Industrial Development Consultants Ltd v Cooley* [1972] 1 WLR 443, the court held that directors must not use their position for personal gain. In a banking context, this means that directors must be transparent about any potential conflicts related to lending transactions, M&A activities, or investment decisions. If a director has a personal financial interest in a client or counterparty, they must disclose this conflict and recuse themselves from any related decision-making.

In banks, conflicts of interest may also arise in the context of financial crime investigations, where directors may be implicated in wrongdoing. The ECCT Act introduced provisions on corporate criminal liability, placing directors at risk of personal liability if they fail to prevent or mitigate financial crime risks. Directors must ensure that investigations into financial crime are independent, and they must avoid influencing the outcome of investigations to protect their own interests.

Internal Accounting and Auditing

Companies are under a statutory duty, pursuant to the Companies Act, to maintain adequate accounting records. It is the responsibility of the directors to ensure that proper accounts are prepared annually and audited by the company's auditors. These accounts must include a profit and loss account for the previous financial year and a balance sheet at the end of that year, which must be approved by the board and signed on its behalf by one of the directors.

Additionally, the accounts must contain a statement confirming that, to the best of each director's knowledge, there is no relevant information of which the company's auditors are unaware and that each director has taken all necessary steps to become aware of any such information and to ensure the auditors are similarly informed. The accounts must also set out any amount which the directors recommend be paid as a dividend.

A strategic report must also be included. This report should offer a fair review of the company's business and that of its subsidiaries over the course of the financial year, as well as an assessment of their financial position at year-end. The Companies Act expressly provides

28 See The Law Commission and the Scottish Law Commission, 'Company Directors: Regulating Conflicts of Interests *(SLC173) (Report)*' (1999) *EWLC* 261.

that the purpose of the strategic report is to assist members in assessing how the directors have performed their duty to promote the success of the company for the benefit of the members as a whole. It should describe the principal risks and uncertainties facing the company and, to the extent required for a proper understanding of the development, the performance or position of the business and provide analysis using financial and other key performance indicators. This includes, where relevant, information relating to environmental matters and employee concerns.

In the case of a quoted company – defined as a company whose equity share capital is officially listed in the UK or which is admitted to trading on the New York Stock Exchange or NASDAQ – additional obligations apply. The directors must prepare a remuneration report, setting out prescribed information concerning directors' pay. Furthermore, the strategic report must include additional disclosures necessary for understanding the development, performance, or position of the business. This includes the main trends and factors likely to influence the company's future performance and position, as well as information on environmental impact, employee matters, social and community issues, and human rights. It must also describe the company's strategy and business model and provide specific gender-related statistics concerning the composition of the board.[29]

Once finalised, the accounts are submitted to the auditors for review. The audited accounts, in their final form, are then presented to the members at the company's general meeting.

In the case of listed companies, the auditing of the company's accounts falls under the oversight of the audit committee. According to the provisions of the Code, this committee should comprise at least three independent non-executive directors, with a minimum of one member possessing recent and relevant financial experience. With regard to internal audit functions, the audit committee is tasked with reviewing the effectiveness of the internal audit processes, recruiting the head of internal audit, and assessing the company's internal control framework and risk management systems. Additionally, the committee is responsible for monitoring the integrity of the company's financial statements, including any formal announcements concerning financial performance. The audit committee also holds primary responsibility for appointing the external auditor and, when requested by the board, provides advice on whether the annual accounts offer a fair, balanced, and understandable representation of the company's financial position from the perspective of its shareholders.

2.3 The Senior Managers and Certification Regime

The Bank of England and Financial Services Act 2016 introduced the SMCR, which has fundamentally reshaped corporate governance in UK banks by imposing personal accountability on senior managers. The regime was developed in response to the failures of governance that contributed to the 2007–2009 global financial crisis, where it was often difficult to identify individual responsibility for significant failures. Under the SMCR, senior managers are required to take personal responsibility for key areas of the business, ensuring that there is clear accountability within the governance structure.[30] By placing greater emphasis on individual accountability and risk management, the SMCR represents a fundamental shift in the regulatory approach to governance within the UK banking sector.

29 Kawamura, A., *Corporate Governance 2015* (Sweet & Maxwell International Series, 2015).
30 Kokkinis, A. and Miglionico, M., *Banking Law: Private Transactions and Regulatory Frameworks* (Routledge, 2021), p. 239.

The SMCR operates through a system of Senior Management Functions, where specific responsibilities are assigned to individuals who must be approved by the PRA or FCA.[31] Each senior manager must submit a Statement of Responsibilities outlining the areas of the business for which they are personally accountable. The purpose of the statement of responsibilities is to provide a clear outline of the areas of the firm's regulated activities for which each senior manager is accountable. For example, in the context of risk management, the senior manager responsible for overseeing the risk function must ensure that the bank's risk frameworks are robust and that potential risks are identified and mitigated effectively.

Furthermore, at all times, credit institutions are required to maintain – as part of SMCR-related obligations – the management responsibilities map. This document is designed to describe the firm's management and governance arrangements. A key purpose of the management responsibilities map is to ensure that, when viewed as a whole, the allocation of responsibilities among the firm's senior managers does not leave any gaps in accountability. It also ensures that the firm maintains a clear and coherent organisational structure.

The SMCR regime also extends beyond senior managers. The Certification Regime applies to individuals who are not senior managers but whose functions[32] have a significant impact on the bank's risk profile. Banks must certify these individuals annually, confirming that they are fit and proper to carry out their roles. This ensures that responsibility for governance is embedded throughout the organisation, rather than being concentrated at the top.

Finally, the Conduct Rules introduced by the SMCR apply to all employees within the firm, setting out high-level standards of behaviour that must be adhered to. This creates a culture of accountability and ethical conduct, aligning with the broader objectives of the UK Corporate Governance Code. The SMCR's focus on individual accountability has made it a model for governance reforms in other jurisdictions, including the Banking Executive Accountability Regime (BEAR) in Australia and similar regimes in Singapore and Hong Kong.

2.4 Senior Management Arrangements, Systems, and Controls

The Senior Management Arrangements, Systems, and Controls (**SYSC**)[33] framework is central to governance, risk management, and internal control regulation for UK financial institutions, forming part of both the FCA Handbook and the PRA Rulebook. SYSC ensures that firms implement sound governance structures, clear senior manager accountability, and effective control systems.

SYSC was introduced to mandate that financial firms maintain systems and controls promoting high governance standards, risk management, and internal oversight. Its objectives include fostering a clear allocation of responsibilities to senior managers, ensuring firms implement adequate internal controls to mitigate risks, and establishing governance structures that align with regulatory expectations in risk management and compliance. SYSC works closely with the SMCR, and it mandates that senior management responsibilities are clearly defined and that managers are accountable for their roles. Under this framework, financial institutions must allocate key governance roles to senior managers, establish board-level

31 Section 60(2A), FSMA.

32 Section 59ZA of FSMA states: "*A function is a 'senior management function', in relation to the carrying on of a regulated activity by an authorised person, if (a) the function will require the person performing it to be responsible for managing one or more aspects of the authorised person's affairs, so far as relating to the activity, and (b) those aspects involve, or might involve, a risk of serious consequences for the authorised person, or for business or other interests in the UK*".

33 See www.handbook.fca.org.uk/handbook/SYSC.pdf (accessed in March 2025).

committees such as audit and risk committees to oversee governance and appoint compliance officers and heads of internal audit who report directly to the board or relevant committee. SYSC 4 requires firms to maintain adequate organisational arrangements, setting general requirements that ensure internal governance and risk management frameworks are both robust and effective. The importance of these practices was highlighted in *Paragon Finance PLC v Nash* [2001] EWCA Civ 1466, where the Court of Appeal emphasised the consequences of inadequate internal controls in a case related to a bank's interest rate increase, underlining the governance principles reinforced by SYSC.

SYSC's risk management requirements, detailed in SYSC 6, require firms to establish effective risk management policies, implement controls, and ensure regular identification and monitoring of risk exposures. Senior management in credit institutions has a general obligation to ensure that adequate risk management systems are in place, as required under Principle 3 of the FCA's Principles for Businesses and Fundamental Rule 5 of the PRA's Fundamental Rules.[34] A key component of an effective risk management framework is stress testing (discussed further in Chapter 7), a method employed to ensure the bank is strong enough to withstand severe scenarios such as a financial crisis, which financial institutions are expected to develop, implement, and integrate into their overall risk management strategy. Senior management must be actively engaged in the stress testing process, particularly in determining the choice of stress scenarios where these are not prescribed, overseeing the testing process, and evaluating the outcomes. They are expected to maintain awareness of potential sources of financial stress and to understand the implications for their institution should these risks materialise.

Firms are also obligated to conduct internal audits and review the adequacy of their systems. A significant case in this area is *Barclays Bank plc v Financial Conduct Authority* [2018] EWHC 3055 (Admin), where Barclays faced sanctions for internal control failures around protecting confidential whistle-blower information. This demonstrates how inadequate governance and compliance mechanisms can lead to regulatory enforcement actions under SYSC.

Finally, SYSC and the SMCR collectively enforce individual accountability among senior managers. Firms must assign Senior Management Functions to senior managers and maintain a clear Statement of Responsibilities for each such senior manager.

In *FCA v Carillion plc* [2022] EWHC 2831 (Ch), governance failures at senior management levels contributing to the company's collapse were highlighted, illustrating how both SYSC and SM&CR can hold senior managers accountable for governance failures, especially in risk management and financial reporting.

2.5 Governance and Risk Management of Ring-Fenced Bodies

From January 2019, the largest UK banks have been required to separate their core retail banking activities from their investment banking operations, a structural reform known as ring-fencing. The objective of ring-fencing is to protect essential banking services – such as deposit-taking and payments – from shocks arising in financial markets and to ensure continuity of service in times of stress. While this regime is discussed in detail within Chapter 7, one should note that corporate governance requirements for ring-fenced bodies (**RFB**s) build upon the PRA's existing rules applicable to all banks but impose additional

34 Fundamental Rule 5 – A firm must have effective risk strategies and risk management systems. See www.bankofengland.co.uk/-/media/boe/files/prudential-regulation/new-bank/fundamentalruleprinciples (accessed in March 2025).

obligations designed to safeguard the independence of RFBs. A fundamental aspect of these requirements is the composition of the board, which must include at least 50% independent NEDs, excluding the chair. Furthermore, the chair must also be an independent NED and cannot simultaneously serve as chair of another group entity, except in the case of a ring-fenced affiliate. To prevent undue influence from the wider banking group, no more than one-third of the board members of an RFB may be current employees or directors of other entities within the same corporate group. To ensure transparency in board appointments, vacancies for independent NEDs must be publicly advertised.

Beyond board composition, RFBs are required to establish separate board committees dedicated to risk, audit, nomination, and remuneration, reinforcing their ability to operate independently from the non-ring-fenced elements of the group. The PRA also mandates that RFBs implement internal governance structures capable of identifying and managing conflicts of interest between their directors or senior management and the broader group. In addition, RFBs must maintain robust risk management and internal audit functions, ensuring that they can make decisions without undue external influence. The heads of risk and internal audit within an RFB must not simultaneously hold equivalent positions in other group entities, except where those entities are also ring-fenced affiliates. These measures collectively strengthen the governance framework of RFBs, ensuring their operational independence and resilience within the broader banking group.[35]

2.6 Requirements for Acquiring or Increasing Control Over a Bank

Further to the implementation of the CRD IV Directive, the UK regulatory framework provides for review of the acquisition of qualifying holdings in credit institutions.[36]

Under Section 178 of FSMA, any person or entity intending to acquire or increase a controlling interest in a UK-based bank must notify the PRA in writing, though this requirement does not extend to foreign banks operating in the UK through branches. The PRA implements a 60-working-day assessment period during which the acquisition cannot be finalised unless prior approval is given within this timeframe.

"Control" is defined as holding shares or voting rights that meet certain thresholds. It encompasses both direct and indirect holdings and aggregates control when acting jointly with others. The notification requirement is triggered when an acquisition results in a holding equal to or exceeding 10% of the total shareholding or voting rights in a UK-authorised entity, its parent, or when the holding grants the acquirer significant influence over the authorised entity. Further, an increase in control occurs if the shareholding or voting rights exceed thresholds of 20%, 30%, or 50% or if the authorised person becomes a subsidiary following the acquisition. Any reduction in control crossing these thresholds similarly requires notifying the PRA in writing. Failing to comply with these notification requirements constitutes a criminal offence.

In reviewing an application, the PRA considers factors such as the applicant's reputation and that of individuals who would have significant influence over the bank's operations, the applicant's financial standing, the bank's ability to meet prudential standards, and any risks

35 Kokkinis, A. and Miglionico, M., *Banking Law: Private Transactions and Regulatory Frameworks* (Routledge, 2021), p. 270.

36 Article 4(1)(36) of Regulation (EU) No 575/2013 (cross-referred by Article 3(1)(33) of the CRD IV) defines as follows: "'qualifying holding' means a direct or indirect holding in an undertaking which represents 10% or more of the capital or of the voting rights or which makes it possible to exercise a significant influence over the management of that undertaking".

associated with the acquisition that may involve terrorist financing or money laundering. The UK imposes no restrictions on foreign ownership of banks, provided that financial sanctions set by the UK, EU, or United Nations are respected. Since November 2024, the PRA and the FCA set out their final policy on the assessment of acquisitions and increases in control.[37] The UK guidance supersedes the EU guidelines on the assessment of acquisitions and increases of qualifying holdings in the financial sector, commonly referred to as the 3L3 Guidelines.[38] These EU guidelines established a common framework for the interpretation and application of assessment criteria by national competent authorities across the EU.

2.7 Statutory and Regulatory Developments

In recent years, the integration of ESG factors into corporate governance frameworks has become a significant focus in the UK (albeit, at the time of writing, the importance of such integration is not universally shared; rather, it is being rejected by other countries, such as the US).[39]

The UK's commitment to green banking and climate-related disclosures further demonstrates the growing importance of ESG in the governance of banks. In April 2019, Sarah Breeden, the Bank of England's Executive Director for International Banks Supervision, provided a more detailed account[40] of the Bank's ongoing initiatives in collaboration with organisations such as the global Network for Greening the Financial System and the domestic Climate Financial Risk Forum. The Bank of England expressed its support for the disclosure standards set by the Task Force on Climate-Related Financial Disclosures (**TCFD**), placing particular emphasis on ensuring that such disclosures are forward-looking, addressing future risks and opportunities rather than merely reflecting current emissions. In this context, the TCFD framework, which the UK has adopted, requires banks to disclose how they assess and manage climate-related risks. This runs counter to the new approach taken in the US on the integration of ESG considerations into corporate governance.[41]

With specific reference to credit institutions, in November 2024, the PRA updated Supervisory Statement SS3/19 "Enhancing banks' and insurers' approaches to managing the financial risks from climate change".[42] According to the supervisory statement, the PRA expects a firm's approach to managing financial risks from climate change to be proportionate to the nature, scale, and complexity of its business. To ensure compliance, the PRA intends to integrate the measurement and monitoring of these expectations into its existing supervisory framework. A firm's board is expected to understand, assess, and oversee the financial risks associated with climate change, ensuring these risks are addressed within the firm's overall business strategy and

37 www.bankofengland.co.uk/-/media/boe/files/prudential-regulation/supervisory-statement/2024/ss1024-november-2024.pdf (accessed in March 2025).

38 See www.esma.europa.eu/sites/default/files/library/jc_gl_2016_01_joint_guidelines_on_prudential_assessment_of_acquisitions_and_increases_of_qualifying_holdings_-_final.pdf (accessed in March 2025).

39 On 9 January 2025, the six largest banks in the US have exited the UN-backed Net Zero Banking Alliance (NZBA).

40 Breeden, S., Avoiding the Storm: Climate Change and the Financial System (Bank of England, 15 April 2019).

41 On 20 January 2025, President Donald Trump issued an executive order titled "Putting America First in International Environmental Agreements" through which the US has ceased or revoked "*any purported financial commitment made by the United States under the United Nations Framework Convention on Climate Change*". see Section 3 (c) www.whitehouse.gov/presidential-actions/2025/01/putting-america-first-in-international-environmental-agreements/ (accessed in March 2025).

42 See www.bankofengland.co.uk/-/media/boe/files/prudential-regulation/supervisory-statement/2024/ss319-november-2024-update.pdf (accessed in March 2025).

risk appetite. The firm's approach should reflect a clear understanding of the distinct characteristics of climate-related financial risks and take a long-term perspective, recognising that such risks may materialise beyond standard business planning horizons. Where appropriate, firms should provide evidence of how they monitor and manage climate-related financial risks in line with their risk appetite statement. Additionally, the PRA expects firms to establish clear roles and responsibilities for the board and its relevant sub-committees in managing climate-related financial risks. Effective governance structures should ensure that climate risks are identified, monitored, and addressed in a manner consistent with the firm's overall risk management framework.

3 REGULATORY FRAMEWORK FOR CORPORATE GOVERNANCE IN THE EU

The governance of financial institutions in the European Union is primarily shaped by three key legislative frameworks: CRD IV and its successors Directive (EU) 2019/878 (**CRD V**)[43] and Directive ((EU) 2024/1619) (**CRD VI**),[44] the Markets in Financial Instruments Directive II (MiFID II),[45] and the Capital Requirements Regulation (**CRR**),[46] subject to the CRR III[47] amendments. MiFID II regulates the conduct of financial firms, with a strong emphasis on governance and transparency. The CRR, working alongside CRD IV and its successors, sets uniform rules for capital requirements, governance structures, and risk management across the EU.

The primary objective of CRD IV was to enhance the resilience of financial institutions by strengthening their governance structures and ensuring that boards of directors and senior management are held accountable for the institutions' risk management practices.[48] CRD V built on the governance reforms introduced by CRD IV. It established more stringent requirements for board independence, remuneration policies, and risk management frameworks, particularly for systemically important financial institutions. CRD V also enhanced the focus on ESG issues in the banking sector, reflecting the growing importance of sustainable finance in corporate governance. CRD VI, which Member States will have to transpose into national law by 10 January 2026,[49] reinforces the fit and proper framework for individuals holding positions of responsibility in credit institutions.[50]

43 Directive (EU) 2019/878 of the European Parliament and of the Council of 20 May 2019 amending Directive 2013/36/EU as regards exempted entities, financial holding companies, mixed financial holding companies, remuneration, supervisory measures and powers, and capital conservation measures.

44 Directive (EU) 2024/1619 of the European Parliament and of the Council of 31 May 2024 amending Directive 2013/36/EU as regards supervisory powers, sanctions, third-country branches, and environmental, social, and governance risks.

45 Directive 2014/65/EU of the European Parliament and of the Council of 15 May 2014 on markets in financial instruments and amending Directive 2002/92/EC and Directive 2011/61/EU (recast).

46 Regulation (EU) No 575/2013 of the European Parliament and of the Council of 26 June 2013 on prudential requirements for credit institutions and investment firms and amending Regulation (EU) No 648/2012.

47 Regulation (EU) 2024/1623 of the European Parliament and of the Council of 31 May 2024 amending Regulation (EU) No 575/2013 as regards requirements for credit risk, credit valuation adjustment risk, operational risk, market risk, and the output floor.

48 The CRR III Regulation ((EU) 2024/1623) and the CRD VI Directive ((EU) 2024/1619) make extensive amendments to the EU's core legislative framework for banks and other credit institutions set out in the Capital Requirements Regulation (575/2013) (CRR) and the CRD IV Directive (2013/36/EU) (collectively "CRD IV"). These amendments reflect the EU's work to implement the final Basel III standards (sometimes referred to as "Basel 3.1" or "Basel IV") as well as various EU-specific reforms unrelated to the Basel standards.

49 Article 2.

50 As set out in revised Article 91 and new Article 91a of the CRD IV.

3.1 Board Composition and Independence

CRD IV places significant emphasis on the composition and independence of boards. It requires that the boards of banks and investment firms include independent NEDs who can provide independent oversight and challenge to the executive management.[51] This is particularly important in ensuring that the decision-making process is not dominated by senior management, thus preventing excessive risk-taking and conflicts of interest.

It[52] also requires that board members shall be of sufficiently good repute,[53] act with honesty, integrity, and independence of mind, and collectively possess the knowledge, skills, and experience necessary for effective governance. This provision, as amended by CRD VI, requires credit institutions and certain companies within their group to assess such suitability both before appointment and on a periodic basis. If an institution determines that a current or prospective member does not meet the suitability criteria, it must prevent the individual from taking up the role or ensure their removal, as appropriate. In the case of large credit institutions and certain group companies, a suitability application must also be submitted to the competent authority prior to appointment. If the competent authority concludes that the individual does not meet the required criteria, it must prevent the individual from serving as part of the management body. The framework also imposes limits on the number of directorships that may be held by members of systemically important credit institutions.

This provision is aimed at addressing governance failures where board members lack the expertise necessary to oversee complex financial institutions. The emphasis is placed not only on a person's knowledge, skills, experience, integrity, reliability, and financial soundness but also on how these attributes are perceived by the market. This is because a key requirement for the proper functioning, protection, and stability of the financial and capital markets is maintaining general confidence in the suitability of credit institutions and in the competence of those responsible for their management. Ensuring trust in the leadership of financial institutions is crucial to maintaining market confidence and preventing instability.[54] Finally, banks need to ensure that board members are qualified and capable of mitigating risks, particularly in large and systemically important financial institutions (**SIFI**s).[55]

In addition to the governance requirements for the management body, a fit and proper framework for key function holders within credit institutions and their group companies has been introduced.[56] These institutions must ensure that key function holders maintain good repute, act with honesty and integrity, and possess the necessary knowledge, skills, and experience to perform their roles effectively. Where an individual is found not to meet these criteria, the institution must take action to prevent their appointment or ensure their removal, as necessary. Key function holders are individuals[57] who exercise significant influence over the direction of an institution but are

51 Under Article 88.

52 Pursuant to Article 91: "*Members of the management body shall at all times be of sufficiently good repute and possess sufficient knowledge, skills and experience to perform their duties. The overall composition of the management body shall reflect an adequately broad range of experiences*".

53 "*The concept of good repute thus refers to the (good) reputation of the credit institution and its shareholders and partners in the eyes of third parties, such as other market participants, in particular creditors and customers. If confidence in that credit institution or in the people acting on its behalf dissipates, or if this confidence is significantly compromised, this triggers an immediate reaction from market participants*". in *Pilatus Bank v ECB (Economic and monetary policy – Single supervisory mechanism – Indictment of the main shareholder in a third country – Opinion)* [2023] EUECJ C-750/21P_O at [128].

54 *Pilatus Bank v ECB (Economic and monetary policy – Single supervisory mechanism – Indictment of the main shareholder in a third country – Opinion)* [2023] EUECJ C-750/21P_O at [127].

55 *PNB Banka v ECB (Economic and monetary policy – Prudential supervision of credit institutions – Judgment)* [2022] EUECJ T-330/19 at [142].

56 Pursuant to Article 91a.

57 As defined under new Article 3(9a) of the CRD IV Directive.

not members of the management body. This includes heads of internal control functions and the chief financial officer, where these individuals are not part of the management body. In addition to the institution's internal suitability assessments, competent authorities will be responsible for evaluating the suitability of an institution's heads of internal control functions and chief financial officer. If they determine that an individual is not fit for the role, they must ensure their removal.

As in the UK, in the context of banks' M&A transactions, the composition of the board and the skills of its members would be a key component for the regulator to allow the proposed merger or acquisition of a credit institution and to determine the suitability of the proposed acquirer and the financial soundness of the proposed acquisition or merger.[58] The primary objective of the assessment is to verify that the proposed acquirer possesses a good reputation and the necessary financial soundness, ensuring that the institution in which the stake is to be acquired continues to meet its prudential requirements. Additionally, the assessment serves to prevent transactions from being financed with the proceeds of illegal activities, thereby safeguarding the integrity and stability of the financial system.[59]

Finally, as discussed within the context of the equivalent regime in the UK, a person wishing to acquire a qualifying holding in a credit institution is subject to a prior assessment, in particular of his or her reputation and financial soundness, in order to ensure the sound and prudent management of the credit institution concerned.[60]

3.2 Risk Management and Internal Controls

CRD IV and CRR require banks to implement robust risk management frameworks. Under Article 76 of CRD IV, banks must establish a risk management function that is independent of the operational units and that reports directly to the board. This function is responsible for identifying, assessing, and mitigating risks across the institution. Additionally, Article 91 of CRD IV mandates that board members and senior managers must have a deep understanding of the risks facing the institution and that they must oversee the implementation of risk management policies.

The importance of such policies was highlighted in the Banco Espírito Santo crisis in 2014,[61] where poor risk management practices led to the bank's downfall. Banco Espírito Santo, one of Portugal's largest banks, failed due to undisclosed loans and risky investments that were not adequately controlled by the board.[62]

CRD V reinforced the requirements for board independence, particularly in SIFIs. It mandated that boards must include a sufficient number of independent directors to ensure that they can effectively challenge executive decisions. This is particularly relevant for large banks, where conflicts of interest and concentrated power at the senior management level can pose significant risks to the institution's stability.

The CRD VI Directive introduces a "fit and proper" framework governing the assessment of individuals holding key roles within banks. This framework includes stricter criteria to evaluate their expertise, integrity, and independence. Moreover, governance

58 According to Article 23(1) and (2) of Directive 2013/36.
59 *PH and Others v ECB (Economic and monetary policy – Prudential supervision of credit institutions – Judgment)* [2024] EUECJ T-323/22 at [63].
60 The mechanism for monitoring qualifying holdings provided for in Article 22 et seq. of Directive 2013/36.
61 Case T-814/14: Action brought on 17 December 2014 – *Banco Espírito Santo v Commission*.
62 See www.bportugal.pt/sites/default/files/faq_bes_20160104_en.pdf (accessed in March 2025).

arrangements shall also include network and information systems that are set up and managed in accordance with the Digital Operational Resilience Regulation (Regulation (EU) 2022/2554),[63] which establishes a comprehensive framework for digital operational resilience for EU financial institutions.

3.3 ESG Considerations

The integration of ESG considerations into corporate governance has become a key focus in the European Union's approach to regulating financial institutions. The EU recognises that ESG factors are crucial for ensuring long-term sustainability and promoting ethical governance. In this respect, CRR III and CRD VI mark a significant shift in EU financial regulation, embedding ESG risk management into the core supervisory and governance frameworks of credit institutions. These measures reinforce the EU's commitment to sustainable finance, ensuring that financial institutions are equipped to identify, assess, and manage the financial impacts of ESG risks in an evolving regulatory landscape. ESG risks, particularly those related to climate change, environmental degradation, and social inequality, have the potential to disrupt financial stability. In response, the EU has embedded ESG considerations into financial regulation through a range of legal frameworks, including the CRD IV and its successors, the Sustainable Finance Disclosure Regulation (Regulation (EU) 2019/2088, SFDR), and the Taxonomy Regulation (Regulation (EU) 2020/852).

The CRD V emphasised the need for financial institutions to integrate ESG risks into their governance and risk management frameworks. CRD V expanded on its predecessor by mandating that banks incorporate ESG risks into their decision-making processes, reflecting the EU's commitment to ensuring that financial institutions contribute to the sustainability agenda. Regulation (EU) 2024/1623 (**CRR III Regulation**)[64] also requires credit institutions to integrate ESG risks into their risk management systems in a consistent and comprehensive manner. Under Article 88 of CRD V, boards of directors were required to oversee the integration of ESG risks into the institution's risk management framework. This included ensuring that governance structures are capable of identifying, assessing, and mitigating risks related to climate change, environmental sustainability, and social issues. Boards are expected to take an active role in managing these risks, ensuring that ESG considerations are embedded in the bank's overall risk profile.

The CRR III Regulation introduces additional measures relating to ESG risk management. It establishes new harmonised definitions of different types of ESG risks,[65] defining ESG risk as

> *the risk of any negative financial impact on an institution stemming from the current or prospective impact of environmental, social, or governance (ESG) factors on that institution's counterparties or invested assets; ESG risks materialise through the traditional categories of financial risks.*[66]

63 Regulation (EU) 2022/2554 of the European Parliament and of the Council of 14 December 2022 on digital operational resilience for the financial sector and amending Regulations (EC) No 1060/2009, (EU) No 648/2012, (EU) No 600/2014, (EU) No 909/2014 and (EU) 2016/1011.

64 Regulation (EU) 2024/1623 of the European Parliament and of the Council of 31 May 2024 amending Regulation (EU) No 575/2013 as regards requirements for credit risk, credit valuation adjustment risk, operational risk, market risk, and the output floor.

65 Under Article 4(1)(52d to 52i).

66 Additionally, credit institutions are now required to consider ESG risks when assessing the value of collateral under Article 210(g). Further obligations include reporting ESG risk exposures to the competent authorities under Article 430 and disclosing ESG risks under Article 449a.

Moreover, the CRR III Regulation imposes reporting obligations on the EBA, requiring it to submit three reports on ESG-related issues to EU authorities, including an assessment of the potential merits of a dedicated prudential treatment for ESG-related exposures.[67]

The CRR III Regulation ESG requirements are aligned with those provided by the CRD VI Directive. Under Article 73, institutions must consider short-, medium-, and long-term ESG risks within their internal capital adequacy assessment processes (**ICAAPs**). Additionally,[68] governance arrangements must integrate ESG risks over the same time horizons. Management bodies are now required[69] to develop forward-looking plans to assess the impact of ESG factors, often referred to as prudential transition plans. These plans must monitor and address financial risks arising from ESG factors and consider the process of regulatory and economic transition towards climate neutrality, aligning with EU and member state regulatory objectives.[70]

Furthermore, the CRD VI Directive mandates that credit institutions establish robust strategies, policies, processes, and systems for identifying, measuring, managing, and monitoring ESG risks over appropriate time horizons.[71] These requirements, set out in Article 87a CRD VI, are to be supplemented by the EBA Guidelines on stress testing methodologies for ESG risks.[72]

The management bodies of credit institutions must collectively possess the knowledge, skills, and experience necessary to understand ESG-related risks and their short-, medium-, and long-term impacts on the institution.[73] Competent authorities have also been given increased supervisory powers under CRD VI. As part of the supervisory review and evaluation process (**SREP**), they must now assess whether credit institutions' governance and risk management frameworks adequately address ESG risks, as well as the extent of their exposure to such risks.[74] Finally,[75] competent authorities are empowered to require credit institutions to take corrective action where they are misaligned with EU ESG policy objectives. This may include adjustments to business models, governance frameworks, and risk management strategies to mitigate ESG-related risks over the short, medium, and long term.

3.4 Role of the European Banking Authority (EBA) in ESG Governance

The EBA plays a central role in promoting the integration of ESG risks into the governance of financial institutions. In its Report on ESG Risks Management and Supervision,[76] the EBA outlined best practices for banks to follow in incorporating ESG risks into their governance frameworks.

67 The final report must be submitted by 31 December 2025, and based on these findings, the European Commission is required to determine, by 31 December 2026, whether to propose new legislative measures under Article 501c.
68 Article 74.
69 Under Article 76.
70 Under Article 76(2).
71 As set out in new Article 87a.
72 Article 100.
73 Article 91(2b).
74 As specified in Article 98.
75 Under Article 104.
76 EBA/REP/2021/18 available at www.eba.europa.eu/sites/default/files/document_library/Publications/Reports/2021/1015656/EBA%20Report%20on%20ESG%20risks%20management%20and%20supervision.pdf (accessed in March 2025).

The EBA issued Guidelines on the Benchmarking of Diversity Practices,[77] which include diversity policies and the gender pay gap under Directive 2013/36/EU and Directive (EU) 2019/2034. These guidelines are intended to ensure a harmonised approach to benchmarking diversity practices, particularly concerning the composition of management bodies, the implementation of diversity policies, and the gender pay gap within institutions and investment firms. The benchmarking process will enable competent authorities to monitor diversity trends over time, identify common practices in diversity policies, and assess gender pay disparities at the level of management bodies. The data collected and analysed will include information on diversity policies and the composition of management bodies, focusing on gender, age, educational and professional background, and the geographical origins of their members. The benchmarking of diversity practices will be based on a representative sample of institutions and investment firms, ensuring a comprehensive and standardised evaluation across the sector.

In January 2025, the EBA took an additional step in strengthening ESG risk management by finalising its Guidelines on the management of ESG risks. Developed under CRD VI, these guidelines aim to ensure the safety and soundness of credit institutions as ESG risks intensify, supporting the EU's transition towards a more sustainable economy. They focus on three key areas. Firstly, they establish minimum methodologies for identifying, measuring, managing, and monitoring ESG risks. Secondly, they introduce requirements for transition plans, obliging institutions to set quantifiable targets and timelines in line with EU sustainability objectives, particularly the 2050 climate neutrality goal. Lastly, they define qualitative and quantitative benchmarks to assess the impact of ESG risks on institutions' solvency and risk profiles in the short, medium, and long term. Rather than imposing rigid obligations, the guidelines adopt a principles-based approach, incorporating proportionality. Larger institutions, as defined under the CRR, must align their transition plans with a scenario limiting global warming to 1.5°C, consistent with the Paris Agreement and EU Climate Law. In contrast, small and non-complex institutions (SNCIs) benefit from simplified requirements, reflecting their lower risk exposure. This proportional approach ensures that ESG-related obligations remain ambitious yet adaptable to the diverse profiles of financial institutions. Proportionality, however, is not based solely on institution size. Some smaller institutions may face higher ESG risks due to sectoral or geographical concentrations. Therefore, risk management approaches must be tailored proportionally to materiality assessments, ensuring effective ESG risk oversight.

A defining feature of the EBA Guidelines on ESG risks is their emphasis on transition planning. Although rooted in prudential banking regulations, they align with broader EU regulatory initiatives. Transition plans fall into two categories: prudential, risk-oriented plans under CRD VI (reported under CRR) and non-prudential, strategy-oriented plans under the Directive on Corporate Sustainability Due Diligence (Directive (EU) 2024/1760) (**CSDDD**)[78] (reported under the Corporate Sustainability Reporting Directive [Directive (EU) 2022/2464] [**CSRD**][79]).

77 See www.eba.europa.eu/sites/default/files/2023-12/213cc021-d991-43ed-977d-c60245301e70/Final%20report%20on%20Guidelines%20on%20the%20diversity%20benchmarking%20exercise.pdf (accessed in March 2025).

78 Directive (EU) 2024/1760 of the European Parliament and of the Council of 13 June 2024 on corporate sustainability due diligence and amending Directive (EU) 2019/1937 and Regulation (EU) 2023/2859.

79 Directive (EU) 2022/2464 of the European Parliament and of the Council of 14 December 2022 amending Regulation (EU) No 537/2014, Directive 2004/109/EC, Directive 2006/43/EC and Directive 2013/34/EU, as regards corporate sustainability reporting.

Under Article 76(2) CRD VI,[80] management bodies must oversee the development and implementation of transition plans. These plans must align with EU climate goals, be based on scientific advisory reports, and ensure consistency across different regulatory frameworks. Supervisory authorities are required to assess and monitor institutions' ESG strategies, risk management practices, and transition plans.

3.5 The Sustainable Finance Disclosure Regulation

Regulation (EU) 2019/2088, or the Sustainable Finance Disclosure Regulation (**SFDR**), introduced mandatory disclosure requirements for financial institutions regarding their integration of sustainability risks. SFDR applies to asset managers, banks, insurers, and other financial market participants, compelling them to disclose how ESG factors are considered in their governance and decision-making processes.

Article 4 of SFDR requires financial institutions to publish a Principal Adverse Impacts statement on their websites, detailing how their operations impact sustainability factors. This includes reporting on issues such as carbon emissions, deforestation, biodiversity loss, and social impacts like labour conditions and human rights. The disclosure must also explain how the institution integrates sustainability risks into its governance framework, providing transparency to stakeholders, including investors and regulators.

Furthermore, financial institutions have to integrate sustainability risk assessments into their decision-making processes. Article 6 of SFDR requires firms to evaluate how ESG risks, such as climate change or social inequality, may impact their financial performance and to develop strategies for mitigating these risks.

Banks, for example, are expected to assess both physical risks (such as damage to assets from extreme weather events) and transition risks (such as regulatory changes that could affect carbon-intensive industries) and to incorporate these risks into their overall risk management frameworks. This reflects the broader shift in EU regulation towards requiring financial institutions to take a proactive approach to managing ESG risks.

3.6 Markets in Financial Instruments Directive II (MiFID II)

MiFID II[81] introduced additional governance requirements for financial institutions in the EU. While MiFID II is primarily concerned with market conduct, transparency, and investor protection, it also imposes significant governance obligations on banks and investment firms.

MiFID II requires financial institutions to establish robust governance arrangements that include clear lines of responsibility and accountability. Article 9 of MiFID II mandates that firms must ensure that senior management is responsible for overseeing the firm's compliance with its regulatory obligationss, including those relating to governance and risk management. Additionally, firms must ensure that their governance structures are transparent and that there are adequate internal controls to manage conflicts of interest and operational risks.

80 "*Member States shall ensure that the management body approves and at least every two years reviews the strategies and policies for taking up, managing, monitoring and mitigating the risks the institution is or might be exposed to, including those posed by the macroeconomic environment in which it operates in relation to the status of the business cycle, and those resulting from the current and short-medium and long-term impacts of environmental, social and governance (ESG) factors*".

81 Directive 2014/65/EU of the European Parliament and of the Council of 15 May 2014 on markets in financial instruments and amending Directive 2002/92/EC and Directive 2011/61/EU (recast).

In *EFSA Securities AB v European Securities and Markets Authority* (2019) ECLI:EU:T:2019:244, the European General Court ruled on the application of MiFID II's governance requirements to investment firms. The case reinforced the principle that senior management must be held accountable for governance failings and that firms must implement adequate systems and controls to manage risks and ensure compliance with regulatory standards.

3.7 The Taxonomy Regulation, the CSDDD, and the CSRD

The Taxonomy Regulation (Regulation (EU) 2020/852)[82] provides a framework for classifying environmentally sustainable economic activities. It is an essential part of the EU's sustainable finance strategy, helping financial institutions and investors identify which activities are aligned with the EU's environmental goals, including those related to climate change mitigation and adaptation.

The Taxonomy Regulation requires financial institutions to report on the extent to which their activities align with the taxonomy's environmental objectives. Under Article 8 of the Taxonomy Regulation, banks and other financial market participants must disclose the percentage of their assets that are environmentally sustainable, according to the taxonomy's criteria.

For example, a bank financing renewable energy projects or energy-efficient buildings must report the proportion of its portfolio that qualifies as "green" under the taxonomy. This disclosure provides transparency to investors and stakeholders, helping them assess the bank's contribution to the EU's climate and sustainability goals.[83]

In terms of non-sector-specific corporate governance, the CSDDD established new obligations for companies within its scope, requiring them to identify and address adverse human rights and environmental impacts resulting from their actions, both within and beyond Europe. The CSDDD applies to companies established under the laws of an EU Member State with more than 1,000 employees and a net worldwide turnover exceeding EUR 450 million in the last financial year.[84] Companies falling within its scope are required to take proactive steps to manage both actual and potential adverse impacts of their activities on human rights and environmental matters. These obligations extend to their own operations, the operations of their subsidiaries, and those of their business partners within their chain of activities. This includes design, extraction, sourcing, manufacture, transport, storage, and supply of raw materials and products, as well as product or service development. It also extends to downstream business partners engaged in the distribution, transport, and storage of the product, but only where these activities are carried out for the company or on its behalf. The due diligence obligations under the CSDDD are "obligations of means" rather than "obligations of result". This means that companies are not expected to guarantee the complete prevention of adverse impacts nor to ensure that they will never occur. However, they are required to take "appropriate measures", meaning measures that are capable of achieving the objectives of due diligence.

The CSRD underpinned by the European Sustainability Reporting Standards, introduced detailed reporting requirements on companies' environmental impact, human rights, social

82 Regulation (EU) 2020/852 of the European Parliament and of the Council of 18 June 2020 on the establishment of a framework to facilitate sustainable investment, and amending Regulation (EU) 2019/2088.

83 See Communication from the Commission – COM(2019) 640 final https://eur-lex.europa.eu/legal-content/EN/TXT/?uri=COM%3A2019%3A640%3AFIN (accessed in March 2025).

84 It will also extend to non-EU companies, defined as those established outside the EU, if they generated a net turnover in the Union exceeding EUR 450 million in the financial year preceding the last financial year. The directive will apply only to those EU and non-EU companies that meet the relevant criteria for two consecutive financial years. Additionally, the CSDDD extends to EU and non-EU ultimate parent companies of corporate groups that, when considered collectively, meet the specified financial and employment thresholds.

standards, and sustainability-related risks. It strengthened and modernised corporate sustainability reporting requirements by introducing amendments to the Accounting Directive,[85] the Transparency Directive,[86] the Audit Directive, and the Audit Regulation.[87] It should be noted, however, that while reporting requirements for emissions in Europe are now clearly defined, such amendments did not prescribe a single measurement methodology. It is, therefore, challenging to determine how to translate these requirements into enforceable contract terms.

The implementation of the CSRD and the CSDDD is now taking place within a new and challenging context.[88] Global trade tensions are intensifying amidst a rapidly evolving geopolitical landscape. Furthermore, the divergent approaches adopted by certain other major jurisdictions with respect to the regulation of corporate sustainability reporting and due diligence give rise to concerns about the potential impact of these EU laws on the competitive positioning of European companies in the global market.[89] As a result, in February 2025, the European Commission finalised its final Omnibus proposal,[90] outlining revisions to the CSRD, the CSDDD, and the Taxonomy Regulation. Companies impacted by CSRD reporting requirements are expected to be significantly reduced by the Commission's proposal.

4 CORPORATE GOVERNANCE IN THE UNITED STATES

Corporate governance in the US financial sector operates under a combination of federal and state-level regulations, with considerable influence from the Dodd-Frank Wall Street Reform and Consumer Protection Act of 2010[91] and the rules established by regulatory bodies such as the Securities and Exchange Commission (**SEC**) and the Federal Reserve. US governance frameworks tend to be more prescriptive than those in the UK and EU, reflecting a preference for rules-based regulation over a principles-based approach.

The Dodd-Frank Act was introduced to address systemic risks and strengthen corporate governance in the financial sector. Title IX of the Dodd-Frank Act focuses on executive compensation, risk management, and board accountability. The Act mandates that financial institutions establish independent risk committees at the board level, staffed with directors experienced in risk management. A notable provision within the Dodd-Frank Act is the Volcker Rule, which restricts banks from engaging in proprietary trading and limits their investments in hedge funds and private equity, requiring boards to implement robust oversight mechanisms to ensure compliance with these restrictions. The importance of governance structures in meeting Dodd-Frank's requirements was tested in *MetLife, Inc. v. Financial Stability Oversight Council,* C.A. No. 15–0045 (D.D.C. Mar. 30, 2016), where MetLife successfully contested its

85 Directive 2013/34/EU of the European Parliament and of the Council of 26 June 2013.
86 Directive 2004/109/EC of the European Parliament and of the Council of 15 December 2004.
87 Directive 2006/43/EC of the European Parliament and of the Council of 17 May 2006. (Audit Directive). Regulation (EU) No 537/2014 of the European Parliament and of the Council of 16 April 2014.
88 And as a result, it has been delayed.
89 As of March 2025, the US Senate was considering a legislative proposal that could alter the corporate sustainability compliance landscape for American businesses operating on a global scale. Introduced by Senator Bill Hagerty, the "Prevent Regulatory Overreach from Turning Essential Companies into Targets Act of 2025" (PROTECT USA Act of 2025) seeks to shield certain US entities from the extraterritorial application of foreign sustainability due diligence requirements, with particular reference to those adopted by the European Union.
90 See https://commission.europa.eu/document/download/892fa84e-d027-439b-8527-72669cc42844_en?filename=COM_2025_81_EN.pdf (accessed in March 2025).
91 124 Stat. 1376 – Dodd-Frank Wall Street Reform and Consumer Protection Act.

designation as a SIFI.[92] The District Court emphasised that cost-benefit analysis constitutes a central component of the administrative process, noting that costs must be weighed against benefits since no regulation can be deemed "appropriate" if it causes significantly more harm than good. On this basis, the Court found it "impossible" to determine whether the Financial Stability Oversight Council's designation of MetLife as a SIFI, in fact, resulted in substantially more harm than benefit. Thus, a regulatory authority must consider whether imposing the costs of additional governance and compliance requirements to a company through a specific designation outweigh the benefits of heightened regulation.

The SEC emphasises board independence as essential to effective governance. Its rules mandate that boards of financial institutions include independent directors unaffiliated with the company, thereby enabling objective oversight. This principle was underscored in *Stanley Lerner, Derivatively on Behalf of Nominal Defendant Citigroup Inc., Plaintiff v Charles O. Prince, III, et al., Defendants, and Citigroup Inc., Nominal Defendant*, 2012 NY Slip Op 22133 [36 Misc 3d 297], where the court evaluated Citigroup's board oversight of risky subprime lending practices, highlighting the necessity for boards to engage in risk management actively and assess management decisions critically.[93]

The New York Stock Exchange (NYSE) and Nasdaq Stock Market (Nasdaq) require that the majority of directors on the board of a listed company must be independent, subject to certain exemptions, such as for "controlled companies" (as outlined later). Both the NYSE[94] and Nasdaq[95] have their own definitions of "independence" that directors must satisfy, although their standards are broadly similar. Additionally, each listed company is required to disclose information regarding the independence of its directors in accordance with Item 407(a) of Regulation S-K.[96]

Under Item 406 of Regulation S-K, the SEC requires companies to disclose whether they have adopted a code of ethics that applies to their principal executive officer, principal financial officer, principal accounting officer and/or controller, as well as individuals performing similar functions. If a company has not adopted such a code, it must publicly explain the reasons for this decision. The code of ethics must include written standards designed to deter wrongdoing.

92 "*FSOC, too, has made the decision to regulate – by designating MetLife. That decision intentionally refused to consider the cost of regulation, a consideration that is essential to reasoned rulemaking. Cf. id. at 2707 ('Consideration of cost reflects the understanding that reasonable regulation ordinarily requires paying attention to the advantages and the disadvantages of agency decisions') (emphasis in original). In light of Michigan and of Dodd-Frank's command to consider all 'appropriate' risk-related factors, 12 U.S.C. § 5323(a)(2)(K), FSOC's position is at odds with the law and its designation of MetLife must be rescinded*". Opinion signed by Judge Rosemary M. Collyer on 30 March 2016.

93 "*Under the two-part test set forth in Aronson v Lewis (473 A2d at 814) demand futility is sufficiently alleged where the allegations raise a reasonable doubt as to whether (1) the majority of directors are independent and disinterested, and (2) where a specific board decision is challenged, that the decision was the product of a valid exercise of business judgment (see also In re Bear Stearns Cos., Inc. Sec., Derivative, & ERISA Litig., 763 F Supp 2d 423, 540–541 [SD NY 2011]). This test requires a fact-intensive determination as to whether the pleadings allege a lack of independence or disinterestedness of a majority of the directors sitting at the time of the commencement of the derivative claim at issue*".

94 Under the NYSE rules, an independent director is defined as someone whom the board of directors affirmatively determines has no material relationship with the company, whether directly or through serving as an officer, partner, or shareholder of an entity that has a relationship with the company (Section 303A.02(a)(i), NYSE Listed Company Manual). The NYSE Listed Company Manual advises boards to "broadly consider all relevant facts and circumstances" when making independence determinations (Commentary to Section 303A.02(a)).

95 Under the Nasdaq rules, an independent director is defined as someone who is neither an executive officer nor an employee of the company and who does not have a relationship that, in the board of directors' opinion, would impair their ability to exercise independent judgment in fulfilling their responsibilities as a director (Rules 5005(a)(20) and 5605(a)(2), Nasdaq Listing Rules).

96 Regulation S-K is a set of SEC rules that establishes the detailed disclosure requirements (excluding financial statements) applicable to registration statements, periodic reports, proxy statements, and other filings made under the Securities Act of 1933 and the Exchange Act of 1934. The SEC forms themselves, such as Form S-1 or Form 10-K, reference specific Items within Regulation S-K.

Both the NYSE and Nasdaq require listed companies (with certain exemptions) to adopt a code of conduct applicable to all directors, officers, and employees.[97] The NYSE mandates that each company adopt corporate governance guidelines outlining the company's corporate governance policies and practices. This requirement does not apply to certain exempted entities, such as controlled companies and foreign private issuers.[98] The corporate governance guidelines must cover several key areas, including qualification standards for directors, their responsibilities, and their access to management and independent advisors. They must also address director compensation, orientation and continuing education for directors, management succession, and annual evaluations of board performance.[99] By contrast, neither Nasdaq nor the SEC imposes a similar requirement.

The SEC defines a code of ethics as a set of written standards reasonably designed to deter wrongdoing and to promote honest and ethical conduct, including the handling of conflicts of interest between personal and professional relationships. It should also promote full, fair, timely, accurate, and understandable disclosure in reports and other documents filed with the SEC or otherwise made public. The code must ensure compliance with applicable laws, rules, and regulations, require prompt internal reporting of any violations to designated personnel, and provide for accountability in complying with its provisions.[100]

Bank directors in the US face unique responsibilities beyond the general fiduciary duties applicable to all corporate directors. They vary based on the type of banking institution, as the US banking system involves different chartering and regulatory authorities. Directors of national banks are subject to federal law and oversight from the Office of the Comptroller of the Currency, though state law may also apply, especially regarding liability standards, which range from gross negligence to simple negligence, depending on the state. Conversely, directors of state-chartered banks are governed primarily by state law but may be subject to federal standards if the bank is a state-member bank within the Federal Reserve System.

Under state law, directors are typically subject to two fundamental fiduciary duties in the performance of their role. The first is the duty of care, which obliges directors to act with diligence and to ensure that they are fully and properly informed when making decisions on behalf of the corporation. This duty requires an active engagement in the affairs of the company and the exercise of sound judgement based on adequate information.[101] The second is the duty of loyalty, which mandates that directors act in the best interests of the corporation rather than pursuing their own personal interests.[102] This duty aims to prevent conflicts of interest and to ensure that directors prioritise the welfare of the company and its shareholders when exercising their decision-making powers. Courts have interpreted the duty of loyalty as encompassing

97 See Lee, P., 'Directors' Duty to Monitor: Experience in the Banking Sector – Part I' (2016) 133 *The Banking Law Journal* 405.

98 See Section 303A.00, NYSE Listed Company Manual.

99 The NYSE requires the CEO of each listed company to certify annually that they are not aware of any violations of the NYSE's corporate governance standards. Additionally, the CEO must promptly notify the NYSE in writing if any executive officer becomes aware of any non-compliance with these standards. In contrast, Nasdaq only requires the CEO to promptly notify it if any executive officer becomes aware of any non-compliance with Nasdaq's corporate governance standards.

100 The SEC mandates that the CEO and CFO of each company certify the company's Form 10-K and Form 10-Q reports under Sections 302 and 906 of the Sarbanes-Oxley Act. The Section 302 certification concerns the accuracy of the report and the company's disclosure controls, procedures, and internal control over financial reporting. The Section 906 certification, meanwhile, confirms compliance with the Securities Exchange Act of 1934 (as amended) and the accuracy of the information provided in the reports.

101 *Francis v. United Jersey Bank*, 432 A.2d 814, 822 (N.J. 1981) (finding a duty to conduct regular review of financial statements) (*Francis*); *Barnes v. Andrews*, 298 F.614, 615 (S.D.N.Y. 1924) (finding a duty to enquire into the corporate business).

102 *Stone v. Ritter*, 911 A.2d 362, 369-70 (Del. 2006).

a duty of oversight, which is firmly rooted in the obligation of directors to act in good faith. This duty recognises that directors cannot fulfil their corporate governance responsibilities in good faith without independent access to and proper consideration of timely and sufficient information to evaluate the company's operations, associated risks, and mitigation efforts. In essence, the duty of oversight requires directors to supervise and monitor the corporation's business activities and ensure compliance with applicable laws.[103] A failure to do so may amount to a breach of fiduciary duty, particularly where directors disregard red flags or fail to engage with material compliance concerns brought to their attention.

The leading case establishing the standard for directors' oversight and monitoring duties is *In re Caremark International Inc. Derivative Litigation*, 698 A.2d 959 (**Caremark**), decided by the Delaware Court of Chancery. This case, along with subsequent decisions that have developed its principles, confirms that directors have a duty to ensure that the company maintains adequate systems and controls – extending to the board level – to provide the board with the information necessary to make well-informed, independent decisions concerning the company's operations, risks, and efforts to mitigate those risks.

In practical terms, this duty of oversight requires directors to ensure the existence of information and reporting systems that are reasonably designed to deliver accurate and timely information to the board. There must also be effective internal compliance controls that capture relevant information about the company's business and compliance with key legal and regulatory obligations and relay this information to the board in the ordinary course of business. Additionally, the board itself must maintain a compliance structure that enables it to consider such information and monitor material compliance risks effectively.[104] Beyond the mere existence of these systems, directors are expected to oversee their operations actively and to engage meaningfully with the information produced. This includes identifying significant risks, following up on issues, and ensuring that the company's response aligns with its legal duties and risk management objectives. To establish a breach of the duty of oversight, it must be shown that directors acted in bad faith by knowingly disregarding their fiduciary obligations. This requires a demonstration that they were consciously aware they were failing to fulfil their responsibilities. Liability may arise where directors failed to act upon clear and substantial red flags, both internal and external, as illustrated *In re Wells Fargo & Co. S'holder Derivative Litig.,* 282 F. Supp. 3d 1074, 1082 (N.D. Cal. 2017). These cases highlight the courts' willingness to impose liability on banks' directors where their inaction reflects a sustained and knowing failure to engage with their oversight duties.[105]

Directors of national and state member banks are elected at annual meetings as per the bank's by-laws (12 U.S.C. § 75) and generally serve terms of one to three years.[106] Upon election, directors must take an oath to manage the bank's affairs faithfully and honestly (12

103 See *In re Caremark International Inc. Derivative Litigation*, 698 A.2d 959 at [970]: "*But it is important that the board exercise a good faith judgment that the corporation's information and reporting system is in concept and design adequate to assure the board that appropriate information will come to its attention in a timely manner as a matter of ordinary operations, so that it may satisfy its responsibility*".

104 *Stone v. Ritter*, 911 A.2d 362, 369-70 (Del. 2006); *Marchand v. Barnhill*, 212 A.3d 805, 820-24 (Del. 2019).

105 *In re Wells Fargo & Co. S'holder Derivative Litig.*, 282 F. Supp. 3d 1074, 1082 (N.D. Cal. 2017) the case ultimately resulted in settlement of claims against directors for personal liability after court denied motion to dismiss based on reasonable inferences that directors knew the company's systems were inadequate at identifying and addressing sales integrity issues and took no action in response to numerous red flags.

106 National banks cap directors' terms at three years (12 U.S.C. § 71), with board size ranging between five and 25 directors, as defined in the bank's by-laws (12 U.S.C. § 71a). Directors' citizenship and residency requirements are specified under federal and state laws; for instance, national bank directors must be US citizens, with a majority residing either in the state where the bank is located or within 100 miles of its office, though the OCC can waive this for a minority of directors (12 U.S.C. § 72).

U.S.C. § 73, 12 C.F.R. § 7.2008).[107] They are expected to have foundational knowledge of the banking sector and its regulatory framework. While they are not required to be experts in all aspects of banking, directors must possess enough knowledge to exercise sound judgement and oversee bank activities effectively. Directors can rely on information provided by qualified officers and employees, assuming they have no reason to question its reliability. Banks may also appoint advisory directors, who offer guidance but do not participate in board votes, generally shielding them from liability for board decisions unless their involvement is comparable to that of full directors.

Directors who are alleged to have breached their fiduciary duties may face civil proceedings in their personal capacity, brought either directly by shareholders or derivatively on behalf of the corporation. In such cases, Delaware courts generally apply one of three standards of review when assessing the legality and propriety of board decisions. The default standard is the business judgement rule, which affords directors a high degree of deference where decisions are made in good faith, on an informed basis, and in the honest belief that the action taken is in the best interests of the company. As noted by the court *In re Citigroup Shareholder Derivative Litigation* 964 A.2d 106, 125 (Del. Ch. 2009), the business judgement rule is essential for promoting the innovative decision-making necessary for a company's long-term success and the benefit of its shareholders. The court explained:

> *[The Business Judgment Rule] is designed to allow corporate managers and directors to pursue risky transactions without the specter of being held personally liable if those decisions turn out poorly. Accordingly, the burden required for a plaintiff to rebut the presumption of the business judgment rule by showing gross negligence is a difficult one, and the burden to show bad faith is even higher.*

In circumstances where there are conflicts of interest or concerns about self-dealing, the court may apply the more exacting standard of entire fairness, which requires directors to demonstrate that both the process and the outcome of the transaction were fair to the corporation. A third standard – enhanced scrutiny – is used in specific contexts, such as change-of-control transactions or defensive measures against takeovers, where the court examines the reasonableness of the board's decision-making and the adequacy of its response to perceived threats. Each standard reflects a different level of judicial intervention, depending on the nature of the alleged breach and the context in which the board acted.[108]

Moreover, directors can face personal liability for fiduciary breaches, legal violations, or unsafe practices. Federal law typically applies a gross negligence standard (12 U.S.C. § 1821(k)) for federally insured depository institution directors, though some states impose a simple negligence standard, which requires reasonable care. In cases of bank failure, the FDIC may pursue negligence or breach of duty claims against directors, especially if their actions contributed to the bank's collapse.

In recent years, there has been a growing emphasis on integrating ESG considerations into US governance, though this is less developed than in the EU, and the approach to such considerations has not been structured thus the different regulatory requirements are somewhat dispersed. For example, some form of public reporting on environmental, labour, or human rights practices is required by relevant governmental agencies to advance their regulatory mission. In this respect, companies must establish monitoring and reporting systems to comply with anti-bribery regulations under the Foreign Corrupt Practices Act[109] and the Environmental Protection Agency enforces

107 For troubled banks, regulatory approval is required for new directors before they assume office, with a mandatory notice to the OCC 90 days prior to assuming directorship (12 U.S.C. § 1831i; 12 CFR § 5.51).
108 *Bamford v. Penfold, L.P.*, No. 2019-0005-JTL [2022] WL 2278867, at [35] (Del. Ch. 24 June 2022).
109 15 U.S.C. §§ 78dd-1, 78m (2012).

various reporting requirements as a matter of environmental regulation and permit enforcement and with respect to greenhouse gas disclosure requirements that apply to certain large emitters.[110]

Despite this hodgepodge legislative approach, in fulfilling their duty of loyalty, directors are also responsible for overseeing key ESG risks facing the organisation, particularly in light of their oversight obligations under the *Caremark* doctrine. This responsibility requires directors to understand the ESG risks specific to their company and to ensure that appropriate systems are in place to identify, monitor, and escalate related concerns. Board members are expected to give due consideration to the ESG-related information presented to them, to recognise potential warning signs, and to follow up appropriately on emerging issues and the organisation's response to them. This forms a critical aspect of the board's broader duty to act in the best interests of the company and its stakeholders.

In 2023, the SEC adopted new rules requiring registrants to disclose material cybersecurity incidents that they experience.[111] Registrants are also obliged to provide annual disclosures of material information relating to their cybersecurity risk management, strategy, and governance. These measures are intended to enhance transparency for investors by ensuring that companies report significant cybersecurity threats and demonstrate how they manage associated risks at both operational and governance levels.

The SEC adopted climate change disclosure rules in March 2024, which "*enhance and standardize climate-related disclosures by public companies and in public offerings*" and reflect the SEC's

> *efforts to respond to investors' demand for more consistent, comparable, and reliable information about the financial effects of climate-related risks on a registrant's operations and how it manages those risks while balancing concerns about mitigating the associated costs of the rules.*[112]

The *City Of New York v. Exxon Mobil Corporation et al* case 2025 N.Y. Slip Op. 25011 exemplifies the significance of ESG. In this instance, although the case was ultimately dismissed in January 2025 by the Supreme Court,[113] New York County, it was alleged that Exxon Mobil and the other defendants misled consumers about the impact of their products on the climate and falsely represented themselves as corporate leaders in the fight against climate change. In particular, the City of New York alleged that the Defendants engaged in deceptive Corporate Greenwashing Statements and product greenwashing by using marketing and public relations campaigns to misrepresent their environmental impact, with the aim of influencing consumers and boosting product sales in New York City.

Such emphasis, at the time of writing, has abated, and a growing backlash against ESG has emerged. In December 2024 and January 2025, several leading US and Canadian banks announced their withdrawal from the Net Zero Banking Alliance, a coalition established to align the banking sector with global climate objectives, reflecting the financial industry's commitment to sustainability. These departing institutions account for 12% of the total assets within the global banking system, highlighting the substantial impact of their withdrawal on the broader sustainability commitments of the sector.[114]

110 40 C.F.R. § 704 (2016).
111 SEC, Press release 2023-139, SEC Adopts Rules on Cybersecurity Risk Management, Strategy, Governance, and Incident Disclosure by Public Companies (26 July 2023), available at www.sec.gov/newsroom/press-releases/2023-139 (accessed in March 2025).
112 SEC, Press release 2024–31, SEC Adopts Rules to Enhance and Standardize Climate-Related Discovery for Investors (6 March 2024), available at www.sec.gov/newsroom/press-releases/2024-31 (accessed in March 2025).
113 Despite the name, it is a court of first instance.
114 See www.abnamro.com/research/en/our-research/esg-strategist-what-does-the-nzba-exodus-tell-us-about-banks-climate (accessed in March 2025).

5 CORPORATE GOVERNANCE IN CHINA

Corporate governance in China is shaped by an intricate mix of laws and regulations issued by the China Banking and Insurance Regulatory Commission, the People's Bank of China, and the Company Law of the People's Republic of China.[115]

The Company Law of the People's Republic of China governs both limited liability companies and companies limited by shares. A listed company is also governed by the Securities Law of the People's Republic of China, 2019 Revision.[116] Furthermore, a company with state-owned capital, whether organised as a limited liability company or a company limited by shares, is also subject to the provisions of the Law of the People's Republic of China on State-Owned Assets of Enterprises 2008.[117]

In response to concerns about banking sector stability, the CBIRC has pursued reforms aimed at enhancing governance and risk management. The Corporate Governance Guidelines for Banking and Insurance Institutions 2021[118] prescribe specific requirements for board composition, risk management practices, and internal controls, including the establishment of risk management committees and a mandate that senior executives possess expertise in managing complex financial risks. The need for these reforms was highlighted by the 2020 collapse of Baoshang Bank,[119] which failed due to governance weaknesses and inadequate risk management. The CBIRC's intervention in Baoshang Bank[120] underscored the necessity of robust governance frameworks, especially for smaller regional banks that may lack the resources and expertise of larger institutions.

In February 2024, under the guidance of the China Securities Regulatory Commission, China's three major stock exchanges issued ESG reporting guidelines. These guidelines mandate companies included in the SSE 180 Index, STAR 50 Index, SZSE 100 Index, and ChiNext Index, as well as companies listed both domestically and overseas, disclose their ESG data starting in 2026. Additionally, the China Securities Regulatory Commission encourages other companies to publish ESG reports on a voluntary basis.

The Ministry of Finance published in 2024 the Basic Guidelines for Corporate Sustainability Disclosure.[121] These guidelines set out general requirements for sustainability information disclosure by Chinese enterprises. Broadly, they align with the International Sustainability Standards Board's disclosure framework, which requires companies to report on governance, strategy, risk and opportunity management, and indicators and targets. However, unlike the International Sustainability Standards Board Standards, which adopt a financial materiality perspective, the Ministry of Finance's guidelines follow the principle of double materiality. This approach considers both the impact of ESG factors on a company's financial performance and the company's impact on ESG outcomes.

115 See unofficial translation available at www.registrationchina.com/articles/law/company-law-of-the-peoples-republic-of-china-2023-revision/ (accessed in March 2025).
116 See https://fyjjxy.zuel.edu.cn/_upload/article/files/68/72/2f6833774fa1b877d91a1fe06d06/addfdf5a-f0b2-4016-bb72-309fa105ff28.pdf (accessed in March 2025).
117 See www.industry.gov.au/sites/default/files/adc/public-record/exhibit_c1.11.2_-_law_of_the_prc_on_the_state-owned_assets_of_enterprises.pdf (accessed in March 2025).
118 The Corporate Governance Guidelines for Banking and Insurance Institutions 2021 have superseded the Corporate Governance Guidelines on Commercial Banks issued in 2013 and the Guiding Opinions Regulating Governance Structure of Insurance Companies, 2006, aiming to consolidate the existing separate regulatory regimes applicable to banking and insurance institutions respectively into one unified regime.
119 See www.pbc.gov.cn/english/130721/3835956/index.html (accessed in March 2025).
120 See https://pidm.gov.my/pidm2022/media/assets/RSP/10-Nationalisation-and-Restructuring-Baoshang-Bank.pdf (accessed in March 2025).
121 Cai Kuai [2024] No. 17.

6 CORPORATE GOVERNANCE IN INDIA

Corporate governance in India operates under the Companies Act 2013, the Banking Regulation Act 1949, and guidelines issued by the Reserve Bank of India, applying a stringent governance framework across both state-owned and private banks.

The Companies Act 2013 introduced critical governance reforms, mandating specific board composition requirements for banks, including the presence of independent directors and the separation of the roles of chairperson and CEO to prevent conflicts of interest. The Companies Act 2013 is supplemented by the Securities and Exchange Board of India (Listing Obligations and Disclosure Requirements) Regulations, 2015 (**LODR Regulations**)[122] applicable to listed companies.

Listed companies and other prescribed companies are required to establish Nomination and Remuneration Committees to assist with the appointment of directors and the determination of their remuneration.[123]

The total managerial remuneration payable by a public company to its directors, including the managing director, full-time director, and manager, is subject to a specified percentage (11%, which may be increased with the approval of the company in a general meeting) of the company's net profits for a financial year.[124] Similar thresholds are set for listed entities under the LODR Regulations for the remuneration of executive and non-executive directors.[125] The Reserve Bank of India's Prompt Corrective Action Framework imposes rigorous governance requirements on banks that breach critical financial thresholds. Any payments exceeding these thresholds require prior approval from shareholders through a special resolution. The annual report must disclose the remuneration paid to directors.[126] Additionally, the board report is required to include information on the ratio of remuneration paid to directors. In the case of listed companies, these disclosures must also comply with the principles set out in the LODR Regulations. Regulation 17 of the LODR Regulations requires the establishment of a code of conduct for the senior management and the board of the company.

The directors of a company owe a fiduciary duty to the company, its shareholders, and its employees as a whole. Section 166 of the Companies Act 2013 enumerates the key directors' duties. Among their statutory duties, directors are required to act in accordance with the company's articles and in good faith to promote its objectives. They must exercise care, skill, and diligence, as well as independent judgement, and act in the best interests of the company, its employees, shareholders, the wider community, and in the protection of the environment.[127] Moreover, every director has to act in the best interests of the company and has to avoid engaging in any activity that may result in actual or potential conflicts of interest, whether direct or indirect. This obligation applies to all directors, including nominee directors. Although Section 149(7) of the Companies Act

122 www.sebi.gov.in/legal/regulations/jul-2024/securities-and-exchange-board-of-india-listing-obligations-and-disclosure-requirements-regulations-2015-last-amended-on-july-10-2024-_84817.html (accessed in March 2025).

123 Section 178 of the Companies Act 2013, read in conjunction with Rule 6 of the Companies (Meeting of Board and its Powers) Rules 2014.

124 I.e., "The total managerial remuneration payable by a public company, to its directors, including managing director and whole-time director, and its manager in respect of any financial year shall not exceed eleven per cent. of the net profits of that company for that financial year computed in the manner laid down in section 198 except that the remuneration of the directors shall not be deducted from the gross profits". Section 197(1) of the Companies Act 2013.

125 Regulation 17(6), LODR Regulations.

126 Section 92 of the Companies Act 2013.

127 Section 166 of the Companies Act 2013.

2013 acknowledges that a nominee director is appointed to protect the interests of the nominating party, it also imposes a fiduciary duty on such directors to act in the best interests of the company to which they are appointed.

This tension was considered in the case of *AES OPGC Holding (Mauritius) v Orissa Power Generation Corporation Ltd.*, [2005] 125 Comp Cas 299, where the court observed that a conflict of interest arises when an individual owes duties to two or more entities and is required to make a decision that may affect all parties to whom they owe allegiance. The court held that, in such circumstances, a director must either recuse themselves from the decision-making process or act solely in the best interests of the company. Failure to do so would amount to a breach of their fiduciary obligations. Accordingly, while a nominee director may, in the ordinary course, act in accordance with the expectations of the party that appointed them, where a conflict arises between that duty and their duty to the company, the latter must take precedence. The fiduciary duty to the company remains paramount and cannot be overridden by the interests of the nominating party.

In addition to these general obligations, the LODR Regulations also outline the specific duties and liabilities of directors and the boards of listed companies.[128] The board is required to prepare an annual report outlining the development and implementation of a risk management policy for the company. This report must include the identification of any elements of risk that could threaten the company's existence.[129] For listed companies, the directors' report must additionally include a management and discussion report, as well as a directors' responsibility statement. Under Section 134(5) of the Companies Act 2013, this statement should address the operations and effectiveness of the internal financial control mechanisms adopted by the company.

Moreover, the top 1,000 listed companies are required to establish a risk management committee.[130] This committee must be constituted by the board, with the majority of its members drawn from the board itself, including at least one independent director. Additionally, the company's auditor is obligated to disclose any instances of fraud identified in the financial statements to the shareholders and to report such matters in the company's accounts to the central government.[131]

The Reserve Bank of India's Guidelines on Fit and Proper Criteria for Directors of Banks[132] ensure that bank directors possess the qualifications and experience necessary to manage complex banking operations. They focus on board accountability, risk management, and internal controls.

7 CORPORATE GOVERNANCE IN JAPAN

In Japan, corporate governance is structured under the Companies Act 2005, the Banking Act, and guidelines issued by the Financial Services Agency. Traditionally, Japanese corporate governance has relied on a consensus-driven approach, with boards primarily comprising insiders closely connected to management.

The introduction of the Corporate Governance Code in 2015 by the Tokyo Stock Exchange marked a significant move towards greater transparency and accountability within

128 Regulations 17 and 25.
129 Section 134(3)(n) of the Companies Act 2013.
130 Regulation 21, LODR Regulations.
131 Section 143(12) of Companies Act 2013.
132 Available at www.pnbindia.in/downloadprocess.aspx?fid=LlY00LHyMpQ7PF4gJtK5Sw== (accessed in March 2025).

Japanese banks, encouraging the appointment of independent directors and the establishment of robust risk management frameworks. However, the strong emphasis on consensus decision-making has sometimes limited board oversight effectiveness. The Toshiba Governance Scandal in 2021, where the board was found to have collaborated with the government to curb shareholder activism, highlighted the need for increased board independence. Although Toshiba is not a banking institution, the scandal influenced governance reform in the financial sector, leading the Financial Services Agency to advocate for stronger board oversight and greater transparency within bank governance structures.

Japanese banks are required by the Banking Act[133] to develop comprehensive risk management frameworks, including the formation of board-level risk management committees. The Financial Services Agency's Comprehensive Guidelines for Supervision of Major Banks[134] specify governance expectations, such as mandating that senior executives possess expertise in risk management and requiring banks to implement transparent governance practices. The Mizuho Financial Group Governance Scandal (2013),[135] in which the bank failed to manage loans linked to organised crime syndicates, underscored the necessity for enhanced governance frameworks in Japanese banks. This incident led the Financial Services Agency to implement stricter governance guidelines, urging banks to establish more independent oversight mechanisms and improve their internal controls.

In March 2023, the Financial Services Agency introduced mandatory sustainability disclosure rules for all listed companies in Japan. Under the new regulations, companies are required to incorporate sustainability information directly into their annual securities reports. These disclosures must adhere to the framework established by the Task Force on Climate-related Financial Disclosures (**TCFD**),[136] with a focus on four key areas: governance, strategy, risk management, and metrics and targets. In addition to these measures, the Tokyo Stock Exchange revised its Corporate Governance Code[137] in June 2021. It now requires companies listed on the Prime Market to disclose climate-related information in line with TCFD recommendations.

Furthermore, the Principles for Responsible Institutional Investors (Stewardship Code)[138] could also be applicable. It encourages – on a voluntary basis – institutional investors, including pension funds, trust banks, and life insurance companies, to foster the sustainable growth of their investee companies through constructive engagement from a medium- to long-term perspective.

8 EXECUTIVE REMUNERATION IN BANKS

In the wake of the global financial crisis of 2007–2009, the G20 countries pledged to reform bank remuneration frameworks in response to widespread criticism that poorly designed compensation structures had encouraged excessive risk-taking within banks, thereby contributing

133 (Act No. 59 of 1 June 1981).
134 Available at www.fsa.go.jp/common/law/guide/en_city.pdf (accessed in March 2025).
135 See www.fsa.go.jp/en/news/2013/20131226-1.html (accessed in March 2025).
136 See https://assets.bbhub.io/company/sites/60/2020/10/FINAL-2017-TCFD-Report-11052018.pdf (accessed in March 2025).
137 See www.jpx.co.jp/english/equities/listing/cg/tvdivq0000008jdy-att/20210611.pdf (accessed in March 2025).
138 See www.fsa.go.jp/en/refer/councils/stewardship/20200324/01.pdf (accessed in March 2025).

to the crisis. If risks are excessive and the firm is to fail, the costs of a financial firm's failure are not borne solely by its shareholders.[139]

In furtherance of this commitment, the Financial Stability Board (FSB) published a set of principles and standards aimed at guiding remuneration practices within the financial sector. These standards were subsequently transposed into European Union law through the CRD IV. As both the UK and EU remuneration frameworks originate from such a common source – the CRD IV – the general requirements governing bank remuneration in the UK and the EU are largely aligned.[140] Although the UK has since ceased to be a member of the European Union, the core principles underpinning remuneration regulation, including the emphasis on sound risk management, proportionality, deferral of variable pay, and governance, continue to reflect their shared origin in CRD IV.

In the UK, these core principles have been incorporated into domestic regulation, namely the SYSC 19D (Dual-regulated firms' Remuneration Code) (**SYSC Remuneration Code**)[141] and the implementation of CRD IV in the Remuneration Part of the PRA Rulebook. Through these provisions, both the FCA and the PRA have developed stringent frameworks to align bankers' remuneration with risk management and long-term financial stability. Put in other terms, if managers have "skin in the game", they would not have the incentive to engage in excessive risk-taking.[142] Moreover, DEI remains a recurring focus for the FCA, which consistently reminds firms of their obligation to uphold gender-neutral pay policies and to ensure that variable pay awards do not discriminate on the basis of any protected characteristic.

8.1 Regulatory Frameworks Governing Remuneration

As discussed previously, the two primary frameworks for bankers' remuneration are the SYSC Remuneration Code and the Remuneration Part of the PRA Rulebook. The SYSC Remuneration Code provides the principles and rules that regulated firms must adhere to when structuring and enforcing remuneration policies. Meanwhile, the Remuneration Part of the PRA Rulebook includes provisions on deferral requirements, as well as clawback mechanisms.

Historically, one of the most significant elements of the UK's remuneration framework was the bonus cap, which limited the ratio of variable remuneration (bonuses) to fixed remuneration (salary). Introduced under CRD IV, this cap limited bonuses to 100% of fixed remuneration or up to 200% with shareholder approval. The bonus cap was introduced to discourage the culture of excessive risk-taking by limiting the potential for large bonuses tied to short-term profits. However, following the UK's exit from the European Union, the PRA and FCA removed the bonus cap as part of post-Brexit reforms. This removal, effective from 31 October 2023,[143] was justified on the grounds that the cap had led to an increase in fixed pay, raising fixed costs for firms and reducing their flexibility. The regulators argued that

139 Armour, J., Awrey, D., Davies, P., Enriques, L., Gordon, J., Mayer, C. and Payne, J., *Principles of Financial Regulation* (Oxford University Press, 2016), p. 382.

140 See Prudential Regulation Authority, *Policy Statement | PS28/21: Remuneration: Identification of Material Risk Takers* (December 2021).

141 See www.handbook.fca.org.uk/handbook/SYSC/19D/1.html (accessed in March 2025).

142 Armour, J., Awrey, D., Davies, P., Enriques, L., Gordon, J., Mayer, C. and Payne, J., *Principles of Financial Regulation* (Oxford University Press, 2016), p. 380.

143 See PS9/23 – Remuneration: Ratio between fixed and variable components of total remuneration ('bonus cap'), PRA policy statement 9/23 and FCA policy statement 23/15, available at (accessed in March 2025). www.bankofengland.co.uk/prudential-regulation/publication/2023/october/remuneration-ratio-between-fixed-and-variable-components-of-total-remuneration (accessed in March 2025).

by removing the cap, firms would regain the ability to adjust remuneration based on performance without the rigidity imposed by higher fixed salaries.

Despite the removal of the bonus cap, firms are still required to ensure that variable remuneration is risk-adjusted and aligned with long-term financial performance. In particular, under the combined regulatory regime provided by the PRA and FCA, banks are obliged to establish, implement, and maintain remuneration policies, procedures, and practices that are consistent with and supportive of sound and effective risk management. The framework is designed to encompass all elements of remuneration that may influence prudent risk-taking behaviour. This includes, but is not limited to, salaries, bonuses, long-term incentive plans, share options, hiring bonuses, severance payments, and pension arrangements.

The overarching aim is to ensure that remuneration structures do not incentivise undue risk-taking and are aligned with the long-term stability and integrity of the financial system.

These principles, which must be applied not only at the individual entity level but also across the group, parent undertaking, and subsidiary undertakings of the banking organisation, require that remuneration policies actively support effective risk management and remain aligned with the bank's stated risk appetite, ensuring that compensation structures do not encourage imprudent risk-taking. In addition, remuneration frameworks must be consistent with the bank's broader business strategy, objectives, and long-term interests, thereby supporting sustainable performance over time.

A strong governance structure is essential to the effective implementation of these requirements. Banks are, therefore, required to maintain a robust oversight framework, including a dedicated remuneration committee responsible for ensuring compliance with applicable regulatory standards. Guaranteed variable remuneration, such as hiring bonuses, is strongly discouraged and may only be permitted in exceptional circumstances, typically limited to the first year of employment.

To align incentives with long-term outcomes, a substantial portion of variable pay must be deferred over a minimum deferral period of up to seven years. Additionally, remuneration must be subject to both *ex ante* and *ex post* risk adjustments. This includes the application of malus and clawback provisions, which enable the reduction or recovery of previously awarded variable pay in light of subsequent risk-related developments.

The regime is also underpinned by the principle of proportionality, ensuring that the application of remuneration requirements is calibrated to the size, complexity, and risk profile of each institution, thereby preventing undue regulatory burdens on smaller firms. Furthermore, variable remuneration must include a significant component paid in shares, share-linked instruments, or equivalent non-cash instruments in order to align employee incentives with the long-term performance of the institution.

Transparency is a further regulatory objective, and banks are required to publicly disclose details of their remuneration frameworks, including aggregate data concerning senior executives and individuals identified as risk-takers. Moreover, remuneration policies must be gender-neutral, ensuring equal pay for equal work and avoiding discriminatory practices. Banks are also required to incorporate ESG considerations into their remuneration frameworks, thereby promoting sustainability and the effective management of long-term risks.

Moreover, under both the UK and EU regulatory frameworks, banks are required to identify individuals qualifying as material risk takers and to apply enhanced remuneration requirements to them. Material risk takers generally include members of senior management, individuals performing control functions, and those responsible for key strategic decisions, significant revenue generation, the management of material assets, or the approval of substantial transactions. In addition, employees whose total remuneration ranks among the highest within the institution may also fall within the scope of material risk taker classification.

The process of identifying material risk takers must be undertaken using both qualitative and quantitative criteria, considering the individual's role, responsibilities, and capacity to influence the institution's overall risk profile.[144] The identification and oversight of material risk takers must be subject to appropriate governance, typically falling within the remit of the bank's remuneration committee where such a body exists. This process must be aligned with both regulatory expectations and the bank's internal risk management framework.

Once identified, material risk takers are subject to more stringent remuneration requirements than other employees. These include higher thresholds for deferral, a greater proportion of variable remuneration delivered in non-cash instruments (such as shares or share-linked instruments), and the application of enhanced risk adjustment mechanisms. Banks are also obliged to include detailed disclosures regarding material risk takers within their public remuneration reports.[145] These disclosures must set out the number of individuals identified as material risk takers, their aggregate remuneration, and the measures taken by the bank to ensure alignment between remuneration outcomes and risk management objectives.

8.2 Key Components of the SYSC Remuneration Code

The SYSC Remuneration Code applies proportionally to firms based on their size, risk profile, and the complexity of their activities. Smaller firms, referred to as Small CRR Firms (those with assets under £4 billion), are exempt from certain remuneration requirements, such as deferral, payment in non-cash instruments, and some malus and clawback provisions.[146] These exemptions recognise that smaller firms pose a less systemic risk and do not require the same level of regulatory oversight as larger, more complex institutions.

The SYSC Remuneration Code requires firms to implement clawback and malus provisions to ensure that remuneration remains aligned with long-term performance and effective risk management. These mechanisms allow firms to adjust or reclaim bonuses if it later emerges that an individual's actions were detrimental to the firm or that performance

144 In the EU, credit institutions must comply with the requirements of Article 38-5 (2) of Commission Delegated Regulation (EU) 2021/923 and use the qualitative and quantitative criteria set out therein when identifying the material risk-takers within the credit institution. Additionally, credit institutions must comply with the requirements of the revised EBA Guidelines on sound remuneration policies (EBA/GL/2021/04) for all staff and for material risk-takers. Credit institutions must also comply with the EBA Guidelines on remuneration policies for sales staff (EBA/GL/2016/06) which set out requirements on remuneration policies and practices to improve links between incentives and the fair treatment of consumers for staff providing products or services to consumers. In this context, Commission Delegated Regulation (EU) No 527/2014 specifies the categories of instruments that appropriately reflect the credit quality of the institution and are intended to be used for the purposes of variable remuneration. Banks must ensure proper application of this regulation.

145 In the EU Commission Implementing Regulation (EU) 2021/637 of 15 March 2021 laying down implementing technical standards with regard to public disclosures by institutions of the information referred to in Titles II and III of Part Eight of Regulation (EU) No 575/2013 of the European Parliament and of the Council and repealing Commission Implementing Regulation (EU) No 1423/2013, Commission Delegated Regulation (EU) 2015/1555, Commission Implementing Regulation (EU) 2016/200 and Commission Delegated Regulation (EU) 2017/2295, sets out implementing technical standards and provides tables and formats for disclosure requirements.

146 See Bank of England's Policy statement 16/23PS – Remuneration: Enhancing proportionality for small firms available at www.bankofengland.co.uk/prudential-regulation/publication/2023/december/remuneration-enhancing-proportionality-for-small-firms-policy-statement (accessed in March 2025).

metrics were misstated.[147] Such provisions have become standard in remuneration policies, and their use is a key tool for regulators to ensure that firms can address risk management failures after the fact.[148]

Clawback enables firms to recover bonuses that have already been paid, typically within a period of up to seven years. In contrast, malus allows firms to reduce or cancel deferred bonuses that have not yet vested should misconduct, risk management failures, or financial misstatements come to light. These provisions serve as essential safeguards, reinforcing accountability and discouraging excessive risk-taking within the financial sector. These provisions were notably enforced in *Galleon Holdings Limited v FCA* [2019] EWHC 2857 (Admin), where senior executives attempted to challenge the FCA's authority to claw back bonuses following the collapse of the firm. The High Court upheld the enforceability of the FCA's clawback provisions, confirming that they play a vital role in ensuring that executives remain accountable for their decisions and that excessive risk-taking does not go unpunished.

One of the central pillars of the remuneration framework is the requirement that a significant portion of bonuses be deferred over a period of three to five years. For senior executives and Material Risk Takers, at least 40% of variable pay must be deferred, with the proportion rising to 60% for particularly high bonuses (defined as those exceeding £500,000). This deferral period ensures that bonuses are not simply tied to short-term performance but are instead aligned with long-term outcomes and the firm's overall risk profile. In addition to the deferral period, at least 50% of both the upfront and deferred components of bonuses must be paid in non-cash instruments, such as shares or equivalent ownership interests. This requirement ensures that senior managers and risk-takers have a vested interest in the firm's long-term success, as the value of their deferred compensation is directly tied to the firm's performance.

Striking the right balance in the length of deferral periods is essential. On the one hand, research conducted by the PRA in 2022 (Measuring the Effects of Bank Remuneration Rules: Evidence for the UK)[149] found that long bonus deferral periods were associated with increases in fixed pay, which could reduce a firm's ability to absorb losses during economic downturns and potentially undermine its safety and soundness. On the other hand, deferral periods must be long enough to allow adverse outcomes to materialise, ensuring that remuneration incentives align with the firm's long-term performance. The PRA assessment suggests that, while no deferral period will capture every potential incident, a five-year deferral window is likely to capture the majority of incidents. This period is considered sufficient for the application of malus and serves as an effective deterrent to reckless behaviour.

The *PRA v Standard Chartered Bank* [2020] EWHC 3001 (Admin) case highlighted the consequences of failing to comply with deferral requirements. The PRA took enforcement action against Standard Chartered for not deferring bonuses for senior managers as required by the PRA Rulebook and CRD IV. The High Court upheld the PRA's decision, emphasising the importance of deferral in promoting sustainable financial performance and discouraging excessive short-term risk-taking.

147 Kokkinis, A. and Miglionico, M., *Banking Law: Private Transactions and Regulatory Frameworks* (Routledge, 2021), p. 238.

148 The PRA's Supervisory Statement 2/17, updated in 2023, reinforces the importance of using clawback and malus where firms suffer material downturns in performance or experience significant governance failures.

149 See www.bankofengland.co.uk/-/media/boe/files/working-paper/2022/measuring-the-effects-of-bank-remuneration-rules-evidence-from-the-uk.pdf (accessed in March 2025).

8.3 Bankers' Remuneration in the European Union

Bankers' remuneration has been one of the EU's most tightly regulated aspects of corporate governance since the global financial crisis of 2007–2009, during which excessive risk-taking and incentives for short-term profits were identified as key contributors to financial instability. These concerns led to widespread reform encapsulated in CRD IV, which introduced comprehensive rules for remuneration in financial institutions.

As in the United Kingdom, banks operating within the European Union are required to establish, implement, and maintain remuneration policies, procedures, and practices that are consistent with and supportive of sound and effective risk management. The EU's remuneration regime mirrors that of the UK in its comprehensive scope, encompassing all elements of remuneration that may influence prudent risk-taking. This includes fixed and variable pay such as salaries, bonuses, long-term incentive schemes, share options, hiring bonuses, severance payments, and pension arrangements.

European banks are likewise subject to a set of core remuneration principles that closely resemble those applied in the UK, with only minimal variations. One such difference is the minimum deferral period for variable remuneration, which, under the EU regime, may extend up to five years. Nonetheless, the overarching objective remains the same: to align remuneration structures with sustainable business performance and effective risk governance.[150]

A significant reform under CRD IV was the bonus cap, which limits variable remuneration to 100% of fixed pay (or up to 200% with shareholder approval). This measure, which the EU has retained under CRD VI, is intended to curb excessive risk-taking by ensuring that bonuses – often linked to short-term profits – do not vastly exceed fixed remuneration. The cap seeks to reduce incentives for executives and material risk-takers to engage in behaviours that might yield short-term gains at the expense of long-term stability.

With CRD V and CRD VI, the EU places greater emphasis on ESG factors in remuneration policies. Article 98 of CRD V requires banks to integrate ESG risks into the structure of variable remuneration, reflecting the EU's commitment to sustainable finance. Article 92 extends ESG integration by requiring that remuneration practices consider ESG objectives alongside financial performance, thereby aligning executive compensation with goals such as reducing environmental impact and improving social governance. Performance-based pay for senior executives and material risk takers, for example, must be tied to sustainability targets like reducing carbon emissions or enhancing diversity, with malus or clawback provisions applied if these targets are not met. This shift encourages long-term, sustainable growth over short-term profit-seeking.

Moreover, CRD VI introduces explicit sanctions provisions for banks that fail to implement a gender-neutral remuneration system or do not adhere to the applicable remuneration requirements. These provisions will become binding once CRD VI is transposed into the domestic law of EU Member States, which must occur no later than January 2026. Previously, in the absence of specific sanctions for remuneration-related breaches, regulatory authorities seeking to penalise a non-compliant remuneration framework would typically have relied on the broader concept of an "improper business organisation" as the legal basis for enforcement action.

Finally, with respect to issuers of crypto assets, Article 45(1) of Regulation (EU) 2023/1114[151] requires that "*Issuers of significant asset-referenced tokens shall adopt, implement and*

150 Kokkinis, A. and Miglionico, M., *Banking Law: Private Transactions and Regulatory Frameworks* (Routledge, 2021), p. 238.

151 Regulation (EU) 2023/1114 of the European Parliament and of the Council of 31 May 2023 on markets in crypto-assets, and amending Regulations (EU) No 1093/2010 and (EU) No 1095/2010 and Directives 2013/36/EU and (EU) 2019/1937.

maintain a remuneration policy that promotes sound and effective risk management of such issuers and that does not create incentives to relax risk standards". To this effect, the EBA has proposed a framework[152] which aims to ensure the risk alignment of variable remuneration for staff whose roles have a material impact on the risks of the issuer or the significant tokens they issue. It includes specific requirements to ensure that variable remuneration remains aligned with risk in the longer term.

9 CONCLUSION

Governance in the banking sector is crucial for maintaining financial stability, mitigating systemic risks, and promoting responsible business conduct. This chapter has explored the key frameworks that shape governance across different jurisdictions, including the UK, EU, US, China, Japan, and India, with a specific focus on the role of individual accountability, risk management, and regulatory compliance. A recurring theme across jurisdictions is the critical role of board oversight and the personal accountability of directors and senior managers. Effective governance frameworks require a delicate balance between collective decision-making and individual responsibility. The integration of ESG considerations into governance frameworks has added further layers of responsibility.

In the UK, the SMCR has brought a significant shift toward individual accountability, holding senior managers directly responsible for their areas of oversight. This has been complemented by statutory duties under the Companies Act 2006, which codify directors' responsibilities, ensuring that they act with care, skill, and diligence, particularly in complex and highly regulated sectors like banking.

The chapter also highlights the diverse approach to governance across different financial markets. While the UK's principles-based approach is characterised by flexible, outcome-focused regulations, other jurisdictions, like the US, India, Japan, and China, adopt more prescriptive rules influenced by their regulatory philosophies and economic structures. In this respect, the EU has implemented rigorous governance standards through principle-driven directives like CRD IV, CRD V, and CRD VI and more prescriptive regulations such as CRR III, focusing on enhancing board independence, risk management, and ESG integration.

152 See Regulatory Technical Standards on governance arrangements for remuneration under MICAR at www.eba.europa.eu/sites/default/files/2024-06/4998fc26-cc88-4ada-835c-292f831a4ccd/Final%20report%20on%20draft%20RTS%20on%20governance%20arrangements%20for%20remuneration%20under%20%20MICAR.pdf (accessed in March 2025).

CHAPTER 5

FINANCIAL CRIME FRAMEWORK

OVERVIEW

This chapter provides a comprehensive examination of the UK's legal and regulatory mechanisms designed to combat financial crimes such as money laundering, terrorist financing, bribery, corruption, sanctions violations, and fraud. It outlines the major statutes that form the cornerstone of the UK's financial crime framework, including the Proceeds of Crime Act 2002 (**POCA**), the Money Laundering, Terrorist Financing and Transfer of Funds (Information on the Payer) Regulations 2017 (**MLR**s),[1] the Bribery Act 2010, and the Sanctions and Anti-Money Laundering Act 2018 (**SAMLA**), among others. Additionally, the roles of the Economic Crime and Corporate Transparency Act 2023 (**ECCTA**) and the National Crime Agency (**NCA**) are considered.

How the Financial Conduct Authority (**FCA**) oversees compliance with financial crime regulations in the banking sector will be discussed. Specifically, Chapter 5 highlights the FCA's powers under the Financial Services and Markets Act 2000 (**FSMA**), its statutory duties, and the requirements imposed on banks to ensure robust systems and controls are in place to prevent and detect financial crime. Further, it presents a number of decisions that illustrate the enforcement of financial crime legislation and the consequences of non-compliance. Notable cases such as *R v Anwoir* [2008] EWCA Crim 1354 (concerning money laundering) and *R v Skansen Interiors Ltd* (a landmark case under the Bribery Act 2010) provide context for the practical application of the legislation discussed.

A significant part of the chapter also explores experiences from significant jurisdictions, global anti-corruption standards, and the international dimension of financial crime regulation. Finally, the chapter discusses the role of financial institutions in complying with financial sanctions imposed by the UK, US, EU, China, and Japan, as well as the enforcement of these sanctions through mechanisms like SWIFT.

1 UK LEGAL FRAMEWORK

The UK's legal framework for financial crime is founded upon a robust array of statutes, regulations, and case law designed to prevent and address illegal activities in the financial services sector. It covers areas such as money laundering, terrorist financing, bribery, fraud, and sanctions violations. Core components of this framework include the POCA, the MLRs, the Bribery Act 2010, and the SAMLA. More recently, ECCTA has further strengthened the UK's measures against financial crime.

2 THE PROCEEDS OF CRIME ACT 2002

POCA is central to the UK's anti-money laundering efforts, providing the legal foundation for confiscating the proceeds of crime and defining a range of money laundering offences. It adopts two approaches: the first involves enforcing anti-money laundering laws through

1 (SI 2017/692).

DOI: 10.4324/9781032662220-6

banks and financial institutions, while the second enforces anti-money laundering laws against them if they are found to be complicit in transferring the proceeds of crime. Under the first approach, the regulation imposes duties on banks and financial institutions to act as gatekeepers, preventing money laundering from occurring and identifying such incidents to assist regulators in enforcement efforts. Under the second approach, banks and financial institutions may be penalised for becoming involved in money laundering, thereby providing a strong incentive for them to take their gatekeeping responsibilities seriously.[2]

Part 7 of POCA addresses the issue of money laundering and is structured around four key elements. First, it establishes the principal money laundering offences. Secondly, it sets out the consent regime, which provides certain defences or pre-emptive shields against liability for some of these offences. Thirdly, it introduces the disclosure regime, which includes an offence of failing to disclose and offers protection from claims for breach of duty for those who make disclosures. Finally, it creates a freestanding offence of "tipping off".[3]

The principal money laundering offences are contained in sections 327, 328, and 329 of POCA. Section 327 makes it an offence to conceal, disguise, convert, or transfer criminal property or to remove criminal property from the UK. This provision applies broadly, targeting anyone who knowingly assists in handling criminal proceeds.

Section 328 extends liability to those who participate in or become involved in an arrangement that they know or suspect, by any means, facilitates the acquisition, retention, use, or control of criminal property by or on behalf of another individual. In this context, the threshold for suspicion is generally regarded as low. Suspicion arises when there is "*a possibility which is more than fanciful that the relevant facts exist*" although "*a vague feeling of unease would not suffice*", as provided by *R (Da Silva)* [2006] EWCA Crim 1654.

Section 329 further establishes that simply acquiring, using, or possessing criminal property constitutes an offence, even where individuals do not directly participate in the laundering process but benefit from crime proceeds. There is no minimum threshold for the value of criminal property, except in cases where the alleged offender is a deposit-taking institution, such as a bank, an electronic money institution (**EMI**), or a payment institution (payment service provider (**PSP**)) that operates an account maintained with it. In such circumstances, if the value of the criminal property concerned is less than £1,000, the *de minimis* exemption applies.[4] POCA also includes civil recovery measures, allowing authorities to reclaim assets derived from unlawful activities on a civil standard of proof where criminal conviction may not be achievable.

Each of the preceding offences is underpinned by the concept of "criminal property", which is defined under section 340(3) of POCA, and it encompasses all property, irrespective of its location. The definition extends to both tangible and intangible property, as well as to pecuniary advantages derived from or connected to criminal conduct. This wide-ranging definition[5] means that even a relatively small amount of criminal property has the potential to contaminate a significantly larger asset or group of assets. For instance, if an individual saves money or reduces expenses through criminal activity, that saving constitutes criminal property. Any property subsequently purchased by that individual could also be deemed

2 Chiu, I. and Wilson, J., *Banking Law and Regulation* (Oxford University Press, 2019), p. 679.

3 *The National Crime Agency v N & Anor (Rev 1)* [2017] EWCA Civ 253 at [9].

4 This exception is provided for under sections 327(2C), 328(5), 329(2C), and 339A of POCA.

5 "*It will therefore be seen that the concept of 'criminal property' is not only very broadly expressed, but it is a fluid one which depends on the state of mind of the alleged offender. The property in question must not only be or represent a benefit from someone's criminal conduct, but the alleged offender must know or suspect that to be the case at the time of carrying out one of the activities prohibited by sections 327 to 329. This means that the same property can be criminal property in the hands of A but not criminal property in the hands of B, depending on their respective states of mind*". in *World Uyghur Congress, R (On the Application Of) v National Crime Agency* [2024] EWCA Civ 715 at [31].

criminal property, as the purchase may have been financed by those illicit savings. The reach of such "extension" was considered in *R v Ahmad* [2014] UKSC 36, where the defendants, convicted of substantial VAT fraud, contested the extent of confiscation orders requiring them to pay amounts equivalent to the entire benefit derived from the fraud, which exceeded their direct financial gain. The Supreme Court upheld the confiscation orders, affirming POCA's broad reach in financial crime cases, and established a precedent for recovering proceeds that reflect the overall benefit to the criminal enterprise rather than being limited to direct financial receipt by individuals.

However, Section 183 of ECCTA 2023 introduced new exemptions to the principal money laundering offences under sections 327, 328, and 329 of POCA, which permit a credit institution to act on behalf of a customer in operating an account or accounts, even where the firm knows or suspects that part – but not all – of the funds or property held constitutes criminal property. This could include actions such as enabling a customer to access money or other property.

These provisions are particularly relevant in situations where a firm holds funds or property for a customer but cannot identify the specific elements of the assets that are criminal in origin. The exemptions do not apply where an action by the firm would reduce the value of the remaining funds or property to below the amount known or suspected to be criminal. In such instances, the firm must submit a request for a Defence Against Money Laundering for the value of the criminal property. Although these exemptions can be used repeatedly for the same account or customer, they cannot be applied to the same transaction. As a result, the exemptions allow for a measured approach to mixed-property transactions, ensuring that the suspected portion is not dissipated while enabling access to the remainder. The mixed-property exemption operates alongside the previously mentioned *de minimis* exemption for low-value transactions.[6]

Under POCA, it is a defence to each of the principal money laundering offences set out in sections 327(2)(a), 328(2)(a), and 329(2)(a) if a person makes an "authorised disclosure" within the meaning of section 338 and obtains "appropriate consent" as defined in section 335. An authorised disclosure, as provided in section 338, involves a disclosure by the alleged offender to a constable, customs officer, or nominated officer, indicating that the relevant property is criminal property. This disclosure must ordinarily be made before the commission of the act, which would otherwise amount to an offence under sections 327, 328, or 329 unless there is a reasonable excuse for failing to make the disclosure beforehand, in which case it must be made as soon as practicable thereafter, as specified in section 338(3).[7] In practical terms, authorised disclosures are usually made to the United Kingdom Financial Intelligence Unit (**FIU**), which operates as part of the National Crime Agency (**NCA**). The FIU functions as an autonomous operational unit tasked with the collection, analysis, and dissemination of intelligence received through suspicious activity reports (**SAR**s). Importantly, there is no requirement for suspicion to be clear, firmly grounded, or directed at specific facts, nor does it need to be based on reasonable grounds. Rather, there must be some degree of satisfaction – less than belief but greater than mere speculation. This principle was reinforced in *David Lonsdale v National Westminster Bank Plc* [2018] EWHC 1843 (QB).[8] Thus, the test incorporates both

6 See explanatory notes: https://publications.parliament.uk/pa/bills/cbill/58-03/0154/en/220154en.pdf (accessed in March 2025).

7 *The National Crime Agency v N & Anor (Rev 1)* [2017] EWCA Civ 253 at [16] and [17].

8 Ibid. at [56]: "*suspicion under POCA is a purely subjective matter. It does not matter whether or not there are reasonable grounds for that suspicion, provided that it is a genuinely held suspicion. The defendant must think that there is a possibility, which is more than fanciful, that the relevant facts exist. A vague feeling of unease would not suffice. But the statute does not require the suspicion to be 'clear' or 'firmly grounded and targeted on specific facts'; or based upon 'reasonable grounds'*".

subjective and objective elements. If a member of staff of a bank genuinely holds a suspicion, they are required to report it, irrespective of whether a reasonable person would have done the same. Conversely, if an honest and reasonable person operating within the regulated sector ought to have formed a suspicion under the circumstances, the member of staff is equally obliged to report.[9] Additional guidance on this subject is provided in sections 6.10 to 6.17 of Part 1 of the Joint Money Laundering Steering Group guidance, which addresses the prevention of money laundering and the combating of terrorist financing.

Once a member of staff determines that they have the requisite knowledge or suspicion of money laundering, the next step is to evaluate whether any of the applicable exemptions or defences under POCA are relevant to the situation. If, after this assessment, the staff member concludes that a report is necessary, they must submit it to their firm's Money Laundering Reporting Officer (**MLRO**). It is then the responsibility of the MLRO to determine whether a disclosure to the NCA is required and, if so, to submit a SAR in compliance with statutory obligations. No offence is committed under sections 327 to 329 or sections 330 or 331 of POCA if two conditions are satisfied. First, the member of staff must know or reasonably believe that the relevant criminal conduct occurred in a specific country or territory outside the United Kingdom. Second, the conduct in question must not have been unlawful under the laws of that country or territory at the time it took place.

Privileged Circumstances

No offence for failing to report under sections 330 or 331 of POCA is committed if the information that gives rise to a staff member's knowledge or suspicion was obtained in "privileged circumstances". Privileged circumstances arise when the information is communicated to the staff member in their capacity as a "professional legal adviser", including an in-house counsel,[10] by a client in connection with the provision of legal advice, by a person seeking legal advice, or by a party in relation to actual or contemplated legal proceedings.

For example, if a bank employee consults an in-house lawyer to determine whether a report should be made to the MLRO, any information disclosed in that context would fall within the privileged circumstances exemption. However, this protection would not extend to information received from an external party, such as a counterparty to a transaction. Importantly, the privileged circumstances exemption under POCA is broader than legal professional privilege. It applies not only to lawyers but also to other professional advisers, including accountants, tax advisers, and auditors, provided the information is obtained within the specified circumstances. However, the exemption does not apply if the communication is made with the intention of furthering a criminal purpose, whether by the client or any other individual.

9 Additional guidance on this subject is provided in sections 6.10 to 6.17 of Part 1 of the Joint Money Laundering Steering Group guidance, which addresses the prevention of money laundering and the combating of terrorist financing, see www.jmlsg.org.uk/guidance/current-guidance/ (accessed in March 2025).

10 One should note that pursuant to Case C-550/07 P, *Akzo Nobel Chemicals and Akcros Chemicals v. Commission* [2010] E.C.R. I-8301 in the EU legal professional privilege would only cover written communications exchanged between a company and an independent lawyer; i.e., a lawyer, registered with the Bar of a European Economic Area Member State, who is not bound to the client by a relationship of employment (an external counsel and not an in-house lawyer).

It is also crucial to note that the privileged circumstances exemption does not extend to the principal money laundering offences set out in sections 327 to 329 of POCA, which apply universally. If a planned transaction or course of action by the bank would constitute one of these offences, disclosure to the NCA under section 338 of POCA remains mandatory. In such cases, even if the reporting obligations under sections 330 or 331 are not triggered, the bank must still request a "defence against money laundering" to ensure compliance with legal and regulatory requirements.

Having determined that authorised disclosure may be appropriate and submitted a SAR if the step that needs to be taken in relation to a customer's transaction or matter would fall within sections 327 to 329 of POCA, a credit institution (through its members of staff) will then need "appropriate consent" before taking that step. Appropriate consent, under section 335 of POCA, may be either expressly given or deemed to have been given; in essence, it refers to an express or deemed confirmation by the NCA or the police that a defence to a principal money laundering offence exists in the event that the proposed activity is undertaken.

Deemed consent can arise in two distinct circumstances. First, if the person making the authorised disclosure does not receive a response within seven days, beginning with the first working day following the disclosure (referred to as "the notice period"), then consent is deemed to have been granted pursuant to section 335(3). Secondly, if the express refusal of consent is communicated within the notice period, a further 31-day "moratorium period" begins on the date when the refusal is received. If no further notice is given to the disclosing party within this moratorium period, consent is again deemed to have been provided. Actual consent may, however, be given at any time during either the notice period or the moratorium period.

These procedural requirements were aptly summarised by case law:

> *Part 7 of POCA Parliament has laid down the relevant procedure and that where a bank suspects the money in the customer's account is criminal property and freezes an account, ordinarily the court should not intervene during the course of the 7 day notice period and 31 day moratorium period. Parliament has entrusted to the NCA the task of deciding whether consent should be given to the carrying out of instructions and to consequent transactions following authorised disclosure. It has also laid down a timetable for that to be done, a timetable which this court has described as being both a "workable" and a "reasonable" balance of conflicting interests.*[11]

Shah and another v HSBC Private Bank (UK) Ltd [2010] EWCA Civ 31

The claimants (Shah) brought an action for damages against HSBC for breach of contract. Shah was an account holder with H and conducted business in Zimbabwe. Over a seven-month period, Shah instructed HSBC on four occasions to transfer funds exceeding $28 million from their account. HSBC, suspecting that the funds constituted criminal property, filed a SAR with the NCA predecessor, the Serious Organised Crime Agency (**SOCA**), as required under POCA, and sought consent to carry out the transactions. Once SOCA granted permission, HSBC processed each transfer. However, on each occasion, there was a delay while HSBC awaited consent. When queried, HSBC informed Shah that the delays were due to its compliance with statutory obligations without providing further details. Shah claimed that these delays caused significant

11 *The National Crime Agency v N & Anor (Rev 1)* [2017] EWCA Civ 253 at [58].

suspicion, which ultimately resulted in the seizure of their assets in Zimbabwe and a financial loss exceeding $330 million.

The central issues before the court were threefold. First, whether HSBC had a genuine suspicion that the transactions in question were connected to money laundering. Secondly, whether the delays arising from HSBC's actions resulted in any loss to Mr Shah. Thirdly, the court was required to consider whether HSBC was under any legal duty to provide Mr Shah with the information he had requested in relation to the transactions.

In its defence, HSBC argued that an implied term in the bank-customer contract allowed it to refuse to process payment instructions in circumstances where it suspected that a transaction involved money laundering and where consent under section 335 of POCA had not yet been granted. HSBC also denied any duty to disclose the information sought by Shah. It was contended that, even if such a duty existed, it was overridden by statutory obligations under sections 333 and 342 of POCA, which prohibit the disclosure of information that could amount to "tipping off" or otherwise prejudice an investigation.

In this context, it was held that "*There is an implied term in the contract that permitted the Defendant to refuse to execute payment instructions in the absence of "appropriate consent" under s.335 POCA where it suspected a transaction constituted money laundering*".[12] Furthermore, the bank was under no obligation to provide the customer with details of its disclosure to SOCA. Where providing such information could constitute a "tipping-off" offence under section 333 of POCA, the bank was legally required to withhold it:

> *The Defendant was not under a duty to provide the Claimants with the information sought. Further or alternatively the Defendant was obliged to refuse to provide the information where the Defendant, its servants or agents, in providing that information might contravene duties under ss.333 and/or 342 POCA.*[13]

Finally, the court held that HSBC's delay in executing the payment instructions did not cause any loss.

This case illustrates the challenges banks face when balancing AML responsibilities with client relationships, affirming the priority of compliance over contractual duties where suspicious activities arise.

As noted previously, it is important to consider that under section 333A of POCA, it is an offence to disclose to any person that a SAR has been submitted to the NCA, the police, or HM Revenue & Customs, or to reveal that an investigation into allegations of money laundering is underway. Such disclosure constitutes an offence if, as a matter of fact, it is likely to prejudice an investigation that is being conducted or might be conducted, regardless of whether the person making the disclosure knows or suspects that it is likely to cause such prejudice.[14] This offence is commonly referred to as "tipping off".[15]

12 Ibid. at [336].
13 Ibid. at [238].
14 Chiu, I. and Wilson, J., *Banking Law and Regulation* (Oxford University Press, 2019), p. 713.
15 In *David Lonsdale v National Westminster Bank Plc* [2018] EWHC 1843 (QB), Mr Lonsdale applied to the High Court to inspect SARs submitted by the bank. This application arose in the context of proceedings for breach of contract, defamation, and breach of the Data Protection Act 1998. The breach of contract claim concerned the bank's failure to execute Mr Lonsdale's instructions following the freezing of his accounts.

In addition, section 342 creates an offence of 'prejudicing an investigation'. A person commits an offence if he knows or suspects that a money laundering investigation is being or is about to be conducted, and he makes a disclosure which is likely to prejudice the investigation.[16]

In *R v Anwoir* [2008] EWCA Crim 1354, the Court of Appeal addressed the challenge of proving that property is criminal in nature without identifying a specific predicate offence. Here, the court affirmed that the prosecution does not need to specify the crime that generated the proceeds but must show that the property could only have originated from criminal activity. This case highlighted POCA's expansive scope in targeting criminal property. *R v Hussain* [2010] EWCA Crim 1627 illustrated the application of POCA's civil recovery regime. Although criminal charges could not sbe brought against Hussain, a civil recovery order was secured, allowing authorities to confiscate assets obtained through fraud. This case underscores POCA's flexibility in addressing financial crime beyond traditional criminal prosecution.

The Singapore International Commercial Court on POCA and SWIFT Instructions

In *Malayan Banking Bhd v Barclays Bank PLC* [2019] SGHC(I) 04, the Singapore International Commercial Court held that Barclays Bank had entered into an implied contract with Maybank to make the payment in accordance with the previously transmitted payment instruction and was not entitled to refuse payment subsequently on the basis of a risk of incurring liability under POC in circumstances where there was a suspected fraud in relation to it. It was further held that Barclays had failed to establish

---

Mr Lonsdale held a mandate for seven accounts with the bank. In March 2017, the bank froze one of these accounts for eight working days, a delay reflecting the time likely required to seek consent from the NCA after submitting one or more SARs. Subsequently, in December 2017, the bank froze additional accounts, leaving Mr Lonsdale unable to access any funds. He initiated legal proceedings on the three causes of action, and in March and April 2018, the bank proceeded to close all seven accounts.

The High Court ultimately ordered the bank to permit Mr Lonsdale to inspect each of the SARs submitted to the NCA in relation to his accounts. The decision was based on the following reasoning:

i) According to the Civil Procedure Rules (CPR 31.14), the default position is that a claimant should be allowed to inspect documents referred to in the defence and counterclaim. As the SARs were referenced by the bank, they fell within this principle.
ii) The bank's argument that complying with the order might require it to commit an offence under section 333A or section 342 of POCA lacked evidentiary support. Furthermore, even if inspection could potentially prejudice an ongoing investigation, the court's order, consistent with a request from the NCA, provided a 14-day period for the bank and the NCA to consider whether objections applied to specific parts of the SARs rather than to the entirety of the documents.
iii) There was no evidence to suggest that the confidentiality of the SARs remained necessary. The SARs had been submitted approximately 16 and seven months, respectively, before the court hearing, and no indication was provided that they were still subject to any ongoing investigative needs.
iv) Inspection of the SARs was deemed essential for the fair resolution of the claim. Their content was directly relevant to determining whether the bank's employees had a genuine suspicion of money laundering, which was a central issue in Mr Lonsdale's breach of contract claim. The SARs were also key documents in the defamation claim, as they were the primary communications alleged to be defamatory.

The court concluded that the question of whether the bank genuinely suspected Mr Lonsdale of engaging in money laundering – a defence to the breach of contract claim – was an evidential matter best resolved at trial. This would enable the court to assess the issue in the context of the facts established at trial, rather than addressing it in the abstract at an earlier stage.

16 *Shah v HSBC Private Bank (UK) Ltd* [2012] EWHC 1283 (QB) at [32].

the existence of a market practice that could be implied by custom or usage as a term of the implied contract:

> *I accept that, prima facie, the relevant person at Barclays who should be produced to give evidence of suspicion of such activity and potential liability is the nominated officer, as set out in Shah and another v HSBC Private Bank (UK) Ltd [2011] EWCA Civ 1154 at [46]–[47], and that Barclays' evidence of the basis of anything other than the initial suspicion, which led to cancellation of the MT 103 STP and the MT 202 COV on the basis of the messages received, is not cogent.*[17]

3 BRIBERY ACT 2010

Given the financial industry's role in facilitating global trade and investment, banks are uniquely positioned to either enable or prevent corrupt activities. As a result, the Bribery Act 2010 imposes significant obligations on banks to prevent bribery in their operations, including those related to their clients, intermediaries, and employees. This regulatory regime extends beyond national borders, reflecting the international scope of modern banking practices.[18] It should be noted that, generally, "*bribery is committed where one person makes, or agrees to make, a payment to the agent of another person with whom he is dealing without the knowledge and consent of the agent's principal*".[19]

3.1 Scope and Application in Banking

The Bribery Act 2010 significantly impacts banks, applying to individuals and organisations involved in both public and private bribery.[20] There are four main offences under the Act relevant to banks: active bribery, passive bribery, bribery of foreign officials, and failure to prevent bribery by commercial organisations.

The offence of offering or giving a bribe (active bribery)[21] may be relevant in banking when financial or non-financial incentives are used to secure business or influence decisions on loans, contracts, or investments. Banks must ensure that employees, agents, and subsidiaries do not engage in bribery, whether dealing with private clients or government officials. To this effect, rigorous anti-bribery compliance is required to prevent such practices.[22]

The accepting of bribes (passive bribery) is also sanctioned;[23] this may pose a significant threat to banks dealing with substantial funds and international transactions. The banking sector's involvement in cross-border financing, project finance, and sovereign debt exposes it to risks of bribery involving foreign public officials. This danger is particularly pronounced in high-risk jurisdictions or sectors prone to corruption. In *SFO v. Glencore Energy (UK) Ltd*

17 Ibid. at [108].
18 Wood, P., *Project Finance, Securitisations and Subordinated Debt* (Sweet & Maxwell, 2019) at [5-039].
19 *Ross River Ltd v Cambridge City FC* [2008] 1 All ER 1004.
20 It should also be noted that in addition to criminal law consequences, bribery has also civil law implications. A claimant seeking a remedy in cases where a bribe is alleged to have been paid may, depending on the specific facts, have other potential causes of action available, such as a claim for breach of fiduciary duty: see *Novoship (UK) Ltd and others v Mikhaylyuk and others* [2012] EWHC 3586 (Comm), Christopher Clarke J at [104].
21 Section 1.
22 Cheung, R., 'Deferred Prosecution Agreements: Cooperation and Confession' (2018) 77(1) *The Cambridge Law Journal* 12–15.
23 Section 2.

[2022] EWCR 2, Glencore Energy UK Ltd (Glencore) was investigated for widespread bribery practices concerning

> bribery offences either committed in Nigeria, or with the intent of *"intending . . . to induce officials of the Nigerian National Petroleum Corporation to perform their functions improperly, or reward them for so doing" in relation to allocation of oil trades and the underlying cargoes. The other five counts on the indictment concern other countries in West Africa.*

This case marks the first instance since the introduction of the Bribery Act 2010 in which a corporate entity has been convicted for the active authorisation of bribery rather than solely for a failure to prevent it:

> *The defendant company played a leading role in organised and planned unlawful activity. . . . For most of the counts, these were not isolated acts of bribery that occurred on single occasions. It is clear that for some counts, the same techniques were used month after month, for the whole period covered by the relevant count in the indictment. Bribery was clearly part of the culture for a number of personnel on the West Africa desk.*[24]

Glencore was sentenced to a total fine of £280,965,092.95 after pleading guilty to seven counts of bribery under the Bribery Act 2010. Mr Justice Fraser, in sentencing Glencore, commented: "*Bribery is a highly corrosive offence. It quite literally corrupts people and companies, and spreads like a disease*".

Section 6 criminalises offering or promising advantages to foreign officials to influence them in their capacity. International banks must ensure their dealings with state-owned enterprises and government entities comply with this provision. The *Serious Fraud Office v Rolls-Royce plc and Rolls-Royce Energy Systems Inc* [2017] Lloyd's Rep. F.C. 249 case,[25] though involving the aerospace industry, exemplifies the significant penalties associated with bribery abroad.

Finally, commercial organisations that fail to prevent bribery by associated persons face strict liability.[26] Banks must have "adequate procedures" to prevent bribery by employees, agents, and third-party partners, including financial intermediaries and consultants. *R v Skansen Interiors Ltd*[27] underscores the necessity for banks to implement comprehensive anti-bribery controls, including client and intermediary due diligence, regular risk assessments, and training. Such necessity is reinforced by the Ministry of Justice's Guidance on the Bribery Act,[28] which outlines essential principles for banks to follow under Section 7 of the Bribery Act 2010 to ensure compliance.[29]

The *Serious Fraud Office v Standard Bank PLC* [2015] Case No U20150854[30] case illustrates the consequences of inadequate controls, as Standard Bank was required to pay fines and improve its compliance program following a Deferred Prosecution Agreement for failing to prevent bribery by a third party in Tanzania. However, to Standard Bank's credit, Lord Justice Leveson provided a comprehensive account of the bank's cooperation with the SFO. He emphasised that the bank had reported its suspicions to the authorities "within days" of

24 See Sentencing Remarks of Mr Justice Fraser on 3 November 2022, at [9], available at www.judiciary.uk/wp-content/uploads/2022/11/Sentencing-Remarks-Glencore.pdf (accessed in March 2025).

25 See www.judiciary.uk/wp-content/uploads/2017/01/sfo-v-rolls-royce.pdf (accessed in March 2025).

26 Section 7 of the Bribery Act 2010.

27 Unreported, Southwark Crown Court (2018). See The Bribery Act 2010: post legislative scrutiny, Chapter 6: Failure to prevent bribery (section 7), at [220], see https://publications.parliament.uk/pa/ld201719/ldselect/ldbribact/303/30309.htm at [277] (accessed in March 2025).

28 See https://assets.publishing.service.gov.uk/media/5d80cfc3ed915d51e9aff85a/bribery-act-2010-guidance.pdf (accessed in March 2025).

29 The inclusion of anti-bribery provisions in contracts could form a part of this strategy, although it will not on its own automatically constitute an adequate procedures defence.

30 See www.judiciary.uk/wp-content/uploads/2015/11/sfo-v-standard-bank_Final_1.pdf (accessed in March 2025).

becoming aware of them, even before its solicitors had commenced, let alone completed, their own internal investigation. Lord Justice Leveson also noted the bank's proactive approach in conducting an investigation through its advisers. This level of cooperation was a key factor in the resolution of the case.

Moreover, in principle, "*failing to prevent bribery is less egregious than an offence of bribery or corruption not least because although it represents a serious failure of corporate governance, the operative minds of the company are not involved in the predicate offence*".[31]

3.2 Extraterritorial Application of the Bribery Act in Banking

A significant aspect of the Bribery Act is its extraterritorial reach, applying to any business with UK operations, even if bribery occurs outside the UK. Multinational banks with UK operations must ensure global compliance with the Act. In *Serious Fraud Office v Sweett Group PLC* (2016),[32] a construction company was prosecuted for failing to prevent bribery by an agent in the UAE, highlighting the Act's global scope. The only defence available to an organisation facing prosecution under Section 7 of the Bribery Act 2010 is to prove, on the balance of probabilities, that it had "adequate procedures" in place at the relevant time to prevent bribery. In the case of *Sweett Group*, the company was unable to rely on this defence due to the inadequacy of its control framework over the activities of its subsidiary, CSI. Reports produced by accounting firm KPMG in 2011 and 2014 highlighted numerous weaknesses and deficiencies in CSI's anti-bribery systems and financial controls. Despite these findings, neither Sweett nor CSI acted to address the identified issues.

4 ANTI-MONEY LAUNDERING FRAMEWORK

The UK's anti-money laundering (**AML**) framework has evolved over decades, largely in response to global standards set by the Financial Action Task Force (**FATF**).[33] Under this framework, financial institutions are obligated to establish comprehensive risk management protocols, report suspicious transactions, and retain accurate customer records to aid in AML compliance.

In addition to POCA, the MLRs,[34] which implemented the EU AML Directives[35] into UK legislation, impose comprehensive AML and counter-terrorism financing (**CTF**) obligations on financial institutions and other regulated sectors in the UK. A core requirement under the

31 Per Sir Brian Leveson P in *Serious Fraud Office v Rolls-Royce plc and Rolls-Royce Energy Systems Inc* [2017] Lloyd's Rep. F.C. 249 at [93].

32 (Crown Ct. (Southwark), 19 February 2016). The SFO opened a criminal investigation into Sweett Group plc in July 2014 in relation to its activities in the United Arab Emirates. The company was charged with an offence under section 7 of the Bribery Act, to which it pleaded guilty on 18 December 2015. On 19 February 2016, it was ordered to pay £2.25 million in fines and confiscation. See https://publications.parliament.uk/pa/ld201719/ldselect/ldbribact/303/30310.htm at [272] (accessed in March 2025).

33 The Financial Action Task Force (**FATF**) is the global money laundering and terrorist financing watchdog. It sets international standards that aim to prevent these illegal activities and the harm they cause to society. See www.fatf-gafi.org/en/home.html (accessed in March 2025).

34 The Money Laundering, Terrorist Financing and Transfer of Funds (Information on the Payer) Regulations 2017 S.I. 2017 No. 692.

35 The latest directive, which was implemented in the UK prior to Brexit, was Directive (EU) 2018/843 of the European Parliament and of the Council of 30 May 2018 amending Directive (EU) 2015/849 on the prevention of the use of the financial system for the purposes of money laundering or terrorist financing, and amending Directives 2009/138/EC and 2013/36/EU.

MLRs is performing adequate customer due diligence, where regulated entities must verify clients' identities, understand the nature of their business relationships, and conduct ongoing monitoring. In higher-risk situations, such as dealings with politically exposed persons (**PEPs**) or jurisdictions with weak AML controls, enhanced due diligence is required.[36]

Under the MLRs, SARs are an essential mechanism. Financial institutions must submit SARs to the NCA whenever they suspect money laundering or terrorist financing activities. This duty aligns with POCA's Section 330, which mandates the reporting of known or suspected money laundering. The MLRs adopt a risk-based approach, encouraging businesses to assess and manage money laundering and terrorism financing risks specific to their sector, implementing suitable controls based on this assessment.

The case of *Shah v HSBC Private Bank (UK) Ltd* [2012] EWHC 1283 (QB) underscored the legal protections available to institutions complying with AML regulations and reinforced the necessity for financial institutions to adhere to their reporting obligations when concerns about money laundering arise. *Shah* clarified that banks must prioritise statutory AML compliance over clients' instructions or contractual obligations.

4.1 MLRs and Cryptoasset Businesses

The FCA is the AML, CTF, and counter-proliferation financing supervisor for certain UK cryptoasset businesses under the MLRs. For the purposes of the MLRs, "cryptoasset" means a cryptographically secured digital representation of value or contractual rights that uses a form of distributed ledger technology and can be transferred, stored, or traded electronically.[37] Businesses within the scope of the regulations are referred to as "relevant persons". Regulation 8(2) and (3) of the MLRs list the types of businesses classified as relevant persons. These include "cryptoasset exchange providers" and "custodian wallet providers". It is important to note that cryptoasset exchange providers and custodian wallet providers are only considered relevant persons if they are operating in the course of a business carried out within the UK, as specified in Regulation 8(1) of the MLRs.

5 ECCTA

ECCTA represents a substantial enhancement to the UK's financial crime framework, particularly by advancing corporate liability and transparency standards. The Act introduces significant new provisions aimed at combating economic crime, thereby reinforcing the accountability of companies and financial institutions.

5.1 Failure to Prevent Offence

ECCTA expands upon existing AML legislation by introducing a new corporate liability for economic crime. Under this provision, companies must demonstrate they have implemented "adequate procedures" to prevent economic crime; failure to do so may result in criminal liability. The aim is to encourage organisations to proactively establish robust internal policies and controls to mitigate the risks of financial crime.

36 Chiu, I. and Wilson, J., *Banking Law and Regulation* (Oxford University Press, 2019), p. 697.
37 This includes a right to, or interest in, the cryptoasset (regulation 14A(3)(c), MLRs).

This provision draws on the framework established by the Bribery Act 2010, which introduced similar requirements to prevent bribery within corporate operations. The Act's failure to prevent offence reflects a growing trend in corporate liability, with emphasis on proactive compliance and accountability for both corporate governance and employee conduct.

Although predating the ECCTA, the case of *R v Skansen Interiors Limited, unreported* [2018][38] provides an instructive precedent for the Act's "failure to prevent" provision. In this case, Skansen Interiors, a small business, was prosecuted under Section 7 of the Bribery Act 2010 for failure to prevent bribery. Despite its limited resources, Skansen was found guilty because it lacked adequate procedures to prevent bribery within its operations (despite some measures being in place). The *Skansen* case serves as a critical example of how courts may apply similar principles under the ECCTA, holding companies accountable regardless of size or resources, provided they fail to meet compliance expectations.

The decision also serves as a reminder that companies which act responsibly by reporting criminal conduct and cooperating with the authorities will not automatically avoid prosecution. In *Skansen*, the Crown Prosecution Service justified the prosecution on the grounds that it would send a clear message to the industry about the critical importance of implementing effective anti-bribery procedures.

5.2 Corporate Transparency

A central tenet of the ECCTA is the requirement for enhanced transparency around beneficial ownership. The act builds upon the foundation laid by the Companies Act 2006, which mandates that companies maintain a Register of People with Significant Control (**PSC**), a key tool in identifying individuals with material control over corporate entities. This complements the obligations introduced under the Small Business, Enterprise and Employment Act 2015 to ensure that individuals cannot obscure their identities behind complex corporate structures.

The PSC regime, which was extended by the Fourth Money Laundering Directive (EU),[39] requires companies to keep a public register of individuals who hold more than 25% of shares, voting rights, or the ability to control the appointment or removal of the board of directors. The PSC aims to prevent criminals from concealing their identities behind opaque corporate structures. This reinforces the need for companies to engage in comprehensive due diligence when onboarding clients or entering into business relationships, a fundamental component of AML compliance.

Under the ECCTA, any changes in the beneficial ownership of a company must be reported to Companies House within 14 days,[40] ensuring that regulators and law enforcement agencies have real-time information about the individuals who control UK companies, thus reducing the risk of money laundering through shell companies or complex ownership structures. These reporting obligations align with FATF recommendations on beneficial ownership transparency, ensuring that the UK remains at the forefront of international AML efforts.

38 A detailed report can be found in the transcript of Iskander Fernandez (Q203) within the House of Lords Bribery Act 2010 Committee, Corrected oral evidence: Bribery Act 2010, Tuesday 11 December 2018 10.30 am available at https://committees.parliament.uk/oralevidence/8818/html/ (accessed in March 2025).

39 Directive (EU) 2015/849 of the European Parliament and of the Council of 20 May 2015 on the prevention of the use of the financial system for the purposes of money laundering or terrorist financing, amending Regulation (EU) No 648/2012 of the European Parliament and of the Council, and repealing Directive 2005/60/EC of the European Parliament and of the Council and Commission Directive 2006/70/EC.

40 Companies House Forms PSC01 – PSC09 should be used to notify Companies House of all changes to PSC information.

Under the ECCTA, companies that fail to register significant controllers or provide false information may face prosecution.[41]

6 REGULATORY REQUIREMENTS AND ENFORCEMENT

The FCA plays a central role in ensuring that credit institutions comply with financial crime regulations, including anti-bribery and anti-corruption measures. Operating under FSMA, the FCA has extensive powers to supervise, investigate, and enforce actions against banks failing to meet regulatory standards. The FCA's framework emphasises robust systems and controls to prevent financial crime, requiring banks to comply with both the Bribery Act and broader financial crime regulations. The FCA also has enforcement powers under FSMA to impose fines, restrict activities, and sanction banks that fail to comply with regulatory requirements. The FCA collaborates with other agencies, including the Serious Fraud Office (**SFO**) and the NCA, in financial crime investigations and prosecutions. An example of such collaboration is the final notice[42] dated 30 January 2017, pursuant to which the FCA imposed a fine of £163 million on Deutsche Bank for failing to maintain AML controls in a "mirror trading" scheme, where clients moved billions of dollars out of Russia undetected. The FCA found that Deutsche Bank's monitoring of suspicious transactions was inadequate, reinforcing the importance of a robust compliance framework for detecting and preventing both money laundering and bribery in banks.

FCA Enforcement Action – Standard Chartered Bank

In 2019, the FCA imposed a significant fine of £102.2 million on Standard Chartered Bank for serious deficiencies in its AML controls. One of the key issues identified was the bank's failure to implement effective risk assessments for PEPs and high-risk jurisdictions, where the risks of bribery and corruption were significantly elevated. Standard Chartered also lacked sufficient oversight and monitoring mechanisms for transactions involving high-risk clients, many of whom were based in jurisdictions with a known prevalence of financial crime. This failure exposed the bank to substantial bribery risks under both the Bribery Act 2010 and broader financial crime regulations. Additionally, the bank's systems for detecting and reporting suspicious transactions were inadequate, in direct contravention of its obligations under POCA. By failing to monitor and report suspicious activity properly, Standard Chartered breached AML regulations and key provisions of the FCA Handbook (SYSC 6.3).

The FCA's enforcement action resulted in one of the largest financial penalties ever imposed in the UK for financial crime failings, underscoring the regulator's commitment to enforcing rigorous anti-bribery and AML standards within the banking sector. Beyond the financial penalty, Standard Chartered was required to overhaul its internal systems and controls, enhance staff training programmes, and implement stricter due diligence measures for high-risk customers.

This case serves as a clear warning to financial institutions about the FCA's stringent oversight and the severe consequences of failing to maintain effective anti-bribery

41 Under Sections 171 to 173.
42 See www.fca.org.uk/publication/final-notices/deutsche-bank-2017.pdf (accessed in March 2025).

and financial crime controls. It also reinforces the expectation that banks must conduct comprehensive risk assessments, apply enhanced due diligence to high-risk clients, and continuously monitor transactions to mitigate bribery and financial crime risks.

The Senior Managers and Certification Regime (**SMCR**), which, as discussed in Chapter 4, addresses the regulation of senior management within financial institutions, is intended to strengthen individual accountability and enhance governance structures within firms.

The SMCR applies to UK-authorised firms and imposes stringent obligations on senior managers to identify, manage, and mitigate risks, including financial crime and bribery risks, within their designated areas of oversight. The Senior Managers Regime requires the most senior individuals within a firm to obtain regulatory approval from the FCA and/or PRA. These individuals are assigned clear responsibilities and may be held personally liable for misconduct, including failures related to anti-bribery controls.[43]

The Certification Regime, which covers specific functions (Certification Functions) that aren't Senior Management Functions, applies to individuals in roles that have the potential to cause significant harm to the firm or its customers, including those responsible for financial crime risk management. These individuals must be certified by their firm as fit and proper,[44] with a particular focus on bribery prevention. In addition, the Conduct Rules apply to most employees within a financial institution, setting a baseline for ethical and professional conduct that directly influences how bribery risks are managed.

6.1 Bribery Risks Under the SMCR

Under the SMCR, senior managers are explicitly responsible for ensuring that their firms comply with the Bribery Act 2010 and other anti-bribery regulations. Bribery risks are particularly relevant for financial institutions that deal with high-risk clients or operate in jurisdictions with a high propensity for corruption.

The SMCR requires senior managers to demonstrate that they have taken "*reasonable steps*" to prevent financial crime, including bribery. This includes implementing effective internal controls, conducting thorough risk assessments, and ensuring that staff are adequately trained in anti-bribery measures. The failure of a senior manager to implement adequate procedures to prevent bribery could result in personal liability under the regime.

The FCA has demonstrated its willingness to take enforcement action against senior managers who fail to meet their obligations under the SMCR. The regime empowers the FCA to impose sanctions on senior managers for misconduct, including fines, suspensions, and prohibitions from holding senior management roles.

On 10 February 2022, the FCA issued a final notice[45] to Julius Baer International Ltd, imposing a fine of £18,022,500 for its involvement in facilitating finder's arrangements between Bank Julius Baer and an employee of several Yukos Group companies. The FCA concluded that Julius Baer International must have been aware of the significant risk that, by

43 Chiu, I. and Wilson, J., *Banking Law and Regulation* (Oxford University Press, 2019), p. 520.

44 See FCA Handbook, FIT 1.3 Assessing fitness and propriety, FIT 1.3.1B: "In the FCA's view, the most important considerations will be the person's: (1) honesty, integrity and reputation; (2) competence and capability; and (3) financial soundness".

45 See Final Notice 139179: www.fca.org.uk/publication/final-notices/julius-baer-international-limited-2022.pdf (accessed in March 2025)

entering into these arrangements, it might be facilitating or participating in financial crime. In particular, "*JBI failed to ensure that it had adequate policies and procedures in place to identify and manage the risks arising in relation to Finders relationships connected to its clients*".[46]

Whether the responsibilities of senior managers in overseeing the bank's conduct in high-risk transactions translate into criminal culpability for the bank, however, could be a different matter under a criminal law analysis.

In *The Serious Fraud Office v Barclays Plc & Anor* [2018] EWHC 3055 (QB), the SFO applied for permission to prefer a voluntary bill of indictment against Barclays. In the aftermath of the 2008 banking crisis, the bank sought to avoid a government bailout by securing fresh injections of capital from alternative sources. Various Qatari entities agreed to provide capital on two occasions in 2008. The bank issued formal prospectuses and subscription agreements, which stated that the Qatari entities would receive a 1.5% commission. However, certain bank directors also arranged two advisory service agreements with the Qatari entities, under which the entities agreed to provide unspecified services in exchange for substantial payments. The SFO argued that the advisory agreements were sham arrangements designed to conceal the provision of higher commissions to the Qatari entities than had been disclosed to the public or to Barclays' shareholders. The SFO further contended that the advisory agreements were interdependent with the prospectuses and subscription agreements, thereby rendering the statements in those documents false. Additionally, it was alleged that the directors intentionally concealed the true purpose of the advisory agreements from the Barclays' board and board sub-committees.

The court examined the principles governing the attribution of the acts, knowledge, or state of mind of individuals within a company to the company itself, thereby potentially rendering it criminally liable. It was held that the dishonest acts of certain bank directors could not be attributed to the bank,[47] as the directors were not the "directing mind and will" of the bank with respect to the relevant acts. The board of directors had retained ultimate authority over these matters:

> *It simply is not acceptable, in my opinion, for the SFO to regard the various resolutions of the Board and of the BFC as, in effect, mere pieces of paper. They are not: they reflect the level of delegation sanctioned by the appropriate organs of the company. Broad appeals to "the realities" and to the "de facto" position cannot overcome that in this case. This is not a matter of form over substance. Rather, in this case, the form is the substance. That the individuals had some degree of autonomy is not enough. It had to be shown, if criminal culpability was capable of being attributed to Barclays, that they had entire autonomy to do the deal in question; and that is not the case here.*[48]

6.2 Adequate Procedures Defence

The SMCR reinforces the obligation for financial institutions to demonstrate that they have "adequate procedures" in place to prevent bribery.[49] The Ministry of Justice has issued guidance on what constitutes adequate procedures, outlining key principles that firms must adhere to in order to mitigate bribery risks effectively.[50]

46 Ibid. at [2.13].
47 Ibid., Lord Justice Davis at [121].
48 Ibid., Lord Justice Davis at [122].
49 As required under Section 7 of the Bribery Act 2010.
50 See https://assets.publishing.service.gov.uk/media/5d80cfc3ed915d51e9aff85a/bribery-act-2010-guidance.pdf (accessed in March 2025).

A fundamental requirement is a top-level commitment, meaning that senior management must take a proactive stance in preventing bribery and communicate this commitment clearly to all employees. Risk assessment is equally critical, requiring firms to conduct comprehensive evaluations of the bribery risks they face and to ensure that these assessments are regularly reviewed.

Additionally, due diligence procedures must be in place to assess third parties with whom financial institutions conduct business, ensuring that appropriate safeguards are implemented to prevent bribery. Finally, ongoing monitoring and review of anti-bribery procedures is essential, allowing firms to verify that their policies remain effective, up to date, and fit for purpose.

7 THE FCA'S ROLE IN COMBATING FINANCIAL CRIME

The FCA's Financial Crime Guide, published in conjunction with its Handbook, provides banks with guidance on implementing anti-bribery measures. The Guide outlines key principles for managing bribery risks, such as conducting risk-based due diligence on clients, particularly those in high-risk jurisdictions, and ensuring that employees are trained to recognise and report suspicious activity. Banks must also establish clear policies for dealing with PEPs and high-risk sectors, as these are often associated with elevated bribery risks.

7.1 FCA Handbook and Financial Crime Compliance

The Senior Management Arrangements, Systems and Controls (**SYSC**) sourcebook within the FCA Handbook mandates banks to implement internal controls to prevent financial crime. SYSC 3.2.6R mandates that firms must have adequate systems and controls in place to prevent the risk of financial crime.

The Handbook's emphasis on financial crime compliance stems from the FCA's statutory objectives under FSMA, which include protecting consumers, enhancing the integrity of the financial system, and promoting competition. The FCA's interpretation of integrity encompasses preventing financial crime, where bribery poses a significant threat not only to individual institutions but to the UK's overall financial stability and reputation.

Under SYSC 6.1.1R, firms must establish, implement, and maintain adequate policies and procedures to ensure compliance with regulatory obligations to counter the risk of financial crime. This includes embedding a culture of compliance with appropriate training, risk management, and reporting mechanisms.

7.2 Anti-Bribery and the Bribery Act 2010

The FCA enforces compliance with the Bribery Act 2010 within regulated firms, ensuring that banks and financial institutions adhere to the legal requirements set out under the Act. Section 7 of the Bribery Act creates a corporate offence of failing to prevent bribery unless the organisation can demonstrate it had "adequate procedures" in place to prevent such misconduct.

The Ministry of Justice's Guidance[51] on the Bribery Act 2010 lays out six key principles for adequate procedures: proportionate procedures, top-level commitment, risk assessment,

51 See https://assets.publishing.service.gov.uk/media/5d80cfc3ed915d51e9aff85a/bribery-act-2010-guidance.pdf (accessed in March 2025).

due diligence, communication, and monitoring and review. The FCA Handbook's SYSC requirements closely align with these principles, reflecting the FCA's focus on ensuring that firms implement effective controls to combat bribery.

SYSC 6.3.7R and 6.3.8G specifically outline that financial firms must assess the risks associated with bribery and have policies and procedures in place to mitigate these risks. These measures should be tailored to the firm's size, nature of business, and geographical scope, recognising that firms operating in higher-risk jurisdictions or sectors will require more robust anti-bribery frameworks.

7.3 FCA's Enforcement Approach to Anti-Bribery Compliance

The FCA has broad enforcement powers under FSMA and uses these powers to sanction firms and individuals who fail to meet regulatory standards, including those related to financial crime. The FCA's enforcement approach to anti-bribery compliance is proactive, with a focus on both prevention and punishment.

The FCA's Financial Crime Guide[52] provides detailed guidance for firms on how to establish systems and controls to prevent financial crime, including bribery. The guide highlights that bribery risks often arise in the context of relationships with third-party agents, contractors, and suppliers, and firms must undertake thorough due diligence in these areas.

Failure to adequately address bribery risks can result in significant financial penalties, reputational damage, and the potential for criminal prosecution.

An FCA's Enforcement Action

The 2021 FCA's enforcement action[53] against **Credit Suisse** is an example of the consequences of shortcomings under the Bribery Act 2010.

Credit Suisse became implicated through its global emerging markets group, based in London, which engaged in trading foreign exchange products, bonds, derivatives, and structured financing, including syndications and the issuance of securities, for failings constituting breaches of Principles 2 and 3 of the FCA's Principles for Businesses and rule 6.1.1R of SYSC.[54]

The failings were tied to three transactions involving two infrastructure projects in Mozambique: one relating to coastal surveillance and the other to the creation of a tuna fishing industry within Mozambican waters. Credit Suisse arranged, facilitated, and provided funding for two loans totalling over USD $1.3 billion to finance these projects. Between October 2012 and March 2016, the FCA found that Credit Suisse failed to maintain adequate financial crime controls, policies, and procedures, including those related to unregulated activities such as corporate lending, to counter the risk of financial crime. The bank failed to sufficiently prioritise the mitigation of financial risks, including corruption risks, in its emerging markets business and lacked a coherent financial crime strategy, as demonstrated by the under-resourcing of its EMEA financial crime compliance team and procedural weaknesses in risk management.

52 See www.handbook.fca.org.uk/handbook/FCG.pdf (accessed in March 2025).
53 See www.fca.org.uk/publication/final-notices/credit-suisse-2021.pdf (accessed in March 2025).
54 See www.fca.org.uk/publication/final-notices/credit-suisse-2021.pdf (accessed in March 2025).

Moreover, senior individuals, committees, and control functions had sufficient information to appreciate the high risk of bribery and corruption associated with the Mozambican loans and a bond exchange tied to government-sponsored projects. Despite this, there was inadequate scrutiny, challenge, and investigation of the numerous warning signs.[55]

Significant kickbacks, estimated at over USD$50 million, were secretly paid by the contractor to members of the Credit Suisse deal team, including two managing directors, to secure the loans on more favourable terms. The Government of Mozambique claimed that the total amount of bribes paid in connection with the two loans was in the region of USD$137 million. Although these employees actively concealed the kickbacks, Credit Suisse's control functions and senior committees should have identified the numerous warning signs of corruption. These employees exploited weaknesses in the bank's approval processes, which lacked effective oversight and challenge, and deliberately withheld material information from colleagues.

The consequences of these tainted transactions were profound, leading to a debt crisis and economic harm for the people of Mozambique. The FCA determined that Credit Suisse failed to adequately prioritise the mitigation of financial risks, including corruption risks, within its emerging markets business.[56] The FCA deemed Credit Suisse's failings "extremely serious", noting that the inadequate consideration and approval of these transactions persisted over an extended period and involved senior individuals and control functions.

As a result, Credit Suisse was fined £147,190,200 for its failings, which formed part of a broader global resolution agreement totalling approximately USD$475 million. This action resulted in a settlement and qualified for a 30% discount under the FCA's executive settlement procedures. It also involved the US Department of Justice, the SEC, and the Swiss Financial Market Supervisory Authority. As part of the resolution, Credit Suisse agreed to write off USD$200 million of debt owed by the Republic of Mozambique.

This case underscores the critical importance of financial institutions implementing robust governance, due diligence, and financial crime risk management frameworks, particularly in high-risk markets.

8 COUNTER-TERRORIST FINANCING FRAMEWORK

CTF measures focus on safeguarding financial systems from misuse in support of terrorist activities. The UK's CTF framework is principally governed by the Terrorism Act 2000 (as amended by the Terrorism Act 2006 and the Counter-Terrorism Act 2008), which criminalises various forms of terrorist financing, supplemented by obligations in the MLRs and the Terrorist Asset-Freezing, etc. Act 2010.

The Terrorism Act 2000 lays out essential provisions targeting terrorist financing. Section 15 criminalises the provision of funds intended for terrorist use, while Section 16

55 Zilioli, C., Bismuth, R. and Thévenoz, L. (eds.), *International Sanctions: Monetary and Financial Law Perspectives* (Brill – Nijhoff, 2024).

56 Ibid. at [5.3]: "*Credit Suisse breached Principle 3 and SYSC 6.1.1R because it failed to sufficiently prioritise the mitigation of financial crime risks, including corruption risks, within its emerging markets business; it lacked an adequate financial crime strategy for the management of those risks, and as a result, the risk management systems it had in place were not adequate*".

broadens this to cover arrangements enabling funds to be made available to terrorist organisations. Section 17 further prohibits the use of money or property for terrorist purposes. These provisions are integral to addressing the financial support of terrorism, as they extend beyond direct funding to arrangements and uses of assets that might support terrorist activities.[57]

Additionally, the Act mandates financial institutions to freeze the assets of individuals and entities designated as involved in terrorism. It also requires them to report any suspicious activities to the NCA, facilitating swift action by authorities. Collectively, these obligations bolster the resilience of the financial sector against terrorist financing risks, ensuring financial institutions play a crucial role in detecting, preventing, and reporting potential threats.

9 GLOBAL PERSPECTIVE ON COUNTER-TERRORIST FINANCING

The FATF is an independent intergovernmental policymaking body which was established in 1989 by the G7 to analyse money laundering trends and techniques and to develop measures to combat money laundering. In 2001, its mandate was expanded to include combating terrorist financing alongside money laundering.

The FATF has established a set of standards that are widely recognised as the international benchmark for combating money laundering, the financing of terrorism, and the proliferation (or spread) of weapons of mass destruction. In 2012, the FATF published a set of guidelines titled *International Standards on Combating Money Laundering and the Financing of Terrorism and Proliferation*.[58] These Standards comprise 40 recommendations, interpretative notes that clarify many (though not all) of the recommendations, a note outlining the legal basis for requirements imposed on financial institutions and designated non-financial businesses and professions, and applicable definitions provided in a glossary.

The primary objective of the Standards is to strengthen international safeguards and further protect the integrity of the financial system. They provide governments with enhanced tools to combat financial crime effectively. Since their initial publication, the Standards have been amended several times to ensure they remain relevant and capable of addressing evolving threats.

Because both the UK and the EU anti-terrorist financing measures derive from the same source and were introduced by the Money Laundering Directives, the AML and CTF standards in the UK and the EU are mostly aligned. Such standards derive from the EU Regulation (EU) 2015/847, which was introduced alongside the Fourth Money Laundering Directive ((EU) 2015/849).[59] Both pieces of legislation shared the common objective of strengthening the EU's AML and CTF framework to enhance its effectiveness. Additionally, they aimed to ensure that the EU framework was fully aligned with the international AML and CTF standards set by the FATF.

However, the EU has adopted measures that significantly amend the EU framework for AML and CTF through the AMLA Regulation (Regulation (EU) 2024/1620), the AML Regulation (Regulation 2024/1624),[60] Regulation (EU) 2023/1113, and the Sixth Money

57 Kokkinis, A. and Miglionico, M., *Banking Law: Private Transactions and Regulatory Frameworks* (Routledge, 2021), p. 197.

58 See www.fatf-gafi.org/content/dam/fatf-gafi/recommendations/FATF%20Recommendations%202012.pdf.coredownload.inline.pdf (accessed in March 2025).

59 As amended by Directive (EU) 2018/843 of the European Parliament and of the Council of 30 May 2018 amending Directive (EU) 2015/849 on the prevention of the use of the financial system for the purposes of money laundering or terrorist financing, and amending Directives 2009/138/EC and 2013/36/EU.

60 Regulation (EU) 2024/1624 of the European Parliament and of the Council of 31 May 2024 on the prevention of the use of the financial system for the purposes of money laundering or terrorist financing.

Laundering Directive (Directive (EU) 2024/1640).[61] This comprehensive framework shall become fully operational by 2028, representing a significant overhaul of the EU's approach to combating financial crime. It aims to modernise the existing regime while achieving greater harmonisation and cooperation among national supervisors and financial intelligence units within the EU. At the heart of this framework is the AMLA,[62] the EU regulatory agency dedicated to combating money laundering and terrorist financing. The AMLA, headquartered in Frankfurt, Germany, is designed to act as a central authority that coordinates all national AML and CTF supervisors – not limited to those in the financial services sector. Its primary objective is to improve the effectiveness and consistency of AML and CTF supervision and enforcement across the EU. While the AMLA will not replace national AML and CTF supervisors, it will have direct supervisory powers over certain high-risk financial institutions. The AML and CTF Single Rulebook introduces a unified EU regulatory framework for AML and CTF.

Moreover, since the flow of illicit money through fund transfers poses a significant risk to the integrity, stability, and reputation of the financial sector and threatens the functioning of the EU internal market, Regulation (EU) 2015/847[63] was introduced[64] with the aim of preventing terrorists and other criminals from exploiting payment systems to transfer funds. Given that criminals can exploit transfers of cryptoassets in much the same way as traditional fund transfers, Regulation (EU) 2023/1113[65] on information accompanying transfers of funds and certain cryptoassets has extended the existing framework to encompass transfers of cryptoassets. This measure aims to support AML and CTF efforts by enabling the identification and tracking of cryptoasset transfers, thereby aligning them with the regulatory framework applicable to traditional financial transactions.

In the US, since the events of 11 September 2001, anti-terrorist financing measures have placed substantial obligations on US lenders to verify the identities of entities and individuals involved in transactions. These requirements are primarily outlined in the USA Patriot Act[66] and the rules enforced by the Office of Foreign Assets Control (**OFAC**), a financial intelligence and enforcement agency of the United States Treasury Department. Additional regulatory obligations, including reporting and transaction restrictions, are imposed under the Bank Secrecy Act and the Trading with the Enemy Act. These measures collectively aim to prevent the misuse of the financial system for terrorist financing and other illicit activities. In particular, the USA Patriot Act plays a key role in CTF, imposing significant obligations on financial institutions to monitor transactions and report any suspicions of terrorist financing. The Act strengthens cooperation between financial institutions and law enforcement, facilitating asset freezing and enforcement actions.

61 Directive (EU) 2024/1640 of the European Parliament and of the Council of 31 May 2024 on the mechanisms to be put in place by Member States for the prevention of the use of the financial system for the purposes of money laundering or terrorist financing, amending Directive(EU) 2019/1937, and amending and repealing Directive (EU) 2015/849.

62 The Authority for Anti-Money Laundering and Countering the Financing of Terrorism (AMLA) is a decentralised EU agency that will coordinate national authorities to ensure the correct and consistent application of EU rules. See www.amla.europa.eu/about-amla_en (accessed in March 2025).

63 Regulation (EU) 2015/847 of the European Parliament and of the Council of 20 May 2015 on information accompanying transfers of funds and repealing Regulation (EC) No 1781/2006.

64 It was amended on 30 December 2024 by Regulation (EU) 2023/1113 of the European Parliament and of the Council of 31 May 2023 on information accompanying transfers of funds and certain crypto-assets and amending Directive (EU) 2015/849.

65 Regulation (EU) 2023/1113 of the European Parliament and of the Council of 31 May 2023 on information accompanying transfers of funds and certain crypto-assets and amending Directive (EU) 2015/849.

66 The Uniting and Strengthening America by Providing Appropriate Tools Required to Intercept and Obstruct Terrorism Act of 2001.

In China, the Counter-Terrorism Law 2015 serves as the primary legal tool for addressing terrorist financing. Financial institutions in China are required to report suspicious transactions related to terrorism, and penalties for non-compliance are severe, with extensive monitoring of cross-border financial transactions.

10 BRIBERY A GLOBAL PERSPECTIVE

The problem of corruption has, for decades, posed a significant challenge to countries worldwide in addressing bribery on a cross-border scale. In 1989, the Organisation for Economic Co-operation and Development (**OECD**) established a working group to examine the national legislation of member countries concerning the bribery of foreign public officials. This initiative led to the signing of the OECD Anti-Bribery Convention in 1997,[67] which sought to encourage states to adopt legislation prohibiting the bribery of foreign public officials within a harmonised framework while also ensuring the monitoring of enforcement efforts in this area. The OECD Anti-Bribery Convention addresses what is referred to in the legal systems of some countries as "active corruption" or "active bribery". This term describes the offence committed by the individual who promises or gives the bribe, as opposed to "passive bribery", which refers to the offence committed by the recipient of the bribe.

In the **US**, the enactment of the Foreign Corrupt Practices Act 1977 (**FCPA**) was a direct response to the widespread foreign bribery by multinational corporations uncovered in the aftermath of the Watergate scandal. As the first statute of its kind globally, the FCPA prohibits US companies, individuals, and foreign entities with a nexus to the United States from offering or paying bribes to foreign public officials. Its aim is to deter the use of corrupt practices to secure or retain business advantages abroad. The FCPA's influence became international in scope following the adoption of the OECD Anti-Bribery Convention in 1997. The FCPA criminalises bribery of foreign officials and requires companies to maintain accurate financial records. One of the key distinctions between the Bribery Act 2010 and the FCPA lies in their scope. The Bribery Act extends to corruption in private-to-private commercial contexts and is not limited to bribery involving public officials. By contrast, the FCPA is primarily focused on bribery involving "foreign officials", and while the broad definition of "foreign official" expands its application, most forms of bribery within the private sector fall outside its ambit. Another notable difference is the approach taken by the two Acts in addressing the nature of bribery. The Bribery Act 2010 covers both "active bribery" (the giving of bribes, also known as the "supply-side of bribery") and "passive bribery" (the receiving of bribes, or the "demand-side of bribery"). In contrast, the FCPA only addresses active bribery involving foreign officials, with no provisions for passive bribery.

The FCPA has been the basis for many high-profile corporate prosecutions, with significant fines imposed for violations. Due to its extensive extra-territorial application, many international companies fall within the scope of the FCPA. While the Bribery Act 2010 applies to bribery both within the domestic sphere and involving foreign elements, the FCPA is limited to bribery involving foreign officials, with domestic bribery in the United States generally addressed under other laws. Since it is perceived that the FCPA "*actively harms American economic competitiveness and, therefore, national security*",[68] on 10 February 2025, a presidential

67 See www.oecd.org/content/dam/oecd/en/topics/policy-sub-issues/fighting-foreign-bribery/Convention%20and%20commentaries%20booklet%202024.pdf (accessed in March 2025).

68 See Pausing Foreign Corrupt Practices Act Enforcement to Further American Economic and National Security available at (accessed in March 2025). www.whitehouse.gov/presidential-actions/2025/02/pausing-foreign-corrupt-practices-act-enforcement-to-further-american-economic-and-national-security/ (accessed in March 2025).

Executive Order[69] was issued instructing the Attorney General to suspend enforcement of the FCPA for a period of 180 days. The purpose of the suspension is to allow the Department of Justice sufficient time to develop and publish revised enforcement guidelines.

Commercial bribery, which is not covered by the FCPA, including that which occurs overseas, can sometimes be prosecuted under other statutes, most notably the Travel Act 1952.[70] The Travel Act prohibits the use of communication and travel facilities to further US state or federal crimes, including private commercial bribery that affects foreign commerce.

To invoke the Travel Act, there must, among other requirements, be a connection to a US state that has an anti-bribery statute criminalising commercial bribery. In recent years, the US government has increasingly utilised the Travel Act to pursue companies and individuals involved in commercial corruption. In addition, corrupt conduct frequently breaches other US laws, including those prohibiting mail fraud and wire fraud, as well as laws targeting money laundering, conspiracy, and aiding and abetting.

Some limited differences between the UK and US approaches also exist with respect to facilitation payments. A facilitation payment is an unofficial and typically small payment made to foreign officials to secure the performance of routine actions. Such payments are generally intended to influence the timing of an action rather than its outcome. In the United States, the FCPA provides a limited exception for payments made to "*expedite or secure . . . routine government action*". In the United Kingdom, facilitation payments are strictly illegal. Making such a payment could result in prosecution under section 1 or section 6 of the Bribery Act 2010. The offence under section 6, which addresses bribing a public official, does not require evidence of improper performance. Furthermore, if the individual making the payment has sufficient connections to a corporate body, the company itself could face prosecution under section 7 of the Bribery Act 2010, which concerns the failure of commercial organisations to prevent bribery.

US anti-money laundering legislation imposes obligations on financial institutions and certain investment advisers to report actual or suspected instances of bribery. Under 31 U.S.C. § 5318(g) and its associated regulations, financial institutions are required to report specific suspicious activities. These institutions include banks, credit unions, securities brokers, and insurance companies, as defined in 31 U.S.C. § 5312(a)(2).

Financial institutions and investment advisers that are registered with or report to the SEC must comply with a range of regulatory obligations. Under 31 CFR § 1010.311, they are required to file a report for every deposit, withdrawal, currency exchange, or transfer involving USD 10,000 or more. In addition, these institutions must submit suspicious activity reports to the Department of the Treasury for any transaction exceeding USD 5,000, where there is knowledge or suspicion that the transaction involves funds derived from illegal activities or is intended to conceal funds or assets linked to such activities. If a transaction has no apparent lawful purpose and lacks a reasonable explanation, it must also be reported. These measures are designed to enhance transparency in financial transactions and combat financial crime by identifying and preventing illicit financial activities.[71]

Moreover, pursuant to the Corporate Transparency Act of 2021, which was enacted as part of the Anti-Money Laundering Act of 2020, certain business entities, defined as "reporting companies", to submit information regarding their "beneficial owners" to the Financial Crimes Enforcement Network (**FinCEN**), a bureau of the US Department of the Treasury, unless an exemption applies. Although this information will not be made publicly available,

69 See www.whitehouse.gov/presidential-actions/2025/02/pausing-foreign-corrupt-practices-act-enforcement-to-further-american-economic-and-national-security/ (accessed in March 2025).
70 18 U.S.C. § 1952.
71 These reporting requirements are codified in 31 CFR § 1020.320(a)(2)(i)-(iii).

FinCEN is authorised to disclose it in specific circumstances. These include disclosure to US federal law enforcement agencies, to certain other enforcement authorities with court approval, and to non-US law enforcement agencies, prosecutors, or judges where the request is made through a US federal law enforcement agency. Additionally, with the reporting company's consent, the information may be shared with financial institutions and their regulators. This obligation was introduced to address the risks posed by anonymous shell companies and opaque ownership structures, which could otherwise be exploited to facilitate money laundering, the financing of terrorism, and other forms of financial crime, although its implementation was suspended in March 2025.[72]

In **China**, there are two primary sources of anti-corruption law. The first is the Criminal Law of the People's Republic of China 2023 (**2023 Criminal Law**). This legislation includes anti-bribery provisions that apply to both Chinese and foreign officials, as well as provisions criminalising commercial bribery. The second is the Anti-Unfair Competition Law 2019, which addresses the administrative offence of commercial bribery, which is regarded as less serious than the criminal offence.

There are also two principal sources of anti-money laundering legislation.

The first is Article 191 of the 2023 Criminal Law concerning offences and dissimulation or concealment of the source and nature of illicit proceeds. Connected guidance on the handling of criminal money laundering cases is set out in the Interpretation of the Supreme People's Court and the Supreme People's Procuratorate on Several Issues Concerning the Application of Law in the Handling of Criminal Money Laundering Cases (2024).[73] This guidance defines the criteria for identifying the offences of self-money laundering and third-party money laundering and offers guidance on how to assess subjective awareness in the context of third-party involvement. It also establishes the thresholds for determining when money laundering offences are deemed to involve "serious circumstances", and it outlines seven specific scenarios that amount to "covering up or concealing the sources and nature of criminal proceeds and gains through other means", and sets out the principles for imposing concurrent punishment where offences of money laundering and those of concealing or disguising criminal proceeds are both committed.

The second is the Anti-Money Laundering Law 2006,[74] which provides a comprehensive framework for the prevention of money laundering, including mechanisms for reporting, investigation, and international cooperation. In particular, the law imposes obligations on financial institutions to implement reporting systems for large-sum transactions and suspicious transactions, forming a key component of China's anti-money laundering regime. Financial institutions in China are required to establish a reporting system for large-sum transactions and suspicious transactions. They must report transactions exceeding a prescribed threshold or those deemed suspicious to an Anti-Money Laundering Information Centre, which is to be established by the State Council and tasked with receiving and analysing such reports.[75] Further strengthening this framework, the Measures for the Supervision and Administration

72 On 2 March 2025, the US Treasury Department announced that, in relation to the Corporate Transparency Act, it will not impose any penalties or fines for breaches of the beneficial ownership information reporting requirements under the current regulatory deadlines. Furthermore, the Treasury confirmed that it will not enforce any penalties or fines against US citizens, domestic reporting companies, or their beneficial owners even after the forthcoming amendments to the rules come into effect. The Treasury also stated that it will be issuing a proposed rule that will revise and narrow the scope of the reporting obligations so that they apply only to foreign reporting companies. See https://home.treasury.gov/news/press-releases/sb0038 (accessed in March 2025).

73 See https://english.court.gov.cn/2024-08/21/c_1014824.htm (accessed in March 2025).

74 See www.pbc.gov.cn/english/130733/2897917/index.html (accessed in March 2025).

75 Articles 10 and 20 of the 2006 Anti-Money Laundering Law.

of Combating Money Laundering and Financing of Terrorism by Financial Institutions[76] were issued by the People's Bank of China. This regulation reiterated the obligation of financial institutions to report large-amount transactions and suspicious transactions.[77]

The Prevention of Corruption Act 1988 serves as the principal anti-corruption legislation in **India**. It criminalises offences committed by public servants in connection with the acceptance or attempted acceptance of any form of undue advantage, defined as anything of value – whether monetary or otherwise – that is not a legal entitlement. In addition to targeting public officials, the Act also provides for the prosecution of individuals who offer bribes, thereby addressing both the supply and demand sides of corruption. Under the Act, a company may be found guilty of an offence if a person associated with the company offers, promises, or provides a financial advantage to a public servant with the intention of obtaining or retaining business or securing an advantage in the conduct of the company's business. Indian anti-corruption laws do not include a specific exception for facilitation payments made to public servants. Strictly speaking, any such payment constitutes bribery. However, in practice, if the amount involved falls below the monetary thresholds prescribed under the relevant conduct rules governing public servants, this may serve as a defence against allegations of bribery for both the public servant and the person making the payment.

Japan's anti-bribery and anti-corruption regime consists primarily of three key pieces of legislation: the Criminal Code,[78] the Act on Punishment of Public Officials Profiting by Exerting Influence (**APPOPEI**),[79] and the Unfair Competition Prevention Act (**UCPA**).[80]

Under the Criminal Code, it is an offence for a person to give, offer, or promise to give a bribe to a public official in connection with their public office or duties.[81] A "bribe" includes both tangible and intangible benefits and must have a direct relationship to the office or duties of the official.[82]

The APPOPEI[83] prohibits the giving (and receiving) of a bribe (or "something of value") to members of parliament, senators, members of local assemblies, or governors of local public entities to induce these public figures to use their influence over other officials to act, regardless of whether such influence violates any law.

The UCPA criminalises the bribery of foreign public officials, including employees of state-owned or state-controlled entities.[84] It is an offence to give, offer, or promise money or any other benefit to a foreign public officer with the intent to influence them to act or refrain from acting in connection with their duties in order to obtain an improper business advantage. This applies specifically in the context of international commercial transactions.

It is important to note that the Criminal Code and the APPOPEI apply only to individuals, whereas the UCPA extends to both individuals and incorporated entities. Neither the Criminal Code nor the APPOPEI provides any specific defences, safe harbours, or exemptions.

Under the UCPA, however, conduct that is lawful under the local regulations of the jurisdiction where it occurs does not give rise to liability. For example, facilitation payments

76 See www.pbc.gov.cn/en/3688241/3688777/3688780/4236224/index.html (accessed in March 2025).
77 See Article 14 of the Measures for the Supervision and Administration of Combating Money Laundering and Financing of Terrorism by Financial Institutions.
78 (Act No. 45 of 1907, as amended).
79 (Act No. 130 of 2009, as amended).
80 (Act No. 54 of 1993, as amended).
81 Article 198.
82 See www.antibriberyguidance.org/qa-relation-bribery-offences-japan/guidance (accessed in March 2025).
83 Under Article 4.
84 Article 18.

permitted under statute or judicial precedent in the jurisdiction of the recipient public official are not punishable under the UCPA. Additionally, the Guidelines for the Prevention of Bribery of Foreign Public Officials,[85] albeit not legally binding, stipulate that liability may not arise where there is a threatened or actual danger to the body or property of an individual or company. The Guidelines also provide commentary on acceptable practices in the context of gifts and services, especially when linked to greetings or social customs. Although the Guidelines do not specify a monetary threshold, they serve as a practical de facto standard.

11 FINANCIAL SANCTIONS AND CREDIT INSTITUTIONS

The nature of sanctions regimes has evolved significantly over time. Historically, a serious diplomatic dispute would often result in the complete severance of commercial and financial ties with the government concerned, extending to all of its nationals, irrespective of their individual status or responsibility for the underlying conflict. In contrast, the modern approach is far more targeted, focusing on political leaders and their associates who are directly involved in or responsible for the issue at hand.[86] These sanctions are intended to combat illegal activities, such as terrorism financing, money laundering, and human rights violations. This shift ensures that sanctions are more precisely directed, minimising unintended consequences for the wider population while increasing pressure on key decision-makers. Credit institutions, given their role as intermediaries in financial markets, are on the front line of ensuring compliance with financial sanctions. Failure to comply can result in severe legal, financial, and reputational consequences.

11.1 The UK's Financial Sanctions Regime

The UK's financial sanctions regime is implemented through a combination of primary legislation and statutory instruments, which together provide the legal framework for enforcement. The key pieces of primary legislation include SAMLA, the Counter-Terrorism Act 2008, and the Anti-Terrorism, Crime and Security Act 2001.[87] The Foreign, Commonwealth & Development Office (FCDO) has overall responsibility for the UK's policy on sanctions and embargoes.

In its March 2021 publication, "Global Britain in a Competitive Age: The Integrated Review of Security, Defence, Development and Foreign Policy",[88] the UK government outlined its intention to utilise the UK financial sanctions regime as part of an integrated strategy to advance UK values and interests. This approach is aimed at addressing key challenges such as state threats, terrorism, cyber-attacks, and the use and proliferation of chemical weapons.

SAMLA empowers the UK[89] government to impose financial sanctions, travel bans, and trade restrictions, particularly targeting individuals and entities involved in terrorism, human rights abuses, or activities posing a threat to UK national security. These sanctions

85 Issued by the Ministry of Economy, Trade and Industry and based on Article 18 of the UCPA, www.meti.go.jp/policy/external_economy/zouwai/pdf/GuidelinesforthePreventionofBriberyofForeignPublicOfficials.pdf (accessed in March 2025).
86 Proctor, C., *The Law and Practice of International Banking* (Oxford University Press, 2015) at [47.10].
87 Proctor, C., *The Law and Practice of International Banking* (Oxford University Press, 2015) at [47.11].
88 See https://assets.publishing.service.gov.uk/government/uploads/system/uploads/attachment_data/file/975077/Global_Britain_in_a_Competitive_Age-_the_Integrated_Review_of_Security__Defence__Development_and_Foreign_Policy.pdf (accessed in March 2025).
89 Under Section 1 of SAMLA.

may encompass measures like asset freezes and prohibitions on providing funds or economic resources to designated persons.[90]

In *Youssef v Secretary of State for Foreign and Commonwealth Affairs* [2016] UKSC 3, Youssef, subject to a UN sanctions regime for alleged associations with terrorism, challenged the legality of these sanctions. The Supreme Court held that while the UK was bound to implement UN sanctions, the Foreign Secretary bore a responsibility to ensure these sanctions aligned with UK legal standards, including fairness and justice principles. This case underscored the necessity of balancing the UK's international obligations with the protection of domestic legal rights when enforcing sanctions.

Similarly, in *European Court of Justice in Kadi v European Commission* (C-402/05 P),[91] the European Court of Justice held that sanctions imposed by the UN Security Council on suspected terrorists must be balanced against fundamental rights, such as the right to due process and the right to effective judicial review. Thus, the court annulled the freezing of Mr. Kadi's assets, finding that the EU's implementation of UN sanctions did not meet EU standards for fundamental rights protection:

> *The contested regulation, in so far as it concerns Mr Kadi, was adopted without furnishing any guarantee enabling him to put his case to the competent authorities, in a situation in which the restriction of his property rights must be regarded as significant, having regard to the general application and actual continuation of the freezing measures affecting him. It must therefore be held that, in the circumstances of the case, the imposition of the restrictive measures laid down by the contested regulation in respect of Mr Kadi, by including him in the list contained in Annex I to that regulation, constitutes an unjustified restriction of his right to property.*[92]

These cases reflect the tension between CTF and sanctions measures and individual rights, a theme that continues to influence both EU and UK legal frameworks on terrorism financing.

The Office of Financial Sanctions Implementation (**OFSI**), part of HM Treasury, is empowered to impose monetary penalties for breaches of financial sanctions.[93] The penalty can range from 50% of the total value of the breach to £1 million, whichever is greater. When determining the appropriate penalty, OFSI considers several factors to ensure the penalty is proportionate to the circumstances of the case. Notably, OFSI may apply reductions to the penalty amount in situations where the breach has been voluntarily disclosed, reflecting the regulator's emphasis on encouraging transparency and cooperation.[94]

To assist firms in complying with the sanctions regime, the Foreign, Commonwealth and Development Office maintains a publicly accessible sanctions list. This list sets out the details of individuals and entities designated under regulations made pursuant to SAMLA.

90 Zilioli, C., Bismuth, R. and Thévenoz, L. (eds.), *International Sanctions: Monetary and Financial Law Perspectives* (Brill – Nijhoff, 2024).
91 Judgment of the Court (Grand Chamber) of 3 September 2008 In Joined Cases C-402/05 P and C-415/05 P.
92 Ibid. at paras 369 and 370.
93 Under section 146 of the Policing and Crime Act 2017.
94 The maximum penalties for offences related to breaches of financial sanctions have been established under the Policing and Crime Act 2017 and the European Union Financial Sanctions (Enhanced Penalties) Regulations 2017 (SI 2017/560). If convicted on indictment, the maximum sentence is seven years' imprisonment. In cases of summary conviction, the maximum penalty is six months' imprisonment.

It encompasses not only financial sanctions but also designations relating to trade, transport, and immigration measures, thereby providing a centralised resource to support compliance across the full spectrum of UK sanctions. In addition, OFSI maintains two key lists of financial sanctions targets, one of which is the "consolidated list". This list encompasses all regimes, entities, and individuals subject to an asset freeze under UK financial sanctions legislation and the United Nations, and it provides detailed information to assist in identifying financial sanctions targets sanctions (including targets relating to retained EU law), such as aliases, dates of birth, passport details, nationality, and last known addresses. The other list maintained by OFSI is a separate list of individuals and entities subject to specific capital market restrictions. Unlike the consolidated list, this list focuses exclusively on those targeted by measures that restrict access to financial markets, such as limitations on dealing with certain financial instruments.[95]

It is an offence to make economic resources available, directly or indirectly, to a designated person if the individual knows or has reasonable cause to suspect that the resources are being made available in such a way that the designated person is likely to use them to obtain funds, goods, or services.

As a starting point, one should note that these offences require either knowledge or reasonable cause to suspect as their mental element. The Supreme Court considered the concept of reasonable cause to suspect in the context of section 17 of the Terrorism Act 2000, which creates an offence where a person has "reasonable grounds to suspect" that money provided to another might be used to fund terrorism. In *R v Lane and Letts* [2018] UKSC 36, the Court held that this test involves an objective assessment, covering those who, based on the information available to them, had reasonable cause to suspect that the funds might be used for terrorist purposes. While the offence has a strong objective component, it is not an offence of strict liability, as the accused's state of mind and the information they possessed are critical factors in determining liability.

Moreover, it is important to understand who a "designated person" is. Under section 9 of SAMLA, it is defined as either a person who has been designated by an appropriate minister for the purposes of the relevant regulations or any provision thereof or a person who has been designated pursuant to any provision made under section 13 of SAMLA, which relates to individuals or entities named in United Nations Security Council resolutions. The term "person" is interpreted broadly and includes not only natural persons but also any organisation, association, or combination of persons. Both the Secretary of State and the United Nations have the authority to designate individuals or entities for the purposes of sanctions.

These sanctions' restrictions will extend not only to designated individuals or entities but also to those bodies – whether incorporated or unincorporated – that are owned or controlled, directly or indirectly, by such targets. For the purposes of assessing whether an entity is owned or controlled by a designated person, the UK regime applies a series of criteria. These include where the person, whether directly or indirectly, holds more than 50% of the shares or voting rights in the entity or has the right to appoint or remove a majority of its board of directors. In addition, the test may be met where it is reasonable to expect that the person is able to ensure that the affairs of the entity are conducted in accordance with their wishes. Control may also be inferred where a designated person is found to have use of, or access to, another person's bank accounts or economic resources, particularly if such resources are being used to circumvent the effect of financial sanctions. Where any of the ownership or control criteria

95 See www.gov.uk/government/publications/financial-sanctions-general-guidance/uk-financial-sanctions-general-guidance (accessed in March 2025).

are satisfied, and the person exercising such control is a designated target, the financial sanctions apply in full to the entity in question.

The meaning of control was addressed in the context of the Russia (Sanctions) (EU Exit) Regulations 2019, which imposed financial restrictions are imposed in relation to designated persons, who are also referred to in this context as asset freeze targets. The regime prohibits any dealings with funds or economic resources that are owned, held, or controlled by a designated person. In addition, it is unlawful to make funds or economic resources available, either directly or indirectly, to or for the benefit of such persons. In *Thomas & Ors v PJSC National Bank Trust* [2025] EWHC 75 (Ch), the Trustees in Bankruptcy of two Russian individuals were concerned regarding the status of National Bank Trust (NBT) following *obiter dicta* remarks made in *Mints* [2023] EWCA Civ 1132, in which the Court of Appeal suggested that NBT is controlled by a designated person. In *Thomas & Ors,* the High Court was of the view, relying on OFSI confirmation of NBT not being owned or controlled directly or indirectly by Mr Putin, that: "

> *Although it is possible, given the nature of Mr Putin's political position, that he may in the future seek to control the affairs of NBT in some relevant way, there is no evidence that he could do so without third-party consents, a breach of the law, or consequences which might cause him not to seek such control. The absence of evidence of potential de facto control in the present case is significant. If there were such evidence, OFSI would no doubt take a different position. . . . Overall, and to use the language of Regulation 7(4), it does not seem to me that it is reasonable, having regard to all the circumstances, to expect that Mr Putin and/or Ms Nabiullina would (if they chose to) be able, in most cases or in significant respects, by whatever means and whether directly or indirectly, to achieve the result that the affairs of NBT are conducted in accordance with their wishes.*

Thomas & Ors underscored the critical importance of continued and enhanced monitoring by credit institutions. Even where an entity is not expressly designated under the UK sanctions regime, it may nevertheless fall within the scope of the regime by virtue of being 'owned or controlled' by a designated person. This heightened monitoring obligation is essential to ensure compliance with the sanctions framework and to mitigate the risk of inadvertently engaging in prohibited transactions. Additionally, the facts of each case and the available exemptions will need to be carefully scrutinised.[96]

Chapter 5[97] of SAMLA outlines the reporting obligations to OFSI. Specific reporting requirements apply to both "relevant institutions" and "relevant businesses or professions". A "relevant institution" includes any person who has been granted permission under Part 4A of FSMA to carry out regulated activities. A "relevant business or profession" refers to businesses engaged in certain financial activities, such as operating a currency exchange office, transmitting money (or any representation of monetary value) by any means, or cashing cheques payable to customers. These entities and professionals are required to comply with the reporting obligations set out in the guidance to ensure proper adherence to the UK's financial sanctions regime.

OFSI administers and enforces sanctions, while the FCA ensures that credit institutions have adequate controls and systems to prevent sanctions breaches.

96 It is worth noting that the Sanctions (EU Exit) (Miscellaneous Amendments) (No. 2) Regulations 2024, which came into effect on 5 December 2024, have been extended to incorporate a new insolvency licensing purpose. Under this amendment, payments made directly or indirectly to a designated person may be permitted, provided that such payments are credited to a frozen bank account. This change introduces a degree of flexibility within the existing sanctions regime, particularly in the context of insolvency proceedings, while ensuring that the designated person remains effectively restricted from accessing or using the funds.

97 See www.gov.uk/government/publications/financial-sanctions-general-guidance/uk-financial-sanctions-general-guidance#reporting-to-ofsi (accessed in March 2025).

Financial sanctions typically entail asset freezing, transaction prohibitions, and heightened due diligence requirements. Asset freezing mandates that credit institutions restrict access to the assets of individuals or entities listed on the UK's sanctions lists, effectively barring them from accessing or managing funds within the UK or internationally. Transaction prohibitions require banks to block transactions involving sanctioned parties, halting the transfer of funds, securities, or financial instruments. Additionally, enhanced due diligence is essential for clients or transactions tied to high-risk countries or sanctioned entities; institutions must enforce Know Your Customer (**KYC**) procedures and employ sanctions screening systems to detect and report any suspicious activity.[98]

The FCA's oversight includes supervising banks' implementation of sanctions compliance and examining the adequacy of their internal systems, risk assessments, and transaction monitoring capabilities. In cases of non-compliance, the FCA has the authority to impose significant fines on institutions and may hold senior executives personally accountable under the SMCR. Furthermore, the FCA provides guidance to help institutions understand their obligations under the UK sanctions framework and underscores the importance of staff training to detect and prevent sanctions violations.

Sanctions and Human Rights Violations

In 2012, the United States Congress enacted the Russia and Moldova Jackson-Vanik Repeal and Sergei Magnitsky Rule of Law Accountability Act (commonly referred to as the Magnitsky Act). This legislation empowers the US government to deny visas and freeze the financial assets of Russian officials believed to be implicated in human rights violations.

A comparable mechanism has since been incorporated into UK law through section 1(7) of SAMLA. This provision was implemented by the Global Human Rights Sanctions Regulations 2020.[99] The regulations establish a targeted sanctions regime with the express purpose of deterring and providing accountability for acts that, if perpetrated by or on behalf of a State, would constitute serious breaches of specified human rights. Importantly, such acts may be carried out not only by States but also by non-state actors. The Global Human Rights Sanctions Regulations 2020 confer authority upon the Secretary of State to designate individuals who are or have been involved in such conduct. Persons so designated may be subject to travel bans and financial sanctions, including the freezing of funds and economic resources. This framework underscores the UK's commitment to the promotion of human rights through the use of autonomous sanctions measures.

11.2 The EU's Financial Sanctions Regime

The European Union plays a significant role in the global effort to impose and enforce financial sanctions as part of its broader Common Foreign and Security Policy. Financial sanctions[100] are typically proposed by the European External Action Service, the EU's diplomatic

98 Kokkinis, A. and Miglionico, M., *Banking Law: Private Transactions and Regulatory Frameworks* (Routledge, 2021), p. 183.
99 (SI 2020/680).
100 See www.eeas.europa.eu/eeas/european-union-sanctions_en (accessed in March 2025).

arm responsible for foreign policy implementation. Consensus among EU member states is necessary for sanctions adoption. Once the Council of the European Union approves these proposals, they are implemented through Council Regulations, which are immediately enforceable across all EU member states and do not require national legislation. The legal basis for these sanctions lies in Article 29 of the Treaty on the European Union[101] and Article 215 of the Treaty on the Functioning of the European Union,[102] empowering the EU to impose economic sanctions directly.

The EU's financial sanctions regime serves as a critical component of its foreign policy, designed to safeguard international stability, human rights, and the rule of law. Financial institutions play a vital role in enforcing these sanctions and must sustain rigorous compliance frameworks to navigate the complexities of EU regulations. Coordination with international sanctions frameworks is essential for effectiveness. The EU often aligns its sanctions with those of the United Nations and other allies, such as the US and UK, to ensure comprehensive enforcement and prevent circumvention by targeted parties. EU sanctions frequently mirror UN mandates; however, the EU maintains autonomy to impose sanctions independently when required. Nevertheless, inconsistencies occasionally emerge between EU sanctions and those of other jurisdictions, particularly the US, complicating compliance for EU businesses and financial institutions that must navigate potentially conflicting legal requirements.

The EU Blocking Statute was enacted to mitigate the impact of extraterritorial sanctions imposed by third countries, especially the US.[103] This statute, codified in Council Regulation (EC) No 2271/96, was notably relevant after the US withdrew from the Joint Comprehensive Plan of Action in 2018, re-imposing sanctions on Iran that affected many EU companies with ties to both regions. The Blocking Statute prohibits EU companies from adhering to extraterritorial sanctions without explicit authorisation from the European Commission, ensuring that EU entities cannot terminate contracts solely due to US sanctions that the EU does not also impose. It further allows EU companies to recover damages from those enforcing such sanctions, compensating for economic losses due to compliance with third-country sanctions. Each EU member state enforces penalties for companies that breach the statute, though these penalties vary by jurisdiction, creating complex compliance obligations for businesses with dual interests in the EU and the US.

EU sanctions operate through several mechanisms. Asset freezes form the core of these measures, restricting designated individuals[104] and entities from accessing or transferring their financial resources within the EU or through EU nationals or entities. Financial institutions in the EU are also prohibited from conducting transactions or providing financial resources to sanctioned parties, covering services like fund transfers, loans, and securities issuance. Additionally, restrictions on specific financial services, especially within the banking sector, are common.

Enhanced due diligence requirements further require EU banks and financial institutions to scrutinise dealings with clients from sanctioned regions or industries, ensuring no inadvertent facilitation of prohibited transactions. This process includes systematic screening

101 OJ C 202, 7.6.2016.

102 OJ C 202, 7.6.2016.

103 Viterbo, A., 'The Enforcement of Extraterritorial Sanctions: Asset Freezes and International Monetary Law' in *The Cambridge Handbook of Secondary Sanctions and International Law* in Ruys, T., Ryngaert, C. and Silvestre, F. R. (eds.) (Cambridge University Press, 2024), pp. 287–304.

104 "*There is therefore a rational link between the targeting of leading businesspersons operating in economic sectors providing substantial revenue to the government*" in *Mazepin v Council (Common foreign and security policy – Restrictive measures taken in respect of actions undermining or threatening the territorial integrity, sovereignty and independence of Ukraine – Freezing of funds – Judgment)* [2023] EUECJ T-282/22 (8 November 2023).

against the EU's Consolidated List of Sanctions, which lists individuals, entities, and sectors subject to sanctions.

A prominent example of EU sanctions in action is its response to Russia's actions in Ukraine. Following the annexation of Crimea in 2014, and significantly intensified in 2022 with Russia's full-scale invasion, the EU imposed comprehensive sanctions on Russian individuals, entities, and sectors. The scope of these measures includes asset freezes and travel bans on thousands of Russian individuals, preventing them from accessing EU-held financial assets or conducting financial transactions. Additionally, sectoral sanctions target vital aspects of the Russian economy, such as energy, finance, and defence. Restrictions on financial markets prevent Russian state-owned enterprises and banks from accessing EU capital markets, barring them from issuing new debt or equity in the EU and restricting loans and credit arrangements. Enhanced due diligence obligations further require financial institutions to closely monitor transactions involving Russian counterparts, with thorough sanctions screening and reporting requirements.[105]

Impact of Financial Sanctions on the SWIFT Network

The SWIFT (Society for Worldwide Interbank Financial Telecommunication) network plays a critical role in facilitating cross-border financial transactions and has become a key instrument in the enforcement of international financial sanctions.

The role of SWIFT in sanctions enforcement was highlighted most prominently in the case of Russia following its invasion of Ukraine in 2022. In response to Russia's military aggression, a coalition comprising the United States, European Union, United Kingdom, Canada, and Japan imposed sweeping sanctions on Russian individuals, entities, and sectors.

On 2 March 2022, the European Union amended its sanctions regulations under Council Regulations (EU) 2022/345 and 2022/398, prohibiting EU-based entities, including the Belgium-based SWIFT system, from providing specialised financial messaging services to seven key Russian banks: Otkritie, Novikombank, PSB, Rossiya, Sovcombank, VEB, and VTB Bank. The prohibition, which took effect on 12 March 2022,[106] also extended to any Russian subsidiaries directly or indirectly owned by more than 50% of these banks. This measure was later expanded on 3 June 2022, when additional Russian and Belarusian banks were disconnected from SWIFT[107] as part of broader sanctions responding to Belarus's role in supporting Russia's invasion of Ukraine. Although Russian banks technically remained free to conduct cross-border transactions using alternative methods, their exclusion from SWIFT caused severe disruptions, rendering such transactions cumbersome and inefficient. Trade, particularly in key export sectors such as oil and gas, was directly impacted as payments were delayed or blocked, hampering Russia's commercial relationships with foreign buyers. The financial markets within Russia also suffered considerable instability, with the

105 Lonardo, L., 'Challenging EU Sanctions against Russia: The Role of the Court, Judicial Protection, and Common Foreign and Security Policy' (2023) 25 *Cambridge Yearbook of European Legal Studies* 40–63.

106 See https://eur-lex.europa.eu/legal-content/EN/TXT/PDF/?uri=CELEX:32022R0345&from=EN (accessed in March 2025).

107 See Council Regulation (EU) 2022/879 of 3 June 2022 amending Regulation (EU) No 833/2014 concerning restrictive measures in view of Russia's actions destabilising the situation in Ukraine, available at https://eur-lex.europa.eu/legal-content/EN/TXT/HTML/?uri=CELEX:32022R0879&from=EN#d1e787-53-1 (accessed in March 2025).

rouble experiencing sharp depreciation and heightened volatility. The central bank's ability to manage liquidity and engage with foreign exchange markets was significantly hindered by its disconnection from SWIFT. In response, Russia sought to expand the use of alternative payment systems, including its domestic *System for Transfer of Financial Messages* and *China's Cross-Border Interbank Payment System* (CIPS),[108] as well as turning to cryptocurrencies and barter arrangements. However, these alternatives lacked the global reach, efficiency, and scale of SWIFT.

The repercussions of these sanctions extended beyond Russia. Given Russia's role as a major supplier of energy and commodities, its exclusion from SWIFT had disruptive effects on global markets. International buyers and suppliers faced delays and uncertainty in settling transactions, with energy markets and commodity prices experiencing significant volatility.

The case of SWIFT's role in Russian sanctions offers important lessons on the power of financial infrastructure in the enforcement of international sanctions. First, it demonstrates the leverage that access to SWIFT provides to sanctioning countries, allowing them to isolate targeted states from the global financial system and severely constrain their economic capabilities. Second, it highlights the economic isolation that results from exclusion from SWIFT, with Russia's case exemplifying how critical international financial messaging systems are to a country's economic stability. Third, while Russia's attempts to build and use alternative systems like SPFS and CIPS illustrate efforts to bypass sanctions, these alternatives have not yet matched the global reach and effectiveness of SWIFT, limiting their utility.

Finally, the use of SWIFT sanctions has also prompted Russia and its affiliates to explore other means of sanctions evasion. On 25 March 2024,[109] 13 entities and two individuals were sanctioned for their roles in Russia's financial services and technology sectors, including virtual asset services used to circumvent US sanctions. Several of these entities were engaged in developing and providing virtual asset platforms designed to facilitate transactions outside of the formal banking system. Notably, although the virtual assets market currently lacks the scale to enable large-scale sanctions evasion, there is evidence that sanctioned Russian entities have used cryptocurrencies, such as Tether, to access international markets and pay for restricted goods and technology.[110]

108 CIPS Co., Ltd. (CIPS) operates under the supervision and administration of the People's Bank of China, in accordance with relevant rules and regulations, including the *Business Rules on the Cross-border Interbank Payment System (CIPS)*, the *Guidelines on Business Operation of CIPS*, and the *CIPS Participants Agreement*.

CIPS is responsible for the operation, maintenance, and development of the CIPS platform, as well as providing services to its participants. Its functions include product innovation, implementation of standards, market expansion, and other related activities. CIPS offers a range of services to both domestic and international financial institutions and other entities authorised by the People's Bank of China. These services include cross-border RMB clearing and settlement, data processing, IT support, services entrusted by shareholders, and other business activities approved by the People's Bank of China. See: www.cips.com.cn/cipsenmobile/7242/7247/index.html (accessed in March 2025).

109 See https://home.treasury.gov/news/press-releases/jy2204 (accessed in March 2025).

110 Institute for Financial Integrity, Russian Use of Crypto for Sanctions Evasion on the Rise: What Financial Institutions Should Know, Including Risk Mitigation Measures (21 May 2024).

11.3 US Financial Sanctions Regime and OFAC's Role

The United States operates one of the most extensive financial sanctions regimes globally, administered by OFAC. OFAC enforces sanctions to advance US foreign policy and national security goals, addressing issues such as terrorism, drug trafficking, human rights abuses, weapons proliferation, and threats to global peace arising from aggressive state actions.

These sanctions are typically comprehensive, covering trade, investment, and financial services. OFAC targets individuals, companies, and organisations involved in illicit activities, with Specially Designated Nationals (**SDN**) sanctions prohibiting US persons from transacting with these designated parties. Additionally, sectoral sanctions focus on specific industries within countries, exemplified by sanctions on Russia's energy, defence, and financial sectors under the Countering America's Adversaries Through Sanctions Act of 2017.[111] The US also employs secondary sanctions, a unique feature extending sanctions to non-US entities, penalising foreign firms and financial institutions engaged in business with sanctioned countries or entities, as seen with sanctions on Iran, where non-US banks transacting with Iranian companies faced US penalties.

As the primary agency enforcing these sanctions, OFAC operates under laws such as the International Emergency Economic Powers Act and the Trading with the Enemy Act alongside presidential executive orders. OFAC's key responsibilities include maintaining and updating sanctions lists, notably the SDN list, issuing licenses that permit specific transactions with sanctioned parties, and enforcing compliance through investigations and penalties.

A critical factor in the effectiveness of the US sanctions regime is the global dominance of the US dollar, the primary reserve currency in world trade. Due to US dollar clearing practices, foreign banks settling dollar transactions typically interact with US banks or correspondent accounts, which brings these transactions under OFAC's jurisdiction. This structure enables OFAC to monitor and, when necessary, block transactions that contravene US sanctions, even if conducted by non-US entities. Through secondary sanctions, foreign banks, companies, and individuals face exclusion from the US financial system if they engage with entities on the SDN list or sanctioned countries, which is a significant penalty for multinational companies or financial institutions dependent on dollar transactions.

The "long arm" of US law extends not only to US entities but also to foreign institutions conducting dollar-denominated transactions or engaging with US persons. This reach is illustrated by the BNP Paribas's enforcement action.[112] The French credit institution was fined $8.9 billion for conspiring to violate the International Emergency Economic Powers Act and the Trading with the Enemy Act.[113] The offence involved processing billions of dollars in transactions through the US financial system on behalf of Sudanese, Iranian, and Cuban entities, all of which are subject to US economic sanctions.[114] These penalties were applied not

111 Public Law 115–144.

112 See www.dfs.ny.gov/system/files/documents/2020/04/ea140630_bnp_paribas.pdf (accessed in March 2025).

113 *"From 1997 to 2007, in criminal violation of U.S. sanctions that were intended to stop Sudan's terrorist activities and human rights abuses and of New York law, Defendant BNP Paribas, S.A., along with its affiliates Defendants BNP Paribas, S.A. New York Branch and BNP North America, Inc., (collectively 'BNPP') secretly conspired with the rogue government of Sudan and gave it forbidden access to the U.S. financial markets and U.S. dollar clearing services in New York. By 2007, BNPP facilitated an astonishing quarter of Sudan's exports and a fifth of its imports. BNPP's financial transactions for the government of Sudan, along with some other illicit transactions with Iran and Cuba, totaled as much as $190 billion dollars"*. Case 1:16-cv-03228-AJN Document 49 Filed 01/20/17, available at www.justsecurity.org/wp-content/uploads/2019/05/Paribas_second_amended_complaint.pdf (accessed in March 2025).

114 See plea agreement www.justice.gov/sites/default/files/opa/legacy/2014/06/30/plea-agreement.pdf (accessed in March 2025).

because the transactions occurred within US borders but because they involved US dollars, thus falling under OFAC's jurisdiction.

For financial institutions, compliance with OFAC's sanctions regime is essential. Banks must establish rigorous internal controls, sanctions screening, and transaction monitoring systems to avoid processing payments involving sanctioned parties. Failure to comply with OFAC regulations can result in severe fines, reputational damage, loss of business, and restricted access to the US financial system. Compliance requirements include sanctions screening, where banks cross-reference customers and transactions against OFAC's lists, particularly the SDN list. Banks are obligated to block any transactions involving sanctioned parties and report these to OFAC, submitting regular compliance reports. Additionally, financial institutions must conduct thorough due diligence, particularly for high-risk industries and regions, and they are required to audit compliance programmes and train staff on sanctions laws.

Breach of US Financial Sanctions by Standard Chartered Bank

A prominent case of sanctions breaches by a credit institution is that of Standard Chartered Bank, which was subject to substantial penalties for breaching US sanctions against Iran. Between 2009 and 2014, Standard Chartered processed over $600 million in transactions involving Iranian clients in violation of US sanctions. These transactions, carried out through the bank's Dubai branch, often involved US dollar payments, thereby bringing the bank within the jurisdiction of OFAC due to its extraterritorial reach.

As a consequence, in 2019, Standard Chartered was fined £102.2 million by both the FCA and OFSI, in addition to nearly $950 million in penalties imposed by US regulators, including OFAC, the Department of Justice, and the New York Department of Financial Services.[115] The case highlighted the strong cooperation between UK and US authorities in enforcing sanctions compliance. Beyond the significant financial penalties, Standard Chartered suffered reputational damage, attracting widespread negative media attention and public criticism. The bank was also required to overhaul its sanctions compliance frameworks and to submit to ongoing regulatory scrutiny.

OFAC's role in maintaining sanctions lists, investigating violations, and imposing fines has solidified its influence in global financial regulation, affecting financial institutions, companies, and individuals worldwide. On 13 January 2025, OFSI and OFAC published a memorandum of understanding (**MoU**)[116] aimed at strengthening cooperation and coordination between the two agencies. This development marks a significant step towards enhancing the enforcement of financial sanctions and promoting a more consistent transatlantic approach to sanctions compliance. The MoU sets out a framework for improved information sharing between OFSI and OFAC and provides for the conduct of joint investigations and enforcement

115 See FCA's Decision Notice dated 5 February 2019 at www.fca.org.uk/publication/decision-notices/standard-chartered-bank-2019.pdf (accessed in March 2025).

116 See https://assets.publishing.service.gov.uk/media/6784f604f0528401055d2309/OFAC-OFSI_Information_Sharing_MOU_-_signed.pdf (accessed in March 2025).

actions. By formalising collaboration between the two authorities, the MoU holds the potential to address this disparity and foster closer alignment in the enforcement and implementation of UK and US sanctions regimes.

11.4 China's Evolving Sanctions Framework

China's financial sanctions framework, while historically less developed than those in the UK, EU, and US, has been expanding in recent years. Traditionally, China aligned its sanctions policy closely with the United Nations; however, its domestic approach is undergoing significant changes.

One notable development is the establishment of the Unreliable Entity List and the Anti-Foreign Sanctions Law, which allow China to counter foreign sanctions targeting Chinese entities. Through these mechanisms, China can impose counter-sanctions on foreign companies or individuals considered to be acting against its national interests. Additionally, to mitigate its reliance on the global SWIFT network and reduce vulnerabilities to potential sanctions, China has been developing its Cross-Border Interbank Payment System, which provides an alternative framework for international transactions.

11.5 Interplay of Sanctions and Payment Obligations

The English Court of Appeal decision in *Celestial Aviation Services Ltd v Unicredit Bank SA* [2024] EWCA Civ 628, pertaining to payment obligations under standby letters of credit issued by Sberbank, a designated Russian entity, and confirmed by Unicredit in the context of leasing arrangements between Irish aircraft lessors and Russian airline operators which were terminated as a result of sanctions, underscore the compliance challenges faced by banks in adhering to conflicting legal obligations.

The Irish lessors, upon expansion of the sanctions regime to civilian aircraft, terminated the lease and, as beneficiaries of the standby letters of credit, submitted demands for payment. It was not in dispute that the claimants' demands were valid and that Unicredit was contractually liable, subject only to the effect of sanctions law. Unicredit contended that payment was prohibited under Regulation 28 of the Russia (Sanctions) (EU Exit) Regulations 2019,[117] arguing that compliance with its contractual obligations would amount to the commission of a criminal offence. The central issue thus became the interpretation and application of Regulation 28(3)(c), which provides that:

> *A person must not directly or indirectly provide financial services or funds in pursuance of or in connection with an arrangement whose object or effect is . . . directly or indirectly making restricted goods . . . available . . . to a person connected with Russia, or . . . for use in Russia.*

Unicredit had sought and obtained licences from the UK sanctions authorities – the OFSI and the Export Control Joint Unit (ECJU) – under Regulations 11,[118] 13[119] and 28 in order to make the payments in question. Following the grant of those licences, the payments

117 (SI 2019/855).

118 Regulation 11(1) provides that: "*A person ('P') must not deal with funds or economic resources owned, held or controlled by a designated person if P knows, or has reasonable cause to suspect, that P is dealing with such funds or economic resources*".

119 Regulation 13(1) provides that "*A person ('P') must not make funds available to any person for the benefit of a designated person if P knows, or has reasonable cause to suspect, that P is making the funds so available*".

were made. However, the claimants contended that such licences had not been necessary and that the applications for them were misleading, particularly in suggesting that a licence to pay the lessors should be conditional upon the grant of a licence permitting payment by Sberbank to Unicredit.

The Court of Appeal's ruling provided significant clarification on three key aspects of the United Kingdom's autonomous sanctions framework.

First, the Court of Appeal confirmed that the UK's prohibition on the provision of financial and ancillary services may extend to transactions relating to Russia – even where the underlying sales or exports predated the imposition of the relevant sanctions. This interpretation underscores the retrospective reach of certain sanctions-related restrictions, particularly where ongoing financial or contractual obligations arise after the sanctions regime has come into force.

Secondly, the Court of Appeal offered guidance on the statutory defence under section 44 of SAMLA, which provides a general defence to liability for acts undertaken in the reasonable belief that they were necessary to comply with UK sanctions. The Court found that this defence is to be interpreted broadly, thereby affording parties a degree of latitude to adopt a cautious or conservative reading of the sanctions regulations without automatically incurring civil liability.

Thirdly, the judgement addressed the extent to which foreign sanctions – specifically United States sanctions – may be relied upon to argue that a contract has become unlawful to perform. The Court considered the interaction between obligations under English law and potential exposure under foreign sanctions regimes, as well as the limited circumstances in which foreign legal constraints may justify the non-performance of contractual duties governed by English law. In this respect, it was discussed whether the question of illegality under the US sanctions regime was engaged under the *Ralli Bros* principle (*Ralli Bros v Compañia Naviera Sota y Aznar* [1920] 2 KB 287) on the basis that effecting payment in US dollars required the involvement of a correspondent bank in the United States. The *Ralli Bros* principle is triggered in circumstances where the performance of a contractual obligation is not unlawful under English law but is illegal in the jurisdiction where performance is to occur. This principle has often been invoked by parties seeking to justify the non-performance of contractual obligations on the grounds that their counterparties are subject to United States sanctions.

Lady Justice Falk examined[120] the application of the *Ralli Bros* principle and distilled it into two distinct elements. The first concerns whether the act of performance would, in fact, be unlawful in the place of performance. The second considers whether the non-performing party has made "reasonable efforts" to avoid such illegality, including, for example, by applying for and pursuing a licence from the relevant sanctions authority that would permit lawful performance.

Having determined that the terms of the letters of credit did not permit payment to be made in cash or in a currency other than US dollars, the Court of Appeal proceeded to assess whether Unicredit had taken reasonable steps to avoid any alleged illegality associated with making the payments. Lady Justice Falk held that, although Unicredit had submitted a licence application to OFAC, the scope of that application was unduly narrow, being focused solely on authorising payment by Sberbank rather than addressing Unicredit's own payment obligations under the letters of credit.

The Court of Appeal's decision highlights the far-reaching nature of the United Kingdom's restrictions on ancillary financial services. These restrictions may apply even in relation to transactions entered into prior to the imposition of the relevant trade sanctions, thereby significantly extending the scope of regulatory exposure. Conversely, the Court of

120 Ibid. at [106].

Appeal's interpretation of the statutory defence under section 44 of SAMLA provides a measure of reassurance. The judgement confirms that the defence is capable of accommodating a conservative approach to the interpretation of sanctions prohibitions.[121]

Finally, the Court of Appeal's reaffirmation of the *Ralli Bros* principle also carries important implications for parties operating in the context of multijurisdictional sanctions regimes. The decision confirms that foreign sanctions may, in certain circumstances, render the performance of an English-law contract illegal and that this may provide a legitimate basis for non-performance. At the same time, the judgement provides important clarification as to the limits of contractual flexibility in accommodating payments to persons designated under US sanctions law. It establishes a clear benchmark for the degree of effort required to overcome such sanctions and identifies the steps that must be taken – such as the scope and substance of any licence applications – in order to rely successfully on such defences in future disputes.

12 CONCLUSION

Financial institutions are at the forefront of preventing money laundering, bribery, and sanctions violations, acting as a critical line of defence against financial crime. As financial crime becomes increasingly sophisticated and global in nature, institutions must continuously adapt their internal controls, risk assessments, and due diligence processes to mitigate these risks. The regulatory oversight provided by the FCA, in combination with robust international cooperation, ensures that the UK remains at the forefront of global efforts to combat financial crime. The evolving landscape, particularly with the introduction of new legislation like the ECCTA, means that institutions must stay abreast of regulatory changes to remain compliant and avoid the severe penalties associated with financial crime violations.

Within this context, due consideration should be given by credit institutions to the international dimension of financial crime regulation, particularly with regard to the extraterritorial application of the Bribery Act 2010 and the role of financial sanctions in global geopolitical conflicts.

The UK's financial crime framework, supported by stringent legislation and active regulatory oversight, ensures that the country remains at the forefront of international efforts to combat financial crime. However, conflicting sanctions regimes, particularly between the UK, US, and the EU, can pose significant challenges for credit institutions operating across multiple jurisdictions.

121 Ibid. at [130].

CHAPTER 6

THE PRUDENTIAL REGULATION OF BANKS

OVERVIEW

The prudential regulation of banks is a cornerstone of financial stability, ensuring that banks operate in a safe and sound manner and are capable of absorbing shocks that may threaten the broader financial system. Prudential regulation primarily focuses on managing the risks inherent in banking activities,[1] including credit risk, market risk, operational risk, and liquidity risk, to name a few. Where risks are excessive and the firm fails, the costs of a financial firm's failure are not borne solely by its shareholders.[2]

Bank capital requirements serve as a fundamental pillar of contemporary banking regulation, mandating that banks maintain a minimum level of capital in relation to loans, securities, and other assets on their balance sheets. This capital acts as a buffer to absorb losses – such as those resulting from loan defaults – thereby safeguarding depositors and other creditors. Well-capitalised and liquid banks are better able to absorb losses and continue lending in adverse conditions, thereby mitigating the impact of shocks on the broader economy and avoiding the pro-cyclicality that can worsen financial crises.

International banking supervision has become increasingly critical as the world's financial markets have become more interconnected. Banks operating across multiple jurisdictions expose themselves and their home countries to a variety of risks, including systemic risks that can impact global financial stability. Insufficient capital levels were widely regarded as a contributing factor to the 2007–2008 financial crisis and the ensuing global recession. In response, regulators worldwide implemented stricter regulations to fortify the banking sector and reduce the likelihood of future crises.

A key aspect of these regulatory reforms was the enhancement of capital standards, requiring banks to hold not only more capital but also capital of higher quality, ultimately bolstering the resilience of the global financial system. Moreover, the 2007–2009 global financial crisis starkly highlighted the need for better-coordinated international banking supervision. In response, global regulatory bodies such as the Basel Committee on Banking Supervision (**BCBS**)[3] and the Financial Stability Board (**FSB**) have played instrumental roles in developing international standards for supervision and regulation.

The *Basel Accords*, produced by the BCBS, have set minimum standards for bank capital adequacy, stress testing, and market liquidity, guiding regulatory policy worldwide. While these standards are not legally binding, they have been adopted in most major jurisdictions, including the UK, EU, US, China, India, and Japan, either directly or through transposed domestic legislation.

1 REGULATION

The function of regulation has been effectively summarised by Armour, Awrey, Davies, Enriques, Gordon, Mayer, and Payne in *Principles of Financial Regulation* as "*an exercise in*

1 Finance must be understood as being predicated on risk and "*all investment involves risk*" (Lord Nicholls in *Royal Brunei Airlines v Tan* [1995] AC 378).
2 Armour, J., Awrey, D., Davies, P., Enriques, L., Gordon, J., Mayer, C. and Payne, J., *Principles of Financial Regulation* (Oxford University Press, 2016), p. 382.
3 Its 45 members comprise central banks and bank supervisors from 28 jurisdictions.

DOI: 10.4324/9781032662220-7

economics – applying the analytic tools of economics to determine the legal and regulatory framework best suited to correcting the failures of a financial system".[4]

The role of improving the functioning of the financial system is entrusted, according to Llewellyn, to the regulatory and supervisory services, where the former is defined as prescriptive, and the latter involves the exercise of allowable discretion, even when both services may be supplied through the same regulator.[5]

A number of other definitions abound in the financial literature. Generally, they advance the view that regulation of the financial systems alters outcomes by controlling the actions of financial institutions and market mechanisms, where control means "*power to decide resource, allocation, production and consumption in a manner that displaces the market as an institution*".[6]

These definitions conceive of only two perspectives: the allocation of scarce resources by the state versus free market mechanisms and the equation of supervisory or prudential measures with highly restrictive financial systems. These theories do not provide any guidance as to the optimum regulatory policy for an economy or a financial system.

Prior to the 2007–2009 financial crisis, there has been a trend emerging based on Stiglitz's[7] neo-liberal views, which now favours an effective and systemically sound regulatory system that ought to encourage innovation focusing on "*the real risks people face*".[8] This perspective advocates deregulation of financial markets as a prescription to promote economic growth and development.[9]

On this basis, two main theories were born which influenced the regulatory system: (a) regulation is counterproductive in achieving its own economic goals of efficient resource allocation and its social goals of protecting the public and private interests; (b) the free market mechanism, including self-regulation by experts, will always produce an outcome closer to Pareto optimality (a situation is said to be Pareto efficient or optimal if there is no way to rearrange things to make at least one person better off without making anyone worse off) and will be more likely to promote the enforcement of agency relationships.[10] These theories had a major limitation in that they were not considered in the context of a global financial system; rather, their application was conceived to a national system taken in isolation. As a result, the possibility that a systemic crisis in an interlinked global financial system could spread across several markets and thus affect the stability of the entire financial system was not considered.

With the benefit of hindsight, it is clear that one of the key purposes of regulation should be to prevent or at least contain systemic risks and the possibility of contagion, as opposed to making each individual player address risk more sensibly. The systemic problem stems from the fact that the actions of each individual financial institution impinge on all other banks and that the crisis in one financial system can, as the 2007–2009 financial crisis has shown, quickly spread to others.

4 Armour, J., Awrey, D., Davies, P., Enriques, L., Gordon, J., Mayer, C. and Payne, J., *Principles of Financial Regulation* (Oxford University Press, 2016), p. 51.
5 Llewellyn, 'Banking in the 21st Century: The Transformation of an Industry' in Edey, *The Future of the Financial System*, Proceeding of a Conference. Economic Group, Reserve Bank of Australia, Alken Press.
6 Curie, 'Toward s a General Theory of Financial Regulation: Predicting, Measuring and Preventing Financial Crisis' *Working Paper No. 142* (University of Technology, 2005).
7 See Stiglitz, 'Towards a New Paradigm for Development: Strategies, Policies, and Processes' *Prebisch Lecture* at UNCTAD, Geneva (19 October 1998).
8 See Stiglitz, 'Testimony before the House Committee on Financial Services' *House Committee on Financial Services* (21 October 2008), p. 18.
9 Alexander, 'Establishing a European Securities Regulator: Is the European Union an Optimal Regulation Area?' *The Cambridge Endowment for Research in Finance, University of Cambridge, Working Paper No. 7.*
10 Curie, 'Towards a General Theory of Financial Regulation: Predicting, Measuring and Preventing Financial Crisis' *Working Paper No. 142* (University of Technology, 2005).

It should be noted, however, that the purpose of regulation is to reduce the level of risk, but there are instances in which even the best-designed regulation and the most effective regulator cannot avoid risk altogether. This is because even if a potential risk is spotted in a regulated entity, it would be uncommon for a regulator to dictate how a firm should operate its business, particularly in such a complex business environment such as banking. Additionally, "too often the focus has been on the risks of a decision taken rather than the lost opportunity of taking none".[11]

2 GLOBALISATION AND CROSS-BORDER BANKING RISKS

As banking has become increasingly globalised, financial institutions have expanded their operations across borders, enabling them to access new markets and enhance profitability. While globalisation of financial markets has enabled broader economic integration, it has also occurred against a political backdrop that has, in recent years, seen a resurgence of nationalist approaches to trade and finance. Moreover, the inherently international nature of banking markets contrasts with the limited territorial jurisdiction of national authorities, creating gaps in supervision that can heighten systemic risk. Furthermore, the globalisation of banking has also introduced new risks. Currency risk and political risk are now significant concerns for banks with operations in multiple countries. Additionally, regulatory arbitrage – where banks seek out jurisdictions with less stringent regulations – poses a challenge to maintaining consistent supervision.

This dynamic has underscored the need for a more coordinated global approach to the supervision of international banking groups, leading to calls for the creation of an international supervisory body. Such a body would be responsible for developing global regulatory standards and coordinating their consistent implementation by national authorities, thereby helping to address the supervisory challenges posed by cross-border banking activities.[12] However, the most challenging issue is not so much whether an international regulator would be beneficial but whether, given the practical realities of world politics, national governments would be willing to support it.[13] Given the vast differences in political regimes and national interests worldwide, it would appear almost impossible to achieve an international agreement to transfer power to a global organisation, with all the associated implications of relinquishing sovereignty and autonomy.

In response to these concerns, the BCBS published in 1992 a set of minimum standards for the supervision of international banking groups.[14] These standards aimed to ensure a robust and cooperative framework for the oversight of banks operating across multiple jurisdictions.

The first standard required that all international banking groups and international banks were supervised by a home country authority capable of exercising effective consolidated supervision, thereby ensuring that the group as a whole was subject to oversight that considered risks throughout its global operations. Furthermore, the establishment of any cross-border banking entity had to be subject to the prior consent of both the host country supervisory authority and the home country authority of the bank or, if different, the wider banking group.

11 See www.fca.org.uk/publication/corporate/our-strategy-2025-30.pdf at p. 3 (accessed in March 2025).

12 Chiu, I. and Wilson, J., *Banking Law and Regulation* (Oxford University Press, 2019), p. 211.

13 Bollen, R., 'The International Financial System and Future Global Regulation' (2008) *Journal of International Banking Law and Regulation* 458.

14 Basel Committee on Banking Supervision, *Minimum Standards for the Supervision of International Banking Groups and Their Cross-Border Establishments* (July 1992), available at www.bis.org/publ/bcbsc314.pdf (accessed in March 2025).

This requirement aimed to ensure that both sets of supervisors can assess and manage any prudential concerns before allowing the bank to operate in the host jurisdiction. Additionally, supervisory authorities had to be empowered to obtain relevant information from cross-border banking establishments of the banks or banking groups for which they serve as the home country supervisor. This provision was essential to ensure that home country supervisors had sufficient visibility over the global operations of their banks, enabling them to assess risks comprehensively and intervene when necessary. Finally, where a host country supervisory authority found that these minimum standards were not being satisfactorily met, it could have imposed restrictive measures that were necessary to address its prudential concerns. This could have included prohibiting the establishment of new banking entities or limiting existing operations, thereby protecting the stability of the host country's financial system.

2.1 Systemic Risk and the "Too Big to Fail" Problem

One of the most significant challenges in international banking was the "too big to fail" phenomenon. Banks that were systemically important due to their size, complexity, and interconnectedness could pose a substantial risk to the global financial system if they fail. The collapse of Lehman Brothers in 2008 demonstrated the catastrophic consequences that the failure of a large, interconnected bank could have on the global economy.[15]

In response to the 2007–2009 financial crisis, global regulatory bodies, including the FSB, have developed frameworks for the supervision and resolution of global systemically important banks (**G-SIBs**). These frameworks included stricter capital requirements and resolution planning to ensure that G-SIBs could be wound down in an orderly fashion without threatening global financial stability.

3 THE NATURE OF PRUDENTIAL REGULATION

Prudential regulation is the cornerstone of financial regulation, aimed at maintaining the safety and soundness of financial institutions and protecting the stability of the financial system. It focuses on ensuring that banks and other financial institutions manage risks effectively and hold sufficient capital and liquidity to absorb potential losses. This is fundamentally important in a business model which involves transforming short-term deposits into long-term loans, which means that the majority of its capital is raised through debt; therefore, banks are, by their nature, highly leveraged.[16]

A prudential framework encompasses both the establishment of regulatory requirements and the supervisory enforcement of those requirements. Its primary objective is to ensure that financial firms manage their risk-taking activities effectively and maintain adequate levels of capital and liquidity. By doing so, the framework seeks to promote the resilience of individual institutions and safeguard the stability of the broader financial system. In this context, prudential regulation operates at two distinct levels: micro-prudential and macro-prudential. Both approaches are critical for ensuring the resilience of the financial system, but they differ in their focus, tools, and objectives.

15 Armour, J., Awrey, D., Davies, P., Enriques, L., Gordon, J., Mayer, C. and Payne, J., *Principles of Financial Regulation* (Oxford University Press, 2016), p. 374.

16 Armour, J., Awrey, D., Davies, P., Enriques, L., Gordon, J., Mayer, C. and Payne, J., *Principles of Financial Regulation* (Oxford University Press, 2016), p. 374.

Micro-prudential regulation focuses on the safety and soundness of individual financial institutions. Its primary objective is to ensure that each bank, insurance company, or financial firm is well-capitalised, solvent, and capable of managing its own risks. By focusing on the health of individual institutions, micro-prudential regulation aims to reduce the likelihood of firm-specific failures that could negatively impact depositors, creditors, and other stakeholders.[17]

In contrast to micro-prudential regulation, **macro-prudential regulation** takes a broader, system-wide approach. It aims to ensure the stability of the entire financial system by addressing risks that could accumulate across multiple institutions or sectors. Macro-prudential regulation seeks to prevent systemic risks – risks that arise when the failure of one institution or market segment could trigger a domino effect, leading to widespread financial instability.

Together, these two forms of regulation are essential for maintaining a stable and resilient global financial system.

3.1 Prudential Regulation: Supervision and Capital Adequacy

The 2008 financial crisis originated in the US as a result of problems in the sub-prime portion of the residential mortgage market. Before 2008, this sector, which represented 10% of the US residential mortgage market, had received little attention from bank management, supervisors, or bank analysts.[18]

However, in August 2007, the news that highly regarded financial institutions held considerable amounts of securitised US sub-prime mortgages caused concerns amongst market participants. This was due to the fact that many credit institutions had used securitised assets as collateral to borrow in wholesale markets, so when the quality of these assets became questionable, wholesale market lending seized up as a result of the lack of confidence in the quality of the underlying assets backing the collateral provided. The problem was further exacerbated by a tightening of the so-called "fair value" or "mark-to-market" accounting rules, whereby banks and other financial institutions valued assets they held (such as securities, portfolios, or loans) based on the daily value of such assets, i.e., the price they would achieve if they were sold on the market at that time, and not at the maturity date of that asset. Such rules determined whether these financial institutions were solvent and fit to continue trading.[19]

For months, credit institutions attempted to address investors' demands for larger capital buffers. However, these attempts proved to be unsuccessful, and

> *in the wake of the Lehman Brothers default on 15 September 2008, the system collapsed. Banks, fearful of their own solvency, all but stopped lending. Issuance of corporate bonds, commercial paper and a wide variety of other securities or financial products largely ceased. Credit-financed economic activity was brought to a virtual standstill.*[20]

The main cause of this "credit crunch", which affected the stability of financial markets, was uncertainty: since no one knew exactly who owned the potential losses from securitised mortgages and other structured financial products, many investors steered clear of them.

17 Kokkinis, A. and Miglionico, M., *Banking Law: Private Transactions and Regulatory Frameworks* (Routledge, 2021), p. 23.

18 Zambelli, M., *The Law of Securitisation in Ireland* (PhD Thesis, Trinity College Dublin, the University of Dublin, 2017), p. 313.

19 See Hall, M., 'The Sub-Prime Crisis, the Credit Squeeze and Northern Rock: The Lessons to Be Learned' (2008) 16(1) *Journal of Financial Regulation and Compliance* 19.

20 'Banks Need More Capital' *The Economist*, 18 December 2008.

Some commentators[21] were of the view that one of the contributors to the capital markets debacle was the then newly implemented (December 2006) framework for banking capital adequacy standards, entitled "International Convergence of Capital Measurement and Capital Standards – A Revised Framework" or Basel II, which had been developed by the BCBS.

3.2 Basel Committee on Banking Supervision

The Basel Committee on Banking Supervision (BCBS), established in 1974, is the principal international body responsible for setting standards for the prudential regulation and supervision of banks.[22] Initially formed in response to financial crises, the BCBS works to enhance financial stability through globally harmonised regulatory standards.

Given the global nature of banking, there is a clear need for a minimum level playing field that applies consistently across jurisdictions. To promote such consistency, the BCBS establishes minimum regulatory standards for internationally active banks. Without such common standards, there is a risk of triggering a "race to the bottom" in which jurisdictions compete to offer the weakest regulatory regimes, undermining the resilience of the global banking sector. Although weaker standards may promote credit expansion and short-term economic growth, they typically encourage excessive risk-taking and the accumulation of dangerous levels of leverage. Such imbalances are often followed by sharp contractions in credit supply, bank failures, systemic financial instability, and severe economic downturns.

These standards have evolved through Basel I, Basel II, Basel III (introduced in response to the global financial crisis of 2007–2009), and Basel IV. Each iteration has brought stronger and more refined rules to ensure the stability of banks and the global financial system. Although these are intended as baseline requirements, many jurisdictions choose to adopt stricter rules, going beyond the Basel minimums to address specific national risks and priorities.

3.3 Legal Status and Structure

The BCBS is based within the headquarters of the Bank for International Settlements (**BIS**) in Basel, Switzerland, and it includes 45 members from 28 jurisdictions, comprising central banks and bank supervisory authorities. It is not an international organisation, and its constituents are not member states but rather representatives of their respective supervisory organisations and central banks.[23] It operates under the umbrella of the BIS but does not have a distinct legal identity from the BIS. Other BIS committees include the Committee on Payments and Market Infrastructures and the Committee on the Global Financial System, which complements the BCBS's work by addressing systemic issues such as payments, clearing, and settlement infrastructures.

The Group of Central Bank Governors and Heads of Supervision (**GHOS**) oversees the BCBS, setting its work programme and providing guidance. The committee itself is responsible for producing the BCBS's standards, guidelines, and sound practices, while

21 *See, for example, Goodhart, 'The Regulatory Response to the Financial Crisis' March 2008,* CESifo Working Paper Series No. 2257. *See also* Proctor, C., *The Law and Practice of International Banking* (Oxford University Press, 2015), p. 124.

22 Ellinger, E. P., Lomnicka, E. and Hare, C., *Ellinger's Modern Banking Law* (Oxford University Press, 2011), p. 77.

23 Chiu, I. and Wilson, J., *Banking Law and Regulation* (Oxford University Press, 2019), p. 195.

sub-committees and task forces carry out specific tasks related to these areas. The BCBS Secretariat, provided by the BIS, supports the committee's operations.

The standards set by the BCBS do not have direct legal effect on their own. However, the BCBS expects its member countries, which include the US, the UK, and the EU, to fully implement its standards within the specified timeframes established by the Committee.

The first step in this direction was the Basel Concordat, which was published in 1975 following the Bankhaus Herstatt's crisis and subsequently revised in 1983 as a result of the insolvency in 1982 of Banco Ambrosiano, an Italian bank.[24] Later, supplements to the Concordat were issued alongside the Basel Core Principles for Effective Banking Supervision, which are widely regarded as the *de facto* minimum standard for sound prudential regulation and supervision of banks and banking systems worldwide.[25]

As a result of the collapse of BCCI,[26] the BCBS reformulated some of the principles of the Concordat and published them as minimum standards for the supervision of international banking groups.[27] The BCBS advocates for a proportionate approach to implementation, encouraging members to tailor their regulatory frameworks according to the relative differences in risk and complexity of banks and the markets in which they operate.[28]

While there is no formal sanction for a country that fails to implement the recommendations of the BCBS, other bodies, such as the Financial Stability Board[29] and the International Monetary Fund, conduct compliance reviews, with the results published alongside recommendations for improvement. This approach serves as an effective soft law mechanism to encourage compliance.

4 EVOLUTION OF THE BASEL STANDARDS

The Basel capital accords are designed to reduce the likelihood of bank failures by establishing a framework for capital adequacy. Central to this framework is the requirement that each asset held by a bank should be weighted according to its risk, which reflects the probability of the counterparty defaulting on its obligations.

The BCBS provides guidance on the application of its standards through the Scope and Definitions chapter (SCO) of the Basel framework. According to SCO10.1, the Basel framework should be applied on a consolidated basis to internationally active banks. While the Basel framework does not formally define the term "bank", the BCBS generally assumes that a bank is an entity that accepts deposits. In its *Core Principles for Effective Banking Supervision*, the BCBS notes that deposit-taking from the public should be restricted to licensed institutions that are

24 Goodhart, C., *The Basel Committee on Banking Supervision: A History of the Early Years* (Cambridge University Press, 2011), p. 104.

25 Goodhart, C., *The Basel Committee on Banking Supervision: A History of the Early Years* (Cambridge University Press, 2011), p. 10.

26 See Chapter 4.

27 Basel Committee on Banking Supervision, *Minimum Standards for the Supervision of International Banking Groups and Their Cross-Border Establishments* (July 1992), available at www.bis.org/publ/bcbsc314.pdf (accessed in March 2025).

28 In a November 2019 newsletter, the BCBS emphasised that a proportionate regulatory framework should appropriately reflect these variations (BCBS: Joint BCBS-BCG statement on proportionality (NL23)).

29 Financial Stability Board, About the FSB: "*The FSB promotes international financial stability; it does so by coordinating national financial authorities and international standard-setting bodies as they work toward developing strong regulatory, supervisory and other financial sector policies.* ***It fosters a level playing field by encouraging coherent implementation of these policies across sectors and jurisdictions.*** *The FSB, working through its members, seeks to strengthen financial systems and increase the stability of international financial markets. The policies developed in the pursuit of this agenda are implemented by jurisdictions and national authorities*", at www.fsb.org/about/ (accessed in March 2025).

subject to bank supervision.[30] This implies that the Basel standards are not necessarily intended to apply to pure investment banks – those that do not engage in deposit-taking activities – although member jurisdictions have the discretion to extend the standards to such institutions.

The term "internationally active" is similarly left undefined in the Basel framework. In an October 2012 report,[31] the BCBS acknowledged that the term is "not specifically defined in the Basel text", leaving its interpretation to national authorities. Some countries apply this classification to banks that exceed certain thresholds of size or cross-border activity, while others extend it to banks with overseas branches or subsidiaries. However, it has cautioned against limiting the definition solely to banks with foreign business locations, as this would conflict with "the spirit of the Basel agreement".[32] Since Basel standards are intended to represent minimum requirements, member jurisdictions are free to expand their scope to cover banks that do not meet the criteria for being internationally active.

5 BASEL I

Basel I, introduced in 1988, was the first international attempt to foster convergence in global banking regulations. Although Basel I was primarily designed for implementation by members of the BCBS, by 2005, it was reportedly implemented in 120 countries.[33]

Its core focus was on credit risk, introducing minimum capital requirements for banks. The accord required that a credit institution's capital ratio – calculated as the institution's capital (the numerator) divided by its risk-weighted assets (the denominator) – must be no less than 8%, expressing the result as a percentage.[34] A firm's total risk exposure amount is, broadly speaking, the sum of its risk-weighted assets (**RWAs**) for credit risk, market risk, and operational risk. Accordingly, institutions must hold sufficient capital to support the risk-weighted value of their assets.

Definition of Regulatory Capital[35]

Capital represents a bank's "own funds" and consists of elements such as ordinary share capital and retained earnings. While it serves as a source of funding for the bank, similar to its liabilities, it is distinct in that it is not borrowed money that must be repaid.

A bank's capital is essentially the difference between the value of its total assets and its total liabilities. This structure means that if the value of the bank's assets declines, the capital can be written down to absorb the losses. As a result, the holders of the bank's capital instruments bear the financial costs of such a decline, underscoring the critical role capital plays in maintaining a bank's resilience and stability.

30 Principle 4 (Permissible Activities): "the taking of deposits from the public is reserved for institutions that are licensed and subject to supervision as banks", (BCP40.11).

31 Available at www.bis.org/bcbs/implementation/l2_eu.htm (accessed in March 2025).

32 See The G20 Research Group at Trinity College at the Munk School of Global Affairs and Public Policy in the University of Toronto, *2017 Hamburg G20 Summit Final Compliance Report*, available at https://g20.utoronto.ca/compliance/2017hamburg-final/2017-g20-compliance-final.pdf (accessed in March 2025).

33 Jones, E. and Zeitz, A., 'The Limits of Globalizing Basel Banking Standards' (2017) 3 *Journal of Financial Regulation* 89, p. 92.

34 In accordance with Article 92(2) of the EU Capital Requirements Regulation (Regulation 575/2013) (**UK CRR**).

35 For an overview of bank capital and the practical issues that banks encounter in relation to their regulatory capital, see Bank of England: Bank capital and liquidity (Quarterly Bulletin 2013 Q3) at www.bankofengland.co.uk/-/media/boe/files/quarterly-bulletin/2013/bank-capital-and-liquidity.pdf (accessed in March 2025).

Only specific loss-absorbing resources qualify as a bank's regulatory capital. These resources are classified into different categories based on their quality and risk profile. The categorisation is primarily determined by whether the resources are considered "going concern" or "gone concern".

"Going concern" resources are designed to enable a bank to continue operating during periods of financial stress, while "gone concern" resources are intended to absorb losses during the resolution process if the bank has failed. This distinction ensures that the bank has sufficient capital to either remain viable in adverse conditions or mitigate the impact of its failure on the financial system.

The concept of RWAs was introduced to ensure that banks maintained adequate capital in proportion to the risk profile of their asset portfolios. An example of risk-weighting under the Basel I framework illustrates how different categories of assets were assigned varying risk weights to calculate a bank's RWAs. **Cash and similar assets**, including exposures to **highly rated sovereign governments**, were assigned a 0% risk weight because they were considered to carry no credit risk; as such, their value was excluded from RWAs. **Residential mortgages** secured by residential property were treated as carrying moderate risk and were assigned a 50% risk weight, meaning that only half of their value was included in the calculation of RWAs. By contrast, **commercial loans**, such as those extended to corporate borrowers, were regarded as high-risk exposures and were therefore assigned a 100% risk weight, resulting in their full value being included in RWAs.

Calculation of Risk-Weighted Assets Under Basel I

Assume a bank holds the following assets within its portfolio:

- Sovereign bonds from a G10 country (AAA rated): £50 million
- Residential mortgages: £100 million
- Unrated corporate loans: £200 million

Each asset class is assigned a risk weight under Basel I as follows:

Sovereign Bonds

Sovereign bonds issued by highly rated G10 countries are considered risk-free and are therefore assigned a risk weight of 0%.

RWAs for sovereign bonds:

£50 million × 0% = £0

Residential Mortgages

Residential mortgages are deemed moderately risky and attract a risk weight of 50% under the Basel I framework.

RWAs for residential mortgages:

£100 million × 50% = £50 million

Corporate Loans

Unrated corporate loans are considered high risk and carry the maximum risk weight of 100%.

RWAs for corporate loans:

£200 million × 100% = £200 million

Total RWAs

- Sovereign bonds: £0
- Residential mortgages: £50 million
- Corporate loans: £200 million

Total RWAs = £0 + £50 million + £200 million = £250 million

Minimum Capital Requirement

In accordance with Basel I, banks must maintain regulatory capital equal to at least 8% of their total RWAs. In this example:

Minimum capital required = £250 million × 8% = £20 million

Accordingly, the bank mu st hold £20 million in regulatory capital to comply with Basel I requirements for the total exposure to a portfolio of £350 million.

Credit commitments, such as lending facilities, also required capital support. Once a credit line is drawn, it becomes a bank asset and is risk-weighted accordingly. However, even undrawn commitments must be assigned a conversion factor to account for the likelihood of future utilisation, with capital requirements adjusted based on the client's creditworthiness.

6 BASEL II

By the late 1990s, weaknesses in Basel I prompted calls for reforms to the standards. A significant concern was that Basel I failed to differentiate the risk levels associated with individual loans adequately. This shortcoming created opportunities for regulatory arbitrage, which banks exploited through various financial techniques.[36] Moreover, Basel I concentrated solely on credit and market risk, overlooking operational risk. It also made little progress in strengthening supervisory institutions or enhancing corporate governance.

The Basel II standards were agreed upon in 2004 after intense and prolonged negotiations. The primary objective of these new standards was to ensure that the regulatory capital held by banks more accurately reflected the actual risks they were undertaking. While Basel II retained certain fundamental aspects of Basel I, it introduced significant changes to the system for risk-weighting assets.

36 Tarullo, D., *Banking on Basel: The Future of International Financial Regulation* (Peterson Institute for International Economics, 2008).

Under Basel II, banks were required to maintain a minimum total capital ratio of 8%, a threshold which remained unchanged from that set under Basel I. This total capital ratio comprised Tier 1, Tier 2, and, in certain cases, Tier 3 capital, all of which were designed to absorb losses and thereby contribute to the stability of the financial system.

Tier 1 capital represents the primary measure of a bank's financial strength and consists predominantly of core capital, including common stock and disclosed reserves. It could have incorporated non-redeemable, non-cumulative preferred stock. Under Basel II, banks had to maintain at least 4% of Tier 1 capital, with a minimum core capital ratio set at 2%. This form of capital was regarded as the most dependable due to its high liquidity and strong loss-absorbing capacity, particularly in times of financial stress.

Tier 2 capital, although considered secondary, remained an essential component of a bank's regulatory capital. It comprised items that were inherently more difficult to value and which could have been redeemable in the future. These included undisclosed reserves, revaluation reserves, general provisions, hybrid instruments, and subordinated term debt, provided such debt had a minimum maturity of five years. While Tier 2 capital was generally seen as less secure than Tier 1, it nonetheless played a vital role in enhancing a bank's capacity to absorb losses beyond those covered by Tier 1.

Tier 3 capital, the least frequently used of the three, comprised short-term subordinated debt, and it was specifically intended to cover market risk. Banks were allowed to utilise Tier 3 capital solely for this purpose, and it had to be combined with Tier 1 and Tier 2 capital to ensure the institution met its overall regulatory capital requirements. Together, these capital tiers constituted an attempt to ensure that banks hold sufficient financial resources to safeguard against unexpected losses, thereby upholding market confidence and protecting the broader financial system. Such an attempt proved ineffective during the global 2007–2009 financial crisis.

Basel II was fundamentally structured around three regulatory pillars,[37] and such a framework has remained largely consistent even with the introduction of Basel III. Pillar 1 set out the method by which financial institutions were required to calculate their eligible capital and, as a result, the minimum capital requirements that must be maintained in relation to their exposure to credit risk, operational risk, and market risk.

Pillar 2 established a supervisory review process that obliged regulators to assess the effectiveness of each financial institution's internal evaluation of its capital adequacy in relation to the risks it faces. This pillar empowered supervisors to intervene when necessary, particularly where deficiencies were identified in how institutions measured or managed their risks. The aim is to ensure that banks maintained capital levels that are appropriate to their risk profile, beyond the minimum levels required under Pillar 1, thereby strengthening overall stability.

Pillar 3 complemented the first two pillars by imposing market discipline through mandatory disclosure requirements. Financial institutions were required to publish detailed information on a bi-annual basis, covering critical areas such as their capital structure, capital adequacy, credit risk mitigation strategies, and securitisation activities. These disclosures were designed to provide market participants with a clear understanding of the bank's risk profile and capital position, promoting greater transparency and allowing investors, customers, and counterparties to make informed decisions.

One of the key innovations of Basel II was that certain financial institutions were permitted to choose between two broad methodologies for calculating their credit risk. The first enabled financial institutions to calculate their risk in a standardised manner supported by

37 Chiu, I. and Wilson, J., *Banking Law and Regulation* (Oxford University Press, 2019), p. 358.

external credit assessments (the Standardised Approach). The second enabled financial institutions to use their own internal credit evaluation systems (the Internal Ratings Based, or "IRB" approach). This second method was subject to the explicit approval of that financial institution's supervisor.

A logical extension of the supervisory approach was the use of banks' own risk measurement systems in the calculation of regulatory capital adequacy.

This approach primarily relied on historical data, which, by its nature, was not a precise indicator of a bank's current risk exposure. Moreover, it had inherent limitations in accounting for unforeseen events that past data could not anticipate. To address these challenges, regulatory frameworks introduced a range of risk assessment methodologies, including the standardised approach, the foundation internal ratings-based (**IRB**) approach, and the advanced internal ratings-based approach.

Under the standardised approach, exposures were classified into distinct risk categories, with three key categories – loans to sovereigns, corporates, and banks – being assigned risk weights based on the external credit ratings of the borrower. Other categories remained subject to fixed risk weights. For instance, loans secured against residential property carried a risk weight of 35%, provided that the loan-to-value (**LTV**) ratio did not exceed 80%.[38] This approach provided a relatively straightforward method for determining capital requirements but was limited by its reliance on external credit assessments and fixed risk weightings.

The foundation IRB approach allowed financial institutions to develop their own models to determine regulatory capital requirements, subject to supervisory oversight. Under this method, lenders were required to estimate the probability of default (**PD**) for each exposure, while regulatory authorities prescribed standardised values for other key risk parameters, including loss given default (**LGD**), exposure at default (**EAD**), and maturity of exposure (**M**). These values were then incorporated into the institution's risk weight function to calculate the appropriate risk weighting for each exposure.

Institutions with more sophisticated risk management capabilities could adopt the advanced IRB approach, which permitted them to estimate all key risk parameters – PD, LGD, EAD, and M – rather than relying on supervisory-set values. For retail portfolios, where the underlying debtors were individual clients rather than corporate entities, the regulatory requirements were slightly less complex. In these cases, institutions needed only to estimate PD, LGD, and EAD, a variation of the advanced IRB approach known as the "retail IRB" approach.[39]

Trading Book and Banking Book

The **trading book** includes financial instruments like derivatives and equities that are actively traded in the market. The capital requirements here cover both market risk (price movements) and counterparty credit risk (distinguished from non-trading credit risk). The objective of trading book capital is to absorb losses from short-term market fluctuations.

38 'Basel II – a guide to new capital adequacy standards for lenders', Council of Mortgage Lenders, February 2008.

39 'Basel II – a guide to new capital adequacy standards for lenders', Council of Mortgage Lenders, February 2008.

The **banking book** includes all exposures not held in the trading book, and its capital requirements are focused on covering unexpected credit losses over a one-year holding period.[40]

7 BASEL 2.5

The 2007–2009 global financial crisis exposed significant weaknesses in the existing international regulatory framework for banking, prompting further revisions to the Basel standards. The risk-sensitivity of Basel II capital requirements came under criticism for exacerbating pro-cyclicality,[41] thereby increasing the likelihood of financial crises. The crisis also underscored the need for better regulation to address risks related to securitisation, counterparty credit exposures arising from derivatives, and repurchase and securities financing transactions. In response, Basel II was supplemented with critical amendments aimed at enhancing risk coverage, addressing areas that had been perceived as insufficiently regulated in the original framework; such supplement was later referred to as "Basel 2.5". While these reforms were primarily targeted at internationally active and systemically significant banks, their impact was broader, particularly within the European Union (and, at the time, the United Kingdom), where they applied to all credit institutions and investment firms.[42]

One of the key areas of reform was the trading book, where capital requirements were adjusted to better reflect the risks associated with trading activities. Another important adjustment was the alignment of capital charges for securitised products within the trading book with those applicable in the banking book, addressing inconsistencies that had previously allowed banks to arbitrage capital requirements between the two books.

Basel 2.5 also introduced stricter capital requirements for re-securitisation positions, reflecting their higher risk profile. Re-securitisations – structured products backed by other securitised assets (see Chapter 14) – exhibited amplified risk during the financial crisis, as losses in the underlying assets had a cascading effect. The revised framework increased capital charges for such exposures to better account for their vulnerability to market disruptions and adverse credit events.

Beyond changes to capital requirements, Basel 2.5 introduced new supervisory guidance under Pillar 2, emphasising improvements in banks' internal governance and risk assessment processes. This guidance was intended to assist financial institutions in better identifying, measuring, and managing risks beyond the minimum capital requirements. Moreover, Basel 2.5 strengthened Pillar 3 disclosure requirements, enhancing transparency by requiring banks to provide more detailed information on their exposures to securitisation risks and the

40 The capital charge for banking book exposures can be calculated using the formula: **Capital Charge = Exposure Amount (EA) x Risk Weight (RW) x General Capital Requirement (GCR)**. For unfunded commitments, a credit conversion factor (CCF) is applied.

41 Procyclicality refers to the tendency of financial variables to move in tandem with the broader economic cycle, fluctuating around a long-term trend. An increase in procyclicality therefore signifies that such fluctuations occur with greater amplitude, amplifying the highs and lows of economic activity. However, once a system becomes destabilised, it departs from the linear regime and begins to exhibit non-linear behaviour, including phenomena such as path dependence, sustained oscillations, and abrupt regime shifts.

42 In the European Union context, Basel 2.5 was implemented through a further amendment to the Capital Requirements Directive (CRD), known as CRD III (Directive 2010/76/EU). This directive applied to all credit institutions and investment firms subject to the MiFID II Directive (2014/65/EU) and the Markets in Financial Instruments Regulation (Regulation 600/2014) (MiFIR).

quality of their capital. These enhanced disclosure obligations aimed to improve market discipline by ensuring that investors and regulators had clearer insights into banks' risk profiles.

Overall, Basel 2.5 represented a transitional regulatory response, addressing critical deficiencies in the Basel II framework while paving the way for more comprehensive reforms under Basel III.

8 BASEL III

Basel III was developed in stages between September 2010 and late 2014, aiming to address the substantial deficiencies that were exposed by the 2007–09 global financial crisis and which were not covered by the Basel 2.5 "fix". Unlike Basel II, Basel III explicitly sought to increase both the quantity and quality of capital held by banks. It also introduced liquidity standards and a range of macroprudential measures designed to mitigate the build-up of systemic risk.[43] In general terms, Basel III is built on the foundation of the Basel II framework, aiming to improve both the quality and quantity of capital, strengthening risk coverage, and introducing new regulatory measures such as capital buffers, a leverage ratio, and enhanced liquidity requirements. These reforms intended to ensure the stability of both individual institutions and the financial system as a whole, and they apply at the micro-prudential (individual firms) and macro-prudential (system-wide) levels.[44]

The quality of regulatory capital has been significantly enhanced, requiring banks to hold a larger proportion of common equity, which consists primarily of common shares and retained earnings. The definition of capital has been streamlined, with Tier 3 capital being eliminated and hybrid financial instruments gradually phased out from Tier 1 capital.

The Basel III Framework

Under the **Basel III framework**, regulatory capital is categorised into different tiers according to its quality and ability to absorb losses, both during ongoing operations and in cases of financial distress. The three main categories – Common Equity Tier 1 (**CET1**), Additional Tier 1 (**AT1**), and **Tier 2** – reflect a hierarchy of capital instruments based on their capacity to absorb risk and support a bank's financial stability.[45]

CET1 represents the highest quality of capital, as it provides immediate loss absorption on a going-concern basis. This category includes common shares issued by the bank, retained earnings, qualifying minority interests (such as common shares in consolidated subsidiaries held by third parties), and certain regulatory adjustments. Given its ability to absorb losses directly and maintain the bank's solvency during periods of financial stress, CET1 forms the core component of a bank's capital structure and is subject to the most stringent regulatory requirements.

AT1 capital also contributes to a bank's ability to absorb losses on a going-concern basis but does not meet the strict criteria required for CET1 classification. It comprises capital instruments specifically designated as AT1, any related surplus, additional qualifying minority interests, and relevant regulatory adjustments. Unlike CET1, AT1

43 Jones, E. and Zeitz, A., 'The Limits of Globalizing Basel Banking Standards' (2017) 3 *Journal of Financial Regulation* 89, p. 97.
44 Chiu, I. and Wilson, J., *Banking Law and Regulation* (Oxford University Press, 2019), p. 371.
45 The specific criteria for CET1, AT1, and Tier 2 capital are detailed in **CAP10**.

often includes perpetual debt instruments, such as contingent convertible bonds, which are designed to convert into equity or be written down when a bank's capital position deteriorates. These instruments provide an additional layer of protection, ensuring that a bank can continue operating while facing financial difficulties.

Tier 2 capital is classified as gone-concern capital, meaning that it absorbs losses only in the event of a bank's failure before depositors and other senior creditors incur losses. It includes subordinated debt and general loan-loss reserves, as specified by the BCBS. Unlike AT1 instruments, which must be perpetual, Tier 2 instruments can have a maturity date, reflecting their role in providing a financial cushion that becomes effective only when a bank is no longer viable.

Total regulatory capital is the sum of CET1, AT1, and Tier 2 capital, net of regulatory adjustments. **Total Tier 1 capital** is the sum of CET1 and AT1 capital, as well as the net of regulatory adjustments.[46]

The Basel framework also includes **regulatory adjustments** and **deductions** from regulatory capital, accounting for uncertainties regarding the realisable value of certain items during periods of financial stress. They are largely applied to CET1 and include significant deductions such as goodwill, other intangible assets, deferred tax assets, and investments in other financial entities.

Under Basel III, significant reforms were introduced to strengthen banks' capital adequacy, risk management, and overall resilience in response to the shortcomings exposed during the global financial crisis. These reforms addressed multiple dimensions, including the quantity and quality of capital, capital buffers, risk coverage, leverage requirements, liquidity standards, and disclosure obligations.

The minimum capital requirements have been increased, with common equity and Tier 1 capital ratios raised to 4.5% and 6%, respectively. However, the overall minimum capital ratio remains at 8%, with additional capital buffers applying to certain institutions to further enhance financial stability.

To reinforce these capital requirements, Basel III introduced two key buffers that operate alongside the higher common equity and Tier 1 capital thresholds: the Capital Conservation Buffer and the Countercyclical Capital Buffer.

Banks classified as G-SIBs were subject to even stricter capital requirements. These institutions had to maintain additional common equity capital layered onto the capital conservation buffer, with the exact amount determined by the institution's systemic importance. This measure ensured that the largest and most interconnected banks hold sufficient capital to absorb losses without destabilising the broader financial system.

Basel III also enhanced risk coverage by addressing areas previously insufficiently regulated under Basel II, particularly counterparty credit risk and over-reliance on external credit ratings. More stringent capital requirements are applied to exposures arising from derivatives, repurchase (repo) transactions, and other securities financing activities, reflecting the heightened risks associated with these transactions.

In addition to risk-based capital requirements, Basel III introduced a leverage ratio to serve as a safeguard against excessive leverage. This leverage ratio acted as a "backstop"

46 (CAP10.2).

to the risk-weighted capital framework, preventing institutions from accumulating excessive debt relative to their capital base. This is because the

> *years preceding the financial crisis were characterised by an excessive build up in institutions' exposures in relation to their own funds (leverage). During the financial crisis, losses and the shortage of funding forced institutions to reduce significantly their leverage over a short period of time. This amplified downward pressures on asset prices, causing further losses for institutions which in turn led to further declines in their own funds. The ultimate results of this negative spiral were a reduction in the availability of credit to the real economy and a deeper and longer crisis.*[47]

Recognising the importance of liquidity in maintaining financial stability, Basel III established two liquidity standards aimed at improving banks' resilience during periods of stress. The Liquidity Coverage Ratio (**LCR**)[48] ensured that banks hold sufficient high-quality liquid assets to meet short-term liquidity needs, while the Net Stable Funding Ratio (**NSFR**) promoted more stable, long-term funding structures, reducing reliance on short-term wholesale funding.

Capital Conservation Buffer, Countercyclical Capital Buffer, Leverage Ratio, and Liquidity Coverage Ratio

Capital Conservation Buffer (CCB): The CCB is an additional buffer of 2.5% of risk-weighted assets that banks must hold in common equity. Its purpose is to absorb losses during periods of financial stress. If a bank's capital ratios fall within this buffer range, its ability to distribute dividends, bonuses, or share buybacks will be restricted. The idea is to ensure that banks retain enough capital to remain solvent during adverse conditions.

Example:

Suppose Bank A has RWA of £100 million. Under Basel III, Bank A is required to hold a minimum of 4.5% in common equity (i.e., £4.5 million). On top of that, the CCB requires Bank A to hold an additional 2.5% (i.e., £2.5 million). If Bank A's capital falls below the combined 7% (4.5% + 2.5%), it would be limited in its ability to make discretionary payments to shareholders and employees.

Countercyclical Capital Buffer (CCyB): The CCyB is designed to protect the banking sector during periods of excessive credit growth. National authorities can impose this buffer (up to 2.5% of RWAs) to require banks to build up additional capital reserves during credit booms, which can then be drawn down in periods of stress.

Example:

In a rapidly growing economy, where credit is expanding at an unsustainable rate, the PRA may impose a 1% countercyclical buffer on top of the CCB. This means Bank A, with £100 million in RWAs, would need to hold an additional £1 million of common equity on top of the CCB, raising its total capital requirement to 8% (7% + 1%).

47 Regulation (EU) No 575/2013 of the European Parliament and of the Council of 26 June 2013 on prudential requirements for credit institutions and investment firms and amending Regulation (EU) No 648/2012 – Recital 90.

48 Chiu, I. and Wilson, J., *Banking Law and Regulation* (Oxford University Press, 2019), p. 413.

A credit institution that fails to meet its buffer requirements must calculate, according to a pre-defined regulatory formula, the maximum amount that it is allowed to pay in the form of dividends, discretionary coupons, or bonuses. This amount is referred to as the maximum distributable amount. The credit institution must also submit a capital conservation plan to its competent authority.

Leverage Ratio: The leverage ratio is a non-risk-based measure that sets a minimum level of capital relative to a bank's total assets and off-balance-sheet exposures. It is designed to prevent banks from becoming excessively leveraged, ensuring they hold sufficient capital against their overall exposure. The Basel III leverage ratio sets a minimum of 3% Tier 1 capital to total exposure.

Example:

If Bank A has £1 billion in total assets and off-balance-sheet exposures, it must hold at least 3% of this amount (£30 million) in Tier 1 capital to meet the leverage ratio requirement, regardless of the riskiness of its assets. This backstop measure ensures that even low-risk activities are adequately capitalised.

The **LCR** requires banks to hold enough high-quality liquid assets (**HQLA**) to cover their net cash outflows over a 30-day stress scenario. For instance, if a bank has €500 million in HQLA and expected outflows of €400 million, its LCR would be 125% (€500m/€400m), comfortably above the minimum requirement of 100%.[49]

Finally, Basel III strengthened market discipline by enhancing disclosure requirements under Pillar 3. Banks had to provide more detailed information on the quality and composition of their capital resources, ensuring greater transparency for investors, regulators, and other market participants. These reforms collectively contributed to a more resilient banking sector capable of withstanding financial shocks and supporting sustainable economic growth.

The BCBS established mechanisms to ensure the full and consistent implementation of Basel III across its member jurisdictions. The Regulatory Consistency Assessment Programme has been central to this effort.[50] It operates through several key components designed to monitor, evaluate, and enforce adherence to the Basel standards. Beyond regulatory alignment, the BCBS also monitored the impact of Basel III reforms on banks. Through these mechanisms, the BCBS ensured the uniform implementation of Basel III and the delivery of its intended benefits in promoting financial stability and resilience.

49 Chiu, I. and Wilson, J., *Banking Law and Regulation* (Oxford University Press, 2019), p. 419.

50 A fundamental aspect of the Regulatory Consistency Assessment Programme (RCAP) is the monitoring of the timely implementation of Basel III by member countries. This process ensures that regulatory reforms are not only adopted but also enforced within the prescribed timeframes. Additionally, the BCBS assesses the consistency of the standards implemented by different jurisdictions, identifying any deviations from the Basel framework and evaluating their significance. This consistency assessment is conducted through two distinct approaches. Jurisdictional assessments examine whether the banking laws and regulations of BCBS member countries align with Basel III requirements, ensuring that national frameworks are appropriately calibrated. In parallel, thematic assessments focus on key regulatory outcomes, such as capital adequacy, RWAs, and other critical prudential metrics, to determine whether the intended objectives of Basel III are being met in practice.

9 BASEL 3.1, FINAL BASEL III OR BASEL IV

The BCBS agreed on a comprehensive package of reforms,[51] referred to as the final Basel III standards, while some commentators have referred to these changes as Basel IV (which also reflects the author's preference) or Basel 3.1,[52] which were intended to supplement and complete the various Basel III reforms introduced incrementally since December 2010. The BCBS set 1 January 2023 as the target date for the implementation of these standards by its members.

The Basel IV standards focused primarily on aspects of the Basel framework that had not been significantly addressed in earlier Basel III reforms, specifically standards initially set out in the Basel II and Basel 2.5 frameworks.[53]

Basel IV included significant revisions to the standardised approach for credit risk, aiming to improve its granularity and risk sensitivity while reducing overreliance on credit ratings. Changes to the IRB approach for credit risk include the removal of the advanced IRB (A-IRB) approach for certain asset classes and the introduction of minimum floor values for bank-estimated parameters used to RWAs.

Regarding market risk, the reforms reflect the outcome of the BCBS's fundamental review of the trading book and include updates to the boundary between the banking and trading books, as well as the introduction of a simplified, standardised approach. The reforms also replace the use of an internally modelled approach for Credit Valuation Adjustment[54] risk – a type of counterparty credit risk that arises in the context of derivatives and other financial contracts – with two standardised approaches.

In terms of operational risk, the previous calculation methods were replaced with a single, risk-sensitive standardised approach. Additionally, a new output floor was introduced to limit the regulatory capital benefits a bank using internal models could derive compared to standardised approaches. The reforms also included the introduction of a leverage ratio buffer for G-SIBs and changes to the exposure measure for calculating the leverage ratio.

Moreover, Basel IV extends the reach of Pillar 2, including specific requirements for managing interest rate risks in the banking book. Furthermore, additional capital requirements will result from the Supervisory Review and Evaluation Process (**SREP**), through which supervisory authorities conduct a comprehensive assessment of the risks to which a credit institution is or may be exposed. This process includes a structured scoring mechanism whereby institutions are evaluated across various risk dimensions – such as governance, capital adequacy, liquidity, and business model sustainability – and assigned scores that inform the imposition of additional capital requirements and qualitative measures.

The BCBS further developed new Pillar 3 disclosure requirements related to market risk and sovereign exposures, which jurisdictions could choose to implement.[55] The package is further complemented by updated regulations on securitisations and large exposures.

51 See www.bis.org/bcbs/publ/d424.pdf (accessed in March 2025).

52 The BCBS discourages the use of the term "Basel IV" because it considers the reforms as revisions to the existing framework rather than the introduction of entirely new elements.

53 Collectively, these latest reforms are encapsulated in the BCBS standard titled *Basel III: Finalising post-crisis reforms (BCBS424)*, issued in December 2017.

54 It reflects the risk of loss caused by changes in the creditworthiness of a counterparty, specifically the risk that the market value of a derivative position deteriorates due to a deterioration in the counterparty's credit quality.

55 Although the reforms concerning market risk and disclosures were developed separately, the BCBS considered them part of the final Basel III standards due to their shared implementation deadline of 1 January 2023.

9.1 Prudential Treatment of Cryptoassets

The rapid growth of cryptoassets and related services has raised concerns about financial stability and the associated risks faced by banks. In response, the BCBS is introducing formal standards for the prudential treatment of cryptoasset exposures by internationally active banks. These standards will be formalised in a new chapter of the Basel framework, SCO60 (Cryptoasset Exposures), which BCBS members are expected to implement by 1 January 2026. Under SCO60, the term "exposure" includes both on- and off-balance sheet amounts that give rise to credit, market, operational, or liquidity risks.[56]

The BCBS has identified several potential risks associated with banks' involvement in cryptoassets. Liquidity risk arises from the difficulty banks may face in converting cryptoassets into fiat currency without incurring significant losses due to the limited liquidity in private markets. Market risk stems from the extreme volatility in the valuation of cryptoassets, which could result in substantial mark-to-market losses. Credit risk may also be present when cryptoassets represent a legal obligation between the issuer and the holder, particularly where the cryptoasset provides a claim on the issuer.

In addition, cryptoassets pose significant cyber and operational risks, as they are susceptible to cyber-attacks, technological vulnerabilities, governance issues, and operational reliability concerns. Legal risks also emerge from the uncertainty surrounding the legal status of cryptoassets, which can create challenges related to consumer protection, the safeguarding of client assets, and compliance with anti-money laundering and counter-terrorist financing requirements. Moreover, banks relying on third-party providers for the development or maintenance of cryptoasset services may face third-party risks, such as operational disruptions or failures by these counterparties.[57]

Recap: The Evolution of Basel Reforms

Basel I (1988): it provided a straightforward regulatory framework for capital adequacy. While its simplicity allowed banks to implement the requirements easily, it also led to significant **regulatory arbitrage**. Banks could achieve substantial reductions in capital requirements without effectively transferring risk. The **overly simplified rules** of Basel I, particularly its "one-size-fits-all" approach, did not account for the varying risk levels of different banking activities, leading to **poor risk management** and encouraging excessive risk-taking.

Basel II (2004): it sought to address the shortcomings of its predecessor by introducing a more **risk-sensitive** framework. It allowed banks to adopt more advanced models for assessing their risks, making capital requirements more closely aligned with actual exposure. However, this flexibility led to **unequal treatment of banks and exposures**, as some institutions were better positioned to exploit these rules than others. While Basel II significantly influenced bank behaviour, it also created **gaps** that

56 As defined in SCO60.4.

57 In this respect, "Cryptoassets are defined as private digital assets that depend on cryptography and distributed ledger technologies (DLT) or similar technologies. Digital assets are a digital representation of value, which can be used for payment or investment purposes or to access a good or service", SCO60 – Cryptoassets exposures, at [60.1], available at www.bis.org/basel_framework/chapter/SCO/60.htm?inforce=20250101&published=20221216 (accessed in March 2025).

sophisticated institutions could exploit, particularly in relation to the **trading book** and risk-weighted assets.

Basel 2.5 fix (2009): these reforms introduced some enhancements to the capital framework, particularly in response to shortcomings revealed during the global financial crisis. A key element of these reforms was the requirement for banks to hold **additional capital to cover default risk** and rating migration risk – that is, the risk that a deterioration in credit ratings could result in substantial mark-to-market losses on trading book positions. Another major component of the Basel 2.5 package was the introduction of a "**stressed value-at-risk**" (stressed VaR) capital charge, thereby ensuring that capital buffers more accurately captured the potential for significant financial stress. Furthermore, the reforms removed the majority of **securitisation exposures** from the scope of internal models, subjecting them to a more conservative capital treatment. This change was intended to address the **regulatory arbitrage** and **undercapitalisation risks** associated with the pre-crisis treatment of complex securitisation instruments under internal modelling approaches.

Basel III (2017): fully implemented in 2023, it responds to the **perceived deficiencies** of Basel II, especially those exposed by the global financial crisis. The reforms place a stronger focus on the **trading book**, **bank liquidity**, and **leverage**, introducing stricter capital and liquidity requirements. Basel III also introduces more stringent leverage ratios and capital buffers, which are expected to increase capital charges significantly. These changes will make certain banking activities more **capital-intensive**, fundamentally altering how banks operate, particularly in high-risk areas.

Basel 3.1, Final Basel III, or Basel IV (2023): it is a collective term referring to regulatory innovations developed by the Basel Committee on Banking Supervision that have not yet been fully incorporated in the UK and in the EU into the CRR and CRD frameworks. Unlike Basel III, which focused primarily on enhancing the quality and quantity of capital and liquidity – thereby strengthening the numerator of the regulatory capital ratio – Basel IV concentrates on the denominator of the ratio. Its primary focus is on the measurement of banks' risk positions, particularly in the areas of credit, market, counterparty, and operational risk under Pillar 1.

The reforms place significant emphasis on standardised approaches, with noticeable restrictions imposed on the use of internal models. Furthermore, the Basel IV framework extends its reach into Pillar 2 and SREP. It also aligns with regulatory disclosure requirements under Pillar 3, thereby enhancing transparency.[58]

10 KEY RISKS COVERED BY THE BASEL FRAMEWORK

In a firm's risk management strategy, three primary categories of risk are central: credit risk, market risk, and operational risk. Each type of risk requires a tailored approach to ensure the firm can effectively mitigate the potential negative impact on its financial stability. Liquidity risk and leverage risk are also of paramount importance.

The Basel frameworks have progressively evolved to address the major risks inherent in banking, establishing regulatory measures to enhance financial stability and resilience. These

58 Chiu, I. and Wilson, J., *Banking Law and Regulation* (Oxford University Press, 2019), p. 432.

risks include credit risk, market risk, operational risk, liquidity risk, and leverage risk, each of which poses distinct challenges to financial institutions.[59]

Credit risk, sometimes referred to as default risk or credit equivalent exposure, arises when a counterparty fails to meet its financial obligations, either through late payment or outright default. This broad category encompasses settlement risk, pre-settlement risk, and delivery risk. The BCBS defines it as the risk that a counterparty will not fulfil its contractual obligations, while Article 4(1) of the retained version of the EU Capital Requirements Regulation (Regulation 575/2013) (**UK CRR**)[60] describes credit risk mitigation as any technique employed to reduce exposure to such risks.

Market risk, also known as replacement risk or price risk, arises from adverse price movements in financial markets. This category includes foreign exchange risk, interest rate risk, basis risk, reinvestment risk, and liquidity risk, all of which can negatively affect a bank's financial standing. The BCBS defines it as the risk to an institution's financial condition resulting from changes in market prices. Banks with significant trading portfolios are particularly exposed to this type of risk, as fluctuations in asset prices can lead to substantial losses.

Operational risk, sometimes referred to as operations risk, is a broad category that encompasses risks arising from inadequate or failed internal processes, systems, people, or external events. This includes model risk, legal risk, reputational risk, business interruption risk, control risk, systems risk, disaster risk, regulatory risk, and political risk. Operational risk can stem from human errors, weak internal controls, IT system failures, transaction processing errors, fraud, external crimes, regulatory breaches, and even unpredictable external shocks such as natural disasters or legal and political changes. The BCBS defines operational risk as the risk of loss resulting from these factors, explicitly including legal risk but excluding strategic and reputational risk. Article 4(1) of the UK CRR similarly categorises operational risk as the risk of loss arising from internal process failures, personnel, systems, or external events, including legal risk.

Liquidity risk refers to the risk that a bank will be unable to meet its short-term financial obligations due to insufficient liquid assets. Basel III introduced two key measures to mitigate this risk: the LCR and the NSFR. As discussed previously, the LCR requires banks to hold a sufficient quantity of high-quality liquid assets to cover short-term liquidity needs, while the NSFR ensures that institutions maintain stable, long-term funding structures, reducing reliance on volatile short-term borrowing. These requirements aim to enhance banks' ability to withstand liquidity shocks and maintain financial stability.

Leverage risk arises when banks accumulate excessive debt relative to their equity capital, increasing their vulnerability to financial distress. To address this, Basel III introduced a non-risk-based Leverage Ratio as a supplementary measure to risk-weighted capital requirements. This ratio acts as a safeguard, preventing banks from engaging in excessive borrowing that could amplify systemic risks in times of financial stress. By limiting overall leverage, the Basel framework ensures that financial institutions maintain a sound capital base and remain resilient during economic downturns.

59 Chiu, I. and Wilson, J., *Banking Law and Regulation* (Oxford University Press, 2019), p. 363.
60 The UK version of Regulation of the European Parliament and the Council on prudential requirements for credit institutions and investment firms (Regulation (EU) No 575/2013) and amending Regulation (EU) No 648/2012, which is part of UK law by virtue of the European Union (Withdrawal) Act 2018.

11 MACRO AND MICRO PRUDENTIAL REGULATION WITHIN THE BASEL FRAMEWORKS

The Basel frameworks integrate both micro- and macro-prudential regulation to ensure a comprehensive regulatory approach. By combining these two perspectives, the Basel frameworks aim to create a banking sector that is both resilient on an institutional level and capable of withstanding broader economic and financial shocks.

11.1 Key Elements of Micro-Prudential Regulation

A fundamental pillar of micro-prudential regulation is capital adequacy, which ensures that financial institutions maintain sufficient capital buffers to absorb losses and continue operating during periods of financial distress. Capital acts as a safeguard against unexpected shocks, and under the Basel III framework, banks are required to hold a minimum level of CET1 capital, along with other types of capital designed to cover various risks. By enforcing these capital requirements, regulators enhance financial institutions' ability to withstand economic downturns and protect depositors and creditors.

Equally important is liquidity management, which requires financial institutions to maintain adequate liquid assets to meet their short-term obligations. Liquidity risk arises when an institution is unable to convert its assets into cash quickly enough to settle its liabilities, potentially leading to insolvency. To mitigate this risk, Basel III introduced the LCR and the NSFR. The LCR ensures that banks hold sufficient high-quality liquid assets to cover short-term liquidity needs, while the NSFR promotes stable long-term funding, reducing reliance on short-term, volatile sources of liquidity. These measures help regulators assess whether institutions can effectively manage liquidity shortfalls and maintain stability during financial stress.

Beyond capital and liquidity, risk management is a core component of micro-prudential regulation. Financial institutions must implement robust risk management systems to identify, assess, and mitigate various risks, including credit risk, market risk, and operational risk. Regulators conduct regular assessments of internal controls, governance frameworks, and risk management processes to ensure institutions comply with regulatory standards. Effective risk management frameworks help prevent excessive risk-taking and enhance institutions' ability to respond to emerging financial threats.

Additionally, **stress testing** is a crucial supervisory tool used to evaluate how financial institutions would perform under adverse economic conditions.[61] By simulating various stress scenarios – such as severe economic downturns, market shocks, or liquidity crises – regulators can identify potential vulnerabilities within institutions and assess whether they have sufficient capital and liquidity to withstand such shocks. Stress testing helps regulators take preemptive action to strengthen financial institutions before crises materialise, thereby reducing systemic risk and enhancing overall financial stability. In the EU, Article 100 of the CRD IV, as amended, requires supervisory authority to conduct stress testing at least on an annual basis on institutions they supervise.

61 Chiu, I. and Wilson, J., *Banking Law and Regulation* (Oxford University Press, 2019), p. 458.

11.2 Key Elements of Macro-Prudential Regulation

Macro-prudential regulation plays a crucial role in safeguarding the stability of the financial system by addressing risks that extend beyond individual institutions. Unlike micro-prudential regulation, which focuses on the resilience of individual banks, macro-prudential oversight aims to mitigate systemic risks that can arise from interconnectedness, procyclicality, and structural vulnerabilities in financial markets.

A key aspect of macro-prudential regulation is **systemic risk monitoring**, which involves identifying and assessing risks across the financial system. Regulators examine how interconnected financial institutions, markets, and sectors can amplify financial instability, particularly during times of economic stress. This includes monitoring excessive credit growth, the formation of asset price bubbles, and risks associated with cross-border banking activities. By analysing these systemic vulnerabilities, regulators can take proactive measures to prevent the accumulation of risks that could trigger financial crises.

To address cyclical risks, macro-prudential frameworks incorporate **countercyclical capital buffers**, which require banks to hold additional capital during periods of excessive credit growth or economic expansion. These buffers are designed to be drawn down during economic downturns, allowing banks to absorb losses and continue lending even in times of stress. By introducing a countercyclical approach to capital regulation, policymakers aim to mitigate the procyclical tendencies of financial markets, reducing the likelihood of boom-and-bust cycles that could destabilise the banking system.[62]

Beyond monitoring risks and addressing cyclical vulnerabilities, prudential regulatory frameworks place particular emphasis on systemically important financial institutions (**SIFI**s) and system-wide stress testing, both of which are essential in preventing financial crises and ensuring economic resilience. These institutions, due to their size, complexity, and interconnectedness, pose a higher risk to the global financial system. The failure of a SIFI could trigger widespread disruptions, leading to financial contagion and economic instability. To mitigate these risks, SIFIs are subject to additional regulatory requirements, including capital surcharges, which require them to hold higher levels of capital to absorb potential losses. They are also subject to enhanced stress testing and heightened regulatory scrutiny, including more stringent supervisory measures to limit excessive risk-taking and prevent systemic failures.

Macro-prudential regulation also incorporates system-wide stress testing to evaluate the resilience of the entire financial system. Unlike stress tests conducted on individual banks, system-wide stress tests assess how the banking sector as a whole would respond to extreme but plausible economic shocks, such as a severe global recession or a sharp decline in asset prices. These tests allow regulators to identify vulnerabilities that may not be apparent when assessing institutions in isolation. By analysing the results, regulators can implement preventive measures, such as adjusting capital requirements, imposing macro-prudential buffers, or strengthening liquidity provisions, to enhance overall financial stability.

System-Wide Stress Testing

System-wide Stress testing is employed by the Bank of England to assess the resilience of the **UK** banking system as a whole in the face of adverse economic scenarios. The objective is to determine whether banks are capable of withstanding severe but

62 Chiu, I. and Wilson, J., *Banking Law and Regulation* (Oxford University Press, 2019), p. 374.

plausible shocks while maintaining their ability to support the real economy. Through this process, the Bank seeks to ensure that financial institutions are positioned to absorb, rather than exacerbate, economic stress, thereby preserving their capacity to continue providing essential financial services to UK households and businesses. For example, the 2025 Bank Capital Stress Test[63] is designed to evaluate the resilience of the UK banking system against a severe and wide-ranging adverse scenario. This scenario includes deep, simultaneous recessions in both the UK and global economies, substantial declines in asset prices, elevated global interest rates, and a stressed level of misconduct-related costs.

In the **European Union**, system-wide stress testing would involve close cooperation between the EBA and the competent authorities (including the Single Supervisory Mechanism – **SSM**, the European Central Bank – **ECB**, and the European Systemic Risk Board – **ESRB**). These stress tests would apply a common macroeconomic baseline scenario alongside a common adverse scenario, covering a two-year period, ensuring a comprehensive evaluation of system-wide financial stability across the European banking sector.

By focusing on the risks posed by SIFIs and conducting comprehensive system-wide stress testing, macro-prudential regulation strengthens the resilience of the financial system, ensuring that it can absorb shocks and continue functioning effectively in times of crisis. These measures are essential in reducing systemic risk, preventing financial contagion, and maintaining confidence in global financial markets.

Key Differences Between Micro and Macro-Prudential Regulation

Aspect	*Micro-Prudential Regulation*	*Macro-Prudential Regulation*
Focus	Individual financial institutions	The entire financial system
Objective	Ensure the soundness of individual institutions	Prevent systemic risks and maintain financial stability
Capital Requirements	Set based on an institution's individual risk profile	Imposed to address system-wide risks, including countercyclical buffers
Stress Testing	Assesses the resilience of individual institutions	System-wide stress tests assess the resilience of the entire financial sector
Scope of Risk Management	Focus on firm-specific risks such as credit risk, market risk, and operational risk	Focus on system-wide risks such as interconnectedness, contagion, and asset bubbles
Regulatory Tools	Capital adequacy requirements, liquidity ratios, internal risk assessments	Countercyclical capital buffers, system-wide stress testing, SIFI surcharges

63 See www.bankofengland.co.uk/stress-testing/2024/boes-approach-to-stress-testing-the-uk-banking-system (accessed in March 2025).

11.3 Key Differences Between Micro- and Macro-Prudential Regulation

While both micro- and macro-prudential regulation aim to mitigate risks in the financial system, they differ in their focus, objectives, and tools.

11.4 Integrating Micro- and Macro-Prudential Regulation

For an effective regulatory framework, both micro-prudential and macro-prudential regulation must work in tandem. The Bank of England, through the Financial Policy Committee (**FPC**), implements both micro-prudential and macro-prudential measures. The PRA focuses on individual banks' capital adequacy and risk management, while the FPC addresses system-wide risks, such as excessive credit growth or asset bubbles. This dual approach ensures that the UK financial system is resilient to both firm-specific and systemic risks.

To address the challenges of cross-border supervision, **supervisory colleges** have been established.[64] These colleges consist of regulators from the home and host countries where an international bank operates. Supervisory colleges facilitate cooperation and information sharing among regulators, allowing for a more coordinated approach to supervising **internationally active banks**.

A **supervisory college** overseeing a G-SIB like HSBC brings together regulators from countries where HSBC has significant operations, including the UK, Hong Kong, and the United States. These regulators work together to assess HSBC's global risk profile and ensure that it meets capital and liquidity requirements in all jurisdictions.

11.5 Home and Host Supervision

In the supervision of international banks, there is a clear division of responsibilities between **home** and **host supervisors**. The home supervisor is responsible for overseeing the bank's consolidated operations, while the host supervisor focuses on the bank's activities within its jurisdiction. This division can create challenges, particularly when there are differing regulatory standards or priorities.

Example: The collapse of **Barings Bank** in 1995, driven by unauthorised trading in Singapore, underscored the risks of inadequate coordination between home and host supervisors. Despite being headquartered in the UK, Barings' failure was triggered by actions in its foreign operations.

It is essential to ensure that supervisors possess the capacity to assess risks comprehensively and effectively challenge banks' practices. Additionally, they must be equipped with a sufficient

64 Chiu, I. and Wilson, J., *Banking Law and Regulation* (Oxford University Press, 2019), p. 215.

range of powers and supported by institutional arrangements that facilitate the implementation of early corrective measures.

12 THE GLOBAL APPLICATION OF THE BASEL BANKING STANDARDS

Basel banking standards have been developed by a selective group of regulators from the world's largest financial centres, while their implementation in jurisdictions beyond these financial hubs is often both shallow and highly selective, reflecting significant variations in the depth and scope of implementation across different regions. However, even within the key financial centres the approaches to prudential regulation can vary significantly across jurisdictions.[65] Such a fragmented global regulatory framework could erode trust in the global financial system and undermine the ability of countries to rely on each other's regulatory systems. This would create inefficiencies by fragmenting capital and liquidity pools, disrupting cross-border financial flows, and ultimately leading to inefficient financing and heightened risks to national economies.[66]

In this context, the prudential frameworks in the UK, EU, US, India, China, and Japan offer key insights into the diverse methods by which banking systems are supervised and maintained and the differences in regulatory priorities and institutional structures.

12.1 The UK's Approach to International Banking Supervision

In the UK, the PRA is responsible for ensuring the safety and soundness of banks operating within its jurisdiction. It employs a risk-based approach to supervision, focusing on the most significant threats to financial stability. Through its SREP, the PRA assesses the risk profile of individual banks to determine whether they maintain adequate capital and liquidity. In addition, the PRA conducts regular stress testing to evaluate banks' resilience to economic shocks.[67]

To support non-systemic banks, the PRA has introduced the Strong and Simple Framework, designed to reduce the regulatory burden on smaller institutions while upholding robust prudential standards. This framework simplifies regulatory requirements for banks that do not pose systemic risks, allowing them to concentrate on their core operations without being subject to disproportionately complex regulatory obligations.

Banks are required at all times to maintain capital resources that are equal to or exceed their base capital resources (**BCR**) requirement, which represents the minimum initial capital necessary at the time of their Part 4A authorisation (see Chapter 3).[68] For the majority of deposit-taking banks, this BCR requirement is set at EUR 5 million. However, for building societies and small specialist banks (**SSBs**), the requirement is the higher of EUR 1 million and £1 million. SSBs are defined as banks that engage in one or more of the

65 Jones, E. and Zeitz, A., 'The Limits of Globalizing Basel Banking Standards' (2017) 3 *Journal of Financial Regulation* 89.

66 Ferreira, C., Jenkinson, N. and Wilson, C., 'From Basel I to Basel III: Sequencing Implementation in Developing Economies' (2019) *WP/19/127* 11.

67 Woods, The Prudential Regulation Authority's Approach to Banking Supervision (July 2023), available at www.bankofengland.co.uk/-/media/boe/files/prudential-regulation/approach/banking-approach-2023.pdf (accessed in March 2025).

68 As set out in Article 93(1) of the UK CRR.

following activities: providing current and savings accounts, lending to SMEs, or issuing loans secured by mortgages on residential property. An SSB will cease to be classified as such once its capital resources reach or exceed EUR 5 million. At that point, the institution will become subject to the standard BCR requirement of EUR 5 million applicable to deposit-taking banks. For investment firms designated by the PRA, the BCR requirement is £750,000.

Own Funds Requirements Under UK CRR

Under the UK CRR, firms are required to maintain compliance with the following own funds' requirements at all times[69]:

- A CET1 capital ratio of 4.5%;
- A Tier 1 capital ratio of 6.0%; and
- A total capital ratio of 8.0%.

The total risk exposure amount represents, in broad terms, the aggregate of the firm's RWAs with respect to credit risk, market risk, and operational risk.[70]

The purpose of minimum capital requirements is to ensure that a bank operates with a sufficient level of capital to safeguard depositors, sustain market confidence, and allow for an orderly resolution in the event of failure without recourse to public funds. These requirements are expressed as capital ratios, which measure a bank's capital relative to its RWAs.

Minimum capital requirements are composed of two elements. The first is the Pillar 1 requirement, which applies uniformly to all banks. The second is the Pillar 2A requirement, which is determined on a firm-specific basis by the PRA, considering the bank's particular risk profile. The PRA refers to the combined total of a bank's Pillar 1 and Pillar 2A requirements as its total capital requirement (**TCR**).

A bank that fails to meet its TCR is not automatically deemed by the PRA to be in breach of the overall financial adequacy rule, nor is it necessarily considered to be failing, or likely to fail, to meet the threshold conditions. However, such a breach would prompt the PRA to assess whether the bank is, in fact, failing or likely to fail to satisfy those conditions and to consider whether further supervisory or regulatory action is warranted.

The PRA imposes Pillar 2A minimum capital requirements on individual banks to address risks that are either not captured or only partially captured under the Pillar 1 framework. These requirements are tailored to the specific risk profile of each institution and, as such, will vary from one bank to another. They are often referred to as a bank's individual capital requirement (**ICR**).

One of the principal risks typically covered under Pillar 2A is interest rate risk in the banking book (**IRRBB**). This risk arises where there is a mismatch between the interest rate characteristics of a bank's assets – such as loans – and the liabilities or funding used to support them, potentially impacting the bank's income and capital.

69 These thresholds are set out in Article 92(1) of the UK CRR.
70 As provided under Article 92(3) of the UK CRR.

When setting a Pillar 2A requirement, the PRA usually specifies that the bank must hold capital equivalent to a particular percentage of its Pillar 1 RWAs, supplemented by one or more fixed add-ons to reflect specific risks. The composition of capital required to meet the Pillar 2A requirement mirrors that of Pillar 1: at least 56.25% must be held in CET1 capital, with no more than 43.75% in AT1 capital and no more than 25% in Tier 2 capital.

The purpose of the **large exposure requirements** is to prevent excessive concentration of risk within a bank's portfolio that could result in disproportionately high losses should a single counterparty or a group of connected counterparties default due to unforeseen events. An exposure is classified as "large" when the total value of a bank's exposures to a client or to a group of connected clients reaches or exceeds 10% of the bank's Tier 1 capital.[71]

A group of connected clients refers to a set of counterparties with such close relationships or interdependencies that, if one were to fail, it is highly likely that the others would also default.[72]

Banks are required to establish robust systems for identifying, managing, monitoring, reporting, and recording all large exposures. They must also report each of their large exposures to the PRA.

A bank is prohibited from maintaining an exposure to a single counterparty or a group of connected counterparties exceeding 25% of its Tier 1 capital. In the case of exposures between two global systemically important institutions (**G-SIIs**), the limit is reduced to 15%. Certain exposures within a bank's trading book may be exempt from the 25% cap, provided specific conditions are met; however, such exposures are then subject to an additional capital requirement.[73]

Any breach of the applicable exposure limits must be reported to the PRA without delay, and the bank is required to rectify the breach promptly.

Firms are required to identify, measure, manage, and monitor liquidity and funding risks across a range of time horizons and under a variety of stress scenarios. To this effect, the PRA requires each bank to maintain, at all times, liquidity resources that are adequate in both amount and quality to ensure that there is no significant risk of being unable to meet its liabilities as they fall due. This requirement is referred to as the overall liquidity adequacy rule (**OLAR**).[74] To comply with OLAR, banks must ensure that their liquidity resources include a sufficient buffer of high-quality, unencumbered assets. This entails maintaining a stock of liquid assets – such as central bank reserves or high-quality government securities – that can be readily accessed to meet obligations as they mature. The purpose of this buffer is to enable a bank to withstand a wide range of severe but plausible stress scenarios, whether institution-specific, market-wide, or a combination of both, and across various time horizons.

Furthermore, banks are required to maintain a prudent funding profile. They should avoid excessive reliance on a narrow range of funding sources, particularly short-term wholesale funding that may become unavailable during periods of market stress. Banks are also

71 In accordance with Part 1.2 of the Large Exposures (CRR).
72 This definition is set out in Article 4(1)(39) of the UK CRR.
73 As detailed in Article 395 of Chapter 4, Large Exposures (CRR).
74 As set out in Internal Liquidity Adequacy Assessment 2.1.

expected to avoid over-reliance on maintaining specific credit ratings to secure funding and to recognise the risks that asset encumbrance may pose to their ability to raise unsecured funding.

FSMA 2023

The UK government has expressed its intention to repeal and replace retained EU financial services law where necessary. Part 1 of the Financial Services and Markets Act 2023 (**FSMA 2023**) establishes a framework for revoking the majority of retained EU law in this area. This includes the UK CRR and other prudential regulations applicable to UK banks, which will be revoked and subsequently replaced by UK-specific legislation and regulations.

Further legislative changes have also been introduced through the Prudential Regulation of Credit Institutions (Meaning of CRR Rules and Recognised Exchange) (Amendment) Regulations 2024,[75] which came into force on 22 November 2024. Among other amendments, these regulations revise the definition of "CRR rules" to include rules that the PRA may introduce to replace provisions of the UK CRR revoked under FSMA 2023.

UK Implementation of Basel IV

The UK has been implementing the Basel IV standards for internationally active banks through the Financial Services Act 2021, which granted HM Treasury the authority to implement the Basel IV standards and outlined the considerations the PRA must address when drafting rules to implement these standards. The specific requirements for firms will be detailed in the PRA Rulebook and other supervisory materials issued by the PRA. Furthermore, HM Treasury will use its powers under FSMA 2023 to revoke provisions of retained EU law within the UK CRR that are no longer required.

Certain smaller UK banks and building societies that choose to participate in the PRA's regime for small domestic deposit takers (SDDTs) will have the option to continue applying Basel III prudential requirements under an interim capital regime. This flexibility will remain in place until the bespoke capital prudential framework for these firms comes into effect. The SDDT regime is part of the PRA's broader initiative to develop a strong and simplified regulatory framework for non-systemic banks and building societies.

In light of the ongoing uncertainty regarding the timing of the implementation of the Basel IV standards in the United States and considering factors related to competitiveness and economic growth, the PRA, in consultation with HM Treasury, has decided to postpone the implementation of these rules to 1 January 2027,[76] subject to any transitional arrangements.

12.2 Prudential Supervision in the European Union and the Basel Framework

The supervisory architecture of a financial system determines how oversight responsibilities and powers are allocated among policy institutions. The core trade-off between decentralised

75 SI 2024/1200.
76 See PRA's press release on 17 January 2025 available at: www.bankofengland.co.uk/news/2025/january/the-pra-announces-a-delay-to-the-implementation-of-basel-3-1 (accessed in March 2025).

(local) and centralised supervision revolves around incentives and information. Central supervisors are better positioned to make decisions that consider the broader banking sector and the wider economy, offering a macroeconomic perspective. In contrast, local supervisors may prioritise local political and economic interests, potentially resulting in biased oversight. However, local supervisors benefit from superior access to detailed, granular information about the banks they oversee and can develop expertise in local conditions. Central supervisors, on the other hand, may encounter difficulties in gathering such information due to physical and institutional distance. This tension underscores the complexities inherent in designing an effective supervisory framework.[77]

In the European Union, the 2007–2009 global financial crisis prompted a vigorous debate on the optimal supervisory structure, with a focus on restoring trust in the banking sector and enhancing the resilience of the financial system. In 2014, the European Single Supervisory Mechanism (**SSM**) was established, assuming centralised supervision of the largest banks within the euro area. The SSM comprises the ECB and the national competent authorities (**NCA**s) of the Member States. The ECB directly supervises "significant" banks within the euro area.[78] All other banks are primarily supervised by national authorities in accordance with ECB guidelines. However, the ECB also exercises oversight of these smaller institutions, relying largely on information provided by national supervisory authorities. Where deemed necessary, the ECB retains the authority to supervise these banks directly.

Implementation of the Basel Framework in the EU: CRD IV

With the introduction of the CRD IV legislative package, consisting of the CRR and the CRD IV Directive, the EU undertook a significant reform of its prudential rules for banks. This package replaced the previous Capital Requirements Directives (2006/48/EC and 2006/49/EC) and incorporated the core elements of the Basel III reforms while also introducing specific EU-focused measures, such as enhancements to disclosure requirements and provisions on remuneration.

While Basel III primarily targeted internationally active and systemically significant banks, in the EU, its provisions have been applied to all credit institutions and investment firms. The EBA has further clarified the application of Basel III through its opinions, such as the guidance on defining a credit institution under Article 4(1) of the CRR.[79]

A key aspect of the CRD IV and Directive (EU) 2019/878 (**CRD V**)[80] packages was the decision to implement the detailed and highly prescriptive Basel III capital requirements through a regulation. This approach aimed to facilitate the consistent application of Basel III, closing potential regulatory loopholes that could arise from divergent national interpretations.

The UK position described previously is the outcome of the implementation of the CRD IV and CRD V packages, which occurred prior to Brexit. As a result, the prudential regime described previously for the UK is reflective of the EU's framework. Some EU-specific requirements are found in article 89 of the CRD IV Directive, which requires firms to provide annual country-by-country reports on a consolidated basis. These reports had to include

77 Gong, D., Lambert, T. and Wagner, W., 'Local Bank Supervision' (28 September 2023), available at https://papers.ssrn.com/sol3/papers.cfm?abstract_id=4586662 (accessed in March 2025).
78 Haentjens, M. and De Gioia-Carabellese, P., *European Banking and Financial Law* (Routledge, 2015), p. 94.
79 (EBA/Op/2014/12).
80 Directive (EU) 2019/878 of the European Parliament and of the Council of 20 May 2019 amending Directive 2013/36/EU as regards exempted entities, financial holding companies, mixed financial holding companies, remuneration, supervisory measures and powers, and capital conservation measures.

detailed information for each country in which a firm operated, such as the name, nature of activities, and geographical location, along with turnover, the number of full-time equivalent employees, profit or loss before tax, taxes paid on profits, and any public subsidies received.

The CRR has imposed uniform requirements for supervisory reporting, including standardised formats, reporting frequencies, and deadlines. Article 101 specifically required firms to report losses incurred from loans secured by immovable property. Credit risk adjustments[81] refer to provisions made for expected loan losses in line with accounting standards. Article 110 further outlined the treatment of general and specific credit risk adjustments, with the EBA tasked with drafting RTS to standardise the calculation of these adjustments across institutions.

The EBA has played a crucial role in the CRD IV and CRD V frameworks. It has been responsible for developing detailed technical standards, including binding regulatory technical standards and implementing technical standards, which are subsequently adopted by the European Commission via delegated regulations. Additionally, the EBA issued guidelines addressing various aspects of the CRD IV and CRD V regimes to ensure consistent application across member states.

Recent Developments: CRR III and CRD VI

The EU began the implementation of this "Basel IV" framework,[82] thereby reaffirming its commitment to upholding international prudential standards. As with earlier iterations of the Basel framework, these enhanced prudential requirements apply to all EU banks – approximately 4,500 institutions – on both a solo and consolidated basis. This broad application is designed to reinforce the resilience of the EU banking system.

The value of this approach was underscored by the banking turmoil experienced in the United States in 2023, where several medium-sized banks, which were not subject to the full Basel III framework, failed. Crucially, the EU banking sector remained stable and avoided contagion, illustrating the importance of maintaining robust prudential safeguards.

In June 2024, two significant legislative acts were published in the Official Journal of the European Union, marking a fundamental shift in the EU's prudential banking framework. Regulation (EU) 2024/1623,[83] known as the CRR III Regulation, amends Regulation (EU) No 575/2013 and introduces substantial new requirements relating to credit risk, counterparty credit risk (CVA risk), operational risk, market risk, and the output floor. Alongside this, Directive (EU) 2024/1619,[84] known as the CRD VI Directive, amends Directive 2013/36/EU, strengthening rules on supervisory powers, sanctions, and the regulation of third-country branches. The CRD VI Directive also introduces explicit provisions addressing environmental, social, and governance (**ESG**) risks in line with the EU's broader sustainability objectives. Member States are required to implement the CRD VI measures by 11 January 2026.

The CRR III Regulation and the CRD VI Directive introduce amendments to the EU's core legislative framework for banks and credit institutions, as set out in the CRR and CRD

81 As defined under Article 4(1)(95).

82 On 1 January 2025.

83 Regulation (EU) 2024/1623 of the European Parliament and of the Council of 31 May 2024 amending Regulation (EU) No 575/2013 as regards requirements for credit risk, credit valuation adjustment risk, operational risk, market risk, and the output floor.

84 Directive (EU) 2024/1619 of the European Parliament and of the Council of 31 May 2024 amending Directive 2013/36/EU as regards supervisory powers, sanctions, third-country branches, and environmental, social, and governance risks.

IV Directive. These include significant revisions to the existing CRR provisions on credit risk and CVA risk, a comprehensive replacement of the operational risk framework, and the transformation of market risk provisions into binding regulatory capital requirements – where previously they had only been applicable for reporting purposes. The CRR III Regulation aims to enhance the sensitivity of risk assessments under both the standardised and IRB approaches. Notably, one of the most important components of these revisions is the introduction of the output floor, a mechanism designed to limit the extent to which banks may reduce their capital requirements through the use of internal models. Credit institutions using internal models must compare the RWAs derived from their internal models to the RWAs calculated under the standardised approach multiplied by a percentage factor. The higher of the two figures is used to determine the total risk exposure amount (TREA) of the institution.[85] Thus, internal model-based calculations are subject to a comparative check, with the higher of the internal model figure or the floor-adjusted standardised figure determining the total risk exposure amount (TREA). The factor will gradually increase, starting at 50% in 2025 and rising to 72.5% by 2030.[86] This measure is intended to reduce excessive variability in capital requirements across banks using internal models, thereby improving comparability and strengthening the overall resilience of the sector.

The second strand of reforms includes EU-specific measures that go beyond the Basel framework.

These encompass the establishment of a new regulatory framework for branches of third-country banks operating within the EU. Under this framework, such branches must obtain authorisation and comply with prudential requirements proportionate to their size and risk profile. Also, these reforms grant expanded supervisory powers to competent authorities, enabling them to oversee significant corporate actions such as acquisitions, divestitures, mergers, and transfers involving credit institutions.

At the same time, simplified reporting obligations have been introduced to reduce the regulatory burden on smaller institutions. These reforms aim to ensure a more robust and transparent regulatory framework across the EU banking sector. Finally, the CRR III Regulation introduces a new Article 501d into the CRR, which requires credit institutions to calculate their own funds requirements for cryptoasset (as defined in the Markets in Cryptoassets Regulation)[87] exposures.[88] High-risk cryptoassets are assigned a risk weight of 1,250%, while tokenised traditional assets are treated as exposures to their underlying assets. All other cryptoasset exposures must be assigned a risk weight of 1,250%. Additionally, the value of a credit institution's total exposure to cryptoassets, other than those referenced in the first two categories, must not exceed 1% of its Tier 1 capital.

As discussed in Chapter 4, governance requirements have also been enhanced.

85 Revises Article 92 of the CRR.

86 Revised Article 465 of the CRR permits member states to adopt a phased approach before the final percentage is reached.

87 Regulation (EU) 2023/1114 of the European Parliament and of the Council of 31 May 2023 on markets in crypto-assets, and amending Regulations (EU) No 1093/2010 and (EU) No 1095/2010 and Directives 2013/36/EU and (EU) 2019/1937.

88 Under the new article 5a "crypto-asset exposure" means an asset or an off-balance-sheet item related to a crypto-asset that gives rise to credit risk, counterparty credit risk, market risk, operational risk, or liquidity risk.

12.3 The United States

In the United States, prudential regulation is primarily governed by the Dodd-Frank Wall Street Reform and Consumer Protection Act of 2010. This landmark legislation was enacted in response to the 2008 global financial crisis and sought to overhaul the US financial regulatory framework to prevent a recurrence of such systemic failures. It introduced enhanced supervision for SIFIs, including both large banks' holding companies and certain non-bank financial companies deemed to pose a risk to financial stability. The Federal Reserve Board (**FRB**) is tasked with supervising these institutions, imposing stringent capital and liquidity requirements, and conducting regular stress tests to assess their ability to withstand economic shocks.[89]

Prudential regulation in the US incorporates the Basel III standards, which were implemented through a series of regulations issued by the FRB, the Office of the Comptroller of the Currency (**OCC**), and the Federal Deposit Insurance Corporation (**FDIC**). However, the US approach diverges from the global framework in some respects. For example, the leverage ratio applied to large US banks is typically stricter than the Basel III standard, reflecting concerns about excessive leverage within the financial system. The Dodd-Frank Act also created the Volcker Rule, which restricts banks from engaging in proprietary trading and limits their relationships with hedge funds and private equity, a measure designed to reduce systemic risk by separating risky trading activities from core banking functions.

Beyond the baseline requirements for CET1, AT1, and Tier 2 capital, US banks are also subject to additional capital buffers aimed at enhancing financial resilience. The CCB, set at 2.5% of risk-weighted assets, applies on top of the minimum capital requirements, restricting capital distributions such as dividends and share buybacks if a bank falls below the required threshold. Furthermore, G-SIBs are subject to additional capital surcharges, reflecting their systemic importance and the potential impact of their failure on financial stability. These measures collectively ensure that US banks maintain a strong capital base, reducing systemic risk and enhancing the overall stability of the banking sector. Foreign banks operating in the United States are also subject to enhanced prudential standards, particularly if they have significant US operations. These standards ensure that foreign institutions maintain sufficient capital and liquidity buffers to support their US activities, aligning with the global objectives of the Basel framework.

Failure to maintain adequate capital results in restrictions on dividend distributions, share buybacks, and other discretionary payouts.[90]

A non-risk-based leverage ratio is also applied to banks. The Supplementary Leverage Ratio requires the largest banks to maintain a minimum ratio of 3% of Tier 1 capital relative to their total leverage exposure, including off-balance-sheet exposures.

US banks are required to meet the LCR and NSFR under Basel III standards. The LCR ensures that banks hold sufficient high-quality liquid assets to meet their short-term obligations, while the NSFR requires banks to maintain stable funding sources for longer-term liabilities. These measures reduce the risks of liquidity shortfalls during periods of market stress.

Under the Dodd-Frank Act, banks with more than $100 billion in assets are subject to annual stress tests conducted by the Federal Reserve. These stress tests assess the ability of banks to maintain sufficient capital during adverse economic scenarios, including recessions

89 Walter, J., 'US Bank Capital Regulation: History and Changes Since the Financial Crisis' (2019) 105(1) *Economic Quarterly* 1–40.

90 Fritsch, N. and Siedlarek, J.-P., 'How Do Banks Respond to Capital Regulation? – the Impact of the Basel III Reforms in the United States' *Working Paper No. 22-11* (Federal Reserve Bank of Cleveland, 2022).

and market crashes. The results of these tests influence decisions about capital distributions and ensure that banks are adequately capitalised to withstand future economic shocks.

Unlike the standardised application of the Basel framework to all kinds of banks in the EU and the UK, in the US, the Economic Growth, Regulatory Relief, and Consumer Protection Act of 2018 modified some of the post-crisis regulations, particularly by raising the asset threshold for enhanced prudential standards from $50 billion to $250 billion. This adjustment was intended to reduce the regulatory burden on smaller banks while maintaining stricter oversight of the largest and most systemically important institutions. However, the 2023 US Banking Crises (see later on) have demonstrated that authorities must not disregard the possibility that banks not formally designated as systemically important may still experience crises with far-reaching consequences for the broader banking sector. Such events can significantly undermine the confidence of depositors, particularly those associated with banks of similar size or business model. Consequently, these institutions should be subject to appropriate and proportionate supervisory measures, supported by an efficient framework for crisis management to mitigate potential risks and maintain financial stability.

In light of the previous, US regulators have proposed the Basel IV reforms, which aim to further enhance capital requirements for large banks, particularly in relation to credit, market, and operational risk;[91] however, at the time of writing, there is still uncertainty surrounding the timing of implementation of such reforms in the US. This uncertainty, as noted previously, triggered a delay in the implementation of the new standard in the UK due to competitive disadvantages concerns.[92] The regulatory divergence between major global financial centres is a particular concern for internationally active banks, as it poses risks to global financial stability.

The 2023 US Banking Crises

In 2023, three mid-sized US banks – Silicon Valley Bank, Signature Bank of New York, and First Republic Bank – failed. These banks often served high-net-worth individuals and engaged in activities such as residential real estate lending, private banking, wealth management, and brokerage services. A key contributing factor to this crisis was the regulatory changes implemented in the United States in 2018.

While the specific causes of their failures varied, they shared common vulnerabilities in their business models: an overreliance on uninsured deposits, which was far greater than that of their peers. These deposits were largely invested in long-term securities with extended maturities, and the banks failed to implement effective liquidity risk management practices to mitigate the associated risks. When interest rates began to rise in 2022, the reversal of the yield curve exacerbated unrealised losses on their long-term securities, while deposit outflows further strained their financial positions. The lack of robust regulatory standards for mid-sized and regional banks left them

91 Board of Governors of the Federal Reserve System, Federal Deposit Insurance Corporation, and Comptroller of the Currency. 2023. "Agencies Request Comment on Proposed Rules to Strengthen Capital Requirements for Large Banks". Joint Press Release. Board of Governors of the Federal Reserve System. July 27, 2023, available at www.federalreserve.gov/newsevents/pressreleases/bcreg20230727a.htm.

92 See PRA's press release on 17 January 2025, available at www.bankofengland.co.uk/news/2025/january/the-pra-announces-a-delay-to-the-implementation-of-basel-3-1 (accessed in March 2025).

particularly vulnerable to these adverse conditions, ultimately contributing to their collapse.[93]

Although none of the banks in question were formally classified as systemically important institutions, their failures nonetheless triggered a contagion effect. This was largely driven by similarities in their business models, as well as geographic or sectoral concentrations, which amplified the risks and spread the impact across interconnected markets and institutions.

12.4 India

In a country like India, where banks dominate the financial sector, banking regulations assume added significance. Prudential regulation is overseen by the Reserve Bank of India, which serves as the central bank and the primary regulator of the banking sector.[94] The Reserve Bank of India has progressively aligned its regulatory framework with the Basel III standards, although with certain modifications to reflect the specific needs of the Indian financial system. Indian banks are required to maintain a CET1 ratio of at least 5.5%, which is slightly higher than the Basel III minimum. Additionally, banks must meet a minimum capital adequacy ratio of 9%, compared to the international standard of 8%, to provide a greater cushion against potential losses. These stricter requirements are designed to mitigate risks in a banking system that serves a large and diverse economy, with significant exposure to agricultural, small business, and infrastructure sectors.

The Reserve Bank of India also imposes a capital conservation buffer of 2.5%, in line with Basel III recommendations, and has introduced the countercyclical capital buffer to protect banks against excessive credit growth during economic booms. Moreover, the Indian regulatory framework requires banks to comply with the LCR and with the NSFR.

One of the unique aspects of India's prudential regulation is the emphasis on financial inclusion and managing the risks associated with rapidly expanding digital financial services. The Reserve Bank of India has introduced measures to enhance the cyber resilience of banks and to supervise the operational risks associated with technology, particularly as digital payments and fintech firms become increasingly integrated with the traditional banking system. The growth of non-bank financial companies (NBFCs) in India has also posed regulatory challenges, leading the Reserve Bank of India to increase its scrutiny of large NBFCs and their linkages to the broader banking system.

12.5 China

China possesses the largest banking sector globally, with assets amounting to approximately $40 trillion as of 2020. In 2015, China introduced reforms aimed at decentralising supervision

93 Trapanese, M. (coord), Albareto, G., Cardillo, S., Castagna, M., Falconi, R., Pezzullo, G., Serafini, L. and Signore, F., 'The 2023 US Banking Crises: Causes, Policy Responses, and Lessons' *No 870 Banca d'Italia, Questioni di Economia e Finanza (Occasional Papers)* (19 July 2024).

94 Srivastava, A., 'The Effectiveness of Prudential Regulations for Banks: Global Perspective and Indian Context' (2019) 48(2) *Prajnan*, available at https://ssrn.com/abstract=3810552 (accessed in March 2025).

for branches of banks classified as "local", while retaining centralised oversight for branches of "national" banks – those directly supervised by the central authority in Beijing.[95]

The China Banking and Insurance Regulatory Commission (CBIRC) is responsible for prudential regulation in coordination with the People's Bank of China, which oversees monetary policy and macroprudential stability. Chinese prudential regulation is largely based on the Basel III framework, with additional measures tailored to the unique characteristics of the Chinese financial system, which is dominated by large state-owned banks.

The regulatory framework mandates that banks maintain a Core Tier 1 capital adequacy ratio of at least 5%, reflecting the highest quality of capital, primarily composed of common equity and retained earnings. Additionally, the Tier 1 capital adequacy ratio, which includes both Core Tier 1 capital and Additional Tier 1 capital, must be no less than 6%. The overall capital adequacy ratio, incorporating Tier 1 and Tier 2 capital, is set at a minimum of 8%.

Banks must also hold a capital conservation buffer of 2.5% of their risk-weighted assets, and a countercyclical capital buffer is applied during periods of excessive credit growth. The CBIRC has implemented stricter requirements for domestic systemically important banks and G-SIBs, which are subject to additional capital and leverage requirements to mitigate their systemic risks.

Liquidity regulation is another key focus of Chinese prudential oversight. On this basis, a commercial bank with total assets of 200 billion yuan or more is required to maintain, on an ongoing basis, an LCR of at least 100%, an NSFR of at least 100%, a liquidity ratio of no less than 25%, and a **liquidity matching ratio**, which measures how well a bank's assets and liabilities match in maturity, of at least 100%. For commercial banks with total assets of less than 200 billion yuan, the applicable standards differ slightly. These institutions must continuously maintain an HQLA adequacy ratio of at least 100%, in addition to meeting the same minimum thresholds for the liquidity ratio (25%) and the liquidity matching ratio (100%).

Chinese regulators have been particularly concerned about the rapid expansion of shadow banking[96] and the risks posed by off-balance-sheet activities, which have led to tighter regulations on wealth management products and other forms of non-traditional banking activities. Moreover, the CBIRC and the People's Bank of China have introduced rules to supervise the risks associated with digital lending platforms, peer-to-peer (P2P) lending, and cryptoassets, reflecting the government's concerns about financial stability in a rapidly evolving market.

12.6 Japan

In Japan, the Financial Services Agency oversees the prudential regulation of banks, with a strong focus on aligning domestic regulations with the Basel III standards. Japan's banking system includes both traditional banks and large financial conglomerates, many of which have significant international operations. Japanese banks are required to maintain a CET1 ratio of at least 4.5%, with higher ratios required for G-SIBs.[97]

95 Gong, D., Lambert, T. and Wagner, W., 'Local Bank Supervision' (28 September 2023), available at https://papers.ssrn.com/sol3/papers.cfm?abstract_id=4586662 (accessed in March 2025).

96 In Li, W., 'China's Shadow Banking in 2020–2022: An Empirical Study' (2024) 11 *Humanit Soc Sci Commun* 282, China's shadow banking is defined as *"those financial businesses that rely on banks' creditworthiness, conduct banking business, but without strict banking regulation. Specifically, they refer to financial businesses beyond banks' traditional on-balance sheet loans and bond investment, which simultaneously have complete function of credit transformation, maturity transformation, and liquidity transformation"*.

97 Hideaki, S., 'Japan: Law & Practice' in *Chambers Global Practice Guides: Banking Regulation 2024*, Nagashima Ohno & Tsunematsu (Chambers and Partners, 2024), available at www.noandt.com/wp-content/

Liquidity regulation is also a key element of Japan's prudential framework. Japanese banks must comply with the Basel III LCR and NSFR's requirements to ensure that they can manage both short-term and long-term liquidity risks. The Financial Services Agency has been particularly focused on the stress testing of Japanese banks, regularly assessing their ability to withstand adverse market conditions, such as prolonged periods of low interest rates and volatile global markets.

In response to the aging population and declining domestic market, Japanese banks have increasingly expanded their operations abroad, particularly in Southeast Asia. This has prompted the Financial Services Agency to enhance its oversight of cross-border banking activities and ensure that Japanese banks maintain adequate risk management practices in their international operations.

13 CONCLUSION

International banking supervision has evolved significantly, particularly in response to the global financial crises of the late 20th and early 21st centuries. The Basel Framework has been central to these regulatory developments, providing a globally recognised structure for regulating capital, liquidity, and risk management, integrating micro-prudential and macro-prudential approaches to banking regulation.

Basel III, in particular, represents a significant enhancement, addressing the weaknesses exposed by the 2007–2009 global financial crisis, such as insufficient capital buffers, inadequate liquidity management, and the lack of a clear framework for managing **SIFI**s. By increasing capital requirements, introducing liquidity standards, and establishing clear rules for leverage ratios, Basel III has fundamentally reshaped how banks manage their risks and how regulators supervise them.

However, the implementation of Basel III has not been without its challenges. One of the critical issues highlighted in the chapter is the need for international coordination in banking supervision. As financial markets have become increasingly interconnected, the activities of multinational banks can create risks that transcend national borders.

Systemic risks, particularly the "too big to fail" problem, remain a critical focus of prudential regulation. Large, interconnected banks, especially G-SIBs, pose unique risks to the financial system due to their size, complexity, and global reach. The regulatory response to this has been the introduction of capital surcharges for G-SIBs, alongside strict resolution planning requirements aimed at preventing the need for government bailouts. These measures are designed to ensure that the failure of a G-SIB can be managed in an orderly fashion without destabilising the entire financial system.

Emerging trends in prudential regulation, such as the ongoing reforms under Basel IV and the increasing focus on climate-related financial risks, illustrate that the regulatory environment is continually evolving. Basel IV aims to address ongoing issues with risk-weighted asset calculations and further strengthen the resilience of the banking sector by reducing variability in banks' risk models and enhancing the standardised approach for credit risk.

uploads/2024/01/cp_gpg_BankingRegulation_2024_Japan_LawPractice.pdf (accessed in March 2025).

CHAPTER 7

BANKS' RECOVERY AND RESOLUTION

OVERVIEW

Banks provide services that are essential to the functioning of the real economy. They also play a crucial role in the transmission of monetary policy. Nevertheless, the failure of a bank – regardless of its size – can have a significant impact on depositors, creditors, and borrowers. Therefore, an effective legal framework for managing non-viable banks is a fundamental component of a jurisdiction's financial safety net.

The UK financial regulatory landscape has undergone significant transformation, particularly in response to the 2007–2008 global financial crisis. This led to the creation of robust frameworks for both the recovery and resolution of banks, with the aim of ensuring the stability of the financial system, protecting depositors, and minimising taxpayer exposure during bank failures.

Chapter 7 delves into the intricacies of the UK's ring-fencing regime, its bank recovery and resolution framework, and its deposit insurance framework, situating it within the broader context of global regulatory practices, including equivalent frameworks in the US, EU, China, India, and Japan. These jurisdictions have each developed a framework to address banks' resolutions, reflecting the global recognition of the importance of such mechanisms in maintaining financial stability.

1 A SPECIAL REGIME FOR BANKS' FAILURES

There is a compelling rationale for subjecting banks to a distinct insolvency, or resolution, regime. Credit institutions perform a unique and systemic role in the national economy. They provide essential services such as the extension of credit, the facilitation of payments, and the maintenance of critical financial infrastructure. Moreover, they play a central role in the transmission of monetary policy. The failure of such institutions can trigger significant disruption and widespread negative externalities, including liquidity shortages, fire sales of assets, and contagion effects transmitted through the interbank market. The global financial crisis, which began in 2007 and intensified during the latter half of 2008, exposed the inadequacy of conventional insolvency frameworks in dealing with failing credit institutions. At that time, authorities were often left with a binary choice: permit the institution to enter corporate bankruptcy or intervene through a public capital injection.

Lehman Brothers' collapse vividly illustrates the systemic consequences of a disorderly bankruptcy; it generated extreme uncertainty across financial markets. This uncertainty contributed to a precipitous decline in global bank equity prices and a surge in interbank lending spreads to unprecedented levels. In parallel, US money market funds, some of which were invested in Lehman's commercial paper, experienced substantial withdrawals. As confidence in these funds eroded, they were compelled to liquidate their holdings, triggering fire sales across the US commercial paper market. The resulting dislocation impaired the flow of short-term funding to corporate borrowers, demonstrating how the failure of a single institution could precipitate far-reaching and destabilising effects across the financial system.

These experiences have underscored that an effective legal framework for managing non-viable banks is a fundamental component of a jurisdiction's financial safety net. Such frameworks must reflect the unique nature of credit institutions and their role in society. General corporate

DOI: 10.4324/9781032662220-8

insolvency regimes are not designed to accommodate the particular risks and public policy concerns associated with bank failures. This is because key aspects of insolvency law – including the grounds for insolvency, the objectives of the process, the available resolution tools, the procedural roles and rights of creditors, and the institutional framework governing the process – are not tailored to the specific characteristics of banks or to the broader public interest concerns linked to their failure.[1]

A specialised resolution regime, according to the Financial Stability Board (**FSB**)'s Key Attributes of Effective Resolution Regimes for Financial Institutions,[2] shall be designed not only to facilitate the orderly resolution of failing firms but also to mitigate systemic risk, preserve financial stability, and minimise reliance on public funds. It could draw inspiration from the core elements which are particularly relevant for systemically important financial institutions (**SIFI**s). Accordingly, resolution regimes are designed to operate independently of and are substantively distinct from, ordinary corporate insolvency procedures, which typically require a more deliberative and consensual approach.

In this respect, since time is of the essence, the banking supervisor is typically better positioned than individual creditors to assess a bank's viability. Given its access to detailed financial and risk-related information, the supervisor is able to identify signs of distress at an early stage and, where necessary, initiate liquidation proceedings to protect financial stability and creditor interests.

In addition to exposing the consequences resulting from the lack of specialised recovery and resolution for credit institutions, the 2007–2009 global financial crisis has highlighted the serious shortcomings in the governance and structure of banks, highlighting the need for fundamental reform in the way banking institutions were structured and organised. Since the crisis, a number of reforms aimed at enhancing the resilience of the financial system, protecting depositors, and reducing the likelihood that the failure of a bank would result in costs being borne by the taxpayer have been introduced in the UK and in other jurisdictions.

2 THE UK RING-FENCING REGIME

One of the key elements of the UK's post-crisis reform is the ring-fencing regime. The Vickers Report, published by the Independent Commission on Banking in 2011,[3] recommended structural reforms to the UK banking sector to prevent a repeat of the financial crisis.[4] One of the report's key recommendations was the introduction of ring-fencing, which would separate critical retail banking services from investment banking by separating them from

1 UNIDROIT Working Group on Bank Insolvency, *Draft Legislative Guide on Bank Liquidation* (UNIDROIT, June 2024) Study LXXXIV, p. 4.

2 'Key Attributes of Effective Resolution Regimes for Financial Institutions' (revised version 2024), available at www.fsb.org/uploads/P250424-3.pdf (accessed in March 2025).

3 'The Independent Commission on Banking: Final Report Recommendations' (September 2011), available at https://webarchive.nationalarchives.gov.uk/ukgwa/20131003105424/https:/hmt-sanctions.s3.amazonaws.com/ICB%20final%20report/ICB%2520Final%2520Report%5B1%5D.pdf (accessed in March 2025).

4 Ibid. at p. 6: "*The recommendations in this report aim to create a more stable and competitive basis for UK banking in the longer term. That means much more than greater resilience against future financial crises and removing risks from banks to the public finances. It also means a banking system that is effective and efficient at providing the basic banking services of safeguarding retail deposits, operating secure payments systems, efficiently channelling savings to productive investments, and managing financial risk. To those ends there should be vigorous competition among banks to deliver the services required by well-informed customers. These goals for UK banking are wholly consistent with maintaining the UK's strength as a pre-eminent centre for banking and finance, and are positive for the competitiveness of the UK economy. They also contribute to financial stability internationally, especially in Europe*".

higher-risk wholesale and investment banking activities.[5] This recommendation was enacted through the Financial Services (Banking Reform) Act 2013, which mandated the creation of ring-fenced banks (**RFBs**). The ring-fencing mandate requires banks to maintain a distinct division between core retail functions, such as deposit-taking, and riskier ventures, like proprietary trading.[6] Only RFBs can perform core banking functions, and these must remain segregated from the wider operations of the banking group. "Part 9B of FSMA prohibits a *"ring-fenced body"*, i.e. a UK based institution which carries on deposit-taking and any other designated *"core activities"* . . ." from carrying on *"excluded activities"*[7] or contravening certain prohibitions".[8] Overall, the ring-fencing framework is designed to ensure that RFBs remain financially and operationally independent from the rest of their banking groups, thereby safeguarding core banking services and protecting financial stability.[9]

This requirement applies to banking groups holding over £25 billion in retail deposits,[10] encompassing major UK banks, including Barclays, HSBC, and Lloyds. The regime has been aptly summarised as conducive to:

> *the separation of its retail banking business from its (potentially riskier) wholesale and investment banking activities. This separation, with ring-fencing, is mandated by statute, and in particular by a new Part 9B which was introduced into FSMA by section 4(1) of the Financial Services (Banking Reform) Act 2013 ("FSBRA"). FSBRA represents a multi-layered response to the financial crisis of 2008 and 2009. It is all part of a package designed to strengthen the UK's larger high-street banks and to provide additional protection to their retail and small business customers. Ring-fencing is an essential part of that response: it is mandatory and has to be effected by 1st January 2019. . . . "Implementation is a highly complex project of national importance. It will be relevant to millions of retail banking customers in the UK". A ring-fencing transfer scheme or "RFTS" is a statutorily-mandated process for implementation of ring-fencing. The process is governed by provisions also newly introduced into Part VII of FSMA by FSBRA. Such a scheme, after*

5 In his Speech in April 2011 Sir John Vickers summarised his proposals: "*Structural reform, in sharp form, would end universal banking and require retail banking and wholesale and investment banking to be carried out by separate banks. This would aim to isolate retail banking services and taxpayers from the risks of global wholesale and investment banking. The Commission's focus is on a combination of these capital and structural approaches, in moderate form*". Speech by Sir John Vickers 11 April 2011.

6 "*It requires UK financial institutions to separate and ring-fence "core activities" from "excluded activities" (sections 142A and 142G of FSMA). The only activity so far designated as a core activity is accepting deposits (section 142B of FSMA). The Financial Services and Markets Act 2000 (Ring-fenced Bodies and Core Activities) Order 2014 (the 'CAO') defines this activity as accepting a 'core deposit'. Paragraph 2 of CAO explains the circumstances in which accepting a deposit is not a core activity. The definition is framed negatively but has the effect that a core deposit is one taken from a retail or small business customer at a branch of a UK bank that is subject to Part 9B of FSMA in the UK or elsewhere in the EEA. The CAO further provides that the ring-fencing regime only applies to an institution if its combined value of core deposits exceeds £25 billion (paragraph 12). 'Excluded activities' include dealing in investments as principal (section 142D of FSMA) and other activities specified in the Financial Services and Markets Act 2000 (Excluded Activities and Prohibitions) Order 2014 (the 'EAPO')*". per Sir Geoffrey Vos in *Barclays Bank Plc And Woolwich Plan Managers Ltd, Re* [2018] EWHC 472 at [10]–[11].

7 *"Excluded activities"* are defined as the regulated activity of dealing in investments as principal and other activities specified by order. Dealing in commodities has also been specified by order as an Excluded Activity.

8 Per Mr Justice Hildyard in *Lloyds Bank Plc & Ors R(ring-fencing transfer scheme) (Rev 1)* [2018] EWHC 1034 (Ch) at [12].

9 Kokkinis, A. and Miglionico, M., *Banking Law: Private Transactions and Regulatory Frameworks* (Routledge, 2021), p. 272.

10 "*A bank will only be designated a RFB if it has (or that bank together with the other UK banks within its group in aggregate have) over £25 billion in core deposits, averaged over a rolling three-year period. To date, the only activity that has been designated as a core activity is the regulated activity of accepting deposits, but only when carried on in specified circumstances. Under the Financial Services and Markets Act 2000 (Ring-fenced Bodies and Core Activities) Order 2014, as amended, a bank will only be deemed to be carrying out the core activity of accepting deposits if it accepts any deposit that is a 'core deposit'. A core deposit is defined, broadly, as a deposit taken from a retail customer or SME customers at a branch in the UK*", per Mr Justice Hildyard in *Lloyds Bank Plc & Ors R(ring-fencing transfer scheme) (Rev 1)* [2018] EWHC 1034 (Ch) at [13].

detailed consideration by statutorily-designated persons, must ultimately be put before the Court for its sanction before it can be given effect.[11]

2.1 Ring-Fenced Banks: Regulatory Framework and Requirements

RFBs are subject to additional regulatory requirements beyond those imposed on authorised deposit-taking institutions. These supplementary obligations are designed to protect RFBs from risks within their groups by limiting their financial and operational reliance on other entities and by ensuring that they have adequate capital and liquidity to withstand financial stress. Therefore, RFBs should interact with their group entities on a third-party basis.

Pursuant to section 142H of FSMA, the PRA is mandated to implement ring-fencing rules designed to safeguard the core activities of an RFB. These rules are set out in the PRA Rulebook, particularly within the Ring-fenced Bodies Part,[12] and they seek to ensure that the RFB's essential banking functions remain insulated from risks arising from other entities in the same banking group. Specifically, the regulations require that the RFB's core activities are not adversely affected by the operations of other group members, that it retains the capacity to make independent decisions without undue influence from affiliated entities, and that it does not depend on resources from other group members that could become unavailable in the event of their failure. Additionally, the ring-fencing framework is designed to enable the RFB to continue performing its core banking activities even in the face of financial distress or insolvency within its wider group. HM Treasury has the authority[13] to specify additional matters that must be addressed in ring-fencing rules or to require the PRA to introduce further rules to reinforce the independence of RFBs from their groups. Furthermore, the PRA is mandated to review its ring-fencing rules every five years to ensure their continued effectiveness.

2.2 Group Structure and Legal Separation

The ring-fencing regime requires a clear legal separation between an RFB and the rest of its corporate group. The structural requirements governing banking groups that include RFBs are set out in Part 9B of FSMA and further elaborated in the Financial Services and Markets Act 2000 (Excluded Activities and Prohibitions) Order 2014, as amended. Under this framework, an RFB must exist as a separate legal entity from any group member that conducts excluded activities. A single entity cannot simultaneously engage in both core and excluded activities,[14] which are defined as the regulated activity of dealing in investments as principal and other activities specified by order, thereby preventing conflicts of interest and ensuring that critical retail banking functions remain insulated from riskier financial activities. Dealing in commodities has also been specified by order as an Excluded Activity. An RFB must not conduct these Excluded Activities, except in certain exempted circumstances specified in the Financial Services and Markets Act 2000 (Excluded Activities and Prohibitions)

11 Per Mr Justice Hildyard in *Lloyds Bank Plc & Ors R(ring-fencing transfer scheme) (Rev 1)* [2018] EWHC 1034 (Ch) at [1] to [5].

12 Further guidance on the PRA's expectations for RFBs is outlined in its supervisory statement on ring-fenced bodies (SS8/16).

13 Section 142I of FSMA.

14 Kokkinis, A. and Miglionico, M., *Banking Law: Private Transactions and Regulatory Frameworks* (Routledge, 2021), p. 268.

Order 2014, as amended.[15] Additionally, RFBs are generally prohibited from maintaining subsidiaries or branches outside the United Kingdom, with limited exceptions for ancillary service undertakings that do not engage in regulated activities.

The PRA has provided further guidance on the structural expectations for banking groups that contain RFBs. It has indicated a preference for a "sibling structure" in which the RFB and non-ring-fenced entities operate as separate affiliates under a common parent rather than existing in an ownership relationship with one another. Although the PRA has not imposed prescriptive rules regarding the precise legal configuration of banking groups, it has made clear that it retains supervisory powers under FSMA to mandate structural changes where necessary to ensure the operational independence of RFBs.

> *There are two basic approaches to structuring a ring-fencing transfer scheme for banking groups that are required to ring-fence their core activities under Part 9B of FSMA. Any entity within the banking group which carries on both core activities and Excluded Activities or business which would breach the Prohibitions. . . . can either: (1) transfer the core activities to a ring-fenced body, leaving the transferor to conduct Excluded Activities and other business which would breach the Prohibitions; or (2) transfer the Excluded Activities and business which would breach the Prohibitions to another entity, leaving the transferor to carry on the core activities as a ring-fenced body. Whereas Barclays chose the first, the Lloyds Group has chosen the second of these options. The choice of this second option means that most of the existing banking business and customers will remain with the Transferors (or entities within its sub-consolidation group).*[16]

The governance requirements for RFBs build upon the PRA's existing rules applicable to all banks but impose additional obligations designed to safeguard the independence of RFBs. Such requirements have been addressed in Chapter 4.

2.3 Prudential and Financial Requirements for RFBs

RFBs are subject to the same prudential requirements as all UK deposit-taking banks but must also adhere to additional standards due to their ring-fenced status. One such requirement is the application of the Other Systemically Important Institutions (O-SII) buffer, which is designed to enhance the resilience of banking groups that contain RFBs, as well as large building societies. Additionally, RFBs that operate within banking groups holding retail deposits of £50 billion or more are subject to the PRA's leverage ratio requirements, which aim to limit excessive leverage and ensure financial stability.[17]

Beyond these specific requirements, the PRA has the authority to impose prudential obligations on an RFB on a sub-consolidated basis. This means that the RFB must meet capital, liquidity, and other prudential requirements independently within its own sub-group rather than relying on the financial position of the broader banking group. These measures are intended to insulate RFBs from risks arising elsewhere in the group and to reinforce their ability to operate as distinct and financially resilient entities.

To prevent excessive risk exposure to non-ring-fenced group members, RFBs must conduct intra-group transactions on an arm's length basis. They must apply the same standards to their dealings with group members as they do to external third parties to ensure their core

15 Per Mr Justice Hildyard in *Lloyds Bank Plc & Ors R(ring-fencing transfer scheme) (Rev 1)* [2018] EWHC 1034 (Ch) at [14].

16 Per Mr Justice Hildyard in *Lloyds Bank Plc & Ors R(ring-fencing transfer scheme) (Rev 1)* [2018] EWHC 1034 (Ch) at [34] and [35].

17 Kokkinis, A. and Miglionico, M., *Banking Law: Private Transactions and Regulatory Frameworks* (Routledge, 2021), p. 270.

activities are not adversely affected. The PRA does not prescribe specific methods for compliance but expects firms to maintain records and evidence that their policies are effectively implemented. Furthermore, they are prohibited from relying on financial support from other group entities and must apply the same risk management standards to intra-group exposures as they would to third parties. Intra-group transactions must be appropriately documented, with clear policies on pricing, approval, and dispute resolution.

The PRA also imposes restrictions on intra-group distributions. An RFB must provide reasonable notice to the PRA before making payments, such as dividends, to other group members. This notification must include evidence that the RFB will maintain sufficient capital resources after the distribution.

RFBs are required to maintain policies and procedures to demonstrate their compliance with ring-fencing rules.

An International Perspective

The potential soundness of the UK ring-fencing approach finds an empirical explanation in the correlation between a higher proportion of bank income derived from non-interest business and a higher likelihood of having received public support during the 2008 financial crisis. This finding suggests that the prudential framework may have incentivised banks to deviate from their core business activities and engage in riskier ventures.[18] On an international level, it should be noted that the insulation of retail banking activities is rare, but it is not unique to the UK. Historically, in the US since 1933, the Glass-Steagall Act was introduced "*to provide for the safer and more effective use of the assets of banks, to regulate interbank control, to prevent the undue diversion of funds into speculative operations, and for other purposes*",[19] thus effectively separating retail banking from investment banking. In 1998, the Federal Reserve Board approved the merger of Travelers, a prominent insurance and securities conglomerate, with Citicorp, the largest bank in the United States. This merger gave rise to Citigroup, the first "universal bank" to operate in the United States since the 1930s. The transaction exploited a temporary loophole in the Bank Holding Company Act of 1956[20] and exerted considerable pressure on Congress to repeal the anti-affiliation provisions of both the Glass-Steagall Act and the Bank Holding Company Act of 1956.

Congress enacted the Gramm-Leach-Bliley Act of 1999,[21] which permitted the establishment of financial holding companies, which were authorised to own banks, securities firms, and insurance companies, thus legitimising Citigroup's universal banking model. The dismantling of the barriers that had historically separated commercial banking from the capital markets culminated in the passage of the Commodity Futures Modernization Act in 2000,[22] which allowed large financial institutions to offer a wide range of over-the-counter derivatives, exempting these instruments from substantive oversight by federal or state regulatory authorities.[23]

18 Maddaloni, A. and Scopelliti, A., 'Rules and Discretion(s) in Prudential Regulation and Supervision: Evidence from EU Banks in the Run-Up to the Crisis' *ECB Working Paper Series No 2284* (May 2019), p. 29.
19 73d CONGRESS. SESS. I. CHS. 87–89. JUNE 15, 16, 1933, [Chapter 89.], available at https://maint.loc.gov/law/help/statutes-at-large/73rd-congress/session-1/c73s1ch89.pdf (accessed in March 2025).
20 12 U.S.C. § 1841, et seq.
21 15 U.S.C. § 6801.
22 7 U.S.C. 1, as Amended Through P.L. 117-339, Enacted January 5, 2023.
23 Crawford, C., 'The Repeal of the Glass-Steagall Act and the Current Financial Crisis' (2011) 9(1) *Journal of Business & Economics Research* 127.

Banks in Japan were generally prohibited from engaging in securities business. However, this prohibition has been gradually relaxed, with the scope of securities activities that banks are permitted to undertake progressively expanding. Securities business, whether conducted directly by banks or through their subsidiaries or the subsidiaries of a Bank Holding Company, is regulated under the Financial Instruments and Exchange Act.[24] Additionally, the Act on the Provision of Financial Services establishes a regulatory framework for "Financial Service Brokerage", designed to facilitate the provision of one-stop services by brokers offering financial products across the banking, insurance, and securities sectors. In the context of securities business, subsidiaries of banks or of a Bank Holding Company may register as "Financial Service Brokers" and engage in a limited scope of securities-related activities.[25]

3 BANKS' RECOVERY AND RESOLUTION PLANNING

Although frequently used interchangeably, Recovery and Resolution Plans are, in fact, distinct and are intended to be deployed at different stages of a SIFI's financial distress. Resolution Plans are designed to enable the effective wind-down of a failing institution in a way that avoids significant disruption to the financial system and ensures that taxpayers are not left to bear the cost. Recovery Plans, by contrast, are forward-looking strategies that outline how an institution can respond swiftly, in an orderly manner, and at minimal cost to periods of extreme stress. These plans detail the range of actions available to restore viability in the face of idiosyncratic, systemic, or combined financial stress events. Recovery planning might have prevented the atmosphere of desperate panic that overwhelmed Lehman Brothers' board, management, and staff in the final days before its collapse and could conceivably have played a role in averting the firm's failure altogether. The early signs of instability in the US housing market, which began to emerge as far back as early 2007, ought to have served as a warning indicator. Had a robust and credible recovery plan been in place – detailing actionable steps to address escalating financial stress – Lehman Brothers may have been better equipped to respond to the unfolding crisis in a structured and controlled manner. In response to the financial chaos that ensued, in 2009, the G20 leaders announced the establishment of the FSB. Comprised of central bank governors and other financial authorities, the FSB was created to identify and address vulnerabilities within the financial services sector. By 2012, the FSB, in collaboration with the Basel Committee on Banking Supervision (**BCBS**), introduced a series of proposals aimed at reducing the likelihood of failure of SIFIs – including major banks, insurance companies, and hedge funds – and, in the event of such failure, mitigating the broader impact on the financial system. Among the key measures was the requirement for SIFIs to develop and submit credible Recovery and Resolution Plans.

The UK's bank recovery and resolution framework is underpinned by the Banking Act 2009, which establishes a comprehensive mechanism for the orderly recovery and resolution of distressed banks. This framework, implemented under the oversight of the PRA and the Bank of England, ensures that banks can recover from financial distress without requiring taxpayer-funded bailouts. It also allows for the resolution of failing banks while ensuring the continuity of essential banking services, particularly to depositors. Such framework is broadly

24 (Act No 25 of 1948).

25 Hideaki, S., 'Japan: Law & Practice' in *Chambers Global Practice Guides: Banking Regulation 2024*, Nagashima Ohno & Tsunematsu (Chambers and Partners, 2024), available at www.noandt.com/wp-content/uploads/2024/01/cp_gpg_BankingRegulation_2024_Japan_LawPractice.pdf (accessed in March 2025).

aligned with the European Union's Bank Recovery and Resolution Directive (**BRRD**),[26] which harmonises recovery and resolution mechanisms across the EU, and the Single Resolution Mechanism (**SRM**),[27] which governs the resolution of banks within the eurozone. The Single Resolution Board (**SRB**)[28] coordinates the resolution of failing banks within the eurozone, ensuring a consistent and harmonised approach across the region.

3.1 Banks' Recovery Planning Framework

Each UK bank is required to produce a recovery plan detailing the measures it would take to restore its financial position following a significant deterioration or a stress scenario. The requirements are closely linked to the broader resolution planning framework, which sets out how banks should prepare for potential resolution.

The PRA's rules on recovery planning are set out in the Recovery Plans Part of the PRA Rulebook, and firms must also comply with the retained EU law version of Commission Delegated Regulation (EU) 2016/1075, which establishes regulatory technical standards (**RTS**) on recovery planning. The PRA's supervisory statement on recovery planning (SS9/17) provides further guidance on how firms should approach these requirements.[29]

The recovery planning framework applies to "CRR firms" as defined within the PRA Rulebook. The framework also applies to qualifying holding companies of CRR firms, known as "qualifying parent undertakings".[30] These entities, along with CRR firms, are referred to as "BRRD undertakings" in recognition of the framework's origins in the BRRD.

The PRA's recovery planning requirements extend to both group recovery plans, which apply at the consolidated level, and individual recovery plans for firms that are not part of a group subject to consolidated supervision. Where the PRA acts as the consolidating supervisor for a banking group, the UK parent undertaking is responsible for preparing the group recovery plan. In cases where the PRA is not the consolidating supervisor, a qualifying parent undertaking[31] must ensure that a group recovery plan is prepared and submitted to the relevant authority.

The PRA has the discretion to apply reduced recovery planning obligations, known as "simplified obligations", to banks whose failure is not expected to have a significant negative impact on financial markets, other institutions, or the broader economy.[32] The PRA expects

26 Directive 2014/59/EU of the European Parliament and of the Council of 15 May 2014 establishing a framework for the recovery and resolution of credit institutions and investment firms and amending Council Directive 82/891/EEC, and Directives 2001/24/EC, 2002/47/EC, 2004/25/EC, 2005/56/EC, 2007/36/EC, 2011/35/EU, 2012/30/EU and 2013/36/EU, and Regulations (EU) No 1093/2010 and (EU) No 648/2012, of the European Parliament and of the Council.

27 Established under Regulation (EU) No 806/2014 of the European Parliament and of the Council of 15 July 2014 establishing uniform rules and a uniform procedure for the resolution of credit institutions and certain investment firms in the framework of a Single Resolution Mechanism and a Single Resolution Fund and amending Regulation (EU) No 1093/2010.

28 Established under Article 42 of Regulation No 806/2014 of the European Parliament and of the Council of 15 July 2014 establishing uniform rules and a uniform procedure for the resolution of credit institutions and certain investment firms in the framework of a Single Resolution Mechanism and a Single Resolution Fund and amending Regulation (EU) No 1093/2010.

29 See SS9/17 available at: www.bankofengland.co.uk/prudential-regulation/publication/2017/recovery-planning-ss (accessed in March 2025).

30 As defined in section 192B of FSMA.

31 Parent undertaking has the meaning given in Article 4(1)(15) of the UK CRR.

32 The criteria for simplified obligations are set out in the retained EU law version of Commission Delegated Regulation (EU) 2019/348, which specifies the quantitative and qualitative factors that determine eligibility.

that banks for which insolvency is the preferred resolution strategy will generally be subject to simplified obligations.

A recovery plan must contain several key elements.[33] The plan must outline appropriate conditions and procedures for the timely implementation of recovery actions, a wide range of recovery options, and scenarios of severe macroeconomic and financial stress relevant to the bank. It must also include a framework of indicators designed to identify points at which recovery actions should be taken, an analysis of the bank's access to central bank facilities, and measures that could be implemented in cases of early intervention.

For group recovery plans, additional requirements apply, including details of measures intended to stabilise the group or specific firms within it, arrangements to ensure coordination between entities within the group, and provisions for intra-group financial support where applicable. The recovery plan should also contain information on the bank's risk management framework, recovery options tailored to stress scenarios, and an assessment of the total recovery capacity the bank could credibly realise. The PRA expects banks to provide self-assessments of their recovery capacity, quantifying their position in terms of common equity tier 1 (**CET1**) capital, leverage ratio, and liquidity coverage ratio.

A well-functioning recovery plan relies on an effective indicator framework that alerts a bank to emerging stress, allowing it to take timely action. The PRA requires banks to include a broad range of indicators beyond regulatory capital and liquidity ratios, incorporating both quantitative and qualitative metrics from their overall risk management framework. The severity of scenarios used in recovery planning is also a key consideration, and banks must ensure that stress scenarios bring them close to their point of non-viability.

Additional expectations relate to governance, communication strategies, and, where relevant, winding down trading activities. The governance framework must include clear decision-making processes, with designated individuals responsible for approving and overseeing the recovery plan. A communication plan must be in place to ensure that timely and appropriate information is shared with stakeholders during a recovery process. For banks with large trading books, recovery plans should also incorporate measures for trading activity[34] wind-down (**TWD**) planning. These requirements apply to firms identified as systemically important that have the wind-down of trading activities as a recovery or post-resolution restructuring option. TWD banks must include trading wind-down as a recovery option, engage in scenario testing, and develop capabilities to execute their trading wind-down plan effectively. In addition to standard recovery planning, the PRA requires non-systemic banks to prepare solvent wind-down (**SWD**) plans to ensure an orderly exit from the market. These plans must demonstrate how the bank could wind down its business while maintaining solvency and repaying all depositors and creditors in full.

33 Including information specified in Section A of the Annex to the BRRD and the supplementary requirements set out in the BRRD RTS.

34 "Trading activities" includes the trading book (as defined in Article 4(86) of Regulation (EU) No 575/2013 of the European Parliament and of the Council of 26 June 2013 on prudential requirements for credit institutions and investment firms and amending Regulation (EU) No 648/2012 and activities carried out in connection with the trading book, such as margin loans and other financing activities carried out in relation to trading, that the firm would consider appropriate to wind-down as part of post-resolution restructuring. For these purposes, "trading activities" do not include banking book activity that the firm would expect to continue after a full wind-down in post-resolution restructuring. Where a legal entity contains only trading activity business, such as a broker-dealer business model, the wind-down of trading activities would likely mean the wind-down of the legal entity. See PRA's statement of policy (SOP) dated 4 March 2025 on Trading activity wind-down available at www.prarulebook.co.uk/guidance/statements-of-policy/sop-trading-activity-wind-down/04-03-2025 (accessed in March 2025).

Recovery plans must be reviewed and updated at least annually[35] to ensure they reflect any material changes to their structure, business, or financial position. Additionally, credit institutions are required to conduct fire drill exercises on their recovery plans before each submission, subject to a minimum of one fire drill every three years. Governance arrangements must be maintained to ensure that the management body oversees the recovery plan, the audit committee periodically reviews it, and an executive director is responsible for its implementation.

3.2 Resolution Planning

The objective of an effective resolution regime is to enable the orderly resolution of financial institutions[36] without causing severe systemic disruption and without imposing losses on taxpayers.[37] Such a regime should ensure the continuity of critical economic functions while adhering to mechanisms that allow shareholders and unsecured, uninsured creditors to absorb losses.[38] This process should have as fundamental objectives value maximisation,[39] depositor protection,[40] the stability of the financial system as a whole, avoidance of the use of public funds and loss to taxpayers, certainty, and predictability.

The design of legal frameworks for managing bank failures varies across jurisdictions. Broadly speaking, jurisdictions may adopt either a single-track regime, where a unified framework applies to all bank failures, or a dual-track regime, which distinguishes between resolution and liquidation or insolvency proceedings. In single-track regimes, the legal framework governing bank failures is typically designed specifically for banks and, in some cases, other financial institutions. Conversely, in dual-track regimes, the liquidation track may be governed by one of three approaches: (i) the general corporate insolvency law; (ii) the general corporate insolvency law with modifications tailored to banks; or (iii) a separate bank-specific liquidation regime.[41]

The UK's – and the EU's – framework for bank resolution, as established in the BRRD, distinguishes between "resolution" and "normal insolvency proceedings". The SRR follows a dual-track regime, whereby resolution is governed by specialised bank resolution laws, while liquidation or insolvency proceedings may be conducted under either general corporate insolvency law or a modified bank-specific insolvency framework.[42] The Bank of England is responsible for establishing a preferred resolution strategy for each bank, typically involving

35 The submission of recovery plans to the PRA is conducted through online submission, and the PRA assesses plans based on criteria set out in the Bank Recovery and Resolution (No 2) Order 2014 (BRRO2).
36 Goode, R. and van Zwieten, K., *Principles of Corporate Insolvency Law* (Sweet & Maxwell, 2019), Chapter 1, Section 5.
37 Banking insolvencies can be very complex: "The BCCI liquidation is even now not complete, and it started over 18 years ago" per Lord Neuberger of Abbotsbury, Master of the Rolls: A judicial perspective on the conduct of claims in the current climate [2009] UKSpeech LHU52 (23 October 2009), p. 5.
38 'Key Attributes of Effective Resolution Regimes for Financial Institutions' (revised version 2024), p. 4, available at www.fsb.org/uploads/P250424-3.pdf (accessed in March 2025).
39 Value maximisation is a fundamental objective of business insolvency laws. The primary aim is to secure the highest possible value from the liquidation estate, thereby ensuring that creditors receive the maximum possible recovery. In certain legal frameworks, a liquidator is explicitly required to wind up the affairs of the insolvent entity in a manner that optimises the value of its assets, ensuring an orderly and efficient distribution to creditors.
40 Depositors generally make up a significant percentage of the creditors of a bank.
41 UNIDROIT Working Group on Bank Insolvency, *Draft Legislative Guide on Bank Liquidation* (UNIDROIT, June 2024) Study LXXXIV, p. 8.
42 UNIDROIT Working Group on Bank Insolvency, *Draft Legislative Guide on Bank Liquidation* (UNIDROIT, June 2024) Study LXXXIV, p. 8.

one of three primary approaches: a bail-in, which reduces or converts the bank's liabilities to absorb losses and recapitalise the institution; a partial transfer, in which parts of the bank's operations are moved to a private purchaser or bridge bank; or insolvency, through the Bank Insolvency Procedure (**BIP**), which ensures prompt depositor compensation by the Financial Services Compensation Scheme (**FSCS**). Banks are required to regularly update their resolution packs, providing the Bank of England with essential information to develop and adjust resolution strategies as the bank's financial structure evolves.

Early Intervention and Supervisory Measures

The PRA can initiate early intervention if a bank shows signs of distress, with the goal of stabilising the institution. Possible measures include imposing restrictions on business activities, such as limiting high-risk operations or prohibiting specific payments like dividends, and implementing governance modifications that require structural or strategic adjustments to improve financial stability. Additionally, the Bank of England holds the authority to remove barriers to resolvability by directing banks to adjust their legal or financial structures to facilitate more effective resolution.

3.3 Resolution of Banks and the SRR

The legislative framework for the SRR has been established under the Banking Act 2009 and supplemented by secondary legislation, including the Bank Recovery and Resolution (No 2) Order 2014.[43] The SRR reflects the measures implemented by the UK in response to the BRRD.

> *The 2009 Act was passed in the wake of the international financial crisis which started in 2008 and included, for the first time, special procedures to deal with insolvent banks. Since that crisis had in part been triggered by the collapse of Lehman Brothers in September 2008, it was appreciated that special insolvency procedures would be needed for investment banks. However, they presented particular problems and the enactment of more general banking legislation could not be delayed while those problems were addressed and resolved. In particular, investment banks hold client assets, often on a very large scale, and existing insolvency procedures as well as the new procedures introduced for banks do not contain provisions to deal adequately with the complex problems which can arise in the event of the insolvency of an investment bank. Accordingly, the Banking Act 2009 made provision in general terms for Regulations to be made dealing with investment banks.*[44]

The SRR is designed to provide a structured mechanism for resolving failing banks. It is intended for use only in situations where a bank's failure is imminent and where the existing powers of the relevant UK authorities – namely, His Majesty's Treasury (**HM Treasury**), the Bank of England, the PRA, and the FCA – are insufficient to address the situation effectively.

The SRR comprises several key components. First, it provides five pre-insolvency stabilisation options, which include: transfer to a private sector purchaser, transfer to a bridge bank, transfer to an asset management vehicle (**AMV**), the bail-in option, and transfer to temporary public sector ownership. In addition to these stabilisation options, the SRR includes two specific insolvency procedures: the BIP and the Bank Administration Procedure (**BAP**).

43 (SI 2014/3348).

44 Per Mr Justice David Richards in *Heis & Ors (Administrators of MF Global UK Ltd.) v MF Global Inc* [2012] EWHC 3068 (Ch) at [35].

The effective operation of the SRR requires close coordination between the Bank of England, HM Treasury, the PRA, and the FCA, with each authority assuming specific responsibilities. The PRA, alongside the Bank of England, is responsible for determining whether the SRR should be triggered for a failing bank. It also oversees the authorisation of bridge banks and the ongoing supervision of institutions within the SRR. The Bank of England is responsible for managing the SRR itself, including selecting and implementing the appropriate resolution tools, except for the temporary public ownership tool, which falls under HM Treasury's remit. HM Treasury also takes the lead on decisions involving public funds and exercises control over temporary public ownership where necessary. Meanwhile, the FCA must be consulted at specified stages of the resolution process to ensure regulatory oversight. The FSCS is also expected to collaborate with the authorities in the implementation of the SRR.

When exercising their powers under the SRR, the relevant UK authorities must consider a set of special resolution objectives as outlined in section 4 of the Banking Act 2009.[45] These objectives include ensuring the continuity of banking services and critical functions within the UK, maintaining financial stability by preventing contagion and upholding market discipline, and fostering public confidence in the financial system. "Critical functions" refer to activities, services, or operations whose discontinuation would likely disrupt services essential to the UK economy or financial stability.

Additionally, the SRR seeks to protect public funds by minimising reliance on extraordinary financial support, safeguarding investors and depositors covered by the FSCS, and ensuring the protection of client assets where applicable. Furthermore, the regime must operate in a manner that does not interfere with property rights in contravention of the Convention rights under the Human Rights Act 1998. Importantly, these objectives are not assigned any specific ranking in terms of priority; rather, section 4(10) of the Act requires that they be balanced appropriately in each case.

Under section 7 of the Banking Act 2009, a specific sequence of events must be followed before a bank enters a resolution. First, the PRA must determine that the bank is failing or is likely to fail based on a pre-resolution valuation (Condition 1). If this condition is met, the Bank of England must then assess whether, given the timing and circumstances, any alternative

45

(1) This section sets out the special resolution objectives.
(2) The relevant authorities shall have regard to the special resolution objectives in using, or considering the use of—
(a) the stabilisation powers, (b) the bank insolvency procedure, or (c) the bank administration procedure.
(3) For the purpose of this section the relevant authorities are – (a) the Treasury, (b) the PRA, (ba) the FCA, and (c) the Bank of England.
(3A) Objective 1 is to ensure the continuity of banking services in the United Kingdom and of critical functions.
(4) Objective 2 is to protect and enhance the stability of the financial system of the United Kingdom, including in particular by – (a) preventing contagion (including contagion to market infrastructures such as investment exchanges, clearing houses, recognised CSDs within the meaning of section 285 of the Financial Services and Markets Act 2000 and central counterparties authorised or recognised in the United Kingdom in accordance with Article 14 or 25 of Regulation (EU) 648/2012 of the European Parliament and the Council of 4th July 2012 on OTC derivatives, central counterparties and trade repositories) as it forms part of assimilated law, and (b) maintaining market discipline.
(5) Objective 3 is to protect and enhance public confidence in the stability of the financial system of the United Kingdom.
(6) Objective 4 is to protect public funds, including by minimising reliance on extraordinary public financial support.
(7) Objective 5 is to protect investors and depositors to the extent that they have investments or deposits covered by the FSCS.
(8) Objective 6, which applies in any case in which client assets may be affected, is to protect those assets.
(9) Objective 7 is to avoid interfering with property rights in contravention of a Convention right (within the meaning of the Human Rights Act 1998).
(10) The order in which the objectives are listed in this section is not significant; they are to be balanced as appropriate in each case.

action – other than resolution under the SRR – is reasonably likely to prevent the bank from failing (Condition 2). If Condition 2 is satisfied, the Bank of England is required to write down or convert the bank's regulatory capital instruments. Under section 6A of the Banking Act 2009, this step must be taken where Condition 1 has been met, and the Bank of England considers that Condition 2 will remain satisfied unless such instruments are written down or converted. If, despite this intervention, the bank remains at risk of failure, the Bank of England must then determine that the use of one or more stabilisation powers is necessary in the public interest, having regard to the special resolution objectives (Condition 3). Finally, the Bank of England must be satisfied that winding up the bank – whether through the BIP or another method – would not achieve the special resolution objectives to the same extent (Condition 4).

Throughout this process, the PRA is required to consult with the Bank of England when considering whether Condition 1 has been met, while the Bank of England must, in turn, consult with the PRA, the FCA, and HM Treasury in relation to the subsequent conditions.[46]

In assessing whether a bank is failing or is likely to fail for the purposes of Condition 1, a number of factors must be considered.[47] A bank is deemed to meet this criterion if it is failing, or is likely to fail, to satisfy the threshold conditions necessary for authorisation under FSMA and if such failure would justify the variation or cancellation of its Part 4A permission by the PRA. Additionally, a bank may be regarded as failing if a pre-resolution valuation determines that its assets are worth less than its liabilities, if it is unable to pay its debts as they fall due (thereby meeting the test for insolvency), or if either of these conditions is expected to apply in the near future. Moreover, the need for extraordinary public financial support can also trigger a determination of failure unless such support is required solely to address a serious disturbance in the UK economy and to maintain financial stability or falls within one of the specified forms of permitted intervention set out in section 7(5E) of the Banking Act 2009, such as an injection of own funds or the purchase of capital instruments on terms that do not confer an undue advantage on the bank.

Pre-Resolution Valuations

Where a bank is at risk of failure, efforts may be undertaken to restore its viability before formal resolution becomes necessary. These include supervisory interventions, such as restrictions on dividend payments to shareholders or bonus payments to senior management, aimed at conserving financial resources. A bank may also take independent action, such as restructuring its finances through a voluntary debt-for-equity swap or selling parts of its business to improve its financial position. A bank's management body is under an obligation to notify the PRA immediately if it believes any of the failure conditions in section 7(5C) have been met. In turn, the PRA must inform the Bank of England if it receives such a notification from a bank or if it independently determines that a bank is failing or likely to fail. These notification

46 In making these assessments, the PRA will regard guidelines issued by the European Banking Authority (**EBA**) prior to 1 January 2021, including those on the interpretation of when a bank should be considered as failing or likely to fail. See "Interpretation of EU Guidelines and Recommendations: Bank of England and PRA approach after the UK's withdrawal from the EU" available at: www.bankofengland.co.uk/-/media/boe/files/prudential-regulation/statement-of-policy/2023/interpretation-of-eu-guidelines-and-recommendations-near-final-december-2023-update.pdf (accessed in March 2025).

47 Notably, section 7(6) of the Banking Act 2009 clarifies that the special resolution objectives are not relevant to the PRA's and the Bank of England's assessment of whether a bank satisfies Conditions 1 and 2. Once all four conditions have been met or a stabilisation power has been exercised, insolvency proceedings against the bank may not be initiated without the Bank of England's consent, in accordance with section 89K(1) of the Banking Act 2009.

requirements are set out in the PRA's Notifications Part[48] and are reinforced by provisions[49] in the Bank Recovery and Resolution (No 2) Order 2014.[50]

Before the Bank of England issues a mandatory reduction instrument or exercises any stabilisation power in respect of a failing bank, it must ensure that a valuation of the bank's assets and liabilities is conducted in accordance with section 6E of the Banking Act 2009. The purpose of this independent valuation is to inform the decision of the Bank of England or the PRA as to whether the bank is failing or likely to fail. In cases of urgency, the Bank of England may carry out a provisional valuation rather than appointing an independent valuer. However, in such instances, an independent valuer[51] must be appointed as soon as practicable.[52] The Banking Act 2009[53] mandates compliance with the methodology set out in the retained EU version of Commission Delegated Regulation (EU) 2018/345, which prescribes regulatory technical standards for conducting valuations in a resolution scenario.

Mandatory Reduction at the Point of Non-Viability

The Bank of England is obligated to write down or convert capital instruments at a bank that has reached the point of non-viability, meaning that it is failing or likely to fail. This process, referred to by the Bank of England as "mandatory reduction", aims to recapitalise the bank and restore its long-term viability by ensuring that shareholders and holders of Additional Tier 1 (AT1) and Tier 2 instruments absorb their share of the bank's losses.[54]

Under section 6A of the Banking Act 2009, the Bank of England must undertake mandatory reduction before it exercises any of the stabilisation options available under the SRR. This power may be applied in conjunction with a stabilisation option where all resolution conditions are met or separately where the bank would remain unviable without a write-down or conversion but could be restored to long-term viability through such a measure. The practical application of these powers is outlined in Chapter 5 of the Bank of England's Code of Practice.

Although mandatory reduction and bail-in may both involve the cancellation, transfer, dilution, reduction, or conversion of capital instruments and relevant internal liabilities, they remain distinct processes. If the Bank of England determines that a greater amount of bail-in liabilities must be reduced or converted beyond what is permitted under a mandatory reduction instrument, it may issue a resolution instrument under section 12A of the Banking Act 2009 instead of relying solely on mandatory reduction.

48 Rules 8.2 and 8.3.
49 Specifically, articles 182 and 183.
50 Articles 46 to 48 of Commission Delegated Regulation (EU) 2016/1075 establish regulatory technical standards under the BRRD, specifying the information that must be provided when making such notifications.
51 The requirements for appointing and, where necessary, removing independent valuers under sections 6E and 48X are set out in section 62A. Independent valuers are also subject to certain provisions in section 55, which grants them the power to apply to the court for access to information relevant to their valuation. To qualify as an independent valuer under section 62A(2), an individual must meet the criteria for independence as defined in the RTS set out in the BRRD. These RTS, detailed in Articles 37 to 41, establish general principles for assessing independence, including the requirement that the valuer possesses the necessary qualifications, experience, and resources, remains structurally separate from the relevant public authorities and the entity being valued, and has no material conflict of interest with either party.
52 As required by section 48X(1).
53 Section 6E(6).
54 Chiu, I. and Wilson, J., *Banking Law and Regulation* (Oxford University Press, 2019), p. 638.

Triggers for Mandatory Transfer, Write-Down, or Conversion

The trigger for the cancellation, transfer, write-down, or conversion of capital instruments and liabilities arises when one of the scenarios set out in section 6A of the Banking Act 2009 applies. These scenarios, referred to as "cases",[55] define the circumstances in which such measures can be taken to ensure the viability of a bank or its group. The **first case** applies where the bank meets all the conditions for resolution, meaning it is failing or likely to fail, and there is no reasonable likelihood that any alternative measure, other than resolution under the SRR, will restore its viability.

The **second case** arises where the bank would no longer be viable unless the write-down power was exercised, and no reasonable prospect exists that any non-resolution measures could restore its viability. The **third case** concerns a situation where the Bank of England determines that the bank's group will not remain viable unless the write-down power is applied to the bank, where that bank is a subsidiary whose Additional Tier 1 (AT1) and Tier 2 capital instruments are recognised for meeting capital requirements both on an individual and consolidated basis. The **fourth case** applies where the Bank of England concludes that the banking group as a whole would not remain viable unless the write-down power is applied to the parent bank, where the parent's capital instruments contribute to the consolidated capital requirements of the group.

The **fifth case** addresses circumstances in which extraordinary public financial support has been provided to the bank, except where such support consists of an injection of own funds or a purchase of capital instruments on terms that do not confer an advantage on the bank. In this case, the Bank of England may determine that a write-down is necessary to address a capital shortfall. Importantly, cases two to five apply where mandatory reduction is used independently of the SRR stabilisation powers, whereas case one applies where the power is used in conjunction with a stabilisation measure other than bail-in.[56]

The Process of Mandatory Transfer, Write-Down, and Conversion

In executing a mandatory reduction, the Bank of England follows a structured process to allocate losses in accordance with the priority of claims. First, it must cancel, severely dilute, or transfer the bank's CET1 instruments, ensuring that losses are borne primarily by the holders of these instruments. If further action is necessary to achieve the special resolution objectives, the Bank of England must write down or convert the principal amount of AT1 instruments into CET1 capital. If these measures are still insufficient, Tier 2 instruments must also be written down or converted to CET1 to the extent required to restore the bank's viability.

As a result, CET1 instruments bear losses in full, while AT1 and Tier 2 instruments absorb losses to the extent necessary to meet the special resolution objectives or up to their full capacity, whichever is lower. In cases where mandatory reduction is applied without the use of a stabilisation power under the SRR (as in the second case), the power must also be applied to the bank's relevant internal liabilities. These are eligible liabilities issued internally between legal entities in a banking group where the issuer is not a resolution entity, often referred to as internal Minimum Requirement for Own Funds and Eligible Liabilities (**MREL**).[57]

55 Kokkinis, A. and Miglionico, M., *Banking Law: Private Transactions and Regulatory Frameworks* (Routledge, 2021), p. 279.
56 Section 81AA.
57 The detailed framework governing the mandatory transfer, write-down, and conversion process is set out in sections 6B and 6C of the Banking Act 2009.

MREL applies to banking groups that include EU (and UK) firms falling within the scope of the BRRD. These entities are required, at all times and both on an individual and consolidated basis, to maintain a minimum level of own funds (i.e., regulatory capital) and eligible liabilities. MREL is expressed as a percentage of either an institution's total risk exposure amount or its total exposure measure. Only specific types of liabilities qualify for the purposes of meeting an institution's MREL obligations. Certain liabilities – referred to as excluded liabilities – are categorically ineligible for this purpose, while others may be excluded at the discretion of the relevant resolution authority.

The Bank of England will adhere to the European Banking Authority's guidelines on the rate of conversion of debt to equity.[58] At least one mandatory reduction instrument will be used to give legal effect to these measures, as demonstrated in the Silicon Valley Bank UK Limited Mandatory Reduction and Share Transfer Instrument 2023, which was issued in March 2023 to write down SVB UK's capital instruments in accordance with sections 6A(2) and 6B of the Banking Act 2009.[59]

The Bank of England also has the power to write down or convert relevant capital instruments or internal liabilities of intermediate holding companies within a banking group. This power applies where a bank is owned by a resolution entity through multiple intermediate holding companies.[60]

3.4 Resolution Tools Available to the Bank of England

The Bank of England is responsible for determining which SRR tool or combination of tools to apply once a bank has been placed into resolution. However, it is required to consult with the PRA and HM Treasury, and any decision to transfer a failing bank into temporary public ownership requires the explicit consent of HM Treasury. Additionally, if HM Treasury has already provided financial assistance to a failing bank, the Bank of England may only exercise a transfer power – whether to a private sector purchaser, a bridge bank, or an AMV – if HM Treasury has recommended it as necessary in order to protect the public interest.

58 See EBA: Final Guidelines: on the rate of conversion of debt to equity in bail-in Opens in a new window (EBA/GL/2017/03). Available at: www.bankofengland.co.uk/-/media/boe/files/paper/2020/december/gl-rate-conversion-debt-to-equity-bail-in.pdf (accessed in March 2025).

59

"*(1) By this Instrument all Shares in issue at the Mandatory Reduction Time are transferred to HSBC.*
(2) By this Instrument:

(a) the principal amount of the Capital Instruments is reduced to zero;
(b) all liabilities owed by Silicon Valley Bank in respect of the Capital Instruments, including accrued interest, are cancelled;
(c) all rights of any holder or beneficial owner of Capital Instruments at any time to or in respect of the Capital Instruments are extinguished and the Capital Instruments are cancelled in full", Section 4 of The Silicon Valley Bank UK Limited Mandatory Reduction and Share Transfer Instrument 2023.

60 As provided under section 81AA of the Banking Act 2009.

Transfer to a Private Sector Purchaser

The transfer to a private sector purchaser tool allows for the sale of part or all of a failing bank's business to a third-party private sector entity. This may involve the transfer of shares in the failing bank or a transfer of its assets and liabilities. Such a transfer may be implemented through either a securities transfer or a property transfer.[61]

Before applying this tool, the Bank of England is required[62] to conduct a marketing process for the sale of the failing bank. This obligation is supplemented by guidance issued by the EBA on circumstances that pose a material threat to financial stability and the effectiveness of the sale of business tools. A notable example of this tool's application occurred in March 2023, when Silicon Valley Bank UK was transferred to HSBC UK Bank plc.

Transfer to a Bridge Bank

Where a private sector sale is not immediately feasible, the authorities may transfer part or all of the failing bank's business to a publicly controlled bridge bank. A bridge bank is a temporary institution created specifically for this purpose and is wholly owned and controlled by the Bank of England. The Banking Act refers to such entities as "resolution companies", a term that also applies to AMVs.

Although there is no statutory time limit on the duration of bridge bank ownership, the expectation is that this is a short-term measure intended to stabilise the failing bank before arranging its eventual sale or wind-down.[63]

Transfer to an AMV

The AMV tool is used to transfer certain assets, rights, and liabilities of a failing bank to a separate entity with the objective of maximising their value through an eventual sale or orderly wind-down. Unlike other stabilisation options, it may only be used in conjunction with another resolution tool.[64] This restriction reflects the fact that AMVs are designed primarily to assist in the restructuring of a failing bank rather than to function as standalone resolution entities.

The use of an AMV is limited to situations where liquidating a bank's assets through normal insolvency proceedings would have adverse effects on financial markets.[65] Additionally, the AMV must be wholly or partially owned by the Bank of England or HM Treasury and controlled by the Bank of England.

In its resolution approach document, the Bank of England notes that AMVs can play a role in both transfer and bail-in resolutions. In a transfer scenario, poor-quality assets may be separated from the remaining bank and moved to an AMV, thereby improving the risk profile of the remaining entity and increasing its attractiveness to potential buyers. In a bail-in,

61 In accordance with section 11 of the Banking Act 2009.
62 Under section 11A of the Banking Act 2009.
63 Governance arrangements for bridge banks are set out in Chapter 9 of the Bank of England's Code of Practice.
64 As specified in section 8ZA(2) of the Banking Act 2009.
65 The circumstances in which this tool may be applied are detailed in EBA guidelines on the impact of asset liquidations under insolvency: available at www.bankofengland.co.uk/-/media/boe/files/paper/2020/december/guidelines%20on%20the%20determination%20of%20when%20the%20liquidation%20of%20asset%20or%20liabilities.pdf (accessed in March 2025).

an AMV may be used to support rapid restructuring by isolating the business lines responsible for the failure, thereby improving the viability of the recapitalised institution.[66]

Bail-In Tool

The bail-in tool is designed to absorb the losses of a failing bank and recapitalise either the existing bank or its successor entity using the bank's own resources. The tool operates by writing down or converting the claims of shareholders and unsecured creditors into equity, thereby restoring solvency while adhering to the established hierarchy of claims in insolvency.

Banks must prepare for potential bail-in by meeting MREL standards and ensuring that non-UK law-governed liabilities recognise bail-in provisions.

Transfer to Temporary Public Ownership

As an option of last resort, the authorities may transfer part or all of a failing bank into temporary public sector ownership. This involves transferring the bank to a nominee of HM Treasury, such as the Treasury Solicitor, or to a company wholly owned and controlled by HM Treasury. Unlike a bridge bank transfer, which may involve only a partial transfer of assets and liabilities, a transfer to temporary public ownership results in the government acquiring full ownership of the failing bank.

Since this option involves the use of public funds, HM Treasury is the sole authority responsible for authorising a transfer into temporary public ownership. Before making such a decision, it must consult with the PRA, the FCA, and the Bank of England.[67] The conditions for transferring a bank to temporary public ownership are more stringent than those governing other resolution tools. In addition to failing banks, HM Treasury also has the power to take bank parent companies – referred to as "holding companies" in the Banking Act – into temporary public ownership.[68]

Moreover, the power to effect a public sector transfer may only be exercised where one of the following two conditions[69] is met: (i) where it is necessary to resolve or mitigate a serious threat to the stability of the UK financial system; or (ii) where HM Treasury has already provided financial assistance to the bank in order to address a systemic risk, or where the Bank of England has provided extraordinary public support to the institution.

Lessons for Crisis Management From Recent Bank Failures

The banking crises of 2023, particularly the failures of Silicon Valley Bank (SVB), Signature Bank, and the intervention in SVB UK, offer valuable insights into crisis management within the financial sector. These cases highlight the importance of swift regulatory intervention, the role of liquidity support, the challenges posed by uninsured deposits, and the effectiveness of different resolution strategies. They also raise critical

66 Governance arrangements for AMVs are set out in Chapter 9 of the Bank of England's Code of Practice.
67 As required under section 9(4) of the Banking Act 2009.
68 The governance arrangements applicable to institutions in temporary public ownership are outlined in Chapter 9 of the Bank of England's Code of Practice.
69 Set out in section 9.

questions about the adequacy of existing frameworks for dealing with mid-sized and smaller bank failures.

A key lesson from the failures of SVB and Signature Bank is the vulnerability of banks with concentrated and uninsured deposit bases. Both institutions suffered rapid and large-scale deposit outflows when confidence in their business models eroded. The speed at which these outflows occurred – exacerbated by digital banking and social media – demonstrates the necessity for banks to maintain strong liquidity management and stress-testing frameworks.

The response of the US authorities also underscores the importance of flexibility in crisis management. The decision to invoke the "systemic risk exception" allowed the FDIC to guarantee all deposits, stabilising confidence and preventing wider contagion. However, this approach raises concerns about moral hazard, as depositors at failed institutions were fully protected, whereas shareholders and certain unsecured creditors bore losses.

The resolution of SVB UK by the Bank of England offers another perspective on crisis management, particularly in the case of mid-sized banks. Ordinarily, SVB UK would have been subject to standard insolvency proceedings, given its size. However, the authorities opted for a resolution due to the bank's significant role in certain market segments.[70] This decision has prompted a reassessment of whether the existing UK framework is sufficiently robust to handle the failure of smaller banks that may not have sufficient bail-inable liabilities to fund resolution. It raises the question of whether alternative mechanisms, such as enhanced liquidity support or a dedicated resolution fund for smaller banks, should be considered to manage such failures without resorting to taxpayer bailouts.

Regulators must ensure that resolution plans are not only well-structured but also actionable under real-world stress conditions. The speed of deposit outflows observed in 2023 suggests that supervisory authorities should consider enhancing early intervention measures to prevent crises from escalating.

Another critical lesson is the need for better coordination between regulatory authorities across jurisdictions. The differing treatment of depositors, capital instruments, and shareholders across the US and the UK in these crises highlights the potential for market uncertainty when resolution frameworks diverge significantly.

4 BANK INSOLVENCY PROCEDURE

The BIP facilitates the orderly liquidation of a failed bank that is not likely to pose a systemic risk and is unlikely to attract a buyer. Unlike standard insolvency under the Insolvency Act 1986, the BIP is specifically tailored to address the unique challenges of winding down banks, prioritising depositor protection. Through the FSCS, depositors receive prompt compensation or have their accounts transferred, ensuring uninterrupted access to their funds.[71]

70 See the Bank of England Report under section 79A of the Banking Act 2009 on the transfer of Silicon Valley Bank UK to HSBC UK available at www.bankofengland.co.uk/paper/2024/report-under-section-79a-of-the-banking-act-2009-on-the-transfer-of-svb-uk-to-hsbc-uk (accessed in March 2025).

71 Arora, A., *Banking Law* (Pearson, 2014), p. 135.

The BIP offers several unique features: it includes an extended moratorium, providing protections similar to those in administrative proceedings; it exempts creditor opt-out provisions, so creditor decision procedures do not apply; and it modifies set-off rules, offering special treatment for deposits within the FSCS limit. Additionally, non-preferential debt ranking follows Insolvency Act 1986 priorities but incorporates specific adjustments under the Banks and Building Societies (Priorities on Insolvency) Order 2018.

More recently, the proposed Bank Resolution (Recapitalisation) Bill sought to expand the SRR, giving the Bank of England greater flexibility to address failures of smaller banks, incorporating lessons learned from the turbulence experienced in the UK banking sector in 2023, particularly following the collapse of Silicon Valley Bank UK.[72]

4.1 Process and Application for Bank Insolvency Order

The bank insolvency process begins with a court order, known as a bank insolvency order, which appoints a bank liquidator to oversee the winding-up of the institution. Applications for this order may be submitted by the Bank of England, the PRA, or the Secretary of State based on three possible grounds: first, that the bank is unable, or likely to be unable, to pay its debts; second, that winding up the bank is in the public interest, even if it is not technically insolvent; or third, that winding up is deemed "fair".[73]

Prior to filing an application, the Bank of England must confirm that the bank has eligible depositors, while the PRA must verify that the bank is failing or likely to fail and that no actions outside the SRR can avert this failure. In some instances, the PRA may apply directly for an insolvency order, provided it has obtained the Bank of England's consent. Additionally, the FSCS is entitled to participate in court proceedings to ensure depositor interests are adequately safeguarded throughout the process.

Once a bank insolvency order is granted, a liquidation committee is formed, consisting of representatives from the Bank of England, PRA, FCA, FSCS, and later, creditor representatives.

4.2 Building Society Insolvency Procedure

The Building Society Insolvency Procedure[74] is similar to the bank insolvency process, but it applies specifically to societies incorporated under the Building Societies Act 1986 and, as with banks, is initiated by a court order following an application from the Bank of England or the PRA. The grounds for application and the steps in the procedure mirror those used in bank insolvency.

Once appointed, the building society liquidator has two key objectives: first, to coordinate with the FSCS to ensure swift depositor compensation or account transfers, and second, to wind up the society's affairs in a way that serves the interests of creditors as a whole. These objectives are pursued concurrently, with depositor compensation taking precedence in the process.

72 See www.bankofengland.co.uk/explainers/what-happened-to-silicon-valley-bank-uk (accessed in March 2025).
73 Section 93(8) of the Banking Act 2009.
74 Established under the Building Societies (Insolvency and Special Administration) Order 2009.

5 BANK ADMINISTRATION PROCEDURE

The pre-insolvency stabilisation options outlined under the Banking Act 2009 enable authorities to intervene in a failing UK bank, facilitating its rescue by transferring part or all of its business to a bridge bank or a private sector purchaser. In instances where only part of the bank's business is transferred, the residual part may be placed into bank administration under Part 3 of the Banking Act 2009. This ensures that essential services, contracts, and systems that are critical for the continuation of the bridge bank or the private purchaser are maintained temporarily by the residual bank, thereby supporting the effective functioning of the entity acquiring the transferred assets.[75]

In certain cases, bank administration may also be employed following the transfer of a failing bank into temporary public ownership or where the Bank of England or HM Treasury implements multiple property transfers in line with the Banking Act 2009 (Bank Administration) (Modification for Application to Multiple Transfers) Regulations 2009.[76] Therefore, unlike the stabilisation options, the BAP does not operate as an independent SRR tool but is generally used alongside a partial transfer in conjunction with either the private sector purchase tool or the bridge bank tool.

The bank administration regime applies to UK-incorporated banks authorised under FSMA to carry out deposit-taking activities. This includes certain investment banks with eligible depositors.[77]

Moreover,[78] bank administration has been extended to include certain systemically important investment firms and banking group companies.

Once the primary objective of facilitating the transfer of part of a failing bank has been fulfilled, bank administration closely mirrors the procedures of Schedule B1 administration under the Insolvency Act 1986 with some modifications to streamline the process for financial institutions. Such modifications are set out under Section 145 of the Banking Act 2009,[79] granting bank administrators certain powers that are typically reserved for liquidators, such as the ability to disclaim onerous property, thereby facilitating the stabilisation of a distressed institution.

One such modification is the application of section 176AZA of the Insolvency Act 1986, which governs and establishes a structured hierarchy of creditors, modifying the ranking of non-preferential debts in financial institution insolvencies. Ordinary non-preferential debts are settled before secondary non-preferential debts, while secondary non-preferential debts take precedence over tertiary non-preferential debts. At the lowest tier, quaternary non-preferential debts rank last, encompassing certain capital instruments such as Common Equity Tier 1, Additional Tier 1, and Tier 2 instruments, as defined under the Banking Act 2009.

The bank administration process begins with a court-issued bank administration order, which can only be requested by the Bank of England.[80] Before applying for this order, two conditions must be met: the Bank of England must have either executed or intend to execute a property transfer involving the bank under one of the SRR stabilisation options, and the Bank of England must be satisfied that the residual bank, as a result of this transfer, is or will likely

75 Proctor, C., *The Law and Practice of International Banking* (Oxford University Press, 2015), p. 255.
76 (SI 2009/313).
77 However, specific exclusions apply, such as credit unions and insurers that accept deposits, as outlined in the Banking Act 2009 (Exclusion of Insurers) Order 2010 (SI 2010/35).
78 As of 1 August 2014.
79 Under section 178 of the Insolvency Act 1986.
80 Section 142 of the Banking Act 2009.

become unable to pay its debts. Additionally, the PRA must give consent for the appointment of a bank administrator.

Once appointed, the bank administrator has two primary statutory objectives. The first is to support the bridge bank or private sector purchaser by ensuring the continuity of essential services and facilities. The second is to fulfil the standard duties of administration, which include either rescuing the residual bank or achieving a more favourable outcome for creditors than immediate liquidation would provide. Although the first objective takes precedence, the administrator is required to work towards both objectives simultaneously.

The bank administrator must agree on a statement of proposals with the Bank of England, setting out how the statutory objectives will be achieved. Only a qualified insolvency practitioner may be appointed as a bank administrator. Specific rules[81] ensure transparency and regulate the flow of information between the Bank of England and the administrator.

The Building Society Special Administration is a variation of bank administration tailored to the legal structure of building societies.[82] This regime functions similarly to bank administration, with the added objective of protecting the interests of building society members and creditors. Finally, the Investment Bank Special Administration Regulations 2011[83] were introduced to handle the unique challenges posed by the insolvency of investment banks. The regime prioritises the return of client assets, the coordination with market infrastructure bodies, and the rescue of the investment bank. The FSCS is also empowered to participate in this process to expedite compensation to clients.

6 BANK'S RESILIENCE AND STRESS TESTING

One of the key tools for the early detection of financial distress in credit institutions is internal stress tests.[84] The term "stress test" is often used to refer to both stress testing and scenario analysis techniques. While both methods are used to assess vulnerabilities under adverse conditions, scenario analysis typically involves a broader range of variables being adjusted simultaneously, providing a more comprehensive assessment of financial resilience.

Since stress tests aim to simulate performance during abnormal market conditions, they provide insights into risks that fall outside those typically captured by standard risk models, such as Value-at-Risk (**VaR**) models. Stress tests may focus on a single variable or involve a complex, integrated scenario. Depending on the scope and objectives, they may be conducted at a business unit level, a financial institution level, or across an entire corporate group. A related approach is reverse stress testing, which requires financial institutions to identify and analyse the scenarios most likely to cause their business model to fail. This process enhances awareness of vulnerabilities, ensuring that firms are better prepared to address potential threats to their financial stability.

81 Such as the Bank Administration (Sharing Information) Regulations 2009 (SI 2009/314).
82 Introduced by the Building Societies (Insolvency and Special Administration) Order 2009 (SI 2009/805) and subsequently by The Building Society Special Administration (England and Wales) Rules 2010.
83 (SI 2011/245).
84 Kokkinis, A. and Miglionico, M., *Banking Law: Private Transactions and Regulatory Frameworks* (Routledge, 2021), p. 288.

7 DEPOSITOR PROTECTION

An effective deposit insurance system or deposit guarantee scheme (**DGS**) is responsible for protecting depositors against the loss of eligible deposits in the event that a bank or other credit institution is unable to meet its financial obligations. The primary objectives of a DGS are to contribute to the financial stability of the jurisdiction in which it operates and to safeguard less financially sophisticated depositors from the risk of losing their deposits when a credit institution fails.

The FSCS serves as the UK's statutory compensation mechanism of last resort, providing compensation to eligible customers of authorised financial institutions when these firms are unable or likely to become unable to meet their financial obligations. Administered by the PRA, the FSCS depositor protection scheme applies in cases where banks, building societies, or credit unions enter default. The Depositor Protection Part of the PRA Rulebook governs compensation for deposits, supported by essential supervisory and policy documents.[85]

For deposit-related compensation, specific conditions must be met: the financial institution in question must be declared in default, and the depositor must hold an eligible deposit. Furthermore, financial institutions are required to comply with FSCS-related disclosure and reporting obligations, including the maintenance of a Single Customer View to facilitate efficient claims processing.[86]

Eligibility for FSCS compensation is conditional on three criteria: deposits must meet the definition of an eligible deposit under the Depositor Protection provisions, they must be held with a member of the UK's DGS or an eligible Gibraltar-based branch, and the institution must be officially declared in default by the PRA or relevant authority.

The standard compensation limit is currently set at £85,000. FSCS protection extends to Temporary High Balances, providing compensation up to £1,000,000 for six months after significant life events, including house sales, personal injury compensation, or divorce settlements. Payments are made in sterling to depositors or designated representatives, with any currency conversion calculated at the prevailing rate on the date of compensation.

The FSCS is required to issue compensation within seven business days following the confirmation of a firm's default, either depositing the funds directly into the depositor's bank account or to an alternative account designated by the depositor.

Case Study: The PRA Enforcement Against HSBC

Since 1 July 2018, HSBC Group's UK operations have been split between ring-fenced (HBUK) and non-ring-fenced (HBEU) entities, which are operationally separate and economically independent; both are wholly owned subsidiaries of HSBC Holdings plc.[87]

In January 2024, the PRA imposed a £57.4 million fine on HBEU and HBUK for significant historical failures in their depositor protection frameworks.

85 Like the PRA Supervisory Statement SS18/15 on Depositor and Dormant Account Protection and the PRA's Statement of Policy on the Deposit Guarantee Scheme.

86 Separate guidance covers FSCS compensation related to insurance contracts or FCA-regulated activities, aligning with the then UK's implementation of the Deposit Guarantee Schemes Directive (DGSD) (2014/49/EU).

87 See PRA Final Notice dated 29 January 2024, available at www.bankofengland.co.uk/-/media/boe/files/prudential-regulation/regulatory-action/final-notice-from-pra-to-hsbc.pdf (accessed in March 2025).

The PRA's investigation revealed that HBEU's mismanagement of depositor protection materially compromised its readiness for resolution. Furthermore, over a 15-month period, HBEU failed to disclose to the PRA significant issues related to the incorrect designation of FSCS-eligible accounts, a breach of its duty to be open and cooperative with the regulator. As a result, both HBEU and HBUK were found to have violated Fundamental Rules 2[88] and 6,[89] along with key provisions in the Depositor Protection Rules (specifically Rules 11, 12, and 14). Additionally, HBEU was deemed to have breached Depositor Protection Rule 50, alongside Fundamental Rules 7[90] and 8. This case marked the first PRA enforcement action concerning a violation of Fundamental Rule 8,[91] which mandates adequate resolution preparedness to mitigate critical service disruption in the event of a failure.

8 CROSS-BORDER ASPECTS OF BANKS' FAILURES

The cross-border nature of banking activities presents significant challenges to the efficient administration of liquidation proceedings.[92] If not effectively managed, these complexities may exacerbate the bank's financial distress and increase the risk of contagion and wider spill-over effects in the financial system. Conversely, effective cross-border cooperation can help mitigate these risks, facilitating an orderly resolution process and enhancing recovery prospects for depositors and other creditors.

Several international standards have addressed cross-border insolvency, including the 1997 UNCITRAL Model Law on Cross-Border Insolvency and the UNCITRAL Model Law on Enterprise Group Insolvency. However, neither of these frameworks is specifically designed to address the unique characteristics of banks and the complexities associated with their failure.[93]

Only the FSB Key Attributes of Effective Resolution Regimes set out high-level principles and legal framework conditions for cross-border cooperation in bank resolution. These principles emphasise that the statutory mandate of a resolution authority should empower and actively encourage it, wherever possible, to pursue a cooperative approach with foreign resolution authorities in order to facilitate an orderly and coordinated resolution process. They

88 "*A firm must conduct its business with due skill, care and diligence*".

89 "*A firm must organise and control its affairs responsibly and effectively*".

90 "*A firm must deal with its regulators in an open and cooperative way and must disclose to the PRA appropriately anything relating to the firm of which the PRA would reasonably expect notice*".

91 "*A firm must prepare for resolution so, if the need arises, it can be resolved in an orderly manner with a minimum disruption of critical services*".

92 "*I would offer just this one (perhaps optimistic) reflection, based on my Lehman experience. That was an international bank failure of hitherto unprecedented proportions, in which the achievement of cross-border dispute resolution without conflict between different jurisdictions was both vital, and unsupported to any great extent by jurisdiction conventions, regulations or treaties. Judges like me and my distinguished colleague Judge Peck from New York, here today, could easily have been, figuratively speaking, at each others' throats. But this simply didn't happen (or at least not in my London-based experience). There was some cross-border judicial consultation, but the main reason why disputes about the insolvency of a global business centred in the USA, the UK, the Far East and elsewhere were (and continue to be) adjudicated without judicial conflict about jurisdiction appears, to me at least, to have stemmed mainly from the professionalism and common sense of the office-holders and major litigants concerned*". Lord Briggs at the P.R.I.M.E. Finance conference, The Hague, The Netherlands: Dispute Resolution in Uncertain Times [2018] *UKSpeech* 180122 (22 January 2018) at [28].

93 UNIDROIT Working Group on Bank Insolvency, *Draft Legislative Guide on Bank Liquidation* (UNIDROIT, June 2024) Study LXXXIV, p. 113.

also include provisions on the legal framework conditions for cross-border cooperation (Key Attribute 7), the establishment of crisis management groups (Key Attribute 8), and the implementation of institution-specific cross-border cooperation agreements (Key Attribute 9).[94] These provisions aim to facilitate coordinated action among resolution authorities in different jurisdictions to ensure the effective management of cross-border bank failures. Furthermore, the FSB Principles set out statutory and contractual mechanisms to ensure that resolution actions undertaken in one jurisdiction can have legal effect in another. These principles are designed to enhance the cross-border enforceability of resolution measures, thereby promoting legal certainty and minimising risks to financial stability.[95]

In response to the 2008 financial crisis, The EU has attempted to address these issues and to provide a level regulatory playing field by implementing a comprehensive regulatory framework, which has the BRRD as one of the core provisions, which led to the establishment of the so-called European Banking Union.

9 THE EUROPEAN BANKING UNION

The UK's bank recovery and resolution framework has been significantly shaped by EU legislation, particularly the BRRD, which was introduced in response to the 2008 financial crisis. The BRRD established a comprehensive approach for managing the recovery and orderly resolution of EU credit institutions and systemically important investment firms.

Complementing the BRRD is the SRM Regulation (806/2014).[96] This regulation applies to all credit institutions in EU member states participating in the SSM, mainly covering eurozone countries. Together, the BRRD and SRM Regulation form critical components of the European Banking Union, a centralised framework designed to ensure stability and uniform supervision across EU banking systems.[97]

The Banking Union emerged as a response to the 2007–2009 financial crisis and the subsequent eurozone crisis of 2009, with a primary objective to address the destabilising feedback loop between banks and sovereign states. During the crises, banks heavily relied on state bailouts, which in turn linked perceptions of national financial instability to the fragility of domestic banks. Such interdependence led to a cycle where deteriorating conditions in banks and sovereign debt markets mutually reinforced each other, exacerbating financial instability within the eurozone. This dynamic underscored the need for a more integrated response, given the interconnectedness of eurozone financial institutions and the risk of banking crises in a one-member state destabilising the entire region. The Banking Union framework applies automatically to all eurozone member states. However, non-eurozone EU member states can opt to participate by entering close cooperation agreements with the ECB, thereby allowing

94 SB (2011) www.fsb.org/uploads/r_111104cc.pdf (accessed in March 2025).

95 'Key Attributes of Effective Resolution Regimes for Financial Institutions' (revised version 2024), available at www.fsb.org/uploads/P250424-3.pdf (accessed in March 2025).

96 Regulation (EU) No 806/2014 of the European Parliament and of the Council of 15 July 2014 establishing uniform rules and a uniform procedure for the resolution of credit institutions and certain investment firms in the framework of a Single Resolution Mechanism and a Single Resolution Fund and amending Regulation (EU) No 1093/2010.

97 According to a 2012 report by the International Monetary Fund (IMF), the European Banking Union addresses critical risks highlighted during the crisis. See www.imf.org/external/pubs/ft/scr/2012/cr12181.pdf (accessed in March 2025).

these countries to benefit from the supervision and resolution mechanisms of the Banking Union without adopting the euro.[98]

The European Banking Union is built on two main pillars: the SSM and the SRM. The first step in establishing the banking union was the creation of the SSM, introduced by Council Regulation (EU) No 1024/2013 of 15 October 2013.[99] This regulation conferred specific tasks on the ECB concerning the prudential supervision of credit institutions.

According to Recital 12 of Regulation (EU) No 806/2014,[100] the SSM was designed to ensure that the EU's prudential supervision policy is implemented in a coherent and effective manner. It aims to guarantee that the single rulebook for financial services is applied consistently across all relevant Member States and that credit institutions are subject to high-quality supervision, free from non-prudential influences.

By centralising supervision, the ECB aims to ensure consistency in regulatory practices across the eurozone. This mechanism was designed to sever the cycle of financial instability between national governments and their banking sectors, minimising mutual financial dependence. These uniform rules and procedures are to be applied by the SRB. The SRB, working alongside the Council of the European Union, the European Commission, and national resolution authorities, operates within the framework of the Single Resolution Mechanism (**SRM**), which is supported by the Single Resolution Fund (**SRF**).

The SRM, established under the SRM Regulation, provides uniform rules and a standardised procedure for the resolution of certain financial entities whose home supervisor is either the European Central Bank or the national competent authority in Eurozone Member States.[101]

The SRB is responsible for determining whether to take resolution action in relation to a financial institution established in a participating Member State,[102] provided that the three conditions are met.[103] The first condition requires that the entity is failing or likely to fail. This assessment is carried out by the ECB, after consulting the SRB, or by the SRB itself.[104] The second condition requires that there is no reasonable prospect that any alternative private sector measures or supervisory actions would prevent the entity's failure within a reasonable timeframe. The third condition requires that a resolution action is necessary in the public

98 Bulgaria and Croatia, for example, entered such agreements in 2020, allowing the ECB to assume supervisory responsibilities over significant institutions within their jurisdictions from 1 October 2020. When Croatia adopted the euro on 1 January 2023, its cooperation agreement was subsequently rendered obsolete.

99 (OJ 2013 L 287, p. 63).

100 Recital 12 of Regulation (EU) No 806/2014 states: "*Ensuring effective resolution decisions for failing banks within the Union, including on the use of funding raised at Union level, is essential for the completion of the internal market in financial services. Within the internal market, the failure of banks in one Member State may affect the stability of the financial markets of the Union as a whole. Ensuring effective and uniform resolution rules and equal conditions of resolution financing across Member States is in the best interests not only of the Member States in which banks operate but also of all Member States in general as a means of ensuring a level competitive playing field and improving the functioning of the internal market. Banking systems in the internal market are highly interconnected, bank groups are international and banks have a large percentage of foreign assets. In the absence of the SRM, bank crises in Member States participating in the SSM would have a stronger negative systemic impact also in non-participating Member States. The establishment of the SRM will ensure a neutral approach in dealing with failing banks and therefore increase stability of the banks of the participating Member States and prevent the spill-over of crises into non-participating Member States and will thus facilitate the functioning of the internal market as a whole. The mechanisms for cooperation regarding institutions established in both participating and non-participating Member States should be clear, and no Member State or group of Member States should be discriminated against, directly or indirectly, as a venue for financial services*".

101 As well as those in non-Eurozone Member States that have entered into close cooperation arrangements under Article 7 of Regulation No 1024/2013 (see recital 15 of Regulation (EU) No 806/2014).

102 Under Article 16(1) of Regulation (EU) No 806/2014.

103 Article 18(1) of Regulation (EU) No 806/2014.

104 It is deemed to be satisfied if the entity is in one or more of the situations listed in Article 18(4) of Regulation (EU) No 806/2014.

interest, that is to say, that it is necessary in order to achieve one or more of the resolution objectives, and winding up of the entity under normal insolvency proceedings would not meet those resolution objectives to the same extent.

In this context,

> *in view of the objective of ensuring the stability of the banking system in the euro area, and having regard to the imminent risk of financial losses to which depositors with the banks concerned would have been exposed if those banks had failed, certain restrictions on the right to property may be justified.*[105]

The SRB is positioned to manage systemic risks effectively and is responsible for the consistent application of resolution tools across member states, supporting the Banking Union's goal of minimising disruption from bank failures.[106]

Additionally, a European Deposit Insurance Scheme (**EDIS**) has been proposed by the European Commission to complement the SSM and SRM by providing liquidity support to national deposit guarantee schemes. However, legislative progress on EDIS has stalled, leaving its adoption and implementation uncertain. If adopted, EDIS would further integrate and stabilise the EU's banking framework by offering additional deposit protection resources and reinforcing financial resilience across member states.

9.1 The BRRD

The BRRD was established to unify crisis management practices across EU member states, empowering national authorities with standardised tools to address financial distress in banks and investment firms. Its framework aims to resolve crises before they escalate into widespread systemic risks, dividing its measures into three key categories: preparatory and preventative measures, early supervisory intervention, and resolution powers and tools.[107] The BRRD framework, along with the relevant legislative measures, serves to enhance both the resilience and the resolvability of financial institutions.

Resolution Authority's Functions

In the European Union, when an administrative authority is entrusted with the resolution function in addition to other functions, it does not need to have a separate decision-making body. In *Getin Holding and Others (Recovery and resolution of credit institutions – Decision to take a crisis management measure in respect of a credit institution – Judgment)* [2024] EUECJ C-118/23, the Court of Justice ruled that:

> *[W]here the national resolution authority also performs "functions of supervision" or "other functions" within the meaning of that provision, and where there are no written internal rules intended to ensure the operational independence of that authority and prevent conflicts of interest between its resolution functions and its other functions, there can nevertheless be compliance with those requirements as the result of the introduction of organisational and other measures that are sufficient for that purpose. That provision does not mean, however, that decisions relating to resolution functions and those relating to the other functions of that authority must be made by different decision-making bodies, or that internal*

105 Judgment of 20 September 2016, *Ledra Advertising and Others v Commission and ECB, C-8/15 P to C-10/15 P*, EU:C:2016:701 at [74].
106 Lo Schiavo, G., *EU Banking Law and Regulation* (Oxford Academic, 2024), p. 262.
107 Chiu, I. and Wilson, J., *Banking Law and Regulation* (Oxford University Press, 2019), p. 609.

functional areas of the same authority are prevented from providing support services both to staff assigned to resolution functions and to staff assigned to other functions, without prejudice to rules on professional secrecy.[108]

The BRRD's preparatory and preventative measures mandate firms to devise recovery plans detailing steps to restore financial health during stress periods. Simultaneously, authorities must develop resolution plans informed by firm-specific data, outlining how to achieve an orderly resolution if recovery fails.

Early supervisory intervention allows authorities to act on emerging crises before they reach critical stages. Resolution authorities are empowered to compel firms to execute their recovery plans, alter business strategies, or replace management with a special manager who can restore stability. These pre-emptive powers enable rapid response to potential issues, ideally preventing firms from reaching a failure point.

As previously considered within the UK regime (which – to date – constitutes an implementation of the BRRD), if a firm is determined to be failing or likely to fail, the BRRD provides a series of resolution tools to ensure an orderly resolution. These tools include the *Sale of Business Tool*, allowing the transfer of a failing firm's assets or shares to another entity; the *Bridge Institution Tool*, creating a temporary entity to maintain essential functions while a lasting solution is found; the *Asset Separation Tool*, isolating non-performing assets to shield healthy parts of the firm; and the *Bail-in Tool*, mandating that creditors and shareholders absorb losses by writing down debts or converting them into equity. To support these mechanisms, firms are required to maintain a minimum level of MREL, ensuring adequate capital reserves for loss absorption during resolution.

The BRRD applies to credit institutions and systemically important investment firms within the EU, covering entities that meet specific capital and systemic risk thresholds as defined in the Capital Requirements Regulation (**CRR III**)[109] and Directive (EU) 2019/2034 (Investment Firms Directive).[110] Beyond standalone institutions, the BRRD extends to relevant entities within corporate groups, including branches, with member states encouraged to apply proportionate measures considering each institution's risk profile, size, and operational model.

Under Article 6(1) of Council Regulation (EU) No 1024/2013, the ECB is to carry out its tasks within an SSM composed of the ECB and national competent authorities and is to be responsible for the effective and consistent functioning of the SSM.[111] The national competent authorities assist the ECB in carrying out the tasks conferred on it by Regulation No 1024/2013 through a decentralised implementation of some of those tasks in relation to less significant credit institutions.[112]

The BRRD establishes frameworks for cross-border crisis management, requiring cooperation between national authorities in different member states. This ensures the coordinated application of resolution tools for financial groups operating across borders, avoiding

108 At [133].

109 Regulation (EU) 2024/1623 of the European Parliament and of the Council of 31 May 2024 amending Regulation (EU) No 575/2013 as regards requirements for credit risk, credit valuation adjustment risk, operational risk, market risk, and the output floor.

110 Directive (EU) 2019/2034 of the European Parliament and of the Council of 27 November 2019 on the prudential supervision of investment firms and amending Directives 2002/87/EC, 2009/65/EC, 2011/61/EU, 2013/36/EU, 2014/59/EU and 2014/65/EU.

111 Judgment of 8 May 2019, *Landeskreditbank Baden-Württemberg v ECB*, C-450/17 P, EU:C:2019:372 at [39].

112 Judgment of 8 May 2019, *Landeskreditbank Baden-Württemberg v ECB*, C-450/17 P, EU:C:2019:372 at [41].

fragmented national responses that could lead to instability in other jurisdictions. Moreover, the BRRD mandated the creation of national resolution funds, which have been financed by contributions from banks and are designed to cover the costs of using resolution tools. These funds are crucial in facilitating the orderly resolution of financial institutions without recourse to taxpayer bailouts.

9.2 The Single Resolution Mechanism

The SRM is a key component of the European Banking Union and applies to all credit institutions established in EU member states participating in the SSM – primarily eurozone members. The SRM centralises the resolution process, ensuring that resolution actions are coordinated at the European level under the leadership of the SRB in conjunction with the European Commission.

The SRB evaluates whether a bank is failing or likely to fail and prepares for its resolution.[113] To support bank resolutions, the SRF provides medium-term funding, with both the SRB and the SRF being financed through contributions from the banking sector.

Under the SRM, the national resolution funds created under the BRRD have been progressively integrated into an SRF, pooling resources from participating member states to strengthen the capacity to manage large-scale bank failures across the eurozone.

The BRRD and SRM Regulation work together within the EU's broader financial stability framework. While the BRRD provides a comprehensive resolution framework for all EU member states, the SRM Regulation specifically applies to banks in the eurozone, centralising resolution responsibilities under the SRB. The resolution tools and powers available under the SRM mirror those under the BRRD, ensuring coherence across the EU, while the SRB assumes functions that would otherwise fall to national resolution authorities in non-eurozone member states.

9.3 Implementation of Financial Stability Board Standards

The BRRD framework also incorporates international standards, particularly the Key Attributes of Effective Resolution Regimes, which represent the global standard for resolving failing financial institutions, especially global systemically important banks (**G-SIBs**). The BRRD reflects these key attributes, ensuring that EU banks are subject to rigorous resolution requirements aligned with global best practices. A notable divergence, however, is that the BRRD applies to a wider range of institutions, including systemically important investment firms, not just G-SIBs.

In response to the evolving financial landscape and global regulatory developments, the BRRD framework was amended in 2019 by the BRRD II Directive[114] and the SRM II Regulation,[115] which implemented the FSB's Total Loss Absorbing Capacity (**TLAC**) standard, which aims to enhance the ability of SIFIs to absorb losses during a crisis, within the EU.

113 In certain circumstances, the European Commission and the Council of the EU can object to a proposed resolution scheme.

114 Directive (EU) 2019/879 of the European Parliament and of the Council of 20 May 2019 amending Directive 2014/59/EU as regards the loss-absorbing and recapitalisation capacity of credit institutions and investment firms and Directive 98/26/EC.

115 Regulation (EU) 2019/877 of the European Parliament and of the Council of 20 May 2019 amending Regulation (EU) No 806/2014 as regards the loss-absorbing and recapitalisation capacity of credit institutions and investment firms.

The TLAC standard mandates that G-SIBs maintain sufficient loss-absorbing capital to support resolution actions, specifically the bail-in tool.[116] The goal is to ensure that G-SIBs have adequate resources for resolution without destabilising the financial system.

The required quantum of TLAC is calibrated by reference to two distinct metrics, and G-SIBs are obliged to satisfy the regulatory minimum under both. The first metric is a risk-based requirement, referred to as the TLAC RWA Minimum. Under this approach, TLAC is expressed as a percentage of the resolution group's risk-weighted assets (RWAs), in accordance with the Basel framework.

The second is a non-risk-based requirement known as the TLAC LRE Minimum. This measure expresses TLAC as a percentage of the resolution group's leverage ratio exposure (LRE) – that is, the aggregate of total non-risk-weighted assets and relevant off-balance sheet exposures. The LRE is the denominator used in the Basel leverage ratio framework and provides a backstop to the risk-based measure, ensuring that capital adequacy is not undermined by excessive leverage or underestimation of risk.

The CRR II Regulation introduced the TLAC requirement as a Pillar 1 requirement, setting minimum standards for both external TLAC and internal TLAC. G-SIBs were required to meet minimum external TLAC levels of 16% of RWAs, rising to 18%, and leverage-based ratios of 6%, increasing to 6.75%. These standards ensure that resolution authorities can use the bail-in tool effectively, with G-SIBs structured to withstand systemic shocks.

MREL, the EU's framework for ensuring institutions have enough loss-absorbing capital, was revised extensively in BRRD II to align with TLAC. While TLAC applies specifically to G-SIBs, the MREL framework is more flexible and applies more broadly to EU credit institutions and investment firms. MREL requires firms to hold a minimum level of their own funds and eligible liabilities (such as subordinated debt) to ensure that resolution tools, including bail-in, can be used effectively.

The moratorium tool[117] empowers resolution authorities to temporarily suspend payment or delivery obligations when a financial institution is in distress. This moratorium can last up to two business days, providing a crucial buffer to stabilise the institution's financial position and evaluate resolution strategies.

Moreover, there is contractual recognition of resolution stay powers, mandating that BRRD institutions include clauses in contracts acknowledging the authority of resolution bodies to limit or suspend certain contractual rights.[118] These provisions specifically target payment and delivery obligations, enforcement of security interests, and termination rights within financial contracts governed by non-EU law. This amendment ensures that third-country governed contracts align with EU resolution powers, enhancing consistency and enforceability in crisis scenarios.

The SRM II Regulation complements the updates under BRRD II, aligning the SRM with BRRD II's revised MREL and TLAC standards. It assigns the SRB responsibilities similar to those held by national resolution authorities under the BRRD.[119]

116 Under the BRRD II Directive, TLAC was integrated into the EU's regime primarily through amendments to the Capital Requirements Regulation (CRR) via the CRR II Regulation (EU 2019/876).
117 Established under Article 33a.
118 Article 71a.
119 By replacing Articles 12 to 12k of the original SRM Regulation with provisions mirroring Articles 45 to 45m of the BRRD, the SRM II Regulation maintains a consistent resolution approach across the eurozone, bolstering the resilience and coherence of the EU's banking resolution framework.

9.4 The Deposit Guarantee Schemes Directive

The Directive (2014/49/EU)[120] (**DGSD**) established a comprehensive framework for deposit protection within the European Union, ensuring a consistent approach across Member States. It requires that banks and other credit institutions participate in a home DGS, which also extends coverage to their branches in other Member States (host states). This ensures that depositors benefit from a uniform level of protection regardless of where a bank operates within the EU.[121]

The DGSD guarantees the rights of depositors to compensation if their deposits with a credit institution become unavailable. In broad terms, it provides compensation for eligible depositors, typically consumers, based on their aggregate deposits with a credit institution up to a specified limit. At present, the coverage level is set at EUR 100,000.

In addition to safeguarding depositors, the DGSD places specific obligations on credit institutions, particularly regarding information disclosure. Credit institutions must provide clear and accurate information to both existing and prospective depositors about their rights to compensation under the relevant DGS.

Under the DGSD, a DGS may take different forms. It may be established as a statutory DGS, a contractual scheme that has been officially recognised as a DGS, or an Institutional Protection Scheme (IPS).[122] A scheme in which member institutions provide mutual support to prevent insolvency which complies with the DGSD.[123] The DGSD allows for the establishment of DGSs that cover multiple Member States, commonly referred to as cross-border DGSs. Each Member State is required to ensure that at least one DGS is introduced and officially recognised within its territory. A DGS may be cross-border or may merge with DGSs in other Member States, provided that it obtains approval from all jurisdictions in which it operates.

If a competent authority[124] identifies problems within a credit institution that could lead to DGS intervention, it must notify the DGS to ensure prompt action can be taken.

The EU's bank resolution framework is undergoing continuous refinement. A central topic in ongoing discussions is the proposed European Deposit Insurance Scheme (**EDIS**), which is intended to provide a common system for the protection of depositors in the SSM. In this respect, EDIS has been proposed to strengthen the resilience of the Banking Union by reducing the dependence of banks on their home Member States and mitigating the risk of national DGSs being overwhelmed by localised financial crises. By providing additional financial support to national DGSs where needed, EDIS would provide a uniform safety net, further supporting the resilience of resolution frameworks by establishing a robust, pan-European deposit insurance system.

10 US REGULATORY FRAMEWORK

In the United States, the regulation and supervision of banking entities are carried out by multiple federal and state agencies, each overseeing specific types of institutions and fulfilling

120 Directive 2014/49/EU of the European Parliament and of the Council of 16 April 2014 on deposit guarantee schemes (recast).
121 Kokkinis, A. and Miglionico, M., *Banking Law: Private Transactions and Regulatory Frameworks* (Routledge, 2021), p. 301.
122 As defined in Article 113(7) of the CRR.
123 IPSs must meet the specific criteria set out in Article 113(7) of the CRR before obtaining such recognition.
124 As defined in Article 4(1)(40) of the CRR.

particular roles in the financial regulatory landscape. The Office of the Comptroller of the Currency (**OCC**) regulates and charters nationally chartered banks, which comprise a large portion of major US banks. The Federal Reserve System (**FRS**) supervises both state-chartered member banks and all bank holding companies (**BHC**s), maintaining an oversight role within its jurisdiction. The Federal Deposit Insurance Corporation (**FDIC**) supervises state-chartered non-member banks and acts as the resolution authority for all insured depository institutions. Additionally, state banking agencies oversee state-chartered banks, working alongside federal agencies to maintain regulatory standards.[125]

The US bank resolution framework is a crucial mechanism for addressing failures of banks and savings associations that hold federally insured deposits.[126] These institutions, classified as insured depository institutions, are subject to oversight by FIDIC, which acts as both a regulator and a resolution authority. The FDIC's role is established under the Federal Deposit Insurance Act of 1950,[127] which provides the statutory basis for handling bank failures and resolving insolvent institutions while minimising disruption to the financial system.

Since its establishment in 1931, the FDIC now insures deposits at eligible institutions and holds the authority to resolve failed banks, managing asset liquidation and debt settlement processes. From 2001 through 2024, there were 567 bank failures in the US, with Washington Mutual Bank's 2008 failure being the largest, involving $307 billion in assets and $188 billion in deposits.[128]

The FDIC insures deposits up to the statutory limit, currently set at $250,000 per depositor, per insured bank, per ownership category. This deposit insurance scheme is intended to prevent bank runs by assuring depositors that their funds are protected in the event of a bank's failure. When an IDI becomes critically undercapitalised or is deemed insolvent, the FDIC intervenes to manage its failure through a structured resolution process.

Rooted in the Federal Deposit Insurance Act[129] and further enhanced by the Dodd-Frank Wall Street Reform and Consumer Protection Act of 2010 (**Dodd-Frank Act**), this process empowers the FDIC to step in as a receiver for failing institutions, such as traditional depository institutions, qualifying financial companies, and SIFIS.

Title II of the Dodd-Frank Act empowers the FDIC to manage the insolvency and liquidation of institutions deemed critical to the stability of the US financial system. It establishes a single-track regime for managing bank failures in the United States. Under this framework, all failed insured depository institutions are either resolved or liquidated in accordance with the provisions of the Federal Deposit Insurance Act, without distinction between resolution and insolvency proceedings. The FDIC acts as the primary authority responsible for administering the resolution process, ensuring the orderly management of failing banks while safeguarding depositors and maintaining financial stability.

125 Armour, J., Awrey, D., Davies, P., Enriques, L., Gordon, J., Mayer, C. and Payne, J., *Principles of Financial Regulation* (Oxford University Press, 2016), p. 343.

126 In the US, insured deposits encompass nearly all deposits held at commercial banking institutions, including checking accounts, savings accounts, money market deposit accounts, and certificates of deposit (CDs), provided they meet the criteria for deposit insurance coverage under the FDIC. The statutory definition of insured deposits is found in 12 U.S.C. § 1813(l), which establishes the scope of FDIC protection. See www.fdic.gov/federal-deposit-insurance-act/section-3-definitions (accessed in March 2025).

127 [64 Stat. 873; 12 U.S.C. 1811 et seq.].

128 See 'FDIC's Bank Failures in Brief – Summary 2024', available at www.fdic.gov/resources/resolutions/bank-failures/in-brief/2024 (accessed in March 2025).

129 12 U.S. Code Chapter 16.

10.1 Pre-Resolution Process

Before the FDIC initiates the resolution process, it must first determine whether a bank meets the criteria for failure. Banks are generally put into resolution if they are found to be critically undercapitalised, with tangible equity less than 2% of total assets. Additionally, state and federal laws provide other grounds for resolution, such as when a bank ceases to meet the requirements for deposit insurance.

The resolution process begins when the bank's regulatory authority issues a notice of critical undercapitalisation or insolvency. At this point, the FDIC works with the bank's board of directors to initiate due diligence and collect the necessary data, including loan and deposit information. This data is used to assess the bank's value and determine the best resolution strategy.

10.2 FDIC's Resolution Process

The FDIC has several resolution strategies at its disposal. A fairly common approach is the Purchase and Assumption transaction, where an acquiring bank purchases the failed institution's assets and assumes its liabilities. Often, the FDIC provides loss-sharing agreements to limit the acquiring bank's potential exposure to losses from these assets.

The resolution process begins with a marketing phase, where the FDIC collects detailed information about the failed bank and markets it to potential acquirers. Qualified bidders conduct due diligence to evaluate the bank's assets and liabilities. The FDIC then undertakes an asset valuation review to determine the most cost-effective resolution method, often weighing offers from bidders against the costs of liquidation.

Once bids are submitted, the FDIC evaluates each one, prioritising those that minimise potential losses to the Deposit Insurance Fund (**DIF**). The FDIC Board of Directors then approves the optimal bid, which is typically followed by the closure of the failed bank at the end of the business day on Friday. The successful bidder assumes control of the bank, with operations generally resuming under new ownership by the next business day.

When no buyer can be found, the FDIC may opt for a deposit payoff, liquidating the bank and directly compensating insured depositors; uninsured depositors may receive a distribution based on the residual value of the liquidated assets. In cases requiring continued operations while seeking a permanent resolution, the FDIC may establish a bridge bank to maintain essential services temporarily.

As the receiver of a failed bank, the FDIC assumes responsibility for settling outstanding obligations and overseeing asset liquidation. In this role, it exercises powers akin to those of a bankruptcy trustee, including repudiating unfavourable contracts, recovering assets through fraudulent transfer claims, and resolving creditor claims. A priority system governs the payment of claims: administrative expenses are settled first, followed by deposit liabilities, other general liabilities, subordinated debts, and finally, shareholder claims.

Following each bank resolution, the FDIC, along with oversight entities like the Office of Inspector General, conducts a post-resolution review. This assessment focuses on the causes of the failure, especially when substantial losses have occurred, aiming to identify supervisory or governance lapses. These reviews provide critical insights that inform and refine future regulatory practices and supervisory frameworks.

The Systemic Risk Exception

In 2023, the failures of Silicon Valley Bank and Signature Bank raised significant policy questions. Both failures prompted the FDIC to establish bridge banks for the institutions and guarantee uninsured deposits under the systemic risk exception.

The systemic risk exception[130] enables the FDIC, in consultation with the Federal Reserve and Treasury Secretary, to take extraordinary steps to prevent the spread of financial instability. This mechanism was invoked in response to the swift collapse of both banks, where regulatory authorities underestimated the speed of deterioration and the potential for contagion.[131] On 10 March 2023, the FDIC was appointed receiver for Silicon Valley Bank by the Commissioner of the California Department of Financial Protection and Innovation. Pursuant to the Resolutions of the Board of Directors of the FDIC, the Director for the Division of Complex Institution Supervision and Resolution was authorised to charter a bridge bank for the resolution of Silicon Valley Bank.[132]

10.3 Deposit Insurance in the US

The FDIC is fundamental to sustaining public confidence in the US banking system by insuring deposits and managing bank failure risks, bolstered by its financial resilience through premiums, special assessments, and federal support.

As the insurer, the FDIC covers deposits up to $250,000 per depositor, per institution, and per ownership category, with this statutory coverage funded by the DIF.

The FDIC insures deposits across various account types at both federal and state-chartered banks and thrifts that meet specific criteria, such as capital adequacy, effective management, and minimal risk to the DIF. Covered accounts include checking and savings accounts, NOW accounts, money market deposit accounts (distinct from non-insured money market mutual funds), certificates of deposit, and certain retirement accounts like IRAs and Keogh plans. However, products like stocks, bonds, mutual funds, annuities, municipal securities, and US Treasury securities are not FDIC-insured once deposited into an account.

11 RECOVERY AND RESOLUTION REGIME FOR BANKS IN CHINA

When a bank is unable to meet its debt obligations or is clearly insolvent, the liquidation of its debts is governed by the Enterprise Bankruptcy Law of the People's Republic of China.[133] Additionally, if the bank's assets are insufficient to cover its liabilities or if it is unlikely to be able to repay its debts, it may also undergo reorganisation under the Bankruptcy Law. The National Financial Regulatory Administration (**NFRA**) is empowered to apply to the courts for either the

130 Pub. Law 102-242.
131 See www.occ.gov/topics/charters-and-licensing/app-to-charter-silicon-valley-bridge-bank-na.pdf (accessed in March 2025).
132 Pursuant to 12 USC 1821(n).
133 'Order of the President of the People's Republic of China No. 54', available at https://english.www.gov.cn/services/doingbusiness/202102/24/content_WS6035f009c6d0719374af97ad.html (accessed in March 2025).

reorganisation or bankruptcy liquidation of a bank. During liquidation, the bank is required to prioritise the repayment of individual savings deposits, following the settlement of liquidation expenses, employee wages, and labour insurance fees.

In situations where a bank faces or may face a credibility crisis that could severely impact the legitimate rights of depositors and other clients, the NFRA has the authority to take over the bank or facilitate its reorganisation. The deposit insurance fund management institution can recommend to the NFRA that appropriate action be taken if a bank is deemed to be experiencing financial difficulties.

Furthermore, when a bank faces payment difficulties that could trigger financial instability, the People's Bank of China may, with the approval of the State Council, inspect and supervise the bank to ensure financial stability. Should a bank be unable to repay its debts, the court can adjudicate the bank as bankrupt with the NFRA's consent. In such cases, the court, in coordination with the NFRA and other relevant authorities, will form a liquidation group to manage the process.

11.1 Obligations to Prepare Recovery Plans

Since June 2021, any bank with a globally adjusted denominator of leverage ratio (on- and off-balance-sheet assets) on a consolidated basis amounting to CNY 300 billion or more at the end of the previous year must prepare recovery and resolution plans.[134]

The NFRA or its local office may also designate other banks, even if they do not meet the CNY 300 billion threshold, to prepare recovery and resolution plans, depending on factors such as the bank's business characteristics, risk profile, and potential spillover effects. G-SIBs and domestic systemically important banks (D-SIBs) are required to meet regulatory requirements for recovery and resolution plans periodically.[135]

11.2 Powers of the Regulator

The Sample Form of the Recovery Plan for commercial banks, set out in the Interim Recovery Measures, outlines multiple resolution instruments available to the NFRA. These instruments allow for a range of recovery options, from creditor bail-ins and shareholder capital investments to the introduction of strategic investors. The plan may also include the disposal of non-performing assets, sales of non-core business units, or even a third-party takeover. Other strategies include acquisition by another institution, establishing bridge institutions, asset transfers to asset management companies, and support from industry protection funds. In cases of severe distress, the bank may enter temporary public ownership through government capital investments, undertake a financial restructuring, pursue mergers or reorganisation, or, as a final measure, face closure or bankruptcy/liquidation.

134 According to the China Banking and Insurance Regulatory Commission issued the Interim Measures for the Implementation of Recovery and Resolution Plans by Banking and Insurance Institutions.

135 See the People's Bank of China (PBC), the China Banking and Insurance Regulatory Commission (CBIRC), and the China Securities Regulatory Commission (CSRC) jointly issued Guidelines on Improving Regulation of Systemically Important Financial Institutions (No. 301 [2018] of the PBC), available at: www.pbc.gov.cn/english/130721/3679855/index.html (accessed in March 2025).

The Administrative Measures for the TLAC requirements[136] apply to Chinese commercial banks identified as G-SIBs, as well as Chinese affiliates designated for the resolution of foreign G-SIBs. The People's Bank of China, NFRA, and the Ministry of Finance jointly oversee these TLAC requirements, including supervision of TLAC-compliant non-capital debt instrument issuance.[137] Chinese banks with overseas branches are also obligated to prepare recovery and resolution plans aligning with their resolution strategies, coordinating closely with host country regulators through joint regulatory discussions.

For the protection of bank customers, the Deposit Insurance Regulation[138] mandates that the Deposit Insurance Fund, financed through insurance premiums, is managed by the Deposit Insurance Fund Management Co Ltd (**DIF Co**), established by the People's Bank of China. All banks in China accepting deposits are required to pay insurance premiums to the DIF Co. This regulation protects depositors for amounts up to CNY 500,000 under several circumstances, such as when the DIF Co takes over a bank, is responsible for its liquidation or when a People's Republic of China court has declared the bank bankrupt and accepted its bankruptcy filing. Additionally, other protective measures may be enacted with State Council approval.

12 RECOVERY AND RESOLUTION REGIME FOR BANKS IN INDIA

Under the provisions of the Banking Regulation Act 1949, the High Court has the authority to order the liquidation or winding-up of banks, whether incorporated in India or established as foreign banks with operations in India. Winding-up proceedings may be initiated by the central government, the Reserve Bank of India, or by the bank itself if the Reserve Bank of India certifies its inability to meet its financial obligations. Furthermore, if the central government finds that a bank's operations are detrimental to depositor interests, it may instruct the Reserve Bank of India to inspect the institution and then proceed with a winding-up application.

The Reserve Bank of India holds the independent authority to initiate winding-up under specific conditions, such as the cancellation of the bank's licence, failure to meet capital and reserve requirements, or if the Reserve Bank of India deems the bank financially incapable of protecting depositor interests. When a winding-up order is issued, the High Court appoints a liquidator to oversee the process, with the Reserve Bank of India eligible to serve as the liquidator if it applies. The liquidator is responsible for managing and realising the bank's assets, verifying creditor claims, and distributing proceeds to creditors in accordance with established priorities.

136 Available at www.pbc.gov.cn/en/3688235/3688609/3688615/4373133/index.html (accessed in March 2025).

137 In April 2022, the Notice on Issuing Non-Capital Bonds for TLAC by G-SIBs was released to provide guidance on bond issuance by Chinese G-SIBs. The issuance of these bonds must include clauses permitting the People's Bank of China or NFRA to write down or convert the bonds into equity upon resolution. Furthermore, all Tier 2 capital instruments must be convertible into common shares at the resolution point to ensure loss absorption.

138 Available at www.pbc.gov.cn/en/3688235/3688414/3688426/3858809/index.html (accessed in March 2025).

It is important to note that while the Insolvency and Bankruptcy Code, 2016 (**IBC**)[139] is regarded as a comprehensive code governing insolvency and bankruptcy proceedings,[140] SIFIs and banks are not specifically governed by it.

12.1 Obligations for Recovery Planning

Banks must maintain a consolidated business continuity plan addressing essential operational and technological aspects, while the Reserve Bank of India may require a corrective action plan under the Prompt Corrective Action Framework. This framework allows the Reserve Bank of India to intervene and take corrective measures to restore the financial health of banks showing signs of distress. The Reserve Bank of India assesses a bank's health through predetermined financial parameters, initiating corrective actions when necessary to prevent further deterioration.

The Prompt Corrective Action Framework enables the Reserve Bank of India to take targeted actions to restore a bank's financial health through mechanisms such as amalgamation, reconstruction, and other strategic interventions. Corrective actions typically fall under supervisory, strategic, governance, capital adjustment, credit and market risk management, and operational restructuring categories, all tailored to the specific challenges facing the bank. Although the Prompt Corrective Action Framework applies to all banks operating in India, there is currently no detailed regulatory process for transferring banking business as part of resolution efforts; such measures remain within the Reserve Bank of India's discretionary authority.

While India has yet to adopt the FSB's TLAC standards, it continues to assess and integrate international regulatory best practices as appropriate, aligning certain aspects with Basel III Capital Regulations.

12.2 Customer Protections in the Event of Bank Failure

The Deposit Insurance and Credit Guarantee Corporation Act of 1961[141] established the Deposit Insurance and Credit Guarantee Corporation (DICGC), a subsidiary of the Reserve Bank of India, to safeguard depositors by insuring bank deposits and guaranteeing credit facilities. All commercial banks, including foreign bank branches, local area banks, regional rural banks, and eligible cooperative banks in India, must register with the DICGC to participate in the deposit insurance scheme. The scheme provides insurance coverage up to INR 500,000 (around USD 6,000) per depositor, per bank.

In the event of a bank's liquidation, amalgamation, or restructuring, the liquidator or CEO of the insured bank must provide a list of depositors and account balances to the DICGC within three months. The DICGC then has two months to distribute pay-outs to insured depositors. Certain deposits are excluded from this coverage, including deposits by foreign

139 "An Act to consolidate and amend the laws relating to reorganisation and insolvency resolution of corporate persons, partnership firms and individuals in a time bound manner for maximization of value of assets of such persons, to promote entrepreneurship, availability of credit and balance the interests of all the stakeholders including alteration in the order of priority of payment of Government dues and to establish an Insolvency and Bankruptcy Board of India, and for matters connected therewith and incidental thereto".

140 Insolvency and Bankruptcy Board of India, *Understanding the IBC: Key Jurisprudence and Practical Considerations – a Handbook* (International Finance Corporation, 2020), p. 56.

141 www.indiacode.nic.in/bitstream/123456789/1655/5/a1961-47.pdf (accessed in March 2025).

governments, central and state governments, inter-bank deposits, and deposits of State Land Development Banks with state cooperative banks.

13 RECOVERY AND RESOLUTION REGIME FOR BANKS IN JAPAN

Japan's framework for bank liquidation, governed by the Deposit Insurance Act,[142] provides structured procedures tailored to various levels of financial crisis. The objective of the Deposit Insurance Act is to establish a deposit insurance system and contribute to the stability of the financial system, thereby protecting depositors and other stakeholders while ensuring the settlement of funds related to failed financial institutions.

The Deposit Insurance Act delineates three primary liquidation regimes. Ordinary Procedures are traditional resolution methods for handling bank failures, while Procedures for Financial Crisis Management are designed as bail-out mechanisms to protect depositors and stabilise the financial system during economic distress. The third regime, Orderly Resolution Procedures, aligns with the FSB's "Key Attributes of Effective Resolution Regimes for Financial Institutions", functioning similarly to a bail-in approach to maintaining systemic stability. Throughout the liquidation process, the Deposit Insurance Corporation of Japan (**DICJ**) plays a pivotal role in ensuring depositor protection and financial stability.

13.1 Obligations for Recovery Plans

In Japan, SIFIs and other critical banks must submit annual recovery and resolution plans as mandated by the Banking Act[143] and the Financial Services Agency guidelines. This requirement is part of a broader effort to ensure that SIFIs maintain preparedness for potential distress scenarios and contribute to the stability of the Japanese financial system.

In cases where a bank faces failure but does not pose systemic risk, Japan typically employs the ordinary procedure under the Deposit Insurance Act. Deposit insurance covers each depositor up to JPY 10 million, providing reassurance within this coverage limit. The ordinary procedure includes two main approaches: the Pay-out Method and the Purchase and Assumption Method. Under the Pay-out Method, depositors are directly compensated through deposit insurance, and the bank proceeds through bankruptcy procedures like civil rehabilitation or corporate reorganisation. Conversely, the Purchase and Assumption Method involves transferring some or all of the failed bank's operations to a financially stable institution, with an appointed administrator managing the bank during this transfer. This method is favoured for its cost-effectiveness, as it enables a more seamless continuation of banking services while limiting disruption for customers.[144]

The Orderly Resolution Regime incorporates elements of the FSB's guidelines to manage systemic risks. Under this regime, the Prime Minister can intervene to stabilise a bank whose failure would disrupt the financial system significantly. For banks not yet in deficit, the Prime Minister may direct the DICJ to oversee the bank's operations, provide liquidity to fulfil obligations, or inject capital as needed. Should a bank fall into deficit, the Prime Minister can

142 (Act No 34 of 1971).
143 (Act No. 59 of 1 June 1981).
144 Hideaki, S., 'Japan: Law & Practice' in *Chambers Global Practice Guides: Banking Regulation 2024*, Nagashima Ohno & Tsunematsu (Chambers and Partners, 2024), p. 12.

direct the DIC to assume control of the bank's assets and operations. Essential contracts may also be transferred to a bridge bank, with financial support provided by the DICJ to ensure the continuity of key banking functions.

Finally, for banks in deficit, the Prime Minister has the authority to implement a contractual bail-in.[145] This mechanism enables the write-down of subordinated bonds, preferred stocks, or subordinated loans, or their conversion into equity, to absorb losses and support recapitalisation. However, bail-ins are limited to scenarios of financial deficit and do not apply to liquidity issues, such as breaches in the Liquidity Coverage Ratio. To prevent systemic disruptions, the Prime Minister may also impose a temporary stay on early termination rights in derivative contracts. This stay would prevent close-out netting actions by temporarily halting early terminations, ensuring that key financial contracts remain operational during critical periods of bank resolution.

13.2 International Cooperation and the Single Point of Entry Strategy

Japan's Financial Services Agency collaborates closely with foreign regulators to manage cross-border resolution for SIFIs, with a preference for the Single Point of Entry's approach resolution strategy. With such an approach, resolution actions are managed by a single authority – typically the regulator of the bank's home country. For Japanese SIFIs, this means that Japanese holding companies bear responsibility for absorbing losses of foreign subsidiaries, aligning with TLAC standards or equivalent requirements in host countries.

Under the orderly resolution regime, the DICJ can facilitate the transfer of essential contracts to bridge banks, which receive financial support from the DICJ to maintain key banking operations. This measure ensures the continuity of critical financial services and safeguards depositor and systemic interests during resolution.

13.3 Customer Protections in the Event of Bank Failure

Japan's deposit insurance system, established under the Deposit Insurance Act, provides a safety net for depositors in the event of bank failure. The DICJ, as a public insurance body, insures deposits held in Japanese-headquartered banks, funded by annual premiums paid by insured institutions.[146] The system covers ordinary deposits but excludes foreign currency and derivative accounts. Settlement-related deposit accounts benefit from full coverage, while all other insured deposit accounts are protected up to JPY 10 million per depositor, per bank.

14 CONCLUSION

Chapter 7 has provided an analysis of the UK's recovery and resolution frameworks for banks, focusing on the ring-fencing regime and the bank recovery and resolution mechanisms introduced following the 2007–2009 global financial crisis. These frameworks were designed

145 Under Articles 102 and 126-2(4) of the Deposit Insurance Act.

146 The mission of the Deposit Insurance Corporation of Japan (DICJ) is to manage the deposit insurance system effectively in pursuit of this objective. See www.dic.go.jp/english/e_kikotoha/page_000049.html (accessed in March 2025).

to ensure the stability of the financial system, protect depositors, and minimise the need for taxpayer-funded bailouts by enforcing stricter regulations on the financial sector.

The UK's ring-fencing regime, established under the Financial Services (Banking Reform) Act 2013, is a key component of this strategy. It mandates the separation of essential retail banking services from riskier wholesale and investment banking activities within large banking groups.

In parallel, the Bank Recovery and Resolution framework, codified in the Banking Act 2009, allows the PRA and Bank of England to intervene in banks facing financial distress, ensuring that they can recover or be resolved in an orderly manner without disrupting critical financial services. The UK's adherence to international standards, such as the FSB's TLAC requirements, aligns the country's framework with global best practices aimed at managing the risks posed by SIFIs.

Furthermore, this chapter has examined equivalent frameworks in other major economies, notably the United States, the European Union, China, India, and Japan. Each jurisdiction has developed recovery and resolution mechanisms that reflect its unique financial structures while adhering to international regulatory standards.

The BRRD and the SRM constitute, amongst the jurisdictions considered in this Chapter, one of the most effective and coherent frameworks for managing banks' failures across member states. In the United States, the FDIC plays a critical role in bank resolution, with the Dodd-Frank Wall Street Reform and Consumer Protection Act[147] establishing the Orderly Liquidation Authority to manage the resolution of SIFIs. China's regulatory regime, managed by the People's Bank of China and the NFRA, focuses on the orderly resolution of SIFIs while integrating key elements of global standards. India, through the Reserve Bank of India, has implemented a Prompt Corrective Action framework for bank recovery, though its approach continues to evolve. Lastly, Japan's framework, overseen by the Financial Services Agency, incorporates the FSB's Key Attributes and TLAC standards, focusing on bail-ins and the resolution of SIFIs.

147 12 USC 5301, 124 Stat. 1376, Public Law 111-203 of 21 July 2010.

CHAPTER 8

AN INTRODUCTION TO BANK LOAN FINANCING

OVERVIEW

Chapter 8 explores the key concepts and structures of bank loan financing. It examines the various reasons borrowers seek loans, whether for business operations, expansion, or specific projects and considers the different types of loan facilities available to meet these needs. The chapter provides a preliminary analysis of loan structures, ranging from bilateral loans to syndicated loan facilities, and discusses the role of financial institutions, intermediaries, and regulatory frameworks in facilitating the flow of funds across multiple jurisdictions.

The discussion extends to a review of the categories of risk in lending, an analysis of the elements of borrowing costs in loan transactions, with particular reference to interest and fees, and an evaluation of the role of sustainable lending practices. The tax implications of lending transactions are also considered, particularly in the context of cross-border lending and the activities of UK and non-UK lenders.

The expansion of cross-border lending in recent decades, despite certain global shifts away from free trade, is also examined. Since cross-border lending presents unique challenges, particularly in relation to country risk, which encompasses political, economic, and legal risks, this chapter evaluates these risks in the context of selected European jurisdictions, including France, Germany, Ireland, and Italy, as well as China, India, and Japan, highlighting some of the regulatory, tax, and legal hurdles foreign lenders must navigate.

1 CORPORATE FINANCE

The financial markets involve a complex web of actors, including individuals, corporations, and financial intermediaries such as commercial banks, investment banks, insurance companies, and pension funds. These intermediaries facilitate the flow of capital from savers and investors to borrowers, either directly or through financial markets.[1] In bank loan financing, intermediaries play a central role in the operation of financial markets, facilitating the flow of capital from those with surplus funds to those in need of financing. Lenders' funds may flow directly from savers to borrowers, known as direct finance, where borrowers receive capital without the involvement of intermediaries. In contrast, intermediated finance occurs when credit institutions act as intermediaries between savers and borrowers. Under this model, the credit institution assumes the credit risk of the borrower, which is a key service provided by banks and other intermediaries. In this context, banks serve as the principal intermediaries, taking deposits from individuals and companies and extending loans to businesses and governments.

Corporate financing primarily takes two forms: equity financing and debt financing, each with distinct characteristics, advantages, and risks.

Equity financing involves raising capital by selling ownership interests in the company, typically through the issuance of equity securities such as shares. In this arrangement, investors provide funds in exchange for shareholder status, granting them potential rights to a portion of the company's profits without any obligation on the company's part to repay the

1 Gullifer, L. and Payne, J., *Corporate Finance Law: Principles and Policy* (Hart, 2020), p. 20.

DOI: 10.4324/9781032662220-9

investment. Shareholders may also influence corporate decision-making, depending on the size of their ownership stake.[2] While equity financing reduces financial risk for the company – since there is no repayment obligation even if the business fails – it also results in the dilution of ownership and control for existing shareholders.

Debt financing, by contrast, involves borrowing funds that must be repaid with interest within an agreed timeframe. This can be achieved through the issuance of debt securities or by obtaining a bank loan. Unlike equity financing, debt financing allows businesses to raise capital without relinquishing ownership, as lenders do not typically acquire management rights or influence over corporate decision-making. However, debt places a financial burden on the company, requiring regular repayments that may strain cash flow, particularly in challenging economic conditions. Since debt financing creates a contractual obligation to repay the borrowed amount with interest, it differs from equity financing, where investors expect returns through dividends or capital appreciation rather than direct repayment.

When a company seeks to raise capital, it must weigh the advantages and disadvantages of using debt financing versus equity financing. While a variety of factors influence this decision, one of the key considerations is the relative cost of each option. Debt financing cost tends to be more straightforward to calculate, with the primary factor being the interest rate at which the company can borrow.

The tax advantages of debt are significant, as the interest paid on loans is deductible against taxable profits, whereas dividends are paid from post-tax earnings. This makes debt financing more cost-effective from a tax perspective, as the company benefits from tax relief on interest payments, lowering the overall expense of the debt. Equity, on the other hand, involves paying returns to shareholders through dividends or share buybacks, neither of which offers tax relief. Shareholders also expect a return on their investment, which may include capital appreciation and future dividends, making the cost of equity potentially higher than the cost of debt.

When interest rates are low, companies may favour borrowing over issuing equity, as it allows them to access capital at a lower cost while also benefitting from tax deductions. However, the decision to use debt financing involves careful consideration of several additional factors beyond cost.

One major factor is the company's existing capital structure. If a company already carries a significant amount of debt, it may face challenges in securing additional debt without offering a higher interest rate or providing additional security to lenders. Companies with high debt-to-equity ratios[3] may find lenders hesitant to extend further credit, particularly if their ability to service the existing debt is already under pressure. For instance, in sectors such as utilities, where companies often have stable cash flows and a large asset base, higher levels of debt might be acceptable. In contrast, start-ups or companies with less predictable revenue streams may face limitations in borrowing, as they are perceived as higher-risk borrowers. Lenders typically assess a company's financial ratios, such as its interest coverage

2 The Companies Act 2006 (Section 560) defines "equity securities" as including both ordinary shares and rights to subscribe for or convert other securities into ordinary shares. Ordinary shares confer ownership rights without any fixed limitations on dividends or capital distributions.

3 The **debt-to-equity ratio** is a measure of a company's financial leverage and shows the degree to which companies finance their activities with equity or with debt. The ratio is calculated by dividing the total debt of financial corporations by the total equity liabilities of the same sector, including investment fund shares. The debt figure comprises several categories of liabilities: currency and deposits, debt securities, loans, insurance, pension, and standardised guarantee schemes, and other accounts payable. The equity component, which forms the denominator, is measured by the market value of shares issued by financial corporations, including investment fund shares.

ratio,[4] to evaluate whether the company can comfortably meet its interest payments. A weak ratio may signal that the company is already overleveraged, limiting its capacity to take on more debt.

Moreover, a company's ability to borrow may be constrained by legal or contractual obligations. Many companies operate under restrictions imposed by their organisational documents, which may set limits on how much debt they can incur. Additionally, existing loan agreements or debt instruments such as indentures often contain covenants that restrict the company from taking on further debt without the lender's consent. Violating these covenants can lead to immediate repayment demands or default, which, in turn, would severely impair the company's financial conditions.

Ultimately, the choice between debt and equity financing is complex, requiring companies to consider not only the cost but also the implications of each option on their financial structure, risk profile, and future flexibility.

The decision on whether to pursue debt or equity financing also interacts with broader corporate governance and control issues. For example, increasing debt levels can shift the balance of power towards creditors, who may impose restrictive covenants on the company's operations. In contrast, equity financing dilutes existing shareholders' ownership, potentially altering control dynamics within the company. This decision becomes even more intricate when companies face unique circumstances, such as financial distress or impending growth opportunities, which may require a more nuanced approach to funding.

2 LOANS: STRUCTURE, TERMS, AND REPAYMENT

A loan is a contractual arrangement in which the lender provides the borrower with the use of funds in exchange for a promise to repay the principal, along with any accrued interest, over a specified period. The terms of repayment (although there may be instances where terms are not formally documented, for example, for an intra-group loan), including the amount and interest rate, are usually pre-determined and outlined in a loan agreement. This document forms the basis of the relationship between the lender and borrower, setting out their respective rights and obligations.[5]

Loans are the most common form of debt financing used by businesses, especially in Europe and Japan, where corporate borrowing tends to rely more on bank loans than in the US. In contrast, the US financial system, though still featuring significant bank lending, is more market-based, with a greater reliance on capital markets for funding.

Loans are generally classified based on their maturity period, which determines the duration for which the borrower is obligated to repay the debt. **Short-term debt** refers to loans with a maturity of less than one year, typically used to finance working capital needs or temporary liquidity shortfalls. These loans are often repaid within a business cycle and may take the form of overdrafts, trade credit, or short-term bank loans.

4 The **interest coverage ratio** (ICR), also referred to as the times interest earned (TIE) ratio, is a key financial indicator used to assess a company's capacity to meet its interest payment obligations from its operating earnings. It is calculated by comparing earnings before interest and taxes (EBIT) to interest expenses, thereby providing a measure of how comfortably a company can service its debt. A higher ICR typically reflects greater financial resilience, although what constitutes an acceptable ratio may vary depending on the specific characteristics of the industry. Sustaining earnings at a level sufficient to cover interest payments is essential for maintaining solvency and protecting shareholder value.

5 Hudson, A., *The Law of Finance* (Sweet & Maxwell, 2013), p. 972.

Intermediate-term debt encompasses loans with a maturity ranging from one to five years. This category is commonly used for financing medium-term investments, such as equipment purchases or business expansion. These loans often involve structured repayment schedules and may be secured or unsecured, depending on the borrower's credit profile and the lender's requirements.

Long-term debt includes loans with a maturity exceeding five years, usually employed to finance significant capital expenditures, such as infrastructure projects, property acquisitions, or corporate development. Given their extended repayment period, long-term loans often involve detailed contractual arrangements and security provisions to mitigate the lender's risk.

Certain types of credit facilities, such as revolving credit or perpetual debt, may not have a fixed repayment date. These structures are tailored to meet the specific financial needs of the borrower, allowing for more flexible repayment arrangements.

2.1 Repayment: Schedules and Types of Loan Facilities

Repayment schedules are a key element of loan facilities. These schedules dictate when and how the borrower is expected to repay the loan. Repayment can either be **on-demand**, where the lender retains the right to demand repayment at any time, as seen in overdraft facilities or **pre-determined**, where the borrower follows a fixed schedule, typically laid out in the loan agreement. Pre-determined schedules are common in term loans, providing borrowers with the predictability necessary for long-term financial planning.

In instances where no specific repayment date is agreed upon, the loan is treated as repayable immediately upon being incurred, as established in *Longstaff International Ltd v Evans* [2001] ALL ER (D) 283.[6] Under the Limitation Act 1980, the limitation period for recovering a debt begins from the date the debt is incurred, creating a potential challenge for lenders seeking timely debt recovery. This is because the general rule is that a claim arising from a contract must be brought within six years from "the date on which the cause of action accrued".[7] However, where a contract is executed as a deed, the limitation period extends to 12 years, although the trigger for limitation remains the same.[8] Notably, the 12-year rule for deeds is subject to any shorter limitation period prescribed by another provision of the Limitation Act 1980.[9]

A specific rule applies to claims for the recovery of money secured by a mortgage or charge; such claims must be brought within 12 years from the date on which the right to receive the money accrued.[10] This extended limitation period applies only to claims for the principal debt. In contrast, claims for interest are subject to a shorter six-year limitation period. A claim to recover arrears of interest must be initiated within six years[11] from the date on which the interest became due. While the general limitation rules under section 5 and section 8, where the relevant trigger is "*the date on which the cause of action accrued*", are generally aligned, the starting point differs. The meaning "*the date on which the cause of action accrued*" has historically created difficulties in legal interpretation, particularly in relation to loans repayable on demand.

6 Proctor, C., *The Law and Practice of International Banking* (Oxford University Press, 2015) at [20.07].
7 Section 5 of the Limitation Act 1980.
8 Section 8(1) of the Limitation Act 1980.
9 Section 8(2) of the Limitation Act 1980.
10 Section 20(1) of the Limitation Act 1980
11 Section 20(5) of the Limitation Act 1980.

Case law initially established that a lender's cause of action arose at the moment the loan was made rather than when a demand for repayment was issued.[12] Section 6 of the Limitation Act 1980 was enacted to reverse the effect of these decisions in respect of loan contracts that are not under specialty (i.e., not executed as deeds), stipulating that, in such cases, the cause of action arises only when a formal demand for repayment is made in writing.[13]

However, it is not clear whether there is a meaningful distinction between "*the date on which the right to receive the money accrued*" and "*the date on which the cause of action accrued*". The difficulty stems from the Court of Appeal's decision in *Hornsey Local Board v Monarch Investment Building Society* (1889) 24 QBD 1, which considered when a local authority had acquired a "present right to receive" certain expenses for pavement works that had been charged on adjoining properties under the Public Health Act 1848.

It was considered that:

> *When, then, does the right accrue to the person or persons in whose favour the charge is imposed to receive the amount secured by the charge? It appears to me that it accrues the moment the charge is imposed on the premises by the statute, that is when the expenses have been incurred and the works completed. It may be that certain things have to be done before the right can be enforced, but the right to receive what is secured by the charge arises concurrently with the charge. The words are "present right to receive", not "present right to recover".*[14]

Hornsey, therefore, established a distinction between "receivability" and "recoverability", confirming that the right to receive a sum may exist even before enforcement is possible. This distinction was reconsidered in *Gotham v Doodes* [2005] EWHC 2576 (Ch) [2007] 1 WLR 86, which concerned a charging order created under section 313 of the Insolvency Act 1986 in favour of a trustee in bankruptcy, where the court concluded[15] that *Hornsey* remains authority for the principle that "*the right of the local board to receive specific sums from individual frontagers was a present right because the only future event on which it could depend was within the power of the local board to procure*".[16]

It should also be noted that if, within a facility agreement, there is no express provision entitling the borrower to make an early repayment (prepayment), the borrower has no legal right to do so.[17] The lender is entitled to rely on the terms of the agreement and its right to receive interest for the full term of the loan. Should the borrower make an early repayment without the lender's consent, such action would constitute a breach of contract, rendering the borrower liable for damages equivalent to any loss incurred by the lender. The lender, however, has a duty to mitigate its losses, which may include redeploying the repaid funds to other investments or uses.

3 INTEREST: THE COST OF BORROWING

Interest rates are a critical element of loan agreements, representing the cost that borrowers must pay for the use of funds. The rate charged by lenders not only reflects the cost of providing

12 This principle was set out in *Re Brown* [1893] 2 Ch 300 and reaffirmed in *MS Fashions v BCCI* [1993] Ch 425, at [447].

13 The operation of section 6 is further explained in *Boot v Boot* (1997) 73 P & CR 137, where Waite LJ provides a useful analysis.

14 At page 11.

15 At [32].

16 Clark, W. and Morgan, J., *Fisher and Lightwood's Law of Mortgage* (LexisNexis, 2014) at [26.34] reference the decision for the principle that "*there can be a present right causing time to start running, notwithstanding there may be no means of immediately enforcing it*". This continues to have significant implications for the interpretation of limitation periods in claims involving secured debts.

17 This principle is supported by *Hyde Management Services Pty Ltd v FAI Insurance* [1979] 144 CLR 541, citing Luxmoor J in *Knightsbridge Estates Trust Ltd v Byrne* [1938] Ch. 741.

the loan but also compensates for operational costs, regulatory expenses, and risk assumed in extending credit. The higher the perceived risk of the borrower, the higher the interest rate.

Understanding the structure of interest rates in commercial lending is essential for both lenders and borrowers, as it directly influences the overall cost of borrowing and the financial exposure of each party. The calculation of interest for a loan facility can be structured in different ways, depending on the agreement between the lender and the borrower. The most commonly used methods include floating rates based on third-party benchmarks, variable rates linked to a specific bank's base rate, and fixed rates for the entire term of the loan. Each method has distinct implications for both parties, particularly in terms of interest rate volatility, predictability, and exposure to market fluctuations.[18] Basis Points (BPS) are the commonly used metric to gauge changes in interest rates. A BPS represents one-hundredth of a percent, or 0.01%.

A **fixed interest rate** remains constant for the entire duration of the loan, providing the borrower with certainty regarding future repayments. This predictability is particularly beneficial for long-term financial planning, especially in an environment where interest rates are expected to rise. However, because fixed rates lock in the borrowing cost when they are set, they tend to be higher than floating rates, particularly when market rates are low, as lenders seek to protect themselves against future fluctuations. In commercial lending, fixed rates are less commonly offered to corporate borrowers, particularly for large loans, as lenders typically prefer the flexibility of floating rates.

By contrast, a **floating interest rate** fluctuates over the life of the loan, typically linked to an external benchmark such as an Interbank Offered Rate (**IBOR**) or a Risk-Free Rate (**RFR**). These rates adjust periodically, reflecting broader market conditions. Floating rates offer borrowers the potential benefit of lower initial costs compared to fixed rates; however, they also introduce the risk that the cost of borrowing may rise if market rates increase. Given their flexibility, floating rates are widely used in commercial lending, particularly in markets characterised by interest rate volatility.[19]

For large commercial loans, floating interest rates generally consist of three key components: a reference rate, mandatory costs, and the lender's margin. The reference rate has traditionally been based on IBORs, such as the London Interbank Offered Rate (**LIBOR**),[20] which represents the average interest rate at which major banks lend to one another on an unsecured basis. However, following the global financial crisis and concerns about the reliability of IBORs, LIBOR has been discontinued, and there has been a transition towards RFRs, which are based on actual overnight transactions rather than estimates. Examples of

18 Adams, D., *Banking and Capital Markets* (College of Law Publishing, 2024), p. 40.

19 Ellinger, E. P., Lomnicka, E. and Hare, C., *Ellinger's Modern Banking Law* (Oxford University Press, 2011), p. 775.

20 "*LIBOR (London Interbank Offered Rate) was, in essence, a benchmark representing the rate at which a bank could borrow money in London at 11am each business day. It was in operation from 1986, and at the relevant time (2006–2010) it was one of the main, if not the main benchmark used for many types of financial transactions (including consumer loans and mortgages, many forms of commercial lending, and derivatives). It was operated by the British Banking Association ('BBA'), a trade association representing the interests of the banking industry operating in London. LIBOR was published each day, in ten currencies, including Sterling, US Dollars and Japanese Yen. Rates would be published for various notional borrowing periods, from overnight to 12 months, known as 'tenors'. The rates were calculated from submissions made from a number of panel banks, appointed by agreement with the BBA, to Thomson Reuters, who conducted the LIBOR setting exercise on behalf of the BBA. In major currencies, such as Sterling, US Dollars and Japanese Yen, there were 16 contributor panel banks. On each business day, each panel bank would submit its estimate of the interest rate that it would be charged if it were to borrow funds from another bank at 11am on the day in question, for the relevant currency and tenors. For each currency/tenor, the submitted rates would be ranked in order, with the highest and lowest quartiles excluded and the mean taken from the middle quartiles (that is, the average of the middle 8 in a 16-bank panel). The 'trimmed mean' average was then published as LIBOR*", in *Hayes & Anor v Rex* [2024] EWCA Crim 304 at [4] per Lord Justice Bean, Lord Justice Popplewell and Mr Justice Bryan.

RFRs include the Sterling Overnight Index Average (**SONIA**) for sterling-denominated loans and the Secured Overnight Financing Rate (**SOFR**) for US dollar loans.[21] These benchmarks are regarded as more transparent and reliable, reducing the risk of manipulation.

In addition to the base rate, lenders often impose **mandatory costs**, which cover expenses incurred due to regulatory compliance, including capital adequacy requirements, liquidity obligations, and deposit insurance schemes. These costs are passed on to the borrower to ensure that the lender recoups the expenses associated with regulatory obligations.

The **lender's margin** represents the profit earned by the lender for providing the loan and is typically expressed in basis points (bps), where 1% equals 100 bps. This margin is influenced by several factors, including the borrower's credit risk, prevailing market conditions, and the competitive landscape of the lending market. Riskier borrowers, such as start-ups with limited financial history, often face higher margins compared to well-established companies with stable earnings. In some transactions, particularly in highly leveraged deals, the margin may be subject to a "margin ratchet" mechanism, which allows for adjustments based on the borrower's financial performance. This means that if the borrower's creditworthiness improves, the interest margin may decrease, whereas if financial conditions deteriorate, the margin may increase.

The Decline of Inter Bank Offered Rates

The transition away from LIBOR and other IBORs, such as the Euro Interbank Offered Rate (EURIBOR)[22] – albeit EURIBOR is still in use – and the Euro Overnight Index Average (EONIA), marks one of the most significant shifts in financial markets in recent decades and it has led to the development and adoption of alternative near RFRs such as the SONIA, the Euro Short-Term Rate (€STR), and SOFR.

The global financial crisis of 2007–2009 raised concerns about the reliability and integrity of IBORs, especially LIBOR. It was revealed that LIBOR submissions,[23] which were based on banks' estimates rather than actual transactions, were susceptible to manipulation.[24] This led to significant reforms aimed at enhancing the transparency

21 The Alternative Reference Rates Committee (ARRC), a committee created by the Federal Reserve, selected SOFR as the proposed benchmark alternative to replace USD LIBOR see www.newyorkfed.org/arrc/sofr-transition (accessed in March 2025).

22 "*EURIBOR (EU Interbank Offered Rate) was devised at the time of the creation of the Euro currency in 1999. It was principally devised by the European Banking Federation ('EBF') representing national banks and the Financial Markets Association ('ACI') representing European Banks. Two entities (EURIBOR – ECF and EURIBOR – ACI) were established, under Belgian law, to supervise the operation of EURIBOR. The purpose of the rate was to provide participants in Euro denominated transactions with a benchmark comparable to those found in many money markets, including LIBOR.*

Like LIBOR, there was a different EURIBOR rate for a range of tenors, from one week to one year. EURIBOR was commonly designated as a reference rate for interest rate swaps or other derivative transactions. For the purposes of setting the daily EURIBOR rate for each 'tenor', submissions were received prior to 11am Brussels time on each day from banks on a designated panel. The number of such panel banks fluctuated from time to time but was generally 48. The EURIBOR daily rate was fixed by averaging the submissions of each panel bank for the respective tenor, but with the highest and lowest 15% of the respective submissions being excluded. The remaining submissions would be averaged and the result rounded to three decimal places, producing the daily rate which was then published by Thomson Reuters. No panel bank was permitted to see any other panel bank's submission during the relevant window before 11am", in *Hayes & Anor v Rex* [2024] EWCA Crim 304 at [8] and [9] per Lord Justice Bean, Lord Justice Popplewell and Mr Justice Bryan.

23 "*The key definition of the LIBOR rate which the panel banks were required to submit was therefore the rate at which that panel bank 'could borrow funds, were it to do so by asking for and then accepting inter-bank offers in reasonable market size, just prior to 11.00 London time*'", in *Hayes & Anor v Rex* [2024] EWCA Crim 304 at [7] per Lord Justice Bean, Lord Justice Popplewell and Mr Justice Bryan.

24 "*In 2012 the LIBOR rigging scandal erupted. It was discovered that a number of banks on the survey panel were engaged in manipulating the various LIBOR benchmarks: rather than submit their genuine assessment of the rate at which they thought they could borrow, they submitted rates that served their own purposes, e.g. assisting their trading divisions which*

and robustness of these benchmarks. Despite these efforts, the underlying market for unsecured interbank lending had diminished, making LIBOR increasingly unreliable as a benchmark.

In response, regulators such as the UK's Financial Conduct Authority (FCA) and the European Securities and Markets Authority (ESMA) accelerated the transition towards RFRs, which are based on actual market transactions and are considered more robust and less prone to manipulation. This led to the development of key regulations, including the EU Benchmarks Regulation ((EU) 2016/1011)[25] and its UK equivalent,[26] to govern the use, provision, and supervision of benchmarks.

LIBOR, which was once the world's most widely used interest rate benchmark, has now been phased out. By 30 September 2024, all 35 LIBOR settings permanently ceased.[27]

The discontinuation of LIBOR necessitated the development of robust alternative benchmarks. In the UK, SONIA was adopted as the preferred RFR, while the US opted for SOFR, and the eurozone moved to €STR (although Euribor is still in use). These RFRs are backward-looking rates based on actual overnight transactions, providing a more accurate reflection of market conditions than IBORs, which rely on estimates.

Key Alternative Benchmarks

i) **SONIA**: administered by the Bank of England, is based on actual transactions in the overnight sterling market. It reflects the average rate at which banks and other financial institutions borrow unsecured sterling overnight. SONIA has been widely adopted in the UK as the primary replacement for sterling LIBOR.
ii) **SOFR**: administered by the Federal Reserve Bank of New York, is based on overnight repurchase agreement (repo) transactions collateralised by US Treasury securities. It has become the standard alternative to USD LIBOR.
iii) **€STR**: administered by the European Central Bank (ECB), reflects the wholesale euro unsecured overnight borrowing costs of banks. It has replaced EONIA and serves as the preferred RFR in the eurozone.

The shift from IBORs to RFRs has had significant implications for loan markets, particularly in terms of how interest is calculated. IBORs were forward-looking rates, meaning they reflected the borrowing cost for a future period. In contrast, RFRs are backward-looking, based on transactions that have already occurred, which presents challenges in calculating interest for loans and other financial products.

---

held LIBOR-tied positions on the markets. The scandal led to fines, prosecutions and reforms on both sides of the Atlantic", in *Leeds City Council & Ors v Barclays Bank Plc & Anor* [2021] EWHC 363 (Comm) at [8]. The scandal fundamentally undermined confidence in LIBOR as a reliable benchmark rate. In its aftermath, global regulators and market participants questioned the appropriateness of continuing to use LIBOR as a reference rate, ultimately leading to its planned phase-out and replacement by alternative, transaction-based benchmarks.

25 Regulation (EU) 2016/1011 of the European Parliament and of the Council of 8 June 2016 on indices used as benchmarks in financial instruments and financial contracts or to measure the performance of investment funds and amending Directives 2008/48/EC and 2014/17/EU and Regulation (EU) No 596/2014 as amended by Regulation (EU) 2021/168 of the European Parliament and of the Council of 10 February 2021 amending Regulation (EU) 2016/1011 as regards the exemption of certain third-country spot foreign exchange benchmarks and the designation of replacements for certain benchmarks in cessation, and amending Regulation (EU) No 648/2012.

26 The Benchmarks (Amendment and Transitional Provision) (EU Exit) Regulations 2019 No. 657.

27 www.bankofengland.co.uk/news/2024/october/the-end-of-libor (accessed in March 2025).

To address the challenges associated with interest rate calculations in the transition from IBORs to RFRs, market participants have adopted various conventions to ensure consistency and accuracy in pricing. One widely accepted approach was the **compounded in-arrears methodology**, which calculates interest based on the compounded daily RFR over the interest period. By compounding daily rates, this approach captures actual market conditions throughout the interest period, reducing reliance on estimations and improving transparency.

In addition to compounded in-arrears calculations, some markets have developed **forward-looking term rates** derived from RFRs, such as Term SONIA and Term SOFR. These rates offer an alternative for specific financial products, including certain loan agreements, by providing an interest rate that is known at the start of the interest period. While forward-looking term rates maintain some of the characteristics of traditional IBOR-based pricing, they are generally less common than compounded in-arrears rates, particularly in wholesale lending markets. Their use is often limited to sectors where certainty over interest payments in advance is essential, such as trade finance or working capital facilities.

3.1 Calculating Interest: Time

The calculation of time in a legal document is ultimately a matter of contractual interpretation, dependent on the intention of the parties in each specific case. In some instances, such calculations are conducted in accordance with market practice or established conventions, which may not necessarily be grounded in case law[28] or statutory provisions.

A key aspect of time calculation in financial agreements is the accrual of interest. While interest rates are typically quoted on an annual basis, interest generally accrues daily, and payments are customarily due at intervals of less than a year.[29] A widely recognised convention in banking practice is that interest "*shall accrue from day to day*", a standard provision in most loan agreements and many other commercial contracts. This means that interest for each day accrues upon the passing of midnight, with fractions of a day disregarded. This is because:

> *Our law rejects fractions of a day more generally than the civil law does . . . The effect is to render the day a sort of indivisible point; so that any act, done in the compass of it, is no more referrible to any one, than to any other, portion of it; but the act and the day are co-extensive; and therefore the act cannot properly be said to be passed, until the day is passed.*[30]

For example, if funds are placed on deposit at noon on a Monday and withdrawn on Tuesday, one day's interest will be payable, regardless of whether the withdrawal occurs before or after noon.[31]

28 See the Irish case of *Irish Bank Resolution Corporation Ltd-v-Morrissey* [2014] IEHC 470 where it was disputed whether the 360/360 convention or the 365/365 method would apply to the calculation of interest under a loan agreement: "*In my judgment, the plaintiff and Mr. Jacobs are correct in construing the total annual interest rate in each facility letter from 2003 (both margin and Euribor) to be an annual rate quoted upon the basis of a 360-day year. This follows from clause 19.2 of the General Conditions as there is no contrary indication in the facility letter. Further, it is agreed that Euribor is and is known to be a 360-day rate. However, in my judgment, they are incorrect in construing the facility letters as permitting 'daily accrual' of interest upon the basis of a 365-day year. Such construction is not warranted by the express terms of the facility letter and is inconsistent with clause 19.2 of the General Conditions*", at [79].

29 Wood, P., *International Loans, Bonds, Guarantees and Legal Opinions* (Sweet & Maxwell, 2019) at [7-005].

30 *Lester v Garland* 33 ER 748 1808 per Sir William Grant MR.

31 See also on this point the Australian case of *Segal v Young* [2001] NSWCA 141, at [19] "*At common law, a day is not divisible and fractions of a day are not recognised*".

To determine how annual interest is allocated across each interest period, the lender and the borrower must agree on a methodology. This is typically achieved through the use of "day count fractions", whereby the calculation of interest for a particular payment period typically follows the formula:

Interest amount = (Principal amount/Notional amount) × Interest rate × Day count fraction

In this formula, the principal or notional amount represents the sum on which interest is calculated, usually expressed in a major currency such as GBP, US dollars or euros. The interest rate, whether fixed or floating, is quoted as a percentage per annum. The day count fraction is a fraction determined by the day count convention agreed upon by the parties in their loan agreement.[32]

Several day count conventions are commonly used in financial agreements. The *30/360* convention assumes that all months have 30 days, and each year consists of 360 days. Under this method, interest accrues at a daily rate equal to 1/360th of the annual interest rate, with each full month always treated as 30 days, regardless of whether it actually has 28, 29, 30, or 31 days. A variation of this, the *30/365* convention, similarly assumes all months have 30 days but considers a full year to have 365 days, meaning that interest accrues at a daily rate of 1/365th of the annual interest rate while still treating each full month as comprising 30 days.

The *Actual/360* convention differs in that it counts the actual number of days in each month but assumes a 360-day year. Interest accrues at a daily rate of 1/360th of the annual interest rate, and the total interest for any given period is calculated by multiplying this daily rate by the actual number of days elapsed. By contrast, the *Actual/365* method also counts the actual number of days in each month but assumes a 365-day year, with interest accruing at a daily rate of 1/365th of the annual interest rate and calculated by multiplying this rate by the actual number of days elapsed.

Finally, the *Actual/Actual* convention provides the most precise calculation, as it accounts for both the actual number of days in each month and the actual number of days in the year. Under this approach, the daily interest rate is derived by dividing the annual interest rate by the actual number of days in the current year. The total interest is then determined by multiplying this daily rate by the actual number of days that have elapsed.

The choice of day count convention can have a significant impact on the amount of interest payable, and it is, therefore, crucial that the parties to a financial contract clearly specify the convention to be applied.[33]

The specific day count convention recommended by the Working Group on Sterling Risk-Free Reference Rates for interest calculated using SONIA compounded in arrears is the same as that previously applied to sterling LIBOR: Actual/365 fixed.[34] This convention has been incorporated into market-standard documentation.

3.2 Selecting Interest Periods

In floating rate facilities, borrowers are often allowed to select the duration of the interest period, typically ranging from one to six months. For instance, a borrower may choose an

32 Odgers, J. and Wilson, I., *Paget's Law of Banking* (LexisNexis, 2023), p. 234.
33 Wood, P., *International Loans, Bonds, Guarantees and Legal Opinions* (Sweet & Maxwell, 2019) at [7-007].
34 See Statement on behalf of the Working Group on Sterling Risk-Free Reference Rates – Recommendations for SONIA Loan Market Conventions www.bankofengland.co.uk/-/media/boe/files/markets/benchmarks/rfr/statement-on-behalf-of-rfrwg-recommendations-for-sonia-loan-market-conventions.pdf (accessed in March 2025).

interest period of one month if they anticipate having excess cash flow to repay the loan early. If the borrower does not select, a default period is usually specified in the loan agreement. In some cases, the interest period may be shortened if it extends beyond the scheduled repayment date.

Interest periods are a critical consideration in managing both the borrower's cash flow and the lender's risk exposure. Longer interest periods may provide cash flow stability for the borrower but increase the lender's exposure to interest rate fluctuations.

3.3 Interest and Default Interest

Interest capitalisation, or the "rolling up" of interest, occurs when unpaid interest is added to the principal balance of a loan instead of being paid on the scheduled interest payment date. This increases the overall principal amount, with interest then being charged on the higher principal balance. Capitalising interest can be advantageous in situations where the borrower has limited or no income during the early stages of the loan, such as in real estate development finance, where the borrower is engaged in property development. Similarly, commitment fees (see what follows) may also need to be capitalised under these circumstances.

If a borrower fails to make a payment on the due date, a facility agreement will typically stipulate that default interest becomes payable from that date. Default interest is charged at a higher rate to compensate the lender for any additional costs arising from the borrower's failure to pay on time. Whether a particular default interest clause constitutes a penalty depends on the facts of the case.[35] If a clause is deemed a penalty, it may be unenforceable or enforceable only up to the amount of the actual loss suffered by the innocent party.

In restating the rule against penalties in *Cavendish Square Holdings BV v Talal El Makdessi and ParkingEye Limited v Beavis* [2015] UKSC 67,[36] Lord Mance reviewed the cases concerning default interest. He identified the size of the uplift as the key consideration, judged at the time the contract was made, typically by comparing the default rate with market rates. Lord Mance indicated:

> *The uplift is conditioned on the breach, but the breach reflects directly upon the continuing appropriateness of the originally agreed interest terms. In substance, the uplift amounts to a variation of the original terms. If on the other hand, it is evident from the size of the uplift that it is in its nature a punishment for or deterrent to breach, rather than an ordinary commercial re-rating to reflect a change in risk (or administration cost), then it will still be disallowed as a penalty.*[37]

In this respect, in *Lordsvale Finance Plc v Bank of Zambia* [1996] 3 All ER 156, a 1% increase in the contracted interest rate was considered reasonable and approved. It was noted:

> *the borrower in default is not the same credit risk as the prospective borrower with whom the loan agreement was first negotiated. Merely for the pre-existing rate of interest to continue to accrue on the outstanding amount of the debt would not reflect the fact that the borrower no longer has a clean record. Given that money is more expensive for a less good credit risk than for a good credit risk, there would in principle seem to be no reason to deduce*

35 In a whole series of cases across the world, courts have taken their cue from Lordsvale and held that provisions in loan agreements for uplifting the interest rate for the future after a default should not be regarded as penalties, save where the uplift is evidently extravagant: see, e.g., *Hong Leuong Finance Ltd v Tan Gin Huay* [1999] 2 SLR 153, *Beil v Mansell* (No 2) (2006) 2 Qd R 499, *PSAL Ltd v Kellas-Sharpe* [2012] QSC 31, *Elberg v Fraval* [2012] VSC 342, *Place Concorde East Ltd Partnership v Shelter Corp of Canada Ltd* (2003) 43 BLR (3d) 54 and, *In re Mandarin Container* [2004] 3 HKLRD 554.

36 At [147-148].

37 Per Lord Mance at [148].

> *that a small rateable increase in interest charged prospectively upon default would have the dominant purpose of deterring default. That is not because there is in any real sense a genuine pre-estimate of loss, but because there is a good commercial reason for deducing that deterrence of breach is not the dominant contractual purpose of the term. . . . There would therefore seem to be no reason in principle why a contractual provision the effect of which was to increase the consideration payable under an executory contract upon the happening of a default should be struck down as a penalty if the increase could in the circumstances be explained as commercially justifiable, provided always that its dominant purpose was not to deter the other party from breach.*[38]

In *Houssein v London Credit Ltd* [2024] EWCA Civ 721, the Court of Appeal held that if the default rate were penal and therefore unenforceable, the standard lower rate set out in the contract would not apply to the outstanding balance as the contract drafting provided that the standard rate and the default rate were exclusive.[39]

3.4 Market Disruption and Fall-Back Clauses

The transition away from LIBOR has raised significant legal issues, particularly concerning legacy contracts that reference LIBOR.[40] Many existing loan agreements, derivatives, and other financial instruments were drafted with LIBOR as the reference rate without adequate provisions for the cessation of LIBOR. To mitigate the risk of disputes, regulators and industry bodies have encouraged the adoption of robust fall-back clauses or at least to include **market disruption clauses** in loan agreements.

In *Blackwater Services Ltd v West Bromwich Commercial Ltd* [2016] EWHC 3083 (Ch), the High Court dealt with the issue of how interest rates should be calculated in the event of market disruption. The loan agreement included a market disruption clause which provided:

> *If at any time the Lender cannot determine or ascertain LIBOR or the Lender is of the opinion that its costs of funding would be in excess of LIBOR, then the Lender (acting reasonably) may determine and certify an alternative basis for calculating the interest rate for the Loan and will notify the Borrower before the next payment date.*

The court held that the use of the term "*certify*" in this context did not impose any formal requirements upon the lender unless the purpose of the provision or the wider legal context clearly necessitated such a requirement. The notifications contained in the letters sent by the lender to the borrower were deemed sufficient, as they specified the alternative basis being adopted by the lender.

The court further held that the term "*basis*" is not a term of art in a banking context requiring a lender to calculate interest by reference to a publicly available, objective standard. The judge clarified that, in this context, the term simply denoted an "*alternative foundation for calculating the interest rate on the facility*", and that the lender's actual cost of funding constituted

38 Per Colman J at pp. 763–764.

39 It was concluded: [72] "*In my judgment, there is no room for an interpretation which allows either the standard rate under clause 6.1 or the default rate under clause 6.6 to spring back if the other rate is not 'applicable'. There is no 'choice' to be made. Whether the standard rate or the default rate applies depends upon the relevant circumstances. If the circumstances are such that default rate interest under clause 6.6 applies, it is 'applicable'. If that is the case, the circumstances will not be such that the standard rate under clause 6.1 applies. They are mutually exclusive. I agree with Mr Cowen, therefore, that one cannot revert back to applying the standard rate pursuant to clause 6.1 if the circumstances are such that clause 6.6 would apply but the provision is found to be unenforceable. Clause 12.5 does not provide for a fall back. The words used cannot bear that interpretation*". . . . [75] "*It follows that I consider that if the default rate of interest is found to be a penalty, in the circumstances of this case, the standard rate of interest will not apply on the sums outstanding after the Repayment Date. Of course, in such circumstances, London Credit may choose to pursue their counterclaim for statutory/equitable interest*".

40 Wood, P., *International Loans, Bonds, Guarantees and Legal Opinions* (Sweet & Maxwell, 2019) at [7-016].

"a legitimate and reasonable alternative basis to have been adopted for calculating the interest rate for the facility".[41]

Fall-back clauses provided for the use of an alternative rate if LIBOR became unavailable (as it permanently did). For example, the Loan Market Association (**LMA**)[42] has developed templates for loan agreements that include provisions for transitioning to RFRs.

One should note, however, that *"benchmarks and their contractually agreed fall-back rates might over time diverge significantly and unexpectedly, and as a consequence, they might no longer represent the same underlying economic reality or lead to commercially unacceptable results"*.[43]

With the increasing use of RFRs such as SONIA and SOFR, market disruption clauses are less likely to be invoked, as these rates are based on actual overnight transactions rather than estimates. However, prudent lenders may still choose to include fall-back provisions, particularly when dealing with complex international transactions or less liquid markets.

4 TYPES OF BANK LOANS AND FACILITIES

Bank loans, also known as loan facilities or credit agreements (in the US), are arrangements whereby lenders provide funds to borrowers under agreed terms and conditions, with an obligation for repayment alongside interest and fees. Such an agreement governs the terms under which the loan is made, detailing the borrowing and repayment procedures, how interest and fees are calculated, and outlining the respective liabilities and obligations of the parties involved.

Loans are categorised based on several features, including the number of lenders, loan duration, security provided, lenders' obligations, and repayment structure.

The first key distinction is the number of lenders involved. A **bilateral loan** involves a single lender and borrower. Due to the involvement of only one lender, bilateral loans are generally simpler, requiring fewer formalities, which reduces both documentation and associated costs. The privacy of bilateral transactions allows for more flexible negotiations, as terms can be tailored to the specific needs of the borrower without adhering strictly to market practices. This can be advantageous in terms of maintaining confidentiality, as information is shared only with one lender, reducing the risk of leaks. However, the reliance on a single lender concentrates risk, often leading to higher interest rates for larger sums, as the lender assumes all the risk and all the regulatory implications associated with the loan.

In contrast, **syndicated loans** involve multiple lenders, typically organised by an agent or arranger, with each lender contributing a portion of the total loan amount.[44] This structure is common for larger deals, as it provides borrowers with access to more capital and spreads the risk among several lenders. The distributed risk often results in lower interest rates compared to bilateral loans. However, syndicated loans come with more complex documentation, higher fees, and reduced borrower confidentiality, as information must be shared with all the participating lenders. Additionally, obtaining consents or waivers in a syndicated facility can

41 Ibid. at [30].

42 Adams, D., *Banking and Capital Markets* (College of Law Publishing, 2024), p. 40.

43 Regulation (EU) 2021/168 of the European Parliament and of the Council of 10 February 2021 amending Regulation (EU) 2016/1011 as regards the exemption of certain third-country spot foreign exchange benchmarks and the designation of replacements for certain benchmarks in cessation, and amending Regulation (EU) No 648/2012 at preamble (12).

44 According to the Hong Kong Monetary Authority, Supervisory Policy Manual CR-S-2 Syndicated Lending, at pp. 3 and 4, available at www.hkma.gov.hk/media/eng/doc/key-functions/banking-stability/supervisory-policy-manual/CR-S-2.pdf (accessed in March 2025): "syndicated loans" refer to *"refers to arrangements whereby multiple lenders advance funds jointly to one or more borrowers (e.g. in the case of lending to different funding vehicles within a borrowing group)"*.

be more challenging, as multiple parties need to agree, unlike the streamlined process in a bilateral facility where only one lender is involved. Syndicated lenders also typically retain the right to transfer their interests, whereas the lender in a bilateral facility is less likely to do so, preferring to refinance the loan if necessary. Multiple lenders are also a feature in a **club deal**, which typically involves a smaller loan than a syndicated one that is pre-negotiated and offered to a group of relationship banks. In some cases, the borrower may take responsibility for arranging the club loan directly. Alternatively, an arranger may be appointed to coordinate the transaction. However, where an arranger is involved, the distinction between the arranger and the other lenders is often minimal. For instance, fees are frequently distributed equally among all participating banks, reflecting the collaborative and balanced nature of the arrangement.

The lender commitment from the onset of the transaction is another characterising factor. **Committed facilities** generally require more time to arrange and document and are typically of longer duration compared to uncommitted facilities. These facilities often include a commitment fee, which is usually calculated as a percentage of the undrawn and uncancelled portion of the facility (this is also the result of the facility attracting prudential capital requirements from the onset). In contrast, with an **uncommitted facility**, the lender is under no legal obligation to provide funds to the borrower and retains full discretion to decide whether or not to lend. Such facilities are usually for a shorter duration, with simpler and quicker documentation processes. The borrower's ability to negotiate terms is often quite limited. However, the borrower lacks certainty that funds will be provided, and the lender may cancel any borrowed funds and demand immediate repayment at any time, at its absolute discretion. While an overdraft facility may be committed, it is typically repayable on demand, making it similar in nature to an uncommitted facility.

Loan duration is another key factor in categorising facilities. **Term loans** involve a commitment by the lender to provide a specified sum of money for a defined period, usually between one and five years. These loans can either be repaid in full at the end of the term or through scheduled instalments. Term loans provide borrowers with certainty regarding repayment, interest rates, and loan amounts, which aids in financial planning. The downside of term loans is that once repaid, they cannot be reborrowed, unlike **revolving credit facilities**, which offer greater flexibility. Revolving credit allows borrowers to draw, repay, and redraw funds up to a specified limit throughout the loan term. This facility operates like a hybrid between a term loan and an overdraft, offering a longer availability period but usually at a higher cost than term loans due to the flexibility provided. Revolving facilities are particularly suited for businesses that have fluctuating cash flow needs.[45]

An **overdraft** is one of the simplest and most accessible forms of finance, often used for short-term cash flow management. Overdrafts are usually (but not always) uncommitted facilities, allowing borrowers to draw funds up to an agreed limit, which are repayable on demand. The lack of commitment from the lender makes overdrafts quick and easy to arrange, though this also introduces uncertainty, as the lender may call for repayment at any time. Moreover, overdrafts typically carry higher interest rates than other loan types, and they usually include "clean-up" provisions requiring the borrower to reduce the outstanding balance periodically. As a result, overdrafts are not suitable for long-term or large-scale financing needs, such as acquisitions.[46]

Certain facilities are designed for specific purposes, such as the **swingline facility** and **standby or bridging facilities**. A swingline facility is a short-term, committed facility often

45 Proctor, C., *The Law and Practice of International Banking* (Oxford University Press, 2015) at [20.14].
46 Proctor, C., *The Law and Practice of International Banking* (Oxford University Press, 2015) at [20.04].

used by companies issuing commercial paper. It provides immediate access to funds, typically for periods no longer than a week, and is often activated in emergencies where the borrower requires urgent liquidity. On the other hand, a standby or bridging facility provides guaranteed funds to cover temporary financing gaps when other planned financing, such as bond issuance, is delayed or falls through. These facilities are intended for short-term use and usually carry higher costs, but they offer critical support during periods of market disruption or financial uncertainty.

Loans can also be distinguished by whether they are secured or unsecured. A **secured loan** requires the borrower to provide collateral, such as real estate, equipment, or receivables, to protect the lender in case of default. Secured loans give the lender priority over unsecured creditors in the event of insolvency and can offer better terms, such as lower interest rates or longer repayment periods, as the lender's risk is mitigated. However, securing a loan can limit the borrower's flexibility, as collateral is often subject to use restrictions. In contrast, **unsecured loans** rely solely on the borrower's creditworthiness and typically come with higher interest rates due to the increased risk for the lender. Unsecured loans are common in investment-grade lending, where the borrower's financial standing is strong enough to forego security.

Another common arrangement is the **guaranteed loan**, where a third party, often the borrower's parent company, guarantees repayment. Guarantees offer lenders additional protection, as they can pursue the guarantor if the borrower defaults. These arrangements are particularly useful in group structures, where assets may be transferred between entities, and a cross-guarantee ensures that the lender can recover funds from any solvent group company. However, guarantees must be carefully structured to avoid falling foul of legal restrictions, such as those related to financial assistance under the Companies Act 2006.

Financial Assistance

It is generally unlawful for a UK public company, or any of its subsidiaries, to provide financial assistance for the purpose of an acquisition of its shares unless a statutory exception applies. This prohibition, set out in section 678 of the Companies Act 2006, extends beyond direct assistance and includes any action taken to reduce or discharge a liability incurred by the purchaser – or any other party – in connection with the acquisition. Similarly, section 679 of the Companies Act 2006 makes it unlawful for a UK public subsidiary to give financial assistance for the purpose of acquiring shares in its private holding company, again subject to limited exceptions. This restriction applies not only to assistance provided at the time of acquisition but also to any assistance given afterwards, including measures to reduce or settle liabilities arising from the acquisition.

Breach of sections 678 or 679 may result in both civil and criminal liability.

In terms of borrowers, **investment grade loans** are those extended to borrowers with a credit rating of BBB – (Standard & Poor's or Fitch) or Baa3 (Moody's) or higher, which typically include loans to governments and established blue-chip companies.[47] These loans generally feature lower interest rate margins, typically ranging from 0% to 1.75% (or 0 to 175

47 INTM524040 – Thin capitalisation: practical guidance: the use of credit ratings: investment grade and non-investment grade credit ratings in HM Revenue & Customs, *International Manual* (first published 9 April 2016, last updated 17 January 2025), available at: www.gov.uk/hmrc-internal-manuals/international-manual/intm524040 (accessed in March 2025).

basis points), depending on the borrower's credit rating. Investment grade loans tend to have fewer covenants compared to more highly leveraged loans, reflecting the lower risk profile of the borrowers. They are also often unsecured, relying instead on the borrower's strong creditworthiness. Investment grade loans serve a variety of general corporate purposes, including financing acquisitions and providing backstop support for commercial paper issued by the borrower. In contrast, **leveraged loans** are made to borrowers with lower credit ratings, typically BB or Ba and below. These loans are considered higher risk and, therefore, command higher interest rate margins, which typically range from 0.75% to 4.5% (or 75 to 450 basis points), depending on the borrower's credit rating or leverage ratio. Leveraged loans are commonly employed to finance acquisitions, particularly in leveraged buyouts, but they are also used for broader corporate purposes. Given their higher risk, leveraged loans typically feature more restrictive covenants and security arrangements than investment grade loans, reflecting the greater need to protect lenders' interests.

Finally, the **repayment structure** of a loan varies. Some loans, such as overdrafts, are repayable on demand, meaning the lender can require repayment at any time. Others, like term loans, have a fixed repayment schedule, either in instalments or as a lump sum at the end of the loan term. Loans can also be **amortised**, meaning that the borrower repays both principal and interest over time, reducing the outstanding balance as the loan progresses.

5 FEES IN THE LOAN MARKET

Beyond interest payments and reimbursing the lender's out-of-pocket expenses, borrowers must also pay various fees, which depend on the nature of the financing arrangement and its terms. In bilateral facilities, these fees are typically outlined in the facility agreement. An arrangement fee compensates the lender for the work involved in structuring the loan, usually paid either upon signing or at the first drawdown, and it applies to the entire facility, regardless of whether it is fully drawn, cancelled, or prepaid.

A **commitment fee**, calculated as an annual percentage of the undrawn portion of the facility, is typically paid quarterly in arrears and ceases once the availability period ends, though if this period is short, the lender may waive the fee. Borrowers have limited room to negotiate fees but may attempt to avoid commitment fees while advances are impossible due to unmet conditions precedent or changed circumstances, though lenders are unlikely to agree to this while future advances remain possible. Borrowers might also seek a refund of any commitment fees paid in advance if the facility is cancelled. In bilateral facilities, fees are rarely detailed in a separate fee letter, except for confidentiality reasons. However, in syndicated transactions, fees such as arrangement, agency, and security trustee fees are often outlined in separate fee letters which are treated as private documents for confidentiality requirements.

6 SUSTAINABLE FINANCE AND LOAN MARKETS

The growing trend towards sustainable finance has influenced the development of loan products that are tied to environmental, social, and governance (**ESG**) criteria.

Green loans and sustainability-linked loans (discussed further in Chapter 13) have become significant as businesses and financial institutions attempt to align with global sustainability goals.

The defining characteristic of a green loan is the requirement that its proceeds be used for environmentally beneficial purposes, such as pollution prevention, sustainable water management, or infrastructure for clean energy vehicles, including related and supporting expenditures, such as research and development (R&D). All designated green projects must demonstrate clear environmental benefits, which should be assessed and, where feasible, quantified by the borrower.[48]

Unlike green loans, which require that the loan proceeds be used exclusively for eligible green projects, sustainability-linked loans have no such restriction and are often structured as general corporate purpose loans. The primary incentive for borrowers to enter into a sustainability-linked loan is the potential for a pricing adjustment based on their performance against agreed sustainability criteria. If the borrower meets its pre-determined sustainability targets, the loan margin typically decreases, providing a financial benefit. Conversely, many agreements include a two-way pricing adjustment, meaning that if the borrower fails to meet its targets, the margin will increase.

Compared to green loans, sustainability-linked loans offer greater flexibility, which has contributed to their growing popularity in recent years. These loans have made the sustainable finance market more accessible, particularly for companies that do not have specific green projects to finance but still wish to demonstrate a commitment to sustainability.[49]

7 SOME TAX ISSUES

The lending and borrowing of money fall under the loan relationship rules in Part 5 of the Corporation Tax Act 2009. These rules[50] provide the framework for the taxation of corporate debt and associated interest payments.[51] Moreover, the UK tax landscape for banks has been influenced by the introduction of a voluntary Code of Practice for Banks by the HM Revenue & Customs (**HMRC**).[52] While adherence to the code is not legally mandated, it is understood that all major banks in the UK have signed up. The code aims to ensure that banks comply with the "spirit of the law" in addition to its strict letter, thereby fostering greater transparency and ethical compliance. The potential impact of this requirement is significant, as it may limit banks' certainty when structuring transactions and increase the need for consultation with HMRC, which could affect transaction timelines. Moreover, the HMRC is empowered to publish an annual report on the code's operation, potentially naming non-compliant entities, thus adding a layer of public accountability for banks that do not adhere to the code's principles.

When entering into a new loan, borrowers must consider several significant issues that could affect their financial and tax positions. The most critical concern, particularly for borrowers, is ensuring that any interest payable on the loan remains deductible for tax purposes. This means structuring the debt to avoid falling foul of anti-avoidance provisions that could treat interest as a non-deductible distribution under sections 1000 and 1015

48 See 'Green Loan Principles' (February 2023), available at www.lma.eu.com/application/files/4716/7715/0338/Green_Loan_Principles_23_February_2023.pdf (accessed in March 2025).

49 See 'Sustainability Linked Loan Principles' (May 2021), available at www.lma.eu.com/application/files/8416/2210/4806/Sustainability_Linked_Loan_Principles.pdf (accessed in March 2025).

50 The treatment of loans between connected parties (i.e., where one company controls the other or they are part of the same group) is outside the scope of this discussion. For the purposes of sections 348 and 466 of the Corporation Tax Act 2010, there is a connection between two companies if one controls the other or both are controlled by a third person. The term "control" is defined in section 472 Corporation Tax Act 2010 and is similar to the definition in section 1124 Corporation Tax Act 2010 in that it requires an ability to secure that the affairs of the company are carried out in accordance with the controlling party's wishes.

51 Southern, D., *Taxation of Loan Relationships and Derivative Contracts – Supplement to the 10th Edition* (Bloomsbury Professional, 2020).

52 See www.gov.uk/hmrc-internal-manuals/banking-manual/bkm500000 (accessed in March 2025).

of the Corporation Tax Act 2010, particularly where results-dependent interest or limited recourse financing is involved. In such cases, borrowers typically seek assurances that any risk of distribution treatment has been mitigated before proceeding.

For lenders, the treatment for the purposes of corporation tax, withholding tax, value added tax, stamp (or transfer) taxes, and certain reporting requirements, with respect to outbound loans (i.e., by UK lenders to non-UK borrowers) and for inbound loans (i.e., by non-UK lenders to UK borrowers) is an issue which is often scrutinised.

The said treatment is dependent upon two distinct scenarios: first, when a UK lender, subject to UK corporation tax, extends a loan to a non-UK borrower who is not tax resident in the UK and does not conduct business there, including loans by the UK permanent establishment of a non-UK resident lender;[53] second, when a non-UK resident lender with no UK presence other than lending to a UK borrower lends to a UK borrower subject to UK corporation tax.

A UK resident lender, or a non-UK resident lender operating through a UK permanent establishment, is subject to UK corporation tax on profits derived from its lending activities.[54] Determining whether a company is a UK tax resident or has a UK permanent establishment involves specific criteria. While lending to a UK borrower does not automatically establish a permanent UK establishment, the presence and involvement of staff in the UK during loan negotiations or management could trigger such an establishment.[55]

The taxation of a lender's profits in the UK is subject to several exceptions. Firstly, a UK resident lender may be exempt from UK tax on the profits derived from its lending activities if the lending occurs through a non-UK permanent establishment and the lender has opted for the "branch profits" exemption.[56] Secondly, interest received by the lender may not be subject to UK tax if the lender is not a bank or an entity engaged in a trade involving the lending of money and if the interest is classified as a distribution for UK tax purposes.

The "UK corporate exemption" from withholding tax, however, does not extend to interest payments made to lenders that are not companies – such as individuals – even if they are UK tax residents or lending through a UK permanent establishment. Further, the rules for determining the place of supply of services for VAT purposes differ based on whether the recipient is a business.

Non-corporation taxpayers, such as individuals, may act in a non-business capacity, and the place of supply of services to non-business recipients is generally where the supplier is based, though exceptions exist (for example, land-related services). Value added tax (**VAT**) charged to non-business persons is often irrecoverable, creating a potential incentive to source services from jurisdictions with lower VAT rates. Additionally, individuals – whether acting as lenders or borrowers – are not subject to the loan relationship regime that applies to

53 Pursuant to Sections 1141 and 1142 of the Corporation Tax Act 2010, a non-UK tax resident company has a UK permanent establishment if either: (a) it has a fixed UK place of business through which its business is wholly or partly carried on. A fixed place of business includes: (i) a place of management; (ii) a branch; (iii) an office; (iv) a factory; (v) a workshop; (vi) an installation or structure for the exploration of natural resources; (vii) a mine, an oil or gas well, a quarry or any other place of extraction of natural resources; and (viii) a building site or construction or installation project. OR (b) An agent acting on behalf of the company has, and habitually exercises in the UK, authority to do business on the company's behalf and that agent is not of independent status acting in the ordinary course of its business. This form of permanent establishment is referred to as a dependent agent's permanent establishment for the exclusion of agents of independent status (including some brokers, investment managers, and Lloyd's agents).

54 As outlined in sections 5 and 19 of the Corporation Tax Act 2009.

55 Southern, D., *Taxation of Loan Relationships and Derivative Contracts – Supplement to the 10th Edition* (Bloomsbury Professional, 2020).

56 Bramwell, R., James, A., Hardwick, M. and Lindsay, J., *Taxation of Companies and Company Reconstructions* (Sweet & Maxwell, 2025), ch R6.

corporation tax payers. Instead, income tax principles govern how interest received by an individual lender is taxed and whether interest payable by an individual borrower is tax-deductible. This distinct tax treatment can affect both the structure and the tax efficiency of the loan arrangement.

7.1 Loan Relationships from a UK Tax Perspective

The loan relationships regime, established under Parts 5 and 6 of the Corporation Tax Act 2009, governs the tax treatment of amounts arising from loans and other financing arrangements for UK corporation tax purposes. This regime provides a comprehensive framework for addressing the tax implications of debt for corporation taxpayers. To qualify as a loan relationship, two key conditions must be satisfied: first, there must be a "money debt", and second, the debt must arise from either a "transaction for the lending of money" or the issuance of an instrument that represents security for the debt or the rights of a creditor in respect of that debt.

A "money debt" is defined as a debt that must be settled either by the payment of money, including foreign currency or by the transfer of another money debt or shares. In addition, the debt amount can fluctuate over time. The "transaction for the lending of money" requirement is generally straightforward for standard lending arrangements but can be more complex for other types of financial transactions. In *HSBC Life (UK) Ltd v Stubbs* [2002] STC (SCD) 9, the court found that economic equivalence to a loan does not necessarily constitute a loan relationship,[57] particularly in cases involving hedging obligations rather than the advancement of money.[58] The nature of the transaction must be examined in detail to determine whether it qualifies as a loan accordingly in *Chow Yoong Hong v Choong Fah Rubber Manufactory* [1962] AC 209, Lord Devlin underscored that the actual nature of an agreement, rather than its form, determines whether it constitutes a loan. A transaction involving an outstanding purchase price, as discussed in *Ramsden v IRC* [1957] 37 TC 619, may not automatically be considered a loan relationship without further evidence of lending.

A debt is also treated as arising from a loan relationship if it involves the issuance of an instrument that represents security for the debt or the rights of the creditor. Although the term "instrument" is not explicitly defined within the loan relationships legislation, it is broadly interpreted to include most written documents issued to secure a debt. However, a legal charge over an asset issued to secure a debt would fall within the scope of the loan relationships regime. Several cases provide examples of what constitutes a loan relationship. For instance, a loan to a subsidiary is considered a loan relationship, while a capital contribution is not. Similarly, a credit facility qualifies, but an outstanding purchase price typically does not unless additional conditions apply. Loan notes also create loan relationships, but dividends on shares do not. In *Greene King plc v HMRC* [2016] EWCA Civ 782, the Court of Appeal confirmed that when a parent company assigns its right to receive interest from a

57 *"It emerges clearly, therefore, that the mere economic equivalence of a transaction to a loan does not show that it is a loan. The authorities show, equally – as Chitty comments – that the concept of 'loan' or 'lending' may vary from statute to statute if a particular meaning is adopted. In the case of Ch II of Pt IV of the 1996 Act, the concept of a 'loan relationship' is certainly unique to this statute but it does not appear that the underlying notion of the lending of money is to be seen in any way differently from that in which it would be seen generally. The contrary is the case; by specifically referring to the concept of 'a transaction for the lending of money', s 81(1)(b) evidently intends to confine a concept whose extent may otherwise be uncertain within well-known and ascertainable bounds . . . In our judgment, it is impossible to conclude that any of the parties to these transactions thought that they were lenders or borrowers, or that they intended that to be the case"*. Ibid. at paras 71 and 73.

58 In *MJP Media Services Ltd v HMRC* [2012] EWCA Civ 1558 the Court of Appeal emphasised the importance of accurately characterising intra-group transactions.

loan to a subsidiary, the amounts received by the subsidiary from the debtor arise from a loan relationship.

7.2 Withholding Taxes

A withholding tax is essentially a mechanism for tax collection, requiring the payor (typically the borrower) to deduct a portion of the payment made to the payee (the lender), which is then paid to the tax authorities. The withheld amount represents the payee's tax liability on that payment.

Jurisdictions impose withholding taxes for several key reasons, primarily to enhance tax collection efficiency, improve cash flow for tax authorities, and mitigate tax evasion risks. One of the main advantages of withholding taxes is that they provide a reliable mechanism for tax authorities to collect revenue, particularly when payments are made to foreign entities. By requiring the payer to deduct tax at the source before remitting funds to the recipient, tax authorities ensure that revenue is collected upfront, reducing the risk of non-compliance.[59]

From a financial market standpoint, withholding taxes is generally viewed unfavourably. While tax authorities benefit from earlier cash flow, the lender suffers a disadvantage by receiving less income upfront, which could have otherwise earned a return. Additionally, withholding taxes are applied on a gross basis, meaning that the tax is deducted without accounting for any expenses incurred by the lender. This can lead to a disproportionately high tax burden for the lender, making the lending arrangement less attractive. The impact is particularly significant when the lender is not subject to tax on a net income basis in the borrower's jurisdiction, as this prevents it from offsetting the withholding tax against local tax liabilities. Additionally, if the lender is unable to claim full foreign tax credit relief in its home country, the withholding tax effectively becomes an unrecoverable cost, further increasing the overall tax liability. The situation is exacerbated when the lender is not eligible for a tax exemption or reduction under an applicable income tax treaty, leaving it exposed to the full withholding tax rate imposed by the borrower's jurisdiction. Loan agreements generally address withholding tax issues through a **"tax gross-up" provision**, which requires the borrower to pay an additional amount to ensure the lender receives the full payment as if no tax had been withheld. This provision is critical in cross-border financing arrangements, where withholding taxes are more likely to apply.[60]

The UK operates a comprehensive system requiring the withholding of tax on payments of interest, particularly where such payments are made by companies. Under section 874 of the Income Tax Act 2007, companies are generally required to withhold income tax at the basic rate of 20% from any payment of "yearly interest". This obligation extends beyond companies to include local authorities, partnerships with a corporate member, and individuals making payments to recipients whose "usual place of abode" is outside the UK. Moreover, under section 874(1) and (2), the obligation to withhold tax is imposed on any party through whom such payments are made.

For these purposes, the definition of "interest" is interpreted broadly, covering not only payments that fall within the conventional meaning of interest but also certain premium payments. The distinction between "yearly interest" and other forms of interest is crucial in determining

59 Southern, D., *Taxation of Loan Relationships and Derivative Contracts – Supplement to the 10th Edition* (Bloomsbury Professional, 2020), Chapter 1, Section I.

60 Proctor, C., *The Law and Practice of International Banking* (Oxford University Press, 2015) at [20.33].

whether withholding tax applies. If a loan is either intended or capable of lasting beyond a year, the interest will be classified as "yearly" and, therefore, subject to withholding tax.

For withholding tax to apply, the interest must arise in the UK. In other words, it must have a "UK source", as confirmed in *Westminster Bank Executor and Trustee Co and Channel Islands Ltd v National Bank of Greece SA* [1971] AC 945, where it was determined that the location of the source of the interest is pivotal in determining whether UK withholding applies. However, the imposition of UK withholding tax does not require the recipient to be within the UK tax charge concerning the interest itself. This point was explored in *Hargreaves Property Holdings Ltd v HMRC* [2024] EWCA Civ 365, which involved an arrangement involving cycles of loan assignments, repayments, and repeated advances. The central issue was whether the exemption from withholding tax in section 933 of the Income Tax Act 2007 could be applied when the recipient of the interest was a UK-resident entity. The court found that it could not because the recipient had no real beneficial entitlement to the interest.

7.3 US Federal Withholding Tax Rules

Under US law, foreign lenders are subject to a 30% federal withholding tax on US source interest unless an exemption applies. US source interest includes payments made by US corporations, residents, or partnerships, as well as by US branches of foreign corporations. Foreign lenders generally incur this tax at the time interest is paid, or in the case of original issue discount (OID), when the debt is redeemed or sold.

Two key exemptions from the US federal withholding tax on interest apply to certain foreign lenders, reducing or eliminating their tax liability under specific conditions.

The portfolio interest exemption provides relief from withholding tax on non-contingent US-source interest payments made to foreign lenders, provided that specific requirements are met. One of the primary conditions is that the lender must be unrelated to the borrower, meaning it cannot own 10% or more of the borrower's voting shares. This exemption is particularly significant in cross-border lending, as it facilitates access to the US debt market by reducing the tax burden on foreign investors.

Another important exemption applies to effectively connected income. Foreign lenders that are engaged in a US trade or business may qualify for a withholding tax exemption if the interest income they receive is deemed to be effectively connected with that business. Instead of being subject to withholding tax, these lenders are taxed on a net income basis, similar to US residents, allowing them to deduct expenses associated with earning the interest income. This treatment ensures that foreign lenders with a substantial business presence in the United States are taxed in a manner consistent with domestic entities rather than facing automatic withholding.

Loan agreements are often structured to ensure that payments qualify for the portfolio interest exemption, which typically requires the loan to be in "registered form" and for lenders to provide IRS Form W-8BEN to certify non-US status. If a lender cannot qualify for this exemption, the loan agreement must address the potential 30% withholding tax and include provisions to mitigate its impact, either through gross-up obligations or treaty-based tax reductions.

The Foreign Account Tax Compliance Act 2010 (**FATCA**) adds another layer of complexity, imposing a 30% withholding tax on certain payments made to foreign financial institutions or non-financial foreign entities that do not comply with FATCA's information reporting requirements. This tax applies to payments of US-source interest, even if the lender would otherwise qualify for an exemption under other tax provisions, such as the portfolio interest exemption. Loan agreements, therefore, typically include provisions that specifically carve out FATCA-related withholding from gross-up obligations and require foreign lenders to provide documentation demonstrating FATCA compliance.[61]

8 CROSS-BORDER LENDING: EXPANSION, RISKS, AND LEGAL CHALLENGES

Despite recent shifts away from globalisation and free trade in certain sectors, cross-border lending has witnessed a significant surge over the past two decades, evidenced by the dramatic rise in both the volume of loans and the number of market participants involved in these transactions. According to data from the Bank for International Settlements, the outstanding stock of cross-border loans has increased from approximately $1.7 trillion in 1995 to over $41 trillion as of September 2024.[62]

Cross-border lending presents unique challenges, particularly when it comes to understanding the creditworthiness of a borrower and assessing country risk. Country risk comprises a blend of political, economic, and legal risks, the significance of which varies depending on the country. A crucial aspect of country risk is legal risk, which encompasses the possibility that the legal environment in a foreign jurisdiction may adversely impact the enforceability of loan agreements or the overall recovery process for lenders. Legal risk, alongside tax considerations, is central to structuring cross-border loan transactions, as it defines the degree to which lenders can rely on the enforceability of the "pile of paper" that constitutes the loan agreement.

In the context of cross-border lending, legal risk can be broadly divided into two categories: enforcement risk and law reform risk. Enforcement risk refers to the ability of a lender to enforce loan agreements, obtain judgements, and recover debts in the borrower's jurisdiction. This risk is exacerbated when a foreign jurisdiction's legal system does not align with international norms or when legal institutions are weak, inefficient, or subject to political influence. For example, a US lender seeking to enforce a loan agreement against a non-US borrower may rely on either the courts of New York or the courts in the borrower's home jurisdiction. In both scenarios, the lender is exposed to the legal institutions of the borrower's jurisdiction, which may create significant uncertainty if these institutions lack independence or are prone to corruption. Even in jurisdictions that have modernised their commercial laws, enforcement risk may remain high if their legal institutions have not fully developed.

Law reform risk arises when the legal framework in a borrower's jurisdiction changes in ways that negatively impact the lender's rights or expectations. This risk is heightened in periods of systemic crisis, where governments may alter laws to protect domestic interests, often to the detriment of foreign creditors. A notable example occurred during Argentina's 2002 financial crisis, when the government enacted laws that converted US dollar-denominated obligations into Argentine pesos, significantly diminishing the value of foreign lenders' loans due to an unfavourable fixed exchange rate. Lenders exposed to such risks must factor in the potential for sudden and arbitrary legal changes when assessing the pricing of loans and may seek to mitigate these risks through specific structuring measures.

While measuring legal risk is not an exact science, various tools can provide a relative sense of one country's legal risk compared to another. Sovereign ratings, for instance, offer

61 Proctor, C., *The Law and Practice of International Banking* (Oxford University Press, 2015) at [20.35].
62 See the BIS' Statistical release: BIS international banking statistics and global liquidity indicators at end-September 2024, available at www.bis.org/statistics/rppb2501.pdf (accessed in March 2025).

a systemic view of a country's economic health and potential for systemic stress, which can indirectly affect legal risk. However, sovereign ratings are not always accurate indicators of a country's enforcement risk, as they primarily reflect the likelihood of default on sovereign debt rather than the efficiency or fairness of legal institutions. Sovereign bond spreads and credit default swap (**CDS**) prices can similarly provide insights into a country's economic stability, but they do not always correlate directly with legal risks in private lending. More specialised analyses, such as recovery rates after default, may offer better insights into the strength of legal institutions, although recovery outcomes are influenced by numerous factors beyond legal risk, including the nature of the default and the composition of the borrower pool.

Given these measurement limitations, lenders often turn to practical tools to mitigate legal risk in cross-border transactions. The inclusion of both governing law and jurisdiction clauses in their contract avoids potential legal uncertainty. Lenders frequently prefer loan agreements governed by New York or English law, as these legal systems are considered stable, sophisticated, and predictable. However, while the loan agreement may be governed by such laws, collateral agreements are generally subject to the law of the jurisdiction in which the collateral is located, which can expose lenders to the legal risks of the borrower's home country. To manage this, lenders may seek additional security, such as requiring guarantees from entities in risk-free jurisdictions or pledging assets located outside the borrower's jurisdiction to avoid reliance on local courts for enforcement.

In any event, clearly defined governing law and jurisdiction clauses provide certainty and predictability, reducing the risk of procedural complications and ensuring that any disputes are resolved efficiently and in accordance with the agreed legal framework.[63] A well-drafted governing law clause is crucial in minimising uncertainty and reducing the risk of costly disputes over which substantive law governs the parties' contractual rights and obligations. Agreeing on jurisdiction at the outset of a contractual relationship allows the parties to determine which country's courts will have the authority to hear disputes arising from the contract. It may be added that the effectiveness of a jurisdiction clause depends on the practical ability to serve proceedings on the defendant within that jurisdiction. The rules governing whether a claim may be served outside the jurisdiction – either with or without the court's permission – are complex, and the procedure involved can be both costly and time-consuming. To circumvent the difficulties associated with serving proceedings abroad, it is common practice, where a party to an agreement containing an English jurisdiction clause does not have a registered office in England and Wales, for the other party to require the appointment of a process agent. This agent is authorised to accept service of proceedings within the jurisdiction. For instance, in a scenario where an English lender extends credit to a foreign borrower, it is standard for the loan agreement to include, as a condition precedent, evidence that a process agent has been duly appointed and has accepted such an appointment.

In some cases, partnering with multilateral development banks or export credit agencies (ECAs) can provide added comfort to lenders in high-risk jurisdictions. The involvement of these quasi-governmental institutions may reduce the risk of arbitrary legal reforms or unfair treatment in the event of restructuring, given their political influence. However, private lenders should be aware that multilateral institutions may have broader objectives beyond financial recovery, such as maintaining diplomatic relations or promoting environmental or social policies, which can sometimes complicate negotiations.

63 See, for example, *Berrocal v Warner Chappell Music Ltd (unreported)*, 3 October 2017, (IPEC), where the defendants unsuccessfully argued that a New York governing law clause could also be construed as a New York jurisdiction clause.

Exchange control risk is also a critical consideration in cross-border financing, as it refers to the potential limitations and regulatory hurdles imposed by a jurisdiction on the movement of foreign currency across its borders. Many countries implement exchange controls to regulate the inflow and outflow of foreign currency, maintain economic stability, and protect domestic currency reserves. For lenders and borrowers involved in international transactions, this risk manifests in various ways, including restrictions on the transfer of loan proceeds, repayment of debt, or enforcement of security. Exchange control regulations can delay or prevent the conversion of local currency into foreign currency or restrict the repatriation of funds by foreign lenders, creating significant obstacles to fulfilling loan obligations. In some jurisdictions, foreign exchange transactions require prior approval from the central bank or relevant authorities, and any violation of these controls can result in severe penalties, including fines or nullification of the contract. Moreover, sudden changes in exchange control policies, often triggered by economic or political instability, can further exacerbate these risks by unexpectedly altering the terms under which cross-border payments are made. As a result, lenders must carefully assess the regulatory environment of the borrower's jurisdiction, including the likelihood of exchange controls being enforced or tightened, and implement strategies such as offshore escrow accounts or securing guarantees from entities in more stable jurisdictions to mitigate exchange control risk in cross-border financing arrangements.[64]

Understanding the full array of potential critical junctures remains a crucial aspect of assessing and managing legal risk in cross-border lending transactions. A few selected cross-border issues on loans with respect to selected European jurisdictions, such as China, India, and Japan, are now considered.

9 FRANCE, GERMANY, IRELAND, ITALY, AND THE EU

Cross-border lending presents a number of regulatory challenges and requirements across different jurisdictions. Each of these jurisdictions has its own legal framework governing the ability of foreign lenders to operate within its borders, as well as the conditions under which security interests and guarantees can be granted. Understanding these frameworks is essential for foreign lenders seeking to engage in lending activities, take security, or enforce guarantees in these jurisdictions.

Under French law, any entity that engages in lending on a habitual basis as part of its business must obtain a licence[65] unless it qualifies for an exemption under one of the exceptions to the general requirement. French case law has established that lending on a "habitual basis" requires at least two credit transactions by a lender. A breach of the banking licence requirement constitutes a criminal offence. However, French law provides numerous exemptions to the licensing requirement.

Among these exemptions are credit transactions carried out by certain mutual funds and alternative investment funds. In addition, commercial companies may provide loans of less than three years to micro, small, and medium-sized enterprises with which they have economic links, provided that such lending is incidental to their principal business activities. Further exceptions apply to companies that grant repayment grace periods or advance

64 Basel Committee on Banking Supervision, *Supervisory Guidance for Managing Risks Associated with the Settlement of Foreign Exchange Transactions: Consultative Document* (August 2012).

65 See https://acpr.banque-france.fr/fr/professionnels/lacpr-vous-accompagne/banque (accessed in March 2025).

payments to their contractors, engage in cash management transactions with affiliated companies under common control, or issue financial securities such as bonds, provided that credit transactions do not constitute a regular part of their business.

There are no significant restrictions on the granting of security interests in favour of foreign lenders, although certain types of security, such as Dailly assignments of receivables,[66] can only be granted to licensed or passported institutions.[67] Importantly, there are no exchange control restrictions in France that limit payments to foreign lenders under a security document, guarantee, or loan agreement. However, one should be mindful of potential issues surrounding financial assistance: Article 430–19 of the French Companies' Law provides that a (*société anonyme*) public limited company shall not, directly or indirectly, advance funds, extend loans or provide security with a view to the acquisition of its own shares by a third party.

Finally, French law deems a loan usurious where the overall effective interest rate at the time of granting exceeds by more than one-third the average effective rate applied during the previous quarter by credit institutions or finance companies for transactions of the same nature involving similar risks. This threshold is determined by the administrative authority, following consultation with the Comité Consultatif du Secteur Financier.[68] If a contractual loan is deemed usurious, any excess amounts collected[69] are automatically deducted from the ordinary interest and, if necessary, from the principal of the debt. Where the principal and interest of the loan have been fully repaid, any undue amounts collected must be reimbursed, with statutory interest accruing from the date of payment.[70]

In Germany, foreign lenders must navigate a slightly different regulatory landscape. While obtaining security or guarantees from German obligors does not require a banking licence, lending, and financial services may require authorisation, particularly for non-EU lenders, who must obtain a licence to lend in Germany.[71] Additionally, while Germany does not impose exchange controls, obligations that contravene exchange control regulations of an International Monetary Fund (**IMF**) member state may not be enforceable. German law imposes stringent restrictions on the provision of financial assistance by a company and its subsidiaries in connection with the acquisition of its own shares. This includes, in particular, the granting of security interests over the company's or its subsidiaries' assets – such as pledges over bank accounts, transfers of assets by way of security, or share pledges over subsidiary entities – when provided as collateral to third parties. Such arrangements are considered forms of financial assistance. As a general rule, financial assistance of this nature is only permissible in the case of a limited liability company (*Gesellschaft mit beschränkter Haftung*, or GmbH), and even then, it is subject to a critical limitation: the assistance must not result in the company's assets being reduced below the level of its stated share capital. In other words, the assistance must not impair the company's non-freely available equity.

Under German law, the charging of excessive interest is prohibited, particularly where the lender obtains monetary advantages that are clearly disproportionate to the performance

66 "Dailly" assignments are security interests where a company makes an outright transfer of any claims it may have over identifiable receivables arising out of its professional activity. They are only available where the beneficiary of the assignment is a credit institution (see Section II) that has extended the financing secured by the security interest.

67 Article L313-23 of the French Monetary and Financial Code.

68 Article L313-5-1 of the French Monetary and Financial Code.

69 Under Articles L. 313-4 and L. 313-5-1 of the French Monetary and Financial Code.

70 Article L313-5-2 of the French Monetary and Financial Code.

71 Böhm, K. and Prechtel, A. (eds.), *Banking Business in Germany* (PricewaterhouseCoopers GmbH Wirtschaftsprüfungsgesellschaft, 2023), p. 169.

provided.[72] This prohibition applies when the lender secures such advantages by exploiting the weak position of the borrower or otherwise acts with a "reprehensible state of mind". As a general principle, a court will deem a monetary advantage disproportionate if the interest rate is at least double the prevailing market rate for a comparable credit facility. Where both of these elements are established, the contract is deemed void under German law.

Ireland offers a relatively straightforward regime for foreign lenders. There are no exchange controls that restrict payments to foreign lenders, and foreign lenders are generally not required to obtain a licence to take security over Irish assets, although they may need regulatory authorisation depending on the specifics of their activities. Non-EU lenders may need to consider whether they require a licence to purchase loans made to Irish borrowers, but in practice, such licences are often unnecessary if the transaction is passive or not conducted on a regular basis. On the other hand, the Central Bank Acts 1942 to 2015 (as amended) ("**Central Bank Acts**")[73] require that any person who carries out "banking business" must obtain authorisation from the Central Bank.[74] The Irish High Court's decision in *Vesta Mortgage Investments Limited v Devine*[75] clarified that by purchasing and enforcing certain "*facilities together with related security and other rights*",[76] Vesta Mortgage Investments Limited was

> *not engaged in any regulated activity which requires a banking licence. It does not carry on "banking business" within the meaning of the Central Bank Act 1971, and, in particular, it does not receive monies from members of the public on deposit or as repayable funds.*[77]

sFurther, Section 82 of the Companies Act 2014 prohibits any Irish incorporated company, public or private, from directly or indirectly providing financial assistance for the purpose of an acquisition (by subscription, purchase, exchange or otherwise) of shares in itself or in its holding company.

Italy's regulatory framework is more restrictive in relation to lending activities. Loans to the public can only be made by banks and authorised financial intermediaries registered with the Bank of Italy (*Banca d'Italia*).[78] In addition to these entities, certain other institutions,

72 It may also be a criminal offence under Section 291 of the German Criminal Code: "*(1) Whosoever exploits the predicament, lack of experience, lack of judgment or substantial weakness of will of another by allowing material benefits to be promised or granted to himself or a third person*

1. *for the rent of living space or additional services connected therewith;*
2. *for the granting of credit;*
3. *for any other service; or*
4. *for the procurement of one of the previously indicated services, which are in striking disproportion to the value of the service or its procurement, shall be liable to imprisonment not exceeding three years or a fine. If more than one person contribute as providers of benefits, procurers or in other ways, and if the result is thereby a striking disproportion between the sum of the material benefits and the value of the services the 1st sentence above shall apply to each of the persons who exploits the predicament or other weakness of the other for himself or a third person in order to obtain excessive material benefits.*

(2) In especially serious cases the penalty shall be imprisonment from six months to ten years. An especially serious case typically occurs if the offender

1. *by the offence places the other in financial hardship;*
2. *commits the offence on a commercial basis;*
3. *accepts promissory notes representing usurious material benefits*".

73 References in this thesis to the Central Bank Acts, as amended, shall be understood as referring to the Central Bank Acts, as amended by the Finance (Miscellaneous Provisions) Act 2015 (37/2015), enacted on 20 November 2015 and including all statutory instruments up to and including the European Union (Deposit Guarantee Schemes) Regulations 2015 (S.I. No. 516 of 2015).

74 See, e.g., section 5 of the Central Bank Acts.

75 *Vesta Mortgage Investments Limited v Devine & anor* [2014] IEHC 109.

76 *Vesta Mortgage Investments Limited v Devine & anor* [2014] IEHC 109 [2].

77 *Vesta Mortgage Investments Limited v Devine & anor* [2014] IEHC 109 at [8].

78 See www.bancaditalia.it/compiti/vigilanza/accesso-mercato/index.html?com.dotmarketing.htmlpage.language=1 (accessed in March 2025).

such as insurance companies and credit funds, are expressly permitted to engage in lending under the applicable regulations. EU banks that have been authorised to grant loans in their home country are automatically permitted to operate in Italy without the need for additional authorisation. However, under certain circumstances, a single lending transaction may be permitted even where the lender is not a registered financial institution. Such transactions are generally allowed, provided that they are not conducted on a professional basis, are individually negotiated, and are not standardised. While the regulation of lending activities is subject to strict controls, there are no specific restrictions on the ability of foreign lenders to take security interests in Italy.

Limitations on financial assistance are also an issue with an Italian company. Since the acquisition or the subscription by such a company of its own shares, for a joint stock company (*società per azioni or S.p.A.*), or quotas, for a limited liability company (*società a responsabilità limitata or S.r.l.*), is prohibited by Article 2358 of the Italian Civil Code (in relation to joint stock companies (*S.p.A.*)) and by Article 2474 of the Italian Civil Code (in relation to limited liability companies (*S.r.l.*)). The prohibition on financial assistance in Italy could encompass all forms of indirect financing, the refinancing of existing loans originally granted for acquisition purposes, and any loans, guarantees, or security provided by a company for the benefit of third parties, where such measures are intended to facilitate the purchase or subscription of the company's own shares or quotas. With respect to joint stock companies (*S.p.A.*), there is, in principle, an exception available in the form of a so-called "whitewash" procedure. This procedure may be used where the financial assistance does not exceed the amount of distributable profits and available reserves and must be authorised by a resolution of the shareholders.[79]

It should be noted that under Italian usury law,[80] the total cost of a loan to the borrower must not exceed a specified threshold, which is updated quarterly for each type of loan or credit facility.[81] Failure to comply with these usury thresholds may result in criminal liability for the lender and could render the loan agreement null and void.

While in **Europe**, most major decisions regarding the structure and content of rules governing financial market activity are now made at the EU level, with the domestic laws of Member States playing an increasingly subsidiary role,[82] there is no harmonised approach among EU member states regarding the regulation of core banking services provided by non-EU firms. To address this issue, Directive (EU) 2024/1619 (CRD VI)[83] will introduce minimum regulatory requirements for the provision of banking services in the EU by non-EU firms. In most cases, the new rules – which will come into effect on 11 January 2027 – will require non-EU firms to establish a third-country branch,[84] with CRD VI setting out provisions for both the licensing of such branches and their ongoing compliance obligations. The new rules apply to non-EU firms

79 This regime was introduced by Legislative Decree No. 142 of 4 August 2008, which implemented Directive 2006/68/EC and amended Article 2358 of the Italian Civil Code accordingly.

80 Law No. 108 of 7 March 1996.

81 Pursuant to article 2(1) of Law No. 108 of 7 March 1996: "*The Minister of the Treasury, after consulting the Bank of Italy and the Italian Foreign Exchange Office, determines on a quarterly basis the average global effective interest rate applied by banks and financial intermediaries registered in the lists maintained by the Italian Foreign Exchange Office and the Bank of Italy, pursuant to Articles 106 and 107 of Legislative Decree No. 385 of 1 September 1993. This rate, expressed on an annual basis, includes commissions, remuneration of any kind, and expenses, excluding taxes and duties, and is calculated based on interest rates applied during the previous quarter for transactions of the same nature. The average values resulting from this assessment, adjusted to reflect any changes in the official discount rate that have occurred since the reference quarter, are published without delay in the Official Gazette*".

82 Haentjens, M. and De Gioia-Carabellese, P., *European Banking and Financial Law* (Routledge, 2015), p. 96.

83 Directive (EU) 2024/1619 of the European Parliament and of the Council of 31 May 2024 amending Directive 2013/36/EU as regards supervisory powers, sanctions, third-country branches, and environmental, social, and governance risks.

84 Article 21c.

that provide core banking services to customers in one or more EU member states. These services are defined as: (i) accepting deposits or other repayable funds; (ii) lending, including both consumer credit and corporate lending; and (iii) the provision of guarantees or commitments.

10 CHINA

When a Chinese borrower seeks to obtain financing from a foreign lender, several regulatory requirements must be satisfied to ensure the lawful execution and performance of the loan agreement.

Any borrowing incurred by a PRC enterprise in the form of "senior bonds, perpetual bonds, capital debentures, medium-term notes, convertible bonds, exchangeable bonds, finance leases and commercial loans" is subject to the Foreign Debt Measures. In addition, foreign debt incurred by overseas enterprises or branches that are "controlled" by a PRC enterprise[85] and foreign debt indirectly incurred by a PRC enterprise[86] are subject to regulation.

The Foreign Debt Measures provide valuable clarification on the definition of "control" for the purposes of determining whether an overseas enterprise falls within the scope of the regulations. Under Article 2, an overseas enterprise will be deemed to be directly or indirectly "controlled" by a PRC enterprise if the PRC enterprise either (i) holds more than 50% of the voting rights in the overseas enterprise or (ii) has the capacity to direct the operation, finance, human resources, technology, and other significant matters of the overseas enterprise.

The Foreign Debt Measures introduce a "review and approval" regime for the regulation of Foreign Debt. All enterprises are subject to a consolidated reporting requirement, meaning that the ultimate domestic holding company is responsible for submitting Foreign Debt registration applications to the National Development and Reform Commission (**NDRC**) on behalf of the entire corporate group.[87]

Exchange controls in China impose restrictions on payments made to foreign lenders under a loan agreement, security document, or guarantee. Any such payment, whether in foreign currency or renminbi, must be subject to State Administration of Foreign Exchange (**SAFE**) registration, and the guarantor's account bank in China may need to conduct a thorough examination and give its consent before the payment can be processed.[88] SAFE approval may also be required, depending on the circumstances. This requirement ensures that payments to foreign lenders are made in accordance with China's foreign exchange control regime, which aims to regulate and monitor cross-border financial transactions.[89]

11 INDIA

External Commercial Borrowings (**ECBs**) are loans or credit facilities provided by foreign lenders to Indian borrowers, governed by the Foreign Exchange Management Act, 1999 (**FEMA**) and the rules and regulations issued under it, including the Master Direction on External Commercial Borrowings, Trade Credit, Borrowing and Lending in Foreign Currency by Authorised Dealers and Persons other than Authorised Dealers (**ECB Guidelines**).[90]

85 The Control Limb, under Article 2.
86 The Indirect Borrowing Limb, under Article 33.
87 Article 11.
88 See www.pbc.gov.cn/english/130733/2830262/index.html (accessed in March 2025).
89 See www.safe.gov.cn/en/MajorFunctions/index.html (accessed in March 2025).
90 As of 26 March 2019.

India operates as an exchange-controlled economy, and under FEMA, there are various restrictions on the inflow and outflow of foreign exchange. The ECB Guidelines regulate multiple aspects of ECBs, including the amount of external commercial borrowing that can be raised, the interest rates and fees that can be paid, and the conditions for prepayment and security creation.

ECBs can be structured as either foreign currency denominated or rupee denominated, with specific provisions governing each type. The ECB Guidelines also stipulate eligibility criteria for both borrowers and lenders. Indian entities that are eligible to receive foreign direct investment under exchange control regulations can raise ECBs, though limited liability partnerships are excluded. Eligible foreign lenders must be residents of the Financial Action Task Force or International Organization of Securities Commissions compliant countries. Pricing for ECBs is capped based on benchmark rates.

The ECB Guidelines also impose restrictions on the prepayment of ECBs, especially if the prepayment does not comply with the minimum average maturity period, which generally must be at least three years. If a borrower seeks to prepay an ECB before fulfilling the minimum average maturity requirements or if an Indian borrower needs to make indemnity payments to a non-resident entity, prior approval from the Reserve Bank of India is mandatory.[91]

The ECB Guidelines also place restrictions on the types of assets that can be used as security for ECBs, with the authorised dealer bank's consent generally required for creating any security interest or providing a guarantee.[92]

End-use restrictions further limit how ECBs can be utilised. Except for certain exceptions tied to the borrower's nature of business and the tenor of the facility, ECBs cannot be raised for real estate activities, investments in the capital market, general corporate or working capital purposes, or for repaying rupee loans. An exception exists for Indian subsidiaries of foreign parent companies, which can raise ECBs for general corporate or working capital purposes provided the minimum average maturity of the ECB is at least five years. Foreign equity holders may provide such loans if they hold at least 25% direct equity, 51% indirect equity, or belong to the same group company with a common overseas parent.

Foreign lenders are not required to obtain specific approval or licences to lend to Indian borrowers or to enforce their rights under a loan agreement. However, Indian borrowers must obtain a loan registration number from the Reserve Bank of India before drawing down on any ECB.

The ECB Guidelines also regulate the creation of security for securing ECBs. Borrowers generally need the authorised dealer bank's consent to create security interests or provide guarantees. ECBs may be secured against immovable property, movable assets, financial securities (such as shares), or personal or corporate guarantees, provided these adhere to the conditions specified under the ECB Guidelines.

12 JAPAN

In general, foreign nationals or foreign companies are not restricted under Japanese law from making loans, acquiring security interests, or receiving guarantees, and there are no prohibitions against taking guarantees from foreign subsidiaries of a borrower. However, certain limitations may apply. If the activity of making loans by foreign lenders qualifies as a "money lending business" under the Money Lending Business Act,[93] they must obtain a money lending business licence. Additionally, a foreign bank wishing to engage in the banking business, including lending in Japan, must secure a licence from the Prime Minister, specifying a single branch office

91 See www.rbi.org.in/commonman/english/scripts/Notification.aspx?Id=850 (accessed in March 2025).
92 See www.rbi.org.in/commonman/english/scripts/FAQs.aspx?Id=1999 (accessed in March 2025).
93 Article 2.1.

as the principal base of operations. Certain sector-specific laws, such as the Act on Nippon Telegraph and Telephone Corporation,[94] impose restrictions on the acquisition of rights by foreign nationals or entities. In these cases, even if security interests can be created, foreign entities may be restricted from acquiring secured assets beyond a threshold ratio of voting shares.

There are also requirements to report capital transactions and inward direct investments to the Minister of Finance via the Bank of Japan if these fall under the Foreign Exchange and Foreign Trade Act (**FEFT**),[95] particularly for executing security documents, guarantees, loan agreements, or foreclosures of security. Since 2020, the FEFT has provided exceptions to the reporting requirement for certain inward direct investments, depending on the status of the foreign investor, business type, and voting share structure. Furthermore, certain payments by residents to non-residents must be reported to the Minister of Finance after the fact, although exemptions exist, such as payments not exceeding JPY30 million or loans under JPY100 million. In some cases, the Finance Minister's prior consent is required for transfers of significant funds between Japan and foreign states, especially if such transfers could adversely affect the Japanese financial or capital markets or undermine the objectives of the FEFT.[96]

13 CONCLUSION

Chapter 8 of this book provides an analysis of bank loan financing, with particular emphasis on the globalised nature of these transactions and the complexities they involve. It explores the variety of reasons why borrowers seek loans, including to support business operations, fund growth, or finance specific projects, and outlines the types of loan facilities available to meet these needs. The chapter provides an examination of loan structures, from simple bilateral loans to complex syndicated loans, highlighting the roles that financial institutions, intermediaries, and regulatory frameworks play in facilitating the flow of funds between lenders and borrowers across multiple jurisdictions.

The discussion extends to an evaluation of the advantages and disadvantages of debt and equity financing. The rise of sustainable finance and green loans is addressed.

The chapter also delves into some of the tax issues related to bank lending, particularly the tax treatment of cross-border loans. It highlights the UK's tax framework under the loan relationships regime in Parts 5 and 6 of the Corporation Tax Act 2009, as well as the withholding tax obligations that arise in cross-border transactions, particularly in the UK and the US. These tax considerations are critical for both lenders and borrowers, especially in the context of cross-border lending, where compliance with tax laws in multiple jurisdictions is necessary to avoid pitfalls such as non-deductibility of interest payments or unforeseen tax liabilities.

Cross-border lending presents unique challenges, particularly in managing country risk, which is a mix of political, economic, and legal risks. The chapter considers some of these risks and outlines how lenders can mitigate them through legal strategies such as choosing stable governing laws like New York or English law.

Finally, the chapter provides a comparative analysis of cross-border lending regulations in key jurisdictions, including France, Germany, Ireland, Italy, China, India, and Japan. Each country has its own legal framework governing the ability of foreign lenders to operate, take security, or enforce guarantees. Understanding these regulatory environments is crucial for lenders engaging in cross-border lending.

94 (Act No. 250 of 1952).
95 (Act No. 228 of 1949).
96 Article 21.2.3, FEFT.

CHAPTER 9

CORPORATE LOAN FACILITIES

OVERVIEW

Corporate loan facilities represent agreements between corporate borrowers and lenders, typically financial institutions, that outline the terms under which funds are lent. Such terms include repayment obligations, interest rates, and various conditions that govern the use of the loan. The structure and complexity of loan facilities can vary widely, shaped by factors such as the borrower's financial needs, the loan's purpose, and the relationship between the borrower and lender.

This chapter focuses on bilateral loans, which are typically the product of long-standing banking relationships and involve a direct agreement between a single lender and a single borrower.

The discussion will examine the key elements that underpin bilateral loan agreements, including the practicalities of drafting and negotiating such contracts and the legal principles that ensure their enforceability under English law. Key components such as conditions precedent, representations and warranties, covenants, events of default, and security arrangements will be thoroughly explored. Each of these elements serves to protect both the lender and borrower by clearly outlining obligations, managing risks, and ensuring compliance.

Finally, an analysis of how these legal and financial principles are applied in practice will be provided. By examining common challenges faced by borrowers and lenders, as well as strategies to mitigate risks and ensure compliance with regulatory and contractual obligations, this chapter aims to provide a comprehensive guide to understanding and managing bilateral loan facilities in a corporate context.

1 BILATERAL LOANS

Bilateral loans are a common form of corporate finance, structured between two parties: the borrower, typically a corporate entity, and the lender, usually a credit institution. These loans are favoured for their adaptability. They can range from straightforward overdraft facilities to more complex term loans, often stemming from established banking relationships.[1]

A notable feature of bilateral loans is the borrower's ability to negotiate terms that restrict the lender's ability to assign or transfer its interest, aiming to maintain continuity with a familiar lender and avoid third-party dealings. This preference reflects the borrower's desire to keep the lender's involvement throughout the loan term. For high-value bilateral loans, however, challenges may arise for borrowers due to the increased risk borne by the sole lender. Unlike syndicated loans, where the risk is distributed among multiple lenders, a single lender in a bilateral arrangement assumes the full risk by itself, often resulting in higher margins or stricter terms for the borrower.

The facility agreement is the primary document governing a bilateral loan transaction, setting out all terms upon which the lender agrees to lend. Typically, it details the loan facility type, fund availability, interest rate, repayment schedule, and conditions precedent, which

1 Ellinger, E. P., Lomnicka, E. and Hare, C., *Ellinger's Modern Banking Law* (Oxford University Press, 2011), p. 773.

DOI: 10.4324/9781032662220-10

must be met before the borrower can draw down. Market practices, such as templates from the Loan Market Association (**LMA**), heavily influence the standard terms in international loan agreements.

Several key provisions define the facility agreement. The loan type and purpose specify the facility nature, such as a term loan or revolving credit, along with the intended purpose, which can be general (e.g., for corporate purposes) or specific (e.g., property acquisition). Fund availability terms indicate when and how the borrower may access funds, often tied to specific conditions. The interest rate is generally linked to a reference rate like SOFR or SONIA plus a margin, with the interest calculation method (compounded or simple) specified.

Repayment terms outline the schedule for principal repayment, including provisions for prepayment and consequences for late payments. Conditions precedent ensure specific requirements are met before funds are provided, with the lender generally retaining discretion to assess their fulfilment. Representations and warranties by the borrower serve as assurances about its legal and financial standing, with breaches potentially leading to termination or default. Covenants provide ongoing protections for the lender, requiring the borrower to operate within set parameters, which may include financial ratios,[2] regular updates, and restrictions on additional debt. Events of default establish the circumstances under which the lender can demand immediate repayment, often due to non-payment, insolvency, or covenant breaches.

1.1 Form and Structure of Bilateral Loans

Although an oral contract, including a loan agreement, is legally enforceable, the absence of a written record can create significant challenges when it comes to proving and enforcing the terms.

If no written facility agreement exists, it will be necessary to determine whether an oral contract was formed, which will depend on the available evidence. In such cases, any additional records of the loan and its agreed terms – such as term sheets, email correspondence, letters, or notes from meetings – should be reviewed. These materials can help establish the key terms of the loan, particularly those relating to interest and repayment.

Under English law, certain transactions or circumstances require a contract to be executed as a deed. However, parties may choose to execute a contract as a deed even when not legally required to do so, either as a matter of convention or to obtain other legal benefits associated with a deed. That said, a standard facility agreement typically does not need to be executed as a deed and is usually signed as a simple contract.

2 For example, see *Torre Asset Funding Ltd & Anor v The Royal Bank of Scotland Plc* [2013] EWHC 2670 (Ch) at [16]: "*The finance structure included two principal financial covenants given by Dunedin in respect of each tier of the lending, reflecting the paramount interest of the lenders in the ability of the borrower to service the loans by payment of interest due throughout the life of the loans (and repayment of the loans at maturity) and in having a satisfactory level of security in place should there ever be a need to have resort to it, if the loans were not repaid: (i) an Interest Cover Ratio ('ICR') covenant, regarding the relationship between the income for Dunedin from the Industrious portfolio and the interest payments due to be made by Dunedin to the various levels of lender, and (ii) a Loan to Value ('LTV') covenant, regarding the relationship between the value of the properties in the portfolio charged as security for the loans and the amount outstanding on the loans. The ICR and LTV covenants were more favourable for lenders towards the Senior end of the lending stack (reflecting the reduced level of risk they were taking in relation to the finance structure) and tighter towards the Junior end (reflecting the higher risk lenders took at the lower levels of the stack). If either the ICR covenant or the LTV covenant were breached, that would qualify as an Event of Default, which could lead to the loans to Dunedin being called in (accelerated) and enforcement against the property given as security*".

2 PURPOSE CLAUSES IN LOAN FACILITY AGREEMENTS

A purpose clause in a facility agreement specifies the intended use of the loan proceeds, acting as a key control mechanism for both the lender and the borrower. This clause may outline a general purpose, such as "working capital", or be tailored to specific objectives like financing assets, property, or company acquisitions. By defining the loan's purpose, the clause helps ensure funds are applied appropriately, reducing the risk of misuse and maintaining transparency. It aligns both parties' expectations regarding the loan's objectives and reinforces the commitment to lawful and agreed-upon uses.[3]

For lenders, the purpose clause is vital to ensure that the loan proceeds are not directed towards activities that could contravene legal standards or the lender's credit policy. For instance, a lender's credit committee might approve a loan for a particular type of asset purchase but exclude others.[4]

A standard purpose clause will generally contain a statement specifying the approved use of the loan funds. While some transactions describe the purpose broadly, such as "general corporate purposes", those with specific aims – like acquisition financing – require that the funds be strictly applied to that purpose. Failure to do so may expose the borrower to significant legal repercussions, including potential claims for breach of contract.

Moreover, in certain cases, a purpose clause can give rise to what is known as a *Quistclose* trust, a fiduciary arrangement established when loan funds are provided solely for a specific purpose. Under this trust, the borrower holds the funds for the lender until used for the agreed purpose. Should the borrower fail to apply the funds as specified, the trust ensures that they remain the lender's property, safeguarding them from claims by the borrower's creditors, even in the event of insolvency.

The *Quistclose* trust was first recognised in *Barclays Bank Ltd v Quistclose Investments Ltd* [1968] UKHL 4 and further clarified in *Twinsectra Ltd v Yardley* [2002] UKHL 12. The key elements include a fiduciary duty on the borrower to use funds exclusively for the stated purpose, the lender's retained beneficial interest until proper application, segregation of the funds from the borrower's assets, and an obligation to return the funds if the purpose fails.[5] As with all resulting trusts, a trust in favour of the lender arises when the lender advances funds on terms that do not fully allocate the beneficial interest. It is not a contingent, reversionary, or future interest, nor does it come into existence only upon the failure of the stated purpose. Instead, it functions as a default trust, operating to fill any gap where a portion of the beneficial interest remains undisposed, thereby ensuring that such interest is not left "in suspense".[6]

When a Quistclose trust applies, the borrower must keep the funds separate from its own assets and refrain from alternative uses. If the specified purpose fails, the borrower must return the funds to the lender, but if used correctly, the lender's beneficial interest ends, converting the borrower to ordinary debtor status. Additionally, if loan proceeds are used unlawfully, the loan agreement may be deemed unenforceable, regardless of the lender's awareness. This principle, established in *JM Allan (Merchandising) Ltd v Cloke* [1963] 2 QB 340 and confirmed in *Spector v Ageda* [1973] Ch. 30, illustrates the necessity of clear drafting and vigilant monitoring to prevent unintended liabilities.

3 Hudson, A., *The Law of Finance* (Sweet & Maxwell, 2013), p. 978.

4 Proctor, C., *The Law and Practice of International Banking* (Oxford University Press, 2015) at [20.18].

5 "*Quistclose – type trusts are a species of resulting trust which arise where property (usually money) is transferred on terms which do not leave it at the free disposal of the transferee. That restriction upon its use is usually created by an arrangement that the money should be used exclusively for a stated purpose or purposes*", per Briggs LJ in *Bellis v Challinor* [2015] EWCA Civ 59 at [56].

6 *Twinsectra Ltd v Yardley* [2002] UKHL 12 per Lord Millet at [102].

Should the borrower misuse the loan proceeds, the lender may invoke its right to trace and reclaim the funds based on restitution principles, particularly when the funds have been misapplied in violation of trust or contract terms.[7] Therefore,

> *a Quistclose trust is a default trust, and it can be moulded or excluded by the terms of the parties' agreements. So, a resulting trust, which arises by operation of law, does not arise if it is inconsistent with the instrument or contractual arrangements under which it is said to be created, or with the applicable context.*[8]

Typically, a monitoring clause relieves the lender of any obligation to verify the borrower's use of funds, specifying that the lender holds no responsibility for overseeing or policing their application. A clause of this nature protects the lender from liability if the borrower misuses the funds, with typical language stating: "*The Lender is not obliged to monitor or verify how any amount borrowed under this agreement is used*".

3 CONDITIONS PRECEDENT

A facility agreement typically includes a conditions precedent clause, accompanied by a detailed schedule listing the specific requirements that must be fulfilled before the loan can be drawn down.[9] The conditions precedent serve to ensure that the transaction documents – including guarantees and security documents supporting the borrower's obligations – are properly executed. Additionally, they confirm that all necessary approvals and consents for the transaction have been obtained and that the lender receives essential documents, evidence, and information required for due diligence, regulatory compliance, or other internal purposes. These conditions often reinforce the representations and warranties made by the borrower in the facility agreement, assisting the lender in assessing the borrower's capacity to repay the loan.

The lender generally retains discretion in determining whether the conditions precedent have been satisfied, which is often expressed in the agreement as a requirement that they be met "*in form and substance satisfactory to the lender*". However, this discretion may be subject to implied contractual limitations, requiring the lender to act reasonably when making such determinations. The extent of these limitations depends on the interpretation of the facility agreement, and courts have established that a lender's exercise of discretion must be honest and rational. This principle was affirmed in *Socimer International Bank Ltd v Standard Bank London Ltd* [2008] EWCA Civ 116,[10] where the court held that a lender's discretion is not absolute and must be exercised in good faith.

In this respect, it is particularly helpful the guidance provided by Lady Hale in *Braganza v BP Shipping Ltd* [2015] UKSC 17:

> *Contractual terms in which one party to the contract is given the power to exercise a discretion, or to form an opinion as to relevant facts, are extremely common. It is not for the courts to re-write the parties' bargain for them, still less to substitute themselves for the contractually agreed decision-maker. Nevertheless, the party who*

7 Hudson, A., *The Law of Finance* (Sweet & Maxwell, 2013), p. 648.

8 Per Lady Arden in *Prickly Bay Waterside Ltd v British American Insurance Company Ltd (Grenada) (Rev2)* [2022] UKPC 8 at [35].

9 Proctor, C., *The Law and Practice of International Banking* (Oxford University Press, 2015) at [20.19].

10 Where Rix LJ stated at [66]: "*It is plain from these authorities that a decision-maker's discretion will be limited, as a matter of necessary implication, by concepts of honesty, good faith, and genuineness, and the need for the absence of arbitrariness, capriciousness, perversity and irrationality. The concern is that the discretion should not be abused. Reasonableness and unreasonableness are also concepts deployed in this context, but only in a sense analogous to Wednesbury unreasonableness, not in the sense in which that expression is used when speaking of the duty to take reasonable care, or when otherwise deploying entirely objective criteria: as for instance when there might be an implication of a term requiring the fixing of a reasonable price, or a reasonable time*".

> *is charged with making decisions which affect the rights of both parties to the contract has a clear conflict of interest. That conflict is heightened where there is a significant imbalance of power between the contracting parties as there often will be in an employment contract. The courts have therefore sought to ensure that such contractual powers are not abused. They have done so by implying a term as to the manner in which such powers may be exercised, a term which may vary according to the terms of the contract and the context in which the decision-making power is given.*[11]

3.1 Legal Effect of Conditions Precedent

While the facility agreement typically becomes effective upon execution (including with respect to obligations relating to fees, representations, warranties, and covenants), the lender's obligation to disburse funds only arises after the conditions precedent are fulfilled.

Failure to meet the conditions precedent may lead to delays in drawdown, but the lender retains the right to waive or defer certain conditions, potentially allowing the borrower to proceed with the loan. Waiving conditions may require the lender to reserve certain rights, particularly if the waiver allows for conditions to be met as conditions subsequent within a specified period. Failure to meet such conditions within the timeframe can trigger an event of default.

In *Bryan Court Ltd v National Westminster Bank* [2012] EWHC 2035 (QB), it was held that a lender who waived some conditions precedent was precluded from refusing further advances based on unmet conditions precedent once part of the loan had been disbursed. Moreover, in *Bank of Ireland v AMCD (Property Holdings) Ltd* [2001] 2 All E.R. (Comm) 894, the court established that a loan advanced before the satisfaction of conditions precedent is still governed by the terms of the facility agreement, reinforcing that lenders must adhere to the facility's terms even when waiving conditions.

In transactions involving multiple drawdowns, such as property acquisition facilities or development finance, conditions precedent may apply to each loan. The initial drawdown will typically depend upon the satisfaction of general conditions precedent, while each subsequent drawdown may require specific conditions precedent related to the particular transaction or asset. In property development finance, funds are often drawn down in stages based on certifications by contractors or lenders. Each stage of the project may require its own set of conditions precedent, such as updated reports, security documentation, or evidence of compliance with project milestones.

3.2 Tailoring and Negotiating Conditions Precedent

Conditions precedent in loan agreements vary widely based on factors such as the borrower's profile, the nature of the transaction, and the lender's specific requirements. These conditions must be tailored to reflect the particular needs of the transaction, considering aspects like the borrower's corporate structure, the loan's purpose, and any unique issues identified during due diligence.

In negotiating conditions precedent, lenders typically seek to draft these provisions as broadly and flexibly as possible, often incorporating "sweeper" clauses that permit them to request any additional documentation or assurances they consider necessary. This flexibility allows lenders to maintain discretion in deciding whether conditions have been fulfilled and

11 Ibid. at [18].

to avoid being limited by any materiality qualifications or restrictions on the representations and warranties that need to be satisfied at the time of drawdown. By contrast, borrowers generally seek to achieve clarity and specificity in order to limit the scope of discretionary conditions and to ensure that the requirements for drawdown are based on objective and ascertainable criteria. Borrowers are particularly concerned that the conditions precedent are clearly defined and unambiguous so that the steps required to satisfy them are transparent and not open to subjective interpretation. They also prefer that conditions be framed objectively rather than subjectively so as to promote a reasonable and fair exercise of the lender's discretion.

Another key concern for borrowers is the timing of satisfaction, as they require assurance that the conditions precedent can be fulfilled within a reasonable period to prevent unnecessary delays in accessing the loan. Where the satisfaction of conditions precedent depends on third parties, such as insurers or providers of reports, borrowers are mindful of the need to ensure that such third-party cooperation is secured in a timely manner to avoid impeding the availability of funding.

4 REPRESENTATIONS AND WARRANTIES IN FACILITY AGREEMENTS

Representations and warranties serve as critical assurances regarding the borrower's legal and financial status at the time of the facility agreement execution and throughout its duration. These assurances generally comprise statements of fact or law relating to the present or past circumstances of the borrower and any other obligors involved. Although "representation" and "warranty" are frequently used interchangeably, they differ legally and confer distinct rights and remedies.[12]

Representations, made before contract signing, are typically intended to persuade the other party to enter the agreement. If found false, the lender may pursue a claim for rescission and damages in cases of fraudulent or negligent misrepresentation, as illustrated in cases like *Bisset v Wilkinson* [1927] AC 177 and *Hedley Byrne & Co Ltd v Heller & Partners Ltd* [1964] AC 465. Warranties, by contrast, are contractual assurances of truth at the time of the contract, where a breach entitles the injured party to damages but generally does not allow contract rescission unless the breach undermines the agreement's purpose, as in *Hong Kong Fir Shipping Co Ltd v Kawasaki Kisen Kaisha Ltd* [1962] 2 QB 26. If breached, the innocent party can seek compensation for losses incurred but must continue fulfilling contractual obligations.

In practice, these distinctions are not particularly relevant in facility agreements, as detailed contractual remedies apply to both representations and warranties if found incorrect or misleading.[13] Generally, representations and warranties are provided by the borrower and often by other obligors such as guarantors or security providers. They are generally made at the

12 Proctor, C., *The Law and Practice of International Banking* (Oxford University Press, 2015) at [20.39].

13 "*The question of whether a clause is a condition is a matter of construction. The court must look at the contract, in light of the surrounding circumstances, and decide whether the intention of the parties, as gathered from the instrument itself, will best be carried out by treating the particular promise as a warranty sounding only in damages or a condition in respect of which the failure to perform relieves the innocent party of further performance under the contract. Thus it is a question of identifying the intention of the parties on the true construction of the contract. Where, upon the true construction of the contract, the parties have not made the term a condition, it will be innominate if a breach may result in trivial, minor or very grave consequences. Unless it is clear that a term is intended to be a condition or (only) a warranty, it will be innominate. The courts should not be too ready to interpret contractual clauses as conditions. The modern approach is that a term is innominate unless a contrary intention is made clear*", in *EMFC Loan Syndications LLP v The Resort Group Plc* [2021] EWCA Civ 844 at [89].

signing of the facility agreement, although lenders often require certain representations to be reaffirmed throughout the loan's term, especially at critical points such as drawdowns, interest payment dates, or even daily in "evergreening" clauses[14] to ensure compliance at all times.

They serve several key functions. They complement due diligence by verifying the borrower's financial and legal status, aid in disclosing any information relevant to the lender's decision, allocate risk between parties, enable ongoing monitoring by repeating representations over the loan's life, and facilitate enforcement when a misrepresentation or warranty breach constitutes an event of default. Additionally, they may act as conditions for drawdowns, where an untrue representation allows the lender to withhold funding until the issue is resolved. The consequences of a misrepresentation can be severe, often triggering an event of default under the agreement if it meets the parties' stipulated materiality threshold. Remedies may include facility termination, drawdown refusal, or security enforcement. Additionally, for fraudulent or negligent misrepresentations, the lender may pursue rescission and damages, as in *Derry v Peek* [1889] UKHL 1 for fraudulent misrepresentation and *Hedley Byrne & Co Ltd v Heller & Partners Ltd* [1964] AC 465 for negligent misrepresentation.

Representations and warranties are heavily negotiated, with lenders seeking broad and recurring representations while borrowers seek to limit their scope. Typical negotiation points include materiality thresholds to limit breaches to significant issues, knowledge qualifiers to limit liability, and carve-outs for specific information disclosed during due diligence.

Their scope is also tailored to suit the specific transaction, influenced by factors such as the borrower's corporate structure, business sector, and lender-specific requirements. The borrower's industry, for example, may necessitate additional representations on environmental compliance, while recent regulatory developments have led lenders to include representations addressing anti-corruption and sanctions concerns. Standard representations and warranties found in facility agreements include assertions on the borrower's status and legal power, compliance with laws, necessary authorisations, absence of litigation, the accuracy of financial statements, and confirmation that no event of default has occurred.

5 COVENANTS IN FACILITY AGREEMENTS

Covenants, or undertakings, are critical promises made by a borrower within a facility agreement, requiring them to undertake or refrain from certain actions throughout the facility's term. Violations can trigger severe repercussions, including events of default, suspension of further loan advances, or even acceleration of the repayment obligation.[15]

Covenants are typically classified into three main categories: non-financial covenants, information covenants, and financial covenants.

Non-financial or operational covenants concern the borrower's internal business conduct and activities, imposing certain restrictions to protect the lender's interests. These may include restrictive covenants, such as a negative pledge prohibiting the creation of additional security interests over the borrower's assets, and positive covenants, which require the borrower to undertake particular actions. Through these covenants, the borrower's legal, operational, and corporate structure is preserved, thereby ensuring the borrower adheres to an agreed framework of responsible conduct.

14 A clause that is automatically extended without amendment, year over year, unless one of the parties provides notice in writing that it is not to be renewed.

15 Hudson, A., *The Law of Finance* (Sweet & Maxwell, 2013) at [32-18].

Information covenants are essential for providing transparency into the borrower's financial condition and operational status. The borrower must regularly supply updates, such as financial reports, management accounts, and notifications of significant events, including litigation or defaults. By furnishing these updates, the borrower enables the lender to monitor its ongoing ability to fulfil its loan obligations, ensuring that any emerging risks are promptly identified. The scope and frequency of these covenants typically reflect the borrower's credit standing, the loan's magnitude, and the lender's appetite for risk.[16]

Financial covenants are specifically crafted to assess the borrower's financial performance, ensuring it remains aligned with the projections presented to the lender when the facility was first granted. These covenants commonly include measures such as leverage ratios, interest coverage ratios, and minimum net worth or net asset value requirements.[17] Through these financial metrics, the lender gains an early indicator of the borrower's financial trajectory, allowing for interventions that can mitigate potential losses and preserve the facility's stability.

5.1 Importance and Purpose of Covenants

Unlike shareholders, lenders lack direct control over the borrower's business operations, and covenants provide an indirect method for safeguarding their investment. By ensuring that the borrower operates within set financial and operational boundaries, covenants reduce the risk of default, preserving the stability of the lender's capital.[18] Additionally, they play an essential role in monitoring borrower performance. Information and financial covenants allow lenders to observe the borrower's status throughout the loan period, enabling early detection of potential financial or operational issues. This ongoing oversight helps the lender identify areas of concern promptly, thereby ensuring that any intervention occurs before minor issues escalate into more significant problems.

Covenants also facilitate risk allocation, as they transfer part of the burden of unforeseen risks or poor business decisions to the borrower. This structure holds the borrower accountable for adhering to the agreed covenants, which, if violated, may lead to legal consequences. In this way, lenders can limit their exposure to specific risks associated with the borrower's operational choices or market fluctuations, strengthening the lender's financial security.

Furthermore, covenants serve as an early warning system. By alerting lenders to any breach or potential deterioration in the borrower's financial health, covenants enable the lender to act pre-emptively. A breach may trigger an event of default, empowering the lender to undertake corrective actions such as suspending advances or demanding repayment. This capability allows the lender to respond proactively, minimising the potential impact of emerging risks.

Through enforcement and control, covenants also give lenders a degree of influence over the borrower's actions without direct involvement in day-to-day management. Restrictive covenants can prevent the borrower from engaging in activities that might threaten the loan's security, such as incurring further debt or disposing of essential assets, thereby maintaining the lender's position.

16 Proctor, C., *The Law and Practice of International Banking* (Oxford University Press, 2015) at [20.40].

17 See The Association of Corporate Treasurers, *A Borrower's Guide to the LMA's Investment Grade Agreements* (ACT 6th Edition, November 2022), p. 261, available at www.treasurers.org/system/files/The%20ACT%20Borrower%E2%80%99s%20Guide%20to%20the%20LMA%E2%80%99s%20Investment%20Grade%20Agreements%20-%20Final.pdf (accessed in March 2025).

18 *Torre Asset Funding Ltd & Anor v The Royal Bank of Scotland Plc* [2013] EWHC 2670 (Ch) at [6].

Finally, covenants can function as a draw-stop mechanism, halting further loan advances if the borrower breaches an agreement or encounters a possible event of default. This feature enables the lender to pause funding, addressing any issues before disbursing additional resources. Through these multiple functions, covenants provide lenders with a structured way to protect their interests while supporting the stability and viability of the lending relationship.

5.2 Consequences of Breaching a Covenant

A breach of covenant typically triggers an event of default under a facility agreement, often allowing for a grace period within which the borrower may cure the breach without further repercussions. If the borrower fails to remedy the breach within this period, the lender may exercise various rights as outlined in the agreement. These rights generally include the suspension of further advances, where the lender can withhold additional funds under the facility, thereby halting any further loan disbursements. Another common remedy is the acceleration of the loan, which allows the lender to demand immediate repayment of the outstanding balance, effectively terminating the original repayment schedule and bringing forward the repayment obligation. Additionally, if the loan is secured, the lender may move to enforce its security interests.

The lender's ability to act on these rights depends largely on the breach's severity and materiality, as well as the particular terms of the facility agreement. In assessing whether to act, the lender also considers whether the breach materially affects the borrower's financial position. In some cases, a covenant breach may not only impact the lender but also involve other creditors or regulatory bodies, especially in instances where the borrower maintains underfunded pension schemes. Under the Pensions Act 2004, for instance, a breach of a banking covenant coupled with an underfunded pension scheme may necessitate notification to The Pensions Regulator.[19] Such regulatory requirements underscore the broader implications a covenant breach can have beyond the lender-borrower relationship, affecting a wider network of stakeholders and obligations.

5.3 Tailoring and Negotiating Covenants

Covenants in a facility agreement are usually negotiated and tailored to fit the specific transaction, the borrower's profile, and the lender's requirements. Lenders tend to impose broad and comprehensive covenants to secure protection, while borrowers aim to narrow their scope to maintain operational flexibility. Tailoring covenants involves balancing these opposing interests, ensuring that the borrower can proceed with regular business activities without undue limitations while still safeguarding the lender's interests. In this respect, some key considerations emerge. First, business objectives must be aligned. Borrowers need to evaluate how the covenants fit with their current operations and future goals. Overly restrictive covenants may impede daily activities or long-term plans, especially if the borrower anticipates significant changes in its corporate structure or intends to expand its business.

Second, the practicality of monitoring covenants is crucial. Borrowers should ensure that compliance is manageable over the life of the facility. Lenders often require periodic financial

19 As specified in sections 69–70 of the Act.

and operational updates, so borrowers must confirm that they can generate these reports within the required timeframes without excessive administrative burden.

Third, covenants often include materiality and exceptions. Borrowers typically seek to introduce materiality thresholds or exceptions to avoid triggering default for minor breaches. Materiality qualifications focus on significant issues, while specific exceptions (such as for asset disposals or new borrowing) allow routine transactions without lender consent. Examples include de minimis thresholds, permitting certain activities up to a specific limit, and carve-outs for intra-group transactions or typical business operations.[20]

Finally, covenants must be consistent with other provisions, ensuring that exceptions to certain requirements are aligned with authorisation stipulations. This consistency avoids potential conflicts within the agreement's terms, creating a cohesive framework that is more manageable and predictable for both parties.

5.4 Common Covenants in Facility Agreements

Facility agreements commonly include a range of covenants designed to protect the lender's interests and ensure the borrower maintains financial stability throughout the loan term. One of the most significant is the **negative pledge** (discussed further in Chapter 10), which restricts the borrower from creating security interests over its assets to secure further indebtedness. This provision safeguards the lender by preventing other creditors from taking priority over the borrower's assets in the event of insolvency. However, exceptions such as permitted security or *de minimis* baskets provide the borrower with limited flexibility to engage in secured transactions within defined parameters.

Another key covenant relates to the **disposal of assets**, which limits the borrower's ability to sell or transfer significant assets, thereby preserving the asset base required to generate revenue for servicing the loan. Exceptions to this restriction typically include disposals of trading stock, disposals made for fair value, and intra-group transfers. Similarly, **borrowing restrictions** are commonly included to restrict the borrower from incurring additional debt during the facility's term, mitigating the risk of excessive leverage. Certain exceptions may be negotiated, such as allowances for pre-approved credit lines or *de minimis* borrowings.

Compliance with laws is a standard requirement in facility agreements, obliging the borrower to adhere to all applicable legal and regulatory obligations, particularly those that impact its ability to fulfil its commitments under the agreement. This covenant often includes specific provisions relating to anti-corruption and sanctions compliance. Lenders may also impose restrictions on **changes to the borrower's business activities** to ensure that the credit risk remains aligned with the lender's initial assessment. This is particularly relevant where the borrower's business operations form a fundamental part of the lender's risk evaluation.

Financial reporting requirements are another essential component of a facility agreement, ensuring that the lender has access to up-to-date information on the borrower's financial position. The standard form of this covenant usually requires the borrower to provide its audited financial statements within a specified period, often 180 days after the end of the financial year, as well as half-yearly financial statements within 90 days after the end of each half-year. Where group accounts are required, the borrower must deliver consolidated financial statements alongside the individual audited financial statements for each obligor,

20 Proctor, C., *The Law and Practice of International Banking* (Oxford University Press, 2015) at [20.39].

including guarantors and security providers. Additionally, the borrower may be required to supply quarterly financial statements, management accounts, and financial projections or cash flow forecasts to provide the lender with a clearer and more frequent view of the borrower's financial position.[21]

The financial information covenant is closely linked to the financial covenants clause, as financial covenants – such as leverage ratios and interest coverage ratios – are generally tested using the financial statements delivered by the borrower. Without a proper financial information covenant, financial covenants would be largely ineffective. In practice, lenders usually require more frequent reporting for non-investment-grade borrowers, often quarterly, to ensure closer monitoring, whereas investment-grade borrowers may be subject to less frequent reporting, such as half-yearly tests.

6 EVENTS OF DEFAULT

An event of default in the context of a facility agreement refers to specific events, conditions, or circumstances that, if they occur, provide the lender with the right to demand early repayment of the facility or to enforce other remedies, even though the facility is not ordinarily repayable on demand.[22]

The events of the default clause serve several important functions. Firstly, it acts as a powerful deterrent to the borrower by imposing sanctions that encourage compliance and the avoidance of triggering an event of default. It also broadens the scope of remedies available to the lender beyond common law provisions for breach of contract or misrepresentation, which can be limited. Under common law, the right to terminate a contract for breach depends on the nature of the term breached – whether it is a condition, warranty, or innominate term. Similarly, remedies for misrepresentation vary based on whether the misrepresentation was fraudulent, negligent, or innocent. An event of default clause thus allows the lender to respond more comprehensively to risks arising during the term of the facility.[23] It effectively penalises the borrower for triggering an event of default and provides the lender with the ability to block further utilisations, thereby limiting its exposure to additional risk. This clause could allow a lender to act proactively, addressing financial issues as soon as they are identified rather than waiting for a more severe deterioration in the borrower's position.[24]

In addition to events of default, some facility agreements include "review events". These are situations that require the borrower to engage in discussions with the lender regarding potential remedial actions or alternative solutions. While these review events do not immediately give rise to enforcement rights, they may lead to consultations on restructuring or rescheduling the debt. The lender may then explore various actions, such as requesting further investigations at the borrower's expense, demanding additional security, imposing drawstops, reducing the working capital facility, increasing the interest margin, or potentially escalating the situation to an event of default, which could trigger the enforcement of security.

Certain occurrences that do not involve borrower fault may instead be classified as mandatory prepayment events rather than events of default. This distinction is often made to avoid triggering cross-defaults under other financing documents. A common example is a change of control, which is typically handled as a mandatory prepayment event. Similarly, illegality

21 Proctor, C., *The Law and Practice of International Banking* (Oxford University Press, 2015) at [20.41].
22 Hudson, A., *The Law of Finance* (Sweet & Maxwell, 2013) at [33–28].
23 Gullifer, L. and Payne, J., *Corporate Finance Law: Principles and Policy* (Hart, 2020), p. 223.
24 Proctor, C., *The Law and Practice of International Banking* (Oxford University Press, 2015) at [20.46].

may be addressed in this manner, with the borrower seeking to characterise it as a mandatory prepayment event to prevent broader consequences under the facility agreement.[25]

As a matter of contract law, the consequences of an event of default, as well as the remedies available to the lender, are typically outlined in the facility agreement itself and may include the right to accelerate the loan and demand immediate repayment, enforce security, or cancel any undrawn commitments. These remedies exist in addition to the lender's common law rights, which might include claims for damages or injunctive relief, but non-contractual remedies are generally limited to breaches of contract, as opposed to non-breach events of default.

A facility agreement also distinguishes between an event of default and a potential event of default, the latter being a condition that, with the passage of time or issuance of notice, could escalate into an event of default if not remedied. For example, a failure to pay interest by the due date typically becomes an event of default only if payment is not made within a grace period, which is often negotiated by the borrower to ensure additional time to comply with the agreement before remedies are triggered. The scope of events of default is typically defined to apply to the borrower, any obligor, and their subsidiaries, although carve-outs for dormant subsidiaries or specific exclusions may be agreed.

Once an event of default occurs, the lender is entitled to invoke key rights under the facility agreement, such as accelerating the loan, cancelling undrawn commitments, or enforcing any security over the borrower's assets. These actions are enforceable under English law, provided they do not impose penalties, such as charging for unearned future interest.[26] Additional consequences may include the borrower being prevented from further borrowings, making dividend payments, or accessing certain accounts.

Generally, the lender's right to enforce remedies requires that the event of default remains "continuing". The facility agreement typically defines this term, meaning the default has not been waived or remedied.[27] Even in the absence of an explicit waiver, a lender's conduct may result in the waiver being implied, and estoppel may also prevent the lender from relying on an event of default if its actions contradict its intent to enforce it.

The lender's discretion in exercising rights is pivotal. While facility agreements often provide a wide range of options, including the ability to declare defaults and accelerate loans, lenders typically avoid immediate enforcement unless necessary to avoid being seen as acting unreasonably or in bad faith. Instead, lenders often negotiate solutions such as waivers, standstill agreements, or amendments to the facility agreement to address a borrower's non-compliance. Courts generally enforce acceleration clauses as long as the lender exercises its rights within the bounds of contractual and common law requirements, but they may find a lender liable for breach if it accelerates a loan without proper grounds or in bad faith. Negotiating flexibility within the event of a default clause is crucial, as a borrower will seek to limit the circumstances in which it could be required to make an early repayment, while lenders will want to include broad default provisions to protect their position and ensure they have early warning of financial distress. For instance, certain events, such as insolvency or changes in the borrower's financial condition, may trigger defaults even if the borrower has not breached the agreement.[28]

Specific events of default, such as non-payment or non-compliance with covenants, are standard, but parties must negotiate materiality thresholds, grace periods, and the extent of

25 Haentjens, M. and De Gioia-Carabellese, P., *European Banking and Financial Law* (Routledge, 2015), p. 184.
26 See *The Angelic Star [1988] 1 Lloyd's Rep. 122, ZCCM Investments Holdings plc v Konkola Copper Mines plc* [2017] EWHC 3288 (Comm).
27 *Mardorf Peach & Co Ltd v Attica Sea Carriers Corporation of Liberia (The Laconia)* [1977] AC 850; *Lombard North Central plc v European Skyjets Ltd* [2022] EWHC 728 (QB).
28 Adams, D., *Banking and Capital Markets* (College of Law Publishing, 2024), p. 92.

lender discretion in determining whether a default has occurred. The inclusion of misrepresentation clauses also serves to protect lenders from incomplete, untrue, or misleading statements made by the borrower in connection with the finance documents. In addition, financial covenant breaches, cessation of business, insolvency, cross-default, and enforcement of security are commonly listed events of default, all of which are tailored to the specific borrower and transaction. Importantly, events of default that involve insolvency, such as those referring to a borrower's inability to pay its debts or the commencement of insolvency proceedings, are often drafted broadly, covering both cash-flow insolvency and balance-sheet insolvency.[29]

Section 233B of the Insolvency Act 1986 (**IA 1986**) prohibits the termination of certain contracts solely on the grounds that the company receiving the supply has entered into insolvency proceedings. This prohibition applies to terminations either automatically, at the supplier's discretion, or by giving notice. However, these protections do not extend to contracts for the supply of goods or services involving certain financial institutions, such as banks, insurers, or investment firms, where either the company or the supplier is one of these specified institutions.[30] There is a further exemption in Part 3 of the same schedule that applies to "financial contracts", covering services such as lending (including factoring and commercial financing), financial leasing, and the provision of guarantees or commitments.

Due to these exemptions, a lender under a facility agreement retains the ability to enforce its rights during a borrower's insolvency process.

Moreover, the Part A1 moratorium provides financially distressed eligible entities with a temporary reprieve from creditor enforcement actions, allowing time for the entity to restructure and potentially rescue the business. During the moratorium, the company remains under the control of its directors but is overseen by an appointed insolvency practitioner known as a "monitor".

Key restrictions imposed on creditors during this moratorium include: (i) preventing creditors from forcing the company into insolvency proceedings;[31] (ii) prohibiting the enforcement of security without court permission (with exceptions for certain types of financial collateral); (iii) disallowing legal proceedings against the company without court permission, except for certain employment claims;[32] (iv) restricting floating charge holders from crystallising their charge or limiting the disposal of charged assets during the moratorium,[33] and invalidating automatic crystallisation clauses during this period;[34] and (v) prohibiting floating charge holders from applying to the court to crystallise the charge or restrict asset disposals.[35]

However, debts or liabilities arising from obligations incurred before the moratorium under financial contracts, including most commercial lending, must continue to be paid.[36] There is no restriction on financial creditors accelerating debt during the moratorium, which could force the monitor to terminate the moratorium if the company cannot meet the accelerated obligations.

29 See *BNY Corporate Trustee Services Ltd v Eurosail-UK 2007-3BL PLC* [2013] UKSC 28 and *Evans v Jones* [2016] EWCA Civ 660.
30 Paragraph 2, Part 2, Schedule 4ZZA, IA 1986.
31 Except for the directors, who retain this power under sections A20 and A24 of IA 1986.
32 Section A21, IA 1986.
33 Section A22(2), IA 1986.
34 Section A22(3), IA 1986.
35 Section A21(2) and (3), IA 1986.
36 Sections A18 and A53(1), IA 1986.

Wrongful Acceleration of the Loan

Under English law, the starting principle is that a contractual agreement is enforceable in accordance with its terms. Consequently, if a company has agreed that a particular act or omission constitutes an Event of Default, the courts are unlikely to look beyond the agreement, and the lender would have the right to accelerate the loan (*Lombard North Central v Butterworth* [1987] QB 527; *Lombard North Central plc v European Skyjets Ltd* [2022] EWHC 728 (QB)). In cases where the Event of Default is clear-cut, such as insolvency or non-payment, the position is straightforward. However, where the alleged default is more subjective or open to interpretation, a borrower may dispute its occurrence or challenge the lender's right to take enforcement action. In such circumstances, the borrower may seek damages or an injunction to restrain the lender from acting unlawfully.

An unjustified declaration of an Event of Default by a lender does not, in itself, constitute a breach of contract; rather, it is merely an ineffective act (*Concord Trust v Law Debenture Trust plc* [2004] EWCA Civ 1001).[37] However, a lender will be in breach of contract if it relies on an unjustified declaration of default as a basis for refusing to honour its obligation to advance further funds. In such instances, the lender will be liable for losses suffered by the borrower as a result of that breach (*Mulvenna v Royal Bank of Scotland* [2003] EWHC Civ 1112).

Similarly, if a lender or security agent wrongfully enforces security, they may be liable for trespass or conversion. Where a borrower suffers financial loss due to the forced sale of assets or the loss of future business profits, the lender may be ordered to pay substantial damages. Additionally, a lender may still face potential liability if a wrongful declaration of default results in adverse reputational consequences for the borrower or triggers a cross-default under other borrowings. This risk arises because cross-default provisions may be activated by a "declared" Event of Default, even where the lender was not justified in making the declaration. As a result, lenders must exercise care and diligence before invoking default provisions, particularly where the consequences may extend beyond the immediate loan agreement.

6.1 Negotiation of an Event of Default Provision

Events of default provisions need to be tailored to the specific circumstances of the transaction, considering factors such as the nature of the borrower and any other obligors, the jurisdiction in which they are established or incorporated, and the type of entity they represent (whether trading or special purpose vehicles). Importantly, the events of default should be limited to circumstances that could materially prejudice the lender's position, either by the borrower failing to meet its obligations or by the lender's risk exposure increasing.

In most agreements, termination upon an event of default is not automatic. Typically, the lender is required to declare the event of default before any termination occurs, allowing the lender discretion as to whether or not to trigger the rights available. In addition, grace periods may be included for remediable defaults, granting the borrower time to address and correct the breach. Automatic termination is not usually in the interests of either party, as it could trigger cross-default provisions in other agreements,[38] potentially pushing the borrower into insolvency.

37 Gullifer, L. and Payne, J., *Corporate Finance Law: Principles and Policy* (Hart, 2020), p. 224.
38 Haentjens, M. and De Gioia-Carabellese, P., *European Banking and Financial Law* (Routledge, 2015), p. 185.

Generally, lenders prefer events of default to be broadly drafted, enabling them to respond to early signs of borrower distress. Borrowers, by contrast, seek to limit the scope of the events of default to minimise the likelihood of premature repayment of the loan. They also seek to remove subjective elements, such as clauses that rely on the lender's opinion or judgement, in favour of more objective criteria. From a borrower's perspective, it is crucial to ensure certainty in determining when an event of default has occurred and to remove any "sweep-up" clauses such as material adverse change events of default.

Lenders, on the other hand, require clarity and certainty in the drafting of events of default, particularly where materiality is concerned. Courts have historically been protective of borrowers, interpreting events of default narrowly. For instance, in *Bank of New York Mellon v GV Films* [2009] EWHC 3315 (Comm), the court considered the validity of an acceleration notice and reinforced the importance of procedural correctness in calling an event of default.

6.2 Events of Default Commonly Included

Non-payment is one of the fundamental events of default[39] and is typically non-negotiable. However, a borrower may negotiate for grace periods in the event of administrative or technical failures. In *Lombard North Central plc v European Skyjets Ltd* [2022] EWHC 728 (QB), Foxton J affirmed that even a small non-payment could trigger an acceleration notice.[40]

Non-compliance with other provisions in the facility agreement, apart from payment or financial covenants, is also a standard event of default. Borrowers may negotiate for grace periods to allow for remediation of defaults. A lender may agree to such grace periods with respect to non-fundamental obligations but may resist including them for more significant breaches.

Cross-default provisions are also typical, whereby an event of default is triggered in one agreement if a default occurs under another. Borrowers may seek to limit cross-default clauses to instances of actual acceleration or material breaches rather than simply any default. Parties' discussions may also focus on excluding immaterial defaults or defaults that are contested in good faith.[41] In *Grupo Hotelero Urvasco SA v Carey Value Added SL* [2013] EWHC 1039 (Comm), the court examined the scope of a rescheduling[42] event of default and considered whether it could be classed as the "roll-over of existing lending into new lending", or it would "constitute negotiations for a debt rescheduling". It determined "*that the evidence shows that the request for an extension was more than a simple roll-over, and happened because of the actual or anticipated financial difficulties which GU faced*".[43]

Insolvency-related events of default are often drafted to capture early warning signs of financial distress. These provisions may include anticipatory defaults, allowing a lender to act before formal insolvency proceedings are initiated. In addition to insolvency itself, there will also be triggers related to insolvency proceedings. This will typically encompass any corporate action, legal proceeding, or procedural step taken in relation to the borrower, with the latter two being particularly significant following the introduction of out-of-court administration appointments under the Enterprise Act 2002. Furthermore, it extends to the enforcement of any security over the borrower's assets, ensuring that secured

39 Chiu, I. and Wilson, J., *Banking Law and Regulation* (Oxford University Press, 2019), p. 139.
40 Adams, D., *Banking and Capital Markets* (College of Law Publishing, 2024), p. 86.
41 Haentjens, M. and De Gioia-Carabellese, P., *European Banking and Financial Law* (Routledge, 2015), p. 185.
42 Where "rescheduling" refers to the formal deferment of debt-service payments and the application of new and extended maturities to the deferred amount.
43 Ibid. at [588].

creditors can take appropriate steps to realise their collateral in the event of default or insolvency.[44] Borrowers often seek to negotiate carve-outs for solvent reorganisations or certain insignificant defaults. In *BNY Corporate Trustee Services Ltd v Eurosail-UK 2007–3BL PLC* [2013] UKSC 28, the Supreme Court clarified the cash flow and balance sheet tests for insolvency, highlighting the importance of assessing the company's ability to pay debts as they fall due and the need for a careful drafting of insolvency-related events of default.[45]

Material adverse change (**MAC**) clauses, often seen as "sweep-up" provisions, allow lenders to respond to unforeseen changes that could affect the borrower's ability to meet its obligations.[46]

6.3 Material Adverse Change

The MAC event of default is designed to capture unforeseen events or circumstances that may not fall within the scope of other specific events of default identified at the time the facility agreement was executed. Due to its inherent vagueness, determining whether a material adverse change has occurred can be challenging, and a lender risks liability if it wrongly calls an event of default under this clause. The uncertainty surrounding what constitutes a material adverse change makes the clause difficult to rely upon with confidence. A lender may opt to draft the clause without requiring any "reasonableness" standard, while a borrower is likely to seek greater certainty by negotiating objective tests or narrowing the scope to events affecting its ability to meet payment obligations or adhere to fundamental covenants.[47]

Notably, a lender cannot rely on a MAC clause for circumstances it was aware of when entering into the agreement. While the applicable principles of contractual construction are not controversial,[48] courts are unable to provide general guidance on the interpretation of

44 Adams, D., *Banking and Capital Markets* (College of Law Publishing, 2024), p. 89.

45 "*Eurosail's ability or inability to pay all its debts, present or future, may not be finally determined until much closer to 2045, that is more than 30 years from now. The complex documentation under which the loan notes were issued contains several mechanisms (identified in para 22(1) to (4) above, the PECO being disregarded for present purposes) for ensuring that liabilities in respect of principal are, if necessary, deferred until the final redemption date, unless the post-enforcement regime comes into operation. The movements of currencies and interest rates in the meantime, if not entirely speculative, are incapable of prediction with any confidence. The court cannot be satisfied that there will eventually be a deficiency*". Per Lord Walker at [49].

46 Chiu, I. and Wilson, J., *Banking Law and Regulation* (Oxford University Press, 2019), p. 139.

47 Adams, D., *Banking and Capital Markets* (College of Law Publishing, 2024), p. 90.

48 "*The applicable principles of contractual construction are not controversial. In summary:– (1) The essential task is 'to determine what the parties meant by the language used, which involves ascertain what a reasonable person would have understood the parties to have meant', per Lord Clarke in Rainy Sky v Kookmin [2011] 1 WLR 2900 at [14]. (2) The objective meaning of the language used in a contract 'has to be assessed in light of (i) the natural and ordinary meaning of the clause, (ii) any other relevant provisions of the [contract], (iii) the overall purpose of the clause and the [contract], (iv) the facts and circumstances known or assumed by the parties at the time that the document was executed, and (v) commercial common sense, but (vi) disregarding subjective evidence of any party's intentions' per Lord Neuberger in Arnold v Britton [2015] AC 1619 at [15]. (3) Words and phrases are not to be considered in narrow isolation: '. . . It has long been accepted that this is not a literalist exercise focused solely on a parsing of the wording of the particular clause but that the court must consider the contract as a whole . . .; and (4) When looking at the wider commercial context, care must be taken to identify the correct context, as observed by Lord Neuberger in Arnold v Britton (above) at [19 & 20]: '. . . commercial common sense is not to be invoked retrospectively. The mere fact that a contractual arrangement, if interpreted according to its natural language, has worked out badly, or even disastrously, for one of the parties is not a reason for departing from the natural language. Commercial common sense is only relevant to the extent of how matters would or could have been perceived by the parties, or by reasonable people in the position of the parties, as at the date that the contract was made' and 'a court should be very slow to reject the natural meaning of a provision as correct simply because it appears to be a very imprudent term for one of the parties to have agreed, even ignoring the benefit of wisdom of hindsight. The purpose of interpretation is to identify what the parties have agreed, not what the court thinks that they should have agreed*'", per Lionel Persey KC in *Finsbury Food Group Plc v Axis Corporate Capital UK Ltd* [2023] EWHC 1559 (Comm) at [115].

MAC clauses, as each case is highly fact-specific and the wording of such clauses varies. However, several cases offer insights into how MAC provisions may be interpreted.[49]

In *Cukurova Finance International Ltd v Alfa Telecom Turkey Ltd* [2013] UKPC 2, the Privy Council held that an event did not need to have an objective adverse effect for a MAC clause to be triggered, provided the lender subjectively believed that such an effect had occurred, and that belief was honest and rational. Similarly, in *Lombard North Central*, where the MAC clause stipulated that "*There shall be default if: (p) in the opinion of the Lender, a material adverse change occurs in the business, assets, condition, operations or prospects of any Group Company or any Credit Support Provider*",[50] the court held that it was unnecessary to demonstrate an objective adverse effect. Borrowers may attempt to negotiate clearer triggers for MAC clauses, using more precise language such as "is reasonably likely to have" a material adverse effect.[51]

Meanwhile, in *Grupo Hotelero Urvasco SA v Carey Value Added SL* [2013] EWHC 1039 (Comm), the High Court provided guidance on interpreting MAC clauses, finding that financial condition should primarily be assessed based on a company's financial information and that any an adverse change would be material if it significantly affects the borrower's ability to repay the loan in question.[52] Furthermore, the court emphasised that changes must not be merely temporary, and the lender cannot rely on facts it knew at the time the agreement was executed. In *Decura IM Investments LLP v UBS AG London Branch* [2015] EWHC 171 (Comm), Burnton J held that a "material adverse effect" meant something that was substantial or significant, as opposed to something of a *de minimis* level.[53]

In other cases, however, the material adverse impact was specifically quantified, in *Kitcatt & Ors v MMS UK Holdings Ltd and Ors* [2017] EWHC 675 (Comm), for example, as being at least 20% in the case of operating income and 10% in the case of revenue. A similar conclusion was reached in *Finsbury Food Group Plc v Axis Corporate Capital UK Ltd* [2023] EWHC 1559 (Comm) upon examination of the meaning of the description of a "*material adverse change in the trading position of any of the Group Companies or their financial position, prospects or turnover" and what is required for the change to occur*".[54]

Since the true construction of a MAC clause must depend upon its drafting and, in common with all questions of contractual construction, the factual matrix of the agreement in question, parties should be careful in assessing that their intentions have been appropriately reflected and that there is clarity as to what would trigger an event of default on the basis of a material adverse change.

Sanctions Provisions in Loan Agreements

Sanctions provisions in facility agreements are critical for lenders to mitigate risks associated with international sanctions regimes (see Chapter 5). Thus, sanctions representations and covenants serve as critical contractual mechanisms that provide lenders with protection and assurance that the borrower is complying with all applicable sanctions

49 Chiu, I. and Wilson, J., *Banking Law and Regulation* (Oxford University Press, 2019), p. 141.
50 *Lombard North Central plc v European Skyjets Ltd* [2022] EWHC 728 (QB) at [119].
51 Proctor, C., *The Law and Practice of International Banking* (Oxford University Press, 2015), p. 411.
52 Per Blair J at [364].
53 At [7] and [31].
54 Ibid. at [11].

laws. These representations are often repeated at various points, such as upon each utilisation of the facility or on each interest payment date.[55]

A typical representation includes a confirmation by the borrower that neither it nor any of its subsidiaries, directors, officers, or employees are subject to sanctions or engaged in any activities that would breach applicable sanctions laws. This assurance usually extends to joint ventures and agents acting on the borrower's behalf, reflecting the need for comprehensive compliance coverage.

In addition, borrowers frequently represent that they are not subject to any ongoing investigations, claims, or proceedings concerning sanctions enforcement by any relevant authority, such as the US Treasury's Office of Foreign Assets Control (**OFAC**) or the European Commission. Finally, they typically confirm that they have established and maintained internal systems and controls aimed at ensuring compliance with applicable sanctions laws and regulations. This representation also includes a commitment to maintain such compliance systems throughout the term of the facility, thereby mitigating the risk of future breaches that could affect both the borrower's operations and the lender's interests.

Borrowers may request qualifications based on their knowledge or awareness, ensuring they are not held liable for activities beyond their control, especially where third-party actions are involved. This is particularly relevant in industries where the borrower might have legitimate business activities in countries that are subject to sanctions but where such activities are permitted under licences (for example, under the United Kingdom's Office of Financial Sanctions Implementation's licences that allow activity prohibited by financial sanctions).

Sanctions covenants extend beyond representations by imposing ongoing obligations on the borrower to ensure compliance with applicable sanctions regimes throughout the duration of the loan. A key aspect of these covenants is the borrower's undertaking not to use the loan proceeds to fund or facilitate any activities involving sanctioned persons or countries. This obligation applies both directly and indirectly, preventing the use of funds in any manner that would breach relevant sanctions laws.

Additionally, borrowers covenant that they will not use funds derived from transactions involving sanctioned persons or countries to repay amounts due under the loan. This assurance is essential for lenders, as it protects them from inadvertently receiving payments that could constitute the proceeds of transactions prohibited under sanctions regimes.

Borrowers also undertake not to enter into any new transactions or business relationships with individuals or entities subject to sanctions.

Moreover, a standard sanctions covenant will require the borrower to notify the lender promptly upon becoming aware of any actual or potential breach of sanctions. Such a requirement enables the lender to evaluate the situation and take appropriate steps to safeguard its position, which may include exercising rights under the facility agreement, such as calling for mandatory prepayment or treating the breach as an event of default.

55 Zilioli, C., Bismuth, R. and Thévenoz, L. (eds.), *International Sanctions: Monetary and Financial Law Perspectives* (Brill – Nijhoff, 2024).

Mandatory Prepayment and Events of Default

Sanctions-related provisions often include mandatory prepayment triggers or events of default. If the borrower breaches a sanctions-related covenant or representation, the lender may require immediate repayment of the loan or may declare an event of default. A typical provision might state that if any of the borrower's business activities are found to involve sanctioned persons or territories, the lender can demand repayment of the entire facility or a portion of it.[56]

In some cases, lenders may prefer that a breach of a sanctions covenant triggers mandatory prepayment rather than an event of default, as this allows for a cleaner exit without the reputational and legal complexities associated with enforcing default remedies.

Illegality and Market Flex Provisions

Lenders may also include illegality clauses that permit them to terminate the facility if, at any point, continuing to lend would result in a violation of sanctions laws. This is particularly relevant where sanctions laws are subject to change, and what was initially permissible at the time of signing may become illegal due to new sanctions or changes in the borrower's circumstances. In such cases, the borrower may be required to repay the loan early or refinance the facility with another lender that is not subject to the same sanctions restrictions.

Additionally, facility agreements often contain market flex provisions allowing the lender to amend the terms of the loan (e.g., pricing or structure) if market conditions change due to sanctions developments. This gives the lender flexibility to respond to shifts in sanctions risk without immediately terminating the facility.

Sanctions Lists and Enforcement

Key to the functioning of sanctions provisions is the inclusion of clearly defined terms that reflect the relevant sanctions regimes. These often include references to sanctions lists such as the UK Sanctions List, the OFAC Specially Designated Nationals List, and the EU Consolidated List of Persons, Groups, and Entities Subject to EU Financial Sanctions.[57]

Where a transaction involves multiple jurisdictions, lenders must ensure that the facility agreement complies with all relevant sanctions regimes. For instance, US lenders will often insist on compliance with OFAC sanctions, even in cases where the borrower has no US operations, because a transaction that involves US dollars may bring the loan within the scope of US jurisdiction.

Enforcing sanctions provisions in facility agreements can be challenging, especially in cases where sanctions are imposed after the facility agreement has been executed. Lenders may find it difficult to recover funds if the borrower becomes subject to sanctions or if the funds have already been transferred to a sanctioned person. In such cases, enforcement may involve complex legal actions, including obtaining licences from sanctions authorities to permit repayments or the realisation of security.

56 Gullifer, L. and Payne, J., *Corporate Finance Law: Principles and Policy* (Hart, 2020), p. 225.

57 https://data.europa.eu/data/datasets/consolidated-list-of-persons-groups-and-%09entities-subject-to-eu-financial-sanctions?locale=en (accessed in March 2025).

7 CHRONOLOGY OF A LOAN FINANCE TRANSACTION

The structure and terms of loan finance transactions can differ significantly based on the needs of the borrower. Despite these differences in complexity, the stages of loan finance transactions and the key finance documents are broadly similar across different types of financing arrangements.[58]

7.1 Commitment and Mandate Letters

A commitment letter, also known as a mandate letter, is a formal document through which a lender specifies the terms under which it is prepared to provide financing to a borrower. Typically accompanied by a term sheet, the commitment letter details the key commercial aspects of the proposed loan. When the borrower signs and returns this letter, it formalises the lender's mandate, essentially securing the lender's role in arranging the financing.

The key terms outlined in a commitment or mandate letter generally include details on fees, specifying the upfront fees due at the outset, with other fees potentially outlined in the term sheet. The letter also addresses the borrower's obligations regarding the provision and distribution of necessary information, including confidential details, which are essential for assessing the financing and finalising terms. Additionally, market flex provisions allow lenders to adjust financing terms in response to shifting market conditions, providing flexibility in structuring the loan. Exclusivity and clear market clauses impose restrictions on the borrower, preventing it from seeking alternative financing from other lenders, thus ensuring that the mandated bank or banks have an exclusive right to arrange the financing. Lastly, the letter typically clarifies the treatment of costs and expenses incurred during the initial stages, setting out how these will be managed between the parties.[59]

Overall, commitment letters play a crucial role in establishing the framework for the eventual loan documentation, providing the borrower with a comprehensive understanding of the lender's terms and conditions for the proposed financing.

7.2 The Term Sheet

A term sheet in a loan finance transaction typically outlines the essential aspects of the deal, such as the parties involved, the loan amount and term, representations, covenants, events of default, as well as guarantees, security requirements, and conditions precedent to loan drawdown.[60] The LMA offers template term sheets designed for syndicated facilities,[61] though many banks have their own internal formats influenced by compliance protocols and credit committee requirements.

It also includes a statement that its terms are indicative only and do not constitute an offer to finance or arrange the facilities. This wording provides the lender or arranger with flexibility

58 Adams, D., *Banking and Capital Markets* (College of Law Publishing, 2024), p. 11.
59 Adams, D., *Banking and Capital Markets* (College of Law Publishing, 2024), p. 14.
60 Chiu, I. and Wilson, J., *Banking Law and Regulation* (Oxford University Press, 2019), p. 137.
61 For example, on 9 January 2025, the Loan Market Association (LMA) published model green loan terms for inclusion in term sheets for transactions structured in accordance with the LMA's recommended forms of facility agreement. The LMA Green Loans Term Sheet complements the LMA's Draft Provisions for Green Loans, which were previously published on 7 November 2024, further enhancing the framework for green lending within the industry.

during subsequent negotiations, ensuring that even if the borrower agrees to the term sheet, the lender or arranger remains under no obligation to provide or arrange the facilities. This is particularly important where the lender or arranger has not yet obtained credit committee approval.

In addition, a term sheet generally specifies that the provision of the facilities remains subject to various conditions, including due diligence on the borrower, credit committee approval (where not yet obtained), the terms and conditions of the commitment letter, and the execution of satisfactory documentation. The requirement for documents to be satisfactory to the lender or arranger further ensures that they retain the discretion to depart from the term sheet during later negotiations.

For the lender or arranger, maintaining maximum flexibility in the term sheet is essential. For example, a term sheet may state that "events of default shall apply, including but not limited to, the following". Such wording provides the broadest possible discretion, preventing any unintended restriction on the lender's rights. However, the more detailed and extensive a term sheet becomes, the more difficult it is in practice for the lender or arranger to deviate from its terms, as the borrower is likely to resist further amendments to terms that have already been negotiated.

A lender may also choose not to include the details of its fees in the term sheet. This could be due to commercial sensitivity or because the fee arrangements are best finalised during the negotiation of the finance documents and the completion of due diligence. Where a formula is used to calculate fees, it is essential that it is accurately drafted to avoid future disputes. The importance of precise drafting was underscored in *ING Bank NV v Ros Roca SA* [2011] EWCA Civ 353, where, albeit on a fairly unusual set of facts, the Court of Appeal held that a bank that had provided an estimate of fees on the basis of a specific method was estopped from subsequently relying on a fees' clause in the final contract that would have allowed it to calculate fees on a different basis.[62]

Care should be taken to ensure that the wording of the provisions is drafted to ensure that the document is not intended to be legally binding except for an agreed period of exclusivity in which to conduct the negotiation.[63] In *RTS Flexible Systems Ltd v Molkerei Alois Muller GmBH* [2010] UKSC 14, Lord Clarke summarised the general principles as follows:

> *Whether there is a binding contract between the parties and, if so, upon what terms depends upon what they have agreed. It depends not upon their subjective state of mind, but upon a consideration of what was communicated between them by words or conduct, and whether that leads objectively to a conclusion that they intended to create legal relations and had agreed upon all the terms which they regarded or the law requires as essential for the formation of legally binding relations. Even if certain terms of economic or other*

62 "*[T]he doctrine of estoppel is a flexible doctrine which can take account of what Lord Wilberforce and Bingham J regarded as the honest and responsible interaction of business parties to a contract. Where there is room for disagreement as to the meaning or effect of a contract but the parties have clearly chosen (or purported to choose) their own understanding of it and have dealt with one another on the basis of that understanding, whether that mutuality is found in a common assumption, or in acquiescence, or in one party's reliance on another's representation, the doctrine of estoppel allows the court in a proper case to give effect to the parties' objectively ascertainable and mutual dealings with one another. This is especially appropriate in a case such as this, where there is room for renegotiation in new circumstances and one party is not obliged to proceed if it chooses not to. Of course, such dealings cannot make a contract out of nothing, where one does not exist, nor can it make a new contract by variation unless the conditions for that are available. However, it can prevent one party from taking advantage of a contractual remedy where an estoppel, reflecting the parties' dealings with one another, would make it unconscionable for that remedy to be exercised. The law should in this way reflect the exigencies and structure of commercial life. The contract is the foundation upon which commercial men operate, and it should remain, for its true construction, unchanged in changing circumstances. However, the parties' dealings with one another in the light of new circumstances may affect their contractual rights so as to make it unconscionable to seek and unjust to permit enforcement of them*". Ibid. at [111] and [112].

63 Chiu, I. and Wilson, J., *Banking Law and Regulation* (Oxford University Press, 2019), p. 156.

significance to the parties have not been finalised, an objective appraisal of their words and conduct may lead to the conclusion that they did not intend agreement of such terms to be a pre-condition to a concluded and legally binding agreement.[64]

Lack of clarity, on the other hand, could lead to unwanted results. In *New Media Holding Company LLC v Ivan Kuznetsov* [2016] EWHC 360 (QB), the High Court held that a document described as a "term sheet" was intended to create legal relations and was, therefore, legally binding. In reaching its decision, the court considered several key factors. The term sheet had been drafted by lawyers and signed by both parties, both of whom were experienced businessmen. Initially circulated as a draft, the term sheet was later amended to include an exclusive jurisdiction clause, specifying that English law would govern the agreement, despite the fact that the company at the centre of the agreement was registered in Latvia. The court was also satisfied that the term sheet was "workable when signed", reinforcing its conclusion that the document carried legal effect. The court emphasised that there is no absolute rule that documents described as "term sheets" must always be regarded as non-binding framework agreements, their legal status depends on the intention of the parties and the specific circumstances surrounding their execution and content. Even where such documents are not legally binding, parties may find it difficult to renegotiate or withdraw from the agreement without damaging commercial relationships or jeopardising their position.[65]

Moreover, in certain European jurisdictions, such as France and Italy, termsheets or heads of terms may be interpreted by the courts as a binding pre-agreement if they contain essential contractual elements, including the identities of the parties, price, and conditions precedent. Consequently, it is crucial that the language used in the term sheet remains clear and consistent in expressing that the document is not intended to be legally binding.

While English law does not impose a general duty to negotiate in good faith, many civil law jurisdictions, including France, Germany, and Italy, recognise such an obligation. In these jurisdictions, the duty to negotiate in good faith typically applies throughout all phases of a commercial relationship, encompassing both the pre-contractual and contractual stages. Signing a heads of terms document can serve to crystallise this duty, making it easier to enforce. For instance, a termsheet that sets out detailed terms agreed in principle could serve as evidence of the proximity of the relationship and the mutual expectations of the parties. This may, in turn, strengthen a claim that a party has failed to negotiate in good faith or has acted inconsistently with the agreed principles. Under New York law, all contracts are deemed to contain an implied covenant of good faith and fair dealing; such obligation would include a promise not to act arbitrarily or irrationally in exercising a discretion contemplated by the contract.[66]

7.3 Credit Committee

The credit committee is an essential part of a bank's internal risk assessment process, ensuring that any proposed lending is consistent with the bank's credit policies and investment strategies.

64 Ibid. at [45]. See also *Astra Asset Management UK Ltd v The Co-Operative Bank Plc* [2019] EWHC 897 (Comm).
65 Ellinger, E. P., Lomnicka, E. and Hare, C., *Ellinger's Modern Banking Law* (Oxford University Press, 2011), p. 790.
66 *Lomas & Ors (Joint Administrators of Lehman Brothers International (Europe)) v Burlington Loan Management Ltd & Ors* [2016] EWHC 2417 (Ch) at [268].

While the credit committee does not interact with clients, it plays a key role in approving the transaction terms.[67]

Credit committees generally comprise executive members with expertise in various risk categories, such as credit, market, operational, or capital adequacy risk. They meet regularly to review and approve new funding proposals or amendments to existing arrangements.

7.4 Due Diligence

Upon receiving instructions, the lender's lawyers initiate the due diligence process, which generally involves several key steps. They begin by conducting searches on Companies House for all obligors, encompassing companies incorporated under the Companies Act 2006 and any overseas companies with a UK establishment. This search includes information on individuals with significant control over a company (PSC), helping to clarify ownership and management structures. Certificates of incorporation, articles of association, and entries in the charges register are also reviewed to ensure that all necessary corporate documentation is in order.

Another crucial component of this phase is verifying that the company possesses both the power and capacity to enter into the transaction, ensuring compliance with corporate governance requirements. Depending on the specifics of the transaction, further searches may be warranted. For instance, lenders are particularly mindful of environmental risks, especially in cases where the borrower's assets include properties or operations with potential environmental liabilities. Due diligence related to anti-corruption and financial sanctions is an essential component, particularly for cross-border transactions, to mitigate the risks of regulatory violations and ensure compliance with international standards.

7.5 The Finance Documents

Once the term sheet is finalised, the lender's lawyers proceed to draft the finance documents, which typically consist of the facility agreement, hedging agreements, security documents, and guarantees. The facility agreement is the central document outlining key loan terms, such as the type of facility, applicable interest rates, repayment schedules, and conditions precedent that must be met for drawdown. For loans with floating interest rates, hedging agreements may also be required to manage interest rate exposure; these often take the form of interest rate swaps. Security documents play a critical role in securing the loan against the borrower's assets, with the type of security varying depending on the nature of the assets involved. Common forms of security include debentures, share mortgages, and property mortgages, each providing the lender with specific rights over borrower assets in case of default.

Additionally, guarantees may be requested to reinforce the borrower's obligations, often involving commitments from parent companies or directors, thereby offering the lender further assurance of repayment. Together, these documents establish a comprehensive framework for the loan, securing the lender's interests while outlining the borrower's obligations and risk management measures.

67 Ellinger, E. P., Lomnicka, E. and Hare, C., *Ellinger's Modern Banking Law* (Oxford University Press, 2011), p. 773.

7.6 Legal Opinions in Finance Transactions

In finance transactions, lenders customarily require legal opinions to ensure that the legal framework of the transaction aligns with their expectations. These opinions (which are discussed in detail in Chapter 13) serve to confirm the validity and enforceability of the transaction and may highlight any legal risks that the lender or other interested parties, such as hedging counterparties, should consider.[68] When a legal opinion is necessary, it is typically stipulated as a condition precedent in the facility agreement. A legal opinion typically includes key statements covering the existence, capacity, power, and authorisation of the parties, the validity and enforceability of the transaction documents, and the lawfulness of the parties' actions.

Legal opinions are generally prepared by the lender's lawyers and addressed directly to the lender.

Where the transaction involves an obligor incorporated in a foreign jurisdiction or assets located overseas, the lender will usually also require legal opinions from local counsel in the relevant jurisdiction(s) to confirm the legal standing of the transaction under applicable foreign law.

7.7 Satisfaction of Conditions Precedent, Completion, and Post-Completion Matters

Although conditions precedent primarily pertains to the drawdown stage, the process of gathering and agreeing upon the form of these conditions begins well in advance of the completion date. Typically, the borrower's solicitors provide the conditions precedent to the lender's solicitors for review and comment before the execution of any documents. The conditions precedent is generally outlined in the facility agreement, often within a specific schedule.[69]

Completion typically refers to the point at which funds are transferred to the borrower. The completion process involves ensuring all conditions precedent are satisfied, updated searches are conducted, and all relevant documents are signed and filed.

In loan finance transactions, the use of "virtual signings and closings" has become common practice to address logistical challenges in obtaining signatures and executing documents. This approach typically involves signing signature pages in advance, which are then attached to the final form of the document once all terms are agreed. However, the effectiveness of this practice was questioned in the case of *R (on the Application of Mercury Tax Group Limited and another) v HMRC* [2008] EWHC 2721 (Admin). Following this decision, it is advisable that final versions of documents be signed rather than using pre-signed pages to avoid issues with enforceability.

Post-completion tasks include registering security, sending notices to relevant parties (e.g., banks or tenants), and perfecting the security. The process concludes with the preparation of a transaction bible containing copies of all signed documents for future reference.

8 CONCLUSION

Loan facilities require careful consideration of numerous legal, financial, and operational factors. These elements must be meticulously addressed within the facility agreement to ensure

68 Adams, D., *Banking and Capital Markets* (College of Law Publishing, 2024), p. 172.
69 Chiu, I. and Wilson, J., *Banking Law and Regulation* (Oxford University Press, 2019), p. 138.

both parties' rights and obligations are clearly defined and enforceable. From the negotiation of the term sheet to the final execution of the loan documents, it is essential that both lenders and borrowers fully comprehend the key components that shape the transaction, including conditions precedent, representations and warranties, covenants, and events of default.

Purpose clauses are a key feature of facility agreements, ensuring that loan proceeds are used as intended and providing critical protections for lenders. In certain circumstances, a *Quistclose* trust may arise, providing additional security if the loan is designated for a specific, exclusive purpose.

Conditions precedent are a fundamental aspect of loan transactions, ensuring that all necessary documents, approvals, and verifications are in place before the lender is obligated to advance funds. These provisions serve to protect the lender by verifying the borrower's capacity and compliance with the facility agreement, thereby ensuring the loan proceeds under the agreed terms.

Representations and warranties are equally important, offering assurances to the lender about the borrower's financial and legal standing. These provisions allow the lender to monitor the borrower's condition throughout the loan term, providing a safeguard against unforeseen risks. Their interplay with events of default and conditions precedent further enhances their significance as tools for managing risk and enforcing compliance.

Covenants in facility agreements provide essential protections to the lender by imposing restrictions on the borrower. These provisions serve to safeguard the lender's capital, monitor the borrower's performance, and provide early warning of potential risks.

The event of a default clause is a critical mechanism for managing lender risk. It functions as a deterrent, encouraging borrower compliance by extending the lender's remedies beyond common law protections. It also provides the lender with the ability to act promptly when financial difficulties arise rather than waiting for a full deterioration of the borrower's financial situation.

Overall, the drafting and negotiation of bilateral loan agreements require a comprehensive approach to managing risks and ensuring that the interests of both the lender and borrower are adequately safeguarded.

CHAPTER 10

SECURITY

OVERVIEW

Loans may be structured as either secured or unsecured, and the distinction between these two types is critical for lenders when considering the risks involved. In unsecured lending, if the borrower defaults or becomes insolvent, the lender stands in line with other unsecured creditors, significantly increasing the risk of losing some or all of the loaned amount. Conversely, secured lending offers the lender a degree of protection, provided that the security has value, is properly registered or perfected, and is immune to being set aside. In such cases, the lender, subject to the applicable rules of priority, is entitled to repayment up to the value of the secured asset and may rank ahead of other creditors in an insolvency or other enforcement scenario.

After considering the rationale for taking security and the general principles of distribution in an insolvency, this chapter delves into the different forms of security available to lenders, including charges, mortgages, pledges, liens, and quasi-security arrangements. It also addresses guarantees and indemnities alongside critical legal issues that may affect the security's enforceability, such as financial assistance, reviewable transactions, financial collateral arrangements, and the implications of insolvency law.

Moreover, this chapter offers an analysis of security interests in the US under the Uniform Commercial Code (**UCC**) framework for creating, perfecting, and prioritising security interests is essential in ensuring that lenders can protect their rights over a borrower's assets, particularly in cases of default or insolvency.

1 WHY TAKE SECURITY?

Security grants a creditor the ability to recover payment through the exercise of proprietary or possessory rights rather than relying solely on the debtor's personal liability. By securing an interest in specific assets (each a "collateral"), the creditor gains an instrument to enforce repayment, ensuring a greater level of protection in the event of default or insolvency.[1] Thus, from a lender's perspective, one of the key objectives of security is to reduce the level of credit risk a borrower may present.[2]

Lenders may extend credit on either a secured or unsecured basis. In cases of unsecured lending, if the borrower defaults or becomes insolvent, the lender ranks alongside other unsecured creditors and may suffer substantial losses.[3] In corporate insolvency, the insolvent company frequently lacks sufficient assets to fully satisfy its liabilities, meaning that one of the primary functions of both administration and liquidation is to realise assets and distribute the proceeds among creditors. This process differs from receivership, where the receiver's principal duty is to repay the secured creditor who appointed them.[4]

1 Ellinger, E. P., Lomnicka, E. and Hare, C., *Ellinger's Modern Banking Law* (Oxford University Press, 2011), p. 811.
2 Haentjens, M. and De Gioia-Carabellese, P., *European Banking and Financial Law* (Routledge, 2015), p. 189.
3 Bamford, C., *Principles of International Finance Law* (Oxford University Press, 2015) at [10.01].
4 Chiu, I. and Wilson, J., *Banking Law and Regulation* (Oxford University Press, 2019), p. 161.

DOI: 10.4324/9781032662220-11

2 PRINCIPLES OF DISTRIBUTION IN AN INSOLVENCY

In an insolvency, under the Insolvency Act 1986 and the Insolvency (England and Wales) Rules 2016[5] (**IR 2016**), the money realised from the assets of a company is applied to meet creditor claims according to a specific order of priority.[6] Generally, after one class of creditor claims is fully satisfied, the remaining realisations are applied to the next class. Ordinarily, creditors within the same class are paid on a *pari passu* basis,[7] meaning that each creditor receives a proportionate share based on the size of their claim. However, creditors may agree to alternative distribution methods, such as a "pay as you go" approach where claims are satisfied as they crystallise.[8] Such an arrangement must be explicitly provided for in the relevant contract, and courts will not lightly infer a deviation from *pari passu* distribution unless clearly expressed in the agreement.[9]

An example of this is *In re Cheyne Finance* [2007] EWHC 2116 (Ch), where all senior creditors ranked equally, although the securities they held bore different maturity dates. Upon the special purpose vehicle (**SIV**),[10] incorporated to buy debt securities, being placed into receivership, noteholders of securities with an early maturity date sought payment of the funds then available on "pay as you go" basis, thereby entitling them to a full recovery. Such an approach would have, however, deprived the other senior noteholders of any funds to pay their securities. As a result, they sought the adoption of a *pari passu* approach, which, while it may not have entitled full recovery for all senior creditors, would have enabled the receiver to pay a reduced sum *pari passu* to all senior creditors at the same time.[11]

5 (SI 2016/1024).

6 Ellinger, E. P., Lomnicka, E. and Hare, C., *Ellinger's Modern Banking Law* (Oxford University Press, 2011), p. 813.

7 The principle "embody 'the fundamental principle of equality'", in *Strategic Value Capital Solutions Master Fund LP & Ors v AGPS BondCo PLC (Re AGPS BondCo PLC)* [2024] EWCA Civ 24 per Lord Justice Snowden at [184]–[185]. This principle is also used in the context of bankruptcy and corporate insolvency in Australia. In a liquidation scenario, application of the *pari passu* principle means that most unsecured creditors rank equally and are entitled to receive the same proportion of what they are owed as each other from any available assets of the company. This principle of equality is reflected in section 555 of the Australian Corporations Act 2001 (Cth) which provides (in part) that "*all debts and claims proved in a winding up rank equally and, if the property of the company is insufficient to meet them in full, they must be paid proportionately*". Similarly, section 108 of the Australian Bankruptcy Act 1966 (Cth) provides (in part) that "*all debts proved in a bankruptcy rank equally and, if the proceeds of the property of the bankrupt are insufficient to meet them in full, they shall be paid proportionately*".

8 Ellinger, E. P., Lomnicka, E. and Hare, C., *Ellinger's Modern Banking Law* (Oxford University Press, 2011), p. 77.

9 In the matter of *Sigma Finance Corporation (in administrative receivership)* [2009] UKSC 2.

10 A Structured Investment Vehicle (**SIV**) is typically funded through a combination of capital provided by the original investors – commonly referred to as capital note holders – and the issuance of short-term debt instruments, such as commercial paper. The business model of an SIV centres on generating profit from the spread between the lower interest paid on its short-term borrowings and the higher returns earned on its long-term investments. These profits are then distributed between the capital note holders and the investment manager, who is responsible for administering the SIV. In many cases, the investment manager is a financial institution or bank. However, SIVs are exposed to a number of significant risks: (a) insolvency, which may occur if the value of the SIV's long-term investments declines substantially, undermining its asset base; and (b) illiquidity, which arises when there is insufficient investor demand for the commercial paper issued by the SIV, making it difficult to refinance maturing obligations. These vulnerabilities became particularly evident during the global financial crisis, when falling asset values and drying up of liquidity rendered many SIVs unsustainable.

11 Goode, R. and van Zwieten, K., *Principles of Corporate Insolvency Law* (Sweet & Maxwell, 2019), Chapter 8, Section 3.

The receivers petitioned the court to interpret the underlying agreement,[12] which resulted in consecutive, contradictory decisions. Initially, the court held that the receivers should adopt a pay-as-you-go approach and thus pay senior noteholders with earlier maturities without regard to a future ability to pay later-maturing senior noteholders. This interpretation stemmed from the wording of the operative clause of the trust deed which required the receivers to make timely payments to the greatest extent possible, and this could only be done by making only those payments then due and payable.

Under the *pari passu* approach, the receivers could have found themselves in a situation where, while trying to pay off all obligations at once, there were insufficient funds to pay maturing senior noteholders. Moreover, the receivers did not offer evidence that Cheyne Finance would be unable to pay later-maturing senior noteholders or, in other words, that the SIV was balance-sheet (but not cash-flow) insolvent. One month later, the same court reversed this decision.[13] The court's action was prompted by new evidence since the receivers had retained the services of an accounting firm to model the future cash flows if Cheyne Finance continued to pay its debts as they fell due. These models showed that after about six months of timely debt-paying, the SIV would become insolvent. Consequently, the court held that although insolvency law made no mention of the ability to make future payments in determining insolvency, such a decision was nevertheless vital because, especially in a case such as this, it made more sense to pay as many creditors as possible while funds were available, as opposed to benefiting certain creditors at the expense of others. In making this determination, the Court relied heavily upon a "*wealth of Australian authority on the question of whether a cash flow or commercial insolvency test permits references to . . . prospective debts*"[14] and held that the receivers should use the *pari passu* method upon the occurrence of an "Insolvency Event" since the court identified an overriding asset management objective in the following proviso

> *[The] Receiver shall, unless and until an Insolvency Event Notice is delivered . . . (a) manage the Security Assets and the business of the Chargor with the objective of arranging for timely payment in full of the Chargor's obligations to the Senior Creditors . . . [and] the other Secured Creditors . . . as and when they fall due for payment.*[15]

While the *Re Cheyne Finance* stands as a stern warning on the consequences of unclear drafting, one should note that the UK Supreme Court has since ruled in a similar SIV case that an SPV's "*ability or inability to pay all its debts, present or future, may not be finally determined until much closer*" to the notes maturity date. This is because the

> *complex documentation under which the loan notes were issued contains several mechanisms . . . for ensuring that liabilities in respect of principal are, if necessary, deferred until the final redemption date, unless the post-enforcement regime comes into operation. The movements of currencies and interest rates in the meantime, if not entirely speculative, are incapable of prediction with any confidence. The court cannot be satisfied that there will eventually be a deficiency.*[16]

12 The relevant provision (clause 12) of the Security Trust Deed read as follow: "*Any moneys received by the Security Trustee or a Receiver after the occurrence of an Enforcement Event shall . . . be applied in the following order of priority:*

a. *[certain expenses and remuneration]*
b. *secondly, in satisfaction of or provision for all Senior Obligations as and when the same become payable and, if more than one such Senior Obligation is payable at the relevant time, pari passu and in proportion to the amounts payable in respect thereof*".

13 *Re Cheyne Finance* [2007] EWHC 2402 (Ch)
14 See for example B*ank of Australasia v Hall* (1907) 4 CLR 1514 at [1527].
15 *Re Cheyne Finance Plc* [2007] EWHC 2402 (Ch) at [63].
16 *BNY Corporate Trustee Services Ltd v Eurosail-UK 2007-3BL PLC* [2013] UKSC 28 at [49] per Lord Walker.

Where the insolvency practitioner realises assets subject to a fixed charge, the proceeds are distributed to the holders of fixed charge security in the order of their priority.[17] The insolvency practitioner's fees and costs incurred in realising the secured assets are deducted from the sale proceeds of those assets, and this amount is agreed upon with the fixed charge holder. In liquidation, the liquidator's remuneration for realising assets "on behalf of" a secured creditor may be determined under rule 18.38 of the IR 2016, which provides a scale-based remuneration.

When a company enters administration or liquidation within 12 weeks of the end of a Part A1 moratorium under the Insolvency Act 1986, certain debts are given priority over other claims. These include moratorium debts – liabilities arising during or after the moratorium – and priority pre-moratorium debts, such as wages, rent, and payments for goods or services supplied during the moratorium.[18] The administrator is responsible for ensuring these debts are paid as a priority, although no specific timescale is provided for this.

The expenses of the insolvent estate are paid before other lower-ranking claims, and there is a statutory hierarchy governing the payment of these expenses. In administration, certain debts arising from contracts adopted by the administrator receive super-priority, ranking ahead of other expenses.[19] These include liabilities arising from contracts of employment adopted by the administrator, although payments for unfair dismissal do not qualify for this status.[20]

After the expenses of the insolvent estate are paid, the insolvency practitioner must satisfy the claims of preferential creditors.[21] These include ordinary preferential debts, such as contributions to pension schemes and wages, as well as secondary preferential debts, which were introduced for certain tax liabilities and deposits protected by the Financial Services Compensation Scheme. Preferential claims rank equally among themselves within each category.

Before distributing proceeds to floating charge holders, the insolvency practitioner must set aside the prescribed part for unsecured creditors.[22] This is calculated as a percentage of the company's property subject to floating charges, up to a maximum of £800,000 for floating charges created on or after 6 April 2020.[23] The prescribed part is not applied to security created under financial collateral arrangements, and certain recoveries from wrongful trading and similar actions are excluded from its calculation (*Re Oasis Merchandising* [1998] Ch 170).[24]

Once preferential debts and the prescribed part have been satisfied, the insolvency practitioner distributes the remaining realisations from assets subject to floating charges to floating charge holders in accordance with their priority.[25] Floating charges created within 12 months of the insolvency are generally void unless they secure new lending.[26]

Unsecured creditors are paid from remaining assets, including the prescribed part, on a *pari passu* basis, subject to certain exceptions, such as deferred claims[27] and specific provisions

17 First-Ranking Claims: Holders of Fixed Charges.

18 Sections A53 and 174A, Insolvency Act 1986: second-Ranking Claims: Moratorium Debts and Priority Pre-Moratorium Debts.

19 Section 115, Insolvency Act 1986 and paragraph 99, Schedule B1, Insolvency Act 1986: third-Ranking Claims: Expenses of the Insolvent Estate.

20 *In the matter of Leeds United Association Football Club Ltd (in administration)* [2007] EWHC 1761 (Ch).

21 Section 175(1), Insolvency Act 1986: fourth-Ranking Claims: Preferential Creditors.

22 Gullifer, L., *Goode and Gullifer on Legal Problems of Credit and Security* (Sweet & Maxwell, 2023) at [5-73].

23 Section 176A, Insolvency Act 1986: Fifth-Ranking Claims: The Prescribed Part.

24 The court will only disapply the requirement to make a prescribed part in exceptional cases (*In the matter of International Sections Ltd (in creditors' voluntary liquidation)* [2009] EWHC 137 (Ch)).

25 Gullifer, L., *Goode and Gullifer on Legal Problems of Credit and Security* (Sweet & Maxwell, 2023) at [5-79].

26 Section 245, Insolvency Act 1986.

27 Under section 74(2)(f) of the Insolvency Act 1986.

for financial institutions.[28] Secured creditors with a shortfall in their recovery from secured assets can claim the remaining debt as an unsecured creditor but cannot participate in the prescribed part.[29]

Shareholders are entitled to any remaining funds after all unsecured creditors have been paid in full, though this is rare in an insolvency.[30] In most cases, shareholders receive nothing unless the company is in solvent liquidation. Furthermore, shareholders must discharge their obligations as contributories before receiving any distribution (*In re Overend Gurney & Co; Grissell's Case* (1866) LR1 Ch App 528).[31]

Insolvency Regimes in the EU

Insolvency regimes with the EU vary significantly at the national level, both in terms of their general structure – which may be administrative or judicial – and in relation to specific aspects such as the hierarchy of claims and the triggers for initiating proceedings.

Regarding triggers for insolvency, they are generally linked to balance sheet insolvency, where liabilities exceed assets, and/or cash-flow insolvency, where the corporate entity is unable to meet its financial obligations as they fall due.[32]

However, the EU introduced Directive (EU) 2019/1023[33] in an attempt to substantively harmonise, to some extent, national insolvency laws. Directive (EU) 2019/1023 established minimum standards for restructuring plans, incorporating class criteria similar to those found in UK schemes of arrangement and, in certain respects, US Chapter 11 proceedings. While the classification of creditors is ultimately determined by national law, the directive required that, at a minimum, secured and unsecured creditors be placed into separate classes.

While EU Member States retained discretion over the majority threshold required for the approval of restructuring plans, an upper limit was imposed. As a result, the required majority must not exceed 75% of the debt, aligning with the threshold in UK schemes of arrangement.[34]

28 Section 176AZA, Insolvency Act 1986: Seventh-Ranking Claims: Unsecured Creditors.
29 *Thorniley v Revenue and Customs Commissioners* [2008] EWHC 124 (Ch).
30 Eighth-Ranking Claims: Shareholders.
31 Claims by shareholders based on misrepresentation rank equally with unsecured creditor claims (*Soden v British & Commonwealth Holdings PLC* [1998] AC 298).
32 Goode, R. and van Zwieten, K., *Principles of Corporate Insolvency Law* (Sweet & Maxwell, 2019), Chapter 15, Section 1.
33 Directive (EU) 2019/1023 of the European Parliament and of the Council of 20 June 2019 on preventive restructuring frameworks, on discharge of debt and disqualifications, and on measures to increase the efficiency of procedures concerning restructuring, insolvency and discharge of debt, and amending Directive (EU) 2017/1132 (Directive on restructuring and insolvency).
34 A scheme of arrangement is a statutory mechanism provided under Part 26 of the Companies Act 2006, allowing a company to enter into a compromise or arrangement with its members or creditors, or with any class of them. The legislation does not limit the scope of matters that may be addressed in a scheme. In principle, it may relate to any issue that the company and the relevant stakeholders are lawfully entitled to agree upon among themselves.

This flexibility means that a scheme of arrangement can be used to implement a wide range of corporate transactions, including internal reorganisations, mergers, and demergers. Provided that the required procedural steps and approvals are secured – namely, approval by a majority in number representing 75% in value of each class of creditors or members voting, and subsequent sanction by the court – a scheme can be an effective and binding tool for achieving complex restructuring objectives. The restructuring plan under Part 26A of the Companies Act 2006 closely resembles the scheme of arrangement process under Part 26, it contains several significant distinctions. Crucially, it is only

3 TAKING SECURITY

In secured lending, the lender benefits from recourse to specified assets of the borrower, provided that the security is correctly registered, perfected, and not vulnerable to challenge. This ensures that the lender is repaid to the extent of the value of the secured asset, ranking ahead of unsecured creditors in an insolvency scenario.

From a commercial perspective, negotiating security involves determining which entities within the borrower's group will provide security and which assets will be charged. Lenders must carefully analyse the transaction structure to ensure that appropriate security is taken and properly documented. Conversely, borrowers typically seek to limit their exposure by minimising the assets subject to security and restricting the extent to which other group entities become liable for the borrower's debts.[35]

Security documentation is usually drafted alongside the facility agreement. Unlike facility agreements, there are no market-standard template security documents, and their contents must be tailored to the specific transaction. Some of the most common security documents in a loan finance transaction include the debenture, which provides security over all of a borrower's assets located in England and Wales, including tangible and intangible property, such as contractual rights and intellectual property. A debenture may also contain fixed and floating charges over specific asset classes, offering comprehensive security to the lender.

Another frequently used security instrument is the mortgage of shares, which enables the lender to sell the borrower's business as a going concern or to assume control in an enforcement situation. Additionally, legal or equitable mortgages over real property provide security over land and buildings, which may be central to the borrower's business or serve as an investment asset. In property finance, such security is fundamental, although it is often taken alongside security over other assets, such as bank accounts.

A charge over cash deposits is another common form of security, frequently used where a parent company provides collateral for a subsidiary's loan or where a borrower secures obligations owed to its lender through funds held on deposit. Each of these security instruments serves a distinct function in loan transactions, ensuring that lenders have adequate recourse in the event of default or insolvency.

It should be noted that the Standards of Lending Practice for Business Customers,[36] issued by the Lending Standards Board, impose certain obligations on financial institutions that subscribe to them, including requirements to provide specific information regarding security for overdrafts, loans, and commercial mortgage products. However, these obligations are limited to business customers with a consolidated turnover of up to £25 million. Financial institutions dealing with larger businesses or entities outside the scope of the standards are not subject to these requirements.

available to companies that are experiencing financial distress, thereby limiting its scope to situations where a company has encountered or is likely to encounter serious financial difficulty. Another key difference lies in its ability to impose a so-called "cross-class cram down", allowing the court to sanction a plan even if one or more classes of creditors or members vote against it, provided certain statutory conditions are met. This mechanism grants the court power to bind dissenting classes where the plan is deemed fair and equitable, and no dissenting class would be worse off than in the relevant alternative. Moreover, unlike schemes of arrangement, where approval requires a majority in number representing 75% in value of each class voting, the restructuring plan requires only a 75% approval in value, without any requirement for a majority in number. This change places greater emphasis on the economic weight of creditors' claims, rather than the number of creditors, making the process more suitable for complex capital structures with large institutional stakeholders.

35 Hudson, A., *The Law on Financial Derivatives* (Sweet & Maxwell, 2017) at [1-25].

36 See www.lendingstandardsboard.org.uk/wp-content/uploads/2024/09/Standards-of-Lending-Practice-for-business-customers-September-2024.pdf (September 2024 version) (accessed in March 2025).

3.1 Charges

In practical terms, most lenders are not inclined to take physical possession of a debtor's assets, nor would a debtor typically be willing to relinquish control of assets that are integral to the day-to-day operation of its business. Thus, lenders commonly seek to secure their interests by obtaining rights over specific assets of the debtor without necessarily taking possession. This is where a **charge** becomes an essential tool.[37]

A charge represents an encumbrance over an asset, providing the lender (the chargee) with an equitable proprietary interest in the charged property. This allows the chargee to have the property appropriated and the proceeds of its sale applied towards the repayment of the debt owed by the debtor (the chargor). However, unlike other security interests, a charge does not confer a right of possession over the asset. In essence, a charge operates as a security interest over the property without requiring the transfer of possession to the lender.[38]

While the term "charge" is often used generically to refer to all types of security interests, strictly speaking, it refers to a contractual arrangement between a creditor and debtor, under which the creditor acquires the right to appropriate and sell the debtor's asset if the debtor defaults on its obligations. The proceeds from such a sale are then used to satisfy the debt. Crucially, the chargee's rights are equitable, meaning the charge creates a proprietary interest in the asset rather than a possessory one. This is distinct from other forms of security, such as mortgages, where possession or ownership of the asset may be transferred.

A charge can be created over any type of asset that equity recognises as property, including intangible property, such as intellectual property or book debts. Furthermore, the legal relationship it establishes is not dependent on the direct connection between the chargee and the underlying debt; thus, a charge can be created in favour of a party other than the creditor to whom the secured liabilities are owed. For example, the case of *Re Lehman Brothers International (Europe) (In Administration)* [2012] EWHC 2997 (Ch) confirmed that a chargee need not be the actual creditor but can instead be a trustee or fiduciary acting on behalf of the creditor.

A charge exists primarily in equity unless it is related to land. In the case of land, the charge must be expressed as a legal mortgage in accordance with section 1(2)(c) of the Law of Property Act 1925 (**LPA 1925**). This distinction between legal and equitable charges is significant, particularly in matters involving insolvency. On the insolvency of a chargor, the status of the charge – whether it is fixed or floating – becomes critical, as this determines the priority of the creditor's claim over the charged assets in relation to other creditors.

3.2 Fixed Charges

A fixed charge is a security interest that attaches immediately to a specific, identifiable asset, granting the lender a degree of control over the charged asset.[39] For a charge to qualify as fixed, the assets must be clearly defined, and the borrower (chargor) must be restricted from disposing of them without the lender's consent. Fixed charges may be created over both existing and future assets, provided that the assets are ascertainable and definite[40] at the time the charge is taken.

37 Ellinger, E. P., Lomnicka, E. and Hare, C., *Ellinger's Modern Banking Law* (Oxford University Press, 2011), p. 842.
38 Gullifer, L., *Goode and Gullifer on Legal Problems of Credit and Security* (Sweet & Maxwell, 2023) at [1-55].
39 Hudson, A., *The Law on Financial Derivatives* (Sweet & Maxwell, 2017) at [15-94].
40 *Tailby v Official Receiver* (1888) 13 App. Cas. 523.

A fixed charge may be created by various entities, including companies, limited liability partnerships (LLPs), traditional partnerships, and individuals. Its defining feature is the degree of control the lender exercises over the charged asset. Control is critical, as a charge may be recharacterised as floating if the lender allows the borrower to freely dispose of the secured asset. Courts have consistently held that the classification of a charge is determined not by the parties' intentions or the label used in the security document but by the substance of the arrangement.

The true nature of the rights and obligations arising from the charge governs its characterisation, rather than its formal designation. Even if a charge is described as floating, it will likely be characterised as fixed where the lender exercises significant control, particularly through prohibitions on asset disposal, as evidenced by the specific rights and restrictions set out in the security documentation.

Restrictions and Control

The distinctive characteristic of a fixed charge is the degree of control exercised by the chargee over the charged assets.[41] In *Re Cosslett (Contractors) Limited* [1998] Ch 495, the court established that a fixed charge requires the lender to maintain sufficient control over the asset, preventing the borrower from disposing of it without consent. In contrast, a floating charge allows the borrower to continue using the charged asset in the ordinary course of business until a crystallisation event occurs. The House of Lords in *National Westminster Bank plc v Spectrum Plus Ltd & Ors* [2005] UKHL 41 reaffirmed that a floating charge does not definitively appropriate the asset to secure the debt until a specific event occurs.

The High Court in *Russell Cooke Trust Company Limited v Elliott* [2007] EWHC 1443 (Ch) addressed whether a security arrangement, described as a floating charge, was, in fact, a fixed charge due to significant restrictions imposed on the borrower's ability to deal with the charged property. The case arose from a lending scheme operated by Elliott's Solicitors plc, in which clients lent money through intermediaries to borrowers, with loans secured by various charges over real property. When the Law Society intervened in 2000 to halt the scheme, a court-appointed trustee was tasked with realising the loans. While most loans were secured by fixed charges over real property (the "**First Charges**"), the dispute focused on seven loans that were additionally secured by charges over other land labelled as floating charges in the documentation, referred to as floating deeds (the "**Deeds**").

Despite being designated as floating charges, the Deeds imposed stringent restrictions on the borrower's ability to deal with the charged property, prohibiting sales, mortgages, transfers, or any form of interest creation, occupation, or possession sharing. The trustee argued that, given these extensive restrictions, the charges were substantively fixed. The High Court agreed, ruling that the Deeds created fixed charges rather than floating charges. The court emphasised that the defining characteristic of a floating charge is the borrower's ability to deal with the charged asset in the ordinary course of business. The court further noted that the substance of a charge prevails over the label attached to it by the parties.[42]

41 Hudson, A., *The Law on Financial Derivatives* (Sweet & Maxwell, 2017) at [15-96].
42 Hudson, A., *The Law of Finance* (Sweet & Maxwell, 2013) at [22-53].

While previous case law, such as *National Westminster Bank plc v Spectrum Plus Ltd*, has primarily concerned instances where charges described as fixed were re-characterised as floating, *Russell Cooke Trust Company Limited v Elliott* demonstrates that the opposite scenario can also occur. Where restrictions on dealing with charged assets are sufficiently severe, a charge labelled as floating may be re-characterised as a fixed charge.

On this basis, in *Rayford Homes Ltd v Bank of Scotland plc and another* [2011] EWHC 1948 (Ch), the court upheld a fixed charge over future-acquired real property, concluding that the borrower could not dispose of the asset without the bank's consent, thereby confirming its fixed nature. This is because a charge of future property is not prevented from being a fixed charge. Therefore, if there is the necessary level of control, the shifting nature of certain assets does, in itself, not preclude the creation of a fixed charge. Moreover, a charge can be fixed despite the borrower's limited ability to deal with the assets under specific circumstances as determined in *Re Avanti Communications Ltd (in administration)* [2023] EWHC 940 (Ch), where the court focused on whether control over the asset was actually exercised in practice. In this case, it was determined that sufficient control had been retained by the lender, particularly as the assets in question were not part of the chargor's circulating capital or fluctuating asset base.

A more recent case, *Re UKCloud Ltd (in liquidation)* [2024] EWHC 1259 (Ch), examined the nature of a charge over intellectual property assets. The case concerned a debenture granted by UKCloud Ltd, which described the charged assets as "*all licences, consents and authorisations (statutory or otherwise) held or required in connection with the company's business or the use of any Secured Asset, and all rights in connection with them*". The court held that this wording suggested an intention to create a fixed charge. However, despite the debenture's wording, the control provisions over the intellectual property addresses were not enforced in practice. Consequently, these provisions were deemed a "sham", and the charge was classified as floating rather than fixed. The court also considered whether the intellectual property addresses constituted "circulating capital", a typical feature of floating charges. While previous case law[43] referred to circulating capital as assets forming part of a company's fluctuating asset pool, the court in *UKCloud Ltd* noted that the intellectual property addresses did not fluctuate in the same way. However, this factor alone was not determinative, as the absence of fluctuating capital characteristics did not necessarily indicate that the charge was fixed.[44]

3.3 Floating Charges

A floating charge is a form of security interest that hovers over a class of assets that may fluctuate over time as part of the borrower's ordinary course of business. These assets typically include stock, receivables, and inventory, which naturally change as business operations continue.[45] The defining feature of a floating charge is that, until certain trigger events occur – such as default or insolvency – the borrower remains free to deal with the assets without requiring the lender's consent. Floating charges can apply to both existing and future assets, meaning that even if no unencumbered assets exist at the time the charge is created,

43 See, for example, *Re Yorkshire Woolcombers Association Ltd* [1903] 2 Ch 284 and *National Westminster Bank plc v Spectrum Plus Ltd & Ors* [2005] UKHL 41.
44 Gullifer, L., *Goode and Gullifer on Legal Problems of Credit and Security* (Sweet & Maxwell, 2023) at [4-21].
45 Gullifer, L., *Goode and Gullifer on Legal Problems of Credit and Security* (Sweet & Maxwell, 2023) at [4-02].

it remains valid and will attach to future assets as they come into existence.[46] In *Re Yorkshire Woolcombers' Association Ltd* [1903] 2 Ch 284 Vaughan Williams LJ held:

> *I do not think that for a "specific security" you need have a security of a subject matter which is then in existence. I mean by "then" at the time of the execution of the security; but what you do require to make a specific security is that the security whenever it has once come into existence, and been identified or appropriated as a security, shall never thereafter at the will of the mortgagor cease to be a security.*[47]

Thus, where a charge is created over an asset, such an asset must be clearly identifiable. This does not mean, however, that it should be in existence when the security is provided. This was confirmed in *SAW (SW) 2010 Ltd v Wilson* [2017] EWCA Civ 1001, where the Court of Appeal upheld the validity of a floating charge even when no unencumbered assets were present at the time of its creation.

While fixed charges may be created by individuals, companies, and partnerships, the creation of a floating charge is more restricted. Under English law, only certain entities can create floating charges, including companies (under the Companies Act 2006), limited liability partnerships (LLPs),[48] farmers,[49] and building societies.[50] However, individuals cannot grant floating charges, as the Bills of Sale Acts of 1878 and 1882 require non-possessory charges over an individual's assets to be registered, which is incompatible with the fluctuating nature of a floating charge.

A floating charge offers several advantages, the most significant being its flexibility. Unlike a fixed charge, it allows the borrower to continue using charged assets in the ordinary course of business, such as selling inventory or using receivables to fund operations. This makes it particularly suitable for trading businesses, where assets are constantly changing. However, this flexibility also introduces risks for lenders, as the borrower could dispose of all charged assets, leaving the lender with little security in the event of insolvency. For this reason, lenders often prefer to take fixed charges over specific assets, such as property or machinery, where feasible.

Nonetheless, floating charges still offer lenders a degree of protection, particularly through crystallisation, where the floating charge converts into a fixed charge, restricting the borrower's ability to dispose of the assets. This can occur either automatically by operation of law or through contractual provisions in the security documentation. Under common law, a floating charge will crystallise in certain circumstances, including insolvency,[51] the appointment of a receiver or administrator over the borrower's assets,[52] or the cessation of business operations.[53]

In addition to common law crystallisation, contractual provisions in security documents often specify predefined trigger events that allow the floating charge to crystallise. These may include the creation of another security interest in favour of a third-party creditor or the commencement of insolvency proceedings. However, automatic crystallisation provisions are subject to statutory restrictions. As discussed in Chapter 9, during a Part A1 moratorium, creditors are temporarily prevented from enforcing security rights, giving notice of crystallisation, or restricting the disposal of charged assets.[54] Despite these restrictions, financial collateral

46 Hudson, A., *The Law on Financial Derivatives* (Sweet & Maxwell, 2017) at [15-98].
47 Ibid. at [294].
48 As per section 15 of the Limited Liability Partnerships Act 2000.
49 Under section 8(1) of the Agricultural Credits Act 1928, which applies to certain agricultural assets.
50 Following legislative changes introduced by the Financial Services (Banking Reform) Act 2013.
51 *Re Crompton & Co Ltd* [1914] 1 Ch 954.
52 *Evans v Rival Granite Quarries Ltd* [1910] 2 KB 979.
53 *Re The Real Meat Company Ltd* [1996] BCC 254.
54 Section A22(2), Insolvency Act 1986.

arrangements, as defined in the Financial Collateral Arrangements (No. 2) Regulations 2003[55] (**FCA Regulations 2003**)[56] remain exempt from crystallisation prohibitions.

3.4 Priority in Insolvency: Fixed vs. Floating Charges

As a general rule, security interests created by companies which are registrable under the Companies Act 2006 and are duly registered in accordance with those provisions will rank in priority according to established principles of law.[57] A fixed security interest will ordinarily take priority over a floating charge, even where the fixed charge is created after the floating charge. This principle was affirmed in *Wheatley v Silkstone and Haigh Moor Coal Company* (1885) 29 Ch D 715. Among fixed charges and legal mortgages, priority is generally determined by the date of their creation, as held in *James v Boythorpe Colliery Co* [1890] 2 Meg 55. In the case of floating charges granted over the entire undertaking of a company, priority likewise follows the order of creation, consistent with the decision in *Re Benjamin Cope & Sons Ltd* [1914] 1 Ch 800.

As a result, in an insolvency, the priority of a floating charge is lower than that of a fixed charge. The proceeds from the sale of charged assets are applied first to fixed chargeholders, who are paid before all other creditors, including preferential creditors. In contrast, floating chargeholders receive payment only after the settlement of fixed chargeholders' claims, the costs and expenses of the insolvency process, and the claims of preferential creditors.

Furthermore, a portion of the floating charge realisations must be set aside for unsecured creditors under the prescribed part mechanism. This prescribed part represents a percentage of the floating charge assets that is ring-fenced for distribution to unsecured creditors, further reducing the amount available to floating chargeholders.

Fixed or Floating?

Book debts refer to unpaid invoices, representing sums owed to a business by its customers. Given that book debts are fluctuating assets, constantly being generated and repaid as part of the ordinary course of business, they are generally more suited to a floating charge. This is because the chargor typically needs to manage and dispose of these debts freely in the ordinary course of its operations. A floating charge allows the chargor to continue using and collecting book debts without the chargeholder's direct intervention until the floating charge crystallises.[58]

55 Implementing the Directive 2002/47/EC of the European Parliament and of the Council of 6 June 2002 on financial collateral arrangements.
56 (SI 2003/3226), as amended.
57 There are several important exceptions and qualifications to these general principles. One such exception arises where security is taken over an asset that requires registration in a specialist register, such as land, intellectual property rights, ships, or aircraft. In these instances, registration must be effected not only at Companies House but also in the relevant specialist asset register. The priority of the security interest in such cases is typically determined by the date of registration in that specialist register, rather than the date of creation alone.
58 Ellinger, E. P., Lomnicka, E. and Hare, C., *Ellinger's Modern Banking Law* (Oxford University Press, 2011), p. 873.

Conversely, for a fixed charge to be valid, the chargeholder must strictly regulate the collection and use of the book debts, and the chargor must be prevented from dealing with the proceeds without the chargeholder's consent.

A similar issue arises with charges over cash deposits held in bank accounts. Whether the charge is fixed or floating depends primarily on the degree of control exercised by the chargeholder over the account. If the chargor retains the ability to withdraw or use the funds freely, the charge is likely to be classified as floating. Conversely, where the chargeholder exercises strict control over withdrawals and the account's operation, the charge may be regarded as fixed.

In the case of current accounts, where the chargor is free to operate the account and withdraw, or deposit funds as necessary, any charge over the account is likely to be floating. This is because the chargeholder does not have sufficient control over the account's operations to constitute a fixed charge. In contrast, a fixed charge may be possible over specific accounts, such as deposit accounts, where the chargeholder exercises strict control over the account, limiting the chargor's access to the funds.

3.5 Mortgages

A mortgage is a security interest involving the transfer of title to an asset as security for specific obligations, typically the repayment of a debt. The transfer of title strengthens the lender's position, enabling them to realise the security while preventing the mortgagor (borrower) from disposing of the asset during the mortgage term.[59] This transfer, however, is subject to an express or implied condition that the asset will be re-transferred once the secured obligations have been fully discharged; therefore, the parties intend the transfer of title to be solely by way of security rather than an absolute conveyance.[60] Mortgages can be created over both tangible and intangible assets, provided the necessary legal requirements are met.[61]

There are two principal types of mortgages under English law: legal mortgages and equitable mortgages. A legal mortgage is the most comprehensive and secure form of security interest, as it involves the transfer of legal title to the mortgagee (lender) while restricting the mortgagor's ability to deal with the asset during the mortgage term. Legal mortgages are widely used for securing substantial obligations, particularly loans for the purchase of real estate.

The formalities for creating a legal mortgage vary depending on the type of asset. In the case of land, a legal mortgage must be created by deed,[62] ensuring its legal validity and enforceability. Under the LPA 1925,[63] a legal mortgagee does not acquire an absolute legal estate in the mortgaged land but is instead treated as if they had been granted a lease for 3,000 years.

For chattels (movable goods), no specific statutory formalities are required, provided there is a valid agreement and an intention to create a legal mortgage.[64] Legal mortgages may be created over documents of title, such as bills of exchange, bills of lading, and bearer securities,

59 Gullifer, L., *Goode and Gullifer on Legal Problems of Credit and Security* (Sweet & Maxwell, 2023) at [1-54].
60 Chiu, I. and Wilson, J., *Banking Law and Regulation* (Oxford University Press, 2019), p. 168.
61 Hudson, A., *The Law of Finance* (Sweet & Maxwell, 2013) at [22-30].
62 Section 52(1) of the LPA 1925.
63 Section 87(1).
64 Ellinger, E. P., Lomnicka, E. and Hare, C., *Ellinger's Modern Banking Law* (Oxford University Press, 2011), p. 821.

as well as transferable intangibles, such as shares. A legal mortgage over registered securities is established by transferring the securities into the mortgagee's name and registering them accordingly. Security over patents is typically effected by means of a legal mortgage, which is created by assigning the patent to the lender by way of security.

A legal mortgage cannot be granted over future property, meaning assets not yet in existence or not owned by the mortgagor at the time of the mortgage's creation.[65] However, an equitable mortgage may be created over it, which becomes effective in equity once the property comes into existence and is acquired by the mortgagor. This principle was established in *Holroyd v Marshall* (1862) 10 HLC 191, confirming that future assets may be charged in equity before they are actually acquired.

An equitable mortgage arises where beneficial title to an asset is transferred to the lender by way of security for an obligation. Unlike a legal mortgage, which involves a formal transfer of legal title, an equitable mortgage typically occurs in situations where the legal formalities for creating a legal mortgage are not fulfilled. Such circumstances include instances where the parties have agreed to create a legal mortgage in the future, but the necessary steps have not yet been completed or where the asset in question is only recognised in equity. In these cases, the mortgagee acquires only beneficial ownership, meaning their security interest is protected in equity but not in law.

The distinction between legal and equitable mortgages remains significant, particularly in insolvency scenarios, where legal mortgagees enjoy stronger rights and priority over equitable mortgagees. However, equitable mortgages still provide valuable security, ensuring that lenders retain recourse to the mortgaged assets even where legal title has not been transferred.

Lender's Remedies – i.e., Security Over Commercial Property

In the event of non-payment of a loan secured on commercial property, a lender has several remedies available to recover the sums secured.[66] The most direct option is to sue the borrower under the covenant to repay the debt; such right remains intact even after exercising the power of sale. If the proceeds from the sale of the secured property are insufficient to discharge the outstanding debt, the lender may still pursue the borrower for the shortfall.[67]

Alternatively, the lender may enforce its security by taking possession of the property, exercising its power of sale, appointing a receiver, or, in rare cases, seeking foreclosure.[68]

The holder of a legal mortgage acquires the right to take possession of the mortgaged property immediately upon the creation of the mortgage unless this right is expressly or impliedly excluded by the terms of the mortgage. Unless otherwise specified in the security document, the right to possession exists even if the secured debt has not yet become due. However, until the lender's power of sale becomes exercisable, possession may only be taken for the purpose of protecting the security and not as a means

65 Bamford, C., *Principles of International Finance Law* (Oxford University Press, 2015) at [10.47].
66 Proctor, C., *The Law and Practice of International Banking* (Oxford University Press, 2015) at [32.01].
67 This principle was affirmed in *Rudge v Richens* (1872–73) LR 8 CP 358.
68 Ellinger, E. P., Lomnicka, E. and Hare, C., *Ellinger's Modern Banking Law* (Oxford University Press, 2011), p. 830.

of enforcing repayment.[69] The statutory power of sale under section 101(1)(i) of the LPA 1925 applies to all mortgages over land, including charges, as the term mortgage under section 205 of the LPA 1925 encompasses a charge. This power arises automatically when the mortgage has been created by deed, and the secured obligations have become due. The lender may exercise the power of sale without the need for a court order, and the sale may be conducted either by private treaty or at auction.[70]

A lender holding a legal or equitable mortgage or a fixed charge will typically have the right to appoint a receiver either through express powers contained in the security document or under statutory powers.[71] The primary function of a receiver is to take control of the secured assets, realise them – usually through sale to a third party – and apply the proceeds to repay the outstanding debt owed by the borrower. Most security documents include an express power allowing the lender to appoint a receiver, commonly referred to as a fixed charge receiver. However, if the security document does not contain such a provision but the security interest was created by deed as a mortgage or charge,[72] the lender can appoint a receiver of the income from the secured asset under the statutory power in section 101 of the LPA 1925. This type of receiver is known as a Law of Property Act receiver. In some circumstances, a lender may also apply to the court for the appointment of a receiver under section 37 of the Senior Courts Act 1981. The court has the discretion to make such an appointment where it considers it just and convenient to do so, although this power is rarely exercised in practice.[73]

When a mortgage is granted over property, the borrower retains the equity of redemption, which is the right to redeem the property by repaying the secured debt. Foreclosure is the legal process by which this right is extinguished, and ownership of the property vests absolutely in the lender. Once foreclosure is complete, the lender becomes the outright owner and may sell the property free from the borrower's rights, including the equity of redemption, as well as the rights of any lower-ranking security holders.

Foreclosure is a remedy available only to holders of a legal mortgage or, in certain circumstances, an equitable mortgage. Specifically, if an equitable mortgage includes an agreement to create a legal mortgage and the property is capable of being subject to a legal mortgage, foreclosure may be granted.[74] However, foreclosure is not available to the holder of a charge or to an equitable mortgage that cannot be converted into a legal mortgage.[75] A lender's right to foreclose arises once the secured obligations have become due and payable.[76]

3.6 Security Assignment

An assignment transfers the right to an asset to a lender, providing security for an underlying obligation. Depending on the formalities observed, an assignment may be either legal

69 See *Western Bank Ltd v Schindler* [1976] EWCA Civ 5.
70 Ellinger, E. P., Lomnicka, E. and Hare, C., *Ellinger's Modern Banking Law* (Oxford University Press, 2011), p. 832.
71 Gullifer, L. and Payne, J., *Corporate Finance Law: Principles and Policy* (Hart, 2020), p. 342.
72 Since mortgage under section 205 of the LPA 1925 includes a charge.
73 Hudson, A., *The Law of Finance* (Sweet & Maxwell, 2013) at [22-38].
74 *Harrold v Plenty* [1901] 2 Ch 314.
75 *Tennant v Trenchard* (1868–69) LR 4 Ch App 537.
76 Hudson, A., *The Law of Finance* (Sweet & Maxwell, 2013) at [22-36].

or equitable. An assignment will qualify as a legal assignment (or statutory assignment) if it complies with the requirements of section 136 of the LPA 1925.[77] To meet these requirements, the assignment must be in writing and signed by the assignor (or mortgagor), ensuring that the transfer of rights is clear and unambiguous. It must also be absolute, meaning it must be unconditional and cover the entire, and in existence at the time, debt or other rights being assigned. In *Forster v Baker* [1910] 2 KB 636, which is considered the precursor to section 136, the court clarified that partial assignments do not meet this criterion. Furthermore, the assignment must not be by way of charge only, distinguishing a true transfer of rights from a situation where rights are merely encumbered as security. Finally, written notification must be given to the third party (the debtor or obligor) against whom the assignor has enforceable rights, informing them that their obligation has been transferred to the assignee. This notification is crucial, as it ensures that the third party recognises the assignee as the new party entitled to enforce the assigned rights.

Once these conditions are met, the assignment takes effect as a legal assignment, granting the assignee (or mortgagee) the right to enforce the assigned rights in their own name without the involvement of the assignor. This is particularly relevant for mortgages over choses in action, such as debts or contractual rights, where compliance with section 136 enables the assignee to pursue claims directly against third parties.

In the case of a security assignment, where an assignee holds security over a chose in action, the assignment will meet the requirement of being absolute if the assignee enjoys full rights to the benefit of the chose in action, and the third party must deal exclusively with the assignee.[78] A mere expectancy, such as payment under a contract yet to be made,[79] is a future chose, whereas sums certain to become payable under an existing obligation are current *choses*.[80] This analysis may present some difficulties where there is an existing legal obligation under which it is uncertain if anything will become due. On the face of it, both a scheme of arrangement and a policy of insurance fall within this category since, in the former case, no dividend may be declared, and in the latter, the risk insured against may never transpire. In *Walker v The Bradford Old Bank* (1862) 10 HLC 191, it was held that, pursuant to Section 25(6) of the Judicature Act 1873, an assignment of an accruing debt arising out of a contract was a debt or a legal *chose* in action. As such, it could be assigned under Section 25(6). Such a result would also make it a current chose assignable in equity. However, it may not apply to the assignment of a future property right. In *Walker,* the right under which the debt arose existed at the time of the assignment; only the amount varied. The effect of an agreement to sell future property rights has been analysed by Lord Westbury in *Holroyd v Marshall* (1862) 10 HLC 191 as follows:

> *If a vendor or mortgagor agrees to sell or mortgage property real or personal, of which he is not possessed at the time, and he receives the consideration for the contract, and afterwards becomes possessed of property answering*

77 Section 136(1) of the Law of Property Act 1925 provides: "*Any absolute assignment by writing under the hand of the assignor (not purporting to be by way of charge only) of any debt or other legal thing in action, of which express notice in writing has been given to the debtor, trustee or other person from whom the assignor would have been entitled to claim such debt or thing in action, is effectual in law (subject to equities having priority over the right of the assignee) to pass and transfer from the date of such notice – (a) the legal right to such debt or thing in action; (b) all legal and other remedies for the same; and (c) the power to give a good discharge for the same without the concurrence of the assignor*".

78 In the US, the position has been summarised in *Titus v. Wallick*, 306 U.S. 282, 288–289 (1939): "*[A]ny form of assignment which purports to assign or transfer a chose in action confers upon the transferee such title or ownership as will enable him to sue upon it. This is true even though the assignment is for the purpose of suit only and the transferee is obligated to account for the proceeds of suit to his assignor*".

79 On this point, see the English case *of Pfeiffer v Arbuthnot* [1988] 1 WLR 150 at page 161.

80 Chitty at [20-028] cites *Shepherd v Federal Commissioner of Taxation* [1965] 113 CLR 385 in support of this proposition.

> *the description in the contract, there is no doubt that a Court of Equity would compel him to perform the contract, and that the contract would in equity transfer the beneficial interest to the mortgagee or purchaser immediately on the property being acquired.*

Since *Holroyd v Marshall*, it has been generally accepted doctrine that an agreement to hold property, which the promisor may afterwards acquire as security for the payment of a debt, operates in equity once the property is acquired to give the stipulated security to the promisee in preference to general creditors.

Therefore, even if the assignor retains an equity of redemption – that is, the right to reclaim the assigned rights once the secured obligation is satisfied – the third party remains obligated to deal solely with the assignee until they are notified of a re-assignment following repayment of the debt.

In practice, the wording for a security assignment could be framed in the following terms:

> *As continuing security for payment and discharge of the Secured Liabilities, each Chargor with full title guarantee assigns absolutely by way of security in favour of the Security Trustee, but subject to the right of such Chargor to redeem such assignment upon the full payment or discharge of the Secured Liabilities, its right, title and interest from time to time in each of the following assets: ×3.3.1 the Specific Contracts; . . . 3.3.4 all rights under any agreement to which it is a party and which is not mortgaged or charged under Clause 3.1 (Mortgages and Fixed Charges), together with all Related Rights in respect of such Charged property provided that each Chargor is entitled until the occurrence of an Event of Default which is continuing to exercise all rights assigned under this Clause 3.3 (Assignments) (subject to the terms of the Secured Finance Documents) and the Security Trustee will reassign any such rights to the extent necessary to enable such Chargor to do so.*[81]

It should be noted that the previous wording includes a proviso for reassignment, which is a fundamental feature of a legal assignment by way of security. This does not invalidate an absolute assignment under section 136 of the LPA 1925. The inclusion of the phrase "with full title guarantee" is significant, as it ensures that the covenants implied under sections 2 and 3 of the Law of Property (Miscellaneous Provisions) Act 1994 apply to the transaction, thereby strengthening the assignor's obligations in relation to the assigned property.

3.7 FCA Regulations 2003 and Financial Collateral

A security financial collateral arrangement involves the creation of a security interest over financial collateral to secure obligations owed to the collateral taker.[82] The enactment of the FCA Regulations 2003 disapplies the requirement for the assignor to execute the assignment in relation to security over financial collateral. Financial collateral includes cash, financial instruments, and credit claims (i.e., claims under loans made by credit institutions). This statutory relaxation facilitates the creation of security over such assets by simplifying formal requirements.[83]

81 In *Mailbox (Birmingham) Ltd v Galliford Try Construction Ltd* [2017] EWHC 67 (TCC) at [18].

82 Gullifer, L. and Payne, J., *Corporate Finance Law: Principles and Policy* (Hart, 2020), p. 322.

83 The FCA Regulations 2003 are set to be revoked under the Financial Services and Markets Act 2023 (**FSMA 2023**), which provides a framework for repealing retained EU financial services law. HM Treasury intends to transfer the relevant provisions into regulator rules or domestic legislation where appropriate. Schedule 1 of FSMA 2023 lists the legislative acts to be repealed, with the FCA Regulations 2003 included in Part 2. However, HM Treasury has stated that revocation will not commence until the regulators have consulted on and finalised replacement rules, meaning the process is expected to take several years.

The FCA Regulations 2003 "*confe[r] on collateral takers the right to enforce the collateral notwithstanding the commencement of insolvency proceedings in respect of the collateral provider*".[84] Thus, as clarified by the Court of Justice of the European Union, under Article 8(1) and (3) of Directive 2002/47,

> *insolvency proceedings cannot have a retroactive effect on financial collateral provided before the commencement of such proceedings. On the other hand, under Article 8(2) of the directive, where collateral has been provided after the commencement of such proceedings, the collateral arrangement will be legally enforceable and binding on third parties only in exceptional circumstances, namely only if the collateral was provided on the day of commencement and the collateral taker provides evidence that he was not aware, nor should have been aware, of the commencement of the proceedings.*[85]

Therefore, holders of financial collateral arrangements entered into at any time prior to the commencement of insolvency proceedings are entitled to enforce their security interests in the financial collateral subject to the arrangement, notwithstanding the company being insolvent.[86] To achieve this, the FCA Regulations 2003 provide for a minimum level of formality, requiring only that there be a written agreement and evidence of provision of collateral. Thus,[87] "*the creation, validity, perfection, enforceability or admissibility in evidence of a financial collateral arrangement or the provision of financial collateral under a financial collateral arrangement*" is not "*dependent on the performance of any formal act*" (such as the execution of any document in a specific form or in a particular manner, the making of any filing with an official body or public body or registration in a public registry).[88]

The collateral must be delivered, transferred, held, or otherwise designated to be in the possession or under the control of the collateral taker. In *Re Lehman Brothers International (Europe) (In Administration)* [2012] EWHC 2997 (Ch), the High Court confirmed that possession or control requires the collateral provider to be dispossessed of the collateral to a sufficient degree. This has raised concerns about the applicability of the FCA Regulations 2003 to floating charges, particularly those over intangible assets, as highlighted in *Gray v G-T-P Group Ltd: Re F2G Realisations Ltd (in liquidation)* [2010] EWHC 1772 (Ch).

Following this case, The Financial Assistance Scheme (Miscellaneous Amendments) Regulations 2010[89] attempted to clarify that possession of intangible financial collateral includes cases where the collateral is credited to an account in the name of the collateral taker, provided the collateral provider's rights are limited to substitution or withdrawal of excess collateral.[90]

Concerns around the application of these regulations have persisted for some time. In November 2016, in the proceedings, *Private Equity Insurance Group SIA v. Swedbank AS*, Case C 156/15, the European Court of Justice (ECJ) decided a reference from the Supreme Court of Latvia, which sought to ascertain

> *whether Directive 2002/47 is to be interpreted as conferring on the taker of financial collateral, such as the collateral at issue in the main proceedings, whereby monies deposited in a bank account are pledged to the*

84 Private Equity Insurance Group SIA v Swedbank AS., Case C-156/15, 10 November 2016, ECLI:EU:C:2016:851 at [26].
85 Private Equity Insurance Group SIA v Swedbank AS., Case C-156/15, 10 November 2016, ECLI:EU:C:2016:851at [46].
86 Wood, P., *Comparative Law of Security Interests and Title Finance* (Sweet & Maxwell, 2019), Part 5, Chapter 51.
87 According to the Regulation 1(1).
88 Judgement of the Court of Justice of the European Union (Case C-156/15), 10 November 2016, ECLI:EU:C:2016:851 at [25].
89 2010 No. 1149.
90 Proctor, C., *The Law and Practice of International Banking* (Oxford University Press, 2015) at [35.01].

> *bank to cover all the account holder's debts to the bank, the right to enforce the collateral, notwithstanding the commencement of insolvency proceedings in respect of the collateral provider.*

It was held that

> *references to the "provision" of financial collateral are to the financial collateral being delivered, transferred, held, registered or otherwise designated so as to be in the possession or under the control of the collateral taker or of a person acting on the collateral taker's behalf.*[91]

In this respect, the CJEU judgement indicated that

> *taker of collateral, such as the collateral at issue in the main proceedings, in the form of monies lodged in an ordinary bank account may be regarded as having acquired "possession or control" of the monies only if the collateral provider is prevented from disposing of them.*[92]

Once again, as discussed in the context of the civil law's equivalent of a fixed charge over bank accounts, the issue of control appears to be of paramount importance.[93] It should be noted that the issue of control is particularly problematic in the context of digital objects since they appear rather fluid and subject to ongoing technological developments. However, as new safety and security frameworks continue to emerge, the understanding of control must adapt accordingly. Innovations such as social recovery wallets and account abstraction techniques are already reshaping the landscape of digital asset security.[94]

One of the primary advantages of the FCA Regulations 2003 is that they modify various statutory formalities and insolvency provisions.[95] Regulation 4 disapplies certain requirements, such as those under the LPA 1925 concerning the assignment of choses in action and the registration of company charges under s. 860 of the Companies Act 2006. Consequently, financial collateral arrangements do not need to be registered at Companies House. Moreover, the registration requirement under section 860 of the Companies Act 2006 does not apply to trusts, whether they take the form of a *Quistclose* trust or a trust with specifically identified beneficiaries. However, distinguishing between certain trusts and charges can be complex. An arrangement in which A grants a charge over property to secure a debt owed to B may closely resemble a declaration of trust by A in favour of himself and B as beneficiaries, with B's entitlement defined by reference to the amount owed by A. For the purposes of determining whether registration is required, a court is likely to adopt a pragmatic approach, focusing on the substance rather than the form of the arrangement. Where the entitlement of the supposed beneficiary is defined by reference to a debt, this may indicate that a charge, rather than a trust, has been created. Additionally, a further factor supporting the inference of a charge is the tax implications for the beneficiary. In the case of a trust, the beneficiary would ordinarily incur an immediate tax liability, making it less likely that they intended to participate in such a structure.[96]

91 Ibid. at [34] to [37].
92 Ibid. at [44].
93 Gullifer, L., *Goode and Gullifer on Legal Problems of Credit and Security* (Sweet & Maxwell, 2023) at [6-40] and [6-41].
94 Law Commission, Digital Assets [2024] EWLC 416 at [5.69], available at www.bailii.org/ew/other/EWLC/2024/LC416.pdf (accessed in March 2025).
95 Hudson, A., *The Law on Financial Derivatives* (Sweet & Maxwell, 2017) at [16-35].
96 *TXU Europe Group Plc (In Administration), R* [2003] EWHC 3105 (Ch) at [26]. Morse, G., *Palmer's Company Law* (Sweet & Maxwell, 2025) at [13.330].

3.8 Equitable Assignment

If an assignment does not comply with section 136 of the LPA 1925, it will instead take effect as an equitable assignment.

Unlike a legal assignment, an equitable assignment has several key distinctions. First, the assignee does not have the direct right to sue the third party (debtor or obligor) in their own name. Instead, the assignor must usually be joined as a party to the legal proceedings, which can complicate enforcement. Secondly, no specific form or statutory requirement exists for creating an equitable assignment. However, there must be a clear intention to transfer or charge the interest or right concerned. This flexibility allows equitable assignments to be created informally, provided the intent to assign is sufficiently clear. Another significant difference is that an equitable assignment allows for the assignment of a future contract[97] "*as soon as it came into existence provided it was sufficiently identifiable under the agreement*".[98]

A legal assignment can generally only be made with respect to existing rights, meaning that taking security over future contractual rights is possible only by way of equitable assignment. Since future rights do not yet exist, they cannot be legally assigned until they come into being. As a result, security over future contracts is limited to equitable remedies, which only take effect once the relevant rights materialise.

3.9 Possessory Securities

Possessory security requires the lender to take possession of the secured asset. Possessory forms of security, such as pledges, involve the transfer of possession without transferring ownership.[99]

A pledge is a form of security created through the delivery of possession of an asset by the pledgor (debtor) to the pledgee (creditor) as security for the repayment of a debt.[100] Only assets capable of physical delivery – or assets represented by documents of title – can be pledged. Examples include goods, documents of title, such as bills of lading, and bearer securities. Debts, being intangible assets, cannot be pledged as they cannot be physically delivered.[101] Delivery of the pledged asset may be either actual (physical transfer)[102] or constructive (for example, by handing over the keys to a warehouse where the goods are stored).

Importantly, while possession of the asset is transferred to the pledgee, ownership remains with the pledgor. This distinguishes a pledge from a mortgage, where title to the asset is transferred to the mortgagee while the mortgagor retains possession.[103]

A third party to whom the debtor purports to sell the asset will not acquire title, even if they provided value for it and acted in good faith unless they fall within the limited exceptions set out in sections 21 to 26 of the Sale of Goods Act 1979. This protection arises because a pledge creates a legal interest rather than merely an equitable interest.[104] As a result, the creditor holding the pledge enjoys certain priority advantages over equitable mortgages and charges. Unlike equitable interests, which can be overridden by a bona fide purchaser who acquires a

97 *Holroyd v Marshall* (1862) 10 HLC 191 (House of Lords).
98 In *Mailbox (Birmingham) Ltd v Galliford Try Construction Ltd* [2017] EWHC 67 (TCC) at [41].
99 Hudson, A., *The Law on Financial Derivatives* (Sweet & Maxwell, 2017) at [15-114].
100 Chiu, I. and Wilson, J., *Banking Law and Regulation* (Oxford University Press, 2019), p. 176.
101 Hudson, A., *The Law of Finance* (Sweet & Maxwell, 2013) at [22-64].
102 *Re Hardwick, ex parte Hubbard* (1886) 17 QBD 690.
103 Gullifer, L., *Goode and Gullifer on Legal Problems of Credit and Security* (Sweet & Maxwell, 2023) at [1-47].
104 Bamford, C., *Principles of International Finance Law* (Oxford University Press, 2015) at [10.61].

legal interest for value without notice of the prior equitable claim, a pledgeholder retains priority over subsequent claimants, reinforcing its superior security position. Furthermore, the creditor's interest in the pledged asset remains effective even if the debtor becomes insolvent or enters administration.[105]

Further, in the event of the debtor's default in payment, the creditor has the right to sell the pledged asset, provided that due notice is given to the debtor.[106] The length of notice varies depending on the circumstances, such as the perishability of the goods. To clarify the parties' rights and obligations, typically, the pledgor and pledgee would enter into a letter of pledge (also known as a memorandum of deposit) detailing the pledgee's rights over the pledged asset and specifying the notice period required for sale.

Although the use of pledges is rare in practice, it retains relevance in certain specialised transactions or jurisdictions where it may play a more significant role.[107]

3.10 Liens

A lien is a security interest that generally arises by operation of law rather than through an express agreement between the parties.[108] In financial transactions where additional security is required, creditors typically prefer to take mortgages, charges, or pledges, or they may seek a third-party guarantee. However, lenders must be aware of the potential impact of liens that may rank ahead of the security they have taken. This is particularly relevant in cases involving maritime liens, which can take priority over a lender's mortgage on a ship.

There are three principal types of lien under English law: the legal (or common law) lien, the equitable lien, and the statutory lien. Additionally, a contractual lien may arise where the parties agree to extend a legal lien by providing specific enforcement rights, such as a power of sale. A contractual lien can also be created where no lien would otherwise exist under common law.[109]

A legal lien grants a creditor the right to retain possession of the debtor's property until the debt is repaid.[110] Unlike a pledge, however, a legal lien does not confer a right of sale, making it a passive security interest aimed at compelling the debtor to repay the debt in order to regain possession of the asset. In this respect, a banker's lien[111] (discussed in Chapter 3) differs from other types of common law liens as a banker's lien entitles, like a pledge, the bank to sell the security.[112] A legal lien can only attach to assets capable of being transferred by delivery. In *Your Response Ltd v Datateam Business Media Ltd* [2014] EWCA Civ 281, the Court of Appeal confirmed that a lien cannot be created over intangibles, such as electronic databases.

There are two types of legal liens: particular liens and general liens.[113] A particular lien entitles a creditor to retain possession of an asset only until a specific debt relating to that

105 Ellinger, E. P., Lomnicka, E. and Hare, C., *Ellinger's Modern Banking Law* (Oxford University Press, 2011), p. 858.
106 *Bassano v Toft and others* [2014] EWHC 377 (QB).
107 Arora, A., *Banking Law* (Pearson, 2014), p. 625.
108 Chiu, I. and Wilson, J., *Banking Law and Regulation* (Oxford University Press, 2019), p. 177.
109 Proctor, C., *The Law and Practice of International Banking* (Oxford University Press, 2015) at [28.31].
110 Bamford, C., *Principles of International Finance Law* (Oxford University Press, 2015) at [10.65].
111 *"It is a general principle in our law that every agent has a lien or right of retention against his principal for the balance due to him, and this right of retention is not confined to moneys collected, such as rents and dividends, but may extend to securities, the precise extent of the lien being determined by the nature or character of the agency. The so-called banker lien is an example of this rule of law, and in this case the decisions establish that a banker has a lien over all such negotiable securities of the customer as are lawfully in his possession and are subject to his control, but this lien may be excluded by agreement, express or implied"*.
112 Ellinger, E. P., Lomnicka, E. and Hare, C., *Ellinger's Modern Banking Law* (Oxford University Press, 2011), p. 864.
113 Hudson, A., *The Law of Finance* (Sweet & Maxwell, 2013) at [22-68].

asset has been repaid. In contrast, a general lien permits a creditor to retain possession of the debtor's property until all outstanding debts owed to the creditor have been discharged. General liens typically arise from long-standing business customs.

An equitable lien arises independently of possession and is created by the court to secure an unpaid debt or obligation over specific assets. Unlike a legal lien, an equitable lien does not require the creditor to be in possession of the asset. A common example is the unpaid seller's lien in real estate transactions, where the seller retains a lien over the property until the purchase price is fully paid. Equitable liens can attach to both tangible and intangible assets, even in the absence of an express agreement between the parties.

A statutory lien arises under the provisions of specific legislation, with its scope and enforcement governed by the terms of the statute that creates it. Common examples include the solicitor's lien over property recovered or preserved in litigation.[114] Other examples include the lien of an unpaid seller of goods under the Sale of Goods Act 1979 and the lien of an airport over unpaid airport charges, as provided for under the Civil Aviation Act 1982.

A contractual lien extends a legal lien through an express agreement between the parties. It may grant the creditor additional enforcement rights, such as the power to sell the asset if the debtor defaults. However, if a contractual lien includes a right of sale, it may be recharacterised as a charge, which would then be subject to registration requirements under the Companies Act 2006.[115] Moreover, a contractual lien may be subordinated to the rights of a party holding a debenture over the same assets, as it occurred in *The Trustees Corporate Trustees Ltd v Capmark Bank Europe PLC* [2011] EWCA Civ 380.

3.11 Security Over Digital Assets

As digital assets such as cryptocurrencies, domain names, and e-money become increasingly prominent in the financial and commercial sectors, lenders are showing greater interest in taking security over such assets.[116] However, the unique nature of digital assets presents significant challenges in determining whether and how security can be created and enforced.

The legal status of digital assets remains an area of ongoing development, particularly with the Law Commission playing a key role in shaping the legal framework. In April 2021, the Law Commission launched a project examining the legal status and treatment of digital assets, culminating in the publication of its final report, which addressed several key legal questions, including the definition of a digital asset, issues surrounding ownership and control, the legal principles governing their transfer, and the broader question of whether digital assets should be recognised as a distinct form of property.[117] As noted in Chapter 2, since digital assets do not fall within the traditional categories of property, the Law Commission published the draft "Property (Digital Assets etc.) Bill" aimed at introducing a third category of property to accommodate digital assets.[118] This statutory recognition is likely to enhance the legal certainty of security arrangements, facilitating more effective lending practices and commercial dealings in the digital asset space.

114 Which is provided for under section 73 of the Solicitors Act 1974.
115 Gullifer, L., *Goode and Gullifer on Legal Problems of Credit and Security* (Sweet & Maxwell, 2023) at [5-15].
116 Gullifer, L., *Goode and Gullifer on Legal Problems of Credit and Security* (Sweet & Maxwell, 2023) at [1-53].
117 See https://webarchive.nationalarchives.gov.uk/ukgwa/20250109172211mp_/https://s3-eu-west-2.amazonaws.com/cloud-platform-e218f50a4812967ba1215eaecede923f/uploads/sites/30/2023/06/Final-digital-assets-report-FOR-WEBSITE-2.pdf (accessed in March 2025).
118 Law Commission, 'Digital Assets *(Law Com No 412) (Final Report)*' [2024] EWLC 416, available at www.bailii.org/ew/other/EWLC/2024/LC416.pdf (accessed in March 2025).

Security Over Cryptoassets

The type of security that can be created over a cryptoasset depends largely on the nature of the cryptoasset and how it is held. As with other intangible assets, such as choses in action (including bank accounts or shares), security over cryptoassets is generally taken by way of a charge.

A charge grants the creditor an equitable proprietary interest in the asset, allowing it to enforce its rights without taking physical possession of the asset. This approach is relevant when dealing with cryptoassets stored in digital wallets.

In instances where a cryptoasset represents bearer securities or another asset capable of being secured by way of a mortgage, it is technically possible to create a mortgage over such a cryptoasset. For a legal mortgage over bearer securities, this would typically require the transfer of the cryptoasset to the mortgagee, analogous to depositing physical bearer securities. This is due to the established principle that a legal mortgage over bearer securities is executed by transferring the asset to the mortgagee.

While less common, it is possible to take a pledge over a cryptoasset if the asset meets the criteria for a pledge, which requires the asset to be transferable by delivery of possession. If a cryptoasset can be delivered in this manner – such as by transferring control of the asset or its associated private keys – a pledge could be created. However, whether cryptoassets are deemed capable of "possession" for the purposes of a pledge will depend on how the courts continue to interpret the legal status of such assets.

A lien cannot be created over a cryptoasset because cryptoassets, being intangible assets, do not meet the requirement for a lien, which must relate to property capable of physical possession. This position was confirmed by the Court of Appeal in *Your Response Ltd v Datateam Business Media Ltd* [2014] EWCA Civ 281, where the court concluded that a lien could not be exercised over intangible assets such as electronic data.

3.12 Security Trusts

Security trusts enable a security trustee to hold security on behalf of multiple lenders or investors, commonly in syndicated loan or club deal transactions.[119] Security trusts provide administrative convenience, allow lenders to regulate enforcement, and offer beneficiaries protection from the security trustee's creditors.[120] The security trustee enforces security on the instruction of the majority of lenders, ensuring that enforcement actions are coordinated and benefit all lenders equitably. These instruments will be further discussed in Chapter 12.

4 SECURITY PERFECTION AND PRIORITY IN LOAN TRANSACTIONS

When a lender takes security for a loan, it must ensure that its interest is protected in the event of default or insolvency of the security provider. The primary objective of the lender is to secure repayment ahead of other creditors.[121] To achieve this, the security interest must be properly

119 Bamford, C., *Principles of International Finance Law* (Oxford University Press, 2015) at [10.69].
120 Hudson, A., *The Law of Finance* (Sweet & Maxwell, 2013) at [22-17].
121 Gullifer, L. and Payne, J., *Corporate Finance Law: Principles and Policy* (Hart, 2020), p. 327.

perfected,[122] making it enforceable against third parties and ensuring that it ranks in priority over competing claims. However, perfection alone does not guarantee validity or priority in all cases, as insolvency laws may still affect the status and enforceability of the security.

The approach to perfecting security depends on the type of security interest, the nature of the asset, and the identity of the security provider.

With respect to possessory security, such as pledges, common law liens, and statutory liens, the secured party has to take and retain possession of the secured asset. These forms of possessory security apply only to assets that can physically be delivered. Constructive possession may also be established by controlling access to the secured asset, for example, by taking possession of warehouse keys that provide access to secured goods. However, possession is not relevant for security over land, as the mere deposit of title deeds does not create an enforceable security interest. Any disposition of an interest in land must be documented in writing, signed by the relevant parties, and incorporate all agreed terms.[123]

In the case of mortgages, legal or beneficial title to the asset must be transferred to the secured party.

Certain security interests must be created in writing and signed by specific parties. A security interest in land or an equitable interest must comply with section 2 of the Law of Property (Miscellaneous Provisions) Act 1989, requiring written documentation signed by the parties. This applies to most equitable mortgages and charges. Similarly, a mortgage or charge over an equitable interest or trust must be in writing and signed by the mortgagor or chargor.[124] However, as discussed previously, the FCA Regulations 2003 disapplied certain formalities[125] for security over financial collateral, including cash, financial instruments, and credit claims.

Where security is taken over choses in action or an equitable interest, notice must be provided to third parties. The timing of notice is crucial in determining priority. In *Dearle v Hall* (1828) 3 Russ 1, the court held that priority is granted to the first party to notify the debtor. Failure to give notice may allow a later assignee to gain priority if they notify the debtor first.[126]

Registration serves as a critical method of perfecting security, particularly in ensuring priority over third parties.[127] Security interests that require registration include mortgages and charges created by companies and LLPs, security over land, intellectual property, ships, and aircraft, and agricultural charges or security given by individuals under the Bills of Sale Act 1878 and the Bills of Sale Act (1878) Amendment Act 1882.

While a failure to register or protect security at the Land Registry or the Land Charges Department generally affects priority rather than enforceability against the borrower, on the other hand, failing to register security granted by a company or an LLP at the Companies House, where registration is required under the Companies Act 2006, would render the security void, in so far as it confers security, against the liquidator, administrator, and any creditor of the company or LLP, other than the lender.[128] This means that while the debt itself remains valid, the lender will lose the benefit of the security and will rank alongside unsecured creditors in any insolvency proceedings.[129]

122 Proctor, C., *The Law and Practice of International Banking* (Oxford University Press, 2015) at [29.24].
123 Under section 2 of the Law of Property (Miscellaneous Provisions) Act 1989.
124 Under section 53(1)(c) of the Law of Property Act 1925.
125 Such as those required under section 53(1)(c) of the Law of Property Act 1925.
126 As demonstrated in *Wilson v Kelland* [1910] 2 Ch 306.
127 Registration falls in two broad categories: under Section 859A of the Companies Act 2006 or in specialised registers.
128 Under section 859H of the Companies Act 2006.
129 Gullifer, L., *Goode and Gullifer on Legal Problems of Credit and Security* (Sweet & Maxwell, 2023) at [5-15].

4.1 Priority of Security Interests

The priority of security interests is a complex area of law, influenced by factors such as the type of security, the timing of its creation, and the order of registration. In insolvency proceedings, secured creditors generally rank ahead of unsecured creditors, although there are numerous exceptions to this principle.[130]

For security interests created by companies, the general rule is that they rank in order of creation. Fixed charges take priority over floating charges, even if the fixed charge was created after the floating charge.[131] Among fixed charges and mortgages, priority is determined by the date of creation.[132] This criterion is also applicable for determining the ranking of floating charges.[133]

However, exceptions exist, particularly where assets require registration in specialist registers, such as land[134] or intellectual property. In such cases, priority is determined by the order of registration rather than the date of creation.[135] Additionally, the *Dearle v Hall* principle applies to assignments of choses in action, meaning that priority is determined by the timing of notice to the debtor.[136]

Lenders can take steps to protect their priority by incorporating a negative pledge (see later on) in loan documents which prohibits the borrower from creating further security interests over their assets.[137]

Marshalling, which is an equitable remedy founded on the principle that a creditor with access to multiple sources for the satisfaction of its debt should not exercise its rights in a way that disadvantages another creditor who has recourse to only one of those sources, may also impact on the enforcement of certain collateral.

Marshalling becomes available where two distinct creditors – typically referred to as A and B – have security over a common pool of the debtor's assets (Assets X), but A also holds security over additional assets not charged to B (Assets Y). If A enforces its security over Assets X without resorting to Assets Y, creditor B, who does not have access to Assets Y, may find itself disadvantaged. In such circumstances, marshalling allows B to look to Assets Y to satisfy any part of its secured debt that cannot be repaid from Assets X due to A's enforcement action.

While there has been some debate as to whether marshalling constitutes a form of equitable subrogation, the courts have clarified that although marshalling may have a subrogative effect – namely, enabling the junior creditor to be treated as if it were entitled to the senior creditor's security – it is conceptually distinct. This was confirmed in *Serious Organised Crime Agency v Szepietowski and others* [2010] EWHC 2570 (Ch). Further clarification was provided by the Supreme Court in *Szepietowski v The National Crime Agency* [2013] UKSC 65, which articulated the test for determining when marshalling is available to a second mortgagee.

130 Proctor, C., *The Law and Practice of International Banking* (Oxford University Press, 2015) at [28.14].
131 As established in *Wheatley v Silkstone and Haigh Moor Coal Company* (1885) 29 Ch D 715.
132 As confirmed in *James v Boythorpe Colliery Co* [1890] 2 Meg 55.
133 As illustrated in *Re Benjamin Cope & Sons Ltd* [1914] 1 Ch 800.
134 The Land Registry does not require a particular form for registration of a mortgage or fixed charge. A legal mortgage of registered land can be in form CH1 but its use is not mandatory (rule 103, Land Registration Rules 2003 (SI 2003/1417) (LRR 2003)).
135 Bamford, C., *Principles of International Finance Law* (Oxford University Press, 2015) at [10.26].
136 Gullifer, L. and Payne, J., *Corporate Finance Law: Principles and Policy* (Hart, 2020), p. 331.
137 Hudson, A., *The Law of Finance* (Sweet & Maxwell, 2013) at [32-42].

Reviewable Transactions in Corporate Insolvency

When a company enters formal insolvency, certain transactions made prior to insolvency can be challenged under the Insolvency Act 1986. These are known as reviewable transactions. The ability to challenge such transactions serves two main purposes: protecting the *pari passu* principle (further discussed in Chapter 12), which ensures that a company's available assets in administration or liquidation are shared equally among unsecured creditors, and maximising returns to creditors by allowing an office holder (such as an administrator or liquidator) to recover assets or reverse transactions that have unfairly diminished the insolvent company's estate.[138]

The Insolvency Act 1986 sets out specific grounds for challenging transactions, including transactions at an undervalue,[139] preferences,[140] extortionate credit transactions,[141] invalid floating charges,[142] transactions defrauding creditors,[143] and contributions from past directors and shareholders.[144]

In addition to these statutory provisions, two common law principles operate to prevent companies from frustrating creditors' rights in insolvency. The anti-deprivation rule ensures that a company cannot structure its affairs in a way that removes assets from the reach of creditors, while *British Eagle International Airlines Ltd v Air France* [1975] 2 All ER 390 (further discussed in Chapter 12) prevents a company from contracting out of insolvency rules in a manner that would undermine the interests of creditors.[145]

Challenging a reviewable transaction typically requires an application to the court by the office holder or another authorised party. If the challenge is successful, the court has broad discretion to undo the effects of the transaction, which may include ordering the return of assets to the insolvent company.[146] For example, if a company has transferred assets at an undervalue,[147] the court may restore those assets to the company's estate, or if a company has made preferential payments to certain creditors, the court may reverse those payments to ensure equal treatment of creditors.

One common example of a reviewable transaction is the creation of a floating charge before insolvency. Under section 245 of the Insolvency Act 1986, a floating charge will be invalid if it was created solely in exchange for prior consideration, such as securing existing loans, goods, or services, rather than new value. Additionally, the charge must have been created within one year before the company's insolvency or within two years if granted in favour of a connected person, such as a director or an associate of the company. The charge will also be invalid if, at the time of creation, the company was unable to pay its debts or became unable to do so as a result of the charge (save where the charge was created in favour of a connected person, in which case the company's ability, or inability, to pay its debts is immaterial).

138 Proctor, C., *The Law and Practice of International Banking* (Oxford University Press, 2015) at [39.01].
139 Section 238.
140 Section 239.
141 Section 244.
142 Section 245.
143 Section 423.
144 Section 76.
145 Goode, R. and van Zwieten, K., *Principles of Corporate Insolvency Law* (Sweet & Maxwell, 2019), Chapter 7.
146 The process for challenging these transactions is governed by the relevant provisions of the Insolvency Act 1986. Typically, an application to the court is required to challenge transactions, such as transactions at an undervalue, preferences, extortionate credit transactions, and transactions defrauding creditors. Given the fact-specific nature of these claims, they often proceed to a full hearing, as the court must examine the evidence comprehensively before reaching a decision. The use of summary judgement in such cases is rarely appropriate, as emphasised in *Philips and another v McGregor-Paterson* [2009] EWHC 2385 (Ch), where the court highlighted the necessity of considering all relevant facts before determining a claim.
147 Gullifer, L., *Goode and Gullifer on Legal Problems of Credit and Security* (Sweet & Maxwell, 2023) at [8-36].

5 QUASI-SECURITY: OVERVIEW AND IMPACT ON SECURED LENDERS

Quasi-security can significantly affect the rights and priority of secured lenders. Therefore, understanding its nature and implications is essential for assessing the true risk and priority ranking of a lender's security interest.[148]

Quasi-security encompasses various financial arrangements that, while not creating a legal security interest, serve a similar economic function. Unlike traditional security, quasi-security does not grant a proprietary interest in the debtor's assets. However, it still enhances a creditor's rights, particularly in insolvency, and can, in some cases, give the creditor priority over secured lenders. These arrangements function by securing the debtor's obligations and ensuring that the creditor has a degree of control over the debtor's financial position. Common forms of quasi-security include negative pledges, finance leasing, sale and leaseback arrangements, hire purchase agreements, conditional sale agreements, factoring, set-off, and retention of title clauses.

As discussed in previous chapters, a negative pledge is a contractual undertaking given by a borrower to a lender not to create, or allow to remain in place, any security over its assets in favour of other creditors. It is a key provision in both secured and unsecured lending arrangements, designed – like other covenants – to afford the lender a degree of control over the borrower's financial conduct.[149] The principal function of a negative pledge is to prevent a borrower from granting security over its assets in favour of other creditors, which would otherwise enhance the position of those creditors to the detriment of the lender relying on the negative pledge. By restricting the creation of competing security interests, the clause helps maintain the lender's relative standing in the borrower's capital structure.

This protection is particularly significant for unsecured lenders, who are otherwise exposed to the risk that the borrower may subsequently grant security to a third party. In the event of the borrower's insolvency, a secured creditor would have priority over the relevant assets, thereby reducing the pool of assets available to satisfy the claims of unsecured creditors. The inclusion of a negative pledge can thus be vital in preserving the unsecured lender's potential recovery by helping to ensure that its position is not eroded by the creation of prior-ranking security interests. Negative pledges are also significant for secured lenders, not only in terms of preserving their priority but also for other practical reasons. A lender holding only a floating charge over a security provider's assets is particularly vulnerable, as a later-created fixed charge will take precedence over the earlier floating charge. This could substantially diminish the value of the lender's security in an enforcement scenario. Even where a lender benefits from a fixed charge or legal mortgage, it will typically seek to include a negative pledge to prevent the borrower from granting further security. Although subsequent security interests would ordinarily rank behind the original charge, assuming that the original has been properly created and perfected, the existence of additional secured creditors may nonetheless adversely affect the original lender.

Negative pledges are typically found in facility agreements and may also appear in security documents. This is because, from a lender's perspective, it is particularly important to ensure that a negative pledge is also set out in the security document so

148 Gullifer, L., *Goode and Gullifer on Legal Problems of Credit and Security* (Sweet & Maxwell, 2023) at [1-31].
149 Gullifer, L., *Goode and Gullifer on Legal Problems of Credit and Security* (Sweet & Maxwell, 2023) at [1-41].

that, upon registration of the security at Companies House, the negative pledge can be publicly noted. Such registration serves to give constructive notice to third parties – including future lenders – of the restriction on the borrower's ability to grant further security, thereby offering additional protection to the lender's position. Thus, if a borrower creates security in breach of a negative pledge and the creditor taking that security has notice[150] of the same, the security may be subordinated to the rights of the original lender. Where the original lender is unsecured, it may seek an injunction to prevent the creation of further security or pursue a tortious claim for inducing a breach of contract if the subsequent creditor had notice of the negative pledge. A breach of a negative pledge often constitutes an event of default under the relevant loan agreement, giving the lender additional remedies.

It is important to bear in mind, however, that a negative pledge is a contractual obligation rather than a legal prohibition. While it affords the lender a measure of protection, it does not prevent the borrower from granting new security in breach of the pledge. The creation of such security would still be legally valid between the borrower and the new secured creditor, although it would give rise to a claim for breach of contract by the original lender.

Finance leasing allows a debtor to finance the acquisition of assets without taking direct ownership during the lease term. In this arrangement, the lessor (often a finance house) purchases the asset and leases it to the lessee (the borrower), who makes payments equivalent to the asset's value plus a return on capital. The lessee has use of the asset without owning it, while the lessor retains title. Since the lessor retains ownership throughout the lease period, the asset is not available as security for any other lender. However, at the end of the lease term, the asset may be sold to the lessee for a nominal value, transferring ownership.

A sale and leaseback arrangement is similar to finance leasing, except that the lessee initially owns the asset. The lessee sells the asset to the lessor (typically a finance house) and then leases it back. This arrangement provides the lessee with immediate liquidity while allowing continued use of the asset during the lease term. As with finance leasing, the lessee does not hold title to the asset during the lease period, preventing its use as security for other loans. The lessor may repossess the asset if the lessee defaults on its lease payments.[151]

Hire purchase is another form of lease agreement where the lessee has the option to purchase the asset at the end of the lease term for a nominal sum. Unlike other forms of leasing, title does not pass automatically to the lessee; it only transfers if the lessee exercises the purchase option. During the hire period, the lessor retains ownership, preventing the asset from being used as security for another lender. However, once the lessee acquires title, the asset becomes available for security. A conditional sale agreement is similar to a hire purchase, with the key distinction that title to the asset automatically passes to the purchaser once all instalments have been paid. Until that time, the seller retains ownership, preventing the asset from being used as security for another lender. Unlike hire purchase, the purchaser does not have an option to acquire title – it transfers automatically upon full payment.[152]

150 For a detailed discussion of the debate about whether registration of a negative pledge at Companies House constitutes notice of that negative pledge, see Gullifer, L., *Goode and Gullifer on Legal Problems of Credit and Security* (Sweet & Maxwell, 2023) at [2-25]–[2-31].

151 Gullifer, L., *Goode and Gullifer on Legal Problems of Credit and Security* (Sweet & Maxwell, 2023) at [5-15].

152 Hudson, A., *The Law of Finance* (Sweet & Maxwell, 2013) at [32-45].

Factoring involves a business assigning its book debts to a factoring company in exchange for immediate payment, typically at a discount. The factoring company then collects the debts as they fall due. Factoring allows businesses to raise cash by selling receivables. Once book debts are factored, they are no longer owned by the original business and, therefore, cannot be used as security for a lender. Lenders taking security over a company's receivables must ensure that these have not already been factored or assigned.

Set-off, as discussed in Chapter 2, arises when competing monetary claims between two parties are offset, resulting in a single net balance owed. If a creditor has a right of set-off against the debtor, that right will generally take priority over a third party's security interest in the debt. For instance, if a bank has a set-off right against a customer's deposits and the customer grants a third party security over those deposits, the bank's set-off right will typically take precedence over the third party's security interest.

Retention of title is commonly used by suppliers to retain ownership of goods delivered to a buyer until payment is made. Under the retention of title clause (also referred to as a "Romalpa" clause, after the leading case on the subject, *Aluminium Industrie Vaasen BV v Romalpa Aluminium Ltd* [1976] 1 WLR 676), the supplier can reclaim the goods if the buyer defaults. The goods cannot be used as security for another lender unless the supplier's retention of title rights is extinguished. Suppliers may enhance retention of title clauses by reserving ownership over the goods until all debts are paid (an all-monies clause) or by claiming rights over proceeds of sale or mixed goods (proceeds of sale clause or mixed goods clause). Care must be taken to ensure these clauses do not inadvertently create a charge, which would require registration under the Companies Act 2006.

6 GUARANTEES AND INDEMNITIES

Lenders will usually seek a guarantee or indemnity as an additional layer of security, particularly when concerns arise regarding the borrower's solvency. A number of loans may be unsecured but are supported by guarantees. Under such a guarantee, the guarantor commits to fulfilling the borrower's obligations if the borrower defaults on repayment of the loan or interest.[153] This arrangement enhances the lender's security, as the guarantor (often more financially stable than the borrower) becomes liable for the debt in place of the borrower. Guarantees are not limited to unsecured loans; they are also used to support secured loans.[154]

A *guarantee* is a secondary obligation, meaning it supports the primary obligation of the borrower. It represents a promise by the guarantor to ensure the borrower fulfils its obligations or to fulfil them if the borrower defaults. The guarantor's liability is contingent upon the borrower's failure to meet its obligations, ensuring the guarantor's responsibility never exceeds that of the borrower. This could include repaying a loan or, in other contexts, fulfilling performance obligations under a contract.[155]

An *indemnity*, by contrast, is a primary obligation that exists independently of the borrower's responsibilities. The indemnifier promises to compensate the beneficiary for losses suffered as a result of specified events. Unlike a guarantee, an indemnity is not contingent on the borrower's default and remains enforceable even if the underlying obligation is set aside.

153 Proctor, C., *The Law and Practice of International Banking* (Oxford University Press, 2015) at [26.24].
154 Hudson, A., *The Law of Finance* (Sweet & Maxwell, 2013) at [22-77].
155 Gullifer, L. and Payne, J., *Corporate Finance Law: Principles and Policy* (Hart, 2020), p. 247.

This makes indemnities particularly robust, as they are not as vulnerable to changes in the primary obligation or underlying contract.[156]

A guaranteed loan facility provides several advantages to a lender, particularly in reducing credit risk exposure. When the guarantor is the borrower's parent company, this arrangement becomes even more valuable, as the parent company is likely to be involved in making significant financial and strategic decisions that affect the borrower. By offering a guarantee, the parent assumes direct accountability for the borrower's financial obligations, ensuring that its decisions remain aligned with the potential impact on the loan.[157]

Moreover, cross-guarantees within a corporate group enhance the lender's protection by allowing guarantees from multiple group companies. This mechanism safeguards the lender in cases where the borrower's assets are transferred to other group entities without obligations to the lender, which would otherwise place the assets beyond the lender's reach in the event of a default. A cross-guarantee enables the lender to claim against any group company that holds significant assets and minimal liabilities, thus improving the chances of recovering the full debt. By offering both the additional security of a guarantee and the strategic oversight of group-wide guarantees, this approach ensures that the lender is protected not only from the borrower's insolvency but also from potential asset transfers within the group, providing a comprehensive safety net across multiple entities.

In many transactions, standard guarantees often combine both a guarantee and an indemnity to maximise protection for the lender. This dual obligation is particularly advantageous as it provides different legal rights and remedies. For example, a combined guarantee and indemnity might read: "*The Guarantor guarantees to the Lender the due performance of the Borrower's obligations and, in addition, agrees to indemnify the Lender for any losses arising from the Borrower's failure to meet those obligations*".

The specific advantages of a guarantee include specific rights automatically granted to the guarantor, such as indemnity, subrogation, and marshalling, which may conflict with the beneficiary's interests. For instance, under the right of indemnity, the guarantor can claim reimbursement from the borrower upon fulfilling the borrower's obligations. Additionally, subrogation allows the guarantor, upon settling the borrower's obligations, to step into the shoes of the lender and benefit from any security held by the lender. Marshalling, a further advantage, permits the guarantor to seek satisfaction from the debtor's other assets where another creditor has already enforced its security over common assets.

On the other hand, indemnities offer certain advantages over guarantees, particularly regarding statutory formalities. Unlike guarantees, indemnities are not subject to the writing and signature requirements imposed by section 4 of the Statute of Frauds 1677, making them easier to enforce in certain situations. Moreover, because indemnities are primary obligations, they remain valid even if the primary obligation is voided or altered. This resilience makes indemnities particularly useful where the underlying agreement might be susceptible to legal challenges.[158]

Despite their differences, guarantees, and indemnities can create legal ambiguities, especially where both are included in a single document. Courts are inclined to construe the terms of such documents in favour of the party assuming the obligations. Therefore, it is critical that the language clearly differentiates between primary and secondary obligations. In cases such as *Fransina Johanna van der Merwe v IIG Capital LLC* [2007] EWHC 2631 (Ch), courts have

156 Proctor, C., *The Law and Practice of International Banking* (Oxford University Press, 2015) at [26.25].
157 Gullifer, L., *Goode and Gullifer on Legal Problems of Credit and Security* (Sweet & Maxwell, 2023) at [8-02].
158 Gullifer, L., *Goode and Gullifer on Legal Problems of Credit and Security* (Sweet & Maxwell, 2023) at [8-12].

scrutinised whether a promise constitutes a guarantee or an indemnity, leaning towards a guarantee unless the language of the document unambiguously states otherwise.[159]

The courts also distinguish between different types of guarantees. A *pure guarantee* obligates the guarantor to ensure the borrower's performance under the primary agreement. If the borrower fails to meet its obligations, the guarantor becomes liable, providing the lender with a claim for damages equal to the loss suffered (the beneficiary accordingly has a duty to mitigate its loss); this latter type of guarantee is also known as a "see to it" guarantee.

Lord Diplock in *Moschi v Lep Air Service Limited* [1973] AC 331, where Mr Moschi guaranteed the performance by a company of its obligation to discharge a pre-existing debt to the respondent at the rate of £6,000 per week subject to a cap on his liability of £40,000, provides a useful summary of the nature of the guarantor's liability under a "see to it" guarantee:

> *it is not an obligation himself to pay a sum of money to the creditor, but an obligation to see to it that another person, the debtor, does something; and that the creditor's remedy for the guarantor's failure to perform it lies in damages for breach of contract only. . . . The legal consequence of this is that whenever the debtor has failed voluntarily to perform an obligation which is the subject of the guarantee the creditor can recover from the guarantor as damages for breach of his contract of guarantee, whatever sum the creditor could have recovered from the debtor himself as a consequence of that failure. The debtor's liability to the creditor is also the measure of the guarantor's.*[160]

Ultimately, the decision to use a guarantee, an indemnity, or a combination of both will depend on the circumstances of the transaction and the level of protection the lender seeks. By combining the benefits of both instruments, creditors can ensure robust security in the event of borrower default or other unforeseen complications in the underlying transaction.

7 CROSS-BORDER SECURITY

Cross-border security involves taking security over assets located or governed by foreign jurisdictions. While English law affords the flexibility of taking security over almost any type of asset, in some overseas jurisdictions, legal frameworks may impose restrictions on securing future or intangible assets. One of the key considerations in such jurisdictions is whether possession of the secured asset can remain with the security provider, prompting the need to explore alternative structures such as finance leases or retention of title arrangements, where the lender holds legal title to the asset while the provider retains usage rights. Trusts, commonly used in English law for structuring security interests, may not be recognised in all jurisdictions or may operate differently. In some cases, a parallel debt obligation structure may address challenges with trust law overseas.

Perfecting security – ensuring its validity and priority – can involve different procedural requirements depending on where the secured asset or security provider is located or the law governing the security document.

In some jurisdictions, enforcement may face additional challenges, including lengthy or costly legal proceedings or restrictions on how enforcement can occur, such as limiting enforcement to public auctions.[161] Additionally, there may be restrictions on the lender's ability to hold the security, requiring an entity based in the overseas jurisdiction to hold it on the lender's behalf. Ensuring that the security provider has the legal capacity to grant security and

159 Hudson, A., *The Law of Finance* (Sweet & Maxwell, 2013) at [22-87].
160 At pages 348H-349.
161 Gullifer, L. and Payne, J., *Corporate Finance Law: Principles and Policy* (Hart, 2020), p. 366.

that "all monies" security will be recognised in the relevant jurisdiction are further important considerations, as some legal systems may require the secured amount to be specified, complicating loans with floating interest rates or multiple currencies. Finally, lenders must evaluate potential practical and legal issues that could arise during enforcement, including the involvement of third parties, costs, and possible restrictions on enforcement rights.

8 SECURITY INTERESTS IN THE US

In the United States, security interests are governed by the UCC. The UCC provides a consistent legal framework for securing personal property and fixtures. Perfection of the security interest is achieved through filing, control, or possession, ensuring the lender's priority over third-party claims.[162]

A security interest provides the lender with a legal right to enforce its claim against the borrower's assets and receive priority over other creditors in bankruptcy or insolvency proceedings.

The Bankruptcy Code, codified as Title 11 of the US Code, outlines two primary types of bankruptcy relief: liquidation and rehabilitation or reorganization. It offers provisions for six different forms of bankruptcy cases. The most relevant chapters for corporate debtors are **Chapter 11** (reorganization) and **Chapter 7** (liquidation).

Chapter 7 provides a process for winding down a business that cannot meet its financial obligations by appointing a bankruptcy trustee to liquidate the debtor's assets and distribute the proceeds to creditors based on the priority rules established in the Code. Secured creditors are generally paid first, while unsecured creditors receive a pro-rata distribution of any remaining funds. The purpose of Chapter 7 is to give the debtor a fresh start by discharging debts while maximising recovery for creditors. The case begins with the filing of a petition, which can be voluntary (initiated by the debtor), involuntary (initiated by creditors), or a conversion from Chapter 11 or 13. Once the case starts, the debtor's assets are turned over to the Trustee, and an automatic stay halts collection efforts. The Trustee liquidates the assets, typically through auction, and distributes the proceeds to creditors, with secured creditors receiving priority. If there are secured creditors, they may seek relief from the automatic stay to foreclose on collateral. Unsecured creditors are paid from the remaining funds, and any outstanding unsecured debts are discharged. Certain creditors, such as those holding administrative claims or priority claims, receive special consideration, and some debts are non-dischargeable. For secured creditors, recovery in Chapter 7 involves balancing the right to full recovery, including interest and legal fees, with avoiding harm to the debtor or other creditors, especially in cases involving time-sensitive collateral such as perishable goods.

A perfected security interest ensures that the lender has enforceable rights over the collateral in the event of default and is protected against competing claims from other creditors if the borrower becomes insolvent. To achieve this, the lender must comply with Article 9 of the

162 Wood, P., *Comparative Law of Security Interests and Title Finance* (Sweet & Maxwell, 2019) at [19-022].

UCC,[163] which governs the creation, attachment, perfection, and priority of security interests in personal property.[164]

For a lender to establish a security interest under the UCC, it must first ensure that the interest is attached to the collateral. Attachment occurs when three key conditions are satisfied: value is given by the lender to the borrower,[165] the borrower has rights in the collateral or authority to transfer them,[166] and the borrower has authenticated a security agreement that sufficiently describes the collateral.[167] A security agreement is the principal document that creates the security interest. While the UCC does not prescribe a specific form, the agreement must contain a granting clause explicitly creating the security interest and a clear description of the collateral.[168] This description must be detailed enough to identify the secured assets. The borrower must also authenticate the agreement, typically by signing it.[169] In some cases, possession or control of the collateral by the lender may satisfy this requirement, particularly for deposit accounts or certificated securities.

Once a security interest has been attached, the lender must perfect it to protect its priority over third parties. The method of perfection[170] depends on the type of collateral and may include filing a UCC-1 financing statement,[171] taking possession of the collateral,[172] obtaining control over the asset,[173] or automatic perfection for certain types of security interests.[174]

Once perfected, the priority of a security interest determines its ranking relative to other creditors' claims. The UCC follows the general principle of first in time, first in right, meaning the first lender to perfect its security interest has priority. A perfected security interest takes precedence over an unperfected one. Where multiple perfected interests exist, priority is determined by the earliest perfection date.[175] Certain security interests, such as Purchase Money Security Interests,[176] may be granted super-priority, meaning they take precedence over earlier-perfected interests if specific statutory conditions are met.[177]

A lender's perfected security interest may be affected by post-closing events, such as changes in the borrower's name or relocation to a different jurisdiction. The UCC requires lenders to take timely action to maintain perfection, such as filing amendments to the UCC-1 financing statement if relevant details change.[178] Additionally, lenders must file continuation statements every five years to prevent their perfected status from lapsing.[179]

163 Wood, P., *Comparative Law of Security Interests and Title Finance* (Sweet & Maxwell, 2019) at [58-021].
164 *USA* in Mellor, T. (ed.), *ICLG – Lending & Secured Finance 2024* (ICLG, 2024). See https://iclg.com/practice-areas/lending-and-secured-finance-laws-and-regulations/usa (accessed in March 2025).
165 UCC § 9-203(b)(1).
166 UCC § 9-203(b)(2).
167 UCC § 9-203(b)(3).
168 UCC § 9-108(a).
169 UCC § 9-102(a)(7).
170 Gullifer, L., *Goode and Gullifer on Legal Problems of Credit and Security* (Sweet & Maxwell, 2023) at [1-59].
171 UCC § 9-310.
172 UCC § 9-313.
173 UCC § 9-314.
174 UCC § 9-309.
175 UCC § 9-322.
176 English law achieves similar commercial results as Purchase Money Security Interests through mechanisms such as: (a) retention of title clauses; (b) fixed charges over specific assets; or (c) chattel mortgages.
177 UCC § 9-324.
178 UCC § 9-507.
179 UCC § 9-515.

9 SECURITY IN FRANCE

In France, real estate encompasses land, buildings, and other constructions attached to land or buildings.[180] Additionally, certain movable assets affixed to land or buildings may be considered immovable by the destination and thus included as part of real estate assets. The most common security interests over such assets are mortgages (*hypothèques*) and "special legal mortgage" (*hypothèque légale spéciale*). Mortgages can secure any debt and are created under a notarial deed, though they incur significant costs due to stamp duty being determined on the secured amount. Lenders' liens, used to secure loans for acquiring real estate, are generally less costly than mortgages. Trusts (*fiducies*) and real estate pledges (*gages immobiliers*) are less commonly used, with trusts requiring the transfer of title to a trustee, leading to associated transfer costs, and pledges involving a transfer of possession to the creditor.[181]

Tangible movable property in France includes machinery, equipment, trading stock, and transportable items such as aircraft, ships, and furniture. The most common form of security over such property is a non-possessory pledge, where possession remains with the pledgor. Possessory pledges, where the creditor holds the property, are less common. For cash deposits, security is typically created through a pledge over a bank account balance or through a pledge over cash (*gage-espèces*), where the creditor can freely dispose of the cash but must return the same amount upon discharge of the secured obligations; a written agreement has to identify the secured obligations.

Security over financial instruments, particularly shares, is typically created through securities account pledges (*nantissement de compte-titres*) or share pledges (*nantissement de parts sociales*). Securities account pledges cover the account in which the shares are registered, as well as a special bank account for related cash proceeds, and extend to additional shares or cash credited during the pledge's duration. In contrast, share pledges apply to non-stock companies and cover only the shares existing at the time of the pledge. A security trust (*fiducie-sûreté*) can also be used to transfer shares to a trustee, with the trustee maintaining them separately from their own estate. For receivables, the most common form of security is a pledge, which can be created over any type of receivables and granted to any creditor. The *Dailly* assignment of receivables is another form of security[182] limited to professional borrowers that benefit certain licensed financial entities. A delegation (*délégation*) allows a debtor to instruct a third party to make payments directly to the creditor.

Intellectual property rights, such as trademarks, patents, designs, and copyrights, are commonly secured through pledges, either individually or as part of a pledge over a business. These pledges must be registered with the relevant intellectual property registry for enforceability.[183]

Certain assets can pose difficulties in creating security interests. For example, future assets may only be pledged if they can be identified, with specific rules for future receivables. Fungible assets, such as goods or commodities, can be pledged under either a possessory or

180 Wood, P., *Comparative Law of Security Interests and Title Finance* (Sweet & Maxwell, 2019), Part 1, Chapter 9.

181 *France* in Mellor, T. (ed.), *ICLG – Lending & Secured Finance 2024* (ICLG, 2024). See https://iclg.com/practice-areas/lending-and-secured-finance-laws-and-regulations/france (accessed in March 2025).

182 "Dailly" assignments are security interests where a company makes an outright transfer of any claims it may have over identifiable receivables arising out of its professional activity. They are only available where the beneficiary of the assignment is a credit institution (see Section II) that has extended the financing secured by the security interest.

183 The establishment of a single Register of Security Interests over Movable Properties through Decree 2021-1887 of 29 December 2021, which came into effect on 1 January 2023, attempted to simplify and centralise the registration process for movable security interests.

non-possessory regime, with differing rules on the secured creditor's ability to dispose of or hold the assets separately.

In terms of formalities, to be enforceable against third parties, mortgages, lenders' liens, and real estate pledges must be registered with the land registry. Trusts over real estate must also be registered with the tax authorities within one month of execution and with the land registry to be valid,[184] while with respect to securities, they must also be registered with the tax authorities and the relevant securities registers. Furthermore, securities account pledges must be registered with the relevant shareholders' accounts, while share pledges must be registered with the commercial court. Pledges over receivables or bank account balances must be notified to the debtor to be enforceable.

10 SECURITY IN GERMANY

In Germany, real estate is recorded as separate plots in the land registers (*Grundbuch*), maintained by local courts, and includes accessory assets serving the economic purpose of the land, as well as buildings and other permanently attached structures.[185] Land can also be subject to heritable building rights (*Erbbaurechte*), which allow the grantee to build on the land and hold ownership of the buildings independently from the land itself. Security over real estate, including heritable building rights, is most commonly taken in the form of a land charge (*Grundschuld*) or, less frequently, a mortgage (*Hypothek*). A land charge is a non-accessory security instrument, meaning it exists independently of the secured claim, can be assigned separately from the claim, and allows enforcement triggers to be set independently; it requires a security purpose agreement (*Sicherungszweckvereinbarung*) to detail the secured obligations. In contrast, a mortgage is an accessory security interest tied to the existence of the secured claim and is only enforceable when the secured claim is due. Mortgages or land charges can be created to secure portfolios of properties, often structured to allow cross-collateralisation across multiple plots.[186]

Security over real estate can be granted either with or without a certificate, with the certificated form offering greater flexibility for assignment, though the uncertificated form is more common to avoid complications if the certificate is lost. The rank of security is determined by the time of registration, and in financing transactions, notarial confirmations are often used to assure lenders of the security's eventual registration rank, as registration can take several weeks.

Security over movable property, such as machinery or inventory, is commonly achieved through either a pledge (*Pfandrecht*) or a security transfer (*Sicherungsübereignung*), with the latter being preferred as it allows the security provider to retain possession of the assets.

Security over financial instruments, particularly shares, is typically granted by way of a pledge or a security assignment, with specific formalities depending on the corporate structure of the entity whose shares are pledged. Pledges over receivables are less common than security assignments, which are often used in financing and insolvency contexts. Security over cash deposits is usually granted through account pledges, and intellectual property rights can be secured through pledges or security assignments, though assignments may incur additional liabilities for the assignee. Security can be granted over future assets, provided they are clearly defined, but insolvency laws prevent the inclusion of assets acquired after insolvency

184 Wood, P., *Comparative Law of Security Interests and Title Finance* (Sweet & Maxwell, 2019) at [13-008].
185 Wood, P., *Comparative Law of Security Interests and Title Finance* (Sweet & Maxwell, 2019), Part 1, Chapter 10.
186 *Germany* in Mellor, T. (ed.), *ICLG – Lending & Secured Finance 2024* (ICLG, 2024). See https://iclg.com/practice-areas/lending-and-secured-finance-laws-and-regulations/germany (accessed in March 2025).

proceedings begin.[187] Security interests over non-transferable assets, such as certain intellectual property rights, cannot be granted.

11 SECURITY IN ITALY

In Italy, real estate assets include the soil, surface, any buildings on the land, and any other asset incorporated into the land. Certain registered movable assets, such as ships, aircraft, and cars, are also treated as immovable for the purposes of transfer and security creation. The most common form of security over land, ships, or aircraft is a mortgage (*ipoteca*),[188] although security can also be taken indirectly through a pledge or assignment of rent receivables from lease contracts or insurance receivables related to real estate. To create a mortgage, a notarial deed must be executed, and the mortgage must be registered with the relevant local real estate registry (or the ships or aircraft registries). Tangible movable property includes assets such as machinery, equipment, and inventory and is typically secured through a pledge. Special liens (*privilegio speciale*) may also be granted under certain conditions, while registered movable assets like ships and aircraft are generally subject to mortgages.[189] A possessory pledge requires the delivery of the asset to the pledgee, while a newly introduced non-possessory pledge allows the pledgor to retain possession, though it cannot be applied to registered movable goods. Financial instruments, including shares, bonds, and fund units, are usually secured by a pledge, perfected through notification to the depositary or by registration if the instruments are dematerialised. Claims and receivables, such as debts or contractual rights, are commonly secured through a pledge or assignment, with perfection requiring notification or acceptance by the debtor. Security over cash deposits is typically achieved by a pledge over the relevant bank account, perfected through notice to the depositary. Intellectual property, including patents, trademarks, and copyrights, can also be secured through a pledge, which must be registered with the Italian Office of Patents and Trademarks to be effective. Security can be granted over future or fungible assets, but the pledge over cash deposits requires periodic updates when the account balance changes, and a pledge over machinery or equipment presents challenges due to the possession requirement, though the non-possessory pledge aims to resolve this issue. The release of security generally follows the same formalities required for its creation, such as executing a deed of release in a notarial form where applicable.

12 SECURITY IN CHINA

Under Chinese law, real estate is broadly defined to include land and fixed objects on the land, such as buildings and forest trees, as well as sea areas. The most common form of security granted over real estate is a mortgage. To create a valid mortgage, the parties must execute a written mortgage agreement. However, merely entering into a mortgage contract does not grant the mortgagee any rights until the mortgage is perfected. For real estate, perfection occurs when the mortgage is registered with the relevant real estate registry, at which point the mortgage becomes valid and enforceable. Specific types of real estate, such as state-owned

187 Wood, P., *Comparative Law of Security Interests and Title Finance* (Sweet & Maxwell, 2019) at [21-007].

188 Article 2808 of the Italian Civil Code regulates mortgages. It grants creditors the right to foreclose on a property that serves as collateral for a loan.

189 *Italy* in Mellor, T. (ed.), *ICLG – Lending & Secured Finance 2024* (ICLG, 2024). See https://iclg.com/practice-areas/lending-and-secured-finance-laws-and-regulations/italy (accessed in March 2025).

land use rights, rural land management rights, and urban buildings, must be registered with the local real estate registration centre to ensure the mortgage's validity.[190]

Tangible movable property, which can include machinery, inventory, ships, aircraft under construction, and means of communication, is also subject to security interests, typically in the form of mortgages or pledges. A mortgage over tangible movable property must be executed in writing, but unlike real estate, registration is not mandatory for the mortgage to be valid. However, an unregistered mortgage cannot be used to defend against third parties acting in good faith.[191] In certain cases, such as with motor vehicles or ships, registration with the appropriate local authority is necessary to perfect the mortgage. For other movable assets, registration may be completed through the unified registration and disclosure system managed by the Credit Reference Center of the People's Bank of China. In contrast, a pledge over tangible movable property requires the transfer of possession to the pledgee, which can be actual or constructive, for the pledge to be perfected.[192]

Financial instruments such as notes, shares, bonds, and certificates of deposit can also be subject to security interests, primarily in the form of pledges. The process of creating a security interest in financial instruments is governed by similar principles, where the pledge is only perfected when the possession[193] or rights over the instrument are transferred or registered, depending on the nature of the asset.

13 SECURITY IN INDIA

Real estate in India encompasses land, whether freehold or leased, along with any buildings or structures attached to it. It also includes anything permanently affixed to the land, as well as rights associated with the land, such as easement rights. Security over real estate is most commonly created through mortgages, which are primarily governed by Section 58 of the Transfer of Property Act 1882, which stipulates:

> *A mortgage is the transfer of an interest in specific immoveable property for the purpose of securing the payment of money advanced or to be advanced by way of loan, an existing or future debt, or the performance of an engagement which may give rise to a pecuniary liability.*

The two prevalent forms of mortgages in India are the English legal mortgage,[194] where the property is transferred to the mortgagee with a condition of reconveyance upon repayment of the debt, and a "*mortgage by deposit of title deeds. Such a mortgage by deposit of title deeds is for all purposes a 'legal mortgage' and not an equitable mortgage*".[195] An equitable mortgage, on the other hand, does not create a charge that can be enforced against third parties (*Right in Rem*). Instead, it only creates a personal obligation (*Right in Personam*) between the parties involved.[196]

190 *China* in Mellor, T. (ed.), *ICLG – Lending & Secured Finance 2024* (ICLG, 2024). See https://iclg.com/practice-areas/lending-and-secured-finance-laws-and-regulations/china (accessed in March 2025).

191 Article 388, 400 and 403, Chinese Civil Code.

192 Article 388, 427 and 429, Chinese Civil Code.

193 Article 429, Chinese Civil Code.

194 *India* in Dewar, J. (ed.), *ICLG – Project Finance 2024* (ICLG, 2024). See https://iclg.com/practice-areas/project-finance-laws-and-regulations/india (accessed in March 2025).

195 See the Indian Supreme Court decision of *The Cosmos Co Operative Bank Ltd vs Central Bank of India* [2025] INSC 243.

196 "*The last part of Section 100 of the Act, 1882 further statutorily recognizes the in personam nature of such 'charge' and provides that they shall not be enforced against any person to whom such property or interest therein has been transferred i.e., to whom it has been mortgaged in terms of Section 58 of the said Act or any other bona-fide transferee who does not have notice of the said charge. Thus, what may be discerned is that, 'equitable mortgages' are very much recognised in India under the nomenclature of 'charge' in terms of Section 100 of the Act, 1882, and the same will be enforceable as far*

Under the Transfer of Property Act 1882, mortgages exceeding INR 100 (other than equitable mortgages) must be executed by way of deed, signed by the mortgagor, attested by two witnesses, and registered with the relevant land registry. For equitable mortgages, the creation is formalised through the deposit of title deeds, often accompanied by a declaration by the mortgagor. Additionally, stamp duty must be paid in accordance with the applicable state laws, and the mortgage must be registered under the Indian Registration Act 1908 within four months of execution. Failure to register renders the mortgage invalid. In certain states, it is mandatory to notify authorities about the creation of equitable mortgages. Further, if the borrower is a company, the mortgage must be filed with the Registrar of Companies and also registered with the Central Registry of Securitisation Asset Reconstruction and Security Interest of India. If the property is leased from the government or a regulatory body, permission from the lessor may be required.

Tangible movable property in India includes assets like plant and machinery, raw materials, trading stock, vehicles, and ships. Security over tangible movable property is often created through mortgages or hypothecation. Mortgages over ships, for example, must follow statutory forms, be attested by witnesses, and be registered with the Mercantile Marine Department. In the case of hypothecation, the security provider executes a deed of hypothecation, creating a charge over the property without transferring possession. Hypothecation of aircraft and vehicles requires specific registrations with relevant authorities like the Director General of Civil Aviation for aircraft and the motor vehicle registry for cars. Similar to mortgages, hypothecation deeds are subject to stamp duty and must be filed with the Registrar of Companies and Central Registry of Securitisation Asset Reconstruction and Security Interest of India.

Security over financial instruments, such as shares, bonds, or mutual fund certificates, is typically created through a pledge. A pledge agreement, often accompanied by a power of attorney, records the arrangement, with the delivery of the financial instruments (physical or constructive) marking the pledge's perfection. If the instruments are in dematerialised form, filings with the depository are necessary. Pledging of shares in a listed company by promoters requires disclosures to the stock exchange and the company itself.

For claims and receivables, security is generally created through a mortgage, hypothecation, or assignment, either by way of security or as an absolute transfer. Assignments are rare in India due to the high stamp duty costs. Cash deposits are typically secured through hypothecation or mortgages.

Intellectual property, including patents, trademarks, and copyrights, can also be secured through assignment, hypothecation, or mortgage. The formalities for securing intellectual property involve executing the relevant agreements and filing with the intellectual property rights office, with mandatory registration for patents, trademarks, and designs.

Certain assets pose difficulties for securing interests, such as future immovable property, where security cannot be created unless the security provider has rights over the property at the time of security creation. Infrastructure assets obtained under government concessions may also require special permissions or be excluded from securitisation, depending on the nature of the concession.

To release a security interest, the satisfaction of charges must be filed with the Registrar of Companies and Central Registry of Securitisation Asset Reconstruction and Security Interest of India. For immovable property, a deed of re-conveyance or release is executed and registered. Ships and aircraft require specific filings with the Mercantile Marine Department

as possible in terms of the procedure and provisions application to a simple mortgage except those without notice of such charge". As per the Indian Supreme Court decision of *The Cosmos Co Operative Bank Ltd vs Central Bank of India* [2025] INSC 243.

and Director General of Civil Aviation, respectively, while intellectual property rights and shares necessitate the execution of release deeds or filings with the relevant authorities.

14 SECURITY IN JAPAN

In Japan, real estate, defined as land and any fixtures on it, is governed under the Japanese Civil Code (*Minpou*) and the Real Property Registration Act,[197] with buildings as the most common type of fixture subject to a separate property registration system.[198] The most common forms of security interests over real estate are statutory mortgages (teito-ken) and umbrella mortgages (which function like a revolving mortgage (ne-teito-ken), which give creditors preferential rights to the value of the property, allowing them to receive payments from the proceeds of its sale. Mortgages and revolving mortgages are created by agreement, not necessarily in writing, and perfected by registration in the relevant property registry.[199] The agreement for a revolving mortgage must specify the scope of claims to be secured and the maximum amount covered. Tangible movable property, which includes items like machinery, equipment, and ships, is subject to security interests such as pledges and security assignments. A pledge is created by an agreement between the creditor and the owner and is perfected by the continuous possession of the pledged property, whereas security assignments are perfected by either delivery[200] or registration if the assignor (grantor of the security assignment) is a corporation.[201] Financial instruments, such as shares and bonds, are commonly secured through pledges or security assignments, with the specific method of creation and perfection depending on whether the instruments are listed, certificated, or dematerialised. Claims and receivables are often secured by either pledges or security assignments, with perfection achieved through notice or acknowledgment to the obligors. Intellectual property, though less commonly used as collateral, can also be subject to pledges or security assignments, but certain rights, like patents or trademarks, cannot be pledged until they are officially registered,[202] while a pledge over copyrights is created by the execution of a granting contract and perfected by the register.[203] Additionally, assets like cash deposits are not recognised as eligible for security under Japanese law, and future or fungible assets may face difficulties in the creation of security unless specifically identified or pooled in a manner recognised by the courts.

15 CONCLUSION

In unsecured lending, a lender stands among other unsecured creditors if the borrower defaults or becomes insolvent, facing a substantial risk of loss. In contrast, security arrangements form the foundation of secured lending, offering critical protection to lenders. A clear understanding of the legal framework governing security interests is essential for structuring effective secured loans.

197 Act No. 123 of 2004).
198 *Japan* in Mellor, T. (ed.), *ICLG – Lending & Secured Finance 2024* (ICLG, 2024). See https://iclg.com/practice-areas/lending-and-secured-finance-laws-and-regulations/japan (accessed in March 2025).
199 Article 177, Japanese Civil Code.
200 Article 178, Japanese Civil Code.
201 Article 3, Act on Special Provisions, etc. of the Civil Code concerning Perfection Requirements for the Assignments of Movables and Claims (Perfection Act).
202 Article 98.1.3, Patent Act; Article 34.4, Trade Mark Act; and Article 35.3, Design Act.
203 Article 77.2, Copyright Act (Chosaku-ken-hou).

The following admirably concise passage from the judgement of Millet L.J. in *Re Cosslett (Contractors) Limited* [1998] Ch 495 may be taken as summarising the key forms of security under English law:

> *There are only four kinds of consensual security known to English law: (i) pledge; (ii) contractual lien; (iii) equitable charge and (iv) mortgage. A pledge and a contractual lien both depend on the delivery of possession to the creditor. The difference between them is that in the case of a pledge the owner delivers possession to the creditor as security, whereas in the case of a lien the creditor retains possession of goods previously delivered to him for some other purpose. Neither a mortgage nor a charge depends on the delivery of possession. The difference between them is that a mortgage involves a transfer of legal or equitable ownership to the creditor, whereas an equitable charge does not.*[204]

A key distinction in security interests lies between fixed and floating charges, primarily in the degree of control the lender exercises over the charged assets. Fixed charges provide lenders with greater control and priority in recovering debts, while floating charges offer flexibility, allowing the borrower to use the charged assets in the ordinary course of business until the charge crystallises. When determining whether a charge is fixed or floating, courts will examine the practical reality of the arrangement rather than merely relying on the labels used in the security documents.

Mortgages offer significant protection by transferring either legal or beneficial title to assets. Legal mortgages provide the most secure interest, but equitable mortgages remain a viable option where formalities are incomplete or the property is recognised only in equity. Legal and equitable assignments also offer security over intangible assets, allowing lenders to recover or enforce rights under assigned contracts if the borrower defaults.

Perfecting security is vital to protect a lender's interest, particularly in insolvency. Methods of perfection – such as possession, transfer of title, notice, and registration – form the legal foundation for establishing and maintaining security interests. Quasi-security, while not creating proprietary interests like traditional security, can still significantly impact lenders, especially in insolvency situations. Lenders must carefully assess any quasi-security arrangements to avoid compromising their priority, while borrowers should be mindful of how such arrangements might limit their ability to use assets as collateral for future loans.

Finally, while the core principles of security remain consistent across jurisdictions, legal and regulatory nuances, particularly in cross-border transactions, must be carefully considered, and lenders must ensure that security interests are correctly structured, perfected, and enforceable. In the United States, the UCC provides a comprehensive framework for creating, perfecting, and determining the priority of security interests in personal property.[205] Similar perfection requirements apply in France, Germany, Italy, China, India, and Japan.

204 Ibid. at p. 508.
205 Wood, P., *Comparative Law of Security Interests and Title Finance* (Sweet & Maxwell, 2019) at [19-036].

CHAPTER 11

SYNDICATED LOAN FACILITIES

OVERVIEW

Syndicated loan facilities are a fundamental component of modern corporate finance, particularly for large-scale transactions that demand substantial capital and require effective risk-sharing mechanisms. By pooling resources, multiple lenders are able to spread the risk of extending finance to a single borrower, making these facilities essential for financing high-value corporate transactions, project financing, and cross-border acquisitions.

The evolution of syndicated loan structures has been shaped by the growing complexity of corporate transactions and the heightened regulatory landscape. This chapter offers an exploration of the essential components of syndicated loan transactions, focusing on the key roles played by lead arrangers, agents, and syndicate members.

In addition, an analysis of the legal frameworks that govern these transactions is provided. The discussion covers the documentation requirements, including the importance of standardised documents developed by industry bodies such as the Loan Market Association (**LMA**) and the Loan Syndications and Trading Association (**LSTA**).

A key benefit of syndicated loans lies in their ability to facilitate access to capital markets, improve liquidity, and mitigate the credit risks faced by individual lenders. The secondary market for syndicated loans, which allows lenders to trade loan exposures, has further enhanced the flexibility and appeal of these instruments. By enabling lenders to manage their portfolios dynamically, the secondary market plays a vital role in maintaining liquidity and ensuring that capital is efficiently allocated across the financial system. This chapter will delve into the mechanics of loan trading, including the transfer of rights and obligations through assignment, novation, and sub-participation, as well as the legal and regulatory complexities involved in these transactions.[1]

1 DEVELOPMENT OF THE MARKET

Syndicated loans were developed as a method to allow lenders to extend large sums of money to a single borrower while spreading the risk across multiple lenders. This structure enabled lenders to diversify their exposure, making it possible to finance substantial loans to sovereign borrowers, particularly during the 1970s and 1980s. However, the landscape shifted dramatically following a series of high-profile sovereign defaults in the early 1980s, and the market gravitated towards using bonds as a more cost-effective solution for rescheduling sovereign loans. As a result, the syndicated loan products originally designed for sovereign borrowers were adapted for large corporate borrowers.[2]

Thereafter, two key developments have significantly influenced the continued expansion of the syndicated loan market. The first is the broadening of the range of borrowers able to access syndicated lending. Initially, such loans were predominantly extended to blue-chip corporations with strong credit ratings. However, as the market became increasingly saturated and prudential

1 Mugasha, A., *The Law of Multi-Bank Financing: Syndicated Loans and the Secondary Loan Market* (Oxford University Press, 2007), p. 99.
2 Hudson, A., *The Law of Finance* (Sweet & Maxwell, 2013) at [33-01].

DOI: 10.4324/9781032662220-12

frameworks in the 1990s imposed limits on the level of exposure a lender could have to a single borrower, the market evolved to include companies with lower credit ratings and less established financial histories. This shift led to the emergence of the leveraged finance market, where higher-risk borrowers were able to obtain syndicated loans, albeit at higher borrowing costs.

The second significant trend has been the development of a secondary market for syndicated debt, which has played a crucial role in maintaining liquidity and enhancing the attractiveness of syndicated loans as an asset class. The establishment of a functioning secondary market necessitated the standardisation of loan documentation in the primary market, ensuring that syndicated loans could be traded efficiently without requiring purchasers to conduct extensive due diligence on each transaction. The LMA and the LSTA have been central to this process, facilitating the creation of standardised documentation for both primary market syndicated loans and secondary market transactions.[3]

2 THE ROLE OF INTERNATIONAL ORGANISATIONS

The expansion of syndicated lending has been significantly facilitated by the involvement of international organisations, particularly credit rating agencies and trade associations. These entities have played a crucial role in both the primary and secondary markets by providing essential credit assessments, standardising loan documentation, and establishing frameworks for efficient debt trading.

Credit rating agencies, such as Standard & Poor's (**S&P**), Moody's Investor Services (**Moody's**), and Fitch Ratings, have been instrumental in assessing the creditworthiness of borrowers and individual lending transactions. Their evaluations provide critical information to lenders and investors in the secondary debt market. From the mid-1980s onwards, agencies such as S&P and Moody's began assigning ratings to syndicated loans, allowing the market to distinguish between investment-grade debt (issued by lower-risk borrowers) and leveraged debt (associated with higher-risk borrowers). Loans with lower credit ratings typically incur higher borrowing costs, with leveraged debt frequently classified as high-risk or high-yield debt. The ability to rate individual syndicated loans has significantly contributed to the development and categorisation of the syndicated loan market, offering investors a clearer understanding of risk exposure.

Trade associations have played an equally vital role by standardising loan documentation and trading processes. These associations operate on a regional basis and include the LMA in Europe, the LSTA in the United States, the Asia Pacific Loan Market Association (**APLMA**) in Hong Kong, Singapore, and Australia, and the Japan Syndication and Loan-trading Association in Japan.[4] Since January 2014, all activities previously conducted by the African Loan Market Association have been fully integrated into and absorbed by the LMA.

3 According to the LMA's Guide to Secondary Market Transactions published in April 2016: "*The Loan Market Association (LMA) is the trade body for the Europe, Middle East and Africa (EMEA) syndicated loan market and was founded in December 1996 by banks operating in that market. Its aim is to encourage liquidity in both the primary and secondary loan markets by promoting efficiency and transparency, as well as by developing standards of documentation and codes of market practice, which are widely used and adopted. Membership of the LMA currently stands at over 600, covering 50+ nationalities, and consists of banks, non-bank lenders, borrowers, law firms, rating agencies and service providers. The LMA has gained substantial recognition in the market and has expanded its activities to include all aspects of the primary and secondary syndicated loan markets. It sees its overall mission as acting as the authoritative voice of the EMEA loan market vis à vis lenders, borrowers, regulators and other interested parties*".

4 "*In 1995 the United States organisation, the Loan and Syndications Trading Association ('LSTA'), issued recommended best practice for loan trading, including standard terms and conditions and standard documentation and forms. The Loan Market Association ('LMA') was formed in London in December 1996, its aims being, among others, to standardise and simplify the sale of loan assets and to establish standard settlement practices, and the LMA too issued standard terms and conditions,*

By developing standardised documentation, these organisations have aligned syndicated loans more closely with bonds and medium-term notes, minimising the need for extensive document review and enabling the growth of a secondary market. The LMA, for instance, has established a comprehensive suite of trading documents for both par and distressed debt and has introduced a loan pricing calculator, further streamlining the trading process. Thus, "*the purpose of LMA standard documentation . . . is to promote certainty and uniformity in lending markets, so as to make agreement of lending documentation more straightforward and to increase the tradability of debt*".[5]

3 THE STRUCTURE AND PROCESS OF SYNDICATED LOAN FACILITIES

Syndicated loan facilities involve a collective lending arrangement in which a group of financial institutions (the syndicate) provides a loan to a borrower under a single loan agreement. These loans are typically arranged by a lead bank or group of banks, known as the lead arranger(s), which structure the deal, negotiate terms with the borrower, and invite other financial institutions to participate in the syndicate.[6] The lead arranger plays a pivotal role not only in underwriting the loan but also in providing a service[7] of orchestrating the syndication process by managing the relationship between the borrower and other lenders.

The process of loan syndication generally unfolds in three distinct phases: the mandate phase, the underwriting and syndication phase, and the closing and post-closing phase.[8]

During the **mandate phase**, the borrower selects the lead arranger(s) and formally mandates them to structure and arrange the loan facility.

The mandate may be secured through competitive bidding or as a result of successful negotiations with the borrower. Once mandated, the arranger is responsible for assembling the syndicate by promoting the loan and securing commitments from other banks willing to participate in the facility.[9] The initial step in this process involves soliciting indications of interest from potential participants. While there is no fixed procedure for

documentation and forms. The Asian Pacific Loan Market Association ('APLMA') based in Hong Kong is directed to trading in the Far East", in *Bear Stearns Bank Plc v Forum Global Equity Ltd* [2007] EWHC 1576 (Comm) at [4].

5 *The Bank of New York Mellon (London Branch) v Truvo NV & Ors* [2013] EWHC 136 (Comm) at [64].

6 According to the Hong Kong Monetary Authority, Supervisory Policy Manual CR-S-2 Syndicated Lending, at pp. 3 and 4, available at www.hkma.gov.hk/media/eng/doc/key-functions/banking-stability/supervisory-policy-manual/CR-S-2.pdf (accessed in March 2025): "*While the structure, pricing, repayment schedule and other terms of syndicated loans can vary, the following common characteristics are usually present:*

- *syndicated loans are normally governed by one set of documentation describing the rights and obligations of the signatories – the borrower and all the lenders (or syndicate members). The latter's obligation to lend is usually several;*
- *one or more lenders are mandated by the borrower to arrange credit facilities on terms agreed between the arranger and the borrower. The arranger may underwrite (i.e. undertake to provide) all or part of the facility amount;*
- *typically, the total amount of a syndicated deal is relatively significant, even though the credit extended by each participant does not generally exceed what it would be prepared to lend on a bilateral basis;*
- *the tenor may well be medium- or long-term, although short-term (under one year) facilities are also common, particularly for trade-related transactions;*
- *the credit facility typically takes the form of a term loan, a revolving credit or a standby letter of credit; and*
- *syndicated lending involves multiple parties (also see subsection 1.3 below), e.g., arrangers, underwriters, sub-underwriters, agents (facility and security), legal counsel and participating lenders. There is no standard terminology, however. Titles such as co-arranger, lead manager and co-lead manager are also found. Such titles do not necessarily correspond to or define the tasks carried out by the parties bearing such titles*".

7 Wood, P., *Law and Practice of International Finance* (Sweet & Maxwell, 2008) at [7-07].

8 Ellinger, E. P., Lomnicka, E. and Hare, C., *Ellinger's Modern Banking Law* (Oxford University Press, 2011), p. 782.

9 Hudson, A., *The Law of Finance* (Sweet & Maxwell, 2013) at [33-05].

doing so, it is common practice to send e-mail communications to prospective lenders. A more targeted approach, however, involves identifying banks that are most likely to be interested and sending them term sheets containing key information about the proposed credit facility, the borrower, and the applicable fees.

Simultaneously, while assembling the syndicate, the arranger engages in discussions with the borrower to negotiate the terms of the loan agreement. The objective is to ensure that a draft agreement is available for review by potential syndicate members as soon as they are identified. Once the syndicate is formed and the terms of the loan agreement have been finalised to the satisfaction of all parties, the transaction is completed by executing the loan agreement. At this stage, the role of the arranger concludes, and ongoing coordination between the lenders and the borrower is assumed by the agent bank, which is specifically appointed for this purpose. It is common practice for the lead arranger to also act as the agent bank, facilitating the administration of the loan following its execution.[10]

The lead arranger undertakes a comprehensive assessment of the borrower's financial position, creditworthiness, and the overall risk profile of the transaction. Following this due diligence process, the lead arranger proposes the loan structure, including the interest rate and key terms. A lender may seek to obtain a sole arranger mandate for two primary reasons. Firstly, acting as the sole arranger allows the lender to retain the full arrangement fee, which is typically calculated as a percentage of the total loan commitment. The specific amount of this fee depends on factors such as the complexity of the transaction, prevailing market conditions, and whether the loan is underwritten. Secondly, securing the role of sole arranger affords the lender a greater degree of control over the syndication process, whereas joint arrangers must coordinate and share decision-making responsibilities. However, joint arranger mandates are common when the borrower has established relationships with multiple lenders and does not have a compelling reason to favour one institution over another.

A loan may be structured either on an underwritten basis[11] or on a **best-efforts** (or best-endeavours)[12] basis. In an underwritten loan, the underwriting lenders – who are typically also the arrangers – guarantee the full loan commitment before syndicating it to other lenders. Should

10 Mugasha, A., *The Law of Multi-Bank Financing: Syndicated Loans and the Secondary Loan Market* (Oxford University Press, 2007) at [3.04].

11 For example, in the application of Basel III, under Regulation (EU) 2024/1623, an underwriting commitment for a syndicated loan is treated as an off-balance sheet exposure. To determine the capital that the underwriting bank(s) must hold against this exposure, a Credit Conversion Factor (the ratio of the undrawn amount of a commitment from a single facility that could be drawn from that single facility from a certain point in time before default and therefore outstanding at default to the undrawn amount of the commitment from that facility) is applied to the total committed amount, resulting in the Exposure at Default (EAD). Article 5 of Regulation (EU) 2024/1623 provides a definition for the term "commitment" as "*any contractual arrangement that an institution offers to a client, and is accepted by that client, to extend credit, purchase assets or issue credit substitutes; and any such arrangement that can be unconditionally cancelled by an institution at any time without prior notice to an obligor or any arrangement that can be cancelled by an institution where an obligor fails to meet the conditions set out in the facility documentation, including conditions that are required to be met by the obligor prior to any initial or subsequent drawdown under the arrangement, unless contractual arrangements meet all of the following conditions: (a) contractual arrangements where the institution receives no fees or commissions to establish or maintain those contractual arrangements; (b) contractual arrangements where the client is required to apply to the institution for the initial and each subsequent drawdown under those contractual arrangements; (c) contractual arrangements where the institution has full authority, regardless of the fulfilment by the client of the conditions set out in the contractual arrangement documentation, over the execution of each drawdown; (d) the contractual arrangements allow the institution to assess the creditworthiness of the client immediately prior to deciding on the execution of each drawdown and the institution has implemented and applies internal procedures that ensure that such an assessment is being made before the execution of each drawdown; (e) contractual arrangements that are offered to a corporate entity, including an SME, that is closely monitored on an ongoing basis*".

12 In contrast to underwritten deals, arranging banks in a best effort syndication generally do not face the same level of capital charge implications during the syndication period

the loan remain undersubscribed, the underwriters are obligated to extend the full underwritten amount to the borrower. Given the greater risk assumed by the underwriters, underwritten loans generally attract higher fees compared to those syndicated on a best-efforts basis.

By contrast, when an arranger acts on a best-efforts basis, it commits only to a specific portion of the loan while endeavouring to secure commitments from other lenders for the remaining amount. However, it does not guarantee that the full loan amount will be raised. In such cases, the borrower assumes the risk that the bookrunner may be unable to arrange sufficient lender commitments, potentially resulting in a shortfall in the funds required.

In the **underwriting and syndication phase**, once the lead arranger and the borrower agree on the loan structure, the syndication process formally begins. The lead arranger invites other financial institutions to participate in the facility, with each agreeing to commit a specified portion of the total loan amount. To facilitate this process, the lead arranger prepares an information or placement memorandum, which provides prospective syndicate members with comprehensive details about the borrower, the loan terms, and the associated risks. This document serves as a crucial tool in attracting participants to the syndicate and expanding upon the initial information circulated in earlier communications.[13]

The final stage, the **closing and post-closing phase**, occurs once the syndicate has been formed and all lenders have confirmed their respective commitments. At this point, the loan agreement is negotiated and finalised, and the transaction is closed. The borrower receives the loan proceeds, and the agent bank assumes responsibility for administering the loan on behalf of the syndicate. The agent bank's duties include managing loan disbursements, collecting repayments, monitoring the borrower's compliance with loan covenants, and serving as the primary point of communication between the borrower and syndicate members. This ongoing administrative role ensures that the syndicate operates effectively throughout the duration of the loan facility.

4 PARTICIPANTS IN SYNDICATED LOANS

A syndicated loan involves multiple participants, each with distinct roles and responsibilities that contribute to the structuring, management, and administration of the loan.[14]

The **lead arranger** is responsible[15] for

> *activities such as putting together a syndicate, seeking to agree a set of provisional terms acceptable to the borrower and attractive to potential participants, acting as principal point of contact between the borrower and syndicate banks, acting as a conduit of information and negotiating legal agreements with the borrower are all typically carried out by MLAs or others but not as agents properly so described.*[16]

This role typically also involves underwriting all or part of the loan, thereby assuming initial credit risk before distributing portions of the loan to other syndicate members. In return for these services, the lead arranger earns underwriting and arrangement fees.[17]

13 Arora, A., *Banking Law* (Pearson, 2014), p. 576.
14 See The Association of Corporate Treasurers, *A Borrower's Guide to the LMA's Investment Grade Agreements* (ACT 6th Edition, November 2022), available at www.treasurers.org/system/files/The%20ACT%20Borrower%E2%80%99s%20Guide%20to%20the%20LMA%E2%80%99s%20Investment%20Grade%20Agreements%20-%20Final.pdf (accessed in March 2025).
15 Hudson, A., *The Law of Finance* (Sweet & Maxwell, 2013) at [33-22].
16 In *Marme Inversiones 2007 SL v Natwest Markets Plc & Ors* [2019] EWHC 366 (Comm) at [444].
17 Chiu, I. and Wilson, J., *Banking Law and Regulation* (Oxford University Press, 2019), p. 149.

Joint arrangers are often appointed in syndicated loan transactions where the borrower maintains strong relationships with multiple lenders and has no strategic advantage in favouring one over the others. By acting as joint arrangers, lenders can share underwriting commitments, thereby reducing their individual exposure. Additionally, joint arrangements often facilitate the syndication process, as potential syndicate members may perceive the transaction as more secure when multiple reputable lenders are involved from the outset. The presence of multiple arrangers signals confidence in the transaction, increasing the likelihood of successful syndication.

Arranger's Liabilities

The role of the arranger in a syndicated loan transaction, particularly in facilitating communication between the borrower and the lenders and, in its capacity as bookrunner, encouraging lender participation, exposes it to significant potential liabilities. Once the facility agreement is executed, a contractual relationship exists between the lenders and the arranger, allowing disputes to be resolved within the framework of the contract. However, before the agreement is signed, no such contractual relationship exists, and any legal action by lenders regarding events occurring during the syndication process would generally have to be based in tort. The extent of the arranger's duty of care to lenders is, therefore, crucial in determining whether lenders can bring a claim against it.[18]

The scope of the standard of care should extend to "*that of a reasonably competent banker specialising in transactions of this nature. This standard was memorably described by Bingham LJ in Eckersley v Binnie [1995–1995] PNLR 348 at [17–34]:*

> *The law requires of the professional man that he live up in practice to the standard of the ordinary skilled man exercising and professing to have his special professional skill. He need not possess the highest expert skill; it is enough if he exercises the ordinary skill of an ordinary competent man exercising his particular art. . . . it follows that a professional man should command the corpus of knowledge which forms part of the professional equipment of the ordinary member of his profession. He should not lag behind other ordinarily assiduous and intelligent members of his profession in knowledge of new advances, discoveries and developments in his field. He should have such awareness as an ordinarily competent practitioner would have of the deficiencies in his knowledge and the limitations on his skill. He should be alert to the hazards and risks inherent in any professional task he undertakes to the extent that other ordinarily competent members of the profession would be alert. He must bring to any professional task he undertakes no less expertise, skill and care than other ordinarily competent members of his profession would bring, but need bring no more. The standard is that of the reasonable average. The law does not require over a professional man that he be a paragon, combining the qualities of polymath and prophet.*"[19]

If a lender joins a syndicate based on the arranger's advice and subsequently finds that the borrower is insolvent or financially weaker than expected, legal action against the borrower may be futile due to its financial distress. In contrast, the arranger, typically a financially robust institution, becomes a more viable target for claims. The duty of care owed by the arranger to the lenders was established in *The Sumitomo Bank Limited*

18 Mugasha, A., *The Law of Multi-Bank Financing: Syndicated Loans and the Secondary Loan Market* (Oxford University Press, 2007), p. 99.

19 Per Mr Justice Males in *Golden Belt 1 Sukuk Company BSC(c) v BNP Paribas* [2017] EWHC 3182 (Comm) at [211].

v Banque Bruxelles Lambert SA [1997] 1 Lloyd's Rep 487, where the arranger was successfully sued for misrepresentation regarding the validity of insurance and full disclosure to insurers concerning the valuation of a mortgaged property, the court held that a duty arises when the person providing advice or information is fully aware of the nature of the transaction, knows that the advice will be communicated to the relevant party, and understands that the recipient is likely to rely on that advice in deciding whether to enter the transaction. While the existence of this duty has been recognised in case law, the precise circumstances that would constitute a breach remain less clearly defined.[20] However, it is well established that an arranger can be held liable for misrepresentation, including negligent misrepresentation, as affirmed in *Hedley Byrne & Co Ltd v Heller & Partners Ltd* [1964] AC 465.

In *UBAF v European American Banking Corp* [1984] QB 713 CA, the Court of Appeal considered a claim concerning an alleged misrepresentation by a lender inviting another lender to participate in an existing loan. Although the case was settled, the lower court suggested that the arranger owed a fiduciary duty to the lenders in the syndicate. This finding, however, has not been widely adopted in subsequent cases and has been heavily criticised.[21]

The scope of an arranger's duty of care was further clarified in *IFE Fund SA v Goldman Sachs International* [2007] EWCA Civ 811, where the Court of Appeal upheld a High Court ruling that imposed strict limits on an arranger's duty to syndicate members. The court dismissed claims that the arranger had a duty of care to disclose additional information provided by auditors regarding the borrower's conduct. It also rejected the argument that the arranger had made implied representations about the borrower's financial condition merely by circulating the information memorandum.

Generally, an arranger's liability is mitigated by the fact that all syndicate participants are experienced professionals and that loan documentation includes disclaimer provisions, which specify that the information provided originates from the borrower and has not been verified by the arranger.

The protection afforded by such disclaimers was considered in *Raiffeisen Zentralbank Osterreich AG v Royal Bank of Scotland plc* [2010] EWHC 1392 (Comm), where the court dismissed a misrepresentation claim against RBS, holding that no representations had been made. It was found that the claimant, Raiffeisen Zentralbank Osterreich AG, was contractually estopped from pursuing its claim due to market-standard arranger disclaimer clauses included in the information memorandum and transaction documents. These disclaimers stated that RBS accepted no responsibility for the information provided.[22]

An arranger will generally be considered to have discharged its duty of care if it has exercised reasonable diligence in preparing the information memorandum and arranging any necessary security or guarantees.

Since it is a party to the facility agreement,[23] non-reliance clauses commonly specify that the arranger is not responsible for the adequacy, accuracy, or completeness

20 Hudson, A., *The Law of Finance* (Sweet & Maxwell, 2013) at [33-25].

21 Arora, A., *Banking Law* (Pearson, 2014), p. 581.

22 Burietz, A. and Mazza, P., 'Lead Arrangers in Syndicated Loans' (5 March 2021) *SSRN Electronic Journal*. 10.2139/ssrn.3798428

23 See The Association of Corporate Treasurers, *A Borrower's Guide to the LMA's Investment Grade Agreements* (ACT 6th Edition, November 2022), p. 224, available at www.treasurers.org/system/files/The%20ACT%20Borrower%E2%80%99s%20Guide%20to%20the%20LMA%E2%80%99s%20Investment%20Grade%20Agreements%20-%20Final.pdf (accessed in March 2025).

of information or the enforceability of transaction documentation. The facility agreement will often also confirm that the arranger may engage in other business with the borrower and its affiliates. Additionally, it is standard practice for the agreement to specify that each lender bears responsibility for conducting its own due diligence and investigations.

Once the loan agreement is executed, the **agent bank** serves as the primary intermediary between the borrower and the syndicate. It is responsible for collecting repayments from the borrower and distributing them to the syndicate members in accordance with their respective participations. The agent plays a critical role in ensuring that all conditions precedent are met before any drawdown takes place, thereby facilitating a structured and coordinated lending process. Moreover, the agent bank monitors the borrower's compliance with covenants and other obligations stipulated in the loan agreement. For these administrative services, the agent bank receives a fee.

The **syndicate members**, or lenders, are financial institutions that commit to funding a portion of the loan. While they do not participate in structuring the transaction, they share in the benefits and risks of the facility. Each lender's risk is limited to its respective contribution, allowing for risk diversification across the syndicate.[24]

What Happens If a Syndicate Member Were to Default?

The primary+ focus of finance documentation has historically been on the credit risk posed by the borrower, with little attention given to the consequences of a finance party's insolvency or failure to perform its obligations. When a lender defaults on its obligation to fund its share of a requested advance, the borrower is not entitled to recover the defaulting lender's share from the other lenders. This is because the obligations of each lender under a syndicated facility agreement are typically expressed to **be several**. Under several liabilities, each party is responsible only for its own designated obligations, with no joint responsibility for the obligations of others. Consequently, if one party fails to fulfil its obligation, the liability does not transfer to the remaining parties, ensuring that each is only accountable for its own commitments.

For example, clause 2.4(a) of the LMA Leveraged Agreement confirms that no lender is responsible for funding any other lender's share of an advance:

> *(a) The obligations of each Finance Party under the Finance Documents are several. Failure by a Finance Party to perform its obligations under the Finance Documents does not affect the obligations of any other Party under the Finance Documents. No Finance Party is responsible for the obligations of any other Finance Party under the Finance Documents.*

This structure can create cash flow difficulties for the borrower, particularly in relation to its day-to-day operations, and may even prevent the completion of a transaction.[25]

24 Payne, J. and Gullifer, L., *Corporate Finance Law: Principles and Policy* (Hart, 2020) at [8.4.6].
25 See The Association of Corporate Treasurers, *A Borrower's Guide to the LMA's Investment Grade Agreements* (ACT 6th Edition, November 2022), p. 379, available at www.treasurers.org/system/files/The%20ACT%20Borrower%E2%80%99s%20Guide%20to%20the%20LMA%E2%80%99s%20Investment%20Grade%20Agreements%20-%20Final.pdf (accessed in March 2025).

Following the collapse of Lehman Brothers in 2008, the LMA responded by revising its Leveraged Agreement to include the Defaulting Lender and Impaired Agent Provisions. These provisions introduced the concepts of a "Defaulting Lender", an "Impaired Agent",[26] and a "Non-Acceptable L/C Lender", helping to mitigate the risks associated with lender insolvency and non-performance. The LMA subsequently issued a users' guide outlining how these provisions could be adapted for use in investment-grade facility agreements.

Under these provisions, a lender is classified as a Defaulting Lender in a range of circumstances. These include failure to fund its share of an advance, failure to provide required cash collateral in respect of a letter of credit, or issuing a notice indicating an intention to default. A lender may also be deemed a Defaulting Lender if it rescinds or repudiates a finance document, fails to issue a letter of credit, or refuses to honour a claim made by a beneficiary under a letter of credit. If the relevant optional language is included in the facility agreement, a lender will also be classified as a Defaulting Lender if it is subject to an Insolvency Event. The definition of an Insolvency Event is broad and encompasses dissolution, the appointment of a liquidator, administrator, or receiver, and an inability to pay debts as they fall due.

The introduction of these Defaulting Lender and Impaired Agent Provisions[27] reflects a shift in syndicated lending practices, acknowledging that lender default and insolvency can have material consequences for borrowers, other lenders, and facility agents. By incorporating these provisions into facility agreements, market participants have been able to mitigate the risks associated with lender non-performance and ensure greater certainty in the administration and execution of syndicated loans.

In larger transactions, a **bookrunner** may be appointed to manage the process of securing commitments from potential syndicate members and overseeing the distribution of the loan. In many cases, the lead arranger assumes this role, although in certain deals, a separate entity may act as the bookrunner. The bookrunner's primary function is to manage the syndication process, which involves marketing the loan to potential syndicate members and coordinating lender participation. After preliminary discussions with prospective lenders, the bookrunner, in consultation with the borrower, prepares an invitation list and distributes formal invitations accompanied by a confidentiality and front-running letter. Lenders that return the signed letter gain access to the information memorandum and may then submit queries or indicate their interest in participating. Prospective lenders express their commitment by submitting statements or letters of intent, often conditional on their approval of the final facility documents. The bookrunner collaborates with the borrower to finalise the allocation of commitments among syndicate members, making adjustments if the loan is oversubscribed or, in rare instances, reducing or withdrawing the loan if it is undersubscribed. Additionally,

26 Wording to deal with such and occurrence will be drafted along the following lines: "*Communication when an Agent is an Impaired Agent If an Agent is an Impaired Agent, the Parties may, instead of communicating with each other through that Agent, communicate with each other directly and (while an Agent is an Impaired Agent) all the provisions of the Interim Finance Documents which require communications to be made or notices to be given to or by the Agents shall be varied so that communications may be made and notices given to or by the relevant Parties directly. This provision shall not operate after a replacement Agent has been appointed*".

27 Replacement language will typically be couched along the following lines: "*Replacement of an Agent (a) The Majority Interim Lenders or the Obligors' Agent may by giving ten (10) days' notice to an Agent which is an Impaired Agent replace that Agent by appointing a successor Agent (which shall be acting through an office in the United Kingdom)*".

the bookrunner advises the borrower on prevailing market conditions to ensure the terms of the loan are sufficiently attractive to secure the necessary commitments.[28]

Market flex refers to the arranger's ability to amend the terms of the facility after signing in order to make it more appealing to lenders in the syndications market, particularly if it is proving difficult to attract sufficient commitments.[29] Although this provision is often unpopular with borrowers, who argue that the arranger, having used its expertise to set the initial pricing, should bear the risk if the pricing is too aggressive for the market, it remains a common feature in larger syndications. Borrowers may seek to limit market flex to adjustments in pricing, such as increases in fees or margins, typically capped at 25–50 basis points, rather than allowing changes to the structure or other terms. Additionally, borrowers may require that market flex only be triggered if the facility cannot otherwise be successfully syndicated, which is usually defined as the arranger being able to reduce its commitment to its target "final hold" amount. In some cases, particularly where the borrower is investment-grade or the associated risks do not warrant such flexibility, the market flex provision may be successfully resisted altogether.

4.1 Agents for the Lender

In a syndicated loan, the agent represents the lenders throughout the facility's term, managing information and cash flows between the lenders and the borrower.[30] Appointed by the arranger and lenders, the agent acts on their behalf but is paid a smaller fee than the arranger and thus does not assume significant risk. The agent's role is primarily mechanical and administrative, with its duties explicitly outlined in the facility agreement, and any fiduciary obligations that might otherwise be implied are typically excluded[31] through the use of express language, which would typically read as follows:

> ***No fiduciary duties*** *(a) Unless otherwise expressly stated in any other Finance Document, nothing in this Agreement constitutes the Agent, the Security Trustee or the Arranger as a trustee or fiduciary of any other person. (b) Neither the Agent, the Security Trustee nor the Arranger shall be bound to account to any Lender for any sum or the profit element of any sum received by it for its own account.*[32]

Agent's Potential Liability

An agent lender may engage with a borrower through multiple departments within the lending institution. If another department advises the borrower on a forthcoming merger or general financing needs, the agent lender may inadvertently acquire notice of an event of default or a potential event of default. This occurs when another part of the lender has actual knowledge of circumstances constituting such an event. However, addressing this issue may be problematic, as disclosing the information to the syndicate

28 Chiu, I. and Wilson, J., *Banking Law and Regulation* (Oxford University Press, 2019), p. 147.
29 Vinter, G., Price, G. and Lee, D., *Project Finance* (Sweet & Maxwell, 2013) at [7-004].
30 Haentjens, M. and De Gioia-Carabellese, P., *European Banking and Financial Law* (Routledge, 2015), p. 188.
31 Bamford, C., *Principles of International Finance Law* (Oxford University Press, 2015) at [7.18].
32 In *Torre Asset Funding Ltd & Anor v The Royal Bank of Scotland Plc* [2013] EWHC 2670 (Ch) at [27].

could constitute a breach of confidentiality. To mitigate this risk, the agent lender's back-office or agency department must be segregated from its front-office or client-facing departments through strictly enforced ethical wall arrangements.

As the agent's role commences only after the facility documents have been executed, its duties are expressly defined within those documents. Additionally, the standard duties and responsibilities of any agent under English law apply, including the implied duty to exercise reasonable care and skill in monitoring the borrower's performance. To protect the agent from undue liability, facility agreements typically include a range of protections. These include provisions stating that the agent may assume there is no event of default unless it has actual knowledge, with some agreements requiring written confirmation. The agent is often expressly excluded from fiduciary liability and any obligations ordinarily imposed by English law on fiduciaries. Furthermore, the agent is entitled to appoint and rely upon the advice of legal, financial, and other professional advisers, with the associated costs being recoverable. The agreement may also include unilateral resignation rights, allowing the agent to withdraw from its role at its discretion.[33]

Additionally, the agent's duties are generally limited to mechanical and administrative functions, ensuring it is not responsible for the effectiveness of the facility documents or the accuracy of information contained within them. Lenders are required to conduct their own due diligence, including Know Your Customer (KYC) checks and credit assessments, and to indemnify the agent against any losses incurred in the performance of its duties. Liability for third-party actions, omissions, or fraud is expressly excluded, and officers, employees, and agents of the agent lender are protected from claims brought by parties other than the agent itself. The agent is not liable for any act or omission unless it results from gross negligence or wilful misconduct.

The terms *wilful misconduct* and *gross negligence* frequently appear in facility agreements, including those published by the LMA. Case law provides guidance on the interpretation of wilful misconduct. In *National Semiconductors (UK) Ltd v UPS Ltd* [1996] 2 LL Rep 212, Longmore J reviewed existing authorities and summarised that wilful misconduct requires either an intention to act wrongfully, a reckless act where the individual is aware of potential loss but disregards the risk, or the taking of a risk that the actor knew should have been avoided.

By contrast, English law does not recognise *gross negligence* as a concept distinct from ordinary negligence.[34] While the term implies a heightened degree of negligence, in practice, it may not add substantive legal value.

The efficacy of standard market clauses limiting an agent's role to mechanical and administrative functions was examined in *Torre Asset Funding Ltd & Anor v The Royal Bank of Scotland Plc* [2013] EWHC 2670 (Ch). The High Court considered provisions related to events of default, the agent's duty to notify lenders of such events, and the dissemination of financial information. The court held that an agent, even if it participated in the events constituting an event of default, was not obliged to notify lenders. Furthermore, if a lender provided the agent with concerning financial information, the agent was not required to share it unless it had been explicitly supplied for distribution to other

33 Burietz, A. and Mazza, P., 'Lead Arrangers in Syndicated Loans' (5 March 2021) *SSRN Electronic Journal*. http://dx.doi.org/10.2139/ssrn.3798428

34 As confirmed by *Moor-Bick LJ in Tradigrain SA v Intertek Testing Systems (ITS) Canada Limited* [2007] EWCA Civ 154.

lenders. This case underscores that courts will narrowly interpret the agent's responsibilities based on the transaction documents.

The agent maintains contact with the borrower, monitors compliance with the facility's terms, and serves as the paying agent for all payments under the facility. Its responsibilities include overseeing the drawdown process, where the agent reviews conditions precedent, confirms interest rates, and manages the disbursement of funds from the lenders to the borrower.[35] In the event of default, the agent is often the first to become aware and must notify the lenders, engage with the borrower to understand the circumstances, and coordinate discussions among lenders to maintain collective bargaining power.[36] The agent acts on instructions from the majority lenders, with major decisions such as waivers or acceleration of the facility, depending on their approval.

Majority Lenders

The term "majority lenders" (or "majority banks") is commonly used to describe a group of lenders who, collectively, hold more than a specified percentage of the total commitments or of the outstanding loan amounts under a syndicated loan agreement. While the requisite threshold will always exceed 50%, the precise figure is typically negotiated and reflects the composition of the syndicate and the divergent interests of the parties involved. For instance, where the acceleration of the loan is subject to the consent of the majority of lenders, the borrower may seek to set the required percentage as high as possible in order to limit the risk of an early demand for repayment. Conversely, where the borrower's request for waivers or consents is at issue, a lower threshold – closer to a simple majority – is likely to be preferred by the borrower, as it facilitates the obtainment of the requisite approval.

The LMA Investment Grade Agreements typically provide that the "Majority Lenders" are those representing 66⅔% of total commitments, which includes both drawn and undrawn commitments.[37] In the investment-grade market, this percentage is almost universally applied.[38] The dynamics within the lending syndicate also play a critical role in determining this threshold. Smaller banks, for example, may wish to avoid a situation in which one or two large lenders, holding substantial proportions of the commitments, are able to dictate decisions without regard to the interests of the minority participants. In such cases, a higher threshold may be negotiated to ensure that some of the smaller lenders are included within the majority.

Where an agreement includes multiple facilities, such as a combination of term and revolving facilities, and lenders do not hold participations in each facility in identical proportions, the determination of Majority Lenders depends on the relative participations of lenders in each facility at the relevant time. While such situations are relatively rare, they may prompt lenders to seek adjustments to the definition of Majority Lenders to ensure a fair and equitable decision-making process.[39]

35 Hudson, A., *The Law of Finance* (Sweet & Maxwell, 2013) at [33-23].
36 Wood, P., *International Loans, Bonds, Guarantees and Legal Opinions* (Sweet & Maxwell, 2019) at [17-003].
37 Wood, P., *International Loans, Bonds, Guarantees and Legal Opinions* (Sweet & Maxwell, 2019) at [18-022].
38 Hudson, A., *The Law of Finance* (Sweet & Maxwell, 2013) at [33-39].
39 See The Association of Corporate Treasurers, *A Borrower's Guide to the LMA's Investment Grade Agreements* (ACT 6th Edition, November 2022), pp. 140–141, available at www.treasurers.org/system/files/

4.2 Security Trustee

In a secured syndicated loan, the security trustee (see Chapter 12) holds the security on trust for the benefit of all lenders and any other entitled parties, such as hedging counterparties.[40] The appointment of a security trustee ensures that one entity manages the administrative aspects of the security, such as holding title deeds and documents, and distributes proceeds to the secured lenders upon enforcement. Additionally, if a lender transfers its interest to another entity, the new lender benefits from the existing security without needing re-registration or new security.[41] The security trustee is also responsible for enforcing or protecting the security but typically will only act upon instructions from a majority of lenders.

5 TYPES OF SYNDICATED LOAN FACILITIES

Syndicated loans can take various forms depending on the borrower's needs and the structure of the transaction. The most common types include[42] a term loan facility providing the borrower with a fixed amount of capital which is commonly employed to finance substantial capital expenditures, including mergers, acquisitions,[43] or large-scale infrastructure developments. A revolving credit facility, by contrast, permits the borrower to draw down, repay, and re-borrow funds as required, up to a specified credit limit. This type of facility is particularly well suited to businesses with variable working capital requirements, offering flexibility in managing short-term liquidity. Letter of credit facilities are frequently utilised in the context of international trade. They serve to guarantee payment to a borrower's suppliers or creditors and are especially valuable in cross-border transactions where the parties may lack established trust. Bridge loans are a form of short-term financing intended to provide interim funding until a more permanent capital source is secured, such as through the issuance of debt or equity instruments. Due to their short tenor[44] and elevated risk profile, bridge loans generally carry higher interest rates.

An Example: A Forward Start Facility

In a forward start facility (**FSF**), a borrower seeks to refinance an existing syndicated loan by entering into a new syndicated loan agreement. This new facility is established before the maturity date of the existing loan, often several months or even over a year in advance. It is designed to secure the borrower's future borrowing arrangements, ensuring that once the existing loan matures, a new facility is already in place. The FSF is committed from the date of signing, but it is not available for drawing until the existing loan matures.

The%20ACT%20Borrower%E2%80%99s%20Guide%20to%20the%20LMA%E2%80%99s%20Investment%20Grade%20Agreements%20-%20Final.pdf (accessed in March 2025).

40 Proctor, C., *The Law and Practice of International Banking* (Oxford University Press, 2015) at [21.49].

41 Haentjens, M. and De Gioia-Carabellese, P., *European Banking and Financial Law* (Routledge, 2015), p. 190.

42 Haentjens, M. and De Gioia-Carabellese, P., *European Banking and Financial Law* (Routledge, 2015), p. 176.

43 Acquisition finance refers to the use of loan facilities to support mergers and acquisitions, often involving significant capital commitments. In this context, syndicated loans are frequently employed and may take the form of term loans, revolving credit facilities, or a hybrid of the two, depending on the borrower's specific financing requirements and the structure of the transaction.

44 Tenor refers to the duration remaining until a financial contract reaches its expiry. The term is sometimes used interchangeably with "maturity", although in certain contexts, distinctions may be drawn between the two.

The FSF typically involves some of the lenders from the existing syndicated loan, though not all. If all lenders were willing to continue, the original loan could simply be extended through an amendment, negating the need for an FSF. The terms of the FSF generally mirror the existing loan, though there are adjustments for factors like the availability period, conditions precedent, pricing, and maturity.

From the lender's perspective, participating in an FSF offers a higher return compared to refinancing close to the loan's maturity date. The borrower, meanwhile, benefits from knowing that the terms and conditions of their future borrowing are fixed, even if the pricing is higher.

As a condition of granting the FSF, the margin and fees under the existing loan are often increased, though these price adjustments benefit only the FSF lenders, leaving the existing loan unamended.

When structuring an FSF, the parties must also address several issues beyond pricing. For instance, the covenant package under the FSF may be more restrictive than that of the existing loan, and the borrower could be bound by these covenants from the FSF signing date. Any breaches of these covenants might even trigger a default under the existing loan. Additionally, cancellations or prepayments of the existing loan typically result in a proportional reduction of the FSF.

Finally, FSFs are distinct from the "amend and extend" approach commonly used in the US syndicated loan market, where loans are extended with the agreement of some lenders and typically require only majority lender approval.

6 LMA DOCUMENTATION AND STANDARDISATION

The role of standardised documentation in syndicated loans cannot be understated. One of the most significant developments in this area has been the contribution of the LMA in producing an extensive set of documents to facilitate debt trades and syndicated loan transactions in the London market and beyond, although it is not unusual for trades to use the LSTA's New York-law documents instead.[45] Such documents are indispensable in ensuring that syndicated loans, particularly those involving cross-border elements, are governed by predictable and consistent terms. This approach helps both sellers and buyers save time and reduce costs associated with drafting and reviewing customised documents.

The LMA has also developed a suite of standardised secondary debt trading documents to facilitate efficient and transparent transactions in the syndicated loan market. Those terms need to be clearly incorporated in the transaction's documents.[46]

These documents are not intended to be used in isolation but as part of a comprehensive package that ensures consistency across all aspects of the loan transaction, from confidentiality obligations to pricing disputes. The adoption of LMA documentation fosters predictability, reduces legal risks, and enhances liquidity within the secondary loan market by providing a well-established framework for market participants.

The documentation governing syndicated loans is inherently complex, reflecting the scale of the transactions and the number of stakeholders involved. As noted previously, the Loan

45 Wood, P., *International Loans, Bonds, Guarantees and Legal Opinions* (Sweet & Maxwell, 2019) at [4-006].

46 "*Nor am I persuaded that the LMA terms are to be incorporated because of a usage or custom. In order for terms to be implied into a contract on this basis, it is not sufficient that there be a mere trade practice, but there must be a usage or custom that is notorious, certain and reasonable: Chitty on Contracts, 29th Ed (2004) Vol. 1 at para 13-018*", in *Bear Stearns Bank Plc v Forum Global Equity Ltd* [2007] EWHC 1576 (Comm) at [145].

Agreement serves as the primary contract, setting out the terms and conditions of the loan, including provisions on interest rates, repayment schedules, financial covenants,[47] and events of default. It also specifies the roles and responsibilities of the agent, lead arranger, and syndicate members. The Information Memorandum, prepared by the lead arranger, provides potential lenders with a comprehensive overview of the borrower's financial condition, the purpose of the loan, and the associated risks. Commitment Letters, signed by syndicate members, outline each lender's agreement to provide a specific portion of the loan and define the terms under which funds are committed. Confidentiality Letters for both the seller and buyer, as well as their respective agents or brokers, alongside Master Confidentiality Undertakings, are provided to ensure the non-disclosure of sensitive transactional details.

Trade Confirmations are available for Bank Debt, Claims, and Risk Participation, providing a formal record of agreed trades. Where the loan is secured, Security Documents establish the collateral pledged by the borrower, which may include real estate, equipment, receivables, or shares in the borrower's subsidiaries. In transactions involving multiple layers of debt, Intercreditor Agreements[48] regulate the relationship between different classes of creditors, such as senior and subordinated lenders (see Chapter 13).

To address termination and disputes in syndicated loans, the LMA has introduced Termination Notices, Buy-in/Sell-out Notices, Purchase Price Notices, and Price Dispute Notices. Funded Participation Agreements, applicable to both par and distressed transactions, enable lenders to participate in syndicated loans under standardised terms. The framework also includes Multilateral and Bilateral Termination and Transfer Agreements, such as novation and assignment, which facilitate the seamless transfer of loan participations, while Multilateral and Bilateral Netting Agreements provide mechanisms for the settlement and netting of obligations among multiple lenders and the borrower.

The Importance of Loan Documentation In *Smith v. Bank of New York Mellon Corporation* [2013] EWCA Civ 379, the court addressed the issue of ambiguous loan documentation in a syndicated loan transaction. The case involved a dispute between a borrower and the syndicate over the interpretation of covenants related to financial ratios. The court held that the ambiguity in the loan agreement could have been avoided had the loan documentation been drafted with greater clarity. This case underscores the importance of precise and unambiguous language in syndicated loan agreements to avoid costly legal disputes.

7 RISK MANAGEMENT IN SYNDICATED LOANS

Syndicated loans involve inherent risks, particularly in cross-border transactions, where lenders must consider the potential for borrower default, currency fluctuations, interest rate volatility, and legal uncertainties regarding enforcement. To mitigate these risks, syndicated loan agreements typically incorporate covenants and protective provisions designed to safeguard

47 *Torre Asset Funding Ltd & Anor v The Royal Bank of Scotland Plc* [2013] EWHC 2670 (Ch).

48 "*In addition to the facility agreements at each tier of the lending stack, each Lender and each Agent was also a party to the Inter-Creditor Deed, which was the principal instrument governing the relationship between the various Lenders, including in relation to their rights with respect to acceleration of repayment by Dunedin and enforcement against security given by Dunedin where an Event of Default occurred. In broad terms, in the case of an Event of Default the most senior Lenders were to have control of the enforcement process until such time as they were repaid, at which point control would pass to the next senior lenders until repaid and so on down the lending stack*", in *Torre Asset Funding Ltd & Anor v The Royal Bank of Scotland Plc* [2013] EWHC 2670 (Ch) at [11].

the interests of the lending syndicate. Such provisions examined in Chapter 9 will be briefly reconsidered in what follows.

Financial covenants impose specific conditions that the borrower must meet to maintain compliance with the loan agreement. These often include maintaining a minimum debt-to-equity ratio, achieving a specified level of earnings before interest, taxes, depreciation, and amortisation (EBITDA), and ensuring adequate liquidity. **Negative pledge** clauses[49] further protect the lenders by preventing the borrower from pledging its assets to other creditors without the consent of the syndicate, thereby preserving the syndicate's priority over the borrower's collateral.

The loan agreement also defines specific **events of default**, which may include the non-payment of interest, breach of financial or operational covenants, or the borrower's insolvency. Upon the occurrence of a default, the syndicate has the right to accelerate the loan, demanding immediate repayment of the outstanding amount. Additionally, **cross-default provisions** ensure that a default on any other loan or credit facility of the borrower constitutes a default under the syndicated loan, thereby protecting the lenders from the risk of broader financial deterioration. These contractual mechanisms collectively enhance the stability and enforceability of syndicated loans, offering lenders a degree of protection against potential financial and legal challenges. However, one should note that

> *the interests of the creditor and borrower are different in respect of this type of provision. The creditor is concerned to safeguard its position prior to the formal commencement of insolvency proceedings. The borrower's concern is not to agree a clause which imposes impractical restrictions on its ability to conduct business.*[50]

Some Considerations for an Incoming Lender

Banks which have been invited to join a syndicate by an arranger often commission legal reviews to assess the terms of the facility agreement and identify any legal risks or unusual provisions. These reviews form a crucial part of the bank's credit committee's decision-making process regarding whether to participate as a lender.[51]

A key aspect of the review is to ensure that the facility agreement clearly outlines the repayment and prepayment mechanisms. While these provisions are generally mechanical in nature, it is important to identify any triggers for repayment or prepayment, as well as any minimum thresholds or notice periods that may apply. Change of control provisions are another area that may be subject to negotiation, even in investment-grade transactions.

Another important focus of the review are the "yank the bank" provisions, which allow borrowers to replace lenders in certain circumstances, such as increased costs[52] or tax gross-up[53] claims. These provisions are often modified in favourable market

49 Wood, P., *International Loans, Bonds, Guarantees and Legal Opinions* (Sweet & Maxwell, 2019) at [11-005].

50 *Grupo Hotelero Urvasco SA v Carey Value Added SL* [2013] EWHC 1039 (Comm) at [573].

51 Wood, P., *International Loans, Bonds, Guarantees and Legal Opinions* (Sweet & Maxwell, 2019) at [35-028].

52 According to the Hong Kong Monetary Authority, Supervisory Policy Manual CR-S-2 Syndicated Lending, at [3.3.3], available at www.hkma.gov.hk/media/eng/doc/key-functions/banking-stability/supervisory-policy-manual/CR-S-2.pdf (accessed in March 2025) **increased costs** means "*the obligation of the borrower to indemnify lenders where market circumstances make it more expensive for lenders to maintain their participations*".

53 According to the Hong Kong Monetary Authority, Supervisory Policy Manual CR-S-2 Syndicated Lending, at [3.3.3], available at www.hkma.gov.hk/media/eng/doc/key-functions/banking-stability/supervisory-policy-manual/CR-S-2.pdf (accessed in March 2025) **tax gross-ups** means "*the obligation of the borrower to increase any payment on which withholding tax or other deductions are levied so that lenders receive the amount they were originally due under the terms of the documentation*".

conditions, and any deviations from the LMA standard should be carefully assessed. Similarly, the right of a borrower to cancel undrawn commitments of a defaulting lender is an important aspect of the facility agreement that warrants attention.

Interest rate provisions are also critical, particularly with the widespread use of risk-free reference rates. It should be clarified how interest periods are selected and whether there is flexibility to adjust them in line with the repayment schedule.

The bank's expectations regarding fees, including commitment, prepayment, and cancellation fees, should be clearly confirmed in the facility agreement. It should be considered whether regulatory costs, such as those arising under the Basel III or CRD IV/V regimes, are included or excluded from the facility agreement's cost clauses. ESG considerations should also be addressed.[54]

The representations and warranties section of the facility agreement is often heavily tailored to the specific transaction. Any carve-outs, additional representations, materiality qualifications, or thresholds that limit the scope of the representations should be identified alongside the representations that are repeated and the frequency with which they must be repeated.

Similarly, the undertakings (or covenants) protect the lender's investment throughout the life of the loan and are typically a major focus of negotiations. In this respect, given the increasing regulatory scrutiny and enforcement actions taken by authorities in both the EU and the US, lenders often seek contractual assurances from borrowers concerning sanctions compliance.

The events of default section is another critical area of the review, particularly with respect to grace periods and cure rights. The events of default which are subject to grace periods, the length of those periods, and the mechanisms for curing defaults should be identified. There should be a clear understanding of what happens if the grace periods expire without the default being remedied or waived.

Provisions concerning the transfer of rights and obligations, which are vital for enabling the bank to trade its loans in the secondary market, should be addressed. The LMA's standard approach promotes a liquid secondary market, but borrowers may negotiate restrictions on transfers, such as requiring the borrower's consent or limiting transfers to approved institutions or sectors.

Set-off clauses, which allow lenders to offset amounts owed by the borrower against amounts owed to the borrower, may be subject to carve-outs. For example, lenders' rights of set-off may be limited to situations where an event of default is continuing. Any restrictions on set-off, especially where the borrower may be prevented from granting set-off rights due to negative pledges in other finance agreements, must be highlighted. If the set-off clause is one-sided, it may be subject to the Unfair Contract Terms Act 1977 (UCTA), which could render it unenforceable if it fails the reasonableness test pursuant to *African Export-Import Bank v Shebah Exploration and Production Co Ltd* [2017] EWCA Civ 845.

Ancillary documents such as notices, fee letters, certificates, and waiver requests may also be relevant to the review, depending on the stage of the transaction. If a legal opinion has been issued with respect to the facility agreement, it should be reviewed to determine whether any legal risks have been identified. However, if the facility agreement is unsigned, no legal opinion is likely to be available.

54 OECD, 'Due Diligence for Responsible Corporate Lending and Securities Underwriting' *OECD Publishing* (2019), available at https://mneguidelines.oecd.org/due-diligence-for-responsible-corporate-lending-and-securities-underwriting.pdf (accessed in March 2025).

8 THE PRIMARY MARKET

The primary loan market consists of direct lending by financial institutions to borrowers, typically through syndicated loans, either at the time the loan is granted or immediately thereafter.[55] This market is broadly categorised according to the creditworthiness of the borrower (as discussed in Chapter 8). **Investment-grade loans** are extended to borrowers with high credit ratings, reflecting a lower risk of default. In contrast, **leveraged loans** are issued to borrowers with lower credit ratings, often carrying a higher risk profile and, consequently, higher interest rates to compensate lenders for the increased credit risk.

Investment-grade syndicated loans are typically extended to sovereign governments, which often enjoy top-tier credit ratings such as AAA from Standard & Poor's (S&P) or Aaa from Moody's, and to blue-chip companies. One of the defining features of the investment-grade loan market is the standardisation of loan documentation, largely influenced by the widespread use of LMA templates for facility agreements. While negotiations remain critical, they tend to focus on a few key elements such as conditions precedent, representations and warranties, covenants, and events of default. Lenders, however, are under pressure to ensure that these documents align with prevailing market standards, as maintaining marketability is essential.

Leveraged loans, in contrast, are typically issued to borrowers with a lower credit rating, usually below BBB – as rated by S&P. The London leveraged loan market is primarily dominated by relationship-based lending, where banks arrange loans for companies with which they have established long-standing ties. The situation in the US is quite different. There, the leveraged loan market is heavily influenced by institutional investors, such as pension funds and hedge funds, who use leveraged loans as a means to diversify and balance risk and reward within their portfolios.[56]

A key distinction between the two markets is the degree of **market flex**. In the US leveraged loan market, there is more flexibility, meaning that in times of heightened risk, such as during an economic downturn, the margin on these loans will increase to reflect the changing risk profile. This feature led to a higher rate of defaults in the US during the last recession compared to the London market.

Leveraged finance is most commonly used for acquisition financing, where the loan is secured to purchase another company. However, it is also used for broader corporate purposes. Institutional investors have become more significant players in the London syndicated loan market, with traditional banks playing a relatively smaller role. This shift has resulted in facility agreements evolving to suit the needs of institutional investors, who typically lack the capacity to monitor the financial health of borrowers as closely as banks. Consequently, there has been a reduced emphasis on financial covenants.

9 THE SECONDARY MARKET

The secondary market for syndicated loans facilitates the sale or transfer of syndicated debt following the completion of the initial syndication.[57] The existence of a liquid secondary market encourages lenders to assume larger commitments during the initial syndication, with the confidence that they can later sell all or part of their exposure if necessary.

55 Kokkinis, A. and Miglionico, M., *Banking Law: Private Transactions and Regulatory Frameworks* (Routledge, 2021), p. 167.

56 Wood, P., *International Loans, Bonds, Guarantees and Legal Opinions* (Sweet & Maxwell, 2019) at [13-006].

57 Mugasha, A., *The Law of Multi-Bank Financing: Syndicated Loans and the Secondary Loan Market* (Oxford University Press, 2007), p. 353.

In the investment-grade lending sector, transactions are typically relationship-driven, making lenders less inclined to sell their holdings.[58] By contrast, in the leveraged finance sector, lenders often participate in syndications with the expectation of subsequently offloading the debt on the secondary market.

Secondary market sales could be driven by various strategic reasons.

9.1 Risk Management

Lenders use the secondary market to manage risk by reducing their exposure to specific borrowers, countries, or market sectors. For instance, lenders may wish to reduce their risk in relation to a single borrower facing potential financial difficulties or in countries with unstable political or economic environments. This can include markets where corporate governance may be less developed or where state intervention and risks like nationalisation can pose significant threats. Similarly, lenders may seek to exit sectors suffering from adverse circumstances, such as declining industries or regions undergoing economic downturns.

9.2 Regulation

Regulatory requirements, such as capital adequacy standards, compel lenders to manage their loan portfolios actively. Many lenders must limit the number of loans on their balance sheets to meet capital requirements set by frameworks such as Basel III and the EU's Capital Requirements Regulation (CRR)[59] and Directive (CRD IV).[60] In this context, the secondary market serves as a crucial tool, enabling lenders to restructure and manage their balance sheets effectively.

9.3 Turnover and Liquidity

In the syndicated debt market, much of the profit is not generated through the margins charged on loans, which are highly competitive, but from fees such as arrangement or agency fees. By selling debt in the secondary market, lenders free up capital, enabling them to arrange new loans and earn further fees, thereby maintaining a high turnover of business.

However, with the increased activity in the secondary market, acting as an agent becomes less attractive to banks that do not expect to hold onto the debt for long periods. As a result, the agency function is increasingly outsourced to specialist service providers, allowing lenders to focus on maintaining liquidity and generating new business.

9.4 Par and Near-Par Debt

Loans traded at or near their face value are classified as par or near-par debt. These are loans that the market considers highly likely to be repaid in full and on time. The secondary market

58 The Joint Money Laundering Steering Group, Syndicated Lending [17.7] in JMLSG Guidance available at: www.jmlsg.org.uk/wp-content/uploads/2020/02/Sector_17-_Final_Version_to_JMLSG_Board_Jan_18.pdf (accessed in March 2025).

59 Regulation (EU) No 575/2013 of the European Parliament and of the Council of 26 June 2013 on prudential requirements for credit institutions and amending Regulation (EU) No 648/2012.

60 As amended by Directive (EU) 2024/1619 of the European Parliament and of the Council of 31 May 2024 amending Directive 2013/36/EU as regards supervisory powers, sanctions, third-country branches, and environmental, social, and governance risks.

for par debt is particularly useful for lenders who wish to adjust their lending portfolios – whether by focusing on specific borrowers or diversifying away from particular countries or industries. Additionally, purchasing such debt can help build relationships with borrowers or syndicate members, especially if the buyer was unable to participate in the original syndication.

9.5 Distressed Debt

Distressed debt refers to loans made to borrowers (including companies, governments, or financial institutions) who are either undergoing insolvency proceedings or facing severe financial difficulties. Such loans are considered unlikely to be repaid in full, and as a result, they are traded at a discount to their face value. Buyers of distressed debt typically bet on the possibility of partial repayment through insolvency proceedings or the eventual recovery of the borrower, which could result in the loan being repaid in full.

9.6 Methods for Trading Loans

> *The LMA terms are intended for use in a market in which loans are traded. A loan may be traded many times, between many different parties, over a number of years. One would not readily infer that a contract for the sale of a loan in a market of that nature was intended to create continuing rights and obligations between the parties to that contract, in respect of payment, which might exist over a substantial period of time.*[61]

Transferring debt in the secondary market or through private transfers necessitates considering several key issues to determine the most appropriate method of transfer. Among the primary factors are the transfer of obligations, the borrower's consent, and the regulatory or commercial objectives of the transaction.[62] These considerations guide lenders and buyers in selecting the optimal mechanism for trading loans, particularly under English law, which allows for different methods such as assignment, novation, and sub-participation. Each method comes with its own set of legal and practical implications, particularly when it involves unfunded commitments or obligations under a facility agreement.

Assignment

Assignment (whose underlying principles have been discussed in Chapter 10 with respect to security assignment) in the context of a facility agreement entails the transfer of a lender's contractual rights to another party.[63] Under section 136(1) of the Law of Property Act 1925, an assignment must satisfy specific conditions to be recognised as a legal (or statutory) assignment. Firstly, it must be documented in writing and signed by the assignor to ensure clarity and enforceability. Secondly, the assignment must encompass the entire debt owed, rather than a partial transfer, to meet the statutory requirements. Thirdly, it must constitute an absolute and unconditional transfer of rights, meaning that it cannot be subject to further conditions or contingencies. If these formalities are not met, the assignment will take effect

61 Per Lord Reed in *Tael One Partners Ltd v Morgan Stanley & Co International PLC* [2015] UKSC 12 at [44].
62 Wood, P., *International Loans, Bonds, Guarantees and Legal Opinions* (Sweet & Maxwell, 2019) at [22-001].
63 Payne, J. and Gullifer, L., *Corporate Finance Law: Principles and Policy* (Hart, 2020) at [9.2.2].

only in equity rather than at law, potentially affecting the assignee's ability to enforce the assigned rights directly.[64]

Additionally, the borrower and any other obligors must receive written notification of the assignment. No particular form is necessary, but the notice must clearly indicate that an assignment has occurred, as established in *Van Lynn Developments Ltd v Pelias Construction Co Ltd* [1968] 1 QB 607, and tell the obligor that the relevant rights are exercisable by the third party as assignee and not merely as an agent for the assignor pursuant to *James Talcott Limited v John Lewis & Co Ltd* [1943] All ER 592. In *Santander UK Plc v Harrison* [2013] EWHC 199 (QB), the High Court examined whether information provided by a lender to borrowers, following a data request under data protection legislation, could constitute valid notice of assignment under section 136 of the Law of Property Act 1925. In this instance, the court opined, *obiter*, that information shared in response to a data protection request did not meet the requirements for notice under section 136. The court reasoned that when information is provided solely to fulfil a statutory data protection request, it is insufficient to communicate an assignment, particularly when it is expressly stated that the information is shared only as a right under data protection legislation. Moreover, the documents in question did not satisfy the *Van Lynn* test, as they merely suggested the possibility of an assignment without explicitly confirming it. In his remarks, the judge extended the reasoning in *Van Lynn*, indicating that section 136 requires the assignee or assignor to take clear, direct steps to notify the debtor of the assignment explicitly. Thus, for an assignment to be legally enforceable, the notice must unequivocally bring the assignment to the debtor's attention.[65]

When the preceding conditions are not met, the assignment becomes equitable rather than legal, meaning only the beneficial interest in the debt is transferred. Notice to the debtor, although unnecessary for the validity of the assignment, is nevertheless important because of the rule in *Dearle v Hall* (1828) 3 Russ. 1, which governs the priority of successive assignments by stipulating that a subsequent legal assignment (where notice to the debtor has been given first) will take priority over a prior equitable assignment. Notice of an assignment can be given by the assignor or the assignee. Further, borrowers who did not receive notice of the assignment can still discharge their debt by paying the original lender (*Bence v Shearman* [1898] 2 Ch 582). Therefore, the assignee faces the dual risk of both borrower default and failure by the assignor to pass on payments, with further complications if the borrower becomes insolvent.

Assignment offers several advantages in transferring a lender's rights without requiring the borrower's consent, providing flexibility in trading. If the assignor retains legal title, there is no need to renew the security for the loan, avoiding delays due to security hardening periods.

However, assignment has notable disadvantages. It will not include liabilities due from the assignor to the debtor as these cannot be assigned and must, instead, be novated.[66] This means that an assignee who takes the benefits under a contract will be required to comply with the obligations upon which those benefits are conditional. Whether or not a benefit is conditional upon an obligation is ultimately a matter of contractual construction; however, for example, it has been held that the assignee of the benefit of a contract to supply goods to a third party is required to comply with the specifications laid down by that third party in the original contract.[67]

Furthermore, it should be noted that whether an assignment of a debt is legal or equitable, the assignee takes subject to equities having priority over its right. This rule is of great

64 Chiu, I. and Wilson, J., *Banking Law and Regulation* (Oxford University Press, 2019), p. 152.
65 Chiu, I. and Wilson, J., *Banking Law and Regulation* (Oxford University Press, 2019), p. 151.
66 *Linden Gardens Trust Ltd v Lenesta Sludge Disposals Ltd* [1993] 3 All ER 417, HL *per Lord Browne-Wilkinson* at page 103B.
67 *Tollhurst's Case* [1903] AC 414.

antiquity[68] and dates as far back as historical records of assignment go. What constitutes equities for this purpose is not entirely clear,[69] and it is not easy to determine which equities the right of the assignee shall be subject. The truth is that the expression "equities" is a loose concept not too happily chosen.[70] However, while the outer limits of what constitutes equities have never been defined with anything nearing precision, such equities could include rights such as charges, encumbrances, options, rights of set-off, liens, and certain court orders obtainable while enforcing judgements (e.g., charging orders and garnishee orders).[71]

Thus, in practice assignment would be unsuitable where the lender has ongoing commitments, such as unfunded commitments in a revolving facility. In this context, the borrower would retain any rights of set-off or counterclaim against the assignor, which may limit the value of the assigned rights for the assignee.[72] Changes to the facility agreement between the assignor and borrower could also impact the assignee without their consent.[73] Due to these limitations, assignment under English law is generally avoided when transferring loans, particularly when complex obligations or rights are involved.

Assignment in the US

An assignment of a loan is the transfer of all or part of the rights and obligations of a lender (the assignor) under a loan agreement to another party (the assignee). It is not subject to the same strict requirements provided by the notion assignment (whether legal or equitable) in England and Wales.

Upon assignment, the assignee replaces the assignor and enters into a direct contractual relationship with the borrower with respect to the assigned portion of the loan. As the new party in privity with the borrower, the assignee acquires all the rights and obligations of a lender under the relevant loan documentation. This includes the right to vote on borrower requests for waivers and amendments, as well as on actions taken by the administrative agent in response to borrower defaults. The assignee is also entitled to indemnification and to exercise rights of set-off against the borrower. In addition, the assignee has the right to bring legal proceedings against the borrower for any breaches of the loan agreement unless the agreement expressly provides otherwise.

In most syndicated loan agreements, the borrower's consent is required before an assignment can occur, except in specific circumstances such as a borrower default or when the assignee is already a lender or is an affiliate or approved fund of a lender. The requirement for borrower consent can complicate the assignment process, as it introduces the possibility of borrower objections. To mitigate delays in obtaining borrower consent, many agreements include deemed consent provisions, whereby the borrower is deemed to have consented if they do not object within a specified period (typically three business days). These provisions are in line with the Model Credit Agreement Provisions published by the LSTA and help streamline the assignment process by reducing potential delays in the secondary loan market.

68 *Peters v Soames* (1701) 2 Vern 428; *Turton v Benson* (1718) 2 Vern. 764.
69 Meagher, R., Gummow, W. and Lehane, J., *Equity: Doctrine and Remedies* (Butterworths, 1984), p. 111 *et seq.*
70 Oditah, *Legal Aspects of Receivables Financing* (Sweet & Maxwell, 1991), p. 225.
71 Oditah, *Legal Aspects of Receivables Financing* (Sweet & Maxwell, 1991), p. 225 *et seq.*
72 *Business Computers Ltd v Anglo-African Leasing Ltd* [1977] 1 WLR 578.
73 *Brice v Bannister* (1877–78) LR 3 QBD 569.

Syndicated loan agreements often require that assignments be made in specified minimum amounts, as set out in the loan agreement. These provisions aim to limit the administrative burden on the administrative agent by preventing the syndicate from becoming unwieldy with too many small lenders. Exceptions to the minimum amount requirements are typically made for assignments to existing lenders, their affiliates, or related funds.

Assignment Documents and Syndicated Loan Provisions

Assignments are typically executed through an assignment and acceptance agreement, which is often included as an exhibit to the loan agreement. Many banks prefer to utilise the standard assignment and acceptance agreement issued by the LSTA to ensure consistency with industry practices.

Syndicated loan agreements include key provisions governing assignments, ensuring clarity in the transfer of lender interests. One fundamental provision concerns the release of the assignor, whereby the assignor is discharged from any obligations related to the assigned interest and bears no liability to the assignee concerning the borrower's creditworthiness. Assignments are typically executed on a "without recourse" basis, meaning that the assignor assumes no ongoing risk with respect to the assigned interest.

Additionally, syndicated loan agreements generally impose restrictions on non-ratable assignments, stipulating that assignments must be proportional. For example, if a lender assigns 50% of its revolving loans, it must also assign 50% of its revolving commitments, ensuring that participation in the facility remains balanced.

Further provisions govern minimum assignment amounts and any associated fees, which are typically outlined elsewhere in the agreement. These provisions collectively ensure that assignments within syndicated loan structures are conducted in an orderly and equitable manner, protecting the interests of both lenders and borrowers.

Not a Security

The US Second Circuit confirmed quite recently in *Kirschner v. JPMorgan Chase Bank, N.A.*[74] that a syndicated loan facility did not meet the legal definition of a security. The Second Circuit began by observing that although the relevant legislation defines a "security" to include "any note",[75] this phrase should not be interpreted in an entirely literal sense. Rather, the court emphasised that only "notes issued in an investment context" qualify as securities, whereas those "issued in a commercial or consumer context" do not fall within this classification. In affirming the district court's dismissal, the Second Circuit ultimately determined that the syndicated bank loan in question bore a strong resemblance to a recognised category of notes that had previously been held not to constitute securities, namely "*loans issued by banks for commercial purposes*". Subjecting syndicated term loans to securities regulation would have imposed additional disclosure and compliance obligations, significantly altering the nature of the syndicated loan market.

74 *Kirschner* v. *JP Morgan Chase Bank, N.A.*, Case No. 21-2726, 2023 WL 5437811 (2d Cir. 24 August 2023).
75 *Kirschner* [2023] WL 5437811, at *7 (citing *Reves*, 494 U.S. at [60]).

Novation

A transfer by way of novation is fundamentally distinct from the assignment of contractual rights.[76] Novation involves the termination of an existing contract and the simultaneous creation of a new one, whereas assignment merely transfers certain rights under an existing contract without extinguishing it.[77] The key distinction between these two mechanisms lies in whether liabilities are transferred alongside rights. In an assignment, only rights are transferred, while liabilities remain with the original party.[78] In contrast, novation transfers both rights and obligations to the new party, provided that all contractual requirements, including consideration, are satisfied. Where the incoming party assumes no obligations, a novation cannot occur due to the absence of consideration.[79]

Novation is particularly valuable in transactions requiring the transfer of both rights and obligations, such as undrawn commitments under revolving credit facilities. As a result, it is the predominant method of loan transfer in the London market. One of its principal advantages is that it enables the transferee to establish a direct relationship with the borrower, thereby eliminating any potential set-off rights or counterclaims that might have been asserted against the original lender. Furthermore, novation removes the loan from the transferor's balance sheet, which can provide regulatory and accounting benefits.

However, novation may also have implications for security arrangements. Since it results in the discharge of the original contract, any associated security may also be extinguished, requiring the security to be re-created. This can reset the relevant time periods for reviewable transactions and potentially alter the priority of security interests. To mitigate these risks, security trustees are frequently used in syndicated lending to hold security on behalf of both existing and future lenders, thereby preserving continuity and avoiding the need to re-establish security each time a loan is transferred.

The LMA Transfer Agreement 2010 Terms go on to define "Novated Assets" and "Novated Obligations" as follows:

> *"Novated Assets" means, subject to [an exception that is not presently material] all of the rights and benefits of the Transferor under or in respect of the Credit Documentation corresponding to the Traded Portion including, without limitation, the rights and interests of the Transferor in and in respect of: (a) the benefit of any guarantee or other assurance against loss given by any Guarantor; (b) the benefit of any other security; and (c) any amounts owing to the Transferor under the Credit Agreement, in each case corresponding to the Traded Portion.*[80]

Consent is critical in novation, and it can be given explicitly or implicitly. In *Habibsons Bank Ltd v Standard Chartered Bank (Hong Kong) Ltd* [2010] EWCA Civ 1335, the court confirmed that express consent given in advance, where the terms of the new contract are sufficiently clear, is valid. Although the decision was not binding, as it was rendered in the context of an interlocutory appeal, it nonetheless offers reassurance that the common practice in many lending transactions of securing prior consent remains effective.[81] Therefore, for a novation to be effective, the agreement of the borrower and all other parties to the facility documentation is required. In many syndicated facility agreements, consent is typically incorporated through a clause in the original agreement allowing for transfers, and the transaction is formalised by signing a

76 Proctor, C., *The Law and Practice of International Banking* (Oxford University Press, 2015) at [22.20].
77 Chiu, I. and Wilson, J., *Banking Law and Regulation* (Oxford University Press, 2019), p. 153.
78 Payne, J. and Gullifer, L., *Corporate Finance Law: Principles and Policy* (Hart, 2020) at [9.2.1].
79 *Rasbora v JCL Marine* [1977] 1 Lloyd's Reports 645 Apr.40.
80 In *GSO Credit – A Partners LP & Ors v Barclays Bank Plc v Barclays Bank Plc & Anor* [2016] EWHC 146 (Comm) at [38]–[41].
81 Wood, P., *International Loans, Bonds, Guarantees and Legal Opinions* (Sweet & Maxwell, 2019) at [22-043].

transfer certificate,[82] which is often standardised through the LMA documentation and signed by the seller, buyer, and agent, in the form attached as a schedule to the facility documentation.

Sub-Participation

Sub-participation (also referred to simply as "participation") is a widely used method for transferring loans or spreading risk in financial markets. The term "sub-participation" lacks a strict legal definition[83] but generally refers to two distinct types of structures: funded participation and risk participation.[84]

> *A sub-participation appears to be a transaction generally used by banks in connection with loans rather than bonds, for the purpose of enabling a lending bank to pass on all or part of the debtor risk in a loan it has made.*[85]

In a **funded participation**,[86] the participant (or sub-participant) makes a payment to the original lender, effectively funding a portion of the loan. This payment can relate either to amounts already drawn by the borrower or to a further drawdown requested by the borrower. The sub-participant receives a fee from the lender, and in return, the lender passes on any interest payments or principal repayments received from the borrower. However, this flow of payments is conditional: the sub-participant only receives these amounts if and when the lender does. Consequently, the sub-participant does not have a direct contractual relationship with the borrower. Instead, it is a creditor of the lender, not the borrower, and relies on the lender to pass along the borrower's payments.[87] This characterisation of sub-participation as a separate debtor-creditor relationship in which the sub-participant acquires no legal or beneficial interest in the underlying loan and no legal relationship with the borrower was also applied by the Privy Council in *Lloyds TSB Bank plc v Clarke and another* [2002] UKPC 27.[88]

Risk participation operates differently.[89] Instead of paying upfront, the sub-participant agrees to pay the lender a specified amount if certain events occur, such as the borrower's

82 The Joint Money Laundering Steering Group, Syndicated Lending [17.7] in JMLSG Guidance available at: www.jmlsg.org.uk/wp-content/uploads/2020/02/Sector_17-_Final_Version_to_JMLSG_Board_Jan_18.pdf (accessed in March 2025).

83 "[A]lthough the term 'sub-participation agreement' is not a legal term of art like 'assignment' or 'trust'. It is, however, a term commonly used in the market", per Lord Hofftman in *Lloyds TSB Bank plc v Clarke and another* [2002] UKPC 27 at [15].

84 Payne, J. and Gullifer, L., *Corporate Finance Law: Principles and Policy* (Hart, 2020) at [9.3.1].

85 *Lloyds TSB Bank plc v Clarke and another* [2002] UKPC 27 at [16] as confirmed in *Yieldpoint Stable Value Fund, LP v Kimura Commodity Trade Finance Fund Ltd* [2024] EWCA Civ 639.

86 "*As explained in the User Guide produced by the LMA, a transfer, by way of novation or assignment, 'is designed to effect a clean sale of the asset from Seller to Buyer', whereas 'the funded participation agreement deals with an ongoing relationship between two parties, the Grantor of the participation (who will usually be the lender of record) and the Participant'. The Comparative Study explains that participation has no technical meaning under English law but 'it normally refers to a back-to-back funding arrangement with a third party. Under English law, a Participation (or sub-participation as it is sometimes called) creates a debtor/creditor relationship between Grantor and Participant rather than a true sale relationship with respect to beneficial ownership of the underlying loans and Commitment*", in *Bear Stearns Bank Plc v Forum Global Equity Ltd* [2007] EWHC 1576 (Comm) at [13].

87 (Funded) sub-participation was considered in *Banca Generali SPA v CFE (Suisse) SA & Anor* [2023] EWHC 323 (Ch) at [14]: "*In the case of a sub-participation, an intermediary acquires a direct interest in a Receivable. That intermediary is typically Silverton Invest Limited and so I will use the expression 'Silverton' to refer to that intermediary. In such cases, CFE does not itself have any direct interest in the underlying Receivable. However, under a sub-participation agreement Silverton, which holds the actual Receivable, provides CFE with an indirect exposure to the performance of the underlying Receivable. In such a case CFE has contractual rights against Silverton, Silverton has contractual rights against the issuer of the Receivable, but CFE has no direct contractual rights against the issuer of the Receivable*".

88 For a comprehensive analysis, see Daley, M., 'Funded Participations – Mitigation of Grantor Credit Risk' (2009) *JIBLR* 288.

89 Arora, A., *Banking Law* (Pearson, 2014), p. 580.

non-payment. The sub-participant does not receive any payments from the lender other than a fee and is only required to provide funds to the lender if the borrower defaults.[90]

As with funded participation, there is no direct contractual relationship between the sub-participant and the borrower. However, once the sub-participant is called upon to reimburse the lender, it acquires rights against the borrower by way of subrogation – essentially stepping into the shoes of the lender and gaining the right to pursue the borrower for the debt.

For lenders, sub-participation offers several significant advantages. One of the primary benefits is risk reduction, as it enables the lender to decrease its exposure to the borrower without the need for an assignment or novation. This is particularly useful when the facility agreement imposes restrictions on transfers or when an assignment or novation would result in adverse tax consequences. Additionally, sub-participation allows the lender to maintain its commercial relationship with the borrower while shifting the risk to a third party. This structure also provides the opportunity for profit retention, as the lender may continue to receive a portion of the margin, generating a financial return despite having transferred the asset. Furthermore, sub-participation offers considerable flexibility, as it can be used both to transfer risk and to sell loan assets as part of the broader syndication process. For participants, sub-participation provides access to loan assets and market sectors that might otherwise be unavailable.[91]

Despite these advantages, sub-participation also presents certain drawbacks.[92] One of the key vulnerabilities of this structure is that the sub-participant assumes a double credit risk – first, the risk that the borrower will default, and second, the risk that the lender may not pass along payments even if the borrower meets its obligations.[93] In the case of risk participation, there is an additional exposure to the possibility that the lender may not pay the agreed fee. The sub-participant is also generally unable to rely on key contractual protections, such as withholding tax gross-up provisions or increased cost clauses, unless these rights are expressly conferred.[94] Rescheduling risk is also a concern, as the borrower may seek to restructure the loan, potentially altering the participant's exposure. While the LMA standard participation agreements contain provisions to mitigate rescheduling risk, these mechanisms require negotiation. Moreover, unless the lender and sub-participant specifically agree otherwise, the sub-participant does not benefit from any security the lender may have negotiated with the borrower.[95]

For the original lender, the primary disadvantage of risk participation is the possibility that the loan remains on its balance sheet rather than being derecognised as intended. There is also a risk of breaching confidentiality obligations if the lender discloses details of the loan to the sub-participant without the borrower's consent.

To address these complexities, the LMA has developed standard documentation for both funded[96] and risk participations, including the *Master Funded Participation Agreement (Par/Distressed)*,

90 Ellinger, E. P., Lomnicka, E. and Hare, C., *Ellinger's Modern Banking Law* (Oxford University Press, 2011), p. 789.

91 Hudson, A., *The Law of Finance* (Sweet & Maxwell, 2013) at [33-42].

92 See LMA, January 2010 (and updated October 2017): 'Funded Participations – Mitigation of Grantor Credit Risk'; The 'Guide to Secondary Loan Market Transactions', published August 2018; and, most recently, a 'Secondary Debt Trading Documentation (Par and Distressed) Users Guide', published January 2021.

93 *Yieldpoint Stable Value Fund, LP v Kimura Commodity Trade Finance Fund Ltd* [2024] EWCA Civ 639.

94 Chiu, I. and Wilson, J., *Banking Law and Regulation* (Oxford University Press, 2019), p. 154.

95 Chiu, I. and Wilson, J., *Banking Law and Regulation* (Oxford University Press, 2019), p. 155.

96 For example, in LMA Funded Participation, the relationship between the Participant and the Grantor in a sub-participation arrangement is fundamentally that of debtor and creditor. The Participant provides the Grantor with an upfront Settlement Amount, along with any expenses due under the Credit Agreement. In return, the Grantor undertakes to pay the Participant a proportionate share of all principal and interest

the *Master Risk Participation Agreement (Par)*, and separate agreements for funded participation in par or distressed trades.[97] These documents establish standardised terms covering critical issues such as information rights, security for undrawn commitments, and voting rights in distressed debt transactions. Confidentiality remains a key consideration, and the LMA forms of confidentiality letter require participants to maintain strict confidentiality, subject to defined exceptions.

Sub-Participation and US Counterparties

The US Dodd-Frank Wall Street Reform and Consumer Protection Act of 2010 (**Dodd-Frank Act**)[98] introduced extensive reforms to the US financial regulatory system, affecting nearly all aspects of the finance industry. Concerns emerged regarding the potential impact of the Dodd-Frank Act on loan participations in Europe, primarily due to the Act's definitions of "swaps", "security-based swaps", and "mixed swaps". Specifically, it was feared that an English-law loan participation, including those structured in accordance with LMA documentation, could fall within the scope of these definitions. If loan participation were classified as a swap, transactions involving the sale or purchase of LMA-style loan participations by or from a US person would become subject to the Dodd-Frank regulatory framework governing swaps.

In July 2012, the US Commodity Futures Trading Commission and the US Securities and Exchange Commission (SEC) jointly adopted rules under Title VII of the Dodd-Frank Act that defined, among other key terms, "swap" and "security-based swap". The accompanying regulatory guidance clarified that loan participations would not be categorised as swaps or security-based swaps – and therefore would not be subject to Title VII regulations – provided that four specific conditions were met. While LMA-funded participations typically meet these conditions, it is unclear whether risk participations involving US counterparties are similarly exempt.

Some sub-participation agreements, including the LMA's standard form, include an "elevation" clause. This provision allows the sub-participant, under certain conditions, to be "elevated" to become a lender under the original facility agreement (i.e., changing the lender of record) or to

received under the loan. Crucially, the Grantor retains both the legal and beneficial ownership of the loan, meaning that the Participant does not acquire direct rights against the Borrower. Consequently, the Participant assumes credit risk not only on the Borrower but also on the Grantor, as payments received depend on the Grantor fulfilling its obligations. From an accounting perspective, sub-participation under UK Generally Accepted Accounting Practice (UK GAAP) or International Accounting Standard (IAS) 39 enables the Grantor to benefit from off-balance sheet treatment, as the transaction is treated as a derivative rather than a loan transfer. However, under United States Generally Accepted Accounting Principles (US GAAP), off-balance sheet treatment requires a "true sale", meaning that the Seller (i.e., the Grantor) must not retain credit risk. This requirement results in LSTA participations involving a transfer of beneficial ownership, distinguishing them from UK market practices.

97 According to Clause 2(a) of the LMA's "Standard Terms and Conditions for Par and Distressed Trade Transactions (Bank Debt/Claims)" dated 20 April 2016: "A binding contract for the sale or participation by the Seller to the Buyer of the Purchased Assets and the Purchased Obligations shall come into effect between the Seller and the Buyer upon oral or, in the absence of such oral agreement, written agreement of the terms on the Trade Date and shall be documented and completed in accordance with these Conditions". See *Astra Asset Management UK Ltd v The Co-Operative Bank Plc* [2019] EWHC 897 (Comm) at [8] and [9].

98 Public Law 111-203 – July 21, 2010.

transfer the loan to a third party, with the sub-participant then entering into a new sub-participation with the third party. Once elevation is completed, the funded participation is terminated, but any rights and liabilities that arose before the termination will remain.[99]

However, elevation may not always be feasible. For example, if the underlying facility agreement includes transfer restrictions, elevation may not be possible, even if the sub-participation agreement includes an elevation clause.

Bankruptcy Risks in the US

In the event of the bankruptcy of either the borrower or the lead lender, the position of the participant becomes uncertain and potentially precarious. Where the borrower is subject to bankruptcy proceedings, participants are not recognised as direct creditors of the borrower. As a result, they lack standing to initiate an involuntary bankruptcy petition, to vote in the proceeding, or to serve on the creditors' committee. Although they may be permitted to participate as a party in interest, such standing is not guaranteed. If they are not granted this status, participants must instead rely on their contractual claims against the lead lender to recover their share of the loan.

The situation becomes further complicated in the event of the bankruptcy of the lead lender, particularly due to the legal uncertainty surrounding the nature of the participant's interest. Key questions arise as to whether the participant is merely a general creditor of the lead lender, whether the participant owns an interest in the underlying debt owed by the borrower, what fiduciary or contractual duties the lead lender owes to the participant, and whether the participation arrangement constitutes a true sale or a loan.

If, in the lead lender's insolvency, the participation is judicially characterised as a loan to the lead lender rather than as a sale of an undivided interest in the borrower's debt, the participant's rights may be significantly impaired. In such circumstances, unless the participant has properly perfected its security interest in the underlying loan receivable, the bankruptcy court may deny the participant any claim to the collateral securing the loan. This could result in a significantly reduced, or even negligible, recovery for the participant.

Other Methods: Credit Derivatives and Securitisation

Other methods for transferring economic interests in loans include synthetic structures such as credit derivatives and securitisation. These mechanisms, which are discussed in more detail in Chapter 14, allow lenders to manage their credit exposure without a direct transfer of the loan itself.

Securitisation is a structured financial transaction whereby a lender, rather than selling an individual loan, packages multiple loans into a pool. These assets are then sold to a special purpose vehicle (**SPV**), which funds the purchase by issuing debt securities to investors. The SPV is a bankruptcy-remote entity designed to isolate the assets from the originator's balance sheet and protect the investors from the originator's insolvency. The SPV generates funds by issuing asset-backed securities, which are serviced by the income stream from the underlying assets. Investors in these securities receive regular payments based on the cash flows of the underlying assets, offering them exposure to these receivables while reducing the originator's

99 Chiu, I. and Wilson, J., *Banking Law and Regulation* (Oxford University Press, 2019), p. 155.

credit risk.[100] The securitisation process provides liquidity to lenders by allowing them to convert illiquid assets into tradable securities, which may be sold to a broad range of investors.

Credit derivatives are financial instruments designed to mitigate or transfer credit risk, enabling lenders to hedge against the possibility of borrower default. One of the most common forms of credit derivative is the credit default swap (**CDS**), in which the protection buyer (in this case, the lender in the underlying transaction) pays periodic premiums to the protection seller in exchange for compensation if a specified credit event occurs, such as the default of a borrower on a loan or bond obligation. These events, often referred to as "credit events", can trigger significant financial obligations under a CDS, with the protection seller either purchasing the referenced obligations at a predetermined price or compensating the buyer for any losses based on the market value of the debt at the time of default.[101] In recent years, the International Swaps and Derivatives Association (**ISDA**)[102] has provided standardised definitions, such as the 2014 ISDA Credit Derivatives Definitions,[103] to guide market participants in determining what constitutes a credit event and the associated triggers. These events may include bankruptcy, failure to pay, restructuring, and acceleration of obligations, although the precise definitions can vary depending on the contract.

In syndicated lending, lenders seeking to hedge their exposure may opt to purchase a credit derivative rather than sell part of the loan. This allows them to maintain their position in the loan while transferring the associated credit risk to a third party. Notably, the borrower – often referred to as the reference entity in a CDS – is typically unaware of the existence of the credit derivative transaction. As the borrower is not a party to the credit derivative, the terms of the derivative contract, including the specific credit events that trigger payment, do not necessarily align with the events of default set out in the borrower's original loan agreement. This distinction underscores the independent nature of credit derivatives in risk management strategies within the syndicated loan market.

Another widely used credit derivative in the syndicated lending market is the collateralised loan obligation or CLO (also considered in Chapter 14). In this structure, a portfolio of loans is transferred to an SPV, which then issues debt securities backed by these loans. This enables lenders to sell portfolios of loans while potentially retaining some exposure to the underlying assets.

Complexity in Loan Trading

Both syndicated and bilateral loans are often accompanied by a variety of complex arrangements, such as security, guarantees, and hedging, which add layers of intricacy to loan trading. These loans may also stem from longstanding customer relationships that are delicate and sensitive, further complicating the transaction process. As a result, trading loans – whether in the secondary market or through private transfer – can be challenging. What follows are key areas of concern that should be considered when trading loans.[104]

100 Payne, J. and Gullifer, L., *Corporate Finance Law: Principles and Policy* (Hart, 2020) at [9.3.2].

101 Proctor, C., *The Law and Practice of International Banking* (Oxford University Press, 2015) at [22.33].

102 As described in *Lomas v JFB Firth Rixson* [2011] 2 BCLC 120 at [53]: *"It is necessary to begin with some preliminary observations about the correct approach to construction. The ISDA master agreement is one of the most widely used forms of agreement in the world. It is probably the most important standard market agreement used in the financial world. English law is one of the two systems of law most commonly chosen for the interpretation of the master agreement, the other being New York law. It is axiomatic that it should, as far as possible, be interpreted in a way that achieves the objectives of clarity, certainty and predictability, so that the very large number of parties using it know where they stand".*

103 Available at: www.isda.org/book/2014-isda-credit-derivative-definitions/ (accessed in March 2025).

104 Hudson, A., *The Law of Finance* (Sweet & Maxwell, 2013) at [33-43].

Transfer Provisions in Finance Documents

While the standardisation of loan documentation has significantly enhanced liquidity and facilitated the transferability of loans in the secondary market, it remains essential to ensure that a loan is structured in a manner that enables efficient trading at the origination stage. Several factors may affect the ease of transfer. The structure of the facility, including multiple utilisations, tranches, or sub-tranches – potentially in different currencies, with varying maturities and interest periods – may introduce complexities that impede the smooth transfer or prompt settlement of loans. Consent provisions also play a crucial role. In Europe, there has been a trend towards increased restrictions on loan transfers within primary loan documents, with more limited categories of permitted transferees and a reduction in deemed consent provisions. These developments have led to delays in the transfer process and, in some cases, have prevented trades altogether.

Another consideration in loan transfers is the imposition of transfer fees. In the European market, it is standard practice to compensate agents for the administrative work involved in processing a transfer. However, excessive transfer fees may deter potential buyers, particularly in an environment where market participants expect agents to facilitate transfers in an efficient and timely manner.

Confidentiality Issues

A transferring lender, particularly a bank, owes a common law duty of confidentiality to its customers, including the borrower. Additionally, facility agreements frequently contain express confidentiality clauses that impose further obligations on the lender. However, despite these restrictions, lenders seeking to transfer or sell a loan must market the facility to potential buyers, which necessitates the disclosure of commercially sensitive information about the obligors and the terms of the facility agreement.[105]

In most cases, the disclosure of such information requires the borrower's consent. Standard syndicated facility agreements often contain express provisions permitting limited disclosure of confidential information to potential transferees, typically subject to the execution of a confidentiality agreement.[106]

Even where borrower consent is obtained, lenders must comply with various requirements governing the disclosure of information. Data protection laws, including the UK General Data Protection Regulation (GDPR)[107] and the UK Data Protection Act 2018,[108] impose strict requirements on the processing and sharing of personal data. Competition law considerations under the Competition Act 1998 further limit the sharing of competition-sensitive information, while insider trading laws prohibit the use of non-public material information in financial transactions, including loan sales.

105 OECD, 'Due Diligence for Responsible Corporate Lending and Securities Underwriting' *OECD Publishing* (2019), p. 21, available at https://mneguidelines.oecd.org/due-diligence-for-responsible-corporate-lending-and-securities-underwriting.pdf (accessed in March 2025).

106 See The Association of Corporate Treasurers, *A Borrower's Guide to the LMA's Investment Grade Agreements* (ACT 6th Edition, November 2022), p. 333, available at www.treasurers.org/system/files/The%20ACT%20Borrower%E2%80%99s%20Guide%20to%20the%20LMA%E2%80%99s%20Investment%20Grade%20Agreements%20-%20Final.pdf (accessed in March 2025).

107 2016 No. 679 or its European source: Regulation (EU) 2016/679 of the European Parliament and of the Council of 27 April 2016 on the protection of natural persons with regard to the processing of personal data and on the free movement of such data, and repealing Directive 95/46/EC.

108 2018 c. 12.

Relationship Management

In many cases, borrowers must be informed that their loans are being sold, especially if the transaction is high-profile. Managing the borrower relationship throughout the sale process is crucial for the seller, as it may need to reassure the borrower regarding confidentiality, loan servicing, and potential cost impacts.[109]

Some lenders may opt to retain a portion of the loan for relationship purposes, providing the borrower with comfort that the original lender remains involved. However, not all buyers, especially non-bank entities like hedge funds, may be interested in assuming undrawn commitments or sharing obligations with other lenders. Prudent borrowers should investigate the buyer's strategy and motives to anticipate any potential renegotiations of loan terms.

Loan Servicing and Further Lending

Unlike distressed debt, performing loans typically involve ongoing servicing obligations and may also include further lending commitments from undrawn facilities. Consequently, buyers acquiring such loans must be prepared to assume various regulatory, operational, and administrative responsibilities. Regulatory approvals may be required, particularly where the buyer intends to engage in lending activities that necessitate authorisation, such as holding a banking licence. In addition, compliance with anti-money laundering (AML) regulations, including Know Your Customer (KYC) checks, is essential to ensure that the borrower meets applicable legal and regulatory standards.

Beyond regulatory compliance, loan servicing functions must also be managed, including the administration of payments and the maintenance of loan accounts. Effective coordination between the seller, buyer, and borrower is particularly crucial when transferring security interests, especially where the security extends to future advances. The process becomes more complex when the loan includes ancillary facilities, such as an overdraft linked to a revolving credit facility, as borrower consent may be required to transfer the associated accounts.

A further complexity arises in relation to undrawn commitments. The lender's obligations under these commitments cannot be transferred through assignment alone, as assignment only transfers rights and not obligations. Instead, a full novation is often required to ensure that both the rights and obligations are effectively transferred to the incoming lender. Without novation, the original lender would remain contractually bound to advance further funds under the facility, even after the transfer of its interest in the loan. In certain cases, sub-participation or synthetic structures may be used to transfer ancillary facilities, although the fluctuating nature of these facilities can pose practical and regulatory capital challenges.

Part Transfers

Under English law, it is not possible to effect a statutory or legal assignment of part of a debt, as the assignee does not acquire both the legal and beneficial interest in the entire debt. Consequently, such an assignment would fail to comply with section 136 of the Law of Property Act 1925.[110] In the context of syndicated loans, any transfer of less than a lender's entire commitment would amount to the assignment of only part of the loan. Given that commitments

109 Payne, J. and Gullifer, L., *Corporate Finance Law: Principles and Policy* (Hart, 2020) at [9.2.4].
110 See *Walter & Sullivan Ltd v J. Murphy & Sons Ltd* [1955] 2 QB 584.

in a syndicated facility are typically several rather than joint, a single lender may assign the entirety of its loan by way of statutory assignment, even if this does not constitute the whole of the borrower's overall debt. However, syndicated lenders that are required for regulatory risk retention purposes or that voluntarily choose to retain a portion of the loan – commonly referred to as keeping "skin in the game" – may be unable to transfer the non-retained portion by way of statutory assignment, as it would represent only part of the debt.

An assignment of part of a debt would, at best, take effect as an equitable assignment. In such cases, the assignee would be unable to enforce the debt independently and would be required to join the assignor in any legal action for recovery, as the original lender would remain the legal owner of the debt.[111] Where an assigned debt is secured or guaranteed, an assignee acquiring only part of the debt would lack the ability to enforce the security, as it would not hold full ownership of the debt with "all legal and other remedies for the same".[112] Additionally, any seller retaining part of the loan would continue to benefit from rights of set-off that would not be available to the assignee. While the possibility of novating part of a debt remains legally uncertain,[113] LMA-based primary documents and secondary trading documents offer greater flexibility, enabling the transfer of part of a debt through novation while allowing original syndicate members to retain portions of the loan.

Taxation and Other Legal Considerations

Several tax issues arise in connection with loan trades, including withholding tax and stamp duty. Under most English-law syndicated facility agreements, lenders may be exempt from the UK withholding tax if they qualify as a UK bank, a UK corporation taxpayer, or are residents in a jurisdiction with a relevant double-tax treaty. However, the facility agreement typically restricts transfers to "qualifying lenders" to avoid triggering withholding tax.

Stamp duty generally does not apply to loan transfers in the UK, as most assignments fall within the loan capital exemption. Novations which create new contracts are not subject to stamp duty. However, in certain multi-jurisdictional transactions, local tax implications that may affect the transaction's economics will have to be considered.

10 PORTFOLIO SALES

In the context of loan trading, portfolio sales involve the transfer of multiple loans, which can include both performing and non-performing loans (NPLs). These transactions differ from single-loan trades due to their scale and the added complexity of managing multiple assets within a single transaction. Although many of the issues arising in portfolio sales mirror those encountered in individual loan trades, there are several additional considerations that must be addressed.

10.1 Regulatory and Management Considerations

A portfolio sale can significantly impact a seller's business, affecting its capital base, employee structure, and overall operations. Regulatory approvals may be required, including under

111 *Re Steel Wing Co. Ltd* [1921] 1 Ch 349.
112 Section 136(1)(b), LPA 1925.
113 *Langston Group Corporation v Cardiff City Football Club Ltd* [2008] EWHC 535 (Ch).

the Transfer of Undertakings (Protection of Employment) Regulations 2006,[114] which protect employee rights when businesses or parts of businesses are transferred. Moreover, large-scale acquisitions involving numerous loans can trigger competition law concerns, requiring a careful assessment of the transaction's impact on market competition. Additionally, the integration of IT and operational systems for both parties can pose challenges, particularly if a new servicing[115] infrastructure needs to be established.

Where the portfolio includes consumer loans, either secured or unsecured, further regulatory considerations come into play. These may include obtaining specific licences or authorisations related to data protection or consumer credit laws.

10.2 Managing Relationships

In a portfolio sale, it is crucial to manage existing customer relationships carefully. Since many customers (especially long-term clients) may feel uneasy about their loans being transferred, relationship managers on the loan origination side will need to cooperate to ensure a smooth transition. The seller's ability to maintain these relationships throughout the transaction process helps ensure that the loan transfer proceeds without degrading the value of the underlying assets.

10.3 Due Diligence and Disclosure

Due diligence is far more extensive and time-consuming in portfolio transactions compared to single-loan sales. The principle of "buyer beware" governs the process, and the warranties provided in the sale and purchase agreement are usually minimal and tightly capped in terms of liability and duration.

The case of *Bibby Factors Northwest Ltd v HFD Ltd* [2015] EWCA Civ 1908 underlined the importance of thorough due diligence when purchasing debt. The Court of Appeal stressed that companies must undertake meticulous investigations into the debt they intend to buy to avoid unforeseen risks. This principle applies equally to loan portfolio purchases, where the complexity and volume of the assets increase the need for rigorous scrutiny.

10.4 Buyer Funding, Co-Investment, and Seller Cooperation

Loan portfolios often offer attractive returns for investors, particularly when structured with higher levels of leverage or through innovative mechanisms like securitisation. Prospective buyers must assess whether the transaction is feasible from a financier's perspective, especially if they intend to use complex funding structures.

In some cases, larger portfolios may require a consortium of investors with varied expertise or regulatory capabilities to come together to acquire the assets. Joint ventures or similar cooperative structures may be formed between the buyer and seller, allowing for continued

114 (SI 2006/246).
115 Portfolio servicing refers to the management of a collection of loans or credit obligations by a servicer. The servicer is the entity responsible for collecting loan payments, maintaining borrower accounts, and ensuring compliance with loan terms.

collaboration during the management or workout of the loan portfolio. Additionally, sellers may agree to provide support by seconding personnel or entering into servicing agreements that ensure smooth operational management post-transfer.

10.5 The Bidding Process

The bidding process is a critical phase in portfolio sales. After selecting the portfolio and determining an appropriate pricing and risk strategy, the seller must run a competitive bidding process to maximise the sale price. This process runs concurrently with the buyer's due diligence and culminates in the selection of preferred bidders. Bidders are typically required to pay deposits, further ensuring their commitment to the transaction. Bid vehicles, often SPVs, are typically used for such transactions, isolating the risk and ensuring the buyer's financial security during the bidding process.

10.6 Documents and Transfer Methods

The standard secondary market trading documents are not entirely suited to portfolio transactions, which involve multiple assets. As a result, the UK market has developed bespoke sale and purchase agreements for portfolio sales, incorporating elements from both corporate asset purchase agreements and LMA secondary debt trading documents to facilitate the transfer.

In such transactions, buyers often seek more extensive indemnity protections. These indemnities compensate for any discrepancies in the portfolio, providing buyers with additional assurances.

Although a clean transfer that moves the loans off the seller's balance sheet is preferred, certain obstacles – such as obligor consent issues, transfer restrictions, or tax considerations – may prevent an outright sale. In these instances, structured alternatives such as funded participation arrangements and synthetic structures may be used until a full transfer can be completed. These structured alternatives provide a means to shift economic risk, with the option to elevate the transaction to a full transfer later on.

11 DISTRESSED DEBT

As noted previously, distressed debt, often referred to as "impaired debt", "sub-performing debt", or "non-performing loans" (NPLs), describes debt that a borrower is unlikely to repay in full by its maturity due to financial distress or insolvency. Debt may also be classified as distressed if it is "value impaired" – for example, if the borrower breaches key covenants in the loan agreement or the lender must extend the repayment date or amend other terms of the loan.

There is no universal international accounting or regulatory standard for defining distressed debt. However, guidance is provided by the Basel Committee on Banking Supervision's *Prudential Treatment of Problem Assets*, which defines[116] "non-performing exposures" based on criteria such as debt being "past-due" or the debtor being "unlikely to pay". Similarly, the European Banking Authority provides a regulatory definition for non-performing loans in

116 See Guidelines on Prudential treatment of problem assets – definitions of non-performing exposures and forbearance available at: www.bis.org/bcbs/publ/d403.pdf (accessed in March 2025).

Commission Implementing Regulation (EU) 2021/451,[117] with key features such as overdue debt and debtor incapacity to repay. Additionally, some market definitions reference the "credit spread", which measures the difference in yield between distressed debt and a risk-free benchmark, such as government bonds or cash.

Distressed debt is actively traded on the secondary market, commonly using LMA standard documentation in the UK. The distressed debt market in the UK emerged in the 1990s, driven by over-leveraged companies encountering financial difficulties. While some lenders opted to reschedule the debt, others chose to sell their loans at a discount to mitigate exposure and recover part of their investment. The aftermath of the 2007–2008 financial crisis, coupled with regulatory changes and liquidity demands, contributed to the growth of this market, with banks selling distressed debt to de-leverage and comply with evolving regulatory frameworks. Lenders are frequently subject to stress tests (see Chapter 7) by regulators to assess liquidity and systemic risk, further driving sales of distressed debt.

The distressed debt market comprises a wide range of participants, reflecting the broader expansion of the leveraged finance sector. Initially dominated by banks, this market has seen increasing participation from institutional investors, hedge funds, and private equity firms, which have since emerged as key purchasers of distressed assets, acquiring non-performing loans from banks and other financial institutions.

In addition to private sector participants, government entities and central banks also play a significant role in the distressed debt market. Government "bad banks", such as Ireland's National Asset Management Agency (**NAMA**), were established in the aftermath of the 2008 financial crisis to manage distressed assets and stabilise financial institutions.[118] Similarly, central banks, including the US Federal Reserve, have engaged in purchasing distressed assets to support financial stability. SPVs issuing collateralised debt obligations (CDOs) have also facilitated investment in distressed debt by repackaging and distributing risk across different tranches of investors.

Companies are often wary of distressed debt investors, fearing that they may be "vulture funds" that will block restructurings or force debt-for-equity swaps. This concern has led borrowers to resist sales of their debt to certain types of investors. Loan agreements often include transfer provisions allowing debt transfers only to "banks or other financial institutions" or approved buyers, as seen in cases such as *Barbados Trust Company Ltd v Bank of Zambia* [2007] EWCA Civ 148 and *Essar Steel Ltd v The Argo Fund Ltd* [2006] EWCA Civ 241.[119] Whether a party qualifies as a "financial institution" or "qualifying lender" for the purposes of a loan agreement is often relevant to the withholding tax position under such agreements. Most distressed debt funds fall within the definitions used in the standard documentation for syndicated debt trading, which generally has broader provisions than earlier case law. In *Hockin v Royal Bank of Scotland plc* [2016] EWHC 925 (Ch), the High Court considered whether a transfer clause in a loan agreement, allowing the lender to assign rights without borrower consent, implied a duty of good faith. The court held that such a duty could not be implied unless necessary to make the agreement work or unless it was "so obvious" it went without saying. The standard drafting of the assignment clause, in this case, did not support such a duty.

117 Commission Implementing Regulation (EU) 2021/451 of 17 December 2020 laying down implementing technical standards for the application of Regulation (EU) No 575/2013 of the European Parliament and of the Council with regard to supervisory reporting of institutions and repealing Implementing Regulation (EU) No 680/2014.

118 Under the National Asset Management Agency Act 2009 Number 34 of 2009. NAMA acquired large portfolios of commercial (real estate) loans secured by land and development property from Anglo Irish Bank, Allied Irish Bank, Bank of Ireland, Irish Nationwide Building Society, and Educational Building Society. The purchase of these assets was financed up to 95% by State-guaranteed bonds.

119 Hudson, A., *The Law of Finance* (Sweet & Maxwell, 2013) at [33-46].

Lenders may sell distressed debt for a variety of reasons, including the need to reduce the administrative burden associated with managing such loans. Additionally, lenders may prefer to realise immediate value by selling distressed debt at a discount rather than holding onto it with uncertain prospects of repayment. Selling distressed debt also enables lenders to free up capital, allowing them to reinvest in more profitable ventures, improving liquidity and potentially generating higher returns.

Regulatory considerations also play a key role in the decision to sell distressed debt. Under UK regulatory capital requirements,[120] banks must manage their loan portfolios to ensure compliance with capital adequacy rules. Disposing of distressed assets assists in meeting these obligations.

Conversely, investors purchase distressed debt for various strategic and financial reasons. Some traders seek to generate a rapid profit by acquiring distressed debt at a discount and reselling it at a higher price, relying on market liquidity to facilitate quick turnover. Investors may also seek to influence a borrower's restructuring by acquiring a significant proportion of its debt, enabling them to shape insolvency proceedings or implement a "loan-to-own" strategy over a longer period.

Distressed debt transactions are typically executed using the same mechanisms as those used for performing loans, including assignment, novation, and sub-participation. The LMA and LSTA have developed standardised documentation for distressed debt trades, providing a structured framework that enhances efficiency and reduces transaction costs for both buyers and sellers. While these standard documents are widely utilised, bespoke arrangements may be necessary for certain sectors, such as real estate, where transactions often involve extensive disclosure requirements and limited warranties.

11.1 Securities Law Issues in Distressed Debt Trading

Buyers of distressed debt typically seek extensive information regarding the debt, the borrower, and any associated security. However, the disclosure of such information is constrained by securities laws and insider dealing regulations. In distressed debt transactions, certain parties may gain access to inside information, necessitating careful compliance with regulatory frameworks. Additionally, holders who acquire such investments, participate in a debt-for-equity swap, or become members of a creditors' or bondholders' committee may also gain access to non-public material information.[121]

Such access creates significant regulatory risks, as holders must ensure that they do not engage in conduct that would breach the UK market abuse regime. Distressed debt traders in the UK, or those trading with UK-based entities, must avoid disseminating false or misleading information related to investments.[122] Under the UK market abuse regime, which is contained

120 The Capital Requirements Directive (Directive (EU) 2013/36, as amended ("CRD IV") which in the EU was subsequently amended by Directive (EU) 2024/1619 ("CRD VI").

121 Hudson, A., *The Law of Finance* (Sweet & Maxwell, 2013) at [33-41].

122 Article 7 of the retained EU law version of the Market Abuse Regulation (596/2014) (UK MAR) sets out the definition of inside information and establishes that it encompasses four distinct types of information, each subject to its own definition. First, it provides a general definition of inside information in relation to financial instruments. In addition to this, it sets out specific definitions applicable to particular contexts. These include inside information relating to commodity derivatives, as well as information concerning emission allowances and auction products based on such allowances. The fourth category concerns information relevant to persons charged with the execution of orders relating to financial instruments, specifically information conveyed by a client that pertains to the client's pending orders in such instruments.

in the retained EU law version of the Market Abuse Regulation (596/2014) (UK MAR),[123] it is unlawful for a trader to knowingly – or in circumstances where they could reasonably be expected to know – distribute false, misleading, or deceptive information. If a trader creates a false or misleading impression about investments or related rights, which induces another party to buy (or refrain from buying) such investments, they could be liable for market abuse. Additionally, if a trader dishonestly conceals material facts or makes deceptive statements, promises, or forecasts, they may be guilty of a criminal offence. Compliance with the FCA's UK Disclosure Guidance and Transparency Rules Sourcebook[124] is also essential, particularly concerning the obligation to disclose inside information in a timely and appropriate manner.

12 CONCLUSION

Syndicated loan facilities remain a cornerstone of modern corporate finance, providing borrowers with access to substantial capital while allowing lenders to diversify and manage their risk exposure. The role of standardisation, facilitated by organisations such as the LMA and the LSTA, has simplified the syndication process and minimised legal risks. This has contributed to the global expansion of syndicated loans, enhancing their efficiency and reliability.

The primary market for syndicated loans is dynamic and influenced by the credit standing of borrowers. The secondary market plays a crucial role in managing risk, enhancing liquidity, and ensuring compliance with regulatory requirements. It enables lenders, particularly in the leveraged finance sector, to sell debt to manage their exposure to specific borrowers, sectors, or regions. The secondary market also provides flexibility for portfolio adjustments and capital optimisation, allowing lenders to free up resources for new loans. Furthermore, it facilitates the trading of both par and distressed debt, with par debt trades focusing on portfolio rebalancing and distressed debt trades centring on risk assessment and recovery prospects through restructuring or insolvency proceedings.

Finally, portfolio sales offer significant opportunities for both sellers and buyers, but they demand meticulous management of legal, regulatory, and operational complexities.

123 UK MAR sets out a regulatory framework on market abuse, as well as measures to prevent market abuse to ensure the integrity of the UK financial markets and enhance investor protection and confidence in those markets. It contains prohibitions on insider dealing, unlawful disclosure of inside information, and market manipulation, and provisions to empower the FCA to prevent and detect these offences. Any transaction, order or behaviour concerning any financial instrument, irrespective of whether or not such transaction, order or behaviour takes place on a trading venue would fall within the remit of UK MAR. Therefore, pursuant to Article 2(3), UK MAR, such remit is extended to off-market and OTC trading.

124 Available at: www.handbook.fca.org.uk/handbook/DTR.pdf (accessed in March 2025).

CHAPTER 12

INTERCREDITOR DEEDS AND SECURITY TRUSTS

OVERVIEW

This chapter explores the key mechanisms used to establish creditor priorities in finance transactions, focusing on intercreditor deeds, deeds of priority, and subordination agreements. It examines the structures employed to create different tiers among various creditor groups with a particular focus on the provisions governing the relationship between senior and mezzanine debt.

In addition, Chapter 12 delves into the function and significance of security trusts, alongside the crucial role of security trustees in finance transactions. Specifically, it examines the use of security trusts in England and Wales to hold security over a borrower's or obligor's assets for the benefit of multiple finance parties, particularly in syndicated loan agreements. Although the focus is on syndicated lending, the principles discussed are equally applicable to securitisation, project finance, and other scenarios involving a collective group of creditors who are entitled to security for the debt owed to them.

1 INSOLVENCY PRINCIPLES AND CREDITORS' ARRANGEMENTS

One goal of the insolvency process is to achieve creditor equality[1] – commonly attempted through a *pro-rata* distribution among creditors. It is a fundamental principle of English insolvency law that the claims of the (unsecured) creditors of an insolvent entity would rank *pari passu*,[2] and in the event of there being insufficient funds to pay all such creditors, they would abate equally.[3] The major qualification to this is that the debts that are validly and effectively secured on the insolvent entity's assets should not be subject to the *pari passu* principle[4] and should rank for payment in order of priority instead.[5] Despite such qualification, it is important to understand what the principle of *pari passu* distribution actually involves.

> *The pari passu principle can be traced back to section 2 of Henry VIII's Statute of Bankrupts 1542 (34 & 35 Henry 8 c.4), under which the assets and debts of a bankrupt were to be identified and appraised, and the assets sold, ". . . for true satisfaction and payment of the said creditors; that is to say, to every of the said creditors, a portion, rate and rate alike, according to the quantity of their debts . . ." In Goode on Principles of Corporate Insolvency Law (5th ed) ("Goode") at [8–02], the principle of pari passu distribution is described*

1 As the Supreme Court has recently put it, the statutory provisions for rateable distribution embody "the fundamental principle of equality" in *Lehman Brothers (International) Europe (in administration) No. 4* [2018] AC 465 at [20] (per Lord Neuberger).

2 "*Thus, the policy of the law in favour of distribution of the assets of an insolvent company in the course of the liquidation process on a pari passu basis between its unsecured creditors is a strong one, and it needs to be shown that special circumstances exist which makes a particular transaction one in the interests of the creditors as a whole before a validation order will be made to override the usual application of the pari passu principle*". In *Express Electrical Distributors Ltd v Beavis & Ors* [2016] EWCA Civ 765 at [20].

3 *Strategic Value Capital Solutions Master Fund LP & Ors v AGPS BondCo PLC (Re AGPS BondCo PLC)* [2024] EWCA Civ 24 at [70].

4 The Privy Council also rejected the argument that it would be unconscionable for the lender's liquidator to retain funds intended for the sub-participant: "*there is nothing unconscionable about requiring [the sub-participant] to share pari passu in the distribution of [the lender's] assets like any other unsecured creditor*", at [27], per Lord Hoffman.

5 Wood, P., *Project Finance, Securitisations and Subordinated Debt* (Sweet & Maxwell, 2019) at [5-027].

DOI: 10.4324/9781032662220-13

> *in these terms, "The most fundamental principle of insolvency law is that of pari passu distribution, all creditors participating in the common pool in proportion to the size of their admitted claims. . . . The principle is based on the notion that losses should be borne by unsecured creditors equally.*[6]

Many scholars believe that insolvency law has a wide role to play and a wide range of interests to accommodate.[7] The contrary view is that it is not for insolvency law to concern itself with employment protection or with wider community interests or to re-order substantive rights acquired under pre-bankruptcy law.[8] Finance practitioners appear to endorse this theory.[9]

To ensure that the pool of assets is dealt with in accordance with the contractual arrangements and to avoid individual creditors taking unilateral action in respect of the pool of assets, a typical loan transaction would seek to put in place an agreement (intercreditor agreement) establishing the ranking of all the creditor parties to the loan transaction and the order in which such creditors will be paid in the event of insolvency. According to such provisions, proceeds from the receivables are allocated first to pay the senior creditors and thereafter to pay more junior creditors[10] (but, usually, subordinated to taxes due to the HM Revenue & Customs, Trustee's expenses, and fees due to other professional advisers).

> *In a general sense the terms "priority" and "subordination" are commonly utilised to describe the ranking of a debtor's indebtedness in circumstances where there is a competition between creditors because there is a shortfall of assets to meet liabilities in an insolvency situation.*[11]

Such a structure reduces the risk of non-payment or delays and losses on collection with respect to the senior creditors since the more junior classes would absorb such a risk first (i.e., they will take the first "hit"). There was a view – supported by somewhat dated case law – that, as a matter of public policy, the principle of *pari passu* distribution to unsecured creditors is to be considered as mandatory and incapable of waiver in any circumstances.[12]

The leading cases in the area of contracting out of the insolvency rules are *British Eagle International Airlines v Compagnie Nationale Air France* [1975] 1 WLR 758 and *National Westminster Bank Ltd. v Halesowen Presswork and Assemblies Ltd* [1972] AC 785. In the *Halesowen* case, the House of Lords decided that the statutory provisions with regard to set-off in insolvency were mandatory and, therefore, could not be contracted out. In the *British Eagle* case, the House of Lords held that if the effect of an agreement is to provide that an asset would be distributed other than in accordance with the statutory rules in relation to the distribution of assets on a liquidation (the *pari passu* rule), it would be contrary to public policy and therefore void. It had been suggested, by way of analogy to the decisions in *British Eagle* and *Halesowen*, that subordination agreements might be contrary to public policy as an attempt to avoid the *pari passu* rule.

6 In *Strategic Value Capital Solutions Master Fund LP & Ors v AGPS BondCo PLC (Re AGPS BondCo PLC)* [2024] EWCA Civ 24 per Lord Justice Snowden at [184]–[185].

7 For an overview of the principal theories advanced, see Finch, *Corporate Insolvency Law: Perspective and Principles* (Cambridge University Press, 2002), Chapter 2.

8 Goode, R., *Corporate Insolvency Law* (Sweet & Maxwell, 2005), p. 41.

9 Gullifer, L., *Goode and Gullifer on Legal Problems of Credit and Security* (Sweet & Maxwell, 2023) at [5-61]. Goode, R. and van Zwieten, K., *Principles of Corporate Insolvency Law* (Sweet & Maxwell, 2019), Chapter 8, Section 3.

10 See *Hayfin Opal Luxco 3 SARL & Anor v Windermere VII Cmbs Plc & Ors* [2016] EWHC 782 (Ch) at [4]: "*Notes in CMBS transactions are typically issued in multiple classes. The allocation of principal receipts on the loans towards payments of principal on the notes is typically governed by complex rules that, in a pre-loan default situation, allocate loan principal receipts to the various classes of notes partly on a sequential basis and partly on a pro-rata basis but, following a loan default, on a fully sequential basis, with the most senior class of notes being paid first in priority and the most subordinate class of notes being paid last in priority*".

11 Per Mr Justice Eder in *The Bank of New York Mellon (London Branch) v Truvo NV & Ors* [2013] EWHC 136 (Comm) at [89].

12 This view is expressed clearly by Peter Gibson J in *Carreras Rothmans Ltd v Freeman Mathews Treasure Ltd* [1985] 1 All ER 155, at [168].

This issue was considered in *Re Maxwell Communications Corp plc (No 2)* [1994] 1 BCLC Ch. D 1, where the question before the court was whether the holder of convertible subordinated bonds could contractually agree not to be repaid until after general unsecured creditors had been repaid in full, the High Court upheld an arrangement by which the rights of a creditor were sought to be subordinated to the rights of other creditors in any insolvency proceedings.[13] This principle was also upheld by the High Court in the context of a securitisation transaction.[14] The outcome can be summarised as follows: "*Commercial parties buying into such traded instruments expect to be bound by the language of them. They are entitled to the certainty and predictability that the adoption of a proper contextual interpretation of the language produces*".[15]

2 METHODS OF RANKING PAYMENTS AND SECURITY

The ranking of payments and security interests can be established through several mechanisms. Structural subordination arises in financing structures where senior-ranking debt is provided to entities that own or are closely linked to entities that own cash-generating assets, while subordinated debt is lent to companies positioned further up the ownership chain. As a result, creditors of the subordinated debt do not have direct recourse to the cash-generating assets. In addition, legal principles, particularly those within insolvency law, establish that the repayment of a company's share capital is generally subordinated to the repayment of its other debts.

Contractual subordination occurs when creditors agree, through the terms of an intercreditor or subordination agreement, that certain debts will be subordinated to others. Security arrangements provide for the prioritisation of secured creditors over unsecured creditors, as secured creditors hold enforceable security interests. Accordingly,

> *i) In high-value finance structures, it is very common for the creditors and debtors to enter into an intercreditor agreement, often based on a form promulgated by the Loan Markets Association (the "LMA"). ii) LMA intercreditor agreements commonly include a detailed contractual regime whereby the security agent is empowered to release and transfer certain types of debt in the event of a security enforcement (known as a "distressed disposal").*[16]

To enable the proper ranking and regulation of debts, all relevant categories of creditors should be parties to the intercreditor deed. In a typical leveraged finance transaction, these categories are generally defined as follows. **Senior debt** (or senior liabilities) includes all amounts due under the senior debt package, covering principal, interest, and fees owed to the senior creditors pursuant to the senior facilities agreement, as well as any ancillary facilities letter and senior fee letters. **Hedging liabilities** encompass amounts owed to hedging counterparties under permitted hedging agreements, which generally relate to both senior and mezzanine debt. **Mezzanine debt** (or mezzanine liabilities), which is a

13 Finch, *Corporate Insolvency Law: Perspectives and Principles* (Cambridge University Press: 2002).

14 "*[T]he structure established by the CTSA is one that depends on written notification of defined and (for the most part) clearly ascertainable events in order to bring about a change of operating state. A structure of that sort has the merits of being clear, certain and relatively simple to operate, all of which are in themselves desirable commercial objectives. The point that one might expect to find machinery for pari passu distribution once insolvency is imminent has force, I acknowledge, but (as I have already suggested in paragraph 48 above) less force than in many commercial contexts precisely because the parties have all agreed to sign up to an investment structure which is "insolvency remote". In those circumstances, it is dangerous to start with assumptions about what the parties must or are likely to have intended, and there is in my judgment no substitute for a close examination of the language of the contractual terms in order to ascertain what their rights may be*", per Mr J. Henderson in *Golden Key Ltd, Re Insolvency Act 1986* [2009] EWHC 148 (Ch) at [98].

15 Per Sir Geoffrey Vos in *Deutsche Trustee Company Ltd v Duchess VI CLO B.V. & Ors* [2019] EWHC 778 (Ch) at [49].

16 *Chaptre Finance PLC, In the Matter Of* [2024] EWHC 2908 (Ch) at [141].

form of junior debt, consists of all obligations owed to mezzanine creditors, including principal, interest, and fees linked to mezzanine financing.[17] **Investor debt** (also referred to as investor liabilities, subordinated debt, or subordinated liabilities) comprises amounts owed to equity investors, typically in the form of loan notes and share capital, with investors often being private equity funds and senior management. Where management's investment consists solely of share capital rather than loan notes, they may not be included as parties to the intercreditor deed. Given the relatively minor value of such investments, senior-ranking creditors generally rely on broader legal principles and borrower group undertakings that restrict dividend payments or share redemptions to protect their priority. **Intra-group debt** (or intra-group liabilities) refers to debts owed between entities within the borrower group.

In simpler financing structures, where there are only two tiers of debt, the intercreditor deed may only distinguish between senior and junior (or subordinated) debt, without the need for further classification.

Where multiple layers of security exist, the intercreditor deed must also establish the order of priority in relation to the security interests.[18] In some cases, a single set of security may be held by a security trustee on behalf of various creditors, including senior, mezzanine, and hedging creditors. In such scenarios, rather than ranking the security itself, the intercreditor deed will specify the priority of the **application of enforcement proceeds**. This hierarchy is often referred to as the "payment cascade" or "payment waterfall".

The payment cascade ensures that, upon enforcement of the security, proceeds are distributed in accordance with the agreed ranking of creditors. For example, senior creditors may be paid first from the enforcement proceeds, followed by mezzanine creditors, and then any remaining parties, such as investors or intra-group lenders, in accordance with their respective priority positions.

In certain transactions, the priority granted to senior creditors may be capped at a specific amount. This cap, often referred to as "senior headroom", limits the amount of debt that ranks above mezzanine or junior debt. If the senior debt exceeds this capped amount, any excess would rank subordinate to the mezzanine debt. This provision is typically included to balance the interests of junior creditors and ensure they receive payment once the senior creditor's capped amount has been satisfied.[19]

The courts have consistently interpreted intercreditor deeds as favouring senior creditors unless explicit provisions state otherwise. In *Rayford Homes Ltd v Bank of Scotland Plc and another* [2011] EWHC 1948 (Ch), the court reaffirmed this approach, underscoring that intercreditor arrangements are generally presumed to prioritise senior creditors. This position was aptly summarised in *CPF One Limited & another v Ortus Secured Finance Limited* [2023] EWHC 2102 Ch:

> *The terms of the Security Trust Deed mean that there was a significant imbalance between the rights of FFF and the rights of OSF. This is not in itself unusual. It is standard practice in syndicated lending for the rights of junior or minority participants to be subordinated to the will of the senior or majority participants; . . . The editors of Paget's Law of Banking 10th Ed at para [11.21] note that, in the context of tiered lending, the law does not generally intervene to protect junior creditors since the risk of being unpaid or outvoted is inherent in the junior or minority position of the junior participant and is part of the commercial risk that that particular creditor has assumed.*[20]

17 Vinter, G., Price, G. and Lee, D., *Project Finance* (Sweet & Maxwell, 2013) at [3-007].
18 Haentjens, M. and De Gioia-Carabellese, P., *European Banking and Financial Law* (Routledge, 2015), p. 190.
19 Wood, P., *Project Finance, Securitisations and Subordinated Debt* (Sweet & Maxwell, 2019) at [10-032].
20 *CPF One Limited & another v Ortus Secured Finance Limited* [2023] EWHC 2102 Ch at [50].

By clearly outlining the ranking of debt and security and providing for any caps on senior debt priority, intercreditor deeds help prevent confusion and disputes during enforcement, ensuring that the rights of all creditors are protected according to the agreed terms.

While subordination in complex financing arrangements varies, a helpful exemplification of such structure is as follows:

> *The Scheme concerns three series of senior secured Notes ("the Existing SSNs"), which have an aggregate principal amount of €1.24 billion plus CHF 250 million.*[21] *. . . The Existing SSNs form part of a wider set of financing arrangements for the Group. The Parent and other Group entities are borrowers under a €150 million revolving credit facility with a group of bank lenders (the "RCF"), which is fully utilised, and they are also borrowers under a €50 million term loan facility (the "Liquidity Facility") advanced by various lenders affiliated to KKR in March 2020. The Existing SSNs, the RCF and the Liquidity Facility share the same guarantee and security package. Guarantees and security have been provided by numerous Group companies. The ranking as between the Existing SSNs, the RCF and the Liquidity Facility is the subject of an intercreditor agreement dated 31 January 2018 ("the Intercreditor Agreement"). Under the terms of that Agreement, the financial liabilities of the Group rank in the following order of priority (in the event that the security is enforced): i) first, the RCF and the Liquidity Facility (on a pari passu basis in the event of any shortfall); and ii) second, the Existing SSNs. The Existing SSN's are therefore contractually subordinated to the RCF Facility and the Liquidity Facility.*[22]

3 INTERCREDITOR ARRANGEMENTS

The primary function of an intercreditor deed is to regulate both the priority of payments and the rights of creditors to enforce security, often in complex, multi-layered debt structures.[23] For an example of such a structure,

> *The Loan, the Junior Loan and liabilities under the hedging arrangements were secured over the assets of the borrowers, including the scheduled properties. The relationship between the Loan, the Junior Loan and the hedging transactions was governed by an Intercreditor Agreement dated 4 August 2006. This provided for the borrowers' liabilities to rank in the following order of priority: first, liabilities under the hedging arrangements; second, the Loan; and, third, the Junior Loan.*[24]

Unlike simpler deeds of priority, intercreditor deeds are more comprehensive. They typically cover not just the ranking of creditors in terms of receiving enforcement proceeds but also regulate the distribution of regular payments (principal, interest, fees) before any enforcement action takes place. Furthermore, intercreditor deeds often stipulate the conditions under which each creditor class can take enforcement actions and the process for instructing a security trustee. In addition to regulating payments and enforcement, intercreditor deeds may impose restrictions on junior creditors, such as prohibiting them from receiving payments until the senior debt is repaid in full, a principle also reflected in *CPF One Limited & another v Ortus Secured Finance Limited* [2023] EWHC 2102 Ch.

Intercreditor arrangements may also regulate multiple structures. For example, a Sharia-compliant lender (see Chapter 14) may participate in a transaction that involves both Sharia-compliant and conventional financing. Key considerations may include the allocation of the borrower's operating income, the distribution of proceeds in the event

21 Mr Justice Adam Johnson in *Selecta Finance UK Ltd, Re* [2020] EWHC 2689 (Ch) at [3] to [4].
22 Mr Justice Adam Johnson in *Selecta Finance UK Ltd, Re* [2020] EWHC 2689 (Ch) at [6] to [9].
23 Proctor, C., *The Law and Practice of International Banking* (Oxford University Press, 2015) at [21.57].
24 *CBRE Loan Servicing Ltd v Gemini (Eclipse 2006-3) Plc* [2015] EWHC 2769 (Ch) at [22].

of default and acceleration, the resolution of disputes and governing law, and the specific rights and restrictions imposed on each lender concerning their respective facilities.[25]

A **deed of priority** (or deed of priorities) is typically less complex than an intercreditor deed and serves the primary function of establishing the ranking of security interests among creditors. It usually applies when multiple secured parties hold different security interests over the same assets, and its main role is to ensure that, in the event of security enforcement, the creditors are paid in an agreed order of priority.

These deeds are particularly focused on the distribution of enforcement proceeds rather than regulating the entire relationship between creditors during the life of the loan. For example, a deed of priority might be used in a simple financing structure where there are only two secured creditors, such as a senior bank lender and a mezzanine lender, and its sole purpose is to regulate the priority of their respective claims over the secured assets.

Because of their narrow focus, deeds of priority do not typically deal with broader issues, such as payment obligations or enforcement rights during the ordinary course of business. They also do not cover unsecured creditors, as they focus solely on the priority of secured claims.

A subordination agreement (or subordination deed) is used to subordinate the claims of one or more creditors to another creditor, typically where junior creditors (such as equity or quasi-equity holders) agree that they will not receive payment until senior creditors have been fully repaid. The subordinated creditors typically agree to defer any payments or enforcement actions until the senior creditors have been satisfied.[26]

A key difference between subordination agreements and intercreditor deeds is that the former may be used when the subordinated creditor does not hold security. For example, in many leveraged finance transactions, subordinated debt is unsecured, and the subordination agreement ensures that the junior creditor's rights are deferred until the senior debt has been discharged.[27]

Subordination agreements can also regulate turnover provisions in an insolvency scenario, ensuring that subordinated creditors must turn over any payments received before the senior debt is paid in full. A clear example of how this works can be seen in *Re SSSL Realisations (2002) Ltd* [2004] EWHC 1760 (Ch), where the court upheld the validity of such subordination clauses. The establishment of such a "turnover" trust does not create a charge over the debts owed by the debtor to the subordinated creditor, provided that the trust does not extend to all monies received from the debtor and held by the subordinated creditor.[28]

3.1 Undertakings From Senior and Mezzanine Creditors

In an intercreditor deed, senior creditors typically undertake several obligations to safeguard the rights of mezzanine creditors, particularly concerning material amendments or waivers to the senior finance documents. These obligations include restrictions on increasing the principal amount of senior debt beyond a specified threshold, modifying the margin or interest rate calculation, increasing fees, or deferring payments beyond a designated period. Senior

25 Dewar, J. and Hussain, M. (eds.), *The Islamic Finance and Markets Law Review* (Law Business Research, 2020), p. 139.
26 Gullifer, L., *Goode and Gullifer on Legal Problems of Credit and Security* (Sweet & Maxwell, 2023) at [1-84].
27 Wood, P., *Project Finance, Securitisations and Subordinated Debt* (Sweet & Maxwell, 2019) at [12-026].
28 See *Manning v AIG Europe UK Ltd* [2004] EWHC 1760 (Ch). See also Morse, G., *Palmer's Company Law* (Sweet & Maxwell, 2025) at [13.331].

creditors are also prevented from obtaining additional security or guarantees unless such benefits are equally extended to mezzanine creditors.[29]

Mezzanine creditors, in turn, agree to subordinate their rights to those of senior creditors until the senior debt has been fully repaid.[30] This subordination entails restrictions on accepting payments, obtaining additional security, accelerating debt repayment, initiating legal proceedings, or enforcing security without satisfying predetermined conditions. Mezzanine creditors are also prohibited from exercising set-off rights or making material amendments to their finance documents without the prior consent of senior creditors. These restrictions frequently extend to junior creditors within the financing structure, who may be subject to even more stringent limitations.

Despite these constraints, the borrower group is generally permitted to make certain payments to mezzanine creditors, such as scheduled interest payments and specified fees. However, these payments are conditional upon the absence of a default under the senior finance documents, continued compliance with financial covenants, and the absence of any notice of acceleration or enforcement issued by senior creditors. Should any of these conditions fail to be met, payments may be blocked, either automatically or upon receipt of a notice from senior creditors.

Mezzanine creditors are generally precluded from accelerating their debt or enforcing their security unless specific circumstances arise. These include instances where senior creditors have already taken similar actions, an insolvency event has occurred within the borrower group, or a standstill period has expired. The duration of a standstill period is typically negotiated and may range from 90 to 150 days, depending on the nature of the default. During this period, mezzanine creditors are restricted from enforcement actions, and any proceeds obtained from enforcement are subject to turnover provisions, ensuring senior creditors receive payment first.[31] Negotiations over intercreditor terms can be contentious, particularly in disputes between senior and mezzanine creditors.

3.2 Investor and Intra-Group Lender Undertakings

If investor debt, such as loan notes, is involved, the intercreditor deed will also bind the investors to undertakings similar to those placed on mezzanine creditors. These often include prohibitions on accepting payments, taking security, or accelerating debt recovery until prior-ranking creditors are repaid in full. Payments to investors are usually limited to fees and, occasionally, interest payments on loan notes, subject to conditions similar to those governing mezzanine payments.

Intra-group lenders are also bound by similar undertakings. They must refrain from accepting payments, taking guarantees, or enforcing their debt until prior-ranking creditors are repaid. Permitted payments to intra-group lenders are typically restricted to payments facilitating the repayment of senior or mezzanine debt, and these conditions may be relaxed if the receiving company has granted equivalent security to that provided by the paying company.

29 Wood, P., *Project Finance, Securitisations and Subordinated Debt* (Sweet & Maxwell, 2019) at [10-026].
30 Vinter, G., Price, G. and Lee, D., *Project Finance* (Sweet & Maxwell, 2013) at [3-008].
31 Vinter, G., Price, G. and Lee, D., *Project Finance* (Sweet & Maxwell, 2013) at [3-008].

3.3 Hedging Counterparty Undertakings

Where hedging arrangements are in place,[32] the intercreditor deed will likely include the hedging counterparty as a party, as they may require payments based on interest or currency fluctuations.[33] Hedging liabilities typically rank *pari passu* with senior debt, and the hedging counterparty undertakes to refrain from independent enforcement actions that might conflict with the senior creditors' plans.

3.4 Subordination on Insolvency

A key feature of an intercreditor deed is subordination upon insolvency, where subordinated creditors agree that their claims are ranked below those of the prior-ranking creditors.[34] This is achieved either by prohibiting subordinated creditors from proving for their claims until the senior debt is fully repaid or through turnover provisions, where proceeds received by subordinated creditors are turned over to prior-ranking creditors. In some cases, subordinated creditors may be required to hold these proceeds in trust for the senior creditors, known as trust subordination.[35]

Trust subordination provisions can create complex legal issues, particularly if the subordinated creditor is in a jurisdiction that does not recognise trusts. In these cases, the prior-ranking creditors may face insolvency risks if they cannot rely on the trust mechanism and are instead left with only a contractual claim against the subordinated creditor.

4 COMMON SECURITY PACKAGE

If a common security package (i.e., the combination of security interests in some or all the borrowers' assets) is to be shared by both senior and mezzanine creditors, all senior and mezzanine creditors must be parties to the intercreditor deed. This is essential, as the deed will include provisions for appointing a security trustee to act on their behalf and hold the security on trust for both groups. However, if separate security packages are provided for the senior and mezzanine creditors, and either the senior or mezzanine debt is syndicated, the senior creditors will typically appoint a senior security trustee, usually under the senior facilities agreement or a separate security trust deed. Likewise, the mezzanine creditors will appoint a mezzanine security trustee, often under the mezzanine facility agreement or a separate security trust deed.

When senior and mezzanine creditors share a common security package, the concept of an "instructing group" is typically employed to determine when and how the security trustee should enforce the security.[36] The security trustee acts based on the instructions of this group. Prior to the full repayment of the senior debt and hedging liabilities, the instructing group generally consists of the majority of senior creditors, often including hedging counterparties. Once the senior debt and hedging liabilities are fully repaid, the instructing group shifts to the majority mezzanine creditors.

32 Hudson, A., *The Law on Financial Derivatives* (Sweet & Maxwell, 2017), p. 148.
33 Wood, P., *Project Finance, Securitisations and Subordinated Debt* (Sweet & Maxwell, 2019) at [10-015].
34 Wood, P., *Project Finance, Securitisations and Subordinated Debt* (Sweet & Maxwell, 2019) at [10-034].
35 Wood, P., *Project Finance, Securitisations and Subordinated Debt* (Sweet & Maxwell, 2019) at [13-005].
36 Wood, P., *Project Finance, Securitisations and Subordinated Debt* (Sweet & Maxwell, 2019) at [10-032].

Disputes may arise between senior and mezzanine creditors over the timing and method of enforcement. In *Saltri III Ltd v MD Mezzanine SA Sicar & Ors* [2012] EWHC 3025 (Comm), the mezzanine creditors argued that the security trustee owed a fiduciary duty to act in the interests of all beneficiaries of the security package,[37] including mezzanine lenders, even though they were not part of the instructing group at the time. The court, however, held that the security trustee's role was governed by the terms of the contract, which stipulated that it could only act on the instructions of the senior lenders. These senior lenders had the right to control both the timing and method of enforcement, even if their actions adversely affected the mezzanine creditors.

5 THE CONCEPT OF SECURITY TRUSTS IN FINANCE TRANSACTIONS

A security trust functions by allowing a security trustee to hold security interests on behalf of lenders or investors, who are the beneficiaries of the trust. This structure is commonly employed in syndicated lending, project finance, securitisation, and corporate bond issuances, among other financial transactions.[38]

The primary purpose of a security trust is to facilitate the centralised management of security interests over a debtor's assets. The security trustee acts as the representative of all creditors with claims over those assets, holding the security interests granted by the debtor or obligor on their behalf. This arrangement streamlines the enforcement and administration of security by establishing a single point of contact between the debtor and its creditors. One of the principal advantages of this structure is its flexibility, particularly in transactions where the composition of creditors may change over time.

In syndicated lending, the security trustee holds the security interests on behalf of all participating lenders, enabling individual lenders to transfer their loans without requiring modifications to the underlying security documentation. This structure enhances liquidity in the syndicated loan market by facilitating secondary market trading, as new lenders can seamlessly replace outgoing ones without incurring the administrative burden associated with transferring security interests.[39] A similar approach is employed in club deals, where a smaller group of banks lends to a borrower, typically in equal amounts. The security trust ensures that each lender holds an equal share in the security package, with the security trustee acting on behalf of all lenders.

In more complex financing arrangements, such as project finance or leveraged finance, multiple layers of debt often exist, with different classes of creditors, including senior, mezzanine, and junior lenders. In such cases, the security trustee holds security interests on behalf of all creditors and ensures that payment priorities, established through mechanisms such as a payment waterfall, are adhered to. This structured approach allows for an orderly distribution of enforcement proceeds in the event of default, ensuring that senior creditors are paid before junior creditors in accordance with the agreed ranking of claims.

Security trusts[40] are also widely employed in securitisation transactions (see Chapter 14). In such arrangements, the security trustee holds security interests over receivables or other

37 Bamford, C., *Principles of International Finance Law* (Oxford University Press, 2015) at [7.79].
38 Proctor, C., *The Law and Practice of International Banking* (Oxford University Press, 2015) at [21.49].
39 A purchaser of security from a trustee need not satisfy itself that the trustee is properly appointed (section 113, LPA 1925).
40 Wood, P., *Project Finance, Securitisations and Subordinated Debt* (Sweet & Maxwell, 2019) at [14-008].

assets that have been transferred to a special purpose vehicle (**SPV**). Acting on behalf of investors who purchase securities issued by the SPV, the security trustee ensures that these investors have a claim over the securitised assets in the event of default. This mechanism provides additional protection to investors and contributes to the structured and efficient administration of securitised assets.

5.1 What Is a Security Trust?

A security trust is a form of express trust. In accordance with general principles of trust law, the settlor (the absolute owner of the property) establishes the trust by transferring or declaring trust over the trust property. To validly create an express trust, the settlor must demonstrate a clear intention to create the trust, and there must be certainty as to the property that will be subject to the trust.[41]

Upon the creation of an express trust, the settlor relinquishes its rights to the trust property, and the beneficiaries acquire a beneficial interest in the property.[42]

In the context of secured syndicated lending, the security trust is established by transferring the trust property – typically the security interest – to the security trustee, who holds it on trust for the benefit of the secured parties. A typical security trust deed might contain an operative clause similar to the following:

> *The security trustee declares that it holds the trust property on trust for the secured parties on the terms contained in this security trust deed.*

Two principal methods may give rise to the creation of a trust in the context of a security trust. Where the security trust is established by way of a declaration of trust by the security trustee, the underlying security documents that create the security interest – being the trust property – must first be duly executed before the trustee can validly declare that it holds the security interest on trust for the secured parties.

Alternatively, where the security trust is constituted through the transfer of property or the grant of a security interest in property to the security trustee, the trust will not be fully constituted until the transfer or other disposition of the relevant property has been properly effected and is legally enforceable. This principle is established in *Milroy v Lord* [1862] 4 De G F & J 264, which confirmed that a trust is only effective once the trust property has been properly transferred to the trustee.

In practice, particularly in England and Wales, the security documents, the security trust deed, and the underlying finance documents are usually executed contemporaneously or within a very short time frame. By ensuring that the security trustee holds the security at the time of the declaration or the property transfer is complete, the trust can be validly constituted without gaps that could undermine the enforceability of the security or the trust arrangement.

In a typical security trust arrangement, the secured parties expressly acknowledge and agree that the security trustee is authorised to act in accordance with the terms set out in the security trust deed, as well as other relevant finance documents. This authority enables the security trustee to manage the trust property and enforce the security for the benefit of the secured creditors, following the procedures and instructions provided in these documents.[43]

41 Wood, P., *Comparative Law of Security Interests and Title Finance* (Sweet & Maxwell, 2019), Part 2, Chapter 12.
42 Wood, P., *Project Finance, Securitisations and Subordinated Debt* (Sweet & Maxwell, 2019) at [11-009].
43 Wood, P., *Comparative Law of Security Interests and Title Finance* (Sweet & Maxwell, 2019), Part 2, Chapter 12.

At common law, the general rule is that trustees are not entitled to charge for their services, as established in *Re White* [1898] 2 Ch 217. However, section 29 of the Trustee Act 2000 provides that professional trustees may charge for their services, and the trust documents specifically outline the fees payable to the security trustee. These fees are often contained in a side letter for reasons of commercial confidentiality.

In some cases, the security trustee may charge additional fees if it is required to act after an event of default or if it must perform duties outside its usual scope. The transaction documents typically provide that the security trustee is to be reimbursed for all fees, costs, and expenses incurred in the performance of its duties, including any additional costs that arise due to extraordinary actions it may need to take.

It should be noted that trusts are not universally recognised across all jurisdictions, and even in those jurisdictions where trusts or trustees are acknowledged as property owners, the legal treatment may differ significantly from the position under English law. A particular challenge may arise in jurisdictions where security is regarded as an accessory to the underlying debt, requiring that it be held directly by the creditors themselves rather than by a trustee on their behalf. Resolving such jurisdictional discrepancies can complicate the structuring and enforcement of security arrangements across different legal systems.

5.2 Advantages of Using a Security Trust

The principal advantages of a security trust include administrative efficiency, the protection of beneficiaries, and the flexibility to manage and enforce security interests in an organised manner.[44] One of the primary benefits is administrative convenience, as a security trust streamlines the management of security interests by centralising them under the control of a security trustee. This is particularly valuable in syndicated lending, where the composition of lenders may fluctuate over time.

A typical security trust structure allows for the inclusion of additional debt obligations, whether owed by existing obligors or new secured parties, within the security package.

English law does not prohibit the establishment of a trust for future beneficiaries, provided that it remains possible to determine whether an entity qualifies as a beneficiary. Accordingly, under a security trust deed and the associated security documents, secured obligations are typically defined to include both liabilities and obligations owed to the original secured parties under the facility documents and any other obligations designated as secured by agreement with the obligors and the security trustee. The definition of secured parties is generally drafted to accommodate future secured parties as well.

The addition of new obligations does not necessitate the re-registration of security at Companies House or the Land Registry, as no new security interest is created – rather, the existing security is simply extended to secure different obligations. The flexibility inherent in a security trust allows for the admission of new obligors and security while ensuring that existing obligors cannot exit the security structure without appropriate safeguards. Secured parties are generally concerned with maintaining or enhancing the security package, as the release of an obligor represents a reduction in credit support.

The practical utility of security trustees in managing the rights of multiple creditors,[45] ensuring that payments are made in accordance with the agreed priority structure. The payment waterfall mechanism, which is typically embedded within security trust deeds, ensures

44 Scott, S., *The Law of Loans and Borrowing* (Sweet & Maxwell, 2024) at [4.298].
45 Gullifer, L. and Payne, J., *Corporate Finance Law: Principles and Policy* (Hart, 2020), p. 373.

that creditors are paid in the correct order, with senior creditors receiving payment before junior creditors. By centralising enforcement powers under the security trustee, individual creditors are prevented from taking unilateral action that could disrupt the agreed order of priority. Enforcement is generally conducted based on instructions from a majority or unanimous decision of the creditors, providing a structured and equitable framework for security realisation.

Another key advantage of a security trust is the protection it affords beneficiaries from the personal creditors of the security trustee. Because the security interests are held separately from the trustee's own assets, the financial difficulties of the trustee do not affect the security. This separation ensures that the creditors' claims remain intact and that the security trust structure does not expose them to additional risks.

5.3 Fiduciary Duties and Security Trusts

As with all trustees, a security trustee is subject to statutory and non-statutory duties, and these bring with them significant responsibilities. Given the onerous nature of the role, a security trustee will often seek to limit its personal liability in cases where it is sued for intentional or negligent breaches of trust.[46]

While a security trust relies on and has to comply with the traditional requirements for the constitution of a trust, it is apparent that a commercial trust has distinct features differentiating it from the traditional trust arrangements.[47] The reason for such a difference lies in the fact that "*where . . . sophisticated parties have chosen to govern their relationship through arm's length commercial contracts, the scope and nature of the duties owed between the parties are shaped by the terms of, and the language used in, those contracts*".[48]

For the same reasons, in *Westdeutsche Landesbank Girozentrale v Islington LBC* [1996] AC 669, Lord Browne-Wilkinson had "*warned against the wholesale importation into commercial law of equitable principles inconsistent with the certainty and speed which are essential requirements for the orderly conduct of business affairs*".[49]

Trustees owe fiduciary duties to the beneficiaries, including acting with skill and care in managing the trust assets.[50] The basis for such duties in a syndicated transaction, was considered by Lord Browne-Wilkinson in *Henderson v Merrett Syndicates Ltd* [1995] 2 AC 145:

> *the extent and nature of the fiduciary duties owed in any particular case fall to be determined by reference to any underlying contractual relationship between the parties. . . . The existence of a contract does not exclude the co-existence of concurrent fiduciary duties (indeed, the contract may well be their source); but the contract can and does modify the extent and nature of the general duty that would otherwise arise.*[51]

In practice, the arrangements entered into in the course of a financial transaction will seek to limit the number of parties that owe fiduciary duties. To achieve this objective, provisions akin to the following will be included:

46 Bamford, C., *Principles of International Finance Law* (Oxford University Press, 2015) at [8.83].
47 The distinct nature of commercial trusts has been aptly summarised by S.I. 'Strong in Arbitration of Trust Disputes: Two Bodies of Law Collide' (2012) 45 *Vanderbilt Journal of Transnational Law* 1157, p. 15 "*as a definitional matter, a commercial trust (also known as a business trust) constitutes 'a trust that implements bargained-for exchange,' in contrast to the kind of donative transfers that are more common in a trust created to pass on family wealth*".
48 *Saltri III Ltd v MD Mezzanine SA Sicar & Ors* [2012] EWHC 3025 (Comm) per Eder J at [123(f)].
49 *Westdeustche Landesbank Girozentrale v Islington LBC* [1996] AC 669.
50 As established in *Armitage v Nurse & Ors* [1997] EWCA Civ 1279.
51 At [206].

> *(a) Unless otherwise expressly stated in any other Finance Document, nothing in this Agreement constitutes the Agent, the Security Trustee or the Arranger as a trustee or fiduciary of any other person. (b) Neither the Agent, the Security Trustee nor the Arranger shall be bound to account to any Lender for any sum or the profit element of any sum received by it for its own account.*[52]

Whilst it may be possible to limit the Trustee's responsibilities when acting in different capacities, the fundamental duties of the Trustee may not be dispensed with. In this respect, the protection of the beneficiaries' interests would be a core obligation under trust law, irrespective of whether such beneficiaries are party to a traditional or a commercial trust arrangement.

Over time, commercial trusts have developed their own rules.[53] The agreements that give rise to such relationships are often the result of a negotiation between sophisticated parties on the basis of accumulated market practice. The key terms on which an agreement is reached are essentially contractual in nature.

As Lord Browne-Wilkinson[54] noted in *Kelly v Cooper* [1993] AC 205:

> *In these situations, it is the contractual foundation which is all-important because it is the contract that regulates the basic rights and liabilities of the parties. The fiduciary relationship, if it is to exist at all, must accommodate itself to the terms of the contract so that it is consistent with, and conforms to them.*

In more recent cases involving the interpretation[55] of trust instruments in the context of structured finance transactions, the commercial nature of such arrangements has not been questioned by the courts.[56]

However, one should be mindful that the view that the court should not interfere with agreements drafted by "*experienced commercial operators advised by expert lawyers*"[57] does not always hold true, as has emerged in the Supreme Court decision in *Re Sigma Finance Corporation* [2009] UKSC 2, which – in overturning the decisions of the lower courts – provided for a purposive approach to the construction of a trust instrument in a structured finance transaction since

52 *Torre Asset Funding Ltd & Anor v The Royal Bank of Scotland Plc* [2013] EWHC 2670 (Ch) at [27].

53 Hudson, A., *The Law of Finance* (Sweet & Maxwell, 2013) at [21-14].

54 Quoting Mason J in *Hospital Products International Pty Limited v US Surgical Corporation* (1984) 156 CLR 41.

55 Particularly helpful in this respect are basic principles of interpretation of financial agreements set out by Richard Snowden in *US Bank Trustees Ltd v Titan Europe 2007-1 (NHP) Ltd* [2014] EWHC 1189 (Ch): "*i) The interpretation of a contract is an objective exercise in which the court's task is to ascertain the meaning that the document would convey to a reasonable person having all the background knowledge which would reasonably have been available to the parties in the situation in which they were at the time of the contract. ii) This exercise of interpretation was described by Lord Clarke in Rainy Sky as a 'unitary' process. The starting point of that process must be the ordinary, natural and grammatical sense of the language used by the parties. The court should not, however, confine itself to a consideration of such language in isolation, but should carry out an iterative process, checking each of the rival meanings of the provision in question against the other provisions of the document and its overall scheme, and investigating their commercial consequences. iii) If as a consequence of this exercise the court concludes that the language used is unambiguous, then the court must apply it, even though some other result might be thought more commercially reasonable, and even if it gives a result that is commercially disadvantageous to one of the parties. The court's function is to interpret the contract, not to rewrite it. iv) In cases where the language used is ambiguous, in the sense that it is capable of bearing more than one ordinary and natural meaning, the court is entitled to prefer the interpretation that is most consistent with business common sense having regard to the commercial purpose of the transaction. v) There may be cases where, even though the language used is unambiguous, it is clear that something must have gone wrong, because the resultant meaning is one that would require the court to attribute to the parties an intention that they plainly could not have had. In such a case, if it is clear both that a mistake has been made in the language used and what a reasonable person would have understood the parties to have meant, the contractual provision must be interpreted in accordance with that meaning*". See also *Deutsche Trustee Company Ltd v Cheyne Capital (Management) UK (LLP) & Anor* [2015] EWHC 2282 (Ch) at [38].

56 See, for example, *In re Cheyne Fin.* [2007] EWHC 2116 (Ch) or *Kahn & Ors v Interested Party A (sub nom. In re Whistlejacket Capital)* [2008] EWCA Civ 575.

57 Per Lord Walker (dissenting) in *Re Sigma Finance Corporation* [2009] UKSC 2 at [34].

"*an over-literal interpretation of one provision without regard to the whole may distort or frustrate the commercial purpose*".[58]

5.4 The Terms of the Trust, Duty of Care, and Trustee's Discretion

The role of the security trustee is primarily governed by the terms of the security trust deed. The trustee holds security on behalf of the secured creditors and is typically authorised to act upon the instructions of the majority of those creditors. However, the trustee's responsibilities extend beyond mere administrative functions; they also involve monitoring the borrower's compliance with the terms of the loan agreement and, where necessary, enforcing the security on behalf of the creditors.[59]

In addition to obligations set out in the trust deed and/or security trust deed, security trustees are subject to statutory duties imposed by the Trustee Act 2000, particularly with regard to the requisite standard of care and skill in managing trust property. Consequently, security trustees must carefully navigate their obligations, balancing the imperative to act in the best interests of the beneficiaries against the constraints imposed by the terms of the security trust deed.

Limitations of Liability

It is standard practice for a security trust deed to incorporate provisions limiting the liability of the security trustee. One common limitation involves the exclusion of the statutory duty of care and skill prescribed by paragraph 7, Schedule 1 of the Trustee Act 2000. Beyond statutory exclusions, security trustees frequently seek further contractual limitations to mitigate the risks inherent in their role.

Among the most prevalent protections is the exclusion of liability for any damage or loss, including consequential loss, arising from acts or omissions under a finance document, save where such damage results from the trustee's own fraud, gross negligence, or wilful default. Furthermore, the trustee is generally shielded from liability for consequences arising from the exercise or non-exercise of rights under a finance document and bears no liability for matters beyond its control, such as force majeure events, including natural disasters and other unforeseeable circumstances.

In addition, where there is a shortfall in recoveries or realisations of the secured assets, the security trustee is not held liable. It is also customary for the trust deed to protect the trustee when acting in accordance with the instructions of the relevant instructing group, and to prevent secured parties from bringing claims against the trustee's officers, employees, or agents. This latter provision is designed to prevent "dog-leg" claims, whereby parties attempt to circumvent trustee liability exclusions by targeting individuals within the trustee organisation.

Although contractual arrangements may limit a trustee's liability for breaches of trust, a security trustee may nevertheless incur personal liability for actions connected with the trust. Such liability may extend to tortious acts, breaches of trust, or issues related to property ownership. While a security trustee can typically seek indemnity from trust assets, this protection is not absolute, and personal liability may arise if the trust assets prove insufficient.

58 Per Lord Collins at [35].
59 *Saltri III Ltd v MD Mezzanine SA Sicar & Ors* [2012] EWHC 3025 (Comm) at [123].

In *Re Pauling's Settlement Trusts* [1964] Ch 303, the court established that trustees could be personally liable for breaches of trust unless excused by the court, thereby highlighting their potential exposure to claims. Additionally, there are judicial limits on the extent to which trustees can exclude liability.

The leading authority in this area, *Armitage v Nurse & Ors* [1997] EWCA Civ 1279, confirmed that trustees may exclude liability for negligence, including gross negligence. However, liability for dishonesty (fraud) cannot be excluded. The judgement clarified that a trustee may commit a deliberate breach of trust in good faith if it genuinely believes it to be in the beneficiaries' best interests, but an exclusion clause will not protect a trustee whose belief is objectively unreasonable. Furthermore, statutory restrictions, such as section 2(2) of the Unfair Contract Terms Act 1977 and section 253 of the Financial Services and Markets Act 2000, may operate to limit the effectiveness of exclusion clauses depending on the circumstances.[60]

Administrative and Managerial Powers

The security trustee is entrusted with a wide range of administrative and managerial powers, whether implied by statute or expressly conferred by the security trust deed. These powers enable the trustee to manage the trust property effectively without requiring constant instruction from the secured creditors.

Such powers typically include the authority to appoint and remunerate independent professional advisers, such as solicitors, surveyors, and accountants, and to act in reliance upon their advice. The trustee may also delegate specific functions to attorneys, agents, custodians, or nominees where appropriate. Furthermore, the trustee is usually empowered to make minor or technical amendments to finance documents, provided such amendments do not materially prejudice the rights or obligations of the secured creditors. Where instructions are absent or delayed, the security trustee retains the discretion to act or to refrain from acting as it considers appropriate in the circumstances. It may also grant waivers or consents to breaches of the finance documents, again provided that no material prejudice to the secured creditors arises as a result.

The exercise of these powers must be carefully calibrated to preserve the trustee's discretion without unduly compromising the rights of the secured creditors.

Applications to the Court

Where the security trustee's express and implied powers are insufficient to manage the trust effectively, it may apply to the court for additional authority. Applications may be made under section 57 of the Trustee Act 1925 for power to deal with trust property or under section 1 of the Variation of Trusts Act 1958 to vary the terms of the trust. However, the broad statutory powers now conferred under the Trustee Act 2000 have significantly reduced the necessity for such court applications.

60 Gullifer, L. and Payne, J., *Corporate Finance Law: Principles and Policy* (Hart, 2020), p. 373.

Indenture Trustee's Duties in the US

In *Cece & Co. Ltd. v. U.S. Bank N.A.*, 2017 NY Slip Op. 05924, the First Department clarified that

> an indenture trustee clearly owes the security holders a duty to perform its ministerial functions with due care. Most importantly, the courts have recognised that even an indenture trustee has a fundamental duty to avoid conflicts of interest. Avoiding conflicts of interest encompasses a trustee's duty not to profit at the possible expense of the beneficiary . . . *[u]nlike an ordinary trustee, the rights, duties and obligations of an indenture trustee are not defined by a fiduciary relationship. Instead, they are defined exclusively by the terms of the agreements by which the relationships were formed*".

In any event, "*There is no doubt . . . that if an indenture trustee owes any fiduciary duties to the beneficiary above and beyond those duties explicitly recited in the trust indenture, they are much more attenuated than those normally owed by trustees*". As confirmed *In re E.F. Hutton Sw. Prop. II, Ltd. v. Union Planters Nat'l Bank, 953 F.2d 963, 969* (5th Cir. 1992).[61]

Following an event of default, the indenture trustee's obligations "come more closely to resemble those of an ordinary fiduciary, regardless of any limitations or exculpatory provisions contained in the indenture", in *Beck v. Manufacturers Hanover Trust Co.*, 632 N.Y.S. 2d 520 (1st Dep't 1995).

5.5 Enforcement of Security and the Role of the Security Trustee

Enforcing security and recovering funds on behalf of the secured parties is a fundamental function of a security trustee. In a security trust arrangement, secured parties do not have a direct contractual relationship with the obligors and cannot individually enforce their rights under the security trust deed. This aspect enhances administrative convenience for the obligors, as they interact with only one entity – the security trustee – rather than a group of creditors, each with potentially conflicting interests.[62]

The security trust deed typically includes an express power granting the security trustee the authority to initiate legal proceedings against the obligors to enforce the security. Any enforcement proceeds are paid directly to the security trustee, who holds these funds on trust for the secured parties. If any secured parties receive proceeds directly, these amounts are generally subject to turnover or trust subordination provisions, which require that such funds be turned over to the security trustee for redistribution according to the terms of the trust deed.

Where the security trustee has discretion in how to enforce the security, and in the absence of explicit direction from the beneficiaries, the trustee must act in accordance with its contractual and fiduciary duties. The trustee must balance its responsibilities to different creditor classes, particularly where subordinated lenders are involved. The extent of the security trustee's duties to these different classes depends on the economic interest of the creditors in the trust property and the terms set out in the trust deed.

61 Robertson, S., 'Debenture Holders and the Indenture Trustee: Controlling Managerial Discretion in the Solvent Enterprise' (1988) 11 *Harvard Journal of Law & Public Policy* 461, 472–473.

62 Gullifer, L. and Payne, J., *Corporate Finance Law: Principles and Policy* (Hart, 2020), p. 422.

In complex enforcement scenarios, particularly where the security trustee also acts as the facility agent or lender, it is crucial for the trustee to act independently and avoid favouring any particular class of creditor. This is particularly challenging in transactions with multiple layers of debt, where the security trustee must navigate potential conflicts of interest[63] and ensure that the enforcement process remains fair to all secured parties.

During enforcement, the security trustee must revisit its indemnity arrangements. The existing indemnity provisions, which cover routine costs and liabilities, may not be sufficient to protect the trustee from the additional risks associated with enforcement action. In some cases, the security trustee may require an additional stand-alone indemnity or additional security to cover enforcement actions. It may also seek pre-funding to cover expenses related to enforcement. Such indemnity may need to persist for a period even after the completion of the enforcement process to cover any liabilities that arise post-enforcement.

In an enforcement scenario, the security trustee must be able to realise the security, including quasi-security such as guarantees, and release any outstanding debt or security claims, applying the proceeds in line with the payment waterfall (see later on). The provisions related to the release of security are, therefore, critical. They must include the release of guarantees and security granted by any company within the obligor group that is sold through a share sale, as well as the release of guarantees and security granted by its subsidiaries. Likewise, they should ensure the release of security over assets sold in an asset sale. Ideally, these provisions should also provide for the automatic release of claims by subordinated lenders against all relevant members of the obligor group. This enables senior lenders to enforce their security and sell the business free from subordinated lenders' claims.[64]

This is essential because senior lenders typically seek to sell the assets or business of the debtor, and such a sale would be complicated if subordinated lenders' claims or security encumber the property. However, the automatic release of claims, in addition to the release of guarantees and security, is not always agreed upon. Subordinated lenders may seek additional contractual protections to ensure that enforcement proceeds are maximised. This could include conditions that disposal proceeds must be received in cash and reflect the fair market value of the assets being sold.

In some cases, enforcement provisions may grant the security trustee the power to undertake a non-consensual restructuring on behalf of certain creditors.

As with many aspects of the security trustee's role, the contractual provisions governing the release of security and asset realisation arrangements are vital, particularly in established markets where such provisions often follow industry-standard terms, such as those developed by the LMA. For instance, the LMA real estate finance intercreditor agreement requires the security trustee to exercise reasonable care to achieve a fair market price, taking prevailing market conditions into account. The LMA documentation also allows the security trustee to appoint a sales advisor who can offer guidance on sales strategies, processes, or valuations, which helps mitigate potential tensions with junior or mezzanine lenders, particularly in share sales.

In *HHY Luxembourg Sarl v Barclays Bank Plc* [2010] EWCA Civ 1248, a dispute arose between the security trustee and the mezzanine lenders regarding whether a release clause permitted the security trustee to release guarantees and security for the entire group or just the holding company being sold. The High Court initially held that the clause limited the release to the holding company. However, the Court of Appeal reversed this decision, ruling that the clause was sufficiently broad to enable releases across the wider group.

63 Wood, P., *Project Finance, Securitisations and Subordinated Debt* (Sweet & Maxwell, 2019) at [11-011].
64 Odgers, J. and Wilson, I., *Paget's Law of Banking* (LexisNexis, 2023), Chapter 11.

5.6 Ranking and Payment Waterfall in Syndicated Lending

In most syndicated lending arrangements, the security trustee holds a single set of securities on behalf of different classes of creditors, including senior and subordinated lenders. In such cases, one of the primary considerations during enforcement is the order of priority in which proceeds from the enforcement are distributed among the creditors. This is known as the payment waterfall or payment cascade.[65]

Before enforcement, any monies received by the security trustee in relation to the secured obligations are held on trust for the secured parties and are distributed according to the underlying finance documents. Upon enforcement, the order of priority for applying the proceeds becomes crucial. A typical payment waterfall in a secured lending transaction might follow this structure:

i) First, payment of any sums owed to the security trustee or any receiver.
ii) Second, payment of costs, expenses, and remuneration incurred by any secured party in connection with the realisation or enforcement of the security.
iii) Third, distribution to the lenders on a rateable basis, proportionate to their exposure.
iv) Fourth, payment to any other person entitled to enforcement proceeds, rateably in accordance with their proportionate exposure.
v) Fifth, any remaining balance is returned to the obligor or as directed by the relevant debtor.

The priority of payments ensures that costs and expenses incurred by the security trustee, including its fees, are satisfied before the proceeds are distributed to the secured parties. Unsecured creditors may also be included in the waterfall in certain cases, although this does not extend the mortgagee's ordinary duties to such creditors or provide them with a direct claim to the proceeds of sale.

The Court of Appeal in *Alpstream AG v PK Airfinance Sarl* [2015] EWCA Civ 1318 has clarified the scope of a mortgagee's duty when selling the mortgaged property, specifically in relation to unsecured creditors.

Generally, a mortgagee selling mortgaged property owes an equitable duty to obtain the best price reasonably obtainable for the property. This duty is owed to parties with a recognised interest in the mortgaged property, such as the mortgagor, subsequent ranking mortgagees, co-mortgagors, or guarantors of the mortgagor's debt.[66]

The case involved a financing arrangement for aircraft purchases, where **P** provided secured senior loans, while **C** provided unsecured, subordinated junior loans to the same debtor, **B**. When B defaulted, P sold the mortgaged aircraft at auction and purchased the assets itself as the sole bidder. C, being an unsecured creditor, claimed that P owed a duty to obtain the best price for the aircraft, as C's recovery was dependent on the residual amount left after the secured creditors were paid. The Court of Appeal ruled that P did not owe any duty to C, as an unsecured creditor, to achieve the best possible price upon the sale of the mortgaged aircraft. A mortgagee's duty of care applies exclusively to those with a direct interest in the mortgaged property,

65 Wood, P., *Project Finance, Securitisations and Subordinated Debt* (Sweet & Maxwell, 2019) at [12-030].
66 As established in *Dean v Barclays Bank plc* [2007] EWHC 1390 (Ch).

including the mortgagor, subsequent mortgagees, co-mortgagors, or guarantors. By contrast, unsecured creditors, even if they may foreseeably suffer financial loss should the mortgaged property be sold at an undervalue, are not owed this duty, as they hold no direct proprietary or security interest in the asset itself. The duty of care imposed upon a mortgagee is grounded in equity rather than tort, and therefore, the mere foreseeability of loss to an unsecured creditor does not establish a cause of action against the mortgagee.

Alpstream provides crucial clarification for both unsecured creditors and mortgagees. For unsecured creditors, it affirms that they cannot challenge a mortgagee's sale on the grounds that the property was sold below market value unless they have a direct interest in the asset. For mortgagees, it underscores that their duty of care in a sale is confined to those with a legal or equitable interest in the property, thus limiting potential liability to other parties affected by the sale.

Additionally, the ruling offers assurance to parties in intercreditor arrangements. Unsecured creditors, who are typically at the bottom of the payment waterfall, cannot claim against the secured assets or the proceeds merely by virtue of their position in the payment waterfall.

In transactions where different security packages exist for senior and subordinated lenders, the security trustee may hold multiple sets of security. In such complex structures, careful consideration is required to ensure the correct order of priority is observed during enforcement. In *Kahn & Ors v Interested Party A (sub nom. In re Whistlejacket Capital)* [2008] EWCA Civ 575, the Court of Appeal clarified the role of a priority clause under a security trust deed. The court held that such a clause serves to determine the priority between different classes of creditors rather than regulating the order of payments to individual creditors within those classes. This decision overturned the first instance ruling and provided important guidance on the interpretation of priority clauses in complex finance structures.

5.7 Release of Security in Enforcement Scenarios

In enforcement situations, it is crucial that the security trustee has the authority to realise the security, including quasi-security interests such as guarantees, and to release any outstanding debt or security claims.[67] Ideally, the release provisions should also ensure that all claims by subordinated lenders against any relevant member of the obligor group are automatically released. This would enable the senior lenders to enforce their security and sell the business free from any encumbrances caused by claims or security held by subordinated lenders.[68]

If the assets remain encumbered by subordinated lenders' security, it could severely restrict the ability of the senior lenders to execute a sale or achieve a favourable outcome in the sale process.

However, it is not always the case that the release of subordinated claims accompanies the release of guarantees and security. Subordinated lenders have increasingly sought additional protections in the intercreditor agreements, particularly to ensure that enforcement proceeds are maximised. These protections may include conditions requiring that the sale proceeds are

67 See *CPF One Limited & another v Ortus Secured Finance Limited* [2023] EWHC 2102 Ch.
68 Wood, P., *Project Finance, Securitisations and Subordinated Debt* (Sweet & Maxwell, 2019) at [5-019].

received in cash and reflect the fair market value of the disposed assets. Additionally, some enforcement provisions allow the security trustee to carry out non-consensual restructuring on behalf of certain creditors.[69]

Given the complexity of the security trustee's role, especially in multi-layered debt structures, the contractual provisions related to the release of security and asset realisation are pivotal. These provisions, particularly in established markets, often follow industry standard terms. For instance, the LMA's real estate finance intercreditor agreement mandates that the security trustee must take reasonable care to secure a fair market price for the assets, considering the prevailing market conditions. Furthermore, LMA documents also grant the security trustee the authority to appoint a sales advisor to provide strategic advice on the sales process and potentially to offer a valuation, reducing the risk of disputes with junior lenders or equity providers who may perceive themselves as disadvantaged, particularly in share sales.[70]

An illustration of the challenges around release provisions is provided by *HHY Luxembourg Sarl v Barclays Bank Plc* [2010] EWCA Civ 1248, where the security trustee and the mezzanine lenders disputed the scope of a release clause. The mezzanine lenders argued that the clause only allowed for the release of security in respect of the holding company being sold, while the security trustee contended that the clause permitted a release of guarantees and security over the broader target group. The High Court initially sided with the mezzanine lenders, limiting the release to the holding company. However, the Court of Appeal overturned this decision, holding that the clause in the intercreditor agreement (ICA) allowed for a more extensive release, covering the entire group of companies:

> *The ICA is one part of a complex financial structure and is itself a complex document. The Group is a complex Group of pan-European companies and subsidiaries; the lenders to the Group probably knew, and would anyway have assumed, that the substantial assets would be likely to lie in the companies in the various jurisdictions where business was done. In those circumstances, it is not at all surprising that Obligors themselves (and any holding company of such Obligor) should be the primary focus of a sub-clause headed "Disposal after Enforcement Action". It is no misuse of language to use the words "disposal of all of the shares in the capital of an Obligor or any holding company of that Obligor" to refer to individual Obligors lower down the company chain and any holding company of such Obligors. It is agreed that the holding company can be both a direct and indirect holding company, and in such circumstances DH7 is indeed the Obligor's holding company and the company the shares in which it is proposed to dispose of.*[71]

5.8 Further Limitations on the Security Trustee's Responsibilities

A key provision found in security trust deeds is often referred to as an "ostrich clause". This clause permits the security trustee to assume that no default or breach of the security trust or other finance documents has occurred unless it has actual knowledge or has been given express notice of such default. Similar provisions are common in agency arrangements, such as syndicated lending agreements, and are sometimes termed "No duty to monitor" clauses. These clauses are designed to limit the active oversight role of the security trustee, relieving it from any obligation to proactively monitor the performance of the obligors or investigate potential defaults.

69 In *CPF One Limited & another v Ortus Secured Finance Limited* [2023] EWHC 2102 Ch the court upheld the commercially agreed position between the parties, making it clear that, beyond the duties expressly set out in the contractual documentation, it is difficult to impose any additional obligations on senior creditors or their agents.
70 Wood, P., *Project Finance, Securitisations and Subordinated Debt* (Sweet & Maxwell, 2019) at [11-009].
71 Ibid. at [22]–[24].

In addition to the presumption that no breach or default has occurred unless formally notified, security trust deeds often impose further limitations on the security trustee's responsibilities. These provisions typically entitle the security trustee to rely on information and certificates supplied by lenders or obligors without conducting independent verification. Furthermore, the trustee bears no responsibility for the terms of the underlying finance documents, the non-performance of obligors, or any credit assessments.

The rationale for such provisions was affirmed in *Torre Asset Funding Ltd v Royal Bank of Scotland Plc* [2013] EWHC 2670 (Ch), where the court held that a facility agent, contractually limited to an administrative role, did not owe a duty to mezzanine lenders to disclose information concerning a potential event of default. The High Court ruled that the agent's responsibilities, as defined by the contractual documentation, shielded it from liability for failing to notify lenders of a default related to the borrower's financial condition.

These provisions are intended to reinforce the passive role of the security trustee, thereby mitigating the risk of "imputed notice" that might otherwise arise if a security trustee's officers, while performing other roles within the transaction, became aware of information potentially relevant to the security trust. However, the security trustee may still be required to disclose non-confidential information that it obtains in the ordinary course of administering the security trust, particularly if such information relates to a potential default or breach.

For large financial institutions that frequently act in multiple capacities (such as security trustee, lender, and hedging counterparty), these provisions necessitate the establishment of robust ethical walls or information barriers to prevent conflicts of interest arising from the receipt of sensitive information in one capacity that could impact another. As noted by some commentators, in some jurisdictions, mere "mechanical reliance" on certificates or information may not be sufficient to exonerate the security trustee from responsibility if it had access to material information.[72] For example, in the US, courts may impose an overriding duty of reasonable diligence on trustees, potentially exposing them to liability despite such exclusion clauses.[73]

The security trustee typically plays a largely administrative or mechanical role in most transactions and is not expected to bear financial risks. Nonetheless, in the performance of its duties, the trustee will inevitably incur costs, expenses, and potential liabilities, particularly where enforcement of the security becomes necessary. Pursuant to section 31 of the Trustee Act 2000, a security trustee is entitled to be indemnified out of the trust property in respect of liabilities, costs, and expenses properly incurred in carrying out its duties and exercising its powers. This right of indemnification arises from the fiduciary nature of the trustee's position rather than any contractual arrangement. However, the trustee is not entitled to indemnification for any costs or liabilities incurred while acting outside the scope of the trust's authority or in breach of trust.[74] According to *Carver v Duncan* [1985] AC 1082, a trustee is entitled to reimbursement for costs reasonably incurred in discharging its responsibilities. This entitlement is further reinforced by the existence of an equitable lien over the trust's capital and income, which enables the trustee to assert priority over the claims of other beneficiaries for the recovery of its expenses.[75] Given these principles, it is common practice for security trustees to ensure that the transaction documents expressly provide for the reimbursement of all fees, costs, and expenses incurred in the performance of their duties. Such recoverable

72 See Wood, P., *Project Finance, Securitisations and Subordinated Debt* (Sweet & Maxwell, 2007).
73 See *Frishmuth v Farmer's Loan and Trust Co*, 95 Fed 5 (S.D.N.Y. 1899).
74 *Leedham v Chawner* (1858) 4 K&J 458.
75 See *Stott v Milne* (1884) LR 25 Ch. D. 710 and *Dodds v Tuke* (1884) LR 25 Ch. D. 617.

expenses typically include management time, legal fees, and other resources expended in the administration and enforcement of the trust arrangements.

Finally, the security trustee may exercise discretion in determining whether to satisfy costs out of the trust's income or capital, depending upon the nature of the expense incurred. Typically, any amounts realised by the trustee through the enforcement or realisation of security are distributed according to a payment waterfall, under which the security trustee's own fees, costs, and expenses are paid in priority before any proceeds are allocated to other creditors. In the event of a shortfall in recoveries, the security trustee may seek recourse to supporting indemnities from the creditors or obligors in order to secure additional recovery. Security trustees often prefer to recover costs on an indemnity basis rather than the standard basis, as this provides a broader right to reimbursement, including costs not strictly necessary or proportionate but reasonably incurred. Some security trust arrangements further contemplate the establishment of a "fighting fund", designed to meet anticipated litigation costs. In such cases, provisions may be included requiring amounts to be retained within the trust for a period of up to six years following the termination of the trust, thereby accounting for any contingent or future claims that may arise.

6 TRUST'S ALTERNATIVE: AGENCY

An agency arrangement may serve as an alternative to a trust in the context of finance transactions.[76] However, in England and Wales, the legal principles governing agencies differ significantly from those relating to trusts. An agent acts on behalf of its principal or principals (such as syndicated lenders) and facilitates contracts with third parties, either by introducing the third party or concluding contracts on behalf of the principal. Crucially, the agent does not contract in its own right but instead represents the principal, typically without incurring personal liability to third parties. Unlike a trustee, an agent's role may not necessarily involve holding or managing rights in or to property. While an agent may owe fiduciary duties to its principals, these duties can also be contractually limited or excluded (as in *Kelly v Cooper* [1993] AC 205 and *Henderson v Merrett Syndicates Ltd* [1995] 2 AC 145).

In contrast, a trustee, although not representing beneficiaries in the same way, owes fiduciary duties to them and is personally liable for contracts entered into on behalf of the trust. A trust also inherently involves rights in or to property, distinguishing it from an agency relationship.[77]

When an agency structure is employed as an alternative to a security trust, certain complexities may arise, even where the debtor grants the agent a security interest or the benefit of a covenant to pay. In such arrangements, the principals hold an undivided share in the security, making them co-owners rather than mere beneficiaries. This structure is further complicated in syndicated lending, where each lender contractually agrees to provide a portion of the loan directly to the borrower. These features can create practical difficulties, particularly when a lender assigns or novates its secured debt. In such cases, the security may be inadvertently discharged, either wholly or partially.[78] Furthermore, lenders may lose their

76 For more on the role of an agent in the context of syndicated lending, the LMA has produced the LMA Guide to Agency Protections, which details the contractual protections afforded to an agent under LMA facility documentation.

77 Hudson, A., *The Law of Finance* (Sweet & Maxwell, 2013) at [34-22].

78 Petrisor, S., 'Considerations Regarding the Concept of Security Agent in Syndicated Loans' (December 2015) 2(2) *Central Bank Journal of Law and Finance* 155.

rights of set-off against amounts owed under the syndicated loan if the agent, acting on their behalf, submits proof of debt in the borrower's insolvency.

7 CONCLUSION

In conclusion, while intercreditor deeds, deeds of priority, and subordination agreements all serve the essential function of establishing creditor priorities, their scope and complexity vary significantly.

The intercreditor deed is indispensable in ensuring clarity regarding the order of payments and enforcement of security. By bringing all relevant parties under a unified framework, it facilitates the orderly and predictable resolution of creditor claims, both during regular operations and in enforcement scenarios. Its importance is amplified in intricate financial structures, where multiple layers of debt and varying creditor interests must be managed.

Equally critical is the role of the security trust, which centralises the management of security interests, providing administrative convenience and ensuring the protection of beneficiaries' rights. However, security trustees must navigate the personal liabilities and statutory duties that come with their role, acting in strict accordance with the security trust deed and the broader legal framework governing trusts.

Ultimately, the enforcement of security by a security trustee in multi-tiered debt structures is a complex and highly contentious process. The trustee must balance the competing interests of creditors, manage conflicts of interest, and ensure that enforcement proceeds are distributed in accordance with the agreed ranking and payment waterfall. In doing so, the security trustee plays a crucial role in the effective administration of syndicated lending transactions, ensuring both the rights of the secured parties and the protection of the trustee through well-considered indemnity provisions.

CHAPTER 13

SUSTAINABLE LENDING, DERIVATIVES, PROJECT FINANCE, AND LEGAL OPINIONS

OVERVIEW

Chapter 13 addresses the significance of Environmental, Social, and Governance (**ESG**) considerations in loan transactions, particularly through the lens of sustainability-linked loans. While the notion of ESG is multifaceted, its primary focus tends to be on assessing whether an economic activity is sustainable for investment decision-making purposes.

The chapter then turns to exploring three critical areas in international banking and finance law: the use of derivatives in loan transactions, the role of loan agreements in project finance transactions, and the issuance of legal opinions within financing arrangements, incorporating both an English and a US law perspective. By covering these three interrelated topics, Chapter 13 provides a comprehensive overview of the key legal and financial mechanisms that underpin modern loan transactions. Each section builds upon the last, offering readers a deeper understanding of how risk management, tailored financial agreements, and legal certainty come together in international banking law.

1 SUSTAINABLE LENDING

On 25 September 2015, the United Nations General Assembly adopted the 2030 Agenda for Sustainable Development, a comprehensive global framework designed to promote sustainable economic, social, and environmental progress. At the heart of this agenda are the Sustainable Development Goals (**SDG**s), which set ambitious targets to address issues such as poverty, inequality, and environmental degradation. Complementing these efforts, the Paris Agreement[1] aims to strengthen the global response to climate change by limiting the increase in global average temperature to well below 2°C above pre-industrial levels while also pursuing efforts to restrict the rise to 1.5°C.[2] These targets are essential for reducing the risks and impacts associated with climate change, requiring coordinated action from governments, financial institutions, and corporate entities worldwide.[3] Therefore, one of the key objectives

1 "*The Paris Agreement is the third treaty in the UN climate regime. It builds upon a complex body of rules and procedures that have developed over 25 years, which together make up the UN climate regime. Its founding Treaty is the United Nations Framework Convention on Climate Change ('UNFCCC'), which was adopted in 1992 and in force from 21 March 1994, the ultimate objective of which is to stabilize greenhouse gas concentrations 'at a level that would prevent dangerous anthropogenic (human induced) interference with the climate system': see Article 2. Actions to implement this objective are based on the principle of common but differentiated responsibilities and capabilities. In particular, developed countries (including the UK) are to take the lead in cutting emissions on the basis that they were largely responsible for climate change: see Articles 3(1) and 4(2). Developed countries are required to finance and provide technology transfer to assist developing countries to mitigate and adapt to climate change: Article 4(3)–(5).*

. . .The Paris Agreement was adopted at the 21st Conference of the Parties to the UNFCCC in 2015. It was initiated by the COP17 (2011) in response to the 'significant gap between the aggregate effect of Parties' mitigation pledges in terms of global annual emissions of greenhouse gases by 2020 and aggregate emission pathways consistent with having a likely chance of holding the increase in global average temperature below 2°C or 1.5°C above pre-industrial levels' (Recital 2 of Decision 1 CP. 17 (UNFCCC Doc. FCCC/CP/2011/9/Add.1)". In *Friends of The Earth Ltd, R. (on the Application of) v The Secretary of State for International Trade Export Credits Guarantee Department (UK Export Finance) ("UKEF") & Anor* [2022] EWHC 568 (Admin) at [13] to [16].

2 See Preamble of Regulation (EU) 2019/2088 of the European Parliament and of the Council of 27 November 2019 on sustainability-related disclosures in the financial services sector.

3 See Preamble of Regulation (EU) 2024/3005 of the European Parliament and of the Council of 27 November 2024 on the transparency and integrity of Environmental, Social and Governance (ESG) rating activities, and amending Regulations (EU) 2019/2088 and (EU) 2023/2859.

DOI: 10.4324/9781032662220-14

of the Paris Agreement is to ensure that financial flows align with pathways leading to low greenhouse gas emissions and climate-resilient development.[4]

Sustainable finance involves integrating ESG considerations into investment decision-making, with the objective of promoting investment in long-term, sustainable economic activities. It further emphasises the necessity for financial institutions and corporate entities to implement robust governance frameworks to mitigate the risks that may affect the stability and resilience of the financial system. Enhanced transparency and disclosure are central to this process, ensuring that market participants can assess and manage sustainability-related risks while facilitating the transition to a more sustainable economy.

While a number of jurisdictions have committed to ESG-driven finance (and some are rescinding such commitment), the European Union has deployed perhaps the most extensive and prescriptive legal frameworks in this field. The EU package of sustainable finance legislation includes: (a) Sustainable Finance Disclosure Regulation (EU) 2019/2088;[5] (b) the Low Carbon Benchmark Regulation (EU) 2019/2089;[6] (c) the Taxonomy Regulation (EU) 2020/852;[7] and (d) Regulation (EU) 2024/3005 on the transparency and integrity of ESG rating activities.[8] This is because the

> *transition to a sustainable economy is key to ensuring the long-term competitiveness and sustainability of the Union economy and the quality of life of citizens in the Union, and to keeping global warming well below the 1,5 degree Celsius threshold. Sustainability has long been at the heart of Union policies and both the Treaty on European Union and the Treaty on the Functioning of the European Union (TFEU) recognise its social and environmental dimensions.*[9]

In this context, as mentioned in Chapter 8, both lenders and corporates have become increasingly mindful of the impact their lending, investment, and business decisions have on climate change and the environment.[10] For lenders, this means balancing their investment objectives and financial returns with a commitment to sustainability. Similarly, companies are seeking to integrate sustainable practices into their business operations while meeting their operational and strategic objectives. As a result, two types of loans have emerged as key instruments for achieving these environmental and social goals: sustainability-linked loans (**SLL**s) and green loans. While both types of loans aim to support environmental objectives, they serve different purposes.

The term "green loan" refers to a loan where the proceeds are expressly designated for environmentally beneficial purposes or projects. Such projects typically include initiatives

4 On 20 January 2025, the United States ceased any commitment to the Paris Agreement and withdrew from it with immediate effect pursuant to the executive order titled "Putting America First in International Environmental Agreements", see www.whitehouse.gov/presidential-actions/2025/01/putting-america-first-in-international-environmental-agreements/ (accessed in March 2025).

5 Regulation (EU) 2019/2088 of the European Parliament and of the Council of 27 November 2019 on sustainability-related disclosures in the financial services sector.

6 Regulation (EU) 2019/2089 of the European Parliament and of the Council of 27 November 2019 amending Regulation (EU) 2016/1011 as regards EU Climate Transition Benchmarks, EU Paris-aligned Benchmarks and sustainability-related disclosures for benchmarks.

7 Regulation (EU) 2020/852 of the European Parliament and of the Council of 18 June 2020 on the establishment of a framework to facilitate sustainable investment, and amending Regulation (EU) 2019/2088.

8 Regulation (EU) 2024/3005 of the European Parliament and of the Council of 27 November 2024 on the transparency and integrity of Environmental, Social and Governance (ESG) rating activities, and amending Regulations (EU) 2019/2088 and (EU) 2023/2859.

9 See Preamble (2) of Regulation (EU) 2024/3005 of the European Parliament and of the Council of 27 November 2024 on the transparency and integrity of Environmental, Social and Governance (ESG) rating activities, and amending Regulations (EU) 2019/2088 and (EU) 2023/2859.

10 OECD, 'Due Diligence for Responsible Corporate Lending and Securities Underwriting' *OECD Publishing* (2019), available at https://mneguidelines.oecd.org/due-diligence-for-responsible-corporate-lending-and-securities-underwriting.pdf (accessed in March 2025).

aimed at pollution prevention and control, the development of infrastructure for clean energy vehicles, or investments in sustainable water management. The defining characteristic of a green loan is the binding commitment to use the proceeds exclusively for a specific project or for activities that contribute to environmental sustainability.

The Green Loan Principles (**GLP**), published by the Loan Market Association (**LMA**), the Asia Pacific Loan Market Association (**APLMA**), and the Loan Syndications and Trading Association (**LSTA**),[11] provide a standardised framework for such loans. These principles define green loans as those made exclusively to finance, refinance, or guarantee new or existing eligible green projects and must align with the GLP's four core components: use of proceeds, process for project evaluation and selection, management of proceeds, and reporting.[12]

Unlike green loans, SLLs do not have a use-of-proceeds requirement and are often structured as general corporate-purpose loans. The LMA, APLMA, and the LSTA have jointly published the Sustainability-Linked Loan Principles (**SLLP**) to provide a standardised framework to promote consistency, transparency, and integrity in the sustainability-linked loan market.

SLLs[13] are designed to incentivise borrowers to improve their sustainability performance by tying loan terms – particularly pricing – to the borrower's achievement of predefined sustainability goals. These goals, referred to as sustainability performance targets (**SPT**s), may encompass a range of environmental or social metrics relating to sustainability risk,[14] such as energy efficiency, water consumption, or the sustainable sourcing of materials. If a borrower meets or exceeds the agreed-upon SPTs, the loan's interest rate typically decreases, providing a financial reward for improved sustainability. Conversely, failure to meet the targets may result in a pricing increase, further motivating borrowers to meet their sustainability commitments.

The following example from case law provides the context in which such arrangements – in connection with financing and a support package – could be considered:

> *UKEF does not allocate public funds to or invest in projects, but provides export credits (through guarantees, insurance, grants or loans) in relation to the supply of UK goods and/or services to overseas buyers, including in relation to projects. . . . As part of its decision-making process, UKEF routinely assesses the statutory basis for support, the export case, the credit risk and environmental, social and human rights ("ESHR") impact considerations. In addition, in the present case officials from the Department for International Development*

11 On 23 February 2023, the LMA, APLMA, and LSTA published updated versions of the GLP, the Social Loan Principles (SLP), and Sustainability-Linked Loan Principles (SLLP), together with updated guidance.

12 Since the initial publication of the GLP, updates in 2018, 2021, and most recently in 2023 have refined the framework, reflecting evolving trends in sustainable finance markets. These updates introduced additional guidance, such as the applicability of the GLP to revolving credit facilities and considerations of social risks during project evaluation. The February 2023 update further aligned the GLP with global developments in sustainable finance, ensuring that transactions completed from March 2023 onwards are assessed under the latest principles.

13 Under Art. 2(17) of Regulation (EU) 2019/2088 of the European Parliament and of the Council of 27 November 2019 on sustainability-related disclosures in the financial services sector "*'sustainable investment' means an investment in an economic activity that contributes to an environmental objective, as measured, for example, by key resource efficiency indicators on the use of energy, renewable energy, raw materials, water and land, on the production of waste, and greenhouse gas emissions, or on its impact on biodiversity and the circular economy, or an investment in an economic activity that contributes to a social objective, in particular an investment that contributes to tackling inequality or that fosters social cohesion, social integration and labour relations, or an investment in human capital or economically or socially disadvantaged communities, provided that such investments do not significantly harm any of those objectives and that the investee companies follow good governance practices, in particular with respect to sound management structures, employee relations, remuneration of staff and tax compliance*".

14 Under Art. 2(22) of Regulation (EU) 2019/2088 of the European Parliament and of the Council of 27 November 2019 on sustainability-related disclosures in the financial services sector "'sustainability risk' means an environmental, social or governance event or condition that, if it occurs, could cause an actual or a potential material negative impact on the value of the investment".

undertook an assessment for the Treasury of the proposed transaction against the OECD Principles and Guidelines to Promote Sustainable Lending Practices in the Provision of Official Expert Credits to Low-Income Countries (the "Sustainable Lending Principles"). That assessment reported on (a) Mozambique's debt sustainability, (b) the Government of Mozambique's efforts in relation to governance and transparency and (c) the Project's positive economic returns.

. . . UKEF assesses the environmental, social and human rights (ESHR) risks and impacts by way of an ESHR review "to be satisfied that these are identified, managed and mitigated in line with local and international ESHR standards". UKEF will not normally provide funding where its "review identifies that the project is unlikely to align with international standards". This is on the basis that to do so would be contrary to the OECD Common Approaches (Recommendation of the Council on Common Approaches for Officially Supported Export Credits and Environmental and Social Due Diligence (Organisation for Economic Co-operation and Development)) and the Equator Principles ("EPs" – a risk management framework adopted by financial institutions for assessing environmental risks in project finance), to which it has committed to comply.

. . .

The OECD Common Approaches and Equator Principles in turn required UKEF to assess whether a project it was proposing to finance complied with host country laws and a list of certain expressly designated "international standards" (§§13 and 21–26 of the OECD Common Approaches and Principle 3 of EP3). That list of designated international standards includes the International Finance Corporation of the World Bank Group's Performance Standards on Social and Environmental Sustainability and the World Bank Group Environmental, Health and Safety Guidelines. The former set of performance standards includes Performance Standard 1 Assessment and Management of Environmental and Social Risks and Impacts.[15]

The preceding discussion highlights the importance of clearly defined sustainability metrics. Due to the divergence and continuous evolution of rating methodologies and rating scales, where an ESG rating serves as the sole key performance indicator (**KPI**), the borrower is expected to justify why this rating provides the most accurate reflection of the core ESG challenges faced by its business. The decision as to whether the selected KPIs relate to environmental (E), social (S), or governance (G) factors – or indeed a combination of all three – is at the discretion of the borrower, subject to agreement with its lenders. Environmental and climate-related KPIs continue to dominate, with the most commonly adopted indicators being those linked to reductions in greenhouse gas[16] or CO_2 emissions. While social and governance KPIs, such as the percentage of women in leadership positions, are becoming increasingly prevalent, they remain significantly less common than environmental KPIs.[17] In practice, the selection of KPIs is highly specific to the individual borrower and the sector in which it operates. The EU has become one of the first jurisdictions to

lay down rules ensuring that ESG ratings provided by ESG rating providers authorised in the Union are of adequate quality, are subject to appropriate requirements that recognise the existence of different business models, and ensure market integrity. Those rules would apply to overall ESG ratings capturing environmental, social and governance factors, and to ratings that only assess a single environmental, social or governance factor or a sub-component of such a factor. Separate environmental (E), social (S) and governance (G) ratings should be provided rather than a single ESG rating that aggregates E, S and G factors.[18]

15 In *Friends of The Earth Ltd, R. (on the Application of) v The Secretary of State for International Trade Export Credits Guarantee Department (UK Export Finance) ("UKEF") & Anor* [2022] EWHC 568 (Admin) at [9], [10].

16 Scope 1, 2, and 3.

17 See also The Association of Corporate Treasurers, *A Borrower's Guide to the LMA's Investment Grade Agreements* (ACT 6th Edition, November 2022), p. 88, available at www.treasurers.org/system/files/The%20ACT%20Borrower%E2%80%99s%20Guide%20to%20the%20LMA%E2%80%99s%20Investment%20Grade%20Agreements%20-%20Final.pdf (accessed in March 2025).

18 See Preamble (26) of Regulation (EU) 2024/3005 of the European Parliament and of the Council of 27 November 2024 on the transparency and integrity of Environmental, Social and Governance (ESG) rating activities, and amending Regulations (EU) 2019/2088 and (EU) 2023/2859.

However, the extent to which this regulatory development might influence the use of ESG ratings as metrics in SLLs remains uncertain.

In this context, the SLLP provides a framework for structuring SLLs, ensuring they are linked to the borrower's overall sustainability strategy and measurable through clear, ambitious, and relevant KPIs. The principles emphasise the importance of reporting and verification, requiring borrowers to regularly report their progress against the agreed SPTs and undergo independent external verification to ensure transparency and accountability. By adhering to these principles, SLLs facilitate a structured approach to promoting sustainable business practices while offering both financial incentives for borrowers and confidence to lenders that sustainability objectives are being met.

This evolution in lending practices has opened up opportunities for companies that may not have specific green projects but still aim to improve their environmental and social impact. As such, SLLs have become a flexible and popular tool, expanding the reach of the sustainable finance market. They provide a bridge for companies to access sustainability-linked finance, fostering environmentally responsible behaviour across various industries, regardless of their involvement in traditionally "green" sectors.[19]

1.1 Performance Indicators in Sustainable Loans

The selection of KPIs is critical in measuring a borrower's sustainability performance. These KPIs must be material to the borrower's business, measurable on a consistent basis, and benchmarked against industry standards to assess the achievement of SPTs. They should be clearly defined, specifying the applicable scope, calculation methodologies, and baselines.

SPTs, in turn, must be ambitious and represent a material improvement in the chosen KPIs. They should be calibrated based on benchmarking against the borrower's peers, industry standards, or science-based targets and aligned with the borrower's overall sustainability strategy. The borrower and lender group must agree on these targets, with the option to engage a sustainability coordinator or external reviewer to ensure appropriateness.

A distinctive feature of SLLs is that the loan's economic terms, such as the interest margin, are tied to the borrower's success in meeting its SPTs. This creates a direct link between sustainability performance and financial outcomes, providing an incentive for borrowers to achieve their sustainability goals.

Reporting is another essential component. Borrowers are expected to provide lenders with regular updates on their performance against the SPTs, at least annually. While public reporting is encouraged, borrowers may opt to share the information privately with their lenders.

Verification plays a key role in ensuring the credibility of SLLs. At least once a year, borrowers are expected to obtain independent and external verification of their performance against the agreed SPTs. This verification should ideally be made publicly available to enhance transparency and accountability in the market.[20]

19 In 2020, the LMA, the APLMA, and LSTA published guidance on the SLLP. In May 2021, following the structural revisions to the SLLP, the LMA, APLMA, and LSTA released updated guidance to reflect the revised principles, incorporating new sections on distinctions between SLLs and social loans. This version was further updated in February 2023 to align with the evolving landscape of sustainable finance. The updated guidance continues to assist borrowers, lenders, and market participants in structuring sustainability-linked loans in accordance with the revised SLLP. Available at: www.lsta.org/content/guidance-on-sustainability-linked-loan-principles-sllp/# (accessed in March 2025).

20 In 2022, the LMA, APLMA, and LSTA published "Guidance for Green, Social and Sustainability-Linked Loans External Reviews". This document provides best practice guidance for borrowers, lenders, and external reviewers to address professional and ethical standards for external reviewers and provide

1.2 Documenting Sustainability-Linked Loans

The SLL market is evolving, and while there is not yet a standardised approach for drafting provisions related to the SLLP within loan agreements, notable progress has been made. The LMA published model provisions for SLLs to be used with their standard loan documentation,[21] marking an important step towards establishing consistent market practices.

In documenting an SLL within a loan agreement, several key drafting points must be considered. First, the agreed KPIs and SPTs for the borrower must be explicitly included, along with a margin adjustment mechanism tied to the borrower's performance. The loan agreement should also set out conditions precedents, representations, and undertakings to ensure that the SPTs are appropriately calibrated and consistent with the borrower's broader sustainability strategy.

The agreement must address reporting obligations, requiring the borrower to regularly provide updates on its progress towards meeting the SPTs. This can be achieved through tailored undertakings and potentially a form of sustainability compliance certificate. Moreover, provisions for independent and external verification of the borrower's performance against its SPTs are essential to ensure transparency and accountability. The role of a sustainability coordinator has become increasingly common in SLL transactions. This role, which is still developing, can vary significantly depending on the transaction and institutions involved.

Beyond LMA provisions, the Chancery Lane Project (**TCLP**) has produced a set of draft clauses, which can be used to incorporate the SLLP into a facility agreement. TCLP is a collaborative initiative involving lawyers from various disciplines and jurisdictions, with the goal of establishing new market standards for addressing climate change risks and issues within contracts and legal frameworks. TCLP's efforts are designed to help law firms and their clients transition towards net zero emissions by embedding climate-conscious provisions in legal documents.[22]

These clauses, designed to work with a standard LMA facility agreement, cover essential elements such as sustainability-linked margin adjustments, sustainability compliance certificates, and obligations relating to the borrower's sustainability strategy. They also address the potential consequences of a borrower's failure to meet sustainability obligations, including the possibility of an event of default, margin increases, or declassification[23] of the loan as an SLL. As the sustainable lending market continues to evolve, tools such as these model clauses and guidelines are invaluable in shaping future lending practices.

recommendations on the organisation, content, and disclosure of their reports. This guidance, updated again in January 2024, remains a voluntary framework but is crucial for fostering integrity and trust in the external review process in sustainable finance. Available at: www.lsta.org/content/guidance-on-green-loan-principles-glp/# (accessed in March 2025).

21 See The Association of Corporate Treasurers, *A Borrower's Guide to the LMA's Investment Grade Agreements* (ACT 6th Edition, November 2022), pp. 83 to 92, available at www.treasurers.org/system/files/The%20ACT%20Borrower%E2%80%99s%20Guide%20to%20the%20LMA%E2%80%99s%20Investment%20Grade%20Agreements%20-%20Final.pdf (accessed in March 2025).

22 These clauses can be found at https://chancerylaneproject.org/clauses/green-loan-starter-pack/ (accessed in March 2025).

23 See also The Association of Corporate Treasurers, *A Borrower's Guide to the LMA's Investment Grade Agreements* (ACT 6th Edition, November 2022), pp. 95 to 96, available at www.treasurers.org/system/files/The%20ACT%20Borrower%E2%80%99s%20Guide%20to%20the%20LMA%E2%80%99s%20Investment%20Grade%20Agreements%20-%20Final.pdf (accessed in March 2025).

2 DERIVATIVES AND LOAN TRANSACTIONS

When a lender contemplates making a commercial loan, it must assess several key considerations, including the risk that the borrower may fail to meet its loan obligations, the potential impact the loan may have on the lender's regulatory capital requirements, and whether the loan will breach any internal or regulatory restrictions imposed on the lender. To navigate these risks, derivatives can serve as useful tools.[24]

A derivative is a bilateral contract, the value of which is derived from the future value of an underlying asset, transaction, or index, such as commodities or exchange rates.[25] The most commonly encountered derivatives in loan transactions are over-the-counter (OTC)[26] derivatives, which are customised agreements tailored to the specific needs of the parties involved. These differ from exchange-traded derivatives, which are standardised and traded on regulated exchanges.

The use of derivatives to hedge risks in loan transactions involves the application of specific financial instruments designed to mitigate key risks faced by both lenders and borrowers.[27]

Interest rate risk arises when loans are subject to variable interest rates that fluctuate in response to market conditions. Given the inherent volatility of floating interest rates, lenders frequently require borrowers to enter into interest rate swaps to mitigate this uncertainty. Under such an arrangement, the borrower exchanges its floating rate liability for a fixed rate by swapping floating cash flows for fixed cash flows. This provides greater certainty regarding the borrower's ability to meet interest obligations and thereby service and ultimately repay the loan in full and on time.

Example of Using an Interest Rate Swap to Minimise Interest Rate Risk

Facts: A loan of £1 million is made by Estrella Bank to Arroyo S.A. at a floating rate of interest.

The interest rate risk: If the base rate underpinning the floating rate of interest rises, Arroyo S.A. may find it difficult to meet its interest obligations. Assuming Arroyo S.A. is comfortable with a fixed rate of 6% per annum, it could manage the risk of exceeding this rate by entering into an interest rate swap with Estrella Bank.

The interest rate swap: Under the swap arrangement:

- Arroyo S.A. pays Estrella Bank a fee to enter into the swap.
- Arroyo S.A. makes fixed rate payments of 6% per annum to Estrella Bank, and Estrella Bank makes floating rate payments to Arroyo S.A. based on the loan's floating rate. These payments are based on a notional amount equal to the loan principal, and the swap's duration will match the loan's term.

24 Hudson, A., *The Law on Financial Derivatives* (Sweet & Maxwell, 2017), Chapter 9.

25 Firth, S., *Firth on Derivatives Law and Practice* (Sweet & Maxwell, 2003) at [1.006].

26 "OTC" transactions are defined by contrast to exchange-traded transactions: "*The terms of exchange-traded derivatives are defined by the exchange on which they are traded. OTC derivatives, by contrast, are concluded bilaterally and their terms are negotiated between the parties to the transaction*", per Mrs Justice Proudman in *Weavering Capital (UK) Ltd & Anor v Peterson & Ors* [2012] EWHC 1480 at [15].

27 Firth, S., *Firth on Derivatives Law and Practice* (Sweet & Maxwell, 2003) at [8.025].

This structure allows Arroyo S.A. to effectively fix the interest rate at 6% per annum. Estrella Bank can further protect its position by entering into a back-to-back swap with another market participant. As a market maker, Estrella Bank may profit from the difference between the fee paid by Arroyo S.A. and the fee it pays for the back-to-back transactions.

Currency risk is a key consideration in cross-border loan transactions, where the loan is denominated in one currency while repayments are made in another. Currency swaps or forward contracts allow parties to lock in an exchange rate for future payments, thereby protecting against adverse fluctuations in foreign exchange rates. This ensures that repayments made in a different currency do not result in unexpected costs or financial losses due to currency devaluation.

Example of Using a Currency Swap to Minimise Currency Risk

Facts: Almeida Corp owns a zinc mine and has borrowed EUR 100 million from Estrella Bank. The loan is in Euros as Almeida can secure favourable funding in that currency. However, the zinc markets where Almeida operates trade in US dollars.

The currency risk: Almeida Corp is concerned that a strengthening of the Euro against the US dollar could make it harder to service its loan from zinc revenues. To manage this risk, Almeida Corp could enter into a currency swap with Estrella Bank.

The currency swap: Assume the exchange rate at the time of the loan is EUR 1 = US$1.20 (EUR 100 million equates to US$120 million). Under the swap:

- Almeida Corp pays Estrella Bank a fee to enter the swap.
- Estrella Bank pays Almeida an amount equal to the Euro interest payment under the loan on each interest payment date.
- Almeida pays Estrella Bank in US dollars at an exchange rate of EUR 1 = US$1.20.
- At loan maturity, Estrella Bank pays EUR 100 million to Almeida, and Almeida pays US$120 million to Estrella Bank.

By entering the swap, Almeida has fixed the exchange rate between its dollar income and Euro liability. Like the interest rate swap, Estrella Bank can protect itself by executing a back-to-back swap with a market counterparty, potentially profiting from the difference between fees.

Credit risk, or the risk of borrower default, can be managed through the use of credit default swaps (**CDS**).[28]

> *Often a lender may wish to obtain protection against default on a loan whilst still retaining entitlement to receipt of interest payments. For example, a bank may wish to obtain insurance against a loan being defaulted on in much the same way that a mortgage company may wish to secure protection for damage to a property*

28 Hudson, A., *The Law on Financial Derivatives* (Sweet & Maxwell, 2017) at [5-161].

against which a loan is secured. The lender accordingly goes into the market as a "protection buyer" and asks a "protection seller" to take on the risk of default in return for the payment of periodic premiums. It "swaps" the risk of default for the payment of those premiums. The protection buyer is known as the long trader and the protection seller as the short trader. A default is known as a "credit event".[29]

Whereas:

The contractual terms of a CDS are usually set out in a "confirmation", which incorporates by reference one or more sets of standard terms such as those published by ISDA (the International Swap and Derivatives Association). However, the terms can be, and in the present case were, customised to a significant degree. The CDS confirmation will list the "credit events" (various categories of adverse development affecting the reference asset) which will trigger an obligation on the protection seller under the CDS.[30]

Pay-outs under the contract will be triggered by credit events in relation to a reference entity or a reference asset.[31]

Typically, credit events include (i) a bankruptcy filing (or similar insolvency process) by the reference entity, (ii) the reference entity's failure to make a payment of interest or principal on a debt obligation, and sometimes (iii) a restructuring of existing debt resulting from the reference entity's distressed condition. The occurrence of a credit event gives the protection buyer the right to "trigger" its remedies under the CDS contract, which can involve either "physical settlement" or "cash settlement". Under physical settlement, the protection buyer delivers a loan or bond of the reference entity to the protection seller, whose notional amount is equal to the notional amount of the CDS; the protection seller, in return, pays the protection buyer the face value for the loan or bond. Under cash settlement, the current market value of a representative debt instrument of the reference entity is determined as a percentage of the par value of the instrument, typically by polling leading dealers of debt instruments; this is referred to as the "recovery rate". The protection seller then pays the protection buyer an amount in cash equal to the notional amount of the CDS minus the notional amount of the CDS multiplied by the recovery rate.[32]

Example of Using a Credit Default Swap to Minimise Credit Risk

Facts: Estrella Bank has provided a loan to Arroyo S.A.

The credit risk: Estrella Bank is concerned that Arroyo S.A. may default on the loan. To hedge against this risk, Estrella could enter into a CDS with a third-party bank, Arcos Bank.

The credit default swap: In exchange for a percentage fee per annum based on the loan's notional amount, Estrella Bank buys protection from Arcos Bank against Arroyo S.A. defaulting, restructuring its debt, or becoming bankrupt. If any of these events occur, Estrella Bank can transfer the loan to Arcos Bank and receive the loan's principal in return. Through this arrangement, Estrella Bank protects itself from

29 Per Mr Justice Kitchin in *Liffe Administration and Management v Pinkava & Anor Rev 1* [2006] EWHC 595 (Pat) at [24] and [25].

30 Per Hamblen J in *Cassa di Risparmio della Republica di San Marino SpA v Barclays Bank Ltd* [2011] EWHC 484 (Comm), at [25] to [26].

31 Bell and Dawson, 'Synthetic Securitization: Use of Derivative Technology for Credit Transfers' (2002) 12 *Duke Journal of Comparative & International Law* 541.

32 Per Hamblen J in *Cassa di Risparmio della Republica di San Marino SpA v Barclays Bank Ltd* [2011] EWHC 484 (Comm), at [27] to [28].

Arroyo S.A.'s default, but the effectiveness of the protection depends on Arcos Bank's creditworthiness.

Commodity risk is particularly relevant in transactions where loan repayments are linked to industries reliant on commodity prices, such as oil or metals. To hedge against price volatility, borrowers or lenders may employ commodity derivatives, such as futures or options, which establish fixed commodity prices. This stabilises costs and revenues associated with the loan, mitigating the impact of unfavourable price fluctuations.

Example of Using a Commodity Derivative to Minimise Loan Risk

Facts: Almeida Corp has borrowed EUR 100 million from Estrella Bank. Almeida's main asset is a zinc mine, and it has entered into offtake agreements to sell its zinc production to market buyers.

The commodity risk: Estrella Bank is concerned that a fall in zinc prices could reduce Almeida's cash flow, making it difficult to service the loan. To manage this risk, Estrella Bank could introduce a series of cash-settled put options in the loan structure.

The Put Option

- Almeida Corp pays a fee to Estrella Bank to enter into the put option.
- At the end of each quarter, Almeida has the right to sell zinc to Estrella at a pre-agreed strike price.
- If the zinc price is below the strike price at the end of the quarter, Almeida will exercise the put option, and Estrella will pay Almeida the difference between the strike price and the market price for the relevant amount of zinc.

By doing so, Almeida Corp can fix the future price of zinc, ensuring that its revenues are sufficient to service the loan. Estrella Bank could execute back-to-back options with other market participants to avoid taking on commodity risk directly.

By integrating these derivative instruments into loan transactions, both lenders and borrowers can effectively manage financial risks, ensuring greater certainty and stability throughout the duration of the loan.[33]

2.1 Using Derivatives to Reduce Regulatory Capital Charges

As discussed in Chapter 6, commercial lenders are subject to minimum regulatory capital requirements designed to protect the financial system from systemic risks and market shocks. However, regulatory capital requirements can place significant constraints on lenders' ability

33 Firth, S., *Firth on Derivatives Law and Practice* (Sweet & Maxwell, 2003) at [1.045].

to lend or engage in other financial transactions. To navigate these constraints, lenders often turn to derivatives, particularly credit default swaps and structured equity derivatives, to reduce the amount of regulatory capital they are required to hold.[34]

CDS are commonly employed by banks and financial institutions to hedge against the risk of default by borrowers. In such arrangements, a lender can transfer the credit risk associated with a loan to a third party in exchange for periodic premium payments.[35] Essentially, by transferring the risk of default to another entity, the lender lowers its own exposure and thus may lower its regulatory capital requirement.

Beyond credit default swaps, structured equity derivatives also offer solutions for managing regulatory capital charges. These derivatives mimic loan transactions but may attract less regulatory capital than a traditional loan.[36]

In an equity swap, a company, instead of borrowing money against its shares, can enter into an agreement with a bank. Under the terms of the swap, the company receives an initial exchange amount equivalent to the loan amount, and in return, the company pays the bank a floating rate. Meanwhile, the bank acquires legal title to the shares for the duration of the transaction, which is more advantageous than merely holding a security interest over the shares. By entering into an equity swap, the lender may reduce the regulatory capital required while still maintaining the essential characteristics of secured lending. Moreover, the bank has the flexibility to deal with the shares during the transaction so long as an equivalent number of shares are returned to the company at the swap's maturity. This structured approach offers both the company and the lender significant flexibility, with the added potential to reduce regulatory capital charges.

Another variation of this structure is the use of a hybrid derivative, combining a prepaid forward contract with an equity swap. In this scenario, the bank would prepay the purchase price for the shares, but instead of taking immediate delivery of the shares, it receives a cash equivalent of their value on a future date. The bank still holds a security interest over the shares, ensuring its protection. To mirror a secured loan, the bank and the company may agree that, at the end of the transaction, any gains in the share price will be repaid to the company, while any losses will be compensated by the company to the bank. This structure allows the company to raise finance against its shares without transferring ownership or voting rights, potentially avoiding stamp duty and capital gains tax, making this structure an appealing alternative to conventional secured lending.

In all these derivative transactions, the central appeal for lenders lies in the possibility of structuring transactions that retain the characteristics of traditional secured loans while potentially benefiting from more favourable capital treatment. In addition, these instruments provide both lenders and borrowers with greater flexibility in managing assets and obligations.

2.2 Using Derivatives to Reduce Credit Risk Concentration

Financial institutions are often subject to stringent internal and external regulations that limit the amount of lending they can extend to a single borrower or industry sector. These limits

34 Nicolò, A. and Pelizzon, L., 'Credit Derivatives: Capital Requirements and Strategic Contracting' *EFMA 2004 BASEL MEETINGS* (March 15, 2006), available at www.bis.org/bcbs/events/rtf06nicolo_etc.pdf (accessed in March 2025).

35 For details on the treatment of risk mitigation in the credit risk framework, see, for instance, paragraph 167 and subsequent paragraphs in www.bis.org/bcbs/publ/d347.pdf (accessed in March 2025).

36 Firth, S., *Firth on Derivatives Law and Practice* (Sweet & Maxwell, 2003) at [8.047].

are designed to prevent an over-concentration of credit risk, which can expose institutions to significant financial vulnerabilities in the event of a default.[37] To manage this risk, many lenders employ CDS as a tool to diversify and limit their credit exposure, enabling them to comply with these regulatory and internal restrictions while maintaining a robust lending portfolio. Credit default swaps provide a means by which lenders can transfer the credit risk associated with a particular borrower or sector to a third party, thereby reducing their direct exposure. By employing CDS, financial institutions can hedge against potential defaults while continuing to lend in sectors or to clients that would otherwise pose excessive credit concentration risks.[38]

As noted previously, a credit default swap works by allowing the lender to pay a periodic premium to a counterparty in exchange for protection against the default of a specific borrower or entity. In the event of a default, the counterparty to the CDS compensates the lender, either by paying the notional value of the loan or by assuming the loan's defaulted obligations. This allows the lender to effectively spread the risk across multiple counterparties, thus minimising the impact of credit concentration. This strategy is particularly advantageous in times of economic uncertainty or when lending in sectors prone to volatility, as the institution is able to hedge its exposure to defaults while continuing to generate income from its loan book.[39]

2.3 Derivatives in Structured Loan Transactions

Credit default swaps are also integral to structured finance transactions, such as synthetic collateralised loan obligations (**CLO**s), which are further discussed in Chapter 14. In these structured deals, CDS can be embedded into bond or loan structures to generate additional income for bondholders or lenders while simultaneously transferring the risk of default on the underlying loans to third parties. This not only enhances returns but also mitigates the credit risk borne by the institution.

3 PROJECT FINANCE AND LOAN AGREEMENTS

Project finance is generally characterised as a financing structure in which the approval of funding is not dependent on the financial stability or creditworthiness of the project sponsor – the entity responsible for initiating the development of the project. Instead, the viability of the financing is assessed primarily on the project's capacity to generate sufficient revenue to service its debt obligations and provide returns on invested capital at a rate commensurate with the project's risk profile.[40] This approach prioritises the project's projected cash flow as the principal source of repayment rather than relying on the assets or financial standing of the sponsors as collateral.[41]

37 Firth, S., *Firth on Derivatives Law and Practice* (Sweet & Maxwell, 2003) at [8.097].

38 Fletcher, G., 'Hazardous Hedging: The (Unacknowledged) Risks of Hedging with Credit Derivatives' (2013–2014) 33 *Review of Banking & Financial Law* 820.

39 Aldasoro, I. and Barth, A., 'Syndicated Loans and CDS Positioning' *ESRB: Working Paper Series No. 2017/58* (November, 2017).

40 It may be defined as "*the raising of funds on a limited-recourse or nonrecourse basis to finance an economically separable capital investment project in which the providers of the funds look primarily to the cash flow from the project as the source of funds to service their loans and provide the return of and a return on their equity invested in the project*". Finnerty, J., *Project Financing: Asset-Based Financial Engineering* (John Wiley & Sons, 2007), p. 1.

41 Gatti, S., *Project Finance in Theory and Practice – Designing, Structuring, and Financing Private and Public Projects* (Academic Press, 2013), ch 1, 1.

It is a method of financing capital-intensive and long-term infrastructure, natural resources, or industrial projects. It has historically been utilised in the context of the Private Finance Initiative (PFI) or Public Private Partnership (PPP) projects, which were typically associated with the delivery of public services, such as building schools, hospitals, or operating prisons. PPP projects are structured on the basis of a contractual or concession agreement between a government or statutory entity and a private sector company, facilitating the delivery of public utility infrastructure services that are accessible through user charges. These projects enable private sector participation in the financing, design, construction, operation, and maintenance of public sector programmes and infrastructure developments. The statutory authority grants licences for the development of such projects under various models, including Build, Operate, Transfer (BOT); Build, Develop, Operate, and Transfer (BDOT); Build, Own, Operate, and Transfer (BOOT); and Toll, Operate, and Transfer (TOT).

A fundamental characteristic of these models is the concept of the "right to use", whereby the private sector's ability to monetise the asset is confined to a specified period. Consequently, if the concession is terminated before the end of its agreed term, the developer is entitled to compensation from the statutory authority in the form of a "termination payment". To enhance the bankability of such concession agreements, the termination payment is almost invariably linked to the "debt due" to the lenders, ensuring that outstanding financial obligations are accounted for in the event of early termination.

An Example of a PPP Project From a Judgement of the Indian Supreme Court[42]

In 2008, Haryana Shehri Vikas Pradhikaran ("HSVP"), the second respondent, issued a Request for Qualification and Request for Proposal ("RFQ/RFP") for developing a metro rail link from Delhi Metro Sikanderpur Station on MG Road to NH-8 ("Project No1"). A Consortium Agreement was entered into on 1 December 2008 between IL&FS Rail Limited ("IRL"), IL&FS Transportation Networks Limited ("ITNL") and DLF Metro Limited in which IRL was identified as the lead member of the consortium. HSVP accepted the bid submitted by the consortium and issued a letter of award of 16 July 2009, subject to the condition that a concession agreement would be executed within 60 days. Pursuant to the letter of award, the consortium incorporated the first appellant, Rapid MetroRail Gurgaon Limited ("RMGL"), under the Companies Act, 1956 (the "Act of 1956") and requested HSVP to accept RMGL as the entity which would undertake, fulfill and exercise the rights of the consortium under the letter of award. 2 On 9 December 2009, HSVP entered into a Concession Agreement with RMGL for the execution of Project No 1 on a design, build, finance, operate and transfer basis. HSVP granted a concession to RMGL for a period of 99 years from the effective date, including the exclusive right, license and authority during the subsistence of the Concession Agreement to implement and operate Project No 1.

A distinguishing feature of project finance is that the revenues generated by the project, once operational, are used to cover its operational costs, repay the financiers, and provide returns to the equity investors. The primary recourse for lenders is the cash flow generated by the project and the project's assets rather than any external assets of the project's equity investors, which makes project finance a form of "non-recourse" or "limited recourse" financing.

42 See Rapid MetroRail Gurgaon Limited Etc. v Haryana Mass Rapid Transport Corporation Limited & Ors Civil Appeals Nos. 925–926 of 2021 at [1].

It is structured around the projected cash flows rather than relying on the value of the assets themselves, meaning that success hinges on the project's ability to generate sufficient income to service its debt.

The borrower in a project finance transaction is typically a special purpose vehicle (**SPV**) created solely for the purpose of owning and operating the project.[43] The SPV has no significant assets other than those directly linked to the project, and at the time debt is advanced, these assets usually consist of contractual rights under various project documents rather than tangible assets. A high debt-to-equity ratio is another hallmark of project finance transactions, with lenders often financing a large proportion of the project's total cost.

Project sponsors, who are typically equity investors in the borrower SPV, may also be parties to key project contracts, such as construction, operations, and offtake agreements. These entities often have a dual interest in the project – seeking returns on their equity investment and, potentially, profits from their involvement in the project's operational contracts. This dual role can create an implicit conflict of interest, as sponsors balance the interests of the project's profitability against their own returns from contractual fees.

An Example of a Project Finance Transaction From a Privy Council Judgement[44]

In January 1997, the Government of Grenada ("the Government") entered into a Memorandum of Understanding with ICSL and the Bank ("the MOU") by which it engaged ICSL to implement and manage the Project via a special purpose development company, which would hold the land on which the stadium was to be constructed and would borrow the moneys needed for carrying out the Project, with financing arranged by the Bank. NS was then incorporated as the special purpose development company. . . .

A suite of detailed agreements was negotiated and put in place on 15 May 1997 to regulate the relevant relationships between the Government, ICS, NS and the Bank, comprising (i) an agreement between the Government, ICS, NS and the Bank, whereby ICS agreed to implement the Project and construct the stadium using finance arranged by the Bank under the Facility Agreement and provided via NS ("the Development Agreement"), (ii) the Facility Agreement, whereby the Bank agreed to arrange funding of the order of US$23m for the Project by lending funds to NS against notes issued by NS, which were placed with investors, and (iii) an agreement between NS and ICS, under which ICS agreed to act as developer to construct the stadium for US$23m ("the Main Construction Contract"). . . .

The MOU, the Development Agreement, the Facility Agreement and the Main Construction Contract contemplated that NS would operate as the special purpose development company for the Project, in that it was established as a company with no other business than to implement the Project, it would be the recipient of the moneys for the Project provided under the Facility Agreement and it would pay out from those moneys sums due to contractors. In this way, the role of NS provided a degree of security for contractors working on the Project, since the funding stream and its operations were entirely dedicated to the Project. Contractors did not have to take the credit risk associated with an operating company carrying on general business activities across a number of projects (which might go wrong and give rise to liabilities) and mixing up its moneys in a general fund available to meet all and any liabilities it might incur.

The site for the Project was vested in NS. Once constructed, the stadium was to be leased to the Government. The site was mortgaged to the Bank as security for the funds advanced to NS under the

43 Böttcher, J. (ed.), *Green Banking: Realizing Renewable Energy Projects* (De Gruyter Oldenbour, 2020), p. 273.
44 National Stadium Project (Grenada) Corp. v NH International (Caribbean) Ltd (Trinidad and Tobago) [2020] UKPC 25.

Facility Agreement. Under the terms of the Development Agreement, if the Government paid off the sums due from NS under the Facility Agreement, the site (with the stadium) would be vested in the Government.[45]

3.1 A Project Finance Loan Facility

The types of assets that are funded through project finance require substantial capital investment and have long operational lives, making the associated financing agreements both intricate and of extended duration. A key feature of project finance is that it is typically structured as a secured non-recourse facility, meaning the repayment of the loan is reliant solely on the revenue generated by the project once it becomes operational. As a result, project finance facility agreements tend to include far more detailed provisions than a conventional corporate loan, particularly around the construction (if applicable) and operation of the assets, rather than focusing on the borrower's balance sheet or business plan.

A project finance facility can be structured as either a bilateral[46] or syndicated facility. However, due to the long tenors and the potential scale of these projects, a syndicated facility is usually the preferred option, even when only a single lender is involved at the outset.

An example of such a facility is provided by case law:

> *This appeal raises a short point of construction of a loan facility agreement dated 4 February 2011 ("the Facility") between various lenders, including the appellants (whom I will call "the Lenders") and the respondent borrower ("the Borrower"). The Facility was for the loan of up to US$500 million to be used to finance the development of phase 1 of the Tonkolili iron ore project in Sierra Leone. Sums advanced under the Facility were to be repaid in 10 monthly instalments between 30 April 2012 and the final repayment date. The interest rate fixed by the terms of the Facility was 11.50%, which would have reflected the risk involved in the project.*[47]

Project finance transactions may involve multiple tranches of funding, each with its own terms and conditions. Given the non-recourse nature of the financing, risk allocation is a central element of any project finance deal, influencing the terms of the finance documents. Such risks are typically identified early in a detailed term sheet or information memorandum,[48] which outlines the key terms and conditions agreed upon by the project sponsor and the lenders.

Common risks in project finance include construction delays, operational inefficiencies, market fluctuations in demand for the project's output (offtake risk), and political or regulatory risks.

45 Per Lord Birggs and Lord Sales in National Stadium Project (Grenada) Corp. v NH International (Caribbean) Ltd (Trinidad and Tobago) [2020] UKPC 25 at [3] to [6].

46 "*The funding arrangement to be implemented under the Facility Agreement was that the Bank would raise money for the Project by arranging a bond issue by NS to private investors and would act as designated Trustee on the investors' behalf in relation to enforcement of the bonds. In anticipation of the issue of bonds by NS, the Bank would advance moneys to NS. This would be done either by providing the moneys directly to NS by way of an ordinary loan, achieved by showing the moneys as a credit in an account of NS with the Bank for NS to use later, or by paying moneys directly to a contractor on the Project on behalf of NS, ie in accordance with NS's instructions . . ., thereby achieving the same result as if the Bank had first provided the money to NS as a loan and NS had itself paid the contractor*". Per Lord Birggs and Lord Sales in *National Stadium Project (Grenada) Corp. v NH International (Caribbean) Ltd (Trinidad and Tobago)* [2020] UKPC 25 at [39].

47 Per Lord Justice Aikens in *BMA Special Opportunity Hub Fund Ltd. & Ors v African Minerals Finance Ltd* [2013] EWCA Civ 416 at [1].

48 Wood, P., *Project Finance, Securitisations and Subordinated Debt* (Sweet & Maxwell, 2019) at [1-003].

3.2 Project Finance Facility Agreement: Main Provisions

A project finance facility agreement is a tailored document.[49] A typical starting point for crafting a project finance facility agreement may involve using a template from the LMA, such as the leveraged finance template or the template for developing markets. However, even when using such a template, significant adaptation will be required to align with the specifics and scale of the project.

A crucial aspect of project finance is the definition and interpretation of key terms, which must remain consistent across the suite of documents supporting the transaction, including security agreements, direct agreements, and any intercreditor arrangements. Given the interconnected nature of these documents, a common framework of definitions is essential for clarity and coherence across the project finance transaction.[50]

Conditions for utilisation of the loan will also be far more extensive in a project finance facility than in a standard corporate loan. The borrower must satisfy numerous conditions precedent before any funds are disbursed, which may include fulfilling construction milestones, obtaining regulatory approvals, or securing key project agreements. These conditions provide lenders with assurances that the project is on track and capable of generating the revenues required to service the loan once operational.

Moreover, the covenants in a project finance facility are quite comprehensive and require the borrower to adhere to a strict set of operational and financial commitments, including detailed reporting on the project's progress, compliance with budgets, and maintaining specific financial ratios. Lenders will often impose specific coverage ratios to monitor the project's ability to generate sufficient revenue to meet its obligations under the facility agreement.

The facility agreement will also address how the project's cash flows are managed. Lenders typically require the borrower to establish secured accounts to ensure that all project revenues are applied in an agreed order of priority, which may include funding operating expenses, making debt service payments, and distributing residual cash to equity investors. The management of these accounts is critical in non-recourse project finance transactions, where lenders rely on the project's revenue stream for repayment.

In cases where the project involves a construction phase, lenders often appoint an independent engineer or project monitor to oversee the progress of the construction, approve funding requests, and certify the completion of milestones. This independent oversight is key to ensuring that the project stays on schedule and within budget, reducing the risk of delays or cost overruns.[51]

49 Vinter, G., Price, G. and Lee, D., *Project Finance* (Sweet & Maxwell, 2013) at [7-004].

50 Please note that "*There has been considerable judicial exposition of these principles by the House of Lords and the Supreme Court in recent years. There is no point in my going over the same ground again at any length. The court's job is to discern the intention of the parties, objectively speaking, from the words used in the commercial document, in the relevant context and against the factual background in which the document was created. The starting point is the wording of the document itself and the principle that the commercial parties who agreed the wording intended the words used to mean what they say in setting out the parties' respective rights and obligations. If there are two possible constructions of the document a court is entitled to prefer the construction which is more consistent with 'business common sense,' if that can be ascertained. However, I would agree with the statements of Briggs J, in Jackson v Dear, first, that 'commercial common sense' is not to be elevated to an overriding criterion of construction and, secondly, that the parties should not be subjected to '. . . the individual judge's own notions of what might have been the sensible solution to the parties' conundrum'. I would add, still less should the issue of construction be determined by what seems like 'commercial common sense' from the point of view of one of the parties to the contract*", per Lord Justice Aikens in *BMA Special Opportunity Hub Fund Ltd. & Ors v African Minerals Finance Ltd* [2013] EWCA Civ 416 at [24].

51 Vinter, G., Price, G. and Lee, D., *Project Finance* (Sweet & Maxwell, 2013) at [5-003].

Events of default in project finance facility agreements are quite detailed. These provisions must account for a wide range of risks, including construction delays, operational failures, regulatory changes, or breaches of key project agreements. The events of default give the lenders the right to exercise remedies, including accelerating the loan or enforcing security if the project is in jeopardy.

Given the long tenor of project finance facilities, lenders will also require the ability to transfer their loan commitments to other financial institutions.

3.3 Project Finance Facility Agreement: The Schedules

A project finance facility agreement, like other facility agreements, typically includes several key schedules that are essential to its structure and function. One of the most important schedules is the list of conditions precedent, which outlines the requirements the borrower must satisfy before any funds are advanced. These conditions are usually divided into two categories: those that apply to the first drawdown and those that must be met for any subsequent drawdowns. The conditions precedent are crucial in protecting the lenders' interests by ensuring that all necessary approvals, documentation, and other preconditions are fulfilled before the loan proceeds are disbursed.

Another vital schedule is the required insurance schedule, which details the types and amounts of insurance coverage that the lenders will require the borrower to maintain. This coverage helps mitigate the risks associated with the project, particularly during its construction and operational phases.[52]

Hedging is another common feature of project finance transactions, particularly when there is a need to manage interest rate, currency, or commodity price risks.[53] The details of the hedging arrangements, which are often necessary to ensure the project's financial stability, are typically included in a dedicated schedule. These hedging arrangements are usually documented using standard ISDA® documentation, which includes an ISDA® Master Agreement, a Schedule to the ISDA® Master Agreement, and one or more confirmations to reflect the specific terms of the hedging strategy.[54]

In addition to these financial and risk management provisions, a project finance facility agreement will typically include a schedule for the compliance certificate. The borrower is required to periodically provide this certificate to the agent, confirming its compliance with the terms of the facility agreement. A standard form of compliance certificate is often included in the agreement as a template, which can be tailored to meet the specific needs of the transaction.

52 "*The relevant background here is that the parties to this contract were commercial entities who employed experienced commercial lawyers to negotiate the terms in very great detail over a period of three months. The contract terms are elaborate and clearly intended to be precise and cover as many eventualities as could be foreseen. The sum involved in the transaction which was governed by the Facility was very large. The project itself was a risky one. At the time the Facility was concluded no production had been started at the Tonkolili iron ore project site, although it was contemplated that production would be under way by November 2011. The Facility was a short term one of only 2 years. Repayments of principal and interest were to be made only in the second year after the Closing Date*", per Lord Justice Aikens in *BMA Special Opportunity Hub Fund Ltd. & Ors v African Minerals Finance Ltd* [2013] EWCA Civ 416 at [25].

53 Vinter, G., Price, G. and Lee, D., *Project Finance* (Sweet & Maxwell, 2013) at [3-014].

54 Vinter, G., Price, G. and Lee, D., *Project Finance* (Sweet & Maxwell, 2013) at [7-014].

3.4 Specialist Project Finance Structures

Specialist project finance facilities often involve unique financing structures or cross-border elements. Many of these facilities pertain to projects located in overseas jurisdictions or sectors like oil, gas, and other commodity-based ventures. These facilities demand careful structuring to account for the legal, regulatory, and commercial challenges inherent in such transactions.

One of the more common specialised structures in project finance is reserve-based lending. This type of financing is frequently used for oil, gas, and commodity-based projects. It is structured as a revolving borrowing base facility, which means the facility's size expands or contracts based on the value of the underlying reserves or collateral. This flexibility is essential in sectors where commodity prices fluctuate, and the value of reserves can vary significantly over time.

Another key component of specialised project finance is the involvement of export credit agencies (ECAs). ECAs play a critical role in many cross-border projects, particularly in emerging markets where political and commercial risks may be heightened.[55] ECAs provide guarantees or insurance to mitigate the risks associated with financing projects in these jurisdictions, making it easier for lenders to extend credit. Their participation can help offset political risks, such as expropriation or changes in law, and provide additional comfort to lenders who may be reluctant to participate in projects in less stable markets.[56] Upon the involvement of an ECA, additional specific requirements often may need to be reflected in the facility agreement, particularly with respect to the terms of repayment and risk allocation.

ESG issues have become relevant in project finance, particularly for projects that are expected to meet specific sustainability or environmental standards. Compliance with these principles may influence the terms of the facility agreement, particularly with respect to reporting obligations, use of proceeds, and performance metrics that track ESG goals.

Cross-border elements are another crucial consideration in project finance transactions, as many projects involve parties or assets located in different jurisdictions. When a project has cross-border aspects, the facility agreement must account for additional legal complexities. For example, parties may need to include clauses that waive sovereign immunity for state-owned counterparties, or they may need to establish offshore accounts to mitigate risks associated with currency controls, unstable banking systems, or substantial exchange risks.[57]

55 For an example of risk faced by a lender in a less than stable jurisdiction: "*Until June 1991 Utexafrica succeeded in making most of the payments required under the Investment Agreement. However, its business was disrupted by the civil unrest which broke out in September of that year and which has continued to plague the country to a greater or lesser degree ever since. Utexafrica's ability to export goods was severely curtailed and apart from two relatively small payments in February 1992 and July 1996 it subsequently failed to meet its obligations under the Investment Agreement. Texaf was unable to purchase goods from Utexafrica to provide the hard currency needed to meet the payments of principal and interest; moreover, it failed to pay sufficient funds into the retention account to enable Utexafrica's obligations to be satisfied. In summary, therefore, nothing has been paid in respect of the instalments of principal which should have been repaid over the six and a half years from June 1992 to December 1998 and virtually nothing in respect of interest accruing due since June 1991*". Per Mr Justice Moore-Bick in *International Finance Corporation v Utexafrica S.P.R.L.* [2001] EWHC 508 (Comm) at [5].

56 Vinter, G., Price, G. and Lee, D., *Project Finance* (Sweet & Maxwell, 2013) at [14-003].

57 For an attempt to mitigate exchange risk: "*Utexafrica also sought the support of the Government of Zaire. In October 1993 the government agreed in principle to guarantee the loan and in June 1994 Utexafrica obtained the government's agreement to undertake the exchange risk, subject to the agreement of IFC as lender. The broad effect of this would have been to enable part of the loan to be paid by Utexafrica in local currency. A meeting was held in Washington in June 1994 to put this proposal to IFC, but it came to nothing because IFC's own constitution prevented it from entering into agreements with governments. The note of that meeting indicates that Mr. Pasquier said that some steps might be taken to ease the exchange of local currency into hard currency at a later date when the political situation had improved and debtors could resume payments*". Per Mr Justice Moore-Bick in *International Finance Corporation v Utexafrica S.P.R.L.* [2001] EWHC 508 (Comm) at [5].

3.5 Security in Project Finance

In project finance, the lenders primarily focus on the project's cash flow and its ability to service the debt. While the project company itself will typically have limited resources, the lenders will still require security over the company's assets. This security ensures that the lenders can control the project and protect it from claims by other creditors if problems arise. The principal assets over which lenders will want to take security typically include the concession agreement or other authorisations to build and operate the project, any sales, offtake, throughput, or other revenue-generating agreements along with the revenues they produce, the project company's accounts and cash flows, subcontracts like construction agreements and operation and maintenance (O&M)[58] agreements (along with performance bonds tied to them), insurance contracts, and in some cases, the land on which the project is situated (if owned or leased by the project company).

In most project finance transactions, security would be held in favour of a security trustee.

When the project company is an SPV, lenders will want to take security over all of its assets to ensure priority over other creditors. If the project company is not an SPV, the lenders will focus on ensuring the relevant assets are protected from claims by other creditors. In addition to securing the project company's assets, lenders will also require security over the shares of the project company, which are often provided by the project sponsors and any intervening entities within the project's corporate structure. This approach ensures comprehensive control of the project's assets and shields them from external interference.[59]

Lenders typically bolster their position with additional forms of support. These include direct agreements, which give lenders step-in rights in relation to key project contracts, and sponsor support, which might take the form of a sponsor support agreement or a guarantee from the project sponsor. These guarantees might be issued with respect to subcontracts where the subcontractor is part of the sponsor's group. Other common forms of support include parent company guarantees, bank guarantees, or letters of credit provided by third parties to safeguard the project further. The use of guarantees in this context is essential in mitigating risks associated with the project's contractual framework.

Enforcing security in project finance is not typically motivated by a desire to liquidate assets to repay debt. Project assets, such as incomplete construction sites or contractual rights, may have limited value outside the context of the completed project. Instead, the lenders are focused on isolating the project and its assets from interference by other creditors.[60] This protection enables lenders to step into the shoes of the project company and take control of the project, allowing them to decide how best to complete it if anything goes wrong.

4 LEGAL OPINIONS

In banking and project finance transactions, lenders typically require legal opinions to confirm that the legal effect of a lending transaction aligns with their expectations. These opinions also highlight potential risks that the lender and other addressees, such as hedging counterparties, should assess further. Typically, a legal opinion is provided by the lender's lawyers and addressed directly to the lender.[61]

58 These agreements ensure the ongoing functionality and upkeep of a project, thereby securing the interests of financiers who have invested substantial resources.
59 Wood, P., *Project Finance, Securitisations and Subordinated Debt* (Sweet & Maxwell, 2019) at [5-028].
60 Vinter, G., Price, G. and Lee, D., *Project Finance* (Sweet & Maxwell, 2013) at [12-014].
61 Wood, P., *International Loans, Bonds, Guarantees and Legal Opinions* (Sweet & Maxwell, 2019), Chapter 24.

4.1 Nature of a Legal Opinion

A legal opinion is a formal letter issued by a lawyer or law firm that provides a legal analysis or conclusions about a specific transaction or matter. Its primary purpose is to inform the addressee of the legal implications and risks associated[62] with a transaction (albeit they are not a substitute for broader legal advice) and to provide assurance on the ability of a party to enter into and perform its obligations under an agreement. Legal opinions often serve as a critical component of finance transactions, where the delivery of such an opinion is a common condition precedent to the advance of a loan or the closing of a deal.

In banking transactions, legal opinions tend to follow a standardised format, addressing key legal issues relevant to the transaction. They will focus on whether transaction documents bind the borrower and other obligors (such as third-party security providers or guarantors) and whether they will be enforceable against them. Other topics commonly addressed include tax implications, such as the absence of stamp duty on the transaction documents and the validity of the governing law and jurisdiction clauses.

When a transaction involves foreign obligors or assets located in other jurisdictions, a foreign legal opinion will also be necessary to cover legal issues relevant to those jurisdictions. In such cases, both foreign and English legal opinions may be required, particularly where English law governs a transaction involving foreign parties or assets. In such instances, care must be taken to ensure that all legal aspects are adequately covered by the various opinions.[63]

It is well established that a party is entitled to rely on the legal advice provided by a reputable foreign law firm without needing to scrutinise the reasoning behind that opinion, as confirmed in *Haugesund Kommune v Depfa ACS Bank* [2009] EWHC 2227 (Comm). This case underscores the weight and credibility of foreign legal opinions in international transactions, reinforcing their significance in cross-border finance deals.

A formal legal opinion should not be confused with other types of legal communications, such as letters of legal advice, reasoned opinions, legal reports, or reports on title.

A letter of legal advice typically addresses a specific point of law, offering guidance or clarification on a legal matter without providing a formal legal conclusion about a transaction. In contrast, a reasoned opinion not only states legal conclusions but also explains the legal analysis behind them, often including detailed qualifications.[64] Reasoned opinions may also be necessary to confirm that a transaction qualifies as a "true sale", a key issue in certain finance structures.[65] For example, in a securitisation, a reasoned opinion might verify that the assets transferred as part of the transaction are legally isolated from the seller's balance sheet, a process known as a true sale. Similarly, a legal report provides a detailed analysis of specific terms within a document, often required as part of due diligence when assessing the legal implications of contractual terms. This type of report focuses on the provisions of a particular document and their potential impact on the transaction rather than offering broader legal conclusions. Lastly, a report on title is distinct from a formal legal opinion, as it focuses on the legal status of real property that is subject to a transaction, such as when the property

62 "*The degree of risk (looked at through the eyes of the reasonably competent solicitor) will dictate the nature of the warning that the client should be given, although other relevant factors for the solicitor to consider and bring to the client's attention in relation to a tax avoidance scheme of this kind will be the likelihood of a challenge to the scheme by the Revenue and the degree of judicial and other scrutiny which the scheme will receive*", per Lord Justice Patten in *Barker v Baxendale Walker Solicitors (a firm) & Anor* [2017] EWCA Civ 2056 at [91].

63 Adams, D., *Banking and Capital Markets* (College of Law Publishing, 2024) at [16.1].

64 Wood, P., *International Loans, Bonds, Guarantees and Legal Opinions* (Sweet & Maxwell, 2019), Chapter 26.

65 Wood, P., *Project Finance, Securitisations and Subordinated Debt* (Sweet & Maxwell, 2019) at [5-077].

is being mortgaged to a lender, and it assesses ownership, encumbrances, and any other issues affecting the property that might impact the lender's security interest.

Each of these forms of legal communication serves a specific purpose and must be distinguished from a formal legal opinion, which is generally required to express binding legal conclusions on the enforceability or legality of the transaction as a whole.

A legal opinion is typically governed by and construed in accordance with the laws of the relevant jurisdiction, such as the laws of England and Wales, as of the date of issuance. This means that the legal conclusions and analyses contained within the opinion are based on the state of the law in that jurisdiction at the time the opinion is issued. It is important to note that laws can evolve or be subject to reinterpretation by the courts, so the opinion reflects the legal position at the specified time.

Liability for a legal opinion arises if the opinion is negligently provided, potentially making the law firm liable to the addressee.[66] However, liability does not automatically follow if the opinion diverges from a subsequent court decision. Law firms typically aim to mitigate liability risks when issuing legal opinions. A common strategy involves stipulating within the opinion that reliance is limited to the original addressee, preventing subsequent parties, such as assignees, from relying on it. Furthermore, if the opinion is disclosed to other parties, such as rating agencies, the opinion will often specify that these parties are not entitled to rely on it. This approach is designed to narrow the law firm's exposure to liability.

Opinion's Liability in the US

According to Section 52 of the Restatement (Third) of the Law Governing Lawyers (2000), the duty of care imposed on legal counsel requires competence and diligence comparable to that expected of attorneys operating in similar circumstances. This standard aligns with the principle of customary practice and imposes a duty of

66 *"In this case, it is not alleged that the Respondents were negligent to take the view of the construction of section 28(4) that they appear to have done. It is accepted that a reasonably competent solicitor with the Respondents' expertise could have done so. The question is whether in the light of all the circumstances no reasonably competent solicitor in the position of the Respondents would have failed to give the specific warning that there was a significant risk that the EBT arrangement would fail to be tax effective because of the post-death exclusion construction. This is the way in which Mr Barker's ground of appeal is founded and it seems to me that it follows that the usual test applies when determining the scope of the solicitor's duty and whether it has been breached. It is important to appreciate that the court is considering what advice ought to have been given by the reasonably competent practitioner in the particular factual circumstances at the time. Of course, the advice which a reasonably competent solicitor would give in the circumstances turns substantially upon the view that he could take of the provision on which it turns. It is also dependent upon whether contrary arguments as to construction are of sufficient significance to require specific mention when taken with the degree of risk inherent in the circumstances and the importance in those circumstances of a balanced view of the provision. As Salmon LJ noted in Dixie v Parsons the question turns in part upon the likelihood or otherwise of a dispute. It seems to me that the following principles are likely to apply: (i) The question of whether a solicitor is in breach of a duty to explain the risk that a court may come to a different interpretation from that which he advises is correct is highly fact sensitive: (Queen Elizabeth, Hermann, Balogun and Levicom cases); (ii) If the construction of the provision is clear, it is very likely that whatever the circumstances, the threshold of "significant risk" will not be met and it will not be necessary to caveat the advice given and explain the risks involved; (iii) However, depending on the circumstances, it is perfectly possible to be correct about the construction of a provision or, at least, not negligent in that regard, but nevertheless to be under a duty to point out the risks involved and to have been negligent in not having done so (Levicom and Balogun cases); (iv) It is more likely that there will be a duty to point out the risks, or to put the matter another way, that a reasonably competent solicitor would not fail to point them out when advising, if litigation is already on foot or the point has already been taken, although this need not necessarily be the case (the Queen Elizabeth case to be compared with Balogun); and (v) The issue is not one of percentages or whether opposing possible constructions are 'finely balanced' but is more nuanced"*, per Lady Justice Asplin in *Barker v Baxendale Walker Solicitors (a firm) & Anor* [2017] EWCA Civ 2056 at [59] to [61].

reasonableness based on the specific circumstances of the case. An opinion giver may be held liable to a third-party opinion recipient if an opinion is negligently provided.[67]

An aggrieved lender may pursue legal action against the borrower's counsel for a legal opinion on several grounds, including fraudulent or negligent misrepresentation, failure to exercise due care in providing the opinion (which constitutes a tortious act), professional malpractice for non-compliance with professional rules governing opinions issued to third parties, or violations of statutory provisions, such as the anti-fraud rules under federal securities laws.

4.2 Structure of a Standard Legal Opinion

A formal legal opinion generally follows a structured and standardised format, allowing the addressee to easily navigate and assess its content. The primary sections of a legal opinion typically include background, definitions, documents examined, enquiries made, assumptions, opinion confirmations, qualifications, and reliance. Each of these sections serves a specific purpose in clarifying the legal analysis and conclusions presented in the opinion.[68]

The **background** section outlines the role of the opinion provider in the transaction, specifying the extent of their involvement and any relevant details about their relationship with the parties or the transaction. This sets the context for the opinion and identifies the scope of the provider's engagement.

Definitions are often included to clarify specific terms used throughout the opinion. This ensures that key legal and technical terms are consistently interpreted by the addressee.

The **documents examined** section lists the transaction documents and any other pertinent documents that were reviewed in forming the opinion, such as the constitutional documents of the obligor. This transparency allows the addressee to understand the basis of the legal conclusions.

In preparing a legal opinion, certain **enquiries** are typically conducted, such as searches at Companies House or other relevant registries. This section details those enquiries, demonstrating the thoroughness of the fact-gathering process, which contributes to the reliability of the opinion.

The **assumptions** section deals with matters that the opinion provider cannot confirm directly, often because they involve facts outside the provider's control or expertise. Commonly, these assumptions cover factual matters, which are excluded from the scope of the opinion.[69] For example, the opinion provider may assume that the documents presented

67 *Prudential Insurance Co. v Dewey Ballantine*, 590 N.Y.S. 2d 831, 605 N.E. 2d 318 (1992).

68 Adams, D., *Banking and Capital Markets* (College of Law Publishing, 2024) at [16.3].

69 "*Each of the legal advisers delivered a formal opinion addressed to BNPP, Citicorp and Golden Belt, confirming the Sukuk to be valid and enforceable under the relevant law. As is standard practice, the opinions were stated to be subject to certain assumptions. The opinion by Norton Rose dealt only with the English law Transaction Documents. It did not even mention the Promissory Note which was not such a document. The assumptions on which the opinion was expressly based included that Saad and Mr Al-Sanea had capacity to execute the English law Transaction Documents, that they had taken all necessary action to authorise such execution, and that they had duly executed each such document.* e *Alliance opinion dealt with, but was not limited to, the Promissory Note. The assumptions on which it was based included that the documents submitted to The Alliance were authentic and true and that all signatures were genuine. Accordingly, the questions whether the signature on the Promissory Note was valid and whether it had been properly executed were not addressed in any of the formal legal opinions. None of the advisers expressed any opinion whether the documents had been validly executed. The legal opinions, therefore, provided no comfort or assurance as to these matters and could not have been understood as doing so. However, as the full list of stated assumptions makes clear, these were not the only questions outside the scope of the legal*

are genuine, signatures are valid, or parties have fulfilled their obligations as warranted in the transaction documents. These assumptions are essential for limiting the opinion provider's liability while ensuring that the opinion can still be delivered on time.[70]

The **opinion confirmations** section contains the legal conclusions, which are typically confined to specific questions of law, not fact. These confirmations answer whether the transaction documents create valid and binding obligations, if the obligors have the capacity to enter into the transaction, and if the documents comply with applicable law. The confirmations provide clarity on the legal status of the transaction and its enforceability.

Qualifications introduce any legal limitations or factors that might affect the conclusions of the opinion. For instance, insolvency laws may impact the enforceability of obligations. This section ensures that the addressee is aware of any circumstances under which the legal conclusions might be subject to modification or challenge.

Finally, the section concerning **who may rely on the opinion** is critical. The opinion will specify which parties are entitled to rely on its conclusions, typically naming the original addressees, such as the lender syndicate, arranger, agent, or security trustee, in cases involving syndicated loans. Reliance is generally restricted to those addressees, and it is common for the opinion to limit reliance by future parties, such as assignees or transferees unless specifically addressed. In some cases, law firms may agree to extend the opinion's reliance to lenders who join the syndicate within a specified timeframe during the primary syndication period, generally up to six months after the signing of the transaction. However, beyond this period, firms usually resist extending reliance to future parties, such as assignees or transferees of the original lenders, and these parties are typically excluded from relying on the opinion.[71]

The opinion should be self-contained, without reliance on external explanations, ensuring that all relevant legal conclusions, assumptions, and qualifications are easily accessible within the document.

4.3 Purpose and Scope of a Legal Opinion

A legal opinion provides specific conclusions of law regarding a party's ability to enter into and perform its obligations under a document, as well as the legal effect of that document. However, it is not a general endorsement of the transaction's overall soundness. The primary purposes of a legal opinion are to state legal conclusions about the capacity of a party to enter into and fulfil its obligations, to inform the addressee about the legal impact of the relevant document, and to identify any legal risks that may require further evaluation. If a significant issue is identified, the transaction might need to be restructured, or the parties may choose not to proceed.

The scope of a legal opinion typically focuses on specific legal issues rather than matters of fact. While the scope will depend on the nature of the transaction and the addressee's requirements, legal opinions generally cover key areas such as the capacity and authority of the parties involved, confirming that an entity is properly incorporated, validly existing, and has the requisite corporate power and authority to enter into the transaction. The opinion will also address whether the relevant documents create legal, valid, binding, and enforceable

opinions". Per Mr Justice Males in *Golden Belt 1 Sukuk Company BSC(c) v BNP Paribas* [2017] EWHC 3182 (Comm) at [53].

70 Wood, P., *International Loans, Bonds, Guarantees and Legal Opinions* (Sweet & Maxwell, 2019), Chapter 25.

71 Wood, P., *International Loans, Bonds, Guarantees and Legal Opinions* (Sweet & Maxwell, 2019), Chapter 26.

obligations.[72] It may additionally cover tax matters, such as the absence of stamp duty, and the governing law and jurisdiction, confirming that the law chosen to govern the documents is a valid choice and that submission to a particular jurisdiction's courts is binding.

4.4 US Legal Opinions in Loan Transactions

In New York, borrower's counsel opinions are typically expected to address the laws of the State of New York, which includes coverage of the Uniform Commercial Code (UCC) of New York, especially where the loan in question is secured. In addition to the application of state law, borrower's counsel is also expected to opine on relevant US federal laws that, in the counsel's experience, customarily apply to finance transactions of the type contemplated by the transaction documents. Collectively, these applicable laws are referred to as the "Covered Law".[73]

When the transaction involves loan parties that are incorporated or organised in the State of Delaware, borrower's New York counsel is generally required to extend their opinion to include certain Delaware-specific laws as part of the Covered Law. These typically include the General Corporation Law of Delaware,[74] the UCC of Delaware, the Delaware Limited Liability Company Act,[75] and the Delaware Revised Uniform Limited Partnership Act.[76]

In the preparation and issuance of third-party legal opinions, both the opinion giver and the counsel representing the opinion recipient typically rely on well-established resources that reflect customary practice and prevailing legal standards. These resources serve as authoritative references, guiding the content, procedures, and legal principles that underpin opinion letters in commercial transactions.

One such key resource is *Laws Commonly Excluded from the Coverage of Third-Party Legal Opinions in U.S. Commercial Loan Transactions* (76 Bus. Law. 889 (2021)), which delineates the legal matters typically excluded from coverage in legal opinions for US commercial loan transactions.[77]

The *TriBar Opinion Committee, Third-Party "Closing" Opinions* (53 Bus. Law. 591 (1998)) remains a fundamental resource for understanding the essential components of legal opinions, the due diligence required, and the importance of precision and clarity in drafting. Similarly, the *ABA Guidelines for the Preparation of Closing Opinions* (57 Bus. Law. 875 (2002)) offer comprehensive guidance on the process of preparing and delivering legal opinions, including examples and explanations of common formulations. Ethical considerations are governed by the *ABA Model Rules of Professional Conduct* (2002), with Rule 2.3 regulating an attorney's responsibilities when providing information to third parties on behalf of a client.[78]

Additionally, legal opinions on security interests under Article 9 of the UCC are addressed in the *TriBar Opinion Committee, UCC Security Interest Opinions – Revised Article 9* (58 Bus. Law. 1450 (2003)), which provides detailed guidance on the structuring and interpretation of

72 Wood, P., *Comparative Law of Security Interests and Title Finance* (Sweet & Maxwell, 2019) at [43-001].
73 Adams, D., *Banking and Capital Markets* (College of Law Publishing, 2024) at [16.7].
74 It can be found in Chapter 15 6 of Title 6 of the Delaware Code.
75 Delaware statutes governing limited liability companies (LLCs) which can be found in Chapter 18 of Title 6 of the Delaware Code.
76 It can be found in Chapters 1, 5, and 6 of Title 8 of the Delaware Code.
77 Additionally, the *Statement of Opinion Practices* (74 Bus. Law. 807 (2019)), issued by the Committee on Legal Opinions of the ABA Section of Business Law, provides an updated framework for contemporary opinion practice, replacing the earlier *Legal Opinion Principles*.
78 Other relevant provisions include Rules 1.2, 1.2(d), 1.6, and 4.1, which address the scope of representation, the prohibition on assisting in fraudulent activities, confidentiality obligations, and the duty of truthfulness in statements to third parties.

opinions in this area. Collectively, these resources form the foundation for third-party legal opinion practice, ensuring consistency, clarity, and adherence to professional standards.[79]

5 CONCLUSION

Chapter 13 has considered the implications of ESG factors in financial transactions. The principles underpinning sustainability-linked loans, as well as their alignment with broader ESG goals, have been considered. These elements mark an important development in how financial institutions respond to the challenges of climate change and social responsibility.

The use of derivatives, loan agreements within project finance, and legal opinions in the context of financing arrangements have then been considered. Together, these topics form the cornerstone of managing risk, structuring complex transactions, and ensuring legal certainty in international banking and finance.

The section on derivatives demonstrated their crucial role in mitigating risks in loan transactions. By employing financial instruments such as interest rates and currency swaps, parties to a loan can protect themselves against market fluctuations, thereby stabilising cash flows and providing greater predictability in servicing debt. The use of credit default swaps and structured derivatives in loan transactions provides lenders with the flexibility to manage credit risk concentration, meet regulatory obligations, and optimise their capital structures.

The examination of loan agreements in project finance transactions highlighted the unique challenges and complexities of this specialised area of finance. Project finance requires a bespoke approach, with agreements that reflect the specific risks associated with capital-intensive, long-term projects. Unlike standard corporate loans, project finance transactions are structured around the project's revenue generation capabilities, necessitating detailed provisions for repayment, prepayment, and security arrangements.

The discussion on legal opinions underscored their vital importance in providing legal assurances to lenders and other parties in financing transactions. Legal opinions serve to confirm the enforceability and validity of the transaction documents, offering crucial reassurance that the legal framework supports the terms of the deal. In this respect, the US approach, particularly under New York law, which is commonly used in international finance, has been addressed.

79 Wood, P., *Comparative Law of Security Interests and Title Finance* (Sweet & Maxwell, 2019) at [58-021].

CHAPTER 14

ALTERNATIVES TO CONVENTIONAL BANK LENDING

OVERVIEW

While traditional bank lending has long served as the foundation of corporate finance, the modern financial landscape has expanded to embrace alternative mechanisms, each tailored to meet diverse and complex capital requirements.

Within this evolution, securitisation, collateralised loan obligations (**CLO**s), Islamic finance, and repurchase agreements (repos) have gained prominence, offering distinct pathways for financing to address the limitations of conventional bank lending. Each of these methods provides distinct advantages in structuring and distributing risk, facilitating liquidity, and catering to a range of regulatory and ethical standards. Securitisation allows the transformation of illiquid assets into tradeable securities, offering capital flexibility and risk dispersion through structured finance techniques. Islamic finance, rooted in Sharia principles, presents a religious, asset-based approach to finance, rejecting interest and speculative transactions while fostering profit-sharing and risk-participation structures. Repos, or repurchase transactions, serve as essential short-term financing arrangements that allow institutions to manage liquidity needs while securing lending with high-quality collateral.

As this chapter will illustrate, the regulatory frameworks governing these instruments have evolved significantly, aiming to enhance transparency, mitigate systemic risk, and protect investors. Securitisation, for example, has faced rigorous scrutiny and standardisation efforts to promote "simple, transparent, and standardised" (STS) structures, particularly within the EU and UK frameworks. Islamic finance, while increasingly standardised, must navigate varied interpretations of Sharia compliance, leading to unique regulatory challenges across jurisdictions. Repos, meanwhile, are governed by frameworks such as the Global Master Repurchase Agreement (**GMRA**), which offers uniformity in an inherently flexible instrument.

By comparing and contrasting these methods, this chapter provides a comprehensive view of how international finance has diversified beyond conventional bank lending, offering new avenues for growth, stability, and risk management.

1 SECURITISATION

The task of defining "securitisation" is complex. Since the term first emerged in the 1970s, participants have continually pushed the limits of product and application innovation, leading to various interpretations and meanings of the term. In academic literature, regulatory frameworks, and case law, securitisation is classified under "structured finance" – a subset of finance focused primarily on risk tranching, achieved through the subordination of different investor classes. Hudson offers a "working definition", describing securitisation as "*the process by which cash receivables or similar assets are grouped together and offered to investors in exchange for capital*".[1]

Although this captures the transactional form, it overlooks essential aspects like credit risk isolation and the intermediary role of a bankruptcy-remote Special Purpose Vehicle (**SPV**).

1 Hudson, A., *The Law of Finance* (Sweet & Maxwell: 2013), p. 1294.

DOI: 10.4324/9781032662220-15

English case law clarifies that while the issuer acts as a "neutral conduit" economically, it is not legally equivalent to such from a regulatory and structural standpoint.[2]

In regulatory terms, The Securitisation Regulations 2024[3] defines securitisation as a

> *transaction or scheme, whereby the credit risk associated with an exposure or a pool of exposures is tranched, having all of the following characteristics – (a) payments in the transaction or scheme are dependent upon the performance of the exposure or of the pool of exposures, (b) the subordination of tranches determines the distribution of losses during the ongoing life of the transaction or scheme, and (c) the transaction or scheme does not create exposures which possess all of the following characteristics – (i) the exposure is to an entity which was created specifically to finance or operate physical assets or is an economically comparable exposure; (ii) the contractual arrangements give the lender a substantial degree of control over the assets and the income that they generate; (iii) the primary source of repayment of the obligation is the income generated by the assets being financed, rather than the independent capacity of a broader commercial enterprise; [whereby] "tranche" means a contractually established segment of the credit risk associated with an exposure or a pool of exposures, where a position in the segment entails a risk of credit loss greater than or less than a position of the same amount in another segment, without taking account of credit protection provided by third parties directly to the holders of positions in the segment or in other segments.*

This layered prioritisation of risk and return is evocatively compared by Barofsky in *Bailout* to "*a bartender pouring a pitcher of beer into mugs lined up on a bar*".[4] In this context, the "*beer in the pitcher*" represents the cash flows in the structured finance transaction.

> *The bartender fills the highest-ranked mug first, then the second highest, and so on down the line until either all . . . mugs are full or the pitcher runs out of beer, which would happen only if a number [of underlying assets stop performing].*[5]

The analogy illustrates how cash flows in securitisation transactions prioritise higher-ranking "mugs" first, ensuring that only when there are performance shortfalls do lower-ranking investors face potential losses.

The focus on tranching underscores the complexity inherent to securitisation but fails to address the role of the SPV as an intermediary between the originator and capital markets, thus narrowing the regulatory view of the transaction.

To capture securitisation's essence, one must focus on the transfer structure to an issuing entity – the SPV – that separates the assets from the originator's insolvency risk, enabling the issuance of securities whose value depends on the assets' performance.[6] Thus, a more precise definition might be that securitisation is a financing tool that allows specific assets or asset pools to be assessed and valued based on their financial performance and credit risk, independently of the originator, through the issuance of securities by an SPV. To refine this definition further, securitisation can be conceptualised as

> *securitisation is a process which allows for intangible assets to acquire, through the intermediation of a special purpose conduit, distinct value and to be employed as collateral and financial support in the process of raising medium-term finance through the issuance of tradeable securities by the conduit.*[7]

In conclusion, this process can be described as *a means of enabling the financial transformation of choses in action, which facilitates its tradability, into transferrable documents of title to which the intangible assets' rights will be attached and whose performance will be dependent upon a segmented exposure through*

2 Hudson, A., *The Law of Finance* (Sweet & Maxwell, 2013) at [44-01].
3 (SI 2024/102).
4 Barofsky, *Bailout: How Washington Abandoned Main Street While Rescuing Wall Street* (Free Press, 2013), p. 83.
5 Barofsky, *Bailout: How Washington Abandoned Main Street While Rescuing Wall Street* (Free Press, 2013), p. 83.
6 Shaw, *International Securitisation* (Macmillan, 1991).
7 Zambelli, M., *The Law of Securitisation in Ireland* (PhD Thesis, Trinity College Dublin, 2017), p. 39.

a bankruptcy remote special purpose entity to the underlying choses in action.[8] As a subsequent step, such physical security can be dematerialised[9] to be traded into an electronic system.[10]

Having identified the nature of securitisation, it is important to understand the legal and regulatory perimeter of this rather complex financial tool. While the Capital Requirements Regulation (**CRR**)[11] has contributed to greater transparency and improved risk assessment in securitisation transactions, Regulation 2017/2402/EU (**EU Securitisation Regulation**)[12] has provided a comprehensive regulatory framework governing securitisation within the European Union (and in the United Kingdom).

A significant aspect of the EU Securitisation Regulation is the introduction of a specific regime for "simple, transparent, and standardised" (STS) securitisations, which aims to establish a general framework for securitisation[13] structures that could be straightforward to assess and understand. The simplicity, standardisation, and transparency criteria[14] define eligible asset classes, transaction structures, and the range of market participants across sectors, aiming to standardise transaction types across the industry.

Repeal and Reform of the UK Securitisation Regulation and Other Retained EU Law in Financial Services

Following the United Kingdom's withdrawal from the European Union, certain EU legislation that had previously applied directly within the UK, alongside domestic legislation implementing EU requirements, was preserved as "retained EU law" under the European Union (Withdrawal) Act 2018 (**EUWA**). The Retained EU Law (Revocation and Reform) Act 2023 establishes a framework for repealing certain retained EU laws while integrating others into UK domestic legislation. While it does not generally repeal retained EU law governing financial services, legislation in this sector, including the

8 Zambelli, M., *The Law of Securitisation in Ireland* (PhD Thesis, Trinity College Dublin, 2017), p. 39.

9 Pursuant to Article 3 of Regulation (EU) No 909/2014 of the European Parliament and of the Council of 23 July 2014 on improving securities settlement in the European Union and on central securities depositories and amending Directives 98/26/EC and 2014/65/EU and Regulation (EU) No 236/2012 OJ L 257, 28.8.2014, "*any issuer established in the Union that issues or has issued transferable securities which are admitted to trading or traded on trading venues, shall arrange for such securities to be represented in book-entry form as immobilisation or subsequent to a direct issuance in dematerialised form*". In accordance with Article 2(1)(4) of the same Regulation "'*dematerialised form' means the fact that financial instruments exist only as book entry records*".

10 Bamford, C., *Principles of International Financial Law* (Oxford University Press, 2015), p. 152.

11 Regulation (EU) No 575/2013 of the European Parliament and of the Council of 26 June 2013 on prudential requirements for credit institutions and investment firms and amending Regulation (EU) No 648/2012.

12 Despite being broadly in line with the EU regime, as of November 2024, the regulatory framework governing securitisation in the United Kingdom comprises several key instruments. The Securitisation Regulations 2024 (SI 2024/102), made under the Financial Services and Markets Act 2000, establish the FCA-PRA regulatory architecture and set out specific securitisation requirements, including investor due diligence obligations applicable to occupational pension schemes. Complementing this is the Securitisation Part of the PRA Rulebook, which applies to PRA-authorised original lenders, originators, sponsors, securitisation special purpose entities (SSPEs), and institutional investors – referred to collectively as "manufacturers" – that are established in the UK. In parallel, the FCA Handbook contains the securitisation sourcebook, which generally applies to all other UK-established original lenders, originators, sponsors, SSPEs, and institutional investors falling outside the PRA's direct remit.

13 Art. 1(1) of the regulation provides: "*a general framework for securitisation. It defines securitisation and establishes due diligence, risk retention and transparency requirements for parties involved in securitisations, such as institutional investors, originators, sponsors, original lenders and securitisation special purpose entities. It also provides a framework for Simple, Transparent and Standardised or 'STS' securitisation*".

14 Detailed in Articles 8 (simplicity), 9 (standardisation), and 10 (transparency) of Regulation 2017/2402/EU.

UK Securitisation Regulation, is undergoing a separate reform process. This reform is being implemented through the Financial Services and Markets Act 2023 (**FSMA 2023**), which provides for the repeal of retained EU financial services legislation and its replacement with a new domestic regulatory framework. Under FSMA 2023, the Financial Conduct Authority (FCA) and the Prudential Regulation Authority (PRA) have been given the responsibility to issue replacement regulations and guidance. This initiative forms part of the UK government's broader programme to establish a "Smarter Regulatory Framework" for financial services.

The UK Securitisation Regulation was repealed and replaced by a new regulatory framework on 1 November 2024. This updated regime consists of the Securitisation Regulations 2024 (as amended) and the Draft Securitisation (Amendment) (No. 2) Regulations 2024, supplemented by rules and guidance issued by the PRA and FCA. These new regulations and supervisory rules took effect alongside the revocation of the UK Securitisation Regulation. However, in order to ensure continuity, the PRA and FCA introduced "grandfathering" provisions, allowing the requirements of the UK Securitisation Regulation to continue to apply to securitisations that closed before 1 November 2024.

While the new securitisation framework retains the overarching policy objectives of the UK Securitisation Regulation, it incorporates several substantive and technical modifications. FSMA 2023 also provides for the repeal and replacement of various other retained EU laws.

The Financial Services and Markets Act 2023 (Commencement No 7) Regulations 2024[15] provided for the revocation, with effect from 1 November 2024, of the Securitisation Regulations 2018,[16] the remaining retained provisions of the EU Securitisation Regulation,[17] and supplementary instruments that had amended or supplemented the Securitisation and Capital Requirements Regulations. These revocations facilitated the implementation of the new UK securitisation framework. As the UK securitisation legislation is repealed and replaced, and as the EU Securitisation Regulation undergoes further revisions, the differences between the UK and EU frameworks are likely to grow.

2 MAIN STRUCTURES IN SECURITISATION

Securitisation began in the United States with the transfer of pools of mortgage assets in the late 70s.[18] Prior to that, credit institutions did not part from the loans they originated but held them to maturity (the so-called "originate to hold" model). Funding for these loans was obtained for the most part by using the account holders' deposits and, more sparingly, by issuing debt obligations such as bonds. However, as credit institutions were unable to maintain the necessary funding level to address the increased number of mortgage applications,

15 (SI 2024/891).
16 (SI 2018/1288).
17 (2017/2402).
18 *"[W]ith the first such transaction generally recognised as having been undertaken by Salomon Brothers 1979"*. See Baig, S., and Choudhry, M., *The Mechanics of Securitization: A Practical Guide to Structuring and Closing Asset-Backed Security Transactions* (John Wiley & Sons Inc., 2013), p. 4. According to Saleuddin, in *"1970 Ginnie Mae issue[d] the first pass-through MBS"* (mortgage backed securities) in Saleuddin, R., *Regulating Securitized Products: A Post Crisis Guide* (Palgrave Macmillan, 2015), p.27.

alternative solutions were sought to finance housing credits. Investment banks devised a circular structure whereby the mortgage loans that had been originated by retail banks could be sold to an entity that would use them as collateral to finance the purchase of the loans from the credit institution itself (this gave rise to the "originate to distribute" model).[19] The first public structured financing took placed in the United States in 1970 with the issuance of "pass-through"[20] securities by the Government National Mortgages Association or "Ginnie Mae".[21] This was the beginning of the securitisation era.[22] In the mid-1980s, thanks to a greater appetite for financial risk and the development of more sophisticated analytical models, securitisation became a well-established source of debt issuance. The categories of the receivables that backed such issuances started to expand to include commercial mortgage loans, commercial and consumer debts, project loans, etc.

Nowadays, at the core of a securitisation transaction is the originator, the entity that generates or owns the income streams (receivables) to be securitised. The originator initiates the incorporation of the SPV, often engaging an arranger to structure the transaction and locate investors to purchase the bonds issued by the SPV. For example, a retail bank acting as an originator might securitise various streams of receivables, such as income from consumer deposits, business loans, or residential mortgage payments. By isolating these cash flows, the bank can use them in a securitisation transaction to optimise its balance sheet and improve liquidity.

The SPV is established as a thinly capitalised entity, with its legal status depending on jurisdictional considerations. Often, SPVs are incorporated offshore in tax-efficient jurisdictions such as Ireland, Jersey, Luxembourg, or the Cayman Islands. This structure ensures the SPV is separate from the originator, both legally and financially. Measures to make the SPV "insolvency remote" include appointing independent directors and including non-petition and limited recourse clauses in key documents, which restrict creditors' claims solely to the assets over which they have security, thereby protecting the SPV from the originator's potential insolvency.[23]

To fund its purchase of receivables, the SPV issues securities, typically in the form of bonds or notes. These securities are often divided into tranches with different risk and return profiles, allowing for varying payment priorities. Senior tranches, for example, generally receive payments first and thus carry a lower interest rate, reflecting their reduced risk. The SPV's acquisition of receivables from the originator is usually carried out via assignment; however, the precise legal mechanics may vary by jurisdiction. Ensuring that this transfer qualifies as a "true sale" is essential to mitigate recharacterisation risk, which could otherwise lead the transaction to be treated as a secured loan rather than a true transfer of ownership.

To meet its obligations to investors, the SPV grants security interests over its assets, effectively collateralising the receivables and other rights. To enhance the creditworthiness of the securities, various credit enhancement techniques may be employed, including over-collateralisation or the issuance of subordinated tranches, both of which help protect senior

19 Schwarcz, S., *Structured Finance: A Guide to the Principles of Asset Securitisation* (Practicing Institute of New York, 2003).

20 In a pass through structure, the SPV issues "Pass Through Notes" in the nature of participation certificates that enable the investors to take a direct exposure on the performance of the securitised assets.

21 Ginnie Mae provides guarantees only, while the Federal Home Loan and Mortgage Corporation (Freddie Mac) originate and package and sell mortgages to investors. Fannie Mae was created in 1938 and became a private corporation in 1968. Freddie Mac was chartered by the US Congress in 1970 as a secondary-market conduit for residential services (see www.fanniemae.com, www.ginniemae.gov, and www.freddiemac.com).

22 Kravitt, J., *Securitization of Financial Assets* (Aspen Law & Business, 1996), p. 21.

23 Ellinger, E. P., Lomnicka, E. and Hare, C., *Ellinger's Modern Banking Law* (Oxford University Press, 2011), p. 882.

tranches from initial losses. To address liquidity risks, cash reserves or third-party liquidity facilities may also be integrated to support timely payments, even if underlying cash flows from receivables temporarily fall short.[24]

Within the securitisation structure, the originator often retains the role of servicing the receivables and collecting payments from the underlying debtors on behalf of the SPV. Collected funds are then distributed through a pre-defined payment waterfall, covering interest, principal, and transaction costs. Any surplus is typically returned to the originator or distributed to holders of junior tranches, enabling efficient cash flow management across the structure.

Credit ratings play a significant role in securitisation, with agencies assessing the risk associated with each tranche. Higher-rated tranches generally attract lower interest rates, reducing borrowing costs for the SPV. Rating agencies evaluate factors like the credit profile of receivables and the transaction's legal integrity to provide investors with insights into risk levels. Regulatory developments have introduced dual ratings for certain structured instruments aimed at preventing over-reliance on a single agency and ensuring more accurate risk assessment.[25]

Regulatory compliance is essential in securitisation, as it typically encompasses requirements for SPV structuring, originator risk retention, consumer protection, and disclosure obligations. For example, the EU's Capital Requirements Regulation and the UK Securitisation Regulation mandate transparency and risk retention, while the underlying consumer credit contracts must also meet jurisdictional standards. Compliance with these frameworks ensures investor protection and market stability.

Dodd-Frank Act and Securitisation

Risk retention, commonly referred to as "skin in the game", constitutes a fundamental aspect of the United States' regulatory reforms in the securitisation sector. It is intended to align the interests of issuers and originators of securitised assets with those of investors in asset-backed securities (ABS). Section 941 of the Dodd-Frank Wall Street Reform and Consumer Protection Act mandates that the sponsor of a securitisation transaction retain a 5% interest in the credit risk of the securitised asset pool. Federal regulators were tasked with determining the specific form of the retained interest and other associated requirements.

US federal regulators adopted final rules governing risk retention requirements for ABS under Section 941 of the Dodd-Frank Act (15 U.S.C. §§ 78c and 78o-11; 79 Fed. Reg. 77602). These rules specify the manner in which risk retention must be implemented and provide further details regarding compliance obligations.

In addition to risk retention requirements, the Dodd-Frank Act introduced enhanced review and disclosure obligations for ABS issuers. These obligations require issuers to conduct thorough asset reviews and disclose relevant information both at the time of issuance and on an ongoing basis throughout the term of the ABS.

2.1 Forms of Securitisation

Having considered the rationale for securitisation and its most common arrangements, it is important to recognise that the securitisation process encompasses a number of

24 Hudson, A., *The Law of Finance* (Sweet & Maxwell, 2013) at [44-11].
25 Hudson, A., *The Law of Finance* (Sweet & Maxwell, 2013) at [44-29].

distinct and notable structures, each serving different commercial purposes and legal functions.[26]

One of the most common forms is traditional securitisation, also referred to as a cash flow or "true sale" securitisation. In this model, assets are transferred outright from the originator to an SPV, which acquires full legal and beneficial ownership. The cash flows generated by these assets are then used to fund payments to investors. The SPV typically issues securities secured on the receivables, meaning that investors bear direct exposure to the cash flows arising from the asset pool. A key feature of this structure is that the SPV is designed to be insolvency-remote, thereby insulating the securitised assets from claims by the originator's creditors in the event of its insolvency. In order for this model to be effective, it must satisfy the "true sale" test (see later on), which requires that there is a clear and enforceable transfer of legal title and risk from the originator to the SPV.

By contrast, synthetic securitisation adopts a different approach, as it does not involve an actual transfer of ownership of the underlying assets. Instead, the SPV obtains economic exposure to a pool of assets through derivative instruments, such as credit default swaps.[27] In a funded synthetic transaction, the SPV issues tranches of securities, and the proceeds from the issuance are used to collateralise the SPV's exposure to the originator's credit risk. Through this structure, the originator retains the assets on its balance sheet while transferring only the credit risk to the SPV and, ultimately, to investors. This mechanism was affirmed in *Belmont Park Investments PTY Ltd v BNY Corporate Trustee Services Ltd and another* [2011] UKSC 38, where the Supreme Court upheld the enforceability of "flip clauses" within swap contracts, thereby confirming the viability of synthetic structures for risk management purposes.[28] Synthetic securitisation is particularly attractive to financial institutions seeking to manage capital efficiently without engaging in outright asset sales.

Another distinctive structure is whole-business securitisation, which involves the securitisation of revenue streams generated by an entire business rather than specific pools of assets. Although less common than other forms of securitisation, this model can be employed by companies whose value resides predominantly in intangible assets, such as intellectual property or brand value, rather than tangible collateral. Consequently, it is particularly effective for businesses with stable and predictable revenue streams coupled with identifiable operating costs. A key structural feature under English law is the protection of investors' rights through mechanisms enabling the appointment of an administrative receiver, thereby preventing the appointment of an administrator only if investors or a security trustee acting on their behalf hold a "qualifying floating charge" over the company's assets. Moreover, the securitisation must qualify as an "exempt capital markets structure" under the Enterprise Act 2002. This designation permits investors to retain essential control rights, preserving the integrity, stability, and enforceability of the securitisation even in the face of potential financial distress.

3 ISSUANCE STRUCTURES IN SECURITISATION

The choice of issuance structure directly impacts a securitisation's flexibility, legal implications, and tax treatment. The main issuance structures are single-issue, multiple issuance,

26 "*Broadly there are three types of securitisation transactions. There are true sale securitisation, synthetic securitisation and whole business securitisation. True sale is the most common form of securitisation; conversely, synthetic securitisation lacks assignment, which differentiates it from the true sale securitisation. Whole business securitisation is also known as corporate securitisation and certain sections of a company's income are ring fenced to be securitised to provide additional benefit to securities holders*". See Akseli, O. and Gray, J., *Financial Regulation in Crisis? The Role of Law and the Failure of Northern Rock* (Edward Elgar Publishing, 2011), p. 2.

27 Hudson, A., *The Law of Finance* (Sweet & Maxwell, 2013) at [44-23].

28 Hudson, A., *The Law of Finance* (Sweet & Maxwell, 2013) at [44-22].

master trust, single-seller and multi-seller conduits, and Structured Investment Vehicles (**SIVs**).

3.1 Single-Issue Structures

In a single-issue structure, an SPV is typically established in a low or non-tax jurisdiction to acquire assets, usually through a novation, assignment, participation, or trust interest. Funding is obtained via the issuance of notes, bonds, or securities in either the public or private debt markets. These SPVs are structured to be "insolvency remote", isolating them from the originator's balance sheet to enhance their creditworthiness. Investors are secured by the SPV's assets through a security trustee, as outlined in *Re Lehman Brothers International (Europe) (In Administration)* [2012] EWHC 2997 (Ch), where the court addressed the importance of structured securitisation in mitigating investor risk in an insolvency context.

3.2 Multiple Issuance Structures

A multiple issuance structure employs a programme format, typically a Euro Medium-Term Note (EMTN) programme, which allows for successive issues of securities backed by different asset pools. This framework affords issuers flexibility in structuring each issuance independently, securing the assets of each series separately. Investors' rights are limited to the specific collateral backing the particular issuance, insulating them from risks associated with other series issued by the SPV.

3.3 Structured Investment Vehicles (SIVs)

SIVs and similar vehicles invest in portfolios of low-risk assets, aiming to profit from the arbitrage between asset returns and the cost of funding. These vehicles are capitalised with both equity and debt, adhering to strict guidelines from rating agencies to maintain high credit ratings. Although SIVs were widely used pre-2008, the financial crisis exposed significant risks associated with their high leverage, and they have since become less common in structured finance.

4 NATURE OF UNDERLYING ASSETS IN SECURITISATION

The asset class underlying a securitisation significantly influences its risk profile, legal requirements, and appeal to investors. The main categories include real estate-backed assets, consumer and commercial receivables, leveraged loan pools, and securities-based assets.

4.1 Real Estate-Backed Assets

Real estate-backed securities (**REBS**), commonly issued as notes or bonds, are secured against portfolios of property-related receivables. These receivables typically arise from the lending operations of banks, building societies, or specialist mortgage lenders who extend loans for property acquisition, with such loans secured by a first-priority mortgage on the acquired property interest. The securitisation of real estate-backed assets gained traction as financial institutions holding substantial mortgage loan portfolios realised they could increase cash flow and enhance mortgage book liquidity by transferring these receivables to the SPVs. The SPVs, in turn, issue bonds backed by these receivables and their underlying security to fund the receivable pools' acquisition.

The securitisation market as we know it today originates from the early Residential Mortgage-Backed Securities (**RMBS**) transactions of the 1970s and 1980s, in which banks sought to transfer repayment rights on residential mortgage loans. These transactions involved securitising loan repayments together with associated security over the property and insurance, thereby creating mortgage-backed securities attractive to a wider investor base. This process allowed banks to free up capital, facilitating further lending while maintaining client relationships and preserving a portion of the economic benefits derived from their mortgage lending business.

Similarly, Commercial Mortgage-Backed Securities (**CMBS**) are based on secured real property rights but differ from RMBS in that their revenue stream is typically derived from lease or licence payments made by commercial tenants. The commercial real estate sector involves risks that are often more complex than those associated with residential mortgages. CMBS structures are sensitive to shifts in industry trends, market sentiment, interest rates, and other factors influencing the underlying business using the commercial property, which may often be purpose-built for specific industries or sectors. Consequently, the commercial property sector carries unique risks, including inaccurate or negligent property valuations. This type of risk was notably addressed in *Titan Europe 2006–3 Plc v Colliers International UK Plc* [2014] EWHC 3106 (Comm), where the High Court held a valuer liable for a negligent property valuation used as collateral for a CMBS loan. This case underscores the criticality for CMBS investors to ensure their payment waterfall is structured such that any recoveries obtained from legal action against a negligent valuer flow through to noteholders. On appeal, however, the Court of Appeal in *Titan Europe 2006–3 Plc v Colliers International UK Plc* [2015] EWCA Civ 1083 overturned the initial decision, finding no negligence on the valuer's part. Nevertheless, the court agreed in obiter with the principle that, in cases of actual negligence, an SPV would possess a cause of action against the valuer, affirming the noteholders' potential recourse.

4.2 Consumer Asset-Backed Securities (ABS)

Consumer ABS transactions pool cash flows from consumer receivables, such as credit card debt, auto loans, and student loans. These pools are often granular, comprising a large number of unrelated obligors, which makes performance projections more statistically reliable. To facilitate securitisation, many originators structure their contracts with future securitisation in mind, ensuring the receivables meet eligibility criteria from the outset.

4.3 Commercial ABS and Trade Receivables

Commercial ABS structures often involve trade receivables from operating companies, a modern adaptation of traditional factoring techniques. Typically short-dated, these receivables generate cash flows within a matter of months through collection from trade debtors, enabling businesses to create liquidity by selling their receivables to an SPV.

Unlike consumer receivables, such as mortgages and personal loans, trade receivables are not generally subject to consumer protection regulation, although specific jurisdictions may regulate their purchase. Trade receivables are often more stable and predictable, as companies are motivated to maintain relationships with key suppliers and avoid payment disruptions that could impact their supply chains. As such, trade receivables securitisation offers a distinct asset class in the securitisation market. Further, for the seller/originator, it serves as an alternative to other forms of receivables financing, such as factoring, forfaiting, or secured loans, while facilitating more extensive and long-term financing options.

The structure of trade receivables securitisation generally involves the originator (seller) transferring receivables to an SPV that secures financing through a combination of loan facilities, asset-backed commercial paper (ABCP), or term debt in the capital markets. In most instances, ABCP conduits – short-term, bank-sponsored debt vehicles – fund the SPV. These conduits issue commercial paper, a short-term debt instrument whose proceeds are invested in trade receivables from the originator. The nature of trade receivables, which fluctuate with business cycles, aligns well with the ABCP conduit structure, as the amount of ABCP in issuance can be tailored to match the value of receivables in the portfolio at any given time. To safeguard liquidity, the sponsoring bank commonly provides backup funding through a liquidity facility, used if commercial paper issuance becomes temporarily unfeasible.

In a standard trade receivables securitisation, receivables are sold to the SPV, with the seller typically continuing to collect and manage payments on behalf of the SPV. The SPV's funding sources may include ABCP conduits, term loans, and market-issued debt. Financing providers seldom cover the receivables' full-face value; rather, the seller often absorbs part of the credit risk by receiving a discounted purchase price or by making a subordinated loan to the SPV, thereby providing what is known as *credit enhancement*. This structure ensures that the seller bears initial losses due to debtor defaults, enhancing the security of the receivables for senior investors.

The receivables pool serves as the securitisation's foundation and must meet specific eligibility criteria to ensure a stable investment profile. A detailed due diligence process, generally performed by the financier, includes examining the nature of the contracts, generating the receivables, debtor profiles, and the seller's underwriting policies. To maintain asset quality, financiers may establish concentration limits to diversify debtor risk and ensure the pool does not become too reliant on individual debtors or specific jurisdictions. For instance, eligible receivables typically exclude overdue payments, receivables owed by high-risk debtors, and those arising from contracts with non-standard terms.

During the *revolving period* – when collections are used to purchase new receivables – the SPV maintains the receivables pool at a constant or gradually increasing level. This period extends until either the transaction's maturity date or the occurrence of an early unwind event. Early unwind protections are integral to the securitisation, as they halt reinvestment in the receivables pool when the associated risk profile becomes unmanageable. Triggers for early unwind may include the seller's insolvency, deteriorating credit enhancement, or failure to meet performance criteria. When early unwind triggers are activated, collections flow first to repay investors, and only residual sums, if any, are remitted to the seller.

Servicing the receivables involves collecting payments and administering receivable accounts, roles typically retained by the seller under a servicing agreement. This agreement delineates the responsibilities and standards the servicer must uphold, particularly regarding reporting and performance benchmarks. If the seller fails to fulfil its servicing obligations or becomes insolvent, a replacement servicer may be appointed. Account control arrangements are crucial for safeguarding collected receivables from seller-related risks. Ideally, debtors would remit payments directly into accounts controlled by the SPV; however, it is more common for payments to continue into seller-held accounts. Account control agreements with third-party banks often facilitate frequent sweeps of the seller's accounts to ensure prompt transfer of funds to the SPV, minimising the risk of commingling assets and protecting the SPV's rights to the funds in the event of the seller's insolvency.

4.4 Asset Finance and Infrastructure Securitisation

Asset-backed financing is also applied to lease receivables, particularly for high-value assets like aircraft or ships. Infrastructure securitisations, commonly structured as public-private partnerships (PPP), are backed by long-term service contracts or concession payments. The cash flow predictability in infrastructure securitisation hinges on the high credit quality of counterparties, often government entities, which supports extended investment horizons.

5 LEGAL CONSIDERATIONS AND REGULATORY ENVIRONMENT

Securitisation transactions must be structured to meet "true sale" requirements, ensuring that the asset pool is legally distinct from the originator and not subject to creditor claims. While the nature of this transfer may appear straightforward, certain commercial aspects of the transaction may raise questions regarding the validity and effectiveness of the transfer. For instance, if the originator receives a servicing fee based on the "profit" generated by the receivables pool or retains a right to repurchase the receivables to terminate the securitisation, it could be argued that the transfer resembles a loan with security rather than a sale. If this were the case, the security interest would be unregistered and, therefore, void against third-party creditors or a liquidator of the originator.

English courts have generally been reluctant to recharacterise a transaction presented as a sale unless it is evidently a sham. The principles governing this issue were set out in *Re George Inglefield Ltd* [1933] Ch 1 and have since been applied in cases such as *Welsh Development Agency v Export Finance Co Ltd* [1992] BC 270 and *Orion Finance Limited v Crown Financial Management Ltd* [1996] BCLC 78.

To ensure that a transaction is recognised as a genuine sale rather than a loan secured by collateral, several key factors must be observed.[29] The sale agreement must explicitly state that the transfer constitutes a sale. The documentation should accurately reflect the distinct legal identities and roles of the parties, ensuring that the transaction is conducted at arm's length and that an appropriate purchase price is agreed upon. Furthermore, the seller must not retain any equity of redemption, as this would suggest the existence of a secured loan rather than an outright sale. The agreement should also demonstrate the transfer of ownership risk to the SPV, reinforcing the true sale nature of the transaction. Additionally, the originator should have no post-transfer rights over funds generated from the transferred receivables, as any such continuing control or benefit could indicate that the transaction is, in substance, a secured financing arrangement rather than a genuine sale.[30]

This structure is reinforced under the UK Securitisation Regulation. Qualifying as an STS securitisation provides preferential regulatory capital treatment, facilitating investor confidence through standardisation.

29 Ellinger, E. P., Lomnicka, E. and Hare, C., *Ellinger's Modern Banking Law* (Oxford University Press, 2011), p. 810.

30 Although courts are typically minded to adhere to the parties' intentions: "*First, I should note that the parties to the Facility are commercial entities, who engaged experienced lawyers during the negotiations of the Facility terms. It seems that the negotiations of the terms took three months and the legal fees paid to the original lenders' six different sets of lawyers totalled about US$1.9 million. The Facility terms themselves are very detailed indeed. The clauses plus the 13 schedules attached to them run to 146 pages. It looks as if the parties did not intend to leave anything to chance and intended the terms to be as precise as possible. On the hearing of the appeal, counsel for both parties urged us to approach the single issue of construction on the basis that the parties and their legal advisers knew what they were doing and that they intended to follow 'commercial common sense' in drafting the terms of the Facility. I am certainly prepared to do so*". *BMA Special Opportunity Hub Fund Ltd. & Ors v African Minerals Finance Ltd* [2013] EWCA Civ 416 at [8].

The EU Securitisation Regulation applies to securitisations where securities were issued on or after 1 January 2019, as well as to any new securitisation position created after this date, subject to specific transitional arrangements. The UK Securitisation Regulation applies on the same basis.

The UK Securitisation Regulation applies directly to originators, original lenders, and sponsors that are either established in or regulated by the UK. While the legislation does not explicitly confine its scope to such entities, several factors indicate that its principal objective is to regulate UK-based market participants. However, the Regulation's investor-related requirements may extend its impact beyond UK borders. For example, where UK investors participate in a securitisation transaction originating in the United States, a US originator may need to comply with certain UK requirements, despite not being directly subject to the Regulation. Such obligations may include adherence to risk-retention rules, credit-granting standards, and specific due diligence measures imposed on investors.

The STS framework places the responsibility for qualification on the transaction parties. To designate a securitisation as STS, parties must ensure the transaction's structural and documentary elements meet all applicable STS criteria.

To support compliance, parties to a securitisation may engage a third-party verifier, who will assess and confirm the transaction's adherence to STS criteria. In the UK, these verifiers must be authorised by the Financial Conduct Authority (**FCA**). However, even if a third-party verifier is involved, primary liability for compliance with STS criteria remains with the originator and sponsor. These entities must submit a notification of STS compliance to the FCA and are subject to sanctions if it is later found that the transaction did not satisfy the necessary criteria.

5.1 The Trust Deed

The trust deed serves as the cornerstone of the transaction's documentary framework, acting as the legal instrument that establishes the securities. It details the SPV's covenant to make the payments specified in the certificates representing the securities, along with other covenants, representations, and warranties provided by the SPV for the benefit of investors. Additionally, the trust deed may constitute the security interest created over the SPV's assets. It defines the relationship between the SPV and the trustee, outlining the trustee's enforcement powers and rights to manage assets within the security package.[31]

The terms and conditions detailed in the prospectus relating to the securities' issuance and the form of certificates representing the securities are typically annexed to the trust deed. A common provision in a trust deed allows the trustee to assume that none of the securities are held by or on behalf of the SPV. This assumption is sometimes broadened to include any securities held by parties that have sold receivables to the SPV for inclusion in the portfolio. The purpose of these provisions is to protect investors by avoiding potential conflicts of interest that may arise between transaction parties holding securities and other investors in the securitisation. However, in *Citicorp Trustee Company Ltd v Barclays Bank Plc & Ors* [2013] EWHC 2608 (Ch), the High Court held that debt securities held or controlled by a party which had sold its loans to a note issuer under a securitisation were not disenfranchised in relation to bondholder votes or directions to the trustee. The court found that, although the bondholder was both an original lender under the loan and a seller of the loan to the SPV, it should be

31 Hudson, A., *The Law of Finance* (Sweet & Maxwell, 2013) at [22-17].

treated as the legal and beneficial owner in its own right. It was not holding the securities in its capacity as seller, and the court found no justification for disenfranchising the bonds.

The trust deed also includes provisions for noteholder meetings, which may be required if the transaction parties seek noteholder approval for amendments to the terms and conditions of the notes. In *Banca Generali SpA v Sovereign Credit Opportunities SA* [2024] EWCA Civ 886, the Court of Appeal addressed the scope of noteholder powers in the context of securitisation transactions, particularly following a default or trigger event. The occurrence of such an event often enables noteholders to direct the issuer in matters impacting the administration of the transaction, including the replacement of agents such as the fiscal agent. The extent of such powers, however, depends on the interpretation of the relevant contractual clauses governing the transaction. In *Banca Generali*, the court held that the service of a trigger notice constituted a significant shift in the balance of power, effectively transferring certain administrative rights to the noteholders who could direct the issuer to replace the fiscal agent.

5.2 Bankruptcy Remoteness

The distinguishing factor for the Notes issued as part of a securitisation transaction is that their capital and interest payments descend from, depend on, and are supported by the assets which have been purchased by the SPV. On this basis, it is essential that the cash flow deriving from the receivables is not interrupted or affected by any externalities (such as the claims of external or internal creditors) and, therefore, that, in addition to being an orphan and independently managed entity, its bankruptcy remoteness is preserved.[32]

Therefore, an essential feature of an SPV is "*ensuring that it could not be wound up*".[33] Thus, should the originator enter an insolvency procedure, its transaction-specific creditors cannot seize the assets of the SPV, and it should be impossible, or at least very unlikely, that the issuer be put into liquidation.

The SPV is a thinly capitalised legal entity which acquires the receivables through the issuance of securities.[34] To a bystander, it appears as a mere connection between the originator and the capital markets which lacks any materiality. The purpose of this structure is to ensure that the SPV is not classified as a subsidiary of the originator, remains unaffected by any insolvency proceedings involving the originator, and does not have its balance sheet consolidated with that of the originator. To make the issuer as bankruptcy remote as possible, its permitted activities need to be restricted to prevent it from incurring liabilities beyond those anticipated within the securitisation. Moreover, one or more directors who are independent of the originator would be appointed to the board of the SPV, with these directors' votes being essential to pass any board resolution that would place the SPV into insolvency proceedings.

In addition, the issuer can also obtain agreements from its creditors that they will not put the vehicle into liquidation in the future, the so-called "non-petition" clauses. To this effect, every party to the transaction will agree not to petition to wind up the SPV. This structuring requirement presents two difficulties. First, it may not be possible to obtain the agreement of

32 This is jargon which means that the SPV is not threatened with potential bankruptcy.
33 *BNY Corporate Trustee Services Ltd v Eurosail-UK 2007-3BL Plc & Ors* [2011] EWCA Civ 227 per Lord Neuberger at [100].
34 In the insurance and reinsurance context, an SPV has been defined by point (26) of Article 13 of Directive 2009/138/EC (as amended) as "*any undertaking, whether incorporated or not, other than an existing insurance or reinsurance undertaking, which assumes risks from insurance or reinsurance undertakings and which fully funds its exposure to such risks through the proceeds of a debt issuance or any other financing mechanism where the repayment rights of the providers of such debt or financing mechanism are subordinated to the reinsurance obligations of such an undertaking*".

all creditors to the proposition and, second, the creditors' agreement in this regard may be held to be unenforceable.[35] Finally, all major transaction documents incorporate limited recourse provisions, ensuring that a counterparty enforcing its rights over the SPV's assets is restricted to the assets actually held by the SPV and covered by the security granted to that counterparty.

However, in *ARM Asset Backed Securities S.A.* [2013] EWHC 3351 (Ch), the High Court held that contractual limited recourse provisions do not prevent a company from being deemed unable to pay its debts and consequently liable to be wound up. The court reached this conclusion by assuming that creditors would submit claims for the full amount of their debts, notwithstanding contractual provisions limiting recourse. A contrasting approach was adopted in *Re Lendy* [2021] EWHC 2285 (Ch), where the court distinguished *ARM* and held that any proof of debt should be valued by the company's administrators in accordance with the investors' limited recourse contractual entitlements. This was the case even if creditors were permitted to submit proofs of debt reflecting the full value of outstanding capital and interest. The decision in *Re Lendy* suggests a more nuanced approach to limited recourse provisions, reinforcing the principle that contractual terms governing creditor entitlements should be considered when assessing a company's solvency in insolvency proceedings.

5.3 Regulatory Framework for Securitisation in the US

The Dodd-Frank Act introduced several key requirements to enhance transparency and investor protection in ABS transactions. Under Rule 193,[36] issuers are required to conduct a review of the securitised asset pool and disclose the "nature" of this review to ensure the material accuracy of asset information. Risk retention requirements under Section 941 of Dodd-Frank, codified in Exchange Act Section 15G,[37] mandate that originators retain at least 5% of the credit risk of ABS transferred to third parties. The final rules issued in October 2014 allow this retention to be held by the sponsor, an originator, or a majority-owned affiliate, provided it meets strict limits on hedging and transfer.[38]

In addition, in November 2023, the SEC adopted Securities Act Rule 192, which prohibits ABS sponsors, placement agents, initial purchasers, and certain affiliates from engaging in conflicted transactions, including short sales or credit default swaps, that would pose material conflicts of interest for investors in ABS transactions, thus covering both registered and synthetic ABS offerings.

Lastly, the FDIC's Securitisation Safe Harbor Rule was introduced post-2008 financial crisis to ensure that FDIC-insured banks holding securitised assets can safeguard those assets from seizure should the bank enter receivership.

Together, these rules reflect an integrated regulatory framework aimed at strengthening the US securitisation market's transparency, accountability, and resilience.

6 COLLATERALISED LOAN OBLIGATIONS

As introduced in Chapter 13, a CLO is a complex, structured finance instrument through which an SPV, often termed an issuer, acquires a portfolio of loans or bonds and issues

35 Doyle, T., 'Structured Finance – Securitisation' in *Banking & Corporate Financial Services, Law Professional Practice Guide – Law Society of Ireland* (Cavendish, 2003), p. 55.
36 17 C.F.R. § 230.193.
37 15 U.S.C. § 78o-11.
38 17 C.F.R. § 246.12.

securities backed by this portfolio. CLOs are segmented into tranches, ranging from senior, mezzanine, junior, to subordinated, each reflecting a distinct level of risk, priority, and return. Therefore, a CLO transaction is, fundamentally, a type of securitisation in which the underlying receivables consist of specific categories of loans.

The SPV funds the acquisition of the loan portfolio by issuing debt securities (referred to as CLO securities), which may be purchased from the originator or acquired on the open market. These CLO securities allow the SPV to finance the purchase of the loan portfolio, enabling it to generate income from the portfolio's cash flow and distribute payments according to a pre-defined "waterfall" structure. This waterfall structure dictates the order of payments, giving senior tranches priority for interest and principal payments, thereby enhancing their credit profile, while subordinated tranches absorb initial losses but offer higher returns.

CLO transactions primarily operate in a "cash flow" model, where interest and principal from the portfolio assets are distributed to satisfy the SPV's debt obligations. Alternatively, "market value" CLOs base payments on the market valuation of assets at specific points, allowing the portfolio manager more flexibility in trading the assets. In "synthetic" CLOs, the SPV gains exposure through credit default swaps without acquiring the loans directly, providing investors exposure to credit risks associated with these assets rather than the actual loans themselves.

Risk is managed through multiple mechanisms, including eligibility criteria for asset selection, portfolio profile tests, collateral quality tests, and coverage tests to ensure the portfolio's quality aligns with investor expectations. These structures are further supported by credit enhancement techniques, such as over-collateralisation, tranching, and retained spread, which mitigate credit risks for senior tranches.

The CLO market is typically segmented into static and dynamic CLOs. In static CLOs, the portfolio assets remain largely fixed, often used for balance sheet management by banks aiming to reduce regulatory capital requirements. Dynamic CLOs, however, involve active management by a portfolio manager who seeks arbitrage opportunities by actively trading the assets within prescribed limits to achieve a higher return than the cost of debt servicing. As a result, dynamic CLOs – often structured as arbitrage CLOs – are primarily intended for profit generation through favourable risk-return differentials on managed portfolios.

7 REPURCHASE AGREEMENTS (REPOS)

Repos have emerged as essential instruments within global finance, providing short-term, collateralised liquidity that can be readily converted into cash. Unlike a traditional secured loan, a repo involves the sale and subsequent repurchase of securities, enabling lenders to manage liquidity efficiently while retaining the collateral's legal title.[39] This contractual arrangement is governed by the GMRA, published by the International Capital Market Association[40]

39 *"The basic structure of securities lending is not in dispute, and was well described in the evidence. Securities lending is an established practice by which a party holding securities, such as a pension fund, insurance company, sovereign wealth fund, or the like, lends them out to another party, such as a bank or a hedge fund, against collateral and in return for a lending fee. . . . For practical reasons, securities lending is commonly performed by the lender's securities custodian, so that loans of securities are negotiated by the same institution as directly holds the securities. . . . Taking collateral from the borrower is an important part of the business, not only to protect the lender, but also to generate income. Securities loans may be made against non-cash or cash collateral. Non-cash collateral is generally in the form of other securities. Typically, securities lending agents agree to indemnify clients against the risk of any decrease in the value of non-cash collateral*", per Mr Justice Blair in *AP-Fonden v Bank of New York Mellon SA/NV & Ors* [2013] EWHC 3127 (Comm) at [36] to [38].

40 Formerly the International Securities Market Association.

(**ICMA**) and the Securities Industry and Financial Markets Association (formerly the Bond Market Association, SIFMA), which outlines the rights and responsibilities of each party.

Repos provide short-term funding solutions for market participants, particularly in high-liquidity markets, with highly liquid securities such as government bonds typically serving as collateral. They are also commonly used in monetary policy, allowing central banks to either inject or withdraw liquidity from the financial system as needed.

Under a classic repo, securities act as collateral, giving the lender (Buyer) recourse in case of non-repayment.[41] Generally, the transaction comprises two simultaneous steps: first, the sale of securities by one party (Seller) to the Buyer on a specified "Purchase Date" for an agreed amount (Purchase Price), and second, the Seller's agreement to repurchase the same or equivalent securities from the Buyer on a predetermined "Repurchase Date" for a set amount (Repurchase Price). The initial securities sold by the Seller are called the "Purchased Securities", typically including bonds or equities, and the securities returned by the Buyer on the Repurchase Date are referred to as "Equivalent Securities".[42]

In this respect, the GMRA stipulates as follows:

> *(a) From time to time the parties hereto may enter into transactions in which one party, acting through a Designated Office, ("Seller") agrees to sell to the other, acting through a Designated Office, ("Buyer") securities and financial instruments ("Securities") (subject to paragraph 1(c), other than equities and Net Paying Securities) against the payment of the purchase price by Buyer to Seller, with a simultaneous agreement by Buyer to sell to Seller Securities equivalent to such Securities at a date certain or on demand against the payment of the repurchase price by Seller to Buyer. (b) Each such transaction (which may be a repurchase transaction ("Repurchase Transaction") or a buy and sell back transaction ("Buy/Sell Back Transaction") shall be referred to herein as a "Transaction" and shall be governed by this Agreement, including any supplemental terms or conditions contained in Annex I hereto, unless otherwise agreed in writing.*[43]

In a standard repo arrangement, the Repurchase Price is higher than the Purchase Price, with the difference representing the "interest" paid by the Seller to the Buyer, effectively compensating the Buyer for lending money. Additionally, the Purchase Price is usually set below the market value of the Purchased Securities, creating a "haircut" or buffer to mitigate the Buyer's exposure to the Seller's credit risk. This gap ensures that the Buyer, acting as the lender, is safeguarded by advancing less than the collateral's market value.

During the term of the repo, further payments may occur between the Buyer and Seller, often related to income from the collateral or margining adjustments. Economically, a repo functions much like a secured loan: the Buyer lends the Purchase Price to the Seller, receiving the Purchased Securities as collateral. At maturity (on the Repurchase Date), the Seller repays the loan with interest by buying back the securities, while the Buyer has recourse to the collateral if the Seller defaults.

Legally, however, a repo is characterised as a "true sale" of securities, with the title transferring from the Seller to the Buyer. This full transfer of the legal and beneficial title to the securities underscores the core nature of repos, which means the Buyer, as the legal owner of the Purchased Securities, has unrestricted rights over them.

The title transfer nature of repos significantly streamlines the collateral realisation process in an enforcement scenario, placing the Buyer in a "super-priority position". If the Seller defaults on its obligations under the GMRA, particularly by failing to repay the loan by paying the Repurchase Price on the Repurchase Date, the Buyer can simply sell the Purchased

41 Gullifer, L., *Goode and Gullifer on Legal Problems of Credit and Security* (Sweet & Maxwell, 2023) at [1-41].
42 Bamford, C., *Principles of International Finance Law* (Oxford University Press, 2015) at [10.73].
43 In *Heis & Ors (Administrators of MF Global UK Ltd.) v MF Global Inc* [2012] EWHC 3068 (Ch) at [12].

Securities to recover the amounts due under the agreement.[44] Under the GMRA, the Seller may substitute equivalent securities for all or part of the Purchased Securities at any time during the repo's term, provided the Buyer consents. If the Buyer agrees, it will transfer the specified amount of the original securities back to the Seller, who must then transfer "New Purchased Securities" of equal or greater market value than the returned securities as of the transfer date. Though this substitution mechanism may initially appear to conflict with the Buyer's legal title to the Purchased Securities, the requirement for the Buyer's consent preserves the transaction's status as a true sale.

Although a variety of securities may be used in repo transactions, highly liquid assets like government bonds (such as UK gilts or US Treasury Bills) are preferred, as they are easily liquidated in case of default. Repos can also involve corporate bonds, structured finance instruments, and equities.

7.1 Structure and Purpose of Repos

Under a classic repo, securities act as collateral, giving the lender (Buyer) recourse in case of non-repayment. The GMRA's standardisation of repo terms mitigates the risk of recharacterisation, distinguishing repos as "true sales" rather than loans.[45]

Repos can take several distinct forms, each serving different market participants and operational needs. Classic repos are structured with fixed terms and a predetermined repurchase date, typically collateralised by high-quality assets. This structure provides security to the buyer while enabling market participants to manage short-term liquidity requirements efficiently.

Tri-party repos involve the appointment of an independent third party to act as custodian, managing the collateral on behalf of both the buyer and seller. This arrangement is particularly advantageous for institutions that lack the operational infrastructure for direct repo management, as the third party assumes responsibility for collateral administration, margining, and substitution requirements.[46]

Buy/sell-back transactions, although economically similar to repos, differ in their legal structure by involving two separate contracts. This bifurcation can complicate the processing of income payments and collateral substitution. Securities lending transactions, while also involving the temporary transfer of securities, are typically driven by a different commercial rationale, as they are primarily structured to facilitate the borrowing of securities for short-term use rather than to provide liquidity.

Repos incorporate various techniques to mitigate counterparty credit risk, which is the risk that a party defaults or becomes insolvent before the transaction completes, thus failing

44 It should be noted that careful drafting is required when describing an event of default. For example, in *Heis and others (administrators of MF Global UK Ltd) v MF Global Inc* [2012] EWHC 3068 (Ch), the High Court was of the view that the UK's special administration regime for investment banks was not "analogous" to liquidation, for the purposes of a standard form event of default in precedent repo documentation. Similarly, in the Australian decisions of *Beconwood Securities Pty Ltd v. Australia and New Zealand Banking Group Pty Ltd* (2008) 66 ACSR 116 and *in Lindholm, In re Opes Prime Stockbroking Ltd* [2008] FCA 1425 the judge held that administrators appointed under the relevant Australian legislation and receivers appointed by secured creditors were not officers analogous to a liquidator. It was held – in the latter case at [61]: "*The function of a liquidator – whether called a liquidator, a trustee, a receiver, a curator or a syndic – is to preside over the death of a company. An administrator appointed in rescue proceedings strives for the opposite result (even though the company may yet in the end die). A receiver appointed by a secured creditor does neither of those things, being largely unconcerned about the fate of the company. From any perspective, the offices are poles apart*".

45 Adams, D., *Banking and Capital Markets* (College of Law Publishing, 2024) at [12.1].

46 Gullifer, L., *Goode and Gullifer on Legal Problems of Credit and Security* (Sweet & Maxwell, 2023) at [6-35].

to fulfil its obligations and thereby causing the non-defaulting party to incur a loss. This risk is distinct from issuer credit risk and market risk.

A key mitigation measure is the *haircut* (or *Margin Ratio* in GMRA terms). A haircut applies a discount to the market value of the Purchased Securities, allowing the Buyer to receive collateral exceeding the cash advanced to the Seller, creating "overcollateralisation". For instance, if the market value of the Purchased Securities is £1,000 and a 10% haircut is applied, the effective repo value would be £900, calculated as follows: Market Value (£1,000) x (100% – Haircut (10%)) = £900. This discount gives the Buyer a buffer should the collateral value decrease, providing some protection in case the Buyer needs to liquidate the securities to recover the value of the amount advanced.

Margining also plays a critical role in counterparty credit risk reduction, requiring parties to transfer collateral periodically. When multiple repos are transacted under the same GMRA, an accumulating exposure can arise if, for instance, one party acts consistently as Buyer, and the haircuts initially applied are insufficient. In such cases, each party's exposure across all repos is assessed, and the party with a Net Exposure may request a *Margin Transfer* from the other. This margin can take the form of either a cash sum (*Cash Margin*) or *Margin Securities*, which are securities agreed upon as acceptable collateral. Due to market fluctuations, Net Exposure may vary daily, potentially reversing which party has the exposure. When one party's Net Exposure increases, it can initiate a margin call to compel the other party to reduce that exposure.

Additionally, *Set-off* reduces counterparty credit risk upon an Event of Default. In such scenarios, all outstanding repos under the GMRA are accelerated, and the Repurchase Date is deemed to have occurred for each transaction. The obligations to deliver securities are replaced by cash payment obligations based on the Default Market Value of the securities.[47] All obligations across different currencies are converted to a single currency (the Base Currency), enabling set-off, where each party's obligations are offset against the other's. The resulting balance, after all debts are netted, is then payable by the party with the larger debt.

7.2 Market Significance and Legal Considerations

Repos play a critical role in facilitating liquidity and ensuring market stability.[48] By structuring repos as true sales, the GMRA safeguards against recharacterisation risk, which could arise when a court deems the transaction to be a disguised grant of security rather than an actual sale and repurchase, as labelled by the parties involved. A determination that a repo constitutes a secured loan rather than a true sale could lead to several adverse consequences. If the transaction is classified as a security arrangement rather than a sale, it may require registration. Additionally, recharacterisation could result in a breach of negative pledge provisions, which typically prohibit the seller from granting security interests without prior consent. Furthermore, if the repo is deemed a disguised security arrangement, either party's ability to engage in secured lending could be restricted.

The risk of recharacterisation is heavily influenced by the governing law of the repo and the jurisdictions of the parties involved, as different legal systems impose varying conditions

47 *"In practice, repo counterparties have flexibility to value the assets and will select a price so as to retain all the collateral pledged to them. That is not in my view right either. Under the GMRA, the value of securities held as collateral is required to be determined as 'the amount which, in the reasonable opinion of the Non-Defaulting party, represents their fair market value'. This is not in the counterparty's discretion"*, in *AP-Fonden v Bank of New York Mellon SA/NV & Ors* [2013] EWHC 3127 (Comm) at [298].

48 Haentjens, M. and De Gioia-Carabellese, P., *European Banking and Financial Law* (Routledge, 2015), p. 211.

for a repo to maintain its status as a true sale. For example, under Spanish netting legislation, a valid repo agreement requires an exchange before the bond reaches maturity.[49] These jurisdiction-specific legal nuances must be carefully considered when structuring and documenting repo transactions to ensure their enforceability as true sales.[50]

English case law suggests that courts, even where they acknowledge that "*'Repo' transactions are regarded as in substance a form of secured lending under which securities are provided as collateral for a loan*",[51] are reluctant to recharacterise repos, generally respecting the contract's express terms and the parties' intentions.[52] These legal principles have also been considered as "good law" in Ireland.[53]

8 ISLAMIC FINANCE

Sharia-compliant finance spans a wide array of financial sectors, including banking, non-bank financial institutions, capital markets, money markets, and insurance. In numerous Muslim-majority countries, assets within Islamic banking have grown more rapidly than conventional banking assets, and there has been a marked increase in interest from non-Muslim jurisdictions, such as the UK, Luxembourg, South Africa, and Hong Kong.[54]

Islamic finance broadly encompasses financial activities that allow individuals, institutions, governments, and financiers to raise capital in ways that conform to Sharia principles. Practically, Islamic finance adapts traditional investment methods to align with Sharia, establishing structures that emulate the economic outcomes of conventional finance across key markets. For example, Islamic finance has become well-established in project and asset financing, especially for infrastructure projects in the Middle East, while the UK's retail market expanded significantly after the 2003 removal of the double Stamp Duty Land Tax on Sharia-compliant mortgages, which led to the licensing of the Islamic Bank of Britain in 2004 and catalysed the growth of Sharia-compliant products offered by major UK banks. Sukuk, the Islamic equivalent of bonds,[55] has rapidly developed as a vital tool for raising capital, representing the most dynamic and innovative segment of the market. Furthermore, a nascent yet evolving market for Sharia-compliant derivatives and structured products is gaining traction as larger conventional banks, often through dedicated Islamic finance units, integrate such products into investment portfolios.

49 Where Royal Decree Law 5/2005, as amended and restated pursuant to Law 7/2011, does not apply, a transfer may amount to a transfer of title as security and, therefore, its validity and effectiveness under the laws of Spain need to be examined under both the Spanish conflicts of laws rules and the principles of Spanish law relating to transfer of title as security. See DLA Piper's legal opinion addressed to the International Swaps and Derivatives Association, Inc. titled "RE: VALIDITY AND ENFORCEABILITY UNDER SPANISH LAW OF COLLATERAL ARRANGEMENTS UNDER THE ISDA CREDIT SUPPORT DOCUMENTS: COLLATERAL PROVIDER INSOLVENCY" www.isda.org/a/B2sEE/Spain-Collateral-Provider-Opinion-ISDA-06092016-Spain-Collateral-Provider-Opinion-ISDA-15-02-2018.pdf (accessed in March 2025).

50 Gullifer, L., *Goode and Gullifer on Legal Problems of Credit and Security* (Sweet & Maxwell, 2023) at [6-36].

51 Per Lord Justice Flaux in *LBI EHF v Raiffeisen Bank International AG* [2018] EWCA Civ 719 at [2]. See also *Lehman Brothers International (Europe) v Exxonmobil Financial Services BV* [2016] EWHC 2699 (Comm) at [2].

52 Haentjens, M. and De Gioia-Carabellese, P., *European Banking and Financial Law* (Routledge, 2015), p. 222.

53 See the Irish High Court decision in *Bank of Ireland v Eteams International Ltd* [2017] IEHC 393.

54 Proctor, C., *The Law and Practice of International Banking* (Oxford University Press, 2015) at [49.01].

55 "*This case is concerned with the duties owed by the defendant bank ('BNPP') as the Arranger of an Islamic financing transaction known as a Sukuk, equivalent in economic effect to a Eurobond issue but structured so as to conform to the principles of Sharia law*". Per Mr Justice Males in *Golden Belt 1 Sukuk Company BSC(c) v BNP Paribas* [2017] EWHC 3182 (Comm) at [1].

Despite its growth – driven in large part by enhanced standardisation in documentation and practices – the Islamic finance industry continues to face several challenges. In particular, the absence of a globally unified interpretation of Sharia principles complicates matters, as market participants frequently need to design innovative solutions to achieve returns that approximate those of conventional finance. As a result of the varied interpretations of Sharia and of the customisation inherent to Islamic finance, transaction costs, timelines, and complexity tend to be higher.

8.1 Principles of Sharia Compliance

For centuries, Islamic jurists have examined the meaning of Qur'anic verses that influence legal rights and obligations to ensure genuine compliance with Islamic principles. Unlike state-based legal systems, Sharia does not seek to establish a fixed body of laws or a single, unified doctrine. Rather, it encompasses a dynamic and interpretative tradition, providing ethical and religious principles that inform both personal conduct and communal life without adhering to the structured characteristics of state legislation.[56]

When evaluating Sharia compliance in commercial transactions, a judge begins by interpreting the relevant religious precept within its broader context. In doing so, he may refer to the consensus of past and contemporary scholars (*ijma*) and apply analogical reasoning (*qiyas*) to derive principles that can be adapted to modern legal realities. *Ijma* requires unanimous agreement among scholars at the level of juristic reasoning (*ijtihad*) in a particular era, typically applied to matters that are unequivocally addressed in the Quran and Sunnah. *Qiyas* permits analogical reasoning to extend established rulings to new issues, enabling Sharia to adapt to novel circumstances.[57]

Over the centuries, this interpretive process has developed into distinct legal schools of thought (*al-madhāhib*), each characterised by the works of its titular head (*mujtahid muṭlaq*), his students of equivalent rank who adopt similar methodologies (*mujtahidūn muntasibūn*), and the later commentators and glossators (*ahl al-tarjīḥ*). The collective body of their writings serves as the primary source for most Islamic legal rulings (*aḥkām*) issued by an Islamic judge (*qāḍī*), as well as for the independent legal opinions issued by eminent jurists (*fatāwā*) provided by an Islamic jurisconsult (*muftī*).[58]

Within this context, *fatwas* provide nuanced and diverse interpretations, reflecting the varied approaches within Islamic jurisprudence. Additionally, the decisions of courts and the legislation of Muslim-majority nations often diverge, further illustrating the plurality of legal perspectives in the application of Islamic financial principles.[59]

This lack of international consensus presents a challenge for the expansion of Islamic finance. In response, many Islamic financial institutions, as well as conventional banks

56 Pirie, F., *The Rule of Laws* (Profile Books, 2022), p. 390.

57 *"Islamic jurists have considered over hundreds of years the meaning of the verses of the Qur'an which affect matters on which legal rights and obligations may arise. The starting point for a judge is the interpretation of a verse, in its whole context, and the judge may resort to the consensus of past and/or present scholars ('imja') and use a form of analytical deduction ('qiyas'), to arrive at principles that can be applied to the realities of the modern world. Judgments should take into account the public good and the prevailing customs in the Saudi community ('urf'). Precedents do not have any legally binding effect, but are treated as a useful, albeit not formally binding, tool by Saudi judges"*. Per Mr Justice Henshaw in *Al Jaber v Al Ibrahim & Anor* [2023] EWHC 2831 (Comm) at [331].

58 Farrar, S., 'Accommodating Islamic Banking and Finance in Australia' (2011) 34(1) *UNSW Law Journal* 413, p. 415.

59 Black, A. and Sadiq, K., 'Good and Bad Sharia: Australia's Mixed Response to Islamic Law' (2011) 34(1) *UNSW Law Journal* 383 p. 390.

participating in Islamic finance through specialised "windows" or advisory services, establish Sharia committees. These committees consist of Islamic scholars who are generally esteemed academics with recognised expertise in Islamic jurisprudence. Sharia committees play a critical role by evaluating proposed financial transactions for compliance with Sharia principles and issuing formal opinions or *fatwas* that confirm a transaction's compliance with Islamic law.

> *In the absence of legal prescription as to what does and what does not constitute "Islamic" banking or finance, most Islamic banks create Religious or Sharia Supervisory Boards*[60] *which review annually the operations of the bank and determine whether or not these have been carried out in accordance with Islamic law.*[61]

A limited pool of qualified Sharia scholars means that many of the same experts often sit on multiple Sharia committees across different financial institutions, fostering a level of consensus on Sharia interpretation within the industry. This shared expertise aids in promoting consistent approaches across Islamic finance, despite the inherent challenges of diverse interpretations.

Islamic finance is based on five key principles.[62] Central among these is the **prohibition of *riba***, or interest. Under Islamic law, earning returns through the payment or receipt of interest is strictly forbidden. Instead, revenue must be derived from profit-sharing arrangements or ownership of tangible assets, with returns generated through legitimate trade or investment activity rather than speculative gain. A second foundational principle is the **avoidance of *gharar***, or excessive uncertainty. Islamic financial transactions must be characterised by clarity and certainty in all material terms, including price, quantity, and delivery. This requirement is more stringent than under conventional finance, where a degree of commercial uncertainty is typically tolerated.

Islamic finance also **prohibits *maisir***, or gambling. Financial products that derive their value primarily from speculation are impermissible, as Sharia seeks to eliminate risk-taking that resembles games of chance. This renders many conventional derivatives and options incompatible with Islamic financial principles in their standard form. Another tenet is the **avoidance of unjust enrichment**. Sharia forbids contractual arrangements that allow one party to exploit the other unfairly, particularly where risk is transferred in a manner that disproportionately benefits the lender. In place of fixed interest obligations, Islamic finance requires risk-sharing mechanisms whereby both parties have a stake in the outcome of the venture.

Finally, **ethical investment** is an essential tenet of Islamic finance. Investments must comply not only with financial regulations but also with moral and ethical standards as defined by Sharia. This excludes investments in industries considered harmful or impermissible, such as those involved in gambling, alcohol production, or other activities deemed unethical in Islamic jurisprudence.

60 "*The Offering Circular included also a 'Pronouncement' of the BNPP Sharia Board. This was a board of Islamic scholars who reviewed 'the structure, mechanism and the documentation for the proposed issuance of the Sukuk' in order to ensure that it was in conformity with the principles of Sharia law. The Board expressed the view that it was. The signed Pronouncement was dated 9 April 2007, well before the issue of the Promissory Note and the other Transaction Documents. It referred repeatedly to the 'proposed issue' of the Sukuk. It was obvious, therefore, that the Pronouncement did not purport to say anything about whether the Transaction Documents including the Promissory Note had been properly executed*". Per Mr Justice Males in *Golden Belt 1 Sukuk Company BSC(c) v BNP Paribas* [2017] EWHC 3182 (Comm) at [35].

61 *Beximco Pharmaceuticals Ltd & Ors v Shamil Bank of Bahrain EC* [2004] EWCA Civ 19 at [8].

62 Proctor, C., *The Law and Practice of International Banking* (Oxford University Press, 2015) at [49.04].

8.2 Some Transaction Structures

While Islamic finance structures vary across jurisdictions, certain fundamental models are widely employed by market participants. The principle of profit and loss sharing underpins Islamic finance, reflecting the Islamic perspective that contractual relationships should be based on equality, with profits and losses distributed fairly among the parties. Sharia does not prohibit the generation of profit; rather, it scrutinises the means by which profit is derived. For instance, the charging of interest is considered exploitative, particularly in circumstances where a client may be experiencing financial hardship, as it allows a financier to increase wealth without effort or risk. Instead, Islamic finance requires that profit must be earned through the assumption of risks and responsibilities as an owner of an asset or as a partner in an enterprise. This distinction underscores the emphasis in Islamic finance on equity rather than debt and its preference for transactions involving tangible assets.[63]

Murabaha

Murabaha, bai salam, istisna'a, ijara, and their variations exemplify asset-based structures, wherein the financier acquires a physical asset and assumes some degree of commercial risk associated with it. In contrast, *mudaraba* and *musharaka* represent risk-sharing structures in which the financier and the customer engage in a joint enterprise, sharing both profits and losses.

In commercial practice, transactions often combine multiple Islamic finance techniques to achieve the desired economic outcome. Large-scale financing arrangements, such as significant infrastructure projects, may incorporate both Sharia-compliant and conventional financing tranches. *Murabaha* is widely employed in trade finance and is increasingly used for acquisition finance in leveraged buyouts. Under a standard *murabaha* arrangement, the financier purchases an asset from a supplier and subsequently sells it to the customer on deferred payment terms with a fixed maturity date.[64] In return for effectively providing financing, the financier receives a deferred sale price comprising the cost price – the amount originally paid by the financier for the asset – plus a pre-agreed premium, typically payable in instalments.

A variation of *murabaha* is reverse *murabaha* or *tawarruq*. In the latter, rather than retaining the asset for use in its business, the customer sells it at the spot price, either back to the original supplier or to a third party. The asset involved is typically a freely tradable commodity, such as platinum or copper, since Sharia law treats gold and silver as currency and prohibits their use in such transactions. Through this structure, the customer can obtain a cash sum in exchange for periodic instalment payments, effectively replicating the economic outcome of interest-bearing loans. It is a fundamental requirement of both *murabaha* and *tawarruq* transactions that the financier must acquire legal title to the asset in question and assume some commercial risk in relation to it. However, in practice, this ownership is often held for a very brief

63 Dewar, J. and Hussain, M. (eds.), *The Islamic Finance and Markets Law Review* (Law Business Research, 2020), p. vii.

64 "*It is not in accordance with Islamic principles for the Bank to provide trade finance by way of short-term interest bearing loans. Accordingly the model used is so-called murabaha agreements: the Bank itself (through CCH as its agent) would buy the goods from the exporter, then, again through CCH as its agent, would sell the goods to the purchaser. The difference between the purchase price and the sale price represented the Bank's profit on the transaction. The agency arrangements with CCH succeeded similar arrangements dating back to the 1980s under which the third defendant and his then business partner, Guvan Nil, the fourth defendant's father, did murabaha deals with the Bank*" per The Honourable Mr Justice Flaux in *Dubai Islamic Bank PJSC v PSI Energy Holding Company BSC & Ors* [2013] EWHC 3186 (Comm) at [3].

period, and in the case of a reverse *murabaha*, the financier typically does not take physical delivery of the asset, merely recording the transfer of commodities as debit and credit entries in its ledger.

In *murabaha* transactions, the customer is frequently appointed as the financier's undisclosed agent to acquire the asset from the supplier on behalf of the financier.[65] This practice is particularly common in trade finance, as it allows the customer to maintain direct relationships with its suppliers. By contrast, in *tawarruq* transactions, the customer is generally not appointed as the financier's agent, as the underlying asset is usually sourced from a broker and is immediately resold by the customer.

Islamic Syndications

Murabaha and *tawarruq* structures are commonly used as Sharia-compliant alternatives to conventional loan facilities, and, like conventional loans, they may be syndicated. Unlike conventional syndicated loans, where each syndicate member extends a separate loan to the borrower under the same facility agreement, a *murabaha* is typically executed by a single financier acting as an agent on behalf of the syndicate members. The relationship between the financiers is governed by a separate agreement, often structured as a *mudaraba* (a technique in which a lender or investor [*rab al maal*] and a borrower or investment manager [*mudareb*] establish a profit-sharing partnership).

Tawarruq has also been adapted, albeit controversially among certain Sharia scholars, to create a "revolving" *tawarruq* facility, which serves as the Islamic finance equivalent of a conventional revolving loan. This facility allows a borrower to draw down, repay, and re-borrow amounts over the facility's term.[66] It operates through a series of back-to-back *murabaha* trades at the same cost price, with corresponding settlement and maturity dates. On each maturity date, the customer notionally settles the deferred sale price under the maturing *murabaha* trade by entering into a new *murabaha* transaction. In practice, the arrangement employs a netting mechanism, whereby rather than actually paying the deferred sale price under the maturing *murabaha* trade, the amount is offset against the proceeds from the new *murabaha* trade. As a result, the customer pays only the benchmark plus margin on each maturity date and defers principal repayment until the final maturity date. It is also possible to structure the facility to amortise by gradually reducing the cost price of each new trade, thereby achieving the same economic effect as a conventional amortising loan.

Murabaha and *tawarruq* agreements are often based on standard loan documentation from the LMA or the Asia Pacific Loan Markets Association (**APLMA**), modified as necessary to ensure Sharia compliance.

Key differences between Islamic and conventional loan documentation include the use of a separate syndicate agreement, which governs the relationship among financiers and addresses matters such as agency appointments, the agent's powers and duties, and internal indemnities. Sharia-compliant syndications differ fundamentally from conventional ones in their reliance on asset-backed structures and profit-sharing arrangements rather than interest-based returns. The structure typically requires multiple contracts, including the syndicate

65 Khanfar, Nehad A. A., 'The Applicability of the Islamic Mortgage Contract Under English Law' (27 November 2009), available at SSRN: https://ssrn.com/abstract=1548869 or http://dx.doi.org/10.2139/ssrn.1548869.

66 Dewar, J. and Hussain, M. (eds.), *The Islamic Finance and Markets Law Review* (Law Business Research, 2020), p. 138.

agreement, a *Murabaha* or *Ijara* contract for asset purchase, and additional documentation to establish compliance. The lead arranger, known as the *Mudarib*, coordinates financing arrangements and manages project investment, sharing returns with syndicate members based on profit-sharing ratios.

In these structures, participants avoid debt instruments and instead focus on equity-like investments, assuming some level of ownership and responsibility over the financed asset. *Mudaraba* and *Musharaka* (joint ventures) are frequently used, with *Mudaraba* being more suitable for larger projects where investors act as silent partners, akin to limited liability shareholders. Whereby

> *A Musharaka arrangement may also be what is known as a diminishing Musharaka under which the customer makes periodic payments under a lease to the bank in return for proportionate increases in his own share in the asset. Under both types of arrangement the customer will have the ultimate right to acquire the asset in question.*[67]

Given the inherent risk-sharing requirements, Islamic syndications often involve rigorous due diligence and higher documentation standards to ensure compliance.[68]

Supplier agreements are also documented separately to avoid any implication that the transaction is merely a disguised loan. The terminology in Islamic finance contracts reflects the nature of the transaction as a sale and purchase rather than a loan; for example, the customer is referred to as the "purchaser" rather than the "borrower", and the financier's return is described as the "profit amount" rather than "interest". In addition, prepayment mechanics differ from those in conventional loan agreements. In a conventional facility, a borrower may prepay a loan to reduce interest costs. However, since the profit amount in a *murabaha* is predetermined, financiers typically have the discretion to grant a partial rebate of the deferred purchase price in the event of early repayment.[69]

Certain conventional finance concepts, such as commitment fees, are prohibited under Sharia principles. Since they compensate lenders for making funds available, they are considered *riba*. To address this, financiers often stipulate short availability periods under *murabaha* arrangements. However, there has been a growing trend, particularly in the Middle East, towards structuring arrangements that enable financiers to earn an equivalent return in a Sharia-compliant manner.

Late payment fees and default penalties in *murabaha* transactions are also contentious. While most Islamic institutions permit them as a means of encouraging timely payment, the amounts collected are typically donated to charity. In some instances, the financier may be entitled to deduct the actual costs resulting from the default before making the donation.

Other Forms of Islamic Finance

A further distinguishing feature of Islamic finance is the requirement for the financier to bear some risk associated with asset ownership. *Ijarah*[70] is a lease-based structure commonly

67 In *Project Blue Ltd v Revenue and Customs* [2016] EWCA Civ 485 at [47].

68 Proctor, C., *The Law and Practice of International Banking* (Oxford University Press, 2015) at [49.44].

69 Wilson, R., *Islamic Finance in Europe* (Robert Schuman Centre for Advanced Studies, 2007).

70 *"[T]he Ijara form of Shari'a financing transaction which was the method utilised in this case does not involve the holding of security by the financial institution in question in the conventional sense of a charge with a power of sale and the retention by the chargor of an equity of redemption enabling the recovery of the property free from the charge on repayment of the loan and any interest and costs. It respects the Islamic prohibition on usury by providing for the property in question to be acquired by the financial institution as its property and then leased to the person seeking the finance in exchange for agreed rental payments which give the financial institution a return on its money. The arrangements will also contain options enabling the*

used in real estate acquisition and other forms of asset finance, including aircraft, ships, and project finance. Under this arrangement, a bank purchases the property and places ownership in a holding subsidiary, subsequently leasing the asset to the buyer through an *ijarah* lease. The title to the property typically remains with the bank until the borrower has fully repaid the cost of the property. During the lease period, the customer pays rent to the bank, which includes the purchase price and the bank's profit. Unlike in a conventional finance lease, where the lessee bears most obligations, the bank, acting as both owner and lessor, is responsible for insuring the asset and undertaking major maintenance. However, these obligations can be contracted out to the borrower, who assumes the role of the lessee. This increased risk exposure may be mitigated by structuring the transaction through an SPV, which acts as a lessor. Additionally, the financier may appoint the customer as its agent to obtain insurance and maintain the asset. The lessee is only liable for rent payments while continuing to use the asset, and the *ijarah* structure cannot become effective until the completion of the leased facility's construction. A key distinction from conventional leasing is that, under *ijarah*, if the property is completely destroyed or condemned, making it unusable for its intended purpose, the rent obligation ceases. The lease-to-purchase model, known as *ijarah wa iqtina*, is also widely used in real estate investment, particularly in the United States.[71]

Sukuk, often referred to as "Islamic bonds", are another key instrument in Islamic finance. Unlike conventional bonds, which represent debt obligations, sukuk confer an undivided ownership interest in an underlying asset, entitling holders to a proportionate share of its returns. For an example of such a structure:

> *The certificates were issued to raise money for investment which was intended to be made in a manner compliant with Islamic religious law (Shari'a). Such certificates are known as sukuk. Sukuk may be issued to finance a variety of different Shari'a-compliant investment activities or structures. One such structure, used in this case, is known as a mudarabah and hence the certificates were described in the listing particulars as sukuk al-mudarabah. A mudarabah is a form of joint venture in which one party (the rab al-maal) invests capital and the other party (the mudarib) invests skill or labour with a view to making a profit which will ultimately be shared between them on an agreed basis.*[72]

8.3 Challenges and Standardisation

While entities like the Accounting and Auditing Organization for Islamic Financial Institutions (**AAOIFI**) have made strides in standardising practices, regional variations persist. For instance, Islamic finance structures that are accepted in one country may face compliance issues in another due to differing interpretations of Sharia principles. This fragmentation has led to a push for greater global standardisation and alignment aimed at making Islamic finance more accessible and cost-effective.

Several prominent financial market bodies, including the International Islamic Financial Market (**IIFM**), the LMA, ICMA, and the International Swaps and Derivatives Association (ISDA), have developed or plan to develop standard form documentation for Sharia-compliant finance transactions. These efforts are challenging due to the significant variation in what constitutes Sharia compliance across different regions, as the restrictions applying to such

property to be acquired by the customer at the end of the rental period or earlier upon terms which provide for the repayment of the balance of any consideration paid by the financial institution for the acquisition of the property and not recovered as rent". In *Project Blue Ltd v Revenue and Customs* [2016] EWCA Civ 485 at [6].

71 Dewar, J. and Hussain, M. (eds.), *The Islamic Finance and Markets Law Review* (Law Business Research, 2020), p. vii.

72 In *Dana Gas PJSC v Dana Gas Sukuk Ltd & Ors* [2017] EWHC 2928 (Comm) at [10].

transactions vary widely. Nevertheless, standardised documents are exceptionally valuable to the growth and accessibility of Islamic finance. Transactions such as *murabaha* and *sukuk*, which are widely used in the market, particularly benefit from such standardisation.

For liquidity management, IIFM has produced the Master Agreements for Treasury Placement (**MATP**), a set of documents for over-the-counter commodity *murabaha* transactions. Available in English, Arabic, and French, these agreements include a Master Murabaha Agreement, a Master Agency Agreement for the purchase of commodities, and a Commodity Murabaha structure memorandum.

Additionally, the Master Collateralized Murabaha Agreement, designed as a Sharia-compliant alternative to repos, supports liquidity management by allowing Islamic financial institutions to access collateralised funds using Sukuk and other Islamic securities.

9 CONCLUSION

In conclusion, securitisation, CLOs, Islamic finance, and repos represent alternative financing mechanisms that expand upon the capabilities of traditional bank lending, providing issuers and investors with innovative tools to meet diverse financial objectives. Each of these models presents unique ways to navigate the complex regulatory, ethical, and liquidity landscapes that define modern finance. Securitisation, with its focus on pooling assets and segmenting risk through tranching and structured finance techniques, offers flexibility for capital mobilisation and risk dispersion.

Islamic finance stands out for its alignment with ethical standards rooted in Sharia principles, promoting risk-sharing and asset-backed structures that eschew interest-based transactions.

Repos, meanwhile, serve as a vital tool for short-term, secured funding, facilitating efficient liquidity management while transferring title to the buyer. The flexibility of repos, which can be tailored to accommodate various forms of collateral and repayment schedules, has positioned them as indispensable tools in institutional cash management and as mechanisms to stabilise financial markets during periods of volatility.

The increasing complexity and regulatory oversight of these alternative financing structures reflects their growing importance within a globalised and interconnected financial system. These regulations underscore the need for continued innovation, transparency, and standardisation to ensure these alternative financing models continue to deliver value in a safe and efficient manner.

CONCLUDING REMARKS

This book has examined the complex legal and regulatory architectures underpinning international banking, providing an understanding of the institutional structures, operative mechanisms, and regulatory challenges that define and influence financial systems.

Each chapter has considered key components of international banking law, from historical foundations to legal structures underpinning modern finance, revealing a landscape defined by complexity, rapid change, and the continuous interplay between legal innovation and regulatory oversight.

These concluding remarks are an attempt to summarise the insights gathered throughout the book, highlighting the critical role of law and regulation in maintaining financial stability, delivering a predictable outcome, and protecting market participants.

THE EVOLUTION OF BANKING LAW: FROM HISTORICAL ORIGINS TO MODERN COMPLEXITIES

Tracing the history of banking law reveals how financial institutions have adapted to an evolving commercial environment, with legal frameworks progressively developed to support and regulate these changes. The early banking systems of Venice and Florence, built on trust and informal practices, set the stage for more formalised financial institutions in England, the US, Europe, and Asia. Over centuries, legal systems have responded to the growing complexity of banking, with incremental legislative milestones helping to shape modern finance.

MONEY AND PAYMENTS: NAVIGATING DIGITAL INNOVATION

The nature of money and the systems that facilitate payment mechanisms have evolved from physical currency and paper-based payment methods to digital assets and cryptocurrencies, reshaping the concept of money and challenging traditional legal frameworks.

The exploration of money, debt, and payment highlights the role of law in shaping the enforceability of transactions across jurisdictions. An examination of the legal structures surrounding set-off and netting arrangements, dematerialised payment systems, and Central Bank Digital Currencies underlines the dual role of law in fostering innovation and protecting market participants. As these developments continue, the legal landscape must adapt to support a secure and efficient payments ecosystem, demonstrating the need for regulatory frameworks that can balance innovation with systemic integrity.

ANTI-FINANCIAL CRIME AND REGULATORY CHALLENGES

The prevention of financial crime, including money laundering, terrorism financing, and sanctions evasion, is another pillar of banking regulation, particularly as financial crime becomes increasingly complex and cross-border in nature. The UK's financial crime framework, supported by legislation such as the Proceeds of Crime Act (POCA) and the Money Laundering Regulations, positions the country at the forefront of global anti-crime efforts.

DOI: 10.4324/9781032662220-16

The EU, the US, and the Chinese frameworks contribute to these efforts, each with a different focus.

THE ROLE OF PRUDENTIAL REGULATION AND CORPORATE GOVERNANCE

A cornerstone of financial stability is the prudential regulation of banks. This regulatory approach, grounded in frameworks like the Basel Accords, has evolved to address the systemic risks associated with globalised finance. The 2007–2009 global financial crisis underscored the vulnerabilities of insufficient capital buffers, weak liquidity management, and inadequate oversight of large financial institutions. The prudential regulatory frameworks in the UK, EU, US, China, India, and Japan reflect a commitment to risk management and financial resilience, with regulators increasingly focused on areas such as leverage, liquidity, and operational resilience.

Corporate governance plays a complementary role in maintaining stability within the banking sector. Governance reforms in the UK and other jurisdictions..

RECOVERY, RESOLUTION, AND SYSTEMIC RESILIENCE

The ability of financial institutions to recover from distress without destabilising the broader economy is a critical focus of modern banking law. Recovery and resolution mechanisms, including the UK's ring-fencing regime and the Bank Recovery and Resolution Directive in the EU, provide structured frameworks for managing the failure of banks. Ring-fencing, which separates retail banking from riskier investment banking activities, aims to protect essential services from market volatility, reducing systemic risk.

Internationally, recovery and resolution frameworks highlight a shared commitment to systemic resilience. As global finance continues to integrate, effective recovery and resolution frameworks remain essential, ensuring that banks can fail safely without triggering widespread economic instability.

LENDING, SECURED TRANSACTIONS, AND CROSS-BORDER FINANCING

The dynamics of corporate lending, secured transactions, and cross-border finance reflect both the complexity of modern banking and the legal structures necessary to support it. In a globalised economy, cross-border lending is critical, enabling businesses to access capital across jurisdictions. However, these transactions come with unique risks, including legal enforceability, exchange control regulations, and tax implications.

Secured transactions, in particular, offer lenders protection in the event of borrower default, with legal structures varying significantly across jurisdictions. Understanding the nuances of security interests, particularly in cross-border contexts, is essential for managing creditor risks. Syndicated loans provide an effective mechanism for pooling resources in large-scale transactions, balancing the needs of multiple lenders while offering borrowers access to substantial capital.

THE ROLE OF ALTERNATIVE FINANCING MODELS

The modern financial landscape is not limited to traditional lending; securitisation, collateralised loan obligations (CLOs), Islamic finance, and repurchase agreements (repos) have emerged as sophisticated financing tools that cater to a range of needs beyond those met by conventional bank loans. These structures provide mechanisms for risk distribution, liquidity management, and regulatory capital optimisation. Securitisation allows financial institutions to transform illiquid assets into marketable securities, enabling capital flexibility and risk dispersion. CLOs similarly distribute loan risks across tranches, catering to investors with varying risk appetites.

Islamic finance, driven by Sharia-compliant principles, provides an ethical alternative to interest-based lending. Its asset-backed, risk-sharing model has gained popularity not only in Muslim-majority countries but also in international financial centres. Repos, meanwhile, serve as essential instruments in money markets, enabling short-term funding and liquidity management. As regulatory frameworks adapt to accommodate these alternative structures, the role of law in ensuring transparency, risk mitigation, and investor protection becomes even more pronounced. Alternative finance thus represents a reflection of the flexibility and adaptability of modern banking law.

A LEGAL FRAMEWORK FOR INTERNATIONAL BANKING

In the journey of modern banking, law and regulation play a fundamental, multi-dimensional role, supporting and stabilising the financial system while accommodating the diverse needs of participants in an increasingly interconnected and volatile global market. The evolution of banking law reveals a process of continual adaptation, driven by the lessons learned from financial crises, the pressures of globalisation, and the unrelenting pace of technological advancement.

The dual role of law, therefore, is to maintain stability while fostering innovation. This balance requires a regulatory framework that is both robust and responsive. Overly rigid laws may stifle innovation and competitiveness, driving businesses to less-regulated markets or shadow banking sectors. Conversely, an under-regulated environment can result in the unchecked growth of risks, potentially culminating in crises that undermine confidence in the financial system. The challenge for international banking law is to evolve as a dynamic framework that accommodates both the need for security and the demands of a fast-paced, global financial marketplace.

THE NEED FOR COHESIVE GLOBAL STANDARDS

In today's interconnected world, the actions of a financial institution in one jurisdiction can have far-reaching implications across the globe, as evidenced by the ripple effects of the 2007–2008 financial crisis. The crisis underscored the critical need for a coordinated global response to systemic risk, driving the development of unified standards under international bodies such as the Basel Committee on Banking Supervision, the Financial Stability Board, and the International Monetary Fund.

These global standards offer a framework for capital adequacy and liquidity, yet each participating country is tasked with implementing these standards within its own regulatory system. While cohesive global standards enhance systemic resilience, they must be balanced with regulatory flexibility, allowing each jurisdiction to address the specific risks and needs of its financial market.

Further convergence, particularly in areas such as anti-money laundering, digital finance, and climate risk, will be essential in promoting a unified approach to the challenges that span national borders. These developments are not without complexity, however, as regulatory divergence can introduce complications for cross-border financial institutions that must navigate conflicting regulatory requirements. International banking law, therefore, faces the challenge of facilitating both harmonisation and jurisdictional specificity – promoting a level playing field while respecting the diversity of national legal systems.

ETHICAL FINANCE AND THE ROLE OF ESG STANDARDS

Despite the global tension on ESG considerations, ESG principles represent a fundamental shift in how finance interacts with society, moving beyond profit maximisation towards broader ethical responsibilities. The incorporation of ESG standards into banking regulation requires an expansion of traditional legal frameworks to include sustainability considerations. This shift is exemplified by the EU's Sustainable Finance Disclosure Regulation (Regulation (EU) 2019/2088) and the UK's Green Finance Strategy, which set requirements for financial institutions to report on their environmental impact and integrate sustainability into their operations. Such initiatives highlight the transformative role of law in ensuring that finance contributes positively to society while protecting the rights of stakeholders and present and future generations.

DIGITAL TRANSFORMATION: NAVIGATING TECHNOLOGICAL INNOVATION AND REGULATORY ADAPTATION

Technology has transformed the banking sector, offering unparalleled opportunities for financial inclusion, efficiency, and innovation. Digital banking, fintech, blockchain, and cryptocurrencies represent new frontiers that require not only legal accommodation but also proactive regulatory oversight. The pace of technological innovation has outstripped that of regulatory development, creating both opportunities and challenges for banking law. The rise of digital assets, such as cryptocurrencies and central bank digital currencies (CBDCs), has sparked a global regulatory conversation about the future of money, with central banks and regulators grappling with how best to incorporate these assets within traditional legal frameworks. Different national approaches to digital assets can give rise to regulatory fragmentation that may result in arbitrage and complicate cross-border transactions.

Therefore, the regulatory challenge posed by digital transformation is twofold: ensuring that new technologies enhance, rather than destabilise, the financial system, and establishing a coherent legal framework that accommodates innovation while protecting consumers. Regulating digital finance involves balancing security, privacy, and financial stability with the need for accessibility and innovation.

FINANCIAL CRIME AND GLOBAL REGULATORY COOPERATION

The fight against financial crime, encompassing money laundering, terrorism financing, bribery, and sanctions violations, is a key area where global regulatory cooperation is crucial.

Financial crime poses risks not only to the integrity of the financial system but also to national security and societal well-being. Laws like the Proceeds of Crime Act 2002, the US's Bank Secrecy Act, and global initiatives led by the Financial Action Task Force reflect a collective commitment to combatting financial crime. However, conflicting regulatory requirements, divergent sanctions regimes, and sudden shifts in regulatory commitments can complicate compliance for institutions operating across multiple jurisdictions.

The extraterritorial reach of anti-money laundering and anti-bribery laws, such as the Bribery Act 2010, underscores the need for banks to navigate an increasingly complex web of international regulations. A cohesive global approach to financial crime regulation or, at least, cooperation amongst regulators, while extremely difficult to achieve in a world that is veering towards de-globalisation, will be instrumental in ensuring that financial institutions can operate in a secure, compliant manner, reducing the risks associated with cross-border financial flows.

RECOVERY, RESOLUTION, AND SYSTEMIC RISK MANAGEMENT

The financial crises of the past decades have underscored the importance of effective recovery and resolution mechanisms in maintaining systemic resilience. The "too big to fail" problem remains a focal point for regulators, with the introduction of Total Loss Absorbing Capacity requirements, recovery plans, and ring-fencing measures aimed at ensuring that large financial institutions can absorb losses and fail without destabilising the broader economy. Recovery and resolution frameworks, as implemented in the UK, EU, US, China, India, and Japan, reflect a collective effort to reduce the risks associated with systemic institutions, thereby enhancing financial stability.

Supervisory coordination, both within and across jurisdictions, is critical in managing systemic risk, particularly as financial institutions operate in multiple countries. International banking law, therefore, must continue to evolve to address these interconnected risks, ensuring that the legal framework supports a resilient, stable, and secure financial system.

THE PATH FORWARD: BALANCING TRADITION AND TRANSFORMATION IN BANKING LAW

The concluding reflections on international banking law highlight an overarching theme: the need for a modern legal framework that balances tradition with transformation. Traditional principles, such as prudential regulation, risk management, and consumer protection, remain as relevant as ever.

In the coming years, international banking law will continue to be tested by new developments, including the rise of artificial intelligence in financial services, the regulatory implications of climate-related risks, sudden policy divergence, and the geopolitical dynamics that shape financial markets. The future of international banking law lies in its ability to adapt to these diverse pressures and to accommodate transformative elements while maintaining the stability and integrity of the financial system.

BIBLIOGRAPHY

BOOKS

- Adams, D., *Banking and Capital Markets* (College of Law Publishing, 2024).
- Akseli, O. and Gray, J. *Financial Regulation in Crisis?: The Role of Law and the Failure of Northern Rock* (Edward Elgar Publishing, 2011).
- Ali, P., *Secured Finance Transactions: Key Assets and Emerging Markets* (Globe Business Publishing, 2007).
- Altamura, C. E., *European Banks and the Rise of International Finance: The Post-Bretton Woods Era* (Routledge, 2016).
- Appleby, J., *Economic Thought and Ideology in Seventeenth-Century England* (Princeton University Press, 1978).
- Armour, J., Awrey, D., Davies, P., Enriques, L., Gordon, J., Mayer, C. and Payne, J., *Principles of Financial Regulation* (Oxford University Press, 2016).
- Arora, A., *Banking Law* (Pearson, 2014).
- Arrighi, G., *The Long Twentieth Century: Money, Power, and the Origins of Our Times* (Verso, 2010).
- The Association of Corporate Treasurers, *A Borrower's Guide to the LMA's Investment Grade Agreements* (ACT 6th Edition, November 2022).
- Bamford, C., *Principles of International Finance Law* (Oxford University Press, 2015).
- Barofsky, N., *Bailout: How Washington Abandoned Main Street While Rescuing Wall Street* (Free Press, 2013).
- Blizzard, K., *The Law of Financial Derivatives in Ireland* (Round Hall, 2011).
- Böhm, K. and Prechtel, A. (eds.), *Banking Business in Germany* (PricewaterhouseCoopers GmbH Wirtschaftsprüfungsgesellschaft, 2023).
- Böttcher, J. (ed.), *Green Banking: Realizing Renewable Energy Projects* (De Gruyter Oldenbour, 2020).
- Braudel, F., *Civilization and Capitalism, 15th–18th Century, Volume II: The Wheels of Commerce* (University of California Press, 1984).
- Breslin, J., *Banking Law* (Round Hall, 2013).
- Breslin, J., *Banking Law – First Supplement* (Round Hall, 2015).
- Breslin, J., *Banking Law in the Republic of Ireland* (Round Hall, 2004).
- Bridge, M., *Personal Property Law* (Oxford University Press, 2015).
- Bridge, M., Gullifer, L., McMeel, G. and Low, K., *The Law of Personal Property* (Sweet & Maxwell, 2017).
- Brindle, M. and Cox, R. (eds.), *Law of Bank Payments* (Sweet & Maxwell, 2017).
- Calnan, R., *Taking Security: Law and Practice* (LexisNexis, 2018).
- Cashill, J., *Popes and Bankers* (Thomas Nelson, 2010).
- Cassis, Y., Schenk, C. R. and Grossman, R. S. (eds.), *The Oxford Handbook of Banking and Financial History* (Oxford University Press, 2018).
- Chernow, R., *The Death of the Banker: The Decline and Fall of the Great Financial Dynasties and the Triumph of the Small Investor* (Vintage Books, 1997).
- Chitty, J., *Chitty on Contracts* (Sweet & Maxwell, 2014).
- Chiu, I. and Wilson, J., *Banking Law and Regulation* (Oxford University Press, 2019).
- Clark, R. and Clarke, B., *Contract Cases and Materials* (Gill & MacMillan, 2008).
- Clark, W. and Morgan, J., *Fisher and Lightwood's Law of Mortgage* (LexisNexis, 2014).
- Cranston, R., Avgouleas, E., van Zwieten, K., Hare, C. and van Sante, T., *Principles of Banking Law* (Oxford University Press, 2018).

- Crockett, A., *Money: Theory, Policy and Institutions* (Thomas Nelson & Sons Ltd, 1973).
- De Roover, R., *The Medici Bank: Its Organization, Management, Operations, and Decline* (New York University Press, 1948).
- Dewar, J. (ed.), *ICLG – Project Finance 2024* (ICLG, 2024).
- Dewar, J. and Hussain, M. (eds.), *The Islamic Finance and Markets Law Review* (Law Business Research, 2020).
- Ehrenberg, R., *Capital and Finance in the Age of the Renaissance: A Study on the Fuggers and Their Connections* (Kelley, 1985).
- Ellinger, E. P., Lomnicka, E. and Hare, C., *Ellinger's Modern Banking Law* (Oxford University Press, 2011).
- Elmgren, K. N., *International Asset Securitisation* (Kluwer, 1995).
- Epstein, S. R., *Genoa and the Genoese, 958–1528* (University of North Carolina Press, 1996).
- Ferguson, N., *The Ascent of Money: A Financial History of the World* (Penguin Books, 2008).
- Ferguson, N., *The World's Banker: The History of the House of Rothschild* (Weidenfeld & Nicolson, 1999).
- Financial Stability Board, *Key Attributes of Effective Resolution Regimes for Financial Institutions* (FSB, 25 April 2024).
- Finch, V., *Corporate Insolvency Law: Perspective and Principles,* (Cambridge University Press, 2002).
- Finnerty, J., *Project Financing: Asset-Based Financial Engineering* (John Wiley & Sons, 2007).
- Firth, S., *Firth on Derivatives Law and Practice* (Sweet & Maxwell, 2003).
- Fox, D., *Property Rights in Money* (Oxford University Press, 2008).
- Fuller, G., *Corporate Borrowing: Law and Practice* (LexisNexis, 2016).
- Gatti, S., *Project Finance in Theory and Practice – Designing, Structuring, and Financing Private and Public Projects* (Academic Press, 2013).
- Gleeson-White, J., *Double Entry: How the Merchants of Venice Created Modern Finance* (W.W. Norton & Co, 2012).
- Goode, R., *Commercial Law* (Penguin, 2021).
- Goode, R., *Corporate Insolvency Law* (Sweet & Maxwell, 2005).
- Goode, R., *Goode on Commercial Law* (Penguin Books, 2016).
- Goode, R., *Legal Problems of Credit and Security* (Sweet & Maxwell, 2003).
- Goode, R. and van Zwieten, K., *Principles of Corporate Insolvency Law* (Sweet & Maxwell, 2019).
- Goodhart, C., *The Basel Committee on Banking Supervision: A History of the Early Years* (Cambridge University Press, 2011).
- Goris, P., *The Legal Aspect of Swaps* (Aspen Publishers, 1994).
- Gorton, G., *The Maze of Banking: History, Theory, Crisis* (Oxford University Press, 2015).
- Gullifer, L., *Goode and Gullifer* on *Legal Problems of Credit and Security* (Sweet & Maxwell, 2023).
- Gullifer, L. and Payne, J., *Corporate Finance Law: Principles and Policy* (Hart, 2020).
- Haentjens, M. and De Gioia-Carabellese, P., *European Banking and Financial Law* (Routledge, 2015).
- Heers, J., *Gênes au XVe siècle* (Flammarion, 1961).
- Hideaki, S., 'Japan: Law & Practice' in *Chambers Global Practice Guides: Banking Regulation 2024*, Nagashima Ohno and Tsunematsu (Chambers and Partners, 2024).
- Hudson, A., *The Law of Finance* (Sweet & Maxwell, 2013).
- Hudson, A., *The Law on Financial Derivatives* (Sweet & Maxwell, 2017).
- Insolvency and Bankruptcy Board of India, *Understanding the IBC: Key Jurisprudence and Practical Considerations – a Handbook* (International Finance Corporation, 2020).
- Kawamura, A., *Corporate Governance 2015* (Sweet & Maxwell International Series, 2015).
- Kern, A., *Principles of Banking Regulation* (Cambridge University Press, 2019).
- King, M., *The End of Alchemy: Money, Banking, and the Future of the Global Economy* (W.W. Norton & Company, 2016).
- Kokkinis, A. and Miglionico, M., *Banking Law: Private Transactions and Regulatory Frameworks* (Routledge, 2021).

- Kothari, V., *Securitisation: The Financial Instrument of the New Millennium, India* (Academy of Financial Services, 1999).
- Lane, F., *Venice: A Maritime Republic* (Johns Hopkins University Press, 1973).
- Lane, F. and Riemersma, J. (eds.), *Economic History* (Homewood, 1953).
- Lo Schiavo, G., *EU Banking Law and Regulation* (Oxford Academic, 2024).
- Mann, F. A., *The Legal Aspect of Money: With Special Reference to Comparative Private and Public International Law* (Oxford University Press, 1992).
- Martin, F., *Money* (Vintage Books, 2013).
- Mellor, T. (ed.), *ICLG – Lending & Secured Finance 2024* (ICLG, 2024).
- Minsky, H. P., *Can "It" Happen Again?* (Routledge Classics, 2016).
- Miskimin, H., *The Economy of Early Renaissance Europe, 1300–1460* (Cambridge University Press, 1975).
- Moloney, N., *EU Securities and Financial Markets Regulation* (Oxford European Union Law Library, 2014).
- Moloney, N., *EU Securities and Financial Markets Regulation* (Oxford University Press, 2016).
- Morse, G., *Palmer's Company Law* (Sweet & Maxwell, 2025).
- Mueller, R., *The Venetian Money Market: Banks, Panics, and the Public Debt, 1200–1500* (Johns Hopkins University Press, 2019).
- Mugasha, A., *The Law of Multi-Bank Financing: Syndicated Loans and the Secondary Loan Market* (Oxford University Press, 2007).
- Neal, L., *The Rise of Financial Capitalism: International Capital Markets in the Age of Reason* (Cambridge University Press, 1990).
- Nishimura, S., Suzuki, T. and Michie, R. (eds.), *The Origins of International Banking in Asia: The Nineteenth and Twentieth Centuries* (Oxford University Press, 2012).
- Nuovo, A., Proot, J. and Booton, D. (eds.), *Competition in the European Book Market* (The Golden Compasses, 2023).
- Odgers, J. and Wilson, I., *Paget's Law of Banking* (LexisNexis, 2023).
- Oditah, F., *Legal Aspects of Receivables Financing* (Sweet & Maxwell, 1991).
- Parks, T., *Medici Money: Banking, Metaphysics, and Art in Fifteenth-Century Florence* (W.W. Norton & Company, 2005).
- Petram, L. O., *The World's First Stock Exchange: How the Amsterdam Market for Dutch East India Company Shares Became a Modern Financial Market* (Columbia University Press, 2014).
- Pirie, F., *The Rule of Laws* (Profile Books, 2022).
- Proctor, C., *The Law and Practice of International Banking* (Oxford University Press, 2015).
- Proctor, C., *Mann on the Legal Aspects of Money* (Oxford University Press, 2012).
- Ruys, T., Ryngaert, C. and Silvestre, F., *The Cambridge Handbook of Secondary Sanctions and International Law* (Cambridge University Press, 2024).
- Scott, S., *The Law of Loans and Borrowing* (Sweet & Maxwell, 2024).
- Shaw, Z., *International Securitisation* (Macmillan, 1991).
- Southern, D., *Taxation of Loan Relationships and Derivative Contracts – Supplement to the 10th Edition* (Bloomsbury Professional, 2020).
- Spufford, P., *Handbook of Mediaeval Exchange* (The Royal Historical Society, 1986).
- Strathern, P., *The Medici: Power, Money, and Ambition in the Italian Renaissance* (Pimlico Edition, 2005).
- Tarullo, D., *Banking on Basel: The Future of International Financial Regulation* (Peterson Institute for International Economics, 2008).
- UNIDROIT Working Group on Bank Insolvency, *Draft Legislative Guide on Bank Liquidation* (UNIDROIT, June 2024) Study LXXXIV.
- Vinter, G., Price, G. and Lee, D., *Project Finance* (Sweet & Maxwell, 2013).
- Von Glahn, R., *Fountain of Fortune: Money and Monetary Policy in China, 1000–1700* (University of California Press, 1996).
- Wechsberg, J., *The Merchant Bankers* (Little, Brown and Company, 1966).

- Whitworth, A., *Regulating Banks: The Politics of Instability* (Agenda Publishing, 2021).
- Wilson, R., *Islamic Finance in Europe* (Robert Schuman Centre for Advanced Studies, 2007).
- Wood, P., *Comparative Law of Security Interests and Title Finance* (Sweet & Maxwell, 2019).
- Wood, P., *The Fall of the Priests and the Rise of the Lawyers* (Bloomsbury, 2016).
- Wood, P., *International Loans, Bonds, Guarantees and Legal Opinions* (Sweet & Maxwell, 2019).
- Wood, P., *Law and Practice of International Finance* (Sweet & Maxwell, 2008).
- Wood, P., *Project Finance, Securitisations and Subordinated Debt* (Sweet & Maxwell, 2019).
- Wood, P., *Regulation of International Finance* (Sweet & Maxwell, 2019).
- Wood, P., *Set-Off and Netting, Derivatives, Clearing Systems* (Sweet & Maxwell, 2019).
- Ziegler, P., *The Sixth Great Power: A History of One of the Greatest of All Banking Families, the House of Barings, 1762–1929* (Alfred A. Knopf, 1988).
- Zilioli, C., Bismuth, R. and Thévenoz, L. (eds.), *International Sanctions: Monetary and Financial Law Perspectives* (Brill – Nijhoff, 2024).

ARTICLES, TRANSCRIPTS, REPORTS, AND WORKING PAPERS

- Adams, R. and Mehran, H., 'Is Corporate Governance Different for Bank Holding Companies?' (2003) 9 *FRBNY Economic Policy Review* 123.
- Aldasoro, I. and Barth, A., 'Syndicated Loans and CDS Positioning' (November 2017) *ESRB: Working Paper Series No. 2017/58.*
- Aldasoro, I., Ehlers, T. and Eren, E., 'Business Models and Dollar Funding of Global Banks' (2018) *BIS Working Paper 48.*
- Alexander, K., 'Establishing a European Securities Regulator: Is the European Union an Optimal Regulation Area?' (2002) *The Cambridge Endowment for Research in Finance, University of Cambridge, Working Paper No. 7.*
- Applegarth, P., 'Credit and Unconscionability – the Rise and Fall of Statutes', speech delivered for the WA Lee Equity Lecture 2020, Supreme Court of Queensland, Brisbane (QSC)' (2020) *Queensland Judicial Scholarship* 13.
- Armelius, H., Guibourg, G., Johansson, S. and Schmalholz, J., E'-Krona Design Models: Pros, Cons and Trade-Offs' (2020) (2) *Sveriges Riksbank Economic Review* 80–96.
- Aurazo, J., Frost, J. and Kosse, A., 'Faster Digital Payments: Global and Regional Perspectives' (December 2024) *BIS Papers No 152.*
- Bank of England, 'Central Bank Digital Currency: Opportunities, Challenges, and Design' (2020) *Bank of England Discussion Paper.*
- Basel Committee on Banking Supervision, 'Basel III: A Global Regulatory Framework for More Resilient Banks and Banking Systems' (2011) *Bank for International Settlements.*
- Basel Committee on Banking Supervision, 'CRE: Calculation of RWA for Credit Risk – CRE50: Counterparty Credit Risk Definitions and Terminology' (Version effective as of 15 December 2019, updated 5 July 2024).
- Basel Committee on Banking Supervision, *Minimum Standards for the Supervision of International Banking Groups and Their Cross-Border Establishments* (Bank for International Settlements, July 1992).
- Basel Committee on Banking Supervision, *Supervisory Guidance for Managing Risks Associated with the Settlement of Foreign Exchange Transactions: Consultative Document* (August 2012).
- BCG [2024], BCG, 'Fortune Favors the Bold' (October 2024) *Global Payments Report.*
- Bell, I. and Dawson, P., 'Synthetic Securitization: Use of Derivative Technology for Credit Transfers' (2002) 12 *Duke Journal of Comparative & International Law* 541.
- Berentsen, A. and Rocheteau, G., 'The Role of Money in Double Coincidence Environments' (2000) University of Lausanne, Faculty HEC, DEEP, *Cahiers de Recherches Economiques du Departement d'Econometrie et d'Economie politique* (DEEP).
- Black, A. and Sadiq, K., 'Good and Bad Sharia: Australia's Mixed Response to Islamic Law' (2011) 34(1) *UNSW Law Journal* 383.

- Blackmore, V. and Jeapes, E., 'The Global Financial Crisis: One Global Financial Regulator or Multiple Regulators?' (2009) 4 *Capital Markets Law Journal* 112, 113.
- Bollen, R., 'The International Financial System and Future Global Regulation' (2008) *Journal of International Banking Law and Regulation* 458.
- Breeden, S., 'Avoiding the Storm: Climate Change and the Financial System' (15 April 2019) *Bank of England.*
- Buckley, R., 'Reconceptualizing the Regulation of Global Finance' (2016) 36(2) *Oxford Journal of Legal Studies* 242.
- Buckley, R. and Nixon, J., 'The Role of Reputation in Banking' (2009) *UNSWLRS* 18.
- Burietz, A. and Mazza, P., 'Lead Arrangers in Syndicated Loans' (5 March 2021) *SSRN Electronic Journal.*
- Chancellor, E., *The Price of Time: The Real Story of Interest* (Penguin Books, 2023).
- Cheung, R., 'Deferred Prosecution Agreements: Cooperation and Confession' (2018) 77(1) *The Cambridge Law Journal* 12–15.
- Clarke, B., 'Duty of Care, Skill and Diligence – from Warm Baths to Hot Water' (2016) 56 *Irish Jurist* 139–160.
- Contract and Commercial Law Committee New Zealand, Working Paper on the Reform of the Moneylenders Act 1908 [1971] *NZCCLRCom* 7.
- Crabbe, L., 'The International Gold Standard and U.S. Monetary Policy from World War I to the New Deal' (June 1989) *Federal Reserve Bulletin.*
- Crawford, C., 'The Repeal of the Glass-Steagall Act and the Current Financial Crisis' (2011) 9(1) *Journal of Business & Economics Research* 127.
- Curie, C., 'Toward s a General Theory of Financial Regulation: Predicting, Measuring and Preventing Financial Crisis' (2005) *Working Paper No. 142*, University of Technology, Sydney.
- Daley, M., 'Funded Participations – Mitigation of Grantor Credit Risk' (2009) *JIBLR* 288.
- European Banking Authority, 'Report on Environmental, Social and Governance (ESG) Risks Management and Supervision' *EBA/REP/2021/18.*
- Farrar, S., 'Accommodating Islamic Banking and Finance in Australia' (2011) 34(1) *UNSW Law Journal* 413.
- Felloni, G., 'The Genoese Assemblies of the Popular Government (1528–1576)' (2009) 16(2) *Financial History Review* 139–159.
- Ferreira, C., Jenkinson, N. and Wilson, C., 'From Basel I to Basel III: Sequencing Implementation in Developing Economies' (2019) *WP/19/127.*
- Ferris, E., 'The Financial Relations of the Knights Templars to the English Crown' (1902) 8(1) *The American Historical Review* 1.
- Feyen, E., Frost, J., Gambacorta, L., Natarajan, H. and Saal, M., 'Fintech and the Digital Transformation of Financial Services: Implications for Market Structure and Public Policy' (2021) *BIS Papers No 117.*
- Flandreau, M. and Ugolini, S., 'Where It All Began: Lending of Last Resort at the Bank of England Monitoring During the Overend-Gurney Panic of 1866' (2011) *Norges Bank Working Paper No. 2011/03.*
- Fletcher, G., 'Hazardous Hedging: The (Unacknowledged) Risks of Hedging with Credit Derivatives' (2013–2014) 33 *Review of Banking & Financial Law.*
- Fratianni, M., 'The Evolutionary Chain of International Financial Centers' (2008) *MoFiR Working Paper No 6.*
- Fratianni, M. and Spinelli, F., 'Italian City-States and Financial Evolution' (2006) 10 *European Review of Economic History.*
- Gelderblom, O. and Jonker, J., 'Completing a Financial Revolution: The Finance of the Dutch East India Trade and the Rise of the Amsterdam Capital Market, 1595–1612' (2004) 64(3) *The Journal of Economic History* 641–672.
- Gong, D., Lambert, T. and Wagner, W., 'Local Bank Supervision' (28 September 2023), available at https://papers.ssrn.com/sol3/papers.cfm?abstract_id=4586662 (accessed in March 2025).

- Hablutzel, P., 'British Banks' Role in U.K. Capital Markets since the Big Bang' (1992) 68 *Chicago-Kent Law Review* 365.
- Haldane, A. G. and May, R. M., 'Systemic Risk in Banking Ecosystems' (2011) 469 *Nature* 351–355.
- Hall, M., 'The Sub-Prime Crisis, the Credit Squeeze and Northern Rock: The Lessons to Be Learned' (2008) 16(1) *Journal of Financial Regulation and Compliance* 19.
- Hanlon, J. and Heywood, R., 'Spectrum Plus and Book Debts: The Final Chapter?' (2006) *Web Journal of Current Legal Issues* 1.
- HM Revenue & Customs, *International Manual* (last updated 17 January 2025), available at www.gov.uk/hmrc-internal-manuals/international-manual/intm524040 (accessed in March 2025).
- The Joint Money Laundering Steering Group, 'Prevention of Money Laundering/Combating Terrorist Financing: Guidance for the UK Financial Sector, Part I' (2023 revised version, June 2023).
- Jones, E. and Zeitz, A., 'The Limits of Globalizing Basel Banking Standards' (2017) 3 *Journal of Financial Regulation* 89.
- Khanfar, Nehad A. A., 'The Applicability of the Islamic Mortgage Contract Under English Law' (27 November 2009). Available at SSRN: https://ssrn.com/abstract=1548869 or http://dx.doi.org/10.2139/ssrn.1548869
- Kregel, J., 'The Economic Problem: From Barter to Commodity Money to Electronic Money' (2021) *Levy Institute Working Paper No. 982*.
- Lane, F., 'Venetian Bankers, 1496–1533: A Study in the Early Stages of Deposit Banking' (1937) 45(2) *Journal of Political Economy* 187–206.
- Lane, P., 'The Digital Euro: Maintaining the Autonomy of the Monetary System' (2025) *Keynote Speech by Philip R. Lane, Member of the Executive Board of the ECB, University College Cork Economics Society Conference 2025*.
- The Law Commission and the Scottish Law Commission, 'Company Directors: Regulating Conflicts of Interests *(SLC173) (Report)*' [1999] EWLC 261.
- Law Commission, 'Digital Assets *(Law Com No 412) (Final Report)*' [2024] EWLC 416.
- Lee, J., 'Should Interest Rates Be Regulated or Abolished? The Case for the Abolition of Usury' (2017) 8 *The Western Australian Jurist* 227.
- Lee, P., 'Directors' Duty to Monitor: Experience in the Banking Sector – Part I' (2016) 133 *The Banking Law Journal* 405.
- Li, W., 'China's Shadow Banking in 2020–2022: An Empirical Study' (2024) 11 *Humanities and Social Sciences Communications* 282.
- Lipton, P., 'The Utilisation of Evolutionary Concepts in Legal History: Company Law as a Case Study' (2020) 46(1) *Monash University Law Review* 58.
- Llewellyn, D., 'Banking in the 21st Century: The Transformation of an Industry' in Edey, *The Future of the Financial System*, Proceeding of a Conference (Economic Group, Reserve Bank of Australia, Alken Press, 1996).
- Lonardo, L., 'Challenging EU Sanctions against Russia: The Role of the Court, Judicial Protection, and Common Foreign and Security Policy' (2023) 25 *Cambridge Yearbook of European Legal Studies* 40–63.
- Lord Briggs, 'Dispute Resolution in Uncertain Times' [2018] *UKSpeech* 180122 (22 January 2018).
- Lord Neuberger of Abbotsbury, 'Master of the Rolls: A Judicial Perspective on the Conduct of Claims in the Current Climate' [2009] *UKSpeech* LHU52 (23 October 2009).
- Lord Neuberger: From Barretry, 'Maintenance and Champerty to Litigation Funding' [2013] *UKSpeech* 130508 (8 May 2013).
- Lord Sales at the Anglo-Australasian Law Society, 'Sydney: Directors' Duties and Climate Change: Keeping Pace with Environmental Challenges' [2019] *UKSpeech* 190827.
- Maddaloni, A. and Scopelliti, A., 'Rules and Discretion(s) in Prudential Regulation and Supervision: Evidence from EU Banks in the Run-Up to the Crisis' (May 2019) *ECB Working Paper Series No 2284*.

- Mahmood, S. K., 'The Long and Short of U.S. Bank Regulations: From the Great Depression to the 2023 Bank Failures' (30 April 2024) *SSRN.*
- Mr Justice Fancourt, 'Forfeiture, Penalties and Damages in Property Law' (2023) *UKSpeech* 6XCWS (10 March 2023).
- Muldrew, C., 'Interpreting the Market: The Ethics of Credit and Community Relations in Early Modern England' (1993) 18(2) *Social History* 163–183.
- Muñoz, M. and Soons, O., 'Public Money as a Store of Value, Heterogeneous Beliefs and Banks: Implications of CBDC' (2024) *Working Paper Series No 146.*
- Munro, J. H., 'The Mediaeval Origins of the Financial Revolution' (2003) 25(3) *International History Review* 505–562.
- Naik, J., 'Beginning of the Early Banking Industry in Mesopotamia Civilization from 8th Century B.C.E.' (10 January 2014).
- Nicolò, A. and Pelizzon, L., 'Credit Derivatives: Capital Requirements and Strategic Contracting' (15 March 2006). *EFMA 2004 BASEL MEETINGS.*
- Nishizaki, K., Sekine, T., Ueno, Y. and Kawai, Y., 'Chronic Deflation in Japan' (2014) *Asian Economic Policy Review* 9.
- Nolan, R., 'Conflicts of Duty and the Morals of the Market Place' (1994) *The Cambridge Law Journal* 53.
- OECD, 'Due Diligence for Responsible Corporate Lending and Securities Underwriting' (2019) *OECD Publishing.*
- Petrisor, S., 'Considerations Regarding the Concept of Security Agent in Syndicated Loans' (December 2015) 2(2) *Central Bank Journal of Law and Finance.*
- Plenderleith, I., 'Review of the Bank of England's Provision of Emergency Liquidity Assistance in 2008–09' (2012) *Documents 8450.*
- Powell, E., *The Evolution of the Money Market, 1385–1915: An Historical and Analytical Study of the Rise and Development of Finance as a Centralised, Coordinated Force* (Routledge, 1966).
- Prudential Regulation Authority, *Policy Statement | PS28/21: Remuneration: Identification of Material Risk Takers* (December 2021).
- Quilter, M., 'Bankruptcy and Order' (2013) 39(1) *Monash University Law Review* 189.
- Quinn, S. and Roberds, W., 'An Economic Explanation of the Early Bank of Amsterdam, Debasement, Bills of Exchange, and the Emergence of the First Central Bank' (2016) 23(1) *Financial History Review* 23–47.
- Quinn, S. and Roberds, W., 'The Evolution of the Check as a Means of Payment: A Historical Survey' (2008) *Economic Review,* Federal Reserve Bank of Atlanta.
- Renda, A., Schrefler, L., Luchetta, G. and Zavatta, R., 'Assessing the Costs and Benefits of Financial Regulation' (10 December 2013) *Study for the European Commission, Secretariat General.*
- Reynolds, R., 'Origins of Modern Business Enterprise: Mediaeval Italy' (1952) 12 *Journal of Economic History* 350.
- Roberds, W. and Velde, F., 'Early Public Banks' (1 August 2014) *FRB Atlanta Working Paper No. 2014–9.*
- Robertson, S., 'Debenture Holders and the Indenture Trustee: Controlling Managerial Discretion in the Solvent Enterprise' (1988) 11 *Harvard Journal of Law & Public Policy* 461, 472–473.
- Reiss-Roy, C., 'An Analysis of the Law and Practice of Securitisation' (2007) PhD Thesis, Institute of Finance Law, University of Wolverhampton.
- Schnabel, I. and Shin, H. S., 'Liquidity and Contagion: The Crisis of 1763' (2004) 2(6) *Journal of the European Economic Association* 929–968.
- Schularick, M. and Taylor, A. M., 'Credit Booms Gone Bust: Monetary Policy, Leverage Cycles, and Financial Crises, 1870–2008' (2012) 102(2) *American Economic Review American Economic Association* 1029–1061.
- Schweikart, L., 'U.S. Commercial Banking: A Historiographical Survey' (1991) 65(3) *The Business History Review* 606–661.

- Sebastianutti, P., 'What Is This Thing Called International Financial Law? Part 3' (2009) 3(3) *Law and Financial Markets Review* 248.
- Silvestri, P., 'Luigi Einaudi's "Scienza delle Finanze" or the Science of Good Government' (2023) 30(5) *The European Journal of the History of Economic Thought*.
- Simmons, A., 'Regulating Libra: Will Legal and Regulatory Uncertainty Prevent the Launch of Facebook's Cryptocurrency Project?' (2021) 16 *Journal of Business & Technology Law* 83.
- Smith, M., 'The Legal Nature of Credit Default Swaps' (2010) *Lloyd's Maritime and Commercial Law Quarterly* 386.
- Sowerbutts, R. and Schneebalg, M., 'The Demise of Overend Gurney' (2016) *The Bank of England Quarterly Bulletin 2016 Q2*.
- Srivastava, A., 'The Effectiveness of Prudential Regulations for Banks: Global Perspective and Indian Context' (2019) 48(2) *Prajnan*.
- Stiglitz, J.,'Testimony before the House Committee on Financial Services' (21 October 2008) *House Committee on Financial Services*.
- Stiglitz, J., 'Towards a New Paradigm for Development: Strategies, Policies, and Processes' (19 October 1998) *Prebisch Lecture* at UNCTAD, Geneva.
- Suri, K., Jaggi, Y. and Choudhary, S., 'A Study on Dynamics of Banking Sector in India' (2022) 9(8) *International Journal of Multidisciplinary Research and Development* 29.
- Trapanese, M. (coord), Albareto, G., Cardillo, S., Castagna, M., Falconi, R., Pezzullo, G., Serafini, L. and Signore, F., 'The 2023 US Banking Crises: Causes, Policy Responses, and Lessons' (19 July 2024) *No 870 Banca d'Italia, Questioni di Economia e Finanza (Occasional Papers)*.
- Wilmarth, A., 'The Transformation of the US Financial Services Industry, 1975–2000: Competition, Consolidation, and Increased Risks' (2002) 2 *University of Illinois Law Review* 215.
- Working Group on E-CNY Research and Development of the People's Bank of China, 'Progress of Research & Development of E-CNY in China' (2021) *BIS Papers No 123*.
- Zambelli, M., 'The Law of Securitisation in Ireland' (2017) PhD Thesis, Trinity College Dublin.

INDEX

Note: Page numbers in **bold** indicate tables in the text, and references following "n" refer notes.